GAIL BORDEN PUBLIC LIBRARY

P9-CRW-233

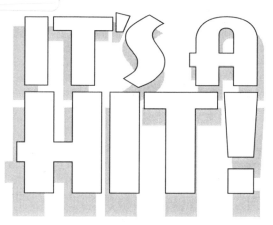

THE *BACK STAGE*® BOOK OF LONGEST-RUNNING BROADWAY SHOWS

1884 TO THE PRESENT

DAVID SHEWARD

BACK STAGE BOOKS

AN IMPRINT OF
WATSON-GUPTILL PUBLICATIONS
NEW YORK

For Jerry, my friend and partner, always

I would like to thank the following for their enormous contributions to this project: Tad Lathrop, Paul Lukas, and Dale Ramsey of Watson-Guptill, who guided this project from its conception to completion; Jay Anning, for the design of the book; the entire staff of the Billy Rose Theatre Collection of the Lincoln Center Library for the Performing Arts; my publisher (Steve Elish), editor (Sherry Eaker) and co-workers (Thomas Walsh, Amy Hersh, Michele LaRue, Ben Alexander, Diane L. Snyder, Bruce Peterson, Jim Contessa, Brian Krall, Steven Jones, Theresa Piti, Julann Gebbie, and the entire staff) at *Back Stage* for their encouragement and support during the writing of this book; the brilliant photographers Martha Swope and Carol Rosegg of Martha Swope Studios, Joan Marcus, and Gerry Goodstein; my friends and fellow theatre mavens Peter Filicha of *Theatre Week* and *The Newark Star-Ledger*, and David Cleaver of Applause Theatre and Cinema Books, who read the manuscript and made many helpful suggestions; Ron and Howard Mendelbaum of Photofest; Ellis Nassour, who generously lent me photos from his extensive collection; my friend Paul J. Ocampo, whose enormous collection of original cast albums and theatre books was a great source of information; and the following theatre artists for lending me their time and insights: Martin Charnin, Harold Prince, Robert Lewis, Kim Hunter, Marian Seldes, Marilyn Cooper, Rosetta LeNoire, and Wendy Wasserstein.

Senior Editor: Paul Lukas
Associate Editor: Dale Ramsey
Designer: Jay Anning
Production Manager: Ellen Greene

CONTENTS

PREFACE

A brief word of explanation about this book: It contains a capsule history of every play, musical, or special attraction that has run on Broadway for over 500 performances. There is a final section with entries on shows with similar off-Broadway runs. Because numerous shows have transferred to Broadway from off-Broadway, those whose *combined* runs were of 500 performances or more are also included. The 500-performance standard is admittedly arbitrary, but it is used by most theatrical recordkeepers as the mark of a long run.

The first section chronicles the years 1884 through 1919. Thereafter the book is divided by decades, from the '20s to the '90s, with a brief introduction to each ten-year period noting major theatrical events, personalities, and influences, as well as some important productions that did not run over 500 times.

Beginning with the 1920–21 season (a theatrical season runs officially from June 1 of one year to May 31 of the next), the author, director, producer, choreographer (in cases of musicals), and principal cast members are listed for each show. The capsule history of the show, including touring productions, motion pictures, and telecasts derived from the Broadway version, follows.

Readers will also find Pulitzer Prize–winning plays, major Antoinette Perry ("Tony") Awards, and New York Drama Critics Circle Awards listed in the back of the book. Please note that the Tony Awards did not begin making formal nominations until the 1954–55 season, when the nominees for Best Play and Best Musical were announced. Thereafter all nominees in all categories were made public.

Finally, for those shows that are still running as this book goes to press, I have given the number of performances up to February 6, 1994, as reported by *Variety*.

1884–1919

Between the 1884–85 season, when *Adonis*, the first long-running Broadway hit on record, opened, and the 1918–19 season, only thirteen shows ran over 500 performances. At that time, an extensive engagement was not needed to recoup investments. Production costs were significantly lower than those of today, so the producer's money could be returned faster. Indeed, a New York run of 100 performances was considered excellent. Since there was no television or cinema, touring companies were guaranteed audiences and, therefore, profits at the box office. Stars like Sarah Bernhardt, Ellen Terry, Henry Irving, Lily Langtry, and Edwin Booth made extensive tours of the country in limited engagements.

Adonis, a musical, opened on September 4, 1884, and ran for 603 performances at the Bijou Opera House. It remained on Broadway for two seasons. The plot, which concerns a statue coming to life, was based on the Pygmalion myth and predated other Pygmalion-based shows, like *One Touch of Venus* and *My Fair Lady*, by sixty years.

Adonis was a variety show; through songs and sketches, it lampooned current events, entertainment fads, and celebrities. Henry E. Dixey, the star and co-author, and William F. Gill, his collaborator, updated their script to reflect new topics in the news as they developed. This practice drew repeat audience members eager to see the fresh material. The production was a hit on the road and in London as well. This style of musical parody was known as "burlesque" long before the word came to connote baggy-pants comics and strip-tease acts.

Adonis's record run remained unbroken until 1891, when theatregoers took *A Trip to Chinatown* (November 9, 1891, Madison Square Theatre, 657 performances). This musical is historically interesting chiefly because of its resemblance to *Hello, Dolly!*—the plot is very similar to that of the Jerry Herman musical of the 1960s.

Both long-running musicals feature a vivacious widow causing trouble for a pompous, middle-class merchant, and both include a scene where two young couples attend the same restaurant as the merchant and wind up with his wallet. The score featured three song hits: "Reuben and Cynthia," "The Bowery," and "After the Ball," a popular tune that was interpolated into the show. (It was later used in another hit, *Show Boat*, with similar success.)

In the interval between *Adonis* and *Chinatown*, David Belasco rose to prominence as playwright, producer, and purveyor of sentiment, two of which were transformed by Puccini into the operatic favorites *Madama Butterfly* and *Girl of the Golden West*. Belasco's main rival for control of Broadway and the country's stages was the monopolistic Theatrical Syndicate, a conglomerate of theatre owners and producers led by Charles Frohman, who ruled the New York theatre with an iron fist. Stars had to agree to the syndicate's terms or the theatre doors were closed to them. Leading men and ladies like Henry Miller, Maude Adams, Ethel Barrymore, and her uncle, John Drew Barrymore II, became the syndicate's chief stars. Because Frohman and his cronies wanted only the most popular fare, experimental works were shunned, and safe, tame comedies embraced. Eventually, independent performers like Minnie Maddern Fiske (known as Mrs. Fiske) and producers like the Shubert brothers (Sam, Lee, and Jacob J.) were able to break the syndicate's grip.

The century would turn before another show exceeded 500 performances. This was *Floradora* (November 12, 1900, Casino Theatre, 553 performances), an English import that had a longer American run than its London engagement. The complicated story involves a beautiful young heiress and a scheme to prevent her from acquiring the rights to a perfume. The musical's main attraction was the famous Floradora sextet who, paired with six gentlemen of the chorus, performed "Tell Me, Pretty Maiden (Are There Any More at Home Like You?)." The "Floradora Girls" became the darlings of the press and public. Millionaires were said to attend the show several times, bringing flowers, gifts, and even deeds of land to their personal favorite Floradoras. Their popularity prefigured the glorification of chorus girls by showman Florenz Ziegfeld in the 1910s and '20s.

Not every hit was a musical. Belasco provided the public with sparkling personalities in plays that were tailored for them. Like glittering jewels in dull cases, Belasco's stars were the important thing, not the hackneyed shows in which they were displayed. One such star was David Warfield, a former comedian with the team of Weber and Fields. A rare male headliner among Belasco's roster of females, Warfield triumphed in *The Music Master* (September 6, 1904, Belasco Theatre, 627 performances). The title character is Anton von Barwig, a down-on-his-luck conductor from Vienna who is reduced to giving music lessons in America while searching for his long-lost daughter. Of

The Floradora Girls.

course, one of his pupils is revealed to be his missing off-spring, now a budding debutante. Von Barwig prepares to make a noble sacrifice for his daughter and quietly return to Vienna so that she may continue to live in comfort. At the last minute, she learns the truth and opens her heart to the father she never knew.

The press castigated the sentimental script but praised Warfield for delivering an honest and deeply felt performance. He stayed with the part for three years and in subsequent revivals until 1916. His career was capped in 1922 by the role of Shylock in Shakespeare's *The Merchant of Venice.*

The Lion and the Mouse (November 20, 1905, Lyceum Theatre, 686 performances) by Charles Klein, author of *The Music Master,* was a melodrama typical of the period, with characters based on journalist Ida Tarbell and tycoon John D. Rockefeller. Shirley Rossmore, a crusading author, assumes another name and goes to work for a despotic millionaire in order to reinstate the good name of her father, a judge whose career was ruined by her employer. She woos the rich man's son and goes through the family

documents, finally finding the evidence to vindicate the judge. Plot mechanisms like this were a staple on the stages of New York; as here, they usually served an emphatically moralistic purpose. *The Lion and the Mouse* was a bigger hit than *Peter Pan,* which opened at around the same time and, obviously, outlived this forgotten show.

The same season saw an elaborate revue entitled *A Society Circus,* which opened on December 15, 1905, and lasted 596 performances. Occupying the huge stage of the Hippodrome Theatre, it bedazzled with acts typical of a circus, including the famous French clown Marceline, elephants, lions, and elaborate production numbers involving golden fountains and airplanes.

Broadway did not see another 500-performance run until Jane Cowl starred in *Within the Law* (September 11, 1912, Eltinge Theatre, 541 performances). Like *The Lion and the Mouse,* this drama focuses on a falsely accused innocent who is ultimately vindicated. Cowl played Mary Turner, whose boss Edward Gilder wrongfully suspects her of theft. After three years of prison, Mary organizes a gang of crooks who keep their capers just within the law. She marries Gilder's son while still harboring a grudge against her father-in-law. When the gang's attempt to rob the Gilder household is foiled, their confession clears Mary's name of the original crime and (surprise!) all ends happily. Cowl made a personal success in the play and went on to become one of the bright stage stars of the '20s.

The same season, another actress emerged to stardom. Laurette Taylor jerked tears and won smiles in *Peg o' My Heart* (December 20, 1912, Cort Theatre, 603 performances), a rags-to-riches confection written for her by her husband J. Hartley Manners. The public gobbled up the story of the guileless Irish girl who comes into money and proves herself cleverer and kinder than the English gentry. Manners wrote two more vehicles for his wife in which simplicity is rewarded with good fortune, *Out There* (1917) and *Happiness* (1918). These were also loved by Taylor's adoring fans, but neither ran as long as *Peg o' My Heart*, which was revived in 1921.

The couple collaborated on one more play, *The National Anthem* (1922), a failure. After that, Manners died and Taylor's career ground to a halt. She began drinking heavily and appeared on the stage less and less frequently. She did regain stardom, however, with her legendary 1944 performance as Amanda Wingfield in Tennessee Williams's *The Glass Menagerie*.

The next long run Broadway offering was a featherweight comedy called *The Boomerang* (August 10, 1915, Belasco Theatre, 522 performances), written by Winchell Smith and Victor Mapes and presented by Belasco. The title refers to the effects of jealousy. In the play, a man visits his doctor complaining of an unknown illness. The physician deduces that the man's malady is caused by his fiancée's flirting. His cure: Make the fiancée jealous by having the patient run after his nurse. The boomerang effect comes into play when the doctor becomes jealous and realizes he's in love with the nurse himself. This kind of mild gag has very rarely served as the basis for a long-run show, but *The Boomerang* played for a year and a half on Broadway.

Most 19th- and early 20th-century actors were closely identified with one role that they played over and over using different names and slightly varied circumstances. Frank Bacon was always known as "Lightnin'" Bill Jones, the protagonist of *Lightnin'* (August 26, 1918, Gaiety Theatre, 1,291 performances), a frontier romp co-authored by Bacon and above-mentioned Winchell Smith. (Play doctor extraordinaire George Abbott, whose reputation for applying his special brand of theatrical medicine to ailing shows would grow with the century, helped with rewriting the script before its original run.) "Lightnin'" is a lovable rascal known to take a nip and spin a tale. The play follows his efforts to win back his fed-up wife and foil some city slickers trying to buy his hotel on the Nevada–California bor-

der. It had the longest run of any production up to the time and held the record until *Abie's Irish Rose* surpassed it in 1925. Bacon played his role throughout the run and died during the national tour. The play was unsuccessfully revived in 1938.

Another popular performer of the day, Fay Bainter, achieved her greatest success in the comedy *East Is West* (December 25, 1918, Astor Theatre, 680 performances). Bainter played Ming Toy, a Chinese girl whose love for an American causes complications for everyone. Anticipating the intercultural romance in *Abie's Irish Rose,* the play was similarly full of stereotypical depictions of its characters. The show owed much of its success to Bainter's bubbling enactment of the Asian daughter—who turns out to be Spanish by birth! Bainter starred in numerous productions through the '20s and went on to Hollywood. The practice of casting white actors in principal Asian roles was a relatively common occurrence until around the 1980s. (In 1991, Asian-American artists made news protesting Englishman Jonathan Pryce's playing a Eurasian in *Miss Saigon*.)

Belasco returned to the hit parade the next season with *The Gold Diggers* (September 30, 1919, Lyceum Theatre, 720 performances), Avery Hopwood's razzmatazz comedy about money-hungry showgirls. The story turns on Stephen Lee, a wealthy man who finds that his nephew is in love with a chorine. Suspecting she is only out for the young man's money, the uncle goes to Jerry Lamarr, an experienced dancer, to check on the nephew's intended. But Jerry gets the uncle drunk and tricks him into proposing to her. All ends happily for both couples when Jerry and Stephen fall in love themselves. The play served as the inspiration for a brace of Depression-era movie musicals from Warner Brothers.

The Gold Diggers was a triumph for Ina Claire, who played Jerry. After starring in a *Ziegfeld Follies*, this play put her over the top as a sharp comedienne. She went on to headline many sophisticated straight plays, and she can be seen as Garbo's rival in the classic film *Ninotchka*.

The Gold Diggers were gum-chewing tough dames. The protagonist of *Irene* (November 18, 1919, Vanderbilt Theatre, 670 performances) was the exact opposite: sweet, pure, but nobody's fool. Edith Day starred in this intimate musical of a poor shopgirl who makes good. Its simple heroine and endearing Harry Tierney–Joseph McCarthy songs ("Alice Blue Gown" was one of the hits) made it the longest running tuner on Broadway until *Pins and Needles* (1939) surpassed it. It launched numerous road companies (at one time seventeen were playing simultaneously across the country) and a smash London production. After the success of *Irene,* a spate of Cinderella-style musicals played on Broadway in the 1920s.

The show was filmed twice. Colleen Moore was Irene in the 1926 silent version, and Anna Neagle gave voice to the 1940 edition. *Irene* resurfaced on Broadway in 1973, when a nostalgia craze prompted a revival with a revised book. Debbie Reynolds starred.

While these thirteen shows ran the longest in the seasons from 1884 to 1919, numerous others were just as popular and influential. The operettas of Victor Herbert, Rudolf Friml, and Sigmund Romberg waltzed onto Broadway, while the musicals of George M. Cohan, Jerome Kern, and Irving Berlin became the forerunners of a distinctly American style of presentation. Ziegfeld's annual *Follies* combined comedy sketches with eye-filling production numbers.

Most successful nonmusical attractions were simple melodramas or light comedies by Edward B. Sheldon, Owen Davis, Avery Hopwood, and Clyde Fitch. The first Pulitzer Prize for drama was awarded in 1918 to *Why Marry?* by Jesse Lynch Williams, a sophisticated comedy about a young woman with modern views on marriage: She believes couples should live together without the benefit of the clergy's approval.

In the next decade, the Roaring Twenties, frivolity would continue to prevail on the New York stage, but Broadway would also begin to show a more serious side.

THE 1920S

The boom in America's prosperity during the 1920s was reflected on Broadway by an increasing number of theatres and the volume of production. Records vary as to the total of theatres, with the reported sum ranging from seventy to eighty, as compared to thirty-five active "Main Stem" theatres today. In 1927–28, production reached an all-time high with 264 attractions. By 1990–91, this figure had shrunk to 27. ☆ Broadway was mainly a place to forget your troubles and have a good time. The tired businessman was the Great White Way's target consumer. *Abie's Irish Rose*, a simple-minded romance of a Jewish man and a Catholic woman, replete with cultural stereotypes, was the longest-running play of the era, much to the amazement of critics who had panned it. Ziegfeld continued to display the greatest talent—Fanny Brice, Will Rogers, Eddie Cantor, Marilyn Miller, and W.C. Fields—as well as innumerable chorus girls' legs. The Barrymores (dashing John, leonine Lionel, and ethereal Ethel), Katharine Cornell, Pauline Lord, Jeanne Eagels, and Ina Claire were also in the galaxy of stars glittering on Broadway. ☆ But more serious subject matter was starting to be explored. Organizations like the Theatre Guild and Eva La Gallienne's Civic Repertory Theatre produced innovative playwrights on the order of Eugene O'Neill (1888–1953), who somberly delved into the psychological conflicts of modern men and women. O'Neill became the predominant playwright of the day and won three of his four Pulitzer Prizes during the '20s, for *Beyond the Horizon* (1920), *Anna Christie* (1922), and the nine-hour marathon *Strange Interlude* (1928). (His fourth was awarded posthumously, in 1957, for his much later autobiographical *Long Day's Journey into Night*.) ☆ On the musical front, frivolity was still king. Plotless revues and slim-storied musicals prevailed, with George and Ira Gershwin, Richard Rodgers and Lorenz Hart, Ray Henderson, B. G. De Sylva and Lew Brown, and Vincent Youmans joining the fraternity of songwriters. The operettas of Sigmund Romberg and Rudolf Friml continued to prove popular. Oscar Hammerstein II and Jerome Kern were pioneers with their 1927 adaptation of Edna Ferber's *Show Boat* (produced by Ziegfeld), in which the story, rather than the musical numbers, drove the show. ☆ By the end of the decade, the party was over. Live theatre would never again be the main entertainment medium in America. The Great Depression shut down several theatres and bankrupted producers, while the novelty of talking pictures began siphoning off audiences.

THE BAT

by Mary Roberts Reinhart and Avery Hopwood, based on Reinhart's short story "The Circular Staircase."

Opened August 23, 1920

867 Performances

The Morosco Theatre

Directed by Collin Kemper

Produced by Wagenhals and Kemper

Cast: Effie Ellsler (Miss Cornelia Van Gorden); May Vokes (Lizzie); Anne Morrison (Miss Dale Ogden); Edward Ellis (Dr. Wells); Richard Barrows (Richard Fleming); Kenneth Hunter (Reginald Beresford); Harry Morvil (Billy); Stuart Sage (Brooks); Robert Vaughan (An Unknown Man).

Mysteries and thrillers rarely achieve long runs on Broadway. The first spine-tingler to run over 500 performances was *The Bat*, based on Mary Roberts Reinhart's short story "The Circular Staircase." Reinhart, one of America's leading mystery writers, adapted her work for the stage with the aid of Avery Hopwood, author of such popular comedies as *The Gold Diggers* and *Getting Gertie's Garter*.

The premise was a simple one, and would be used numerous times in later thrillers: An old spinster rents the isolated home of a man believed to be dead. But it soon appears the man may not be deceased after all, and that stolen bank funds are hidden somewhere in the house. Frightening, unexplained occurrences begin to take place and a masked, shadowy figure is spotted. The old woman hires a detective to get to the bottom of the affair, and others arrive who want to find the money. An easily frightened maid provides comic relief throughout.

This basic plot about a group of people in a spooky house was employed in countless horror films, as well as by the Queen of Mystery herself, Agatha Christie, in one of her most popular spellbinders, *And Then There Were None.*

The Bat scared audiences for over two seasons and proved popular for stock and amateur groups. Its popularity was all the more remarkable for its genre—Broadway would not see another long-running mystery until *Angel Street* opened in 1941. *The Bat* was revived on Broadway in 1937 and again in 1953, and it was filmed in 1915, 1926, 1930, and 1959. The silent film version was seen by a young comic-book artist named Bob Kane, who claimed to have been inspired by the mysterious masked character to create a similarly dark figure (one who fought on the side of good), Batman.

Marilyn Miller as *Sally* entertains the bluebloods at a swank affair.

THE FIRST YEAR

by Frank Craven
Opened October 20, 1920
760 Performances
The Little Theatre
Directed by Michell Smith
Produced by John Golden

Cast: Frank Craven (Thomas Tucker); Roberta Arnold (Grace Livingston); William Sampson (Mr. Livingston); Maude Granger (Mrs. Livingston); Tim Murphy (Dr. Anderson); Lyster Chambers (Dick Loring); Leila Bennett (Hattie); Hale Norcross (Mr. Barstow); Merceita Esmonde (Mrs. Barstow).

Frank Craven wrote and starred in this simple little play chronicling the first year of married life for one Tommy Tucker. Tommy and his bride Grace get through the normal travails of newlyweds, but when an important business dinner is ruined and Grace grows impatient with Tommy's tightwad tendencies, they split. Of course, the play ends happily and the marriage is saved, although the manner in which this occurs is a telling reflection of the money-mad '20s: Tommy manages to make a bundle on a real-estate deal and Grace returns to him. Critics commended the play for its realism in depicting the difficulties of middle-class marriages.

By serving as both the author and star of the show, Craven prefigured such notable playwright-actors as Noël Coward, Ruth Gordon, Athol Fugard, Harvey Fierstein, and others. He later achieved greater renown for playing the Stage Manager in both the stage and film versions of *Our Town*, Thornton Wilder's 1938 Pulitzer Prize–winning paean to the everyday.

SALLY

Book by Guy Bolton
Music by Jerome Kern
Lyrics by Clifford Grey, P.G. Wodehouse, B.G. De Sylva, and Anne Caldwell
Opened December 21, 1920
570 Performances
The New Amsterdam Theatre
Directed and choreographed by Edward Royce
Produced by Florenz Ziegfeld

Cast: Marilyn Miller (Sally Green); Leon Errol (Connie); Walter Catlett (Otis Hooper); Irving Fisher (Blair Farquar); Mary Hay (Rosalind Rafferty); Stanley Ridges (Jimmie Hooper); Dolores (Mrs. Ten Broek); Alfred P. James (Pops); Jacques Rebiroff (Sascha); Phil Ryley (Col. Travers); Alta King (Babe); Betty Williams (Fluff); Barbara Dean (Tot); Vivian Vernon (Kitty); Gladys Montgomery (Pickles); Mary McDonald (Bobby); Frank Kingdon (Richard Farquar); Wade Boothe (Billy Porter); Jack Barker (Harry Burton); Earl Barroy (Ivan).

Young female stars headlining musicals named for their characters were in vogue in the early 1920s. *Irene*, *Sally*, and *Sunny* were the bright young heroines of the Jazz Age, just as the middle-aged Mama Rose, Dolly, and Mame would dominate the late '50s and '60s.

Sally was the first of two such shows to star Marilyn Miller, the decade's dancing darling. She was discovered by the producer of extravaganzas, Florenz Ziegfeld. After starring in the *Follies of 1918*, Miller married chorus member Frank Carter, much to Ziegfeld's displeasure. He hired both to appear in his 1919 version of the Follies and then fired Carter during out-of-town tryouts. Miller was contractually obligated to remain with the show. Carter died soon thereafter in an automobile accident. Although rumors of an affair between Miller and Ziegfeld would persist, Miller blamed Ziegfeld for her husband's death.

In spite of their tense relationship, Ziegfeld searched for a musical story for his latest star. He also wanted to produce separate shows for two comics, Leon Errol and Walter Catlett. He found a vehicle for all three talents in an unfinished musical by Jerome Kern, P.G. Wodehouse, and Guy Bolton called *The Little Thing*. The script went through significant alterations, and Wodehouse, who withdrew during the process, was replaced by three other lyricists, Clifford Grey, B.G. De Sylva, and Anne Caldwell. Kern's score was augmented with a ballet sequence by Victor Herbert.

The final version, called *Sally*, followed the Cinderella formula of *Irene*—and of Miller's offstage experiences. Like *Irene*, Sally is a poor girl in humble circumstances. The audience first discovers her washing dishes in a Greenwich Village joint, advising herself to "Look for the Silver Lining." One of the waiters in the restaurant (Erroll) is actually the exiled Duke of Czechogovinia. A ballerina who was supposed to accompany him to a high-toned Long Island party, where she was to perform, has backed out, and he asks Sally to stand in for her. Predictably, Sally goes along, enchants the bluebloods with her terpsichorean charms, meets the man of her dreams, and (like Miller) is offered a spot in *The Ziegfeld Follies*. Catlett played a comic press agent who aides the heroine in her rise to fame.

Ziegfeld surrounded his star with the same opulence he provided for the *Follies*. He employed the same set designer, Joseph Urban, as well as a small army of famous couturiers for the costumes. Rather than being smothered by all this elegance, Miller shone all the brighter. According to contemporary sources, her acting and singing were so-so, but, as Ziegfeld's wife Billie Burke pointed out, "a delightful thing happens when she comes on stage." Her presence and her dancing had the extra spark that captivated audiences.

Colleen Moore starred in a silent film version of *Sally* in 1925, while Miller did a sound and Technicolor adaptation in 1929. (The silent film does not survive, and there is only one print of Miller's.) A 1948 stage revival with Bambi Lynn and Willie Howard closed after 48 performances. Theatregoers, now accustomed to the strong storylines and believable characters in shows like *Oklahoma!* and *Carousel*, had outgrown the simplicities of *Sally*.

SHUFFLE ALONG

Book by Flournoy Miller and Aubrey Lyles

Music by Eubie Blake

Lyrics by Noble Sissle

Opened May 23, 1921

504 Performances

The 63rd Street Music Hall

Directed by Walter Brooks

Choreographed by Lawrence Deas

Produced by Nikko Producing Co. (Al Mayer)

Cast: Aubrey Lyles (Sam Peck); Flournoy Miller (Steve Jenkins); Noble Sissle (Tom Sharper); Roger Matthews (Harry Walton); Lottie Gee (Jessie Williams); Gertrude Saunders (Ruth Little); Paul Floyd (Jim Williams); Mattie Wilks (Mrs. Sam Peck); Lawrence Deas (Jack Penrose); C. Wesley Hill (Rufus Loose); A.E. Baldwin (Soakum Flat); Billy Williams (Strutt); Charles Davis (Uncle Tom); Bob Williams (Old Black Joe); Ina Duncan (Secretary to Mayor).

Shuffle Along was the first hit musical written, staged, and performed by African-Americans to play over 500 performances. It also began a trend for black musicals on Broadway over the next few seasons and launched the careers of many of those involved. The musical was the result of the collaboration of two vaudeville teams: comics Flournoy Miller and Aubrey Lyles and song-and-dance men Eubie Blake and Noble Sissle.

For many years Miller and Lyles had performed their Southern-style comedy act in blackface (a common practice for black acts of that era) on the circuit of RKO Keith stages. Blake and Sissle, known as The Dixie Duo, performed their own compositions, including Blake's popular ragtime numbers. The four men met in 1920 at a Philadelphia NAACP benefit, where they discussed the idea of merging their talents to create and produce a Broadway show. The last successful Main Stem offering with a black cast had been in 1908, when *Bandanna Land* had starred the famous duo of Bert Williams and George Walker.

The basis for *Shuffle Along* was a sketch from the Miller and Lyles repertoire about a mayoral election in the fictitious locale of Jimtown. Much of the humor was derived from the fracturing of the English language by political rivals Steve Jenkins (Miller) and Sam Peck (Lyles). There was also a love-interest subplot between third candidate Harry Walton and Jessie Williams, daughter of the richest man in town. The duet sung by these two characters at the end of Act I stirred some controversy: It was the first time that African-American lovers had serenaded each other on the Broadway stage without satire or condescension.

Material was incorporated from the trunks of both teams. The plot stopped dead in its tracks in the second act while Blake left his position at the head of the orchestra pit to join Sissle onstage and perform a segment of their vaudeville routine. There was also a twenty-minute, humorous fight sequence danced by Miller and Lyles—a trademark of their act.

The score contained numerous songs that became hits, like "I'm Craving That Kind of Love," the unprecedented Act I finale "Love Will Find a Way," and "I'm Just Wild About Harry." The use of the name Harry for an underdog politician was prescient: thirty years later, the tune had a second life as the campaign song of another dark-horse candidate, Harry Truman.

The chorus girls may have been wild about Harry, but producers were not so enthusiastic about backing an all-black show, claiming that white audiences wouldn't come to see it. Through various vaudeville connections, the creators managed to get an audition with theatrical entrepreneur John Cole and his son Harry. Cole liked what he saw and gave *Shuffle Along* a home, the 63rd Street Music Hall, a somewhat rundown venue away from the main theatre district. He also tossed in some old costumes from two recent flops. Construction work that the Music Hall needed continued even after the opening, and certain numbers were created to make use of available costumes.

During the out-of-town tryout, the company was often short of money. The production arrived in New York $18,000 in debt, but positive audience response and favorable reviews (mostly of the musical numbers—the book was dismissed as clumsy) heated up the box office. It became fashionable to be seen at *Shuffle Along*, especially at Wednesday midnight performances, and white audiences made the trip uptown to attend. Black theatregoers, who up to this point had been restricted to the balcony, were now allowed to purchase choice seats, although the show's management still only allowed one-third of the orchestra to be sold to black patrons. Over the next few years, this final barrier was dissolved and segregation in Broadway seating was eliminated.

Several original company members went on to successful careers, but the biggest stars *Shuffle Along* fostered were in replacement and touring companies. Paul Robeson made his stage debut as a substitute for a member of a vocal quartet. Josephine Baker, who later became a European sensation, was a chorus girl in the touring version. She attracted attention by crossing her eyes and deliberately keeping out of step. Adelaide Hall and Florence Mills became major singers.

There were two subsequent editions of the show, *Keep Shufflin'* (1928) and *Shuffle Along of 1933*, as well as a 1952 Broadway revival featuring Blake and Sissle. This production ran only four performances. Vastly more successful was *Eubie!*, a 1978 songbook revue of Blake and Sissle's music starring Gregory and Maurice Hines. Although *Shuffle Along* would probably be considered offensively stereotypical to a present-day audience, the show's influence is still felt. It was among the first musicals to inject the distinctively American sound of jazz and ragtime into its score when most Broadway musicals were still heavily in debt to European operetta. It also demonstrated that black people could write and perform a hit show that audiences of all races would attend.

BLOSSOM TIME

Libretto by Dorothy Donnelly

Music by Sigmund Romberg, adapted from the music of Franz Schubert

Opened September 29, 1921

576 Performances

The Ambassador Theatre

Directed by J.C. Huffman

Choreographed by F. M. Gillespie

Produced by the Shuberts

Cast: Bertram Peacock (Franz Schubert); Olga Cook (Mitzi Kranz); Howard March (Baron Schober); William Danforth (Herr Kranz); Ethel Branden (Mrs. Kranz); Roy Cropper (Vogl); Dorothy Whitmore (Fritzi); Frances Halliday (Kitzi); Zoe Barnett (Bella Bruna); Emmy Niclas (Greta); Paul Kerr (Kuepelweiser); Eugene Martinet (Von Schwind); Lucius Metz (Binder); Perry Askam (Erkmann); Yvan Servias (Count Sharntoff); Irving Mels (Hansy); Robert Payton Gibbs (Novotny); Mildred Kay (Rose); Erba Robeson (Mrs. Coberg).

The life and work of Franz Schubert provided the basis for *Blossom Time*, the first of Hungarian-born Sigmund Romberg's operettas to run over 500 performances.

Bertram Peacock and Olga Cook in *Blossom Time*.

Romberg contributed to a total of fifty-seven musicals in his career; for *Blossom Time*, he adapted the melodies of Schubert for the Broadway stage. Dorothy Donnelly did the book and lyrics.

The show was based on a Viennese original called *Das Dreimaderlhaus (The Home of Three Girls)* by A. M. Willner and H. Reichnert, with Heinrich Berte's adaptations of Schubert's music. The story was a totally fictionalized account of the composer's life in which young Franz is a shy man whose career is sponsored by Herr Krantz, a wealthy patron of the arts. It so happens that Krantz has three daughters—Mitzi, Kitzi, and Fritzi. The composer becomes smitten with Mitzi and writes a love song for her. In a variation on *Cyrano de Bergerac*, the handsome Baron Schober sings Franz's melody for Mitzi and she is entranced by him.

Because of this development, an anguished Schubert is unable to complete his Eighth Symphony (the famous "Unfinished" Symphony, which contains the melody the show's love song was based upon). He composes a final masterpiece, the *Ave Maria*, and dies of a broken heart.

The Shubert brothers (no relation to the composer) acquired the rights to the Viennese operetta and offered it to Romberg, who had worked for them previously on *The Blue Paradise* (1915), *Maytime* (1917), and the Al Jolson vehicle *Sinbad* (1918).

Some critics objected to the vulgarization of classical themes in a saccharine, untrue love story. But the music's beauty shone through, and Olga Cook, Howard March, and Bertram Peacock (who bore a striking resemblance to Schubert) sang it with feeling. Vulgarization or no, Broadway had not seen the last of shows based on classical music, as the success of such hits as *Carmen Jones* (after Bizet, 1943), *Song of Norway* (from Grieg, 1944), and *Kismet* (derived from Borodin, 1953) attests.

Numerous road companies took *Blossom Time* across the country and occasionally back to Broadway, sometimes playing one- or two-week engagements in New York. The operetta received a total of six New York revivals, the last in 1943.

KIKI

by David Belasco, adapted from the French play by André Picard.

Opened November 29, 1921

600 Performances

The Belasco Theatre

Produced and directed by David Belasco

Cast: Lenore Ulric (Kiki); Sam B. Hardy (Victor Renal); Max Figman (Baron Rapp); Thomas Findlay (Brule); Sidney Toler (Joly); Saxon Kling (Sinette); Thomas Mitchell (Adolphe); Harry Burkhardt (The Doctor); Arline Fredericks (Paulette); Pauline Moore (Lolotte); Florence Lee (Susanne); Gertrude Bond (Claire); Mignon Ranseer (Marcel); Jean Scott (Florine); Frances Kyle (The Cook).

Showman David Belasco knew what the public wanted. His many hits included sentimental melodrama as well as light, clean comedies. One of his biggest successes was *Kiki*, a sanitized adaptation of a French farce by André Picard. Kiki, a lovely chorine stuck on the producer of the show in which she is kicking up her heels, tries everything to win him, including pretending to be in a trance, and eventually gets her man.

The play was dismissed as empty-headed pabulum, but Lenore Ulric's praised performance in the title role made her a star. The original cast also included Sidney Toler, who went on to play Charlie Chan in numerous films, and Thomas Mitchell, whose many movie roles included Scarlett O'Hara's father in *Gone With the Wind* and an Oscar-winning supporting turn in *Stagecoach*.

Kiki was the first French-inspired Broadway hit. Later French comedies that had Broadway success were *Cactus Flower* (1965) and *Forty Carats* (1968); on the dramatic side, Jean Anouilh's plays *Antigone* (1946), *Becket* (1960), and *The Rehearsal* (1963) did well on Broadway. Among French musicals, a show called *Les Misérables* (1987) has sold quite a few tickets.

CHAUVE-SOURIS

Entire production devised by M. Nikita Balieff
Opened February 4, 1922
520 Performances
The 49th Street Theatre
Produced by F. Ray Comstock, Morris Gest

Cast (listed in original program by surnames): Messrs. Balieff, Wavitch, Gorodetsky, Birse, Borco, Davidoff, Kochetovsky, Malakoff, Marievsky, Pons, Stoianovsky, Salama, Dalmatoff; Mesdames Birse, Ershova, Dianina, Karabanova, Deykarhanova, Fechner.

Chauve-Souris was a clever song-and-dance revue put together by exiled Russian performers and hosted by a heavy-set comic named Nikita Balieff. The group, a community of refugees from revolution-torn Russia, had first performed at Balieff's Bat Restaurant in Paris as a means of amusing each other. (The title *Chauve-Souris* is French for "bat.") Balieff organized their acts into a legitimate stage show and put them on in Paris and later London. Morris Gest, a Russian-born American producer, loved the production and brought it to Broadway.

Although *Chauve-Souris* was performed in the native language of the cast, the acrobatics and dazzle of these Muscovites enchanted the Americans. One highlight was "The Parade of the Wooden Soldiers," a production number with the ensemble marching as toys.

Gest also presented a Russian-language repertory season of the Moscow Art Theatre, led by its founder, Constantin Stanislavski.

During the summer of 1922, *Chauve-Souris* moved from the 49th Street Theatre to the Century Roof. The second theatre's smaller seating capacity helped extend the attraction's run. Additional versions of the show opened to acclaim in 1923, 1925, and 1927. A later edition in 1943 had a brief run of 12 performances.

ABIE'S IRISH ROSE

by Anne Nichols
Opened on May 23, 1922
2,327 Performances
The Fulton Theatre
Directed by Laurence Marston
Produced by Anne Nichols

Cast: Robert B. Williams (Abraham Levy); Marie Carroll (Rosemary Murphy); Alfred Wiseman (Solomon Levy); John Cope (Patrick Murphy); Mathilde Cottrelly (Mrs. Isaac Cohen); Bernard Gorcey (Isaac Cohen); Howard Lang (Dr. Jacob Samuels); Harry Bradley (Father Whalen); Dorothy Grau (Flower Girl).

H. L. Mencken regarded this show as a potboiler, calling it "America's third-largest industry." The *New York Globe* labelled it "a dramatization of the Sunday comic strip." The *New York World* sneered that it had "not so much as a single line of honest writing." But *Abie's Irish Rose* survived these critical putdowns to become the all-time record holder for long runs until *Tobacco Road* eclipsed it more than a decade later.

The comedy, which reviewers castigated for its simplistic characterizations and religious stereotyping, poked fun at interfaith intolerance with its story of a Jewish boy falling in love with a Catholic girl. They are initially married by a Protestant minister. To please their respective quarreling families, the couple is later entwined by both a Jewish rabbi and a Catholic priest. Between weddings, there are jokes about the eating habits and broken English of both clans. The play ends with the rabbi and the priest preaching harmony and the arrival of the couple's offspring—twins named Rebecca and Patrick Joseph.

Anne Nichols, a former actress, stated that she wrote the play to promote understanding between followers of different faiths. "My own people hated both the Jews and the Catholics," she told the *New York Times*. "When I was eleven years old I was spanked for giving a Catholic girl a prayer book of her Church for a birthday present. That explains why I knew something of religious intolerance."

She was determined to get her play on Broadway at any cost. *Abie* was first optioned by Oliver Morosco for a run in Los Angeles. When Morosco showed no signs of moving the California company to New York, Nichols mounted a Broadway production with her own funds. When Morosco sued to stop the rival East Coast *Abie*, Nichols countersued for nonpayment of royalties and control of the rights on the West Coast production. She eventually won, only to have her production greeted with hostility by the press.

To keep the show on, Nichols mortgaged her home and the actors took a pay cut. An audience was gradually built up through word of mouth, giving Nichols the last laugh on the critics. She invited each of the reviewers who panned the opening to the closing 2,327th performance. An estimated 11 million people saw the comedy either on Broadway or in the dozens of cities around the world (including Shanghai) where it played.

But all was not rosy for *Abie*. In 1930, Nichols sued Universal Pictures for $3 million over what she saw were similarities between her play and the studio's *The Kellys and the Cohens*. In order to get the "official" version on celluloid, the author signed a contract with Adolph Zucker's Famous Players–Lasky Corporation for $300,000 in exchange for the movie rights on the day the play reached a performance total of 2,000. It was filmed twice (1928 and 1946) with middling results. Again, the critics blasted it, and this time audiences stayed away. A radio series based on the play aired in 1942.

Revivals in 1937 and 1954, both directed by Nichols, were unsuccessful because of the outmoded ethnic humor.

Nichols wanted to be remembered as more than the author of just one play. At one point she announced that a sequel to *Abie* was forthcoming, but she never finished it. Her subsequent output consists of a few forgotten comedies.

SEVENTH HEAVEN

by Austin Strong
Opened October 30, 1922
704 Performances
The Booth Theatre
Produced and directed by John Golden

Cast: Helen Menken (Diane); George Gaul (Chico); Marion Kirby (Nana); Frank Morgan (Brissac); Hubert Druce (Boul'); Fred Holloway (The Rat); Beatrice Noyes (Arlette); Alfred Kappeler (Maximilian Gobin); Bernard Thornton (Recan); Richard Carlyle (Blonde); William Post (Pere Chevillon); John Clements (Sgt. of Police); Harry Forsman (Uncle Georges); Isabel West (Aunt Valentine); Lionel Joseph (Lamplighter).

Sentiment sells. *Seventh Heaven,* John Golden's production of a tearjerker about a Parisian girl of the streets, left neither a dry eye nor an empty seat in the house. Helen Menken was lavishly praised for her performance as Diane, a good-hearted pickpocket (her profession of prostitute, in the original script, was changed). The heroine is saved from being arrested by the sewer-worker Chico, who lies to the police and claims she is his wife. He then takes her to his seventh-floor apartment, which they nickname Seventh Heaven. The two become lovers and perform a marriage ceremony themselves in their walk-up paradise. Then war

separates the common-law couple and Chico is reported missing in action. Four years pass. Diane is about to give her heart to another when she just happens to notice Chico in the street, blinded in the war. Accompanied by the sobs of the audience, Diane and Chico are reunited.

Golden first came across the play in the form of a one-act script. He urged the author to flesh it out to a full-length play, but he didn't like the results. After numerous attempts at interesting other playwrights to do a rewrite, he finally did it himself. Although critics acknowledged the play's obvious tugs at the heartstrings, they admitted to brushing away tears.

Frank Morgan, later known for playing the title role in *The Wizard of Oz*, had a featured role.

The silent film version, released in 1927, became one of the American cinema's perennially favorite tearjerkers. Janet Gaynor won the first Oscar for Best Actress for her performance. (Among Gaynor's rivals for the first Oscar was Gloria Swanson for her Sadie Thompson in the screen version of *Rain*.) The film also won for Best Screenplay (Benjamin Glazer) and Director (Frank Borzage). James Stewart was miscast as the hero of the 1937 remake, with the French Simone Simon more believable as Diane.

Helen Menken and George Gaul are in *Seventh Heaven.*

RAIN

by John Colton and Clemence Randolph, based on the short story by W. Somerset Maugham.

Opened November 7, 1922

648 Performances

The Maxine Elliott Theatre

Directed by John D. Williams

Produced by Sam H. Harris

Cast: Jeanne Eagels (Sadie Thompson); Robert Kelly (Rev. Davidson); Rapley Holmes (Joe Horn); Emma Wilcox (Ameena); Fritz Williams (Dr. McPhail); Shirley King (Mrs. McPhail); Catharine Brooke (Mrs. Davidson); Harry Quealy (Quartermaster Bates); Kent Thurber (Pvt. Griggs); Harold Healy (Corp. Hodgeson); Robert Elliott (Sgt. O'Hara); Kathryne Kennedy (Native Girl); Bhana Whitehawk (Native Policeman); Oka Bunda, Llano Paulo (Natives).

While the heroine of *Seventh Heaven* was innocent of heart, the leading character of *Rain*, another big hit of the 1922–23 season, was her opposite. Sadie Thompson, the harsh, bitter prostitute who sells her favors to off-duty soldiers in the South Seas, is not the self-sacrificing type.

The play's central conflict is between Sadie and the self-righteous Reverend Davidson. A cholera epidemic forces the two together in a Pago Pago hotel during a torrential rainy season. At first, the minister attempts to steer the harlot onto the road to salvation, but he ultimately proves weak in the face of temptation and reveals lust for his prospective convert. The play concludes with Davidson's suicide and Sadie's decision to return to her wanton ways.

Somerset Maugham's short story was rejected by numerous publications because of its frankness. It was finally accepted by George Jean Nathan, one of New York's foremost drama critics, for his magazine *Smart Set*. Playwright John Colton was correcting proofs of the story and saw possibilities in bringing Sadie to the stage. He gained Maugham's permission to dramatize the story. With Clemence Randolph as collaborator, Colton brought the unfinished script to John D. Williams, a producer and director, who immediately gave them a production contract. In order to acquire the services of Jeanne Eagels to play Sadie, Williams gave up control of the production to Sam H. Harris, who had Eagels under contract. Williams remained as director and kept a 25-percent stake in it.

The tryout period in Philadelphia was as stormy as the onstage deluge. The opening night was covered by second-string critics, since another play was opening at the same time. Harris carped about Williams's direction and Eugene Walter, the author of *The Easiest Way*, a popular drama, was asked to do a rewrite. There were more arguments than actual revisions. Williams managed to tighten up the staging, and the show moved to New York.

The sensual Eagels sizzled onstage, and she captured the imagination of Broadway. Sadly, though she could write her own ticket after *Rain*, she took to drink and drugs, ruined her health and professional standing, and died in 1929.

Sadie proved to be more durable. She was played by Tallulah Bankhead in 1935, June Havoc in a 1944 musicalization called *Sadie Thompson*, and Sabra Jones in a 1984 off-Broadway revival. Screen Sadies included Gloria Swanson, Joan Crawford, and Rita Hayworth.

WHITE CARGO

by Leon Gordon

Opened November 5, 1923

686 Performances

The Greenwich Village Theatre

Directed by Leon Gordon

Produced by Earl Carroll

Cast: Richard Stevenson (Longford); Annette Margules (Tondelayo); Conway Wingfield (The Doctor); A.E. Anson (Witzel); Frederick Roland (Ashley); J. Malcolm Dunn (The Missionary); Curtis Karpe (The Skipper); Tracy Barrow (The Engineer); Harris Gilmore (Worthing).

White Cargo is the earliest instance of an off-Broadway production transferring to a Broadway run of over 500 performances. The play opened downtown, in Greenwich Village, and eventually moved uptown to a larger venue.

Like *Rain* and *Tobacco Road*, this Leon Gordon potboiler achieved popularity because of its sensuality and a voyeuristic curiosity on the part of theatergoers. It details the crack-up of Longford, a white Englishman succumbing to the pressures of working on a West African rubber plantation. Upon his arrival, he vows to stay away from booze and the local women. Giving way to the desires of the flesh, but determined to stick to his code of ethics, he marries a seductive but shallow half-French native named Tondelayo. She grows tired of him and, after a year of their disastrous union, Longford goes insane and is shipped back to England. His fellows at the rubber plantation refer to him as so much "white cargo."

Two toned-down films were made from the play, in 1929 and 1942. Hedy Lamarr headlined in the second as the sexy Tondelayo.

THE SHOW-OFF

by George Kelly

Opened February 5, 1924

571 Performances

The Playhouse Theatre

Directed by George Kelly

Produced by Stewart and French, Inc.

Cast: Louis John Bartels (Aubrey Piper); Helen Lowell (Mrs. Fisher); Regina Wallace (Amy); Juliette Crosby (Clara); Guy D'Ennery (Frank Hyland); C.W. Goodrich (Mr. Fisher); Lee Tracey (Joe); Francis Pierlot (Mr. Gill); Joseph Clayton (Mr. Rogers).

You know the type: The braggart who guffaws at his own moronic gags and slaps you heartily on the back. George

Kelly immortalized this archetypal American blowhard with his domestic comedy *The Show-Off*. Subtitled "A Transcript of Life in Three Acts," the play concerns the intrusion of Aubrey Piper, the title character, into an ordinary middle-class Philadelphia family.

Aubrey is a $32-a-week railroad clerk with delusions of grandeur. While spouting clichés and chomping on cigars, he spins tales of his great future in the business world. One of the daughters of the family is in love with him and they marry. The rest of the clan can't stand him, especially the eminently practical mother. In an ironic twist, Aubrey does bring wealth to all his in-laws by the final curtain. The original script reportedly did not have this surprise ending, but allegedly, during out-of-town tryouts, the producer insisted that the twist be added in order to send audiences home with smiles on their faces.

It worked. Theatregoers laughed at the show-off's foolishness and loved the ending. Aubreys were becoming more prevalent in American culture, and Kelly's targeting of the type was warmly welcomed. The role was originated by Louis John Bartels, a vaudevillian comic. He became so closely identified with the part that he was virtually uncastable after the show closed.

The play was thought to be a shoe-in for the 1924 Pulitzer Prize; it went instead to an inferior drama on religious fanaticism, *Hell-Bent fer Heaven*. Kelly, like Bartels, began his career in the theatre as an actor and writer of sketches for vaudeville. His brother Walter was famous on the vaudeville circuit for his comic characterization of a corrupt Virginia judge. One of George's sketches "Poor Aubrey" formed the basis of *The Show-Off*.

The playwright's other hits during the decade included *The Torchbearers* (1922), a take-off on amateur theatricals, and the Pulitzer Prize-winning *Craig's Wife* (1925), a drama of a woman obsessed by social position and her immaculate house; this blistering character study later provided Joan Crawford with one of her bitchier screen roles. Many felt the Pulitzer for *Craig's Wife* was a consolation prize for the one Kelly should have gotten for *The Show-Off*.

The comedy has been revived and filmed a number of times. It reappeared on Broadway in 1932 with Raymond Walburn in the lead, and again in 1950 with Lee Tracey, a supporting player in the original cast, now playing Aubrey. Ellis Rabb's APA Theatre presented an acclaimed production in 1967 with Clayton Corzette in the title role, though Helen Hayes, a guest artist with the company, was the real star as his cantankerous mother-in-law. She took the production on tour the next season to bolster the sagging finances of the APA. The tour was a huge success, returning a profit of $250,000.

The Roundabout Theatre Company did the play twice. In 1978, this off-Broadway company did it in a small Chelsea venue, where Paul Rudd and Polly Rowles played the leads. In 1992, the company had moved to the Criterion Center in the theatre district, and *The Show-Off* was well-received, this time with Pat Carroll, Boyd Gaines, Sophie Hayden, and Laura Esterman.

There are three film versions. They starred Gregory Kelly (1926), Spencer Tracy (1934), and Red Skelton (1947).

ROSE-MARIE

Book and lyrics by Otto Harbach and Oscar Hammerstein II
Music by Rudolf Friml and Herbert Stothart
Opened September 2, 1924
557 Performances
The Imperial Theatre
Directed by Paul Dickey
Choreographed by David Bennett
Produced by Arthur Hammerstein

Cast: Mary Ellis (Rose-Marie LaFlamme); Dennis King (Jim Kenyon); Frank Greene (Edward Hawley); William Kent (Hard-Boiled Herman); Dorothy Mackaye (Lady Jane); Arthur Deagon (Sgt. Malone); Edward Ciancelli (Emile LaFlamme); Pearl Regay (Wanda); Arthur Ludwig (Black Eagle); Lela Bliss (Ethel Brander).

The familiar strains of "When I'm calling you-ooo-ooo" were first heard on Broadway before Nelson Eddy and Jeannette MacDonald preserved them on screen. "Indian Love Call" was one of many popular songs to come from *Rose-Marie*, an operetta set in the Canadian Rockies in which not only does boy get girl, but the Mounties get their man (in this case, woman).

This show also represents one of the earliest attempts to integrate songs into plot. Only five of the numbers were listed in the program because the authors felt that most of the score was interwoven into the story. Oscar Hammerstein II, co-author of the book and lyrics, would later be more successful in seamlessly combining songs and story with *Show Boat* and *Oklahoma!*

The show was produced by Hammerstein's uncle Arthur, who originally had the idea of setting a musical in Canada. He sent his nephew and Oscar's collaborator, Otto Harbach, to Quebec to see an ice carnival that could be used as a model for some of the numbers. The writers didn't care for the ice show, but they soaked up enough Northern atmosphere to invent a story with a Canadian backdrop. Rudolf Friml, Sigmund Romberg's main rival as King of the Operettas, composed the score in collaboration with Herbert Stothart. Friml was responsible for the bulk of the principal songs, while Stothart mostly concentrated on the comedy numbers.

In the story, the singer Rose-Marie LaFlamme is in love with Jim Kenyon, who is wrongfully accused of killing an Indian, Black Eagle. But the deed was done by Black Eagle's wife, Wanda, whom he had caught in a passionate clinch with the hissable villain Edward Hawley. Just as Rose-Marie is about to surrender her virtue to Hawley in order to save her man, the Mounties intervene. The real culprits are captured, and love triumphs. Comic interludes, a necessary element in any such musical, were provided by the trader Hard-Boiled Herman and Lady Jane.

Reviewers and audiences appreciated the show's operatic aspirations as a welcome contrast to the repetitious Cinderella shows and plotless revues of the time. Mary Ellis, who had sung with the Metropolitan Opera, garnered the most raves, as did the musical number "Totem Tom-Tom," in which the chorus girls were dressed as totem poles.

The show went on to record-breaking runs in London and Paris, four road companies (one of which played Broadway in 1927), and three movie adaptations.

A silent 1928 film of *Rose-Marie* necessarily deleted the songs, but starred Joan Crawford in the lead. As previously noted, Nelson Eddy and Jeanette MacDonald sang in the 1936 MGM movie, an adaptation in which the story was totally different from that of the stage version. Here Rose-Marie is an opera singer searching for her criminal brother, and she falls in love with a Mountie who is on the same trail. In the 1954 remake, the plot changed yet again, but the original story was followed more closely. The Mounties were still prominently featured. This time, Howard Keel played a Canadian man in uniform and he sets out to tame wildcat Ann Blyth. Bert Lahr, Fernando Lamas, and Marjorie Main were along for the ride.

THE STUDENT PRINCE

Book and lyrics by Dorothy Donnelly
Music by Sigmund Romberg
Opened December 2, 1924
608 Performances
The Jolson Theatre
Directed by J.C. Huffman
Choreographed by Max Scheck
Produced by the Shuberts

Cast: Howard Marsh (Prince Karl Franz); Ilse Marvenga (Kathie); Greek Evans (Dr. Engel); George Hassell (Lutz); Roberta Beatty (Princess Margaret); Fuller Mellish (Von Mark); W.H. White (Ruder); Violet Carlson (Gretchen); Adolph Link (Toni); Raymond Marlowe (Detlef); Frederic Wolff (Lucas); Paul Kleeman (Von Asterberg); Fred Wilson (Nicolas); Charles Williams (Hubert); Florence Morrison (Grand Duchess Anastasia); John Coast (Capt. Tarnitz); Dagmar Oakland (Countess Leyden); Robert Calley (Baron Arnheim); Frank Kneeland (1st Lackey); William Nettum (2nd Lackey); Lawrence Wells (3rd Lackey); Harry Anderson (4th Lackey); Martha Mason (Premier Dancer); Lucius Metz (Rudolph Winter); Elmer Pichler (Freshman); C. Sparin (Capt. of the Guard).

Three months after *Rose-Marie* opened, the Shuberts and Sigmund Romberg responded with an operetta that equalled the success of the Friml–Hammerstein–Harbach collaboration. *The Student Prince in Heidelberg,* as it was officially titled, had a run of 608 performances, surpassing *Rose-Marie*'s 557, and it toured continuously for almost twenty-five years. There was a very popular Broadway revival in 1943.

Based on the German play *Old Heidelberg* by Wilhelm Meyer-Forster, which had been produced in 1903 on Broadway with Richard Mansfield in the lead, the show was set in 1860 and concerned the romance of a prince and a charming waitress named Kathie. While studying at dear old Heidelberg University, Prince Karl Franz falls for Kathie despite his exalted station. Their affair is cut short when the old king dies and the lad must return to the palace to assume the throne. Once crowned, he is duty-bound to marry Princess Margaret. He returns to the university in a vain attempt to recapture his carefree youth, yet in a development unconventional for its day, the young king returns to his responsibilities and Kathie is left heartbroken.

Dennis King and Mary Ellis in *Rose Marie.*

The unhappy conclusion almost prevented *The Student Prince* from graduating from script to production. The Shuberts insisted the conclusion be changed to a happy one, but Romberg felt just as strongly that the lovers should be poignantly, and realistically, disappointed. It took the threat of legal action on the composer's part to get the producers to agree to his way of thinking.

Romberg collaborated with his *Blossom Time* wordsmith Dorothy Donnelly. Howard Marsh, who was Baron Schober in that show, played the title character. German actress Ilse Marvenga, who played Kathie, drew praise for her outstanding soprano. A 40-member male chorus sang such rousing, red-blooded numbers as the familiar "Drinking Song." Other enduring songs included "Golden Days," Serenade," "Just We Two," and "Deep in My Heart."

"Deep in My Heart" provided the title for a 1954 film biography of Romberg, which featured José Ferrer as the composer.

Like *Rose-Marie, The Student Prince* was in filmed in both silent and sound versions. The 1927 silent movie starred Ramon Navarro and Norma Shearer and was directed by Ernst Lubitsch. The 1954 sound remake had Ann Blyth (who had a busy year, for she also filmed *Rose-Marie*) and Edmund Prudom (for whom Mario Lanza provided the vocals) in the leads. A silent film based on the original straight play was filmed in 1919.

IS ZAT SO?

by James Gleason and Richard Tabor

Opened January 5, 1925

618 Performances

The 39th Street Theatre

No director credited

Produced by Earl Boothe

Cast: James Gleason (Hap Hurley); Robert Armstrong (Chick Cowan); Sydney Riggs (C. Clinton Blackburn); Marie Chambers (Susan Blackburn Parker); Victor Morley (The Major); Jo Wallace (Florence Hanley); John C. King (Robert Parker); Marjorie Crossland (Marie Mestretti,); Tom Brown (Master James Blackburn Parker); Eleanor Parker (Grace Hobart); Duncan Penwarden (Fred Hobart); Jack Perry (John Duffy); Carola Parsons (Angie Van Alsten); William London (Smith).

Actors James Gleason and Richard Tabor were suffering from a condition common in their profession: unemployment. There never seemed to be roles available, so they wrote *Is Zat So?*, a bare-knuckled comedy about a down-at-the-heels boxer and his scrappy manager.

The action begins with Chick Cowan, former contender for the light-heavyweight championship of the world and his manager, Hap Hurley, sitting on a park bench, indulging in a postmortem of their most recent fight, which Chick lost. Now they are broke. With a twist of fate that could occur only on the stage, an alcoholic rich man approaches them and, on learning their trade, sug-

gests they accompany him to his Fifth Avenue penthouse. He will hire them as butler and valet, but they will really be training all the booze out of their new employer.

In their palatial new digs, the rough-edged protagonists find romantic diversion with a nurse and secretary of the household, engage in a drawing-room boxing match for the pleasure of high society, and foil their boss's villainous brother-in-law. The play relied upon the tried-and-true formula of tough, but honest street types mixing with the upper crust and proving themselves to be just as good, if not better, than their well-mannered hosts. There were numerous gags about Chick and Hap murdering the English language, as indicated by the title.

Acting as their own producers, the authors tested the show in such unlikely summer-stock venues as Milwaukee and Worcester, Massachusetts, with Gleason playing Hap and Robert Armstrong as Chick. Their New England engagement bankrupted the playwrights, but the comedienne Fannie Brice, who had seen the show and liked it, gave them $5,000 to keep going. Producer Sam H. Harris expressed an interest and bought an option, but he thought the script needed extensive rewrites. Playwright Owen Davis offered his services, but demanded half the royalties for his efforts. Harris dropped his option, turning to another project.

Producer Earl Boothe and the Shuberts came to the rescue. They didn't think rewrites necessary and presented the play at the Shubert-owned 39th Street Theatre. The boxing community was heavily involved in the Broadway production. The drawing-room match was staged by prizefighter Benny Leonard, who also trained Armstrong. Chick's opponent in the match was played by an actual contendor for the welterweight title, Jack Perry. A dressing room at the theatre was converted into a gymnasium, complete with punching bag. Opening night was attended by a retinue of famous names from the boxing world, including "Gentleman" Jim Corbett. In the spirit of the show, Armstrong challenged critic Frank Vreeland, of the *Telegram-Mail*, to a fight, once the latter's review had appeared in print. Vreeland's reply: "I can't understand it. I'm sure I gave Mr. Armstrong a good notice."

Opening on the same night as the Ruth Gordon vehicle *Mrs. Partridge Presents, Is Zat So?* proved a popular hit that the critics discovered after the audiences. Alexander Woollcott of the *Sun* called it "homely, original, and unpretentious." The producers soon moved it to the larger 46th Street Theatre to accommodate the demand for tickets. A second company then opened in Detroit with co-author Tabor as the fighter. Eventually there were six companies of the comedy, including one in London.

James Gleason, who drew the best notices as Hap, had another success the same season when his play *The Fall*

Guy (co-written with George Abbott) opened in March. Gleason eventually left the theatre and became one of Hollywood's most reliable character actors.

THE VAGABOND KING

Book by Brian Hooker, Russell Janney, and W.H. Post

Music by Rudolf Friml

Lyrics by Brian Hooker

Choreographed by Julian Alfred

Opened September 21, 1925

511 Performances

The Casino Theatre

Directed by Max Figman

Produced by Russell Janney

Cast: Dennis King (François Villon); Carolyn Thomson (Katherine de Vaucelles); Max Figman (Louis XIth); Herbert Corthell (Guy Tabarie); Robert Craik (René de Montigny); Leon Cunningham (Casin Cholet/Astrologer); Catherine Hayes (Margot); Merle Stevens (Blanche); Vivian Kelley (Isabeau); Marius Rogati (Jehan De Loup); Joseph Miller (Trois Echelles); Jane Carroll (Huguette Du Hamel); Mimi Hayes (Jehanneton); H.H. McCullum (Tristan L'Hermite); Bryan Lycan (Thibaut D'Aussigny); Charles Carver (Capt. of Scotch Archers); Olga Treskoff (Lady Mary); Herbert Delmore (Noel Le Jolys); Julian Winter (Oliver Le Dain); Marian Alta (1st Court Lady); Ann Auston (2nd Court Lady); Earl Waldo (Toison D'Or); Tamm Cortez (Queen); Helen Grenelle (Dancer); G.L. Mortimer (Bishop); William Johnson (Hangman); Walter Cross (1st Courtier); John Mealey (2nd Courtier).

In the decade of the operettas, Rudolf Friml followed his *Rose-Marie* with *The Vagabond King*, an adaptation of E.H. Sothern's *If I Were King*, which played on Broadway in 1901. Producer Russell Janney had intended to mount a musical version of the play using a fresh, young team of songwriters, Richard Rodgers and Lorenz Hart, who had already done a song-and-dance version for an amateur production at the Benjamin School for Girls. Future lyricist Dorothy Fields played the lead wearing a beard. But Janney was unable to get enough investments from backers; they considered Rodgers and Hart too green. He hired the more experienced Friml and Brian Hooker.

The plot is sort of a *Student Prince* in reverse. Instead of a sovereign finding love among the common folk, *The Vagabond King* is an ordinary citizen made royal who woos a noble lady. King Louis XI of France decides to make poet-vagabond François Villon king for a day. In return for this boon, Villon must court the disdainful Katherine de Vaucelles and help the real king against the traitorous Duke of Burgundy. If he fails, he will be executed.

Between meetings with Katherine, Villon raises a vagabond army that defeats Burgundy and his followers. Dennis King, fresh from *Rose-Marie*, was the embodiment of derring-do as Villon; he left matinee girls swooning and critics applauding. Friml's score included "Only a Rose," the virile "Song of the Vagabonds," and "Love Me Tonight" (not to be confused with the later Rodgers and Hart number).

Friml and Dennis King offered more dashing French heroics in 1928 with *The Three Musketeers*, a musicalization of the classic Dumas novel. A lavish spectacle produced by Ziegfeld, with King in the lead as D'artagnan, that show ran 318 performances.

Two film versions of *The Vagabond King* were made. The first was one of the earliest talkies, with Dennis King repeating his stage role and Jeanette MacDonald as his leading lady. The second was released in 1956, with the single-named Oreste and Kathryn Grayson toplining, and Rita Moreno and Cedric Hardwicke in support. The same story without music came to the screen in 1928 and 1938.

SUNNY

Book and lyrics by Otto Harbach and Oscar Hammerstein II

Music by Jerome Kern

Opened September 22, 1925

517 Performances

The New Amsterdam Theatre

Directed by Hassard Short, John Tiller, and Fred Astaire

Choreographed by Julian Mitchell, David Bennett, and Alexis Kosloff

Produced by Charles Dillingham

Cast: Marilyn Miller (Sunny Peters); Jack Donahue (Jim Deming); Clifton Webb (Harold Harcourt Wendell-Wendell); Paul Frawley (Tom Warren); Mary Hay (Weenie Winters); Joseph Cawthorn (Siegfried Peters); Cliff Edwards (Sam); Pert Kelton (Magnolia); Esther Howard (Sue Warren); Dorothy Francis (Marcia Manners); Helene Gardner (Mlle. Sadie); Charles Angelo (Bally Hoo); William Ladd (Bob Hunter); Jackie Hurlburt (Jane Cobb); Louis Harrison (Quartermaster); Elmer Brown (1st Ship's Officer); Abner Barnhart (2nd Ship's Officer); James Wilson (Ship's Captain); Jeanne Fonda (Diana Miles); Joan Clement (Millicent Smythe); Don Rowen (Groom); George Olsen Orchestra.

Marilyn Miller returned to Broadway after her triumph in *Sally* to play *Sunny*, a similarly high-spirited girl who gives voice to Jerome Kern's songs. This time she did it without Ziegfeld, who sponsored her earlier hit. The star had married against her mentor's wishes once (see entry on *Sally*). After her first husband's death, Miller married again—this time to Jack Pickford, who had previously stolen another dancer from Ziegfeld. Miller added insult to injury by defecting to Ziegfeld's closest rival on Broadway, Charles Dillingham. For the story, which was merely an excuse to showcase Miller's singing and dancing abilities, Otto Harbach and Oscar Hammerstein came up with the character of Sunny Peters, a circus bareback rider who is performing in England. There Sunny meets and falls in love with Tom Warren, an American tourist. In order to marry Tom, Sunny stows away aboard the ship returning him to the United States. But through a series of complications, Sunny marries Tom's best friend Jim. Yet, in the end, she and Jim amicably divorce and the heroine and the man of her dreams, Tom, are wed.

The loose plot also provided an opportunity for the supporting ensemble to show off its special talents: Dancing comic Jack Donahue, the urbane Clifton Webb, Cliff "Ukulele Ike" Edwards, George Olsen's band, which would later appear in *Good News,* and Pert Kelton, who later played the leading lady's mother in *The Music Man* (and was the very first Alice Kramden opposite Jackie Gleason's Ralph on *The Honeymooners*).

Miller equalled her success in *Sally* with this new show. The hit song was "Who?" which, along with "D'ye Love Me?" and the title song, had audiences humming on the way home. For her two next vehicles, Miller returned to Ziegfeld. She and Jack Donahue were reunited for *Rosalie* (1928), a lighter-than-air romance between a princess and an aviator with songs by the Gershwins and Sigmund Romberg. Ziegfeld followed this up with *Smiles* (1930) in which Miller danced along with the brother-and-sister team of Fred and Adele Astaire. For her final Broadway outing, Miller headlined *As Thousands Cheer* (1933), a revue by Irving Berlin and Moss Hart that satirized newspapers. Clifton Webb, Ethel Waters, and Helen Broderick co-starred.

The film version of *Sunny* was one of Miller's three Hollywood musicals. It was released in 1930. Anna Neagle appeared in the remake in 1940. Miller, who fell ill and died at age 38, was the subject of a 1949 movie musical called "Look for the Silver Lining," named for her signature song from *Sally*. June Haver played her in that film biography, and Judy Garland portrayed Miller in *Till the Clouds Roll By*, a movie of Jerome Kern's life story.

BROADWAY

by Philip Dunning and George Abbott

Opened September 16, 1926

603 Performances

The Broadhurst Theatre

Directed by George Abbott

Produced by Jed Harris

Cast: Lee Tracey (Roy Lane); Sylvia Field (Billie Moore); Robert Gleckler (Steve Crandell); John Wray ("Scar" Edwards); Paul Porcasi (Nick Verdis); Clare Woodbury (Lil Rice); Ann Preston (Katie); Joseph Spurin-Calleia (Joe); Mildred Wall (Mazie Smith); Edith Van Cleve (Ruby); Eloise Stream (Pearl); Molly Ricardel (Grace); Constance Brown (Ann); Henry Sherwood (Dolph); William Foran ("Porky" Thompson); Thomas Jackson (Dan McCorn); Frank Verigun (Benny); Millard Mitchell (Larry); Roy R. Lloyd (Mike).

The gangster films of the '30s can trace their ancestry to a honky-tonk stage melodrama of the '20s named after the street of its setting, *Broadway*. The play contained all the elements movie fans would later cry for in the machine-gun shoot-em-ups starring Humphrey Bogart, Edward G. Robinson, and James Cagney.

Rival bootlegging gangs battle over turf in this show, as chorus girls kick and turn. Hard-boiled dames, bathtub gin, and whizzing bullets were part of the vocabulary. In addition to the rivalry between gangsters, the main plot

dealt with the romantic face-off between hoofer Roy Lane and mobster Steve Crandell for chorine Billie Moore.

The original script, under the title *Bright Lights*, was by Philip Dunning, a former dancer with playwriting ambitions. His real surname was Dunn. He added the "ing" to distinguish himself from his brother Caesar, another dramatist. The producer Jed Harris saw potential in the play, but felt it needed polishing. To do the rewriting, he

Sylvia Field and Lee Tracey grab a moment backstage in *Broadway*.

hired George Abbott, who had collaborated with authors of two previous hits, *The Fall Guy* (1925) and *Love 'Em and Leave 'Em* (1926).

Abbott added plot and speed to Dunning's script and staged it in the rapid-fire style that became a hallmark of his many later productions. Dunning later estimated that there were over 300 entrances and exits during the course of the play, and that no single scene lasted longer than four minutes.

The one hitch in the smooth running of the rehearsals and out-of-town try-out was the casting of the girlfriend of Harris's partner Crosby Gaige. She couldn't act, Abbott reported in his memoirs, but he managed to wring a performance out of her by the time the show opened in Atlantic City.

In New York, Dunning himself had found employment as the stage manager of the hit musical *Sunny*. On opening night, he sneaked away from that show and into *Broadway* to hear the first-nighters' cheers. A long run was guaranteed. Eventually, ten companies were sent out to perform the show, six in the United States and four abroad.

Harris was initially worried that the play was too American to travel. The jazzy slang might be indecipherable to foreign audiences. There was also the matter of the Lord Chamberlain, the official censor of the London stage who was expected to demand changes in the sometimes vulgar patter. But apart from the replacement of a few "God"s with "Gee"s, there were few alterations, and English audiences loved the Yankee jargon.

Abbott's career on Broadway skyrocketed with *Broadway*. As director/producer/playwright, he seemed almost incapable of turning out flops, as evidenced by the number of times his name comes up in the following pages. Throughout the '30s, he specialized in slam-bang farce, then in the '40s, '50s, and '60s, he moved on to musicals, doing an occasional comedy for good measure.

The story was filmed twice by Universal—first in 1929, as one of the earliest talking pictures, then again in 1942. The latter version with movie tough guy George Raft was adapted to mesh with the star's real-life background as a dancer.

A 1978 revival of the show, directed by Robert Allen Ackerman and presented at the Berkshire Theatre Festival, was slated for a Broadway run. William Atherton, Chris Sarandon, and Gilda Radner enacted the three principals. Teri Garr replaced Radner for the production's pre-Broadway Boston tryout, where it closed before reaching New York.

Another production, this one at the Great Lakes Theatre Festival, did transfer to Broadway in 1987. It was again directed by Abbott—at the age of 100, amazingly—but this revival folded in less than a week.

THE LADDER

by J. Frank Davis

Opened October 22, 1926

789 Performances

The Mansfield Theatre

Directed and produced by Brock Pemberton

Cast: Antoinette Perry (Margaret Newell); Vernon Steele (Roger Crane); Hugh Buckler (Stephen Pennock); Irene Purcell (Betty Pennock); Ross Alexander (William Matteson); Edward J. McNamara (Wat of Hampshire); Edgar Stehli (Bellwood); Minnie Milne (Lady Mortimer, etc.); Julius McVicker (Sir John Mortimer, etc.); Carl Anthony (Sir Henry Maule, etc.); Anita Damrosch (Mistress Ellen, etc.); Sallie Sanford (Mistress Judith, etc.); Montague Rutherfurd (Abbot of Winfield, etc.); Leonard Carey (Ensign Marshall); George Carmichael (Brooks).

The Ladder, an unremembered but long-running play, examined the subject of reincarnation for two seasons after it opened in 1926. Strangely enough, the show was plainly a failure.

The Ladder began its ascent to Broadway when millionaire Edgar B. Davis commissioned an author named J. Frank Davis (no relation) to write a play on a subject that fascinated the wealthy man—reincarnation. The financier had made a fortune in South American rubber and Texas oil and now wanted to use his wealth to spread his personal philosophy of the destiny of the human soul.

The playwright Davis derived his title from a poem by Josiah Gilbert Holland: "Heaven is not reached at a single bound,/But we build the ladder by which we rise/From the lowly earth to the vaulted skies,/And we mount to its summit round by round."

The play is set in 1926 in New York. Margaret Newell is in conflict over which of her two beaus to chose. Stephen Pennock is a prosperous but ruthless businessman, while Roger Crane is a noble but somewhat ineffectual artist. One evening after the three have discussed the theory of reincarnation, Margaret stares at an ancient tapestry in Stephen's living room. She wonders what the people were like at the time it was woven. After falling asleep, Margaret imagines herself and her two competing lovers in three different previous lives. They make the same mistakes in medieval Britain, Restoration London, and colonial New York. She awakens in the 20th century and takes Roger's hand, knowing from her metaphysical time trip that he is the right one.

The millionaire Davis contacted a friend, producer-director Brock Pemberton, and persuaded him to mount the play on Broadway. Davis would foot all the bills. Pemberton assembled an admirable cast headed by Antoinette Perry, one of the best-regarded actresses of the '20s. Elaborate scenery and costumes evoked the four time periods. The reviewers praised the acting and the décor, but blasted the play itself. Alexander Woollcott of the *New York World* responded by pronouncing it "a large, richly upholstered piece of nothing at all."

Curiosity about the mystical subject drew audiences for a while, but they eventually began to fall off. This did not prevent Davis from pursuing his self-appointed mission of reaching the public with his message. Free performances were given on Christmas Day. Ads featuring testimonials from clergymen were placed in the dailies. But audiences stayed away.

Davis insisted on continuing the run. Pemberton did not want to appear to be taking the millionaire for a ride by drawing a salary from a show that was losing money, so he resigned. *The Ladder* went on racking up performances before half-empty houses. Davis paid the theatre's rent and the actors' salaries and realized no profit—he was losing $10,000 a week. In 1927, after Thanksgiving, the play was made a free show. Even with a nonexistent admission price, the cast frequently outnumbered the audience. Despite several rewrites and shifts to other theatres, *The Ladder* never caught on. Davis had lost almost a million and a half dollars by the end of the run.

Pemberton and Perry recovered from the disaster and worked together as producer and director on such plays as *Personal Appearance, Harvey,* and *Janie.*

GOOD NEWS

Book by Laurence Schwab and B. G. De Sylva

Music by Ray Henderson

Lyrics by B.G. De Sylva and Lew Brown

Choreographed by Bobby Connelly

Opened September 6, 1927

551 Performances

The 46th Street Theatre

Directed by Edgar MacGregor

Produced by Laurence Schwab and Frank Mandel

Cast: Mary Lawlor (Constance Lane); John Price Jones (Tom Marlowe); Gus Shy (Bobby Randall); Inez Courtney (Babe O'Day); John Grant ("Beef" Saunders); Zelma O'Neal (Flo); Edwin Redding (Bill Johnson); John Sheehan ("Pooch" Kearney); Edward Emery (Charles Kenyon); Shirley Vernon (Patricia Bingham); Don Tomkins (Sylvester); Wally Coyle (Windy); Jack Kennedy (Slats); Ruth Mayon (Millie); The George Olsen Orchestra; Bob Rice, Fran Frey, Bob Borger (Glee Club Trio).

Good News is the prototypical college musical in which the most important question is whether the star quarterback will pass his final exam so he can play in the big game. Football hero Tom Marlowe is failing in astronomy. Campus brain Connie Lane agrees to tutor the athlete. Despite Connie's initial resistance, romance develops. The ballad "The Best Things in Life Are Free" and the zingy dance number "The Varsity Drag" were among the musical highlights. Another was the entrance of the George Olsen Orchestra through the audience at the top of the show. Dressed in collegiate letter sweaters, they led the patrons in various rah-rah cheers before starting up the overture.

Composer Ray Henderson and librettists B.G. De Sylva and Lew Brown had collaborated on several of producer George White's "Scandals" shows, the main rivals to the Ziegfeld "Follies." *Good News* was their first in a series of successful book musicals. None of the later ones played over 500 performances, but all had respectable showings at the box office. These included *Manhattan Mary* (1927), a vehicle for Ed Wynn; *Hold Everything* (1928) with Bert Lahr stealing the show as a punch-drunk boxer; *Follow Through* (1929), a country-club romp that featured the perennial song "Button Up Your Overcoat"; and *Flying High* (1930) with Bert Lahr now starring opposite Kate Smith. De Sylva then left for Hollywood. Brown and Henderson carried on with *Hot Cha!* (1932), this time putting Lahr on a bill with Mexican spitfire Lupe Velez. *Strike Me Pink* appeared in 1933.

Peter Lawford and June Allyson starred in the 1947 MGM movie, which featured new material by Betty Comden and Adolph Green. Tom's weak subject was changed from astronomy to French. Comden and Green wrote a charming new novelty number called "The French Lesson," tailored for Lawford's limited vocal range.

In the midst of the nostalgia craze of the '70s, a revised edition of the show opened on Broadway. Old-timers Gene Nelson and Alice Faye were featured, and this revival included several songs by De Sylva, Brown, and Henderson not in the original show. It ran for two weeks in September 1974.

Other shows in the college (or prep-school) genre include *Leave It to Jane* (1917), *Too Many Girls* (1939), and *Best Foot Forward* (1941). Later musicals mainly inspired by trends among the young were *Bye, Bye, Birdie* (1960) and *Hair* (1968).

SHOW BOAT

Book and lyrics by Oscar Hammerstein II

Music by Jerome Kern

Opened December 27, 1927

572 Performances

The Ziegfeld Theatre

Directed by Florenz Ziegfeld, Sammy Lee, and Zeke Colvan (Oscar Hammerstein II, uncredited)

Choreographed by Sammy Lee

Produced by Florenz Ziegfeld

Cast: Norma Terris (Magnolia Hawks/Kim Ravenal); Howard Marsh (Gaylord Ravenal); Helen Morgan (Julie La Verne); Charles Ellis (Steve Barker); Charles Winninger (Cap'n Andy); Edna May Oliver (Parthy Ann Hawks); Eva Puck (Ellie); Sammy White (Frank); Jules Bledsoe (Joe); Tess Gardella (Queenie); Thomas Gunn (Vallon); Allan Campbell (Windy); Francis X. Mahoney (Rubber Face); Bert Chapman (Pete); Jack Wynn (Jeb/Faro Dealer); Phil Sheridan (Gambler); Jack Daley (Backwoodsman/Jim); Dorothy Denese (La Belle Fatima); Estelle Floyd (Ethel); Annie Hart (Landlady); Annette Harding (Sister); Mildred Schwenke (Mother Superior); Eleanor Shaw (Kim as a child); Robert Farley (Jake); Ted Daniels (Man with Guitar); J. Lewis Johnson (Charlie); Tana Kamp (Lottie); Dagmar Oakland (Dolly); Maurine Holmes (Hazel); Laura Clairon (Old Lady).

Many students of the musical theatre credit Rodgers and Hammerstein's *Oklahoma!* (1943) with starting the trend for musicals in which the songs were expressions of character and story, rather than specialty numbers allowing stars to show off their individual talents. Though *Oklahoma!* went further with its integration of dance into the story and elimination of overelaborate scenery and chorus lines, it was *Show Boat,* produced sixteen years earlier, that first blazed more artistic trails.

The authors and producer of *Show Boat* had previously fed the public's appetite for light entertainment. Oscar Hammerstein had specialized in librettos for love-conquers-all operettas. Jerome Kern supplied the music for charming, fluffy capers. Florenz Ziegfeld had dazzled audiences with opulence but seldom challenged them. With *Show Boat,* they decided to try something different: a musical play dealing with adult themes such as miscegenation and unhappy marriage.

Based on Edna Ferber's novel of life on a riverboat that is also a traveling music hall, the show spans forty years. The story focuses mainly on Magnolia Hawks, daughter of Cap'n Andy and Parthy Ann, owners of the paddlewheel-driven *Cotton Blossom.* Magnolia's marriage to the gambler Gaylord Ravenal is a troubled one. There are subplots involving the mulatto singer Julie, who descends into alcoholism and loses her husband, and Joe, who gives voice to the anguish of black stevedores in the song "Ole Man River."

Through Magnolia's travails, we see a history of show business from the boat itself to turn-of-the-century nightclubs and Broadway and even Hollywood in the '20s. Occasionally, the musical numbers are pure diversions, but most deepen the characterizations. The duet "Make Believe" is not only Magnolia and Gaylord's declaration of first love, but also foreshadowing of the gambler's reckless, fantasy-based life-style. Julie's song "Bill," which was interpolated from another Kern show and has lyrics by P.G. Wodehouse, is a pained cry for her lost love.

In the show's tryout in Washington, D.C., the running time was over four hours. The authors judiciously cut the show down during runs in Cleveland and Philadelphia. In order to open *Show Boat* at the theatre named for him, Ziegfeld moved his well-received *Rio Rita* to the Lyric Theatre. When the *Cotton Blossom* glided onto the stage two days after Christmas 1927, the critics outdid themselves in superlatives. The public kept it running for 571 performances. Ziegfeld even talked about opening a second company in another theatre. This plan never came to fruition, but the touring and London versions were mounted with a success equal to that of the original.

No musical has been reproduced so often or with as many changes as *Show Boat.* There has (by now) been a total of four New York revivals. The first was presented in 1932 by Ziegfeld with most of the original cast; Dennis King came in as Gaylord and Paul Robeson as Joe. A 1946 version was produced by Hammerstein and Kern, with backing from MGM. A new song, "Nobody Else but Me," was added, while three others were dropped. Jan Clayton, Carol Bruce, Charles Fredericks, Buddy Ebsen, Pearl Primus, and Talley Beatty (the last two later became forces in the world of dance) starred.

The Music Theatre of Lincoln Center mounted the 1966 version. "Can't Help Lovin' Dat Man" and "Ole Man River" were rewritten to remove any offensive racial phrasing. David Wayne, Barbara Cook, Stephen Douglass, Constance Towers, William Warfield, Allyn Ann McLerie, Margaret Hamilton, and Rosetta LeNoire were the new stars. A production from the Houston Grand Opera was transferred to Broadway in 1983 with Donald O'Connor, Lonette McKee, Sheryl Woods, Ron Raines, Bruce Hubbard, and Karla Burns.

In addition, there was a major London revival in 1971 starring Cleo Laine, as well as another in 1990; a 1988 production at the Paper Mill Playhouse in New Jersey, later broadcast on PBS, featured material cut from the original Broadway production; and a major studio recording of the score in 1988 also restored the cut songs and was cast from the worlds of opera and musical comedy. Harold Prince staged a Toronto revival in 1993, starring Elaine Stritch and Robert Morse. It was slated for a 1994 Broadway opening.

Show Boat was filmed three times, with a different storyline in each instance. The 1929 Universal movie was a partial talkie with Joseph Schildkraut, Laura La Plante, and Alma Reubens. Universal tried again in 1936 with what many regard as the best of the three. It starred Charles Winninger and Helen Morgan from the original cast, Irene Dunne and Paul Robeson from the national and London companies, and Allan Jones, Helen Wesley, and Hattie MacDaniel. MGM filmed a "sanitized" third version in Technicolor in 1951. Kathryn Grayson, Howard Keel, Ava Gardner, Joe E. Brown, William Warfield, Agnes Moorehead, and Marge and Gower Champion were the stars of this version.

BLACKBIRDS OF 1928

Music by Jimmy McHugh
Lyrics by Dorothy Fields
Opened May 9, 1928
518 Performances
The Liberty Theatre
Produced and directed by Lew Leslie

Cast: Adelaide Hall, Bill Robinson, Aida Ward, Tim Moore, Ruth Johnson, Crawford Jackson, Marjorie Hubbard, Blue McAllister, Eloise Uggams, Lloyd Mitchell, Billie Cortez, George Cooper, Mamie Savoy, Mantan Moreland, Elizabeth Welch, Harry Lucas, Baby Banks, Willard McLean, Philip Patterson, Earl Tucker.

Black musicals re-emerged on Broadway after a two-year absence with *Blackbirds of 1928*. During the early '20s, *Shuffle Along* inspired numerous imitations, but the craze for shows featuring African-American performers faded within a few years. But black shows began appearing in other locales. Harlem nightclubs with well-staged floor shows became the favorite haunts of white sophisticates, so much so that many clubs began discouraging black patrons in favor of their wealthier white counterparts.

Blackbirds began in this Harlem milieu. Lew Leslie, a white producer of previous black shows in London and New York, had presented an earlier version of the show at the Alhambra Theatre at West 126th Street in 1926. Florence Mills, who had headlined in Leslie's London revue *From Dover to Dixie* and in its Broadway cousin *Dixie to Broadway*, became the toast of two continents, and Leslie starred her in the Harlem production. After the engagement there, *Blackbirds* toured Europe. (Also, Leslie produced a companion show in London called *Whitebirds* in 1927.) Continental audiences loved the show as an example of authentic Americana and re-established Mills as an exotic star. No recordings exist of her voice but, reportedly, her sexy renditions of ballads, combined with an incomparable technique, hypnotized theatregoers.

The plan was to bring *Blackbirds* to Broadway, but Mills died at the age of 32 before rehearsals could begin. Leslie held extensive auditions to find the right talent to replace his star. He came up with Adelaide Hall, Aida Ward, Elizabeth Welch, and Eloise Uggams (the mother of Leslie Uggams). Tap dancer Bill "Bojangles" Robinson joined the show in try-out, and though he had only one number ("Doin' the New Low-Down") and it came late in the second act, Robinson received the most glowing notices. He went on to tap in other Broadway shows and in movies and is best remembered for dancing opposite Shirley Temple in a number of her pictures.

The biggest hit of the show was "I Can't Give You Anything but Love," which is still sung in piano bars today. Gossip columnists planted items about the song's origin, stating that Fields and McHugh were on Fifth Avenue watching a young couple in front of a jewelry store. The boy told his girlfriend he'd like to give her diamonds, but he couldn't give her anything but love. According to Allen Woll's book *Black Musical Theater: From "Coontown" to "Dreamgirls,"* the song was used in a previous show called *Delmar's Revels* as a paean to aviator Charles Lindbergh called "I Can't Give You Anything but Love, Lindy."

Mills, the intended star of the show, was memorialized in the number, "A Memory of 1927." Aida Ward sang the song in male attire (one of Mills's trademarks) and then launched into "Mandy, Make Up Your Mind," one of Mills's hits from *Dixie to Broadway*. Other *Blackbirds* songs which

became popular included "Dig-a Dig-a Do" and "I Must Have That Man."

The show also contained a condensation of *Porgy*, DuBose and Dorothy Heyward's straight drama of life in Catfish Row, which was also playing on Broadway. Seven years later, George and Ira Gershwin adapted the play along with DuBose Heyward as *Porgy and Bess*, perhaps the most popular opera written in America.

The one element that critics found wanting was the show's comedy, consisting of worn-out routines about cheating at poker, stealing chickens, and acting scared in a graveyard. It was still common for African-American performers to appear in blackface, too, and they did so here. Such racial stereotypes, unthinkable on the Broadway of the '90s, persisted even when they were hackneyed.

Later *Blackbird* editions were seen in 1930 (with Ethel Waters), 1933 (with Bill Robinson), and 1939 (with Lena Horne).

THE NEW MOON

Book and lyrics by Oscar Hammerstein II and Frank Mandel
Music by Sigmund Romberg and Laurence Schwab
Opened September 19, 1928
509 Performances
The Imperial Theatre
Directed by Edgar MacGregor (uncredited)
Choreographed by Bobby Connelly
Produced by Laurence Schwab and Frank Mandel

Cast: Lvelyn Herbert (Marianne); Robert Halliday (Robert Mission); Gus Shy (Alexander); Max Figman (Vicomte Ribaud); William O'Neal (Phillippe); Marie Callahan (Julie); Pacie Ripple (Monsieur Beaunoir); Edward Nell, Jr. (Capt. Paul Duval); Lyle Evans (Besac); Earle Mitchell (Jacques); Esther Howard (Clotilde Lombaste); Thomas Dale (Fouchette); Lester Dorr (Capt. Dejean); Daniel Barnes (Proprietor of the Taverns); Olga Albani (Flower Girl); Herman Belmonte (A Spaniard); Edith Sheldon (Dancer); Rosita and Ramon (The Dancers); Hernandez Brothers Trio (The Musicians).

Oscar Hammerstein II and Sigmund Romberg joined forces to create *The New Moon*, viewed by many as the best operetta of the decade. After contributing to two rival musicals during the 1924–25 season (Romberg to *The Student Prince*; Hammerstein to *Rose-Marie*), the two united to write *The Desert Song* (1926) which ran 471 performances, just under the 500-mark.

Hopes were high for their second effort together, but during its Philadelphia tryout period *The New Moon* was in danger of a total eclipse. Both Romberg and Hammerstein were at work on other projects simultaneous with the operetta. Romberg was composing the music for *Rosalie*, Ziegfeld's latest vehicle for Marilyn Miller, while Hammerstein was laboring on the book and lyrics of another Ziegfeld production, *Show Boat*. The New Moon suffered, and reviews from the Philly critics were alarmingly bad.

George Gershwin was called in to help out with *Rosalie,* and *The New Moon* closed down for extensive repairs.

The book and score were totally rewritten, and a new cast was hired. When the new *New Moon* opened at the Imperial a year later, it was a hit.

The story takes place in 1788, in the romantically French colony of New Orleans—even though New Orleans was in fact a Spanish property at that time. The leading man, Robert Mission (based on a historical figure), is a nobleman fleeing France on a charge of murder. He escapes to the Louisiana port disguised as a bondsman to M. Beaunoir and falls in love with Marianne, Beaunoir's daughter. Just as the lovers have declared their passion in the duet "Wanting You," Robert is arrested and deported on the ship *The New Moon.*

But Marianne has contrived to be abroad. During the voyage back to France, Robert and the crew mutiny and establish a mini-democracy on a West Indian isle. The French Revolution conveniently frees Robert from his murder rap. He and Marianne are wed, and the island becomes a French republic.

The score included such standards as "Softly, as in a Morning Sunrise," "Lover, Come Back to Me," and "Stout-Hearted Men," another rousing all-male choral number on the order of "The Drinking Song" in *The Student Prince.*

As with many of the operettas of the period, there was more than one film version. Opera stars Lawrence Tibbett and Grace Moore appeared in the 1930 filming, while Jeannette MacDonald and Nelson Eddy harmonized in the second screen adaptation ten years later.

As the American musical theatre evolved, adapting the rhythms of popular music and relying on more realistic storylines, the appeal of the more Old World–style operettas faded. Romberg's efforts during the '30s were mostly unsuccessful, except for his *May Wine* of 1935. There was a brief revival of interest in the form during the '40s, during which the composer had his final triumph, *Up in Central Park* (1945).

STREET SCENE

by Elmer Rice

Opened January 10, 1929

601 Performances

The Playhouse Theatre

Directed by Elmer Rice

Produced by William A. Brady, Ltd.

Cast: Erin O'Brien-Moore (Rose Maurrant); Mary Servoss (Anna Maurrant); Horace Brahan (Samuel Kaplan); Robert Kelly (Frank Maurrant); Beulah Bondi (Emma Jones); Leo Bulgakov (Abraham Kaplan); Eleanor Wesselhoeft (Greta Fiorentino); Hilda Bruce (Olga Olsen); Russell Griffin (Willie Maurrant); Conway Washburne (Daniel Buchanan); T.H. Manning (George Jones); Joseph Baird (Steve Sankey); Jane Corcoran (Agnes Cushing); John M. Qualen (Carl Olsen); Anna Kostant (Shirley Kaplan); George Humbert (Filippo Fiorentino); Emily Hamill (Alice Simpson); Frederica Going (Laura Hildebrand); Eileen Smith (Mary Hildebrand); Alexander Lewis (Charlie Hildebrand); Glenn Coulter (Harry Easter); Millicent Green (Mae Jones); Joseph Lee (Dick McGann); Matthew McHugh (Vincent Jones); John Crump (Dr. John Wilson); Edward Downes (Ofc. Harry Murphy); Ellsworth Jones (Marshall James Henry); Jean Sideny (Fred Cullen); Ralph Willard (Milkman); Herbert Lindholm (Letter Carrier); Samuel S. Bonnell (Iceman/Intern); Rose Lerner (College Girl); Astrid Alwyn (College Girl/Nursemaid); Mary Emerson (Music Student); Joe Cogert (Old Clothes Man); Anthony Pawley (Ambulance Driver/Policeman); Ed. A. McHugh (Furniture Mover); Nelly Neil (Nursemaid); Carl C. Milter, John Kelly (Policemen); Frances F. Golden, Otto Frederick (Apartment Hunters).

Hard-edged realism invaded the lighthearted world of Broadway with Elmer Rice's Pulitzer Prize–winning drama, *Street Scene.* The entire play takes place on the street in front of a shabby walk-up apartment house in "a mean quarter of New York." The main story deals with the Maurrant family. Anna takes refuge from her cruel husband Frank by indulging in a back-street affair with Steve Sankey, the milk collector. Daughter Rose is torn between the attentions of her lecherous boss Mr. Easter and Samuel Kaplan, an intense young man who also lives in the building.

The action takes a violent turn when Frank discovers his wife in the arms of Sankey and kills the lovers. After the murderer is captured, Rose decides she must take her little brother and leave the squalid atmosphere of the city. Sam pleads with her to stay with him. He loves her and they belong together, he says. Rose replies "People should belong to themselves." She reasons that if her parents had truly belonged to themselves, the killings would never have happened. As she leaves, a new couple comes to look at the vacated apartment, and Mrs. Jones, the meddling gossip and Greek chorus of the play, continues her sharp-tongued commentary as the curtain falls.

Throughout the three acts, neighbors, passersby, nursemaids, children, workmen, and other denizens of the neighborhood walk up and down the street. This naturalistic panorama of tenement dwellers was something of a departure for Rice. His first play, *On Trial* (1914), was remarkable for its nonlinear structure: many of the scenes took place out of time-sequence, and the playwright made the first use of the flashback in an American play. In 1923, the most famous Rice work, *The Adding Machine,* an expressionistic fantasy, protested the inhumanities of modern industrial society.

Upon returning from a long sojourn in Europe, Rice was overwhelmed by the vibrancy and variety of life in New York. He decided to move away from experiments with structure and fantasy to realistically capture the flavor of the city. The finished play was turned down by almost every producer in town. The Theatre Guild, which had presented *The Adding Machine,* declared that the new Rice script had "no content." Others called it unreadable and incomprehensible. One producer opened the manuscript, counted the number of characters (over fifty) and rejected it right there. It was finally accepted by William A. Brady, an old showman who had not had a hit in twelve years.

Finding a director was just as difficult as acquiring a producer. George Cukor was the original choice, but he worked on the project for only four days. Rouben Mamoulian was asked to take over, but he never showed up at the theatre. With no one else to turn to, Rice assumed the director's position himself and received accolades from the reviewers for maneuvering the huge cast, coordinating the myriad sound effects of everyday street life, and making it all seem as if it were occuring only a few blocks from the theatre. Rice staged all his own work after that.

The most important element was the set, which Rice had come to regard as a major character. For his design, Jo Mielziner re-created an actual brownstone tenement, 25 West 65th Street. That New York building later toured the country in a successful road version. The London production was equally acclaimed.

Rice created more variations on his *Street Scene* theme. He wrote the screenplay for the 1931 movie adaptation. Rose was played by Sylvia Sydney, who was to become typecast as a street saint. Rice also wrote the book for the musical version of *Street Scene* which premiered in 1947. Kurt Weill composed the music and poet Langston Hughes penned the lyrics. It ran for 148 performances. The New York City Opera added it to its repertory in 1959.

When television was born, Rice submitted a treatment to the fledgling networks for a series based on his play. Just as the original script had been roundly rejected, the series idea was universally passed over. One executive wrote that a weekly show about impoverished city residents would be too depressing to sell advertisers' products.

BIRD IN HAND

by John Drinkwater
Opened April 4, 1929
500 Performances
The Booth Theatre
Directed by John Drinkwater
Produced by Lee Shubert

Cast: Herbert Lomas (Thomas Greenleaf); Jill Esmond Moore (Joan Greenleaf); Charles Hickman (Gerald Arnwood); Amy Veness (Alice Greenleaf); Ivor Barnard (Mr. Blanquet); Charles Maunsell (Cyril Beverly); Frank Petley (Ambrose Godolphin, K.C.); Roddy Hughes (Sir Robert Arnwood).

Englishman John Drinkwater was one of London and Broadway's most serious playwrights. He specialized in biographical drama about such significant historical figures as Abraham Lincoln, Oliver Cromwell, Robert E. Lee, Napoleon, and Mary, Queen of Scots. But his greatest hit,

and the only one to run 500 performances, was an unassuming comedy called *Bird in Hand*. Critics were surprised to find that this dramatist possessed the light touch. The play poked a little fun at British class distinctions, as a lower-class innkeeper objects to his daughter's courtship with the son of the local squire. Three guests at the inn, representing a cross-section of English society, offer amusing advice and counsel on the situation. In the end, the squire himself asks the girl to marry his son.

The play was first staged in 1927 with Laurence Olivier and Peggy Ashcroft. The following year Olivier appeared opposite Jill Esmond Moore, whom he later married.

There was a return New York engagement in 1930 and a failed revival in 1942.

STRICTLY DISHONORABLE

by Preston Sturges
Opened September 18, 1929
557 Performances
The Avon Theatre
Directed by Brock Pemberton and Antoinette Perry
Produced by Brock Pemberton

Cast: Muriel Kirkland (Isabelle Parry); Tullio Carminati (Count Di Ruvo); William Ricciardi (Tomaso Antiovi); Louis Jean Heydt (Henry Greene); Carl Anthony (Judge Dempsey); Edward J. McNamara (Patrolman Mulligan); John Altieri (Giovanni); Marius Rogati (Mario).

A maiden's virtue was the subject of *Strictly Dishonorable*, a play by Preston Sturges which took the same cynical, satiric view of social and sexual mores that his many films did.

The action takes place in a speakeasy and the apartment above it. Dashing opera singer Count Di Ruvo meets Isabelle Parry, a naive but eager young girl from New Jersey. He takes her upstairs to his room in pursuit of yet another sexual conquest. She is more than willing to surrender to him, having just broken off with her stuffy fiancé. But the Count sees that she really is a decent girl and just can't bring himself to "deflower" her. The curtain falls on his heartfelt proposal to Isabelle. Although the comedy ends in a respectable marriage, it attacks the hypocrisy of middle-class values (as represented by Isabelle's jilted boyfriend) and Prohibition. Sturges made the hero Italian, so that his friend Georges Renavent, who had an accent, could play the part.

Sturges wrote the play on his father's living-room table after having been fired from a stage-managing job. The thirty-year-old playwright cockily predicted that he would finish it in thirty days and that it would be a smash hit. At the end of his self-imposed deadline, the play was done. He mailed it to the office of producer Brock Pemberton (for whom he had worked as an assistant stage manager), boasting to his father that an advance check would be in the post the following Saturday. There was a delivery for the young playwright that day, but it was his manuscript, marked "insufficient postage." Once the proper amount had been affixed to the package and Pemberton had received it, Sturges' predictions came true. The producer sent a cable agreeing to mount a production, but added that the script needed some work.

Pemberton collaborated on the direction with his frequent partner Antoinette Perry (for whom the Tony Awards, Broadway's annual prizes, were later named). Georges Renavent was in Hollywood making movies, so the role went to Tullio Carminati. Rehearsals were stormy. There were frequent disagreements, usually over Sturges' refusal to do any more rewrites. There were also clashes over casting. Pemberton and Perry wanted Muriel Kirkland for the ingénue, while Sturges insisted that they hire his current girlfriend or he would make no further rewrites. The producer and director called the young playwright's bluff. They summoned the entire company and announced that because of Sturges' stubbornness, they could not produce the show. Reluctantly, Sturges relented, and Kirkland played Isabelle.

Opening night arrived, and the audience was not laughing right away. Disheartened, Sturges rushed to a speakeasy and proceeded to get smashed. The next morning a friend called asking for a pair of tickets. Thinking it would be no problem since the show was a bomb, Sturges called Pemberton's office with the request. The producer answered, "Are you nuts? We're sold out. We've just turned away 1500 people." It seems that after the playwright's departure, the opening-night audience warmed to the comedy considerably, as did the critics. Brooks Atkinson of the *New York Times* called it "a well-nigh perfect comedy."

Even the stock market crash, which occured a month after the opening, did not affect *Strictly Dishonorable*'s box office. While bankers were on the streets selling apples and most other Broadway attractions were playing to half-empty houses, scalpers were getting $60 for a pair of tickets to the hit comedy. At the show's first anniversary performance, Pemberton, noted for his publicity stunts, could afford to give out individual birthday cakes to each member of the audience.

During this flush of success, Sturges gave an interview in which he stated that he preferred playwriting to writing for the movies, for the theatre was superior to the cinema when it came to snappy dialogue. Ironically, Sturges went on to write and direct some of the wittiest and most popular screen comedies ever, including *The Great McGinty, The Lady Eve, Sullivan's Travels,* and *The Palm Beach Story*. Meanwhile, his plays are only infrequently revived.

Speaking of movies, *Strictly Dishonorable* was brought to the screen in 1931. In 1951, Ezio Pinza and Janet Leigh did an MGM remake that took up where the stage play left off and followed the marriage of the two lead characters.

THE 1930s

A lthough the Depression was paralyzing the nation's economy, Broadway was a treasure house of vital drama, enchanting comedy, and tuneful musicals throughout the decade. Although there were no long-running hits for the first three seasons of the 1930s, many important playwrights, actors, and companies were getting their start. To combat the risks of purely commercial ventures, many theatre organizations sprang up. ✫ The Group Theatre burned brightly and fiercely from 1931 to '41, illuminating the Great White Way with the social protest plays of Clifford Odets (*Waiting for Lefty, Awake and Sing!*). The Federal Theatre employed hundreds of out-of-work actors and writers in its Living Newspapers and other presentations including Orson Welles's voodoo *Macbeth* set in Haiti and featuring an all-black cast. Welles and John Houseman set up their own Mercury Theatre in 1937 and made an impact with a modern-dress *Julius Caesar.* The Playwrights Company, made up of five writers for the stage who pooled their resources to produce their own work and that of others, had a successful first season in 1938 which included Robert E. Sherwood's *Abe Lincoln in Illinois,* Maxwell Anderson's and Kurt Weill's *Knickerbocker Holiday,* and S.N. Berhman's *No Time for Comedy.* ✫ The Theatre Guild continued with productions of Eugene O'Neill's large-scale drama *Mourning Becomes Electra* and his comedy *Ah, Wilderness,* as well as George and Ira Gershwin's *Porgy and Bess.* Thornton Wilder paid homage to the everyday with his *Our Town* and two Georges (Kaufman and Abbott) were the kings of comedy. ✫ In the 1934–35 season, the Pulitzer Prize committee bypassed such worthy candidates as *The Children's Hour, Awake and Sing, The Petrified Forest* and *Valley Forge* to give their award to *The Old Maid,* Zoë Akins's run-of-the-mill adaptation of a story by Edith Wharton. In protest, Broadway reviewers banded together to present their own award for the year's best and formed the New York Drama Critics Circle. The first winner was Maxwell Anderson's verse drama *Winterset* of the 1935–36 season. ✫ Stars such as Alfred Lunt and Lynn Fontanne, Katharine Cornell, Helen Hayes, and Ina Claire dazzled theatregoing audiences with their glamour and expertise, but talking pictures and the radio were beginning to make inroads on the country's limited entertainment dollars.

THE GREEN PASTURES

by Marc Connelly, derived from *Ol' Man Adam and His Chillun,* by Roark Bradford.

Opened February 26, 1930

The Mansfield Theatre

640 Performances

Directed by Marc Connelly

Produced by Laurence Rivers, Inc. (Rowland Stebbins)

Cast: Richard B. Harrison (The Lord); Wesley Hill (Gabriel); Tutt Whitney (Noah); Daniel L. Haynes (Adam/Hezdrel); Charles H. Moore (Mr. Deshee/Isaac); Inez Richardson Wilson (Eve); Lou Vernon (Cain); Dorothy Randolph (Cain's Girl); Edna M. Harris (Zeba); James Fuller (Cain the Sixth); Susie Sutton (Noah's Wife); Milton J. Williams (Shem); Freddie Archibald (Flatfoot); J. Homer Tutt (Ham/High Priest); Stanleigh Morell (Japeth/Joshua/Officer); J.A. Shipp (Abraham/Archangel); Edgar Burks (Jacob); Alonzo Fenderson (Moses); Mercedes Gilbert (Zipporah); McKinley Reeves (Aaron); Arthur Porter (Head Magician); Reginald Fenderson (Candidate Magician); Emory Richardson (First Wizard/Officer); George Randol (Pharaoh); Walt McClane (General); Billy Cumby (Master of Ceremonies); Jay Mondaaye (King of Babylon); Ivan Sharp (First Scout/Gambler/Prophet); Josephine Byrd (Angel/First Cleaner); Florence Fields (Second Cleaner).

Prior to his Pulitzer Prize–winning religious fable *The Green Pastures,* playwright Marc Connelly's Broadway credits were light comedies mostly written in collaboration with George S. Kaufman. This new play was a marked departure from his previous efforts.

Derived from *Ol' Man Adam and His Chillun,* Roark Bradford's retelling of Old Testament stories in African-American dialect and settings, the play travels from the Garden of Eden to the passion of Christ from the point of view of a Southern backwoods preacher explaining the Bible to his Sunday-school class. A benevolent Deity presides over a heavenly fish fry. The decadence of Babylon resembles that of a Harlem nightspot. The Pharaoh's palace is the meeting hall of a mystical fraternal lodge.

The script's broad Amos 'n' Andy–style dialect and the patronizing depiction of blacks as faithful, childlike innocents, date the play and render it offensive to many today. But at the time of its opening it was seen as a novel and charming approach to the Gospels and an excellent means of theatricalizing them.

The all-black play required nearly sixty performers. Connelly explained the casting of the play to the *New York Herald Tribune*: "There is a casting office in Harlem, but it doesn't operate like the ones downtown. When this office looks for a type, there are no files to consult, no list of applicants. Instead, it seems to me the agents just wander around the streets until they find a person who seems to fit."

Richard B. Harrison fit the role of the Lord perfectly. Although he had never acted professionally before, Harrison had toured the country giving readings from the Bible

The story of Moses meeting the Pharaoh is restaged in this scene from *The Green Pastures.*

and Shakespeare. His calm authority served him well and many began to regard him with a reverence befitting his role. He was often asked to baptize children in his Harlem church.

The Green Pastures was never presented in England, because the censorhip authority, the Lord Chamberlain's office, declared it blasphemous for an actor to play God. There was a Swedish production in 1932. The cast of Swedes in blackface was pelted with eggs at one performance for their "religious irreverence." The National Socialist Party was blamed for the incident.

After the play closed on Broadway in 1931, it made five national tours, playing 200 cities in thirty-nine states, with Harrison never missing a performance as the Lord. The tour ran into a few problems. The town of Lubbock, Texas, banned the play since the only building large enough to accommodate the huge production was the local high school. This would have meant the all-black cast would be using facilities meant for the all-white student body. In Tampa, Florida, a local ordinance forbade blacks from buying tickets, so the management sneaked them in disguised as hawkers of refreshments.

After the extensive tour, *Pastures* returned to Broadway in 1935. Harrison himself went to greener pastures during this return engagement. Two other actors who died during the show's run were the original Gabriel, Wesley Hill, who was killed in an auto accident, and his successor Samuel Davis, who succumbed to pneumonia during the tour.

The Green Pastures was adapted for the screen in 1936 with Rex Ingram as the Lord, with Eddie "Rochester" Anderson (famed for his role on Jack Benny's radio and television shows) and Oscar Polk co-starring. The condescending view of African-Americans as simple-minded prevents the film from being screened very frequently. On television, *Hallmark Hall of Fame* presented a version with Frederick O'Neal and Anderson in 1957. It was revived on Broadway in 1951.

SAILOR, BEWARE!

by Kenyon Nicholson and Charles Robinson

Opened September 28, 1933

500 Performances

The Lyceum Theatre

Directed by Kenyon Nicholson

Produced by Courtney Burr

Cast: Bruce MacFarlane (Chester "Dynamite" Jones); Audrey Christie (Billie "Stonewall" Jackson); Edward Craven (Barney Waters); Horace MacMahon (Mattie Matthews); George Heller (Wop Wilchinski); Ross Hertz (Spud Newton); Bradford Hatton (Luther Reed); Don Rowen (Peewee Moore); Murray Alper (Herb Markey); Larry Fletcher (Jake Edwards); Paul Huber (Lt. Loomis); Rod Maybee (Texas Patton); Ann Winthrop (Ruby Keefer); Ann Thomas (Bernice Dooley); Ruth Conley (Hazel De Fay); Josephine Evans (Dode Bronson); Edgar Nelson (Humpty Singer); John Bard (Louie); Harry Hornick (Senor Gomez).

Subtitled "Variations on a Familiar Theme," the raucous comedy *Sailor, Beware!* was a salty, sexually frank yarn which would have been perfectly suitable for the backroom of a bar. Sailor Chester Jones, nicknamed "Dynamite" for his reputation with women, has been set a task by his fellow shipmates while they're on leave in the Panama Canal zone. His mission: to seduce and conquer the intractable but gorgeous Billie Jackson, entertainer and hostess at the Idle Hour Shore Resort. Billie has a nickname, too; she's known as "Stonewall" for her impenetrable defenses against the charms of the male sex.

As "Stonewall" resists the endless advances of "Dynamite," the stakes in the bets among both the sailors and showgirls get higher and higher. Then the inevitable happens: the sexual combatants fall in love and, by order of the Admiral, all bets are off and everybody lives happily ever after.

Sailor, Beware! was one of the many hit comedies of the '30s that were dismissed by critics but loved by the public. Brooks Atkinson of the *New York Times* said, "It makes no pretensions to social significance. . . . It is blandly offered to Broadway as ribald entertainment." The comedy went on to run 500 performances, just qualifying for inclusion in this survey of long-running shows.

Since the play depended so much on broad innuendo, the watered-down movie version starring Lew Ayres was weak. Its tepid gibes could only hint at the heat of the stage production, despite the contribution of Dorothy Parker, one of America's wittiest writers at the time, to the screenplay.

TOBACCO ROAD

by Jack Kirkland, based on the novel by Erskine Caldwell.

Opened December 4, 1933

3,182 Performances

The Masque Theatre

Directed and produced by Anthony Brown

Cast: Henry Hull (Jeeter Lester); Margaret Wycherly (Ada Lester); Maude Odell (Sister Bessie Rice); Sam Byrd (Dude Lester); Ruth Hunter (Ellie Mae); Patricia Quinn (Grandma Lester); Dean Jagger (Lov Bensey); Ashley Cooper (Henry Peabody); Reneice Rehan (Pearl); Lamar King (Capt. Tim); Edwin Walter (George Payne).

A 1941 *New Yorker* cartoon shows an old couple sitting at home as a younger husband and wife get ready for a night on the town. The caption of the older man speaking to his spouse reads: "Mother, do you remember when we went to see *Tobacco Road*?" The longevity of Jack Kirkland's dramatization of Erskine Caldwell's steamy bestseller about dirt-poor Georgia sharecroppers was the subject of many such quips. Lorenz Hart even mentioned it in his lyrics for "Give It Back to the Indians," an ode to Manhattan Island.

James Barton and Margaret Wycherly played the Jeeters when *Tobacco Road* hit the 1000-performance mark.

Despite its later success, Kirkland had a difficult time getting the show produced. Although the language and actions of Jeeter Lester and his family of turnip-eaters would be considered mild by audiences used to David Mamet and Sam Shepard, the producers of 1933 found the material too racy to risk their funds on. Kirkland finally had to do it himself. With his director Anthony Brown as producer, he spent his last $6,000 to make *Tobacco Road* a part of the Great White Way. (It eventually earned back almost 100 times the original investment.) On the last night of Prohibition, *Tobacco Road* opened.

Like its record-breaking predecessor *Abie's Irish Rose, Tobacco Road* received deprecating reviews. Brooks Atkinson of the *New York Times* called it "one of the grossest episodes ever put on the stage. The theatre has never sheltered a fouler or more degenerate parcel of folks." But he admitted it did leave a "vivid impression." Percy Hammond of the *New York Herald-Tribune* genteelly described it as a play "for those who get a naughty thrill from dark disclosures of the primitive human animal while writhing in the throes of gender." But all the critics praised Henry Hull's performance as Jeeter.

Initial receipts were so low at the box office that the landlord at the Masque Theatre forced the production to move. Business picked up at the show's new home, the 48th Street Theatre, when an editorial in the *Daily News* came out comparing the play to the works of Emile Zola and Theodore Dreiser for truthfully depicting the deplorable conditions of its characters.

Tobacco Road was now a *succes de scandale* with the public flocking to see it, expecting obscenity. Another controversy helped the box office: During the first of many national tours, the mayor of Chicago attended a performance and immediately banned it from further showings there. People had to see what was so dirty that it couldn't be seen on the stage in a big city like Chicago. There were further censorship problems in Boston, New Orleans, and Atlanta. In Indiana City, Michigan, where the local fathers had forbidden the Jeeters from setting a bare foot in their town, the play was performed on a showboat moored just outside the jurisdiction of the local government. Despite, or maybe because of, these censorship problems, the various road tours played 327 cities, some for as many as eight times.

The show even inspired congressional action, both praising and damning the production. Representative Kramer of California asked for a Congressional investigation of the economic conditions of citizens living in real-life tobacco roads, while Deen of Georgia attacked the play from the floor of the House while it was playing Washington, D.C. He called the treatment of his home state "untruthful, undignified, undiplomatic, and unfair."

Meanwhile, back on Broadway, the New York company was doing so well that Kirkland was able to move it to the Forrest Theatre and take over the lease. It was an eventful eight-year run. An actress died in her dressing room during a performance, the playwright married a member of the company, and the box office was robbed at gunpoint.

The biggest backstage brouhaha involved James Barton, Henry Hull's successor in the lead role. Ironically, he was called before the board of Equity Actors Association for cursing at fellow cast members offstage and received an offical reprimand from that union. Barton left the company soon after. The role was played on Broadway by five different actors, the last of whom was Will Geer, now best remembered as the grandfather on *The Waltons* television series.

20th-Century Fox released John Ford's film version in 1941. Charley Grapewin (who played Uncle Henry in *The Wizard of Oz*) was Jeeter. *Tobacco Road* reappeared on Broadway a total of four times.

PERSONAL APPEARANCE

by Lawrence Reilly

Opened October 17, 1934

501 Performances

The Henry Miller Theatre

Directed by Brock Pemberton and Antoinette Perry

Produced by Brock Pemberton

Cast: Gladys George (Carole Arden); Philip Ober (Chester (Bud) Norton); Merna Pace (Joyce Struthers); Florence Robinson (Gladys Kelcey); Richard Kendrick (Clyde Pelton); Eula Guy (Aunt Kate Barnaby); Minna Philips (Mrs. Struthers); Otto Hulette (Gene Tuttle); Phil Sheridan (Johnson); Dorrit Kelton (Jessie); John Jones (Henry Bush).

In the fall of 1934, producer Brock Pemberton, who had not had a project on the boards since the hit *Strictly Dishonorable* closed two seasons before, announced he would be back on Broadway with five new shows. All the gossip columns carried the news of Pemberton's return, which included mounting three comedies: *Personal Appearance,* *To My Husband,* and *The Nude in Washington Square,* as well as historical dramas based on the lives of French revolutionary and murderess Charlotte Corday and the Empress Josephine.

Of these five, only the first, a broad swipe at Hollywood by Lawrence Reilly, a new playwright from Pennsylvania, materialized on stage. Like *Strictly Dishonorable,* it was staged by Pemberton and Antoinette Perry. It also ran for more than a year. The *Personal Appearance* of the title refers to a tour being made by movie siren and former waitress Carole Arden to publicize her latest cinematic opus, *Drifting Lady.*

The play opens with the theatre audience watching the last reel of this epic on a giant movie screen. Then Arden makes a live appearance, thanking her public, ever the gracious star. But when her expensive sportscar breaks down in Nowheresville, Pennsylvania, we see the real Carole: profane, short-tempered, and lusty. At first she wants to blow this hick burg, but then finds herself attracted to the local gas station attendant and sets her cap for him. The mechanic's fiancée, however, is determined to fight for her man. Therein lies the comedy, and Broadway audiences enthusiastically ate it up.

They also found Gladys George appetizing as the glamorous film actress. Talking pictures were still relatively new, and the public was fascinated by them. Reilly exploited this fascination and poked fun at the pomposity of moviemaking and movie stars. Long before Marilyn Monroe wiggled down the pike, Carole Arden was one of the first "dumb blondes." One of the play's most frequent sources of laughs were the malapropisms that sprang from her lips like "I must retire now and commute with myself for a moment."

Pemberton launched a clever publicity campaign, quoting obscure critics in his ads. He even printed a rave from a reviewer for the *New York Journal,* a Chinese-language publication, in the original Chinese script.

During the run of the show, Gladys George was the subject of some ugly publicity when her husband sued for divorce. He claimed he had caught her "entertaining" an actor in her hotel room late at night. She maintained the actor only came over to help her put a bandage on her wounded cat. Pictures of George with the feline and bandage in question were in all the papers, garnering scads of free publicity for the show.

At the time, George was herself under contract to MGM as a result of making a splash in another Main Stem show, *The Milky Way.* Pemberton managed to get a suspension for her. She is best known today for her supporting role in the film classic *The Maltese Falcon.*

The play was brought to the screen in 1936, as a vehicle for the legendary femme fatale Mae West, under the new title of *Go West, Young Man.* Randolph Scott was her grease-monkey love interest, and this movie about the movies enjoyed a moderate success.

THE CHILDREN'S HOUR

by Lillian Hellman

Opened November 20, 1934

691 Performances

Maxine Elliot's Theatre

Produced and directed by Herman Shumlin

Cast: Anne Revere (Martha Dobie); Katharine Emery (Karen Wright); Robert Keith (Dr. Joseph Cardin); Aline McDermott (Mrs. Lily Mortar); Florence McGee (Mary Tilford); Eugenia Rawls (Peggy Rogers); Katherine Emmett (Mrs. Amelia Tilford); Barbara Beals (Rosalie Wells); Elizabeth Seckel (Evelyn Munn); Lynne Fisher (Helen Burton); Jacqueline Rusling (Lois Fisher); Barbara Leeds (Catherine); Edmonia Nolley (Agatha); Jack Tyler (Grocery Boy).

Twenty-nine-year-old Lillian Hellman made a scandalous debut on Broadway with *The Children's Hour,* her scalding drama about a pair of teachers accused by a malicious student of being lesbian lovers. Hellman handled the controversial topic with restraint rather than sensationalism, and sophisticated Broadway audiences greeted the play enthusiastically.

The Children's Hour details the damage done when spiteful Mary Tilford whispers to her influential grandmother that her headmistresses Martha Dobie and Karen Wright are involved in "unnatural acts." Unable to disprove the lie, Martha and Karen lose their school and a subsequent libel case. At the play's conclusion, Martha confesses she does have more than friendly affection for Karen, then goes offstage to shoot herself. This set a pattern for future homosexual stage and movie characters to meet an untimely end, usually at their own hand. (This suicide fate was not altered until later, from the 1960s on,

J. Robert Keith, Anne Revere, Florence McGee, Katherine Emery, and Katherine Emmet
in a tense scene from Lillian Hellman's *The Children's Hour*.

in plays like *The Boys in the Band* and *Torch Song Trilogy*, which offered a more understanding alternative.)

The idea for the play was suggested to Hellman by her companion, the mystery writer Dashiell Hammett. He had come across a book of famous court cases entitled *Bad Companions* by William Roughead. One chapter chronicled an 1810 Scottish libel suit involving a young girl falsely naming two of her teachers lesbians. (The writing of this play is dramatized, incidentally, in a brief scene in the film *Julia*, based on Hellman's memoirs; in frustration, Hellman (played by Jane Fonda) throws her typewriter out the window.)

Once the play was finished, the young playwright took it to producer-director Herman Shumlin, for whom she had been reading scripts. Without telling him the name of the author, Hellman stated that she thought it the best play she had read in a long time and that he should produce it immediately. Shumlin read it and concurred.

The Broadway stage was far ahead of motion pictures when it came to adult themes such as homosexuality. The first Broadway attraction with a lesbian character, called *The Captive*, was presented in 1926. Although it received good notices, the police raided the show and arrested the leading ladies.

Lee Shubert, who owned the theatre in which *The Children's Hour* was presented and who had money in the show, feared another *Captive* incident with the cast, and possibly himself, landing in the slammer. Shumlin assured his backer that that wasn't going to happen by preventing the conservative Commissioner of Licenses, the city official with jurisdiction over plays and theatres, from seeing the play until after it had opened and the reviews were out. If they were as positive as Shulman predicted, an attempt by the Commissioner to close the show would cause a public outcry.

The reviews were everything the playwright and producer could have hoped for, with Robert Benchley of *The New Yorker* calling it "the high-water mark of the season." There was no trouble from the Commissioner. However, there was a censorial glitch when a national tour was planned and *The Children's Hour* earned the epitaph "banned in Boston." Shumlin offered to give a special performance before the mayor, but was turned down. A similar censorship issue arose when the play was to be produced in England. The Lord Chamberlain, the British equivalent of the Commissioner of Licenses, forbade the play from being presented on the London stage. He stated to Hellman that, while there was "a male homosexual problem" in Britain, there were to his knowledge no lesbians in the country. Hellman reported falling off her chair laughing. This obstacle was skirted by having the play performed at a "private theatrical club" rather than on a commercial stage.

A "cleaned-up" version of the play, entitled *These Three*, was brought to the screen in 1936. All references to lesbianism were replaced by accusations of Martha having sex with Karen's fiancé Joseph. William Wyler directed Merle Oberon, Miriam Hopkins, and Joel McCrea in the leads. Since the central theme of the play was not lesbianism, but the power of a lie to destroy lives, the story held up, and the film was a success. In 1961, Wyler directed a more faithful film version with the original title and homosexual content restored. Audrey Hepburn, Shirley MacLaine, James Garner, and Miriam Hopkins (this time as Martha's meddling aunt) headlined.

The stage version was revived in 1952 with Hellman directing and Kim Hunter and Patricia Neal as the accused teachers. The parallels between little Mary's whispers and the red-baiting of Senator Joe McCarthy made the production especially timely.

THREE MEN ON A HORSE

by John Cecil Holm and George Abbott

Opened January 30, 1935

835 Performances

The Playhouse Theatre

Directed by George Abbott

Produced by Alex Yokel

Cast: William Lynn (Erwin Trowbridge); Sam Levene (Patsy); Shirley Booth (Mabel); Joyce Atling (Audrey Trowbridge); Fleming Ward (Clarence Dobbins); James Lane (Harry); Millard Mitchell (Charlie); Teddy Hart (Frankie); Richard Huey (Moses); Edith Van Cleve (Gloria); Garson Kanin (Al); Frank Camp (Mr. Carver); J. Ascher Smith (Tailor); Nick Wiger (Delivery Boy); Margaret Smithers (Motel Maid).

George Abbott continued his streak of successful play doctoring with *Three Men on a Horse*, an uproarious comedy smash of race tracks and gambling fever. As with his previous hit *Broadway*, Abbott rewrote the work of another play-wright, staged it, and made it into an audience-pleaser. This was a profitable pattern he would repeat again and again.

This play was originally called *Hobby Horses*, the sole work of John Cecil Holm. Warner Brothers had promised to invest in the show, but wanted the script to be polished up. Abbott, who considered the basic premise strong, but the structure, especially the resolution, weak, tightened up the dialogue and further exaggerated the characters to farcical proportions. He renamed the show, and Warners liked the new title, but suggested a slight variation: *Three on a Horse*. They hoped to cash in on the popularity of a recent movie hit, *Three on a Match*. Abbott fought for his version and won.

The story concerns Erwin Trowbridge, a shy writer of greeting cards with an incredible knack for selecting winning horses. But he is so timid, he would never dream of actually putting money on any of his hunches and only picks the ponies for fun. By chance, he runs into a bar and encounters a gang of unsuccessful gamblers. They discover his amazingly accurate track record and decide to cash in on this phenomenon.

After absconding with Erwin to a motel, the gamblers place bet after bet and rake in piles of winnings. The spell is broken when Erwin places his own money on a nag that wins only because of a disqualification. Sure he's lost his golden touch, he returns to his job and spouse.

Abbott was assisted by Robert Griffith, who would go on to become a famous producer in his own right. He would later join Harold Prince in producing such musical hits as *The Pajama Game, Damn Yankees,* and *Fiorello!* Another Abbott associate, Garson Kanin, who later wrote and directed *Born Yesterday*, had a bit part in *Three Men on a Horse*.

The reviews were positive, but not ecstatic, so it was hardly clear that the show would sustain a long run. But good word of mouth eventually led to a strong box office return. The motion picture rights were sold before the play's financial status was established, so they went for the relatively modest price of $75,000.

But the continued success of the Broadway run made up for this low sale. There were also three touring companies and a London production.

Sam Levene reprised his role of Patsy, the head gambler, many times and appeared in the 1936 film with Frank McHugh, Joan Blondell, Teddy Hart, and Guy Kibbee. There were two stage-musical adaptations, *Banjo Eyes* (1941), with Eddie Cantor and Virginia Mayo, and *Let It Ride* (1961) starring Levene and George Gobel. Neither of these succeeded. The original version has been a popular choice for summer stock and amateur groups. There have been two Broadway revivals. A 1969 remounting, directed by Abbott himself, featured Levene (again), Jack Gilford,

Dorothy Loudon, Hal Linden, and Butterfly McQueen. The second revival was in 1993, by Tony Randall's National Actors Theatre, with Randall and his longtime television co-star, Jack Klugman.

DEAD END

by Sidney Kingsley

Opened October 28, 1935

687 Performances

The Belasco Theatre

Directed by Sidney Kingsley

Produced by Norman Bel Geddes

Cast: Theodore Newton (Gimpty); Gabriel Dell (T.B.); Billy Halop (Tommy); Huntz Hall (Dippy); Bobby Jordan (Angel); Charles R. Duncan (Spit); Joseph Downing ("Babyface" Martin); Martin Gabel (Hunk); Charles Bellin (Philip Griswald); Bernard Punsly (Milty); Elspeth Eric (Drina); Carroll Ashburn (Mr. Griswald); Louis Lord (Mr. Jones); Margaret Mullen (Kay); Cyril Gordon Weld (Jack Hilton); Marjorie Main (Mrs. Martin); Sheila Trent (Francey); George Cotton (Doorman); Marie R. Burke (Old Lady); George N. Price (Old Gentleman); Charles Benjamin (Chauffeur); Margaret Linden (Lady with Dog); Sidonie Espero (Governess); Robert J. Mulligan (Officer Mulligan); Richard Clark (Chauffeur); Harry Selby (Plainclothesman); Philip Bourneuf (Interne); Lewis L. Russel (Medical Examiner); Bernard Zaneville (Sailor); Leo and David Gorcey (Second Avenue Boys). Future film director Sidney Lumet had a bit part.

As the curtain rose at the Belasco Theatre for the premiere of Sidney Kingsley's *Dead End*, the audience found itself sitting in the East River. On the stage was producer-designer Norman Bel Geddes's painstakingly detailed re-creation of a New York waterfront, containing an exclusive new high-rise apartment surrounded by squalid tenements. A gang of scruffy urchins scrambled onto the set and proceeded to

The Dead End Kids attempt to cool off in *Dead End*.

dive into the orchestra pit, accompanied by realistic sounding splashes. They emerged dripping wet, having been doused by stagehands. Other lifelike sound effects such as riverboat whistles, police car reports, and a party aboard an offstage yacht, issued from loudspeakers concealed in an onstage lamppost and steam shovel. The background sounds never ceased throughout the three acts.

Clearly similar to Elmer Rice's *Street Scene*, this play offered a realistic, if unseemly, slice of slum life. Kingsley, like his contemporary, Clifford Odets, specialized in plays of social protest. He had won the Pulitzer Prize in 1934 for *Men in White*, in which the playwright turned his scalpel upon corruption in a big city hospital. *Dead End* was followed by *Ten Million Ghosts* (1936), an attack on munitions manufacturers. The premise in *Dead End*, that poverty breeds crime, was demonstrated by the lawless ways of the boys who could grow up to become like Babyface Martin, a ruthless killer who revisits his old neighborhood. Instead of a hero's welcome, he finds his former girlfriend a prostitute and his mother destitute and full of hate for him. The second act climaxes with Babyface riddled with bullets by G-men, and Tommy, one of the young gang, nearing arrest for stabbing a wealthy tenant of the high-rise. Kingsley drew the parallel of Babyface's fate foreshadowing Tommy's.

The show was an immediate hit. Productions costs of $19,000 (a fortune in 1935) were paid off in only two weeks. Brooks Atkinson of the *New York Times* called it "an enormously stirring drama, a contribution to public knowledge."

At one point the onstage world of the streets struck a little too close to home for the production. Edward Furman was a street kid with no acting experience who played Spit in the road company of *Dead End*. He ad-libbed obscenities onstage, sexually harassed an actress in the company, and was subsequently arrested and put under observation at Bellevue Hospital. His case was later dismissed, but he was dismissed from the company as well.

Dead End came to the screen in 1937, directed by William Wyler with a somewhat watered-down screenplay by Lillian Hellman. Sylvia Sydney, Joel MacCrea, and Humphrey Bogart were the top-billed players, but the real stars of the film were the Dead End Kids, many of whom had been in the play. The Kids, led by Leo Gorcey and Huntz Hall, appeared in seven Warners Brothers gangster films, including *Angels With Dirty Faces* and *Angels Wash Their Faces*. As the East Side Kids and the Bowery Boys, they subsequently made a series of shorts for Monogram Studios from 1940 to 1957. Mostly low-budget comedies with the Kids as happy-go-lucky, harmless hooligans, these light two-reelers were a far cry from Kingsley's indictment of persistent slum conditions.

In 1960, a revival was mounted by the off-Broadway Equity Library Theatre, but withdrawn before the opening by Actors Equity Association, the actors' union that sponsored the production, on the grounds that it wasn't professional enough. The cast, which included Dustin Hoffman and Ron Leibman, disagreed and put on the show themselves at the 41st Street Theatre. Kingsley gave his approval, waived his royalties, and the production was well received.

BOY MEETS GIRL

by Samuel and Bella Spewack

Opened November 27, 1935

669 Performances

The Cort Theatre

Produced and directed by George Abbott

Cast: Allyn Joslyn (Robert Law); Jerome Cowan (J. Carlyle Benson); Joyce Arling (Susie); James MacColl (Rodney Bevan); Royal Beal (C.F. Friday); Charles McClelland (Larry Toms); Everett H. Sloane (Rosetti); John Clarke (Major Thompson); Peggy Hart (Peggy); Lea Penman (Miss Crewes); Garson Kanin (Green); Maurice Sommers (Slade); Helen Gardner (Nurse); Perry Ivins (Doctor); Edison Rice (Chauffeur); Philip Faversham (Young Man); George W. Smith (Studio Officer); Robert Foulk (Cutter); Marjorie Lytell (Another Nurse).

Hollywood has been the target of many a wisecracking Broadway playwright's barbs. *Once in a Lifetime, Merton of the Movies, Personal Appearance,* and *Speed-the-Plow* are a few of the comedies that have savaged the movie capital. The longest-running show of this genre is *Boy Meets Girl,* by Samuel and Bella Spewack, with 669 performances.

The story concerns Robert Law and J. Carlyle Benson, two screwball screenwriters constantly playing practical jokes on the studio bigwigs. During the course of their antics, they befriend a commisary waitress who is pregnant without benefit of a husband. The writers conspire to make the girl's baby a sensational child star by pairing him with a dimwitted movie cowboy. This cowpoke finds himself upstaged by the photogenic infant and plots to become his legal guardian—thereby getting access to the child's salary—by marrying the waitress. Law and Benson manage to foil the actor's scheme, marry the girl to the right man, and obtain lifetime contracts for themselves in the bargain.

Robert Law and J. Carlyle Benson were presumably based on two men who were considered Hollywood's Katzenjammer Kids, Ben Hecht and Charles MacArthur, who wrote the hit play *The Front Page* and were legendary movie-writing cut-ups themselves. (All the parties involved, the Spewacks and Hecht and MacArthur, denied this, but tongues continued to wag.)

The husband and wife playwrights had plenty in common with Hecht and MacArthur. Both pairs of writers began as newshounds and spent time on Broadway and in Hollywood. The Spewacks met when they were writing for the *New York World* and married when they were nineteen years old. Samuel Spewack eventually became an overseas correspondent and wired reports from Russia and Germany. When he returned to the States, he collaborated with his wife on *Clear All Wires,* a comedy about an American correspondent in Russia. While that show was not a smash, it did get the Spewacks noticed, and they were hired to write for Metro-Goldwyn-Mayer.

After six years on the West coast writing screenplays such as *The Cat and the Fiddle, Should Ladies Behave?,* and *Rendezvous,* the Spewacks used their experiences in Movieland as the basis for a stage satire on the studio system's idea of a storyline: "Boy meets girl. Boy loses girl. Boy gets girl."

The couple took their script to George Abbott, Broadway's top director. He decided to produce as well as to direct it—the first time he had worn both these particular hats. This was a busy year for Abbott. His *Three Men on a Horse,* which he had directed and co-authored, was still running, and he staged *Boy Meets Girl* at the same time as Billy Rose's production of the Rodgers and Hart and Hecht and MacArthur musical, *Jumbo.* Abbott would rehearse *Boy Meets Girl* during the day and then rush over to the Hippodrome and put *Jumbo* through its paces at night. The former was a hit; the latter closed after five months.

In addition to his usual lightning-fast pacing, Abbott placed musicians in the boxes to play during set changes. "I often wondered what theatre boxes were for," the director said, "and now I know. It's something in which to hide musicians."

The movies which were its source for ridicule became the medium for *Boy Meets Girl* in 1938, when the screen version was released. It starred James Cagney and Pat O'Brien as the screenwriters with Marie Wilson, Ralph Bellamy, Penny Singleton, and a young man named Ronald Reagan in supporting roles. There were Broadway revivals in 1948 and 1976. The latter was presented as a part of the Phoenix Theatre's repertory season. It was directed by John Lithgow and starred Lenny Baker, Charles Kimbrough, and Mary Beth Hurt.

VICTORIA REGINA

by Laurence Housman

Opened December 26, 1935

517 Performances

The Broadhurst Theatre

Produced and directed by Gilbert Miller

Cast: Helen Hayes (Victoria); Vincent Price (Prince Albert); Babette Feist (Duchess of Kent); Lewis Casson (Lord Melbourne); E. Bellenden-Clarke (Lord Conyngham); Harry Plimmer (Archbishop of Canterbury); George Macready (Prince Ernest); Albert Froom (Mr. Richards); Oswald Marshall (Mr. Anson); Mary Heberden (Lady Muriel); Renee Macready (Lady Grace); James Bedford (Mr.

Oakley); Cherry Hardy (Duchess of Sutherland); Helen Trenholme (Lady Jane); Tom Woods (General Grey); James Woodburn (John Brown); George Zucco (Lord Beaconsfield); Herschel Martin (Sir Arthur Bigge); Felix Brown (An Imperial Highness); Gilbert McKay (His Royal Highness); Mary Forbes (1st Princess); Shirley Gale (2nd Princess); Elizabeth Munn (3rd Princess); Alfred Halton (Footman); Mary Austin (Maidservant); Arthur Gould-Porter (1st Queen's Gentleman); Edward Martin (Usher); Mary Newnham-Davis (Lady-in-Waiting); Fothringham James (2nd Queen's Gentleman); Edward Jones (3rd Queen's Gentleman); Robert Von Rigel (Footman).

Helen Hayes is, unfortunately, best remembered today as an impish character actress specializing in cute little old ladies. In her heyday, she was called the First Lady of the American Theatre and respected as the queen of the American stage. She aptly achieved her greatest triumph as a most royal figure, Queen Victoria, in the biographical pageant *Victoria Regina*.

The author, Laurence Housman (brother of the great poet A.E. Housman), originally published this vast stage work as a collection of thirty scenes, more literary than theatrical, from the life of England's beloved queen. The stage version consisted of eleven of the scenes. The London production was presented at a private theatrical club. A commercial mounting was forbidden by the Lord Chamberlain—an office that long operated as a censor—since it was considered disrespectful to portray, even in a respectful manner, royalty who had lived within the past century.

Helen Hayes as Queen Victoria in *Victoria Regina*.

Pamela Stanley was Victoria and a young American actor named Vincent Price played Prince Albert.

The producer Gilbert Miller saw potential in the play. Since a profitable run was not possible in London, he offered it to Helen Hayes as a vehicle for Broadway. Hayes had some experience playing queens. She had recently enacted the title role in Maxwell Anderson's *Mary of Scotland* and had a great success. She was somewhat reluctant at first, regarding Victoria as something of a pill, compared to the passionate Mary. But after reading the script and seeing that Housman portrayed his subject as a strong, intelligent woman, rather than as stuffy or priggish, Hayes agreed to play her. Price was engaged to repeat his role of Albert.

Victoria was more challenging than Mary, Queen of Scots, for the role required that Hayes age as she went from the teenaged Victoria's ascension to the throne to the stately matriarch's celebration of her Diamond Jubilee. Actor Charles Laughton suggested to Hayes that she put two slices of apple in her cheeks to puff them out with agedness. But the apples always wound up eaten, so cotton was used instead.

Audiences were scarcely able to recognize her as she progressed through the monarch's reign. At one performance during the last scene, a gentleman in the audience could be heard asking his companion, "Who is that? That can't be Miss Hayes." On the strength of this performance, Noël Coward called her "the greatest living actress."

Hayes was a busy radio actress as well as a stage star. During the run, she was contracted to appear in two weekly radio series. The first was aired live on Tuesday nights, so the play was presented as a matinee so as not to conflict with it. But *Bambi,* the second series, was broadcast live on a Monday night, when the star had to do both her radio show and an evening performance. Every Monday night, Hayes would first get made up, do the radio show from 8:00 to 8:30 P.M. at the studio, and then, with a policeman riding shotgun on the running board of her car, rush back to the theatre in time for her first entrance at 8:40.

Royalty visiting New York would invariably attend a performance of *Victoria Regina* and then call on the leading lady's dressing room. This happened so often that the management hired an expert on royal etiquette for such backstage visitations. After the Broadway run, there was an extensive national tour. In the tradition of the day, the New York star traveled with the play so that all the country could see her.

The play was finally done in Britain when King Edward VIII lifted the ban on productions dealing with the royal family. Pamela Stanley got to play the Queen, this time for a general audience rather than for a private club. The production tied in with the 100th anniversary of Victoria's coronation and the recent coronation of George VI (following the abdication of his brother Edward).

Hayes repeated her legendary impersonation of the queen on both radio (on *The Theatre Guild of the Air*, in 1947) and television (on *Robert Montgomery Presents*, in 1951). Julie Harris later played Victoria for television for a *Hallmark Hall of Fame* production, in 1961.

The romance of Victoria and Albert, incidentally, was the subject of two unsuccessful musicals, *Love Match*, which closed on the road in 1968, and *H.R.H*, a London show that folded after four months in 1972.

YOU CAN'T TAKE IT WITH YOU

by George S. Kaufman and Moss Hart
Opened December 14, 1936
837 performances
The Booth Theatre
Directed by George S. Kaufman
Produced by Sam H. Harris

Cast: Henry Travers (Martin Vanderhof); Josephine Hull (Penelope Sycamore); Margot Stevenson (Alice); Jess Barker (Tony Kirby); Frank Wilcox (Paul Sycamore); George Tobias (Boris Kolenkhov); Paula Trueman (Essie); George Heller (Ed); Ruth Attaway (Rheba); Oscar Polk (Donald); Frank Conlan (Mr. DePinna); William J. Kelly (Mr. Kirby), Virginia Hammond (Mrs. Kirby); Hugh Rennie (Henderson); Mitzi Hajos (Gay Wellington); Anna Lubowe (Olga).

George S. Kaufman and Moss Hart's classic comedy of nonconformity takes place in the Sycamore family's living room, or as the authors described it, the "every-man-for-himself room," where each household member pursues his or her own eccentric hobby without disturbing the others. Grandpa collect snakes, Penny writes plays, Essie practices ballet, and so on and so forth.

Conflict comes into this happy nest when "normal" daughter Alice falls in love with Tony, the boss's son at the Wall Street firm where she alone in the family holds down a regular job. Despite Alice's protests, the boy's parents are invited over for dinner—and pandemonium reigns.

This gentle farce was perfect for a population still reeling from the Depression. Evidently the family had no money problems. The household appeared to be supported by Grandpa's fortune and Alice's wages. Audiences escaped into a comfy world where one was free from worry about work and government bogeymen from the IRS and the FBI could be laughed away.

Kaufman and Hart had previously collaborated on *Once in a Lifetime* (1929) and *Merrily We Roll Along* (1934). Hart had since provided the book for *Jubilee*, a Cole Porter musical, while Kaufman had penned *First Lady* (with Katherine Dayton), *Bring on the Girls* (with Morrie Ryskind) and *Stage Door* (with Edna Ferber).

To work on a third play together, Kaufman journeyed to Hollywood where his partner had a screenwriting

A typical evening at the Sycamores is interrupted by the arrival of some stuffed shirts in *You Can't Take It with You*.

assignment. Hart wanted to dramatize Dalton Trumbo's satirical novel *Washington Jitters*, but Kaufman found it too fanciful to be staged. Instead, he suggested they develop a vague idea of Hart's about a crazy family that did whatever they damned well pleased. The collaborators spent ten days drafting each of the three acts. The play was finished in a month. Several different titles like *Foxy Grandpa, Grandpa's Other Snake, Money in the Bank*, and *The King Is Naked* were considered before settling on the simple *You Can't Take It with You.*

Despite uncertainty about the title, the authors were certain about their play's potential—so much so that they had producer Sam Harris begin casting it before they were even finished writing it. They specifically asked for reliable character actors Josephine Hull, George Tobias, Frank Conlan, and Oscar Polk. For the important role of Grandpa Vanderhof, the head of the clan, Kaufman and Hart engaged Henry Travers themselves in California. Travers is best remembered today as the apprentice angel Clarence in the Frank Capra motion picture *It's a Wonderful Life.*

Kaufman and Hart were absolutely correct; not only did the show pack the Booth Theatre, but it won critical plaudits. There was some consternation when the play received the 1937 Pulitzer Prize. Many reviewers felt the award should not be bestowed on a frivolous comedy, albeit a good one. These detractors have since been proven short-sighted, for this play has outlived many a serious drama like *High Tor*, the highly regarded New York Drama Critics Critic's choice of the same season.

You Can't Take It with You was not as successful in London, where it had a miserable one-week run in 1938. Apparently the London audience judged it to be too American in its humor.

The film version came out in 1938 while the play was still running—the first time this had occured—yet neither suffered at the box office. The film rights had been bought by Harry Cohn for Columbia (just beating out Louis B. Mayer at MGM) at $200,000. Frank Capra, a master of sentimental film comedy, directed. The movie starred James Stewart, Jean Arthur, Lionel Barrymore, Edward Arnold, Spring Byington, and Ann Miller. It received the Oscar for Best Picture and Best Director.

Ellis Rabb's Association of Producing Artists (APA) Theatre had a hit with a revival starring Rosemary Harris in 1965, which Rabb directed. There was also a television production in the 1980s with Art Carney, Jean Stapleton, Blythe Danner, Barry Bostwick and Mildred Natwick. The next Broadway revival was in 1983 with Ellis Rabb directing a cast that featured Jason Robards, Elizabeth Wilson, James Coco, Colleen Dewhurst, and later George Rose. This version was also filmed.

BROTHER RAT

by John Monks, Jr. and Fred F. Finklehoff

Opened December 16, 1936

577 Performances

The Biltmore Theatre

Produced and directed by George Abbott

Cast: Eddie Albert (Bing Edwards); Frank Albertson (Billy Randolph); José Ferrer (Dan Crawford); Kathleen Fitz (Kate Rice); Curtis Burnley Railing (Mrs. Brooks); Wyn Cahooh (Joyce Winfree); Anna Franklin (Jenny); Mary Mason (Claire Ramm); Richard Clark (Harley Harrington); Robert Foulk (A. Furman Townsend, Jr.); Gerard Lewis ("Newsreel" Scott); Robert Griffith ("Tripod" Andrews); Ezra Stone (Grant Bottome); David Hoffman (Slim); Vincent York (Lt. "Lace Drawers" Rogers); Carroll Ashburn (Col. Ramm).

Just two days after *You Can't Take It with You* opened, *Brother Rat*, another smash comedy, began a long run on Broadway. This production was part of a bargain George Abbott had made with the public to produce one hit comedy a season. In 1934–35, he did *Three Men on a Horse*; the following fall, *Boy Meets Girl*. His 1936 comical obligation to Broadway came from an unlikely source.

John Monks, Jr., and Frank Finklehoff, both twenty-six years old, showed up at Abbott's office with a script for a comedy about life at their alma mater, Virginia Military Institute. Called *Brother Rat*, after an affectionate greeting for a freshman, the play centered around three cadets. Star athlete Bing Edwards has been secretly married to Kate Rice, who is now pregnant. The action of the play follows the efforts of Bing's two roommates, Billy Randolph and Dan Crawford, to help their pal win a cash prize for being the school's best athlete and to keep the secret until graduation. Naturally, everything works out by the final curtain. While Bing fails to win their school's athletic prize, the young couple receives $300 for having the class's first baby.

While they were still in the academy, Monks and Finklehoff, known as the jokesters and bad boys of VMI, decided to dramatize certain of their school experiences while in the local jail nursing wounds after a fight. They wrote during off-hours in school, went their separate ways after graduation (Monks tried his hand at writing professionally, and Finkenhoff became a lawyer), joined forces again, and made an effort to sell their script. Using titles such as *When the Roll Is Called* and *Stand at Ease*, the fledgling dramatists revised their play thirty-two times before arriving at *Brother Rat*. They showed it to thirty-one producers before George Abbott.

To give youth a chance, Abbott agreed to produce and direct the play. He resolved to hire a young cast. "They're playing the part of Virginia Military Institute cadets—college men and prom trotters—and we'll not have a middle-ager in the crowd," he declared. The cast included such future stars as Eddie Albert and José Ferrer. Their co-star Frank Albertson had already achieved fame in the movies, opposite Katharine Hepburn, in *Alice Adams*.

The two young authors went back to VMI, in Lexington, Virginia, to get the blessing of cadet captains and officers. Their efforts were heartily endorsed, so several of them were bussed in for the tryout engagement in Baltimore, where the theatre was decked in red and lemon, the school colors.

Despite the cadets' enthusiasm, early signs were not good for *Brother Rat*. It was produced right after Abbott had a flop with *Sweet River*, an adaptation of *Uncle Tom's Cabin*. Two other military academy plays, *Honor Bright* and *So Proudly We Hail* had failed earlier that season. While the earlier plays stood as indictments of military schools as breeding fascism and cruelty, *Brother Rat* was, clearly, an easy romp through the rites of passage in late adolescence and early adulthood. *Newsweek* magazine compared the three plays, stating that in the comedy "none of the characters has a neurosis . . . and one scene actually shows a boy studying for an examination. Most important, the two young authors have succeeded in writing dialogue that might be spoken at any preparatory school."

The critics agreed that the comparison of similar shows helped, rather than hurt, *Brother Rat*. Many also commented on the freshness of having the characters being played by actors close to the correct age.

The play was filmed in 1938, with Eddie Albert repeating his stage role; co-starring were Ronald Reagan and (his then wife) Jane Wyman. It was remade as a movie musical in 1952. This version, called *About Face*, featured Gordon MacRae, Eddie Bracken, and Joel Grey.

THE WOMEN

by Clare Boothe Luce

Opened December 26, 1936

657 Performances

The Barrymore Theatre

Directed by Robert B. Sinclair

Produced by Max Gordon

Cast: Margalo Gillmore (Mary Haines); Ilka Chase (Sylvia Fowler); Phyllis Povah (Edith Potter); Jane Seymour (Nancy Blake); Adrienne Marden (Peggy Day); Margaret Douglass (Countess De Lage); Betty Lawford (Crystal Allen); Audrey Christie (Miriam Aarons); Jessie Busley (Mrs. Morehead); Anne Teeman (Jane); Ethel Jackson (Mrs. Wagstaff); Ruth Hammond (Olga); Charita Bauer (Little Mary); Mary Cecil (Maggie); Marjorie Main (Lucy); Eloise Bennett (Euphie); Mary Stuart (1st Hairdresser); Jane Moore (2nd Hairdresser); Ann Watson (Pedicurist); Eileen Burns (Miss Fordyce); Doris Day (1st Saleswoman); Jean Rodney (2nd Saleswoman); Lucille Fenton (Head Saleswoman/Nurse); Beryl Wallace (First Model); Martina Thomas (3rd Saleswoman); Joy Hathaway (Fitter); Beatrice Cole (2nd Model); Arlene Francis (Princess Tamara/Helene); Anne Hunter (Exercise Instructress); Virgilia Chew (Miss Watts); Mary Murray (Miss Trimmerback); Marjorie Wood (Sadie); Lillian Norton (Cigarette Girl).

Though there had been many plays on Broadway with all-male casts, Clare Boothe Luce's *The Women* was only the second to feature an all-female ensemble. The first had appeared in 1930, *Nine 'til Six*, about the workers in a dress shop. In *The Women*, thirty-five actresses played forty authors, hair-

dressers, cooks, models, secretaries, salesclerks, housekeepers, and so on—the entire spectrum of the upper middle class feminine world in 1936. The plot revolved around saintly Mary Haines's discovery of her husband's affair with guttersnipe Crystal Allen and the subsequent breakup of the Haines marriage. But the energy of the play derived from the author's acid satire on gossipy Park Avenue matrons, exemplified by the catty Sylvia Fowler, Mary's professed friend and the worst tongue wagger of them all.

The author, a reporter for *Vanity Fair* and the wife of *Time* magazine publisher Henry Luce, had one other show to her credit, a flop called *Abide with Me*. Yet her producer Max Gordon asked to see the author's next work. The novelty of a show featuring a cast with only women appealed to him, so he agreed to put it on.

The production was a huge one. The play's twelve scenes required twenty-seven stagehands. The thirty-five actresses, each of whom needed several changes of costume, needed 250 gowns and 200 pairs of shoes. There were over 1,000 props. The roles called for an army of understudies, many of whom played smaller roles, and a second company of standbys, in case the first group had to go on. One busy actress covered thirteen parts.

There were rumors that Broadway's hottest writing team, Kaufman and Hart, had a hand in the script. Both had money in the show and were often seen at rehearsals during the Philadelphia tryout. Kaufman maintained that they had only offered suggestions. According to Kaufman biographer Scott Meredith, when asked if he had indeed secretly written the play, the master playwright and wit quipped "Of course. What would be more natural than that I should write a smash and sign it Clare Boothe Luce?"

Luce was criticized for attacking her own sex by depicting almost all the characters as shallow and selfish. In a preface to the published version of the play, the author explained that her work was not about all females: "The women who inspired this play deserved to be smacked across the head with a meat axe. And that, I flatter myself, is exactly what I smacked them with. They are vulgar and dirty-minded and alien to grace, and I would not if I could . . . gloss over their obscenities with a wit which is foreign to them."

The London production almost didn't come off since the Lord Chamberlain objected to a character's contemptuous attitude towards motherhood. But he relented and the British production was mounted by Gilbert Miller and Jack Buchanan in 1937 with an American cast.

Luce wrote three other comedies after *The Women*, none as successful. She later turned from playwriting to politics and served as a Congresswoman and Ambassador to Brazil.

Filmed in 1939 with a screenplay by Anita Loos and direction by George Cukor, the MGM movie of *The*

Betty Lawford and Margalo Gillmore are being listened to by the entire staff of a dress shop in *The Women*.

Women featured Norma Shearer, Joan Crawford, Paulette Goddard, Rosalind Russell, and Joan Fontaine. A remake in 1956, entitled *The Opposite Sex*, added songs and a few male characters. June Allyson, Joan Collins, Dolores Gray, Ann Sheridan, Joan Blondell and Ann Miller were the new generation of gossips.

A Broadway revival of the play, directed by Morton Da Costa, was mounted in 1973. The cast that reached New York included Kim Hunter, Myrna Loy, Alexis Smith, Dorothy Loudon, Rhonda Fleming, and Jan Miner. (Lainie Kazan was fired in Philadelphia for refusing to wear a blond wig as Crystal.) This time the play ran afoul of Seventies sensitivities. Feminists complained about the play's portrayal of females as either domestic saints or bitches; Gloria Steinem called it a "minstrel show." The revival closed after 63 performances.

ROOM SERVICE

by John Murray and Allen Boretz

Opened May 19, 1937

500 Performances

The Cort Theatre

Produced and directed by George Abbott

Cast: Sam Levene (Gordon Miller); Eddie Albert (Leo Davis); Teddy Hart (Fakur Englund); Philip Loeb (Harry Binion); Donald MacBride (Gregory Wagner); Margaret Mullen (Christine Marlowe); Alexander Asro (Sasha Smirnoff); Betty Field (Hilda Manney); Cliff Dunstan (Joseph Gribble); Philip Wood (Simon Jenkins); Jack Bryne (Timothy Hogarth); Hans Robert (Dr. Glass); Ralph Morehouse (Senator Blake); William Mendrek (Bank Messenger); William Howard (Senator Blake's Secretary).

The George Abbott hit parade marched on with *Room Service*, another farcical smash from the master director–play doctor. This play, as originally produced by Sam H. Harris, had folded in Philadelphia. Abbott's assistant, Garson

Kanin, convinced his boss that the comedy should be salvaged. Abbott took Kanin's advice and rewrote the script, taking no credit as co-author.

Abbott also recast the play with many actors from his recent productions. Sam Levene and Teddy Hart (brother of lyricist Lorenz Hart) were brought in from *Three Men on a Horse*, and Eddie Albert, from *Brother Rat*.

Levene again played a schemer, Gordon Miller, a would-be Broadway producer intent on mounting a play by an unknown, Leo Davis, just off the bus from Oswego, New York. Miller and Davis and their director and an assistant are trappped in a suite at the Great White Way Hotel. They can't leave, for the bill has not been paid. The crux of the comedy is Miller's numerous attempts to get out of the room to get his show on the road and hotel owner George Wagner's efforts to stop him and collect payment.

The plot was very basic, but Abbott pulled every gag he could with his slam-bang staging. Reviewers acknowledged that the premise was weak, but that the theatrical magician Abbott had created theatrical magic again.

For the screen rights, RKO paid a record $255,000 and filmed the play as a vehicle for the Marx Brothers in 1938. Lucille Ball and Ann Miller led the female cast. The material was recycled as a movie musical in 1944 under the title *Step Lively*. Frank Sinatra crooned while George Murphy and Adolphe Menjou clowned.

There was short-lived revival in 1953, notable chiefly for providing the young Jack Lemmon with his Broadway debut. Two revivals off-Broadway featured Ron Leibman, in 1970, and Mark Hamill, in 1986.

PINS AND NEEDLES

Sketches by Arthur Arent, Marc Blitzstein, Emanuel Eisenberg, Charles Friedman, and David Gregory

Music and lyrics by Harold Rome

Opened November 27, 1937

1,108 Performances

The Labor Stage

Directed by Charles Friedman

Choreographed by Gluck Sandor and Benjamin Zemach

Produced by the International Ladies Garment Workers Union

Cast: Lydia Annucci, Sol Babchin, Sadie Bershadsky, Anne Brown, Sam Dratch, Zilla Edinburgh, Al Eben, Anthony Fazio, Tillie Feldman, Irene Fox, Sandra Gelman, Eugene Goldstein, Hyman Goldstein, Enzo Grassi, Nettie Harary, Hattie Hausdorf, Lynne Jaffee, Harry Kadison, Hyman Kaplan, Rose Kaufman, Bella Kinburn, Al Levy, May Martin, Murray Modick, Betty Morrison, Miriam Morrison, Jean Newman, Rose Newmark, Olive Pearman, Joseph Roth, Ruth Rubinstein, Fred Schmidt, Moe Schreier, Paul Seymour, Isaac Sides, Sidney Sklar, Mae Spiegel, Millie Weitz, Beatty Uretsky.

Today, the only musical connection most people make with the International Ladies Garment Workers Union (ILGWU) is the TV commercial in which we are advised to "Look for the Union Label." But in 1937, the union was responsible for the longest-running Broadway musical up to that time. The show was *Pins and Needles*, a political revue with a completely amateur cast of union garment workers.

The ILGWU had purchased the Princess Theatre, the home of many Jerome Kern musicals, and renamed it the Labor Stage. (Kern, as it happened, had composed "Look for the Silver Lining," which was the basis for the union's above-mentioned song). Louis Schaeffer, the union's official in charge of theatrical activities, commissioned director Charles Friedman to stage a show for the amusement of the membership and for recruitment purposes. Friedman asked several of his friends to contribute, including composer Harold Rome, who was making his professional debut, and writer Arthur Arent, who penned *One Third of a Nation*, the Federal Theatre's most successful "Living Newspaper" production. Marc Blitzstein, whose labor musical *The Cradle Will Rock* opened in the same season, wrote sketches for the show.

The revue had a definite leftist slant, as some of its song titles suggest: "Sing Me a Song of Social Significance," "Big Union for Two," and "It's Better With a Union Man." International politics were also fair game for parody. "Four Little Angels of Peace Are We" presented Hitler, Mussolini, Neville Chamberlain, and an unnamed Japanese leader claiming to be ministers of peace while sowing destruction.

Because of their daytime jobs, the cast could only come to rehearsals three nights a week, so it was a year before the show was ready to open. Even so, there was an unexpectedly favorable response from the critics, and the show became such a big hit that it switched its weekends-only schedule to a full eight performances a week. This meant that cast members had to decide if they wanted to be actors or to retain their jobs in the garment industry. Schaeffer worked out a deal which allowed the *Pins and Needles* ensemble to perform in the show and return to their factory jobs once the run was complete. Of course, this meant that they all had to join Actors Equity, another union. They became the first union cardholders to have membership in both the American Federation of Labor (A.F.L., Equity's parent organization) and the Commission of Industrial Organizations (C.I.O., the ILGWU's parent). This, of course, was decades before the two labor giants merged.

Even the carriage trade it taunted flocked to see the show. One letter requesting tickets was sent to the box office from 1194 Park Avenue; it read: "Please disregard the address long enough to send me four tickets to your show."

There was a special performance in the nation's capital to celebrate the 25th anniversary of the Department of

Labor's founding, but Secretary Frances Perkins had to censor certain scenes that poked fun at government officials who would be in the audience. These controversial segments were restored for a command performance at the White House for President and Mrs. Roosevelt, who laughed heartily at all the Washington references.

New material was constantly being put in to reflect changes in current events, and so the title was changed to *New Pins and Needles* and *Pins and Needles of 1939* during its three-year run. When Stalin and Hitler signed their Soviet–Nazi treaty, Stalin was targeted in *The Red Mikado*, which also satirized *The Hot Mikado* and *The Swing Mikado*, two recent attempts at modernizing the Gilbert and Sullivan operetta. When British Prime Minister Neville Chamberlain caved in to Hitler, he became the subject of the sketch "Britannia Waives the Rules."

During the run, the production moved to the larger Windsor Stage so that a top ticket price of $1.65 could be instituted.

Other revues attempted to copy the *Pins and Needles* success by using a political theme and the talents of Harold Rome: *Sing Out the News* (1938) and *Let Freedom Ring* (1942). These, however, were not as popular. There have been other musicals with labor or political themes, but not until the '60s, with the revolutionary *Hair*, has one been as overt in its left-wing viewpoint.

WHAT A LIFE

by Clifford Goldsmith
Opened April 13, 1938
538 Performances
The Biltmore Theatre
Produced and directed by George Abbott

Cast: Ezra Stone (Henry Aldrich); Betty Field (Barbara Pearson); Lea Penman (Mrs. Aldrich); Arthur Pearson (Mr. Nelson); Ruth Matteson (Miss Shea); Edith Van Cleve (Miss Pike); William Mendrek (Mr. Patterson); Eddie Bracken (Bill); Maidel Turner (Miss Eggleston); Daniel Ocko (Mr. Vecchitto); Elena Salvatore (Gertie); Vaughan Glaser (Mr. Bradley); Joyce Arling (Miss Wheeler); James Corner (George Bigelow); Jack Bryne (Mr. Ferguson); Butterfly McQueen (Mary).

What a Life, a gentle snapshot of 1930s adolescence, became the first Broadway show to inspire both a hit radio and movie series. Ezra Stone, an assistant to George Abbott, played Henry Aldrich, a teenage boy who is constantly tripping over trouble—the prototype for a long line of adolescent stumblejohns—from the comic strips' Archie Andrews to, more recently, Neil Simon's Eugene Jerome, of his 1980s *Brighton Beach* trilogy. The play's slight plot turned on Henry's efforts to go to the Spring Dance. All three acts took place in a high school principal's office, where Henry often found himself.

The radio series was created in order to boost the Broadway show, but it soon overshadowed and outran it.

The cry of "Henry! Henry Aldrich!" and Henry's quavering response of "Coming, Mother!" was soon as familiar to American households as Franklin Roosevelt's salutation, "My friends." Ezra Stone became typecast as Henry in the stage and radio versions and never broke out of the mold. Paramount's 1939 movie of *What a Life* cast Jackie Cooper as Henry, with Betty Field as his girlfriend and Vaughan Glaser as his short-tempered principal (repeating their Broadway roles). Paramount then launched a series of mildly funny Henry Aldrich films to rival MGM's popular Andy Hardy series. Jimmy Lyndon played Henry through most of the comedies. And finally, a television *Aldrich Family* series debuted on NBC in 1949.

HELLZAPOPPIN'

Sketches by Ole Olsen and Chic Johnson
Music by Sammy Fain
Lyrics by Charles Tobias
Addtional songs by Annette Mills, Teddy Hall, Don George, Paul Mann, Stephen Weiss, and Sam Lewis
Opened September 22, 1938
1,404 Performances
The 46th Street Theatre
Directed by Edward Dowling
Produced by Olsen and Johnson

Cast: Olsen and Johnson, Barto and Mann, Shirley Wayne, Hal Sherman, The Radio Rogues (Sidney Chatton, Jimmy Hollywood, Eddie Bartel), Ray Kinney and the Aloha Maids, Bettymae and Beverly Crane, The Charioteers, Walter Nilsson, Berg and Moore, Reed, Dean and Reed, Whitey's Steppers, Billy Adams, The Starlings, Dorothy Thomas, Roberta and Ray, Hardeen.

Olsen and Johnson, a pair of old-style vaudeville comics, proved that their lowbrow antics were anything but out of date by producing, writing, and starring in *Hellzapoppin'*, a wacky revue that surpassed *Pins and Needles* to become the longest-running musical of its time.

Subtitled "A Scream-Lined Revue," *Hellzapoppin'* had everything. Just to name a few of the attractions, there was cyclist Walter Nilsson, whose vehicle sported square wheels, sister act Bettymae and Beverly Crane, magician Hardeen (Houdini's brother), an African-American singing group called The Charioteers, comedy violinist Shirley Wayne, and a trio of celebrity impersonators called The Radio Rogues. But what really drew the crowds were the unexpected screwball antics, usually involving members of the audience.

Once the lights dimmed, the show began with a phony newsreel. Hitler was seen speaking with a Yiddish accent and Mussolini with a deep Southern dialect. Then Roosevelt appeared talking gibberish. Each extolled the virtues of the show the audience was about to see. What followed was mayhem of the highest order, punctuated by the occasional variety act to give the audience a chance to catch its breath.

There were many members of the cast planted in the audience. A ticket scalper was heard trying to sell tickets to *I Married an Angel*, another show on Broadway. A woman continuously roamed up and down the aisles yelling for someone named Oscar. A gorilla suddenly abducted a screaming young lady from her box seat and dragged her out of the theatre. A man in the front row won fifty pounds of ice in an onstage raffle and the prize was dumped into his lap. The lights suddenly blacked out, and a voice over the loudspeaker announced that the audience was about to be pelted with spiders. This was followed by showers of rice.

The critical fraternity, with the exception of powerful columnist Walter Winchell, of the *New York Mirror* (who was impersonated by The Radio Rogues in the show), frowned upon these shenanigans. Brooks Atkinson of the *New York Times* was particularly vehement. He stated in his notice that Olsen and Johnson had "stood on the corner of the street and stopped every third man. Those were the actors. Taking an old broom, they went up to the attic and swept out all the gags in sight. Those were the jokes." Olsen and Johnson got their revenge at one Thursday midnight show, adding a sketch in which actors playing the New York critics were hit with cream pies and soaked with seltzer water.

Despite getting a journalistic razzing, *Hellzapoppin'* remained a smash. The closest thing to a controversy in this show was a song about Abraham Lincoln sung by The Charioteers. The lyrics contained a direct quote from the 16th president about the people's right to overthrow the government. A few right-wingers mistook this for communist propaganda.

Jackie Gleason and Lew Parker (later seen on television's *That Girl*) headed the national company. The show was brought to the screen in 1941 with Martha Raye joining Olsen and Johnson to run amok in a movie studio. In the same year, a second Broadway edition entitled *Sons o' Fun* was created and made almost as big a hit. An updated version of *Hellzapoppin'* starring Jerry Lewis and Lynn Redgrave was attempted in 1977, but it closed out of town in Boston. A similar vaudevillean venture entitled *Sugar Babies* opened on Broadway in 1979, with Mickey Rooney and Ann Miller; it, too, was a hit.

THE MAN WHO CAME TO DINNER

by George S. Kaufman and Moss Hart
Opened October 16, 1939
739 Performances
The Music Box Theatre
Directed by George S. Kaufman
Produced by Sam H. Harris

Cast: Monty Woolley (Sheridan Whiteside); Edith Atwater (Maggie Cutler); Theodore Newton (Bert Jefferson); Carol Goodner (Lorraine Sheldon); John Hoysradt (Beverly Carlton); David Burns (Banjo); Mary Wickes (Miss Preen); Virginia Hammond (Mrs. Ernest Stanley); George Lessey (Mr. Stanley); Ruth Vivian (Harriet Stanley); Gordon Merrick (Richard Stanley); Barbara Wooddell (June Stanley); Dudley Clements (Dr. Bradley); Michael Harvey (Sandy); George Probert (John); Mrs. Priestly Morrison (Sarah); Barbara Adams (Mrs. Dexter); Edmonia Nolley (Mrs. McCutcheon); LeRoi Operti (Prof. Metz); Carl Johnson (Mr. Baker); Harold Woolf (Expressman); Edward Fisher (Westcott).

During the '20s and '30s, Alexander Woollcott was one of the most famous men in the world. Wit, critic, author, lecturer, and radio personality, Woollcott was among the most influential tastemakers of the period. Today he is perhaps best known as the inspiration for Sheridan Whiteside, the cantankerous title character in Kaufman and Hart's enduring farce on celebrity, *The Man Who Came to Dinner.*

Edith Atwater, Monty Woolley, and John Hoysradt in *The Man Who Came to Dinner.*

The heavy-set, acerbic Woollcott was great friends with Kaufman and Hart, and he asked them to write a play for him. He had appeared in two Broadway productions, *Brief Moment* (1931) and *Wine of Choice* (1938), and in the film *The Scoundrel*, playing witty "buttinsky" variations on himself.

The plot came to the authors when Woollcott visited Hart's farm in Bucks County, Pennsylvania. After making himself unwelcome and demanding, Woollcott inscribed the guest book with: "This is to certify that I had one of the most unpleasant evenings I can ever recall having spent." Kaufman asked Hart, "What if he had broken his leg and had to stay all summer?" They developed a storyline about Sheridan Whiteside, their stand-in for Woollcott, breaking his leg at the home of Mr. and Mrs. Stanley, who live in an Ohio town along his lecture circuit. He then proceeds to take over the home and the lives of the helpless homeowners.

There is a romance between Whiteside's secretary and a local reporter, but the main fun is the invasion of the mad world of international show business into a staid middle-class home. Every famous name of the day, from Walt Disney to Gertrude Stein, either drops by the house or telephones to pay their respects to Whiteside. Some characters were thinly disguised caricatures of members of the authors' celebrity set. Gertrude Lawrence was the model for man-eating actress Lorraine Sheldon. Noël Coward served as the basis for erudite, effete Beverly Carleton, who sang a Cowardesque song supplied by Cole Porter. Movie comic Banjo, whose brothers were named Whacko and Sloppo, was really Harpo Marx. (Kaufman had written for the Marx Brothers.)

The co-authors had a heavy workload with *The Fabulous Invalid*, *Sing Out the News*, and *The American Way* all in the works during the writing of *The Man Who Came to Dinner*. Finally, Woollcott decided not to play the role, claiming that he did not wish to exploit his own personality. After Robert Morley and Adolphe Menjou turned it down or proved too busy, Monty Woolley was cast. The only problem during tryouts occured when one scene was not working; the character of artist Miguel Santo, apparently based on Picasso, had to be written out of the show in New Haven.

The New York production was a triumph, and many other versions were mounted. Robert Morley did play the title role in London. Clifton Webb was the Chicago Whiteside.

Woollcott himself finally played it, too—playing himself, that is—in the West Coast production. He had a heart attack a few weeks into the run and Kaufman, who had appeared in his and Hart's *Once in a Lifetime*, took the train cross-country to play the role for a few days. Kaufman also played Whiteside in a historic production at the Bucks County Playhouse which also featured co-author Moss Hart as Beverly Carlton and Harpo Marx speaking his first lines onstage as Banjo.

The 1941 movie version had Monty Woolley repeating his Broadway role. Jimmy Durante, as Banjo, and Bette Davis, in a rare comedy turn as Whiteside's secretary, were featured.

A misbegotten 1967 musicalization called *Sherry!* starred Clive Revill (he replaced George Sanders, who left the cast in Boston) and closed after 63 Broadway performances.

Television's *Hallmark Hall of Fame* gave *The Man Who Came to Dinner* the all-star treatment in 1972, with Orson Welles, Joan Collins, Lee Remick, Don Knotts, and Marty Feldman in the leads. Mary Wickes, who originated the role of Miss Preen, Whiteside's put-upon nurse, in the Broadway and film versions, repeated her role. Ellis Rabb, who has had hits with revivals of other Kaufman works— *You Can't Take It With You* and *The Royal Family*—staged the show and starred as Whiteside in the most recent Broadway production of this show; this was in 1980 at the Circle in the Square. The Royal Shakespeare Company mounted a London version in 1989, with Gene Saks directing and John Wood in the lead.

LIFE WITH FATHER

by Howard Lindsay and Russel Crouse, based on the book by Clarence Day.

Opened November 8, 1939

3,224 Performances

The Empire Theatre

Directed by Bretaigne Windust

Produced by Oscar Serlin

Cast: Howard Lindsay (Father); Dorothy Stickney (Vinnie); John Drew Devereaux (Clarence); Teresa Wright (Mary); Richard Simon (John); Raymond Roe (Whitney); Larry Robinson (Harlan); Ruth Hammond (Cora); Richard Sterling (The Rev. Dr. Lloyd); Katherine Bard (Annie); Dorothy Bernard (Margaret); Portia Morrow (Delia); Nellie Burt (Nora); A.H. Van Buren (Dr. Humphreys); John C. King (Dr. Somers); Timothy Kearse (Maggie).

Among all the nonmusical long-run shows, *Life with Father* ranks as the record-holder; its eight-year run still holds after more than four decades. When you count the musicals, its record is still impressive. Only *A Chorus Line*, *Oh! Calcutta!*, *42nd Street*, *Grease*, *Fiddler on the Roof*, and *Cats* have run longer.

Like several later comedies (*My Sister Eileen*, *Junior Miss*), *Life with Father* first appeared on the pages of *The New Yorker* as a series of articles. Clarence Day's reminiscences of his growing up in Victorian-era New York centered on his crusty father ruling over his loving, cleverer wife and his four sons. Producer Oscar Serlin recognized the potential for a film or stage play in Day's pieces and obtained an option from the author's widow on the material.

Father Howard Lindsay (standing) makes a point at the breakfast table while mother Dorothy Stickney urges their youngest to listen in *Life with Father,* the longest-running play in Broadway history.

Serlin first conceived of a Paramount film with W.C. Fields as Father. He commissioned a screenplay tailored to Fields's talents, but Mrs. Day, sensing that the bulbous-nosed comedian did not present the right image, nixed the project. Undaunted, Serlin brought the property to Howard Lindsay, who had read the Day articles to his wife, actress Dorothy Stickney, while her eyes were bad. Lindsay enthuiastically assented to tackling the assignment of adapting the material to the stage. He brought in Russel Crouse, his collaborator on the books of three previous musicals, including *Anything Goes.* Crouse also had written three books on the American Victorian era, so he was an expert on the period.

Without an advance from the producer or the Day family, Lindsay and Crouse spent two years on their stage adaptation, most of the time talking and working out the scenes. Nothing was committed to paper until it had been meticulously plotted beforehand. Unlike the Fields movie script, the new version proved to be satisfactory to the Day family, and production was allowed to proceed.

The first choice for the roles of Father and Mother Day were Alfred Lunt and Lynn Fontanne, Broadway's most celebrated acting couple. While Lunt was enchanted with the idea of playing the blustering patriarch, the elegant Fontanne could not see herself as the mother, who hides her ability to manage Father behind an ingenuous persona.

Walter Connolly, Roland Young, John Halliday, and Walter Huston also rejected the leading role. It finally fell to Lindsay himself to enact Father opposite his wife as Mother. This was not so undesirable, for the co-author had wanted to play it all along.

Investors were hard to come by. They couldn't imagine much mileage in the pleasant snapshot of family life in the 1880s. An offer came to mount the play at a summer theatre in Skowhegan, Maine, but there was still no money. Lindsay was so determined to get *Life with Father* on and to act in it that he and Stickney mortgaged their home and anything of value they owned. After the summer stock run, on a shoestring budget, enough backers were attracted to attempt a New York mounting.

Bretaigne Windust, who had made a hit with his staging of Robert E. Sherwood's drama, *Idiot's Delight*, signed on as director. There were few cast changes from Skowhegan. A young Montgomery Clift almost played Clarence, but he was judged too sophisticated for the virginal eldest son, so John Drew Devereaux from the summer cast repeated the role. Mrs. Day was at all the rehearsals to ensure that the sacred memory of her husband's work was never compromised. As owner of fifty percent of the rights, she was also protecting her financial interests.

After a week's tryout in Baltimore, the show opened at the Empire Theatre on Broadway. Before the premiere, Lindsay remarked to Crouse, "We've got a nice little comedy here. We might even get six months out of it." What they got was one of the longest Broadway runs in history. At the closing performance, Lindsay and Stickney sent a telegram to the company reading "Better luck next time." In fact, in 1948, the authors penned a sequel entitled *Life with Mother*. The second play on the Days had a modest success and ran 265 performances.

William Powell starred with Irene Dunne in the 1947 film of the play with a young Elizabeth Taylor. A television series based on the play ran from 1953 to 1955, with Leon Ames and Lurene Tuttle as Father and Mother.

THE 1940s

The harsh realities of World War II sent audiences to Broadway in search of gentle comedies and backward glances at pleasanter eras in the recent past. Broadway complied with hits like *Arsenic and Old Lace, Blithe Spirit, Junior Miss, Harvey, I Remember Mama,* a new edition of the *Ziegfeld Follies,* and *Oklahoma!* The last named was a milestone musical which marked the beginning of the partnership of Richard Rodgers and Oscar Hammerstein II, the most influential songwriting and producing team of this era and perhaps the century. There was the occasional wartime drama from Lillian Hellman (*Watch on the Rhine, The Searching Wind*), but comedy was the dominant box office force during the first half of the '40s. ✦ After the war ended in 1945, we were ready for a more probing look at ourselves. Emerging playwrights like Tennessee Williams and Arthur Miller provided it with their powerhouse dramas. Elia Kazan staged most of these authors' first Broadway efforts, commencing his reign as the theatre's top director. Eugene O'Neill's sombre *The Iceman Cometh* was respected by critics but did not have a long run. It was to have a second life years later off-Broadway. ✦ Even musicals and comedies cut a little deeper: *South Pacific* and *Finian's Rainbow* dealt with racism. Lindsay and Crouse turned from nostalgia in *Life with Father* to examine Presidential politics in *State of the Union.* Garson Kanin's *Born Yesterday* took the cliché role of the dumb blonde and gave her a more meaningful twist, as well as supplying an excellent starring vehicle for young Judy Holliday. Mary Martin and Ethel Merman also came into their own as queens of musical comedy. ✦ In 1947, the American Theatre Wing started handing out the Antoinette Perry Awards (later nicknamed the Tonys) for outstanding stage work. The ceremony was held at a small dinner party at the Waldorf Astoria. There was no list of nominees, only winners. (Complete lists of nominees were not included in the Tony ceremonies until 1956.) Female winners received silver compact cases and the men got engraved golden bill clips. What began as a private little gathering for theatre folk grew into an annual nationally telecast event, the outcome of which could mean box office life or death for many productions.

SEPARATE ROOMS

by Joseph Carole and Alan Dinehart, Alex Gottlieb, and Edmund Joseph

Opened March 23, 1940

613 Performances

The Maxine Elliott Theatre

Directed by William B. Friedlander

Produced by Bobby Crawford

Cast: Alan Dinehart (Jim Stackhouse); Lyle Talbot (Don Stackhouse); Glenda Farrell (Pam); Mozelle Britton (Linda); Austin Fairman (Gary Bryce); James Robbins (Scoop Davis); Madora Keene (Leona Sharpe); Jack Smart (Taggart).

The public's fascination with celebrity and gossip spawned two long-running comedies during the 1939–40 season. One was Kaufman and Hart's witty and elegant *The Man Who Came to Dinner* (above). The other was *Separate Rooms*, a somewhat more sordid take on the private world of show biz that had less longevity. While the former play has been produced countless times, *Separate Rooms* has had no major revivals.

The action takes place in a New York townhouse shared by two brothers, Don and Jim Stackhouse. Don, a Broadway playwright, is married to Pam, the star of his latest hit. But she insists on a "separate rooms" arrangement and galavants around town with a former lover. Jim, a scandal-sheet gossip columnist, gathers enough information about his sister-in-law to blackmail her into performing her wifely duties. But Pam has the last laugh by pulling the same trick on Jim and forcing him to marry his loyal secretary Linda.

With four playwrights receiving credit in the program (a record for a straight play), the show previewed under the title of *Thanks for My Wife* in Chicago. When it opened in New York, reviews were mixed. The play's long run was attributed to a low ticket-price policy, the presence of B-movie stars Glenda Farrell and Lyle Talbot, and the numerous double entendres and sexual innuendoes which peppered the dialogue.

PANAMA HATTIE

Book by Herbert Fields and B.G. De Sylva

Music and lyrics by Cole Porter

Choreographed by Robert Alton

Opened October 30, 1940

501 Performances

The 46th Street Theatre

Directed by Edgar MacGregor

Produced by B.G. De Sylva

Cast: Ethel Merman (Hattie Maloney); James Dunn (Nick Bullett); Arthur Treacher (Vivian Budd); Joan Carroll (Geraldine Bullett); Betty Hutton (Florrie); Pat Harrington (Skat Briggs); Frank Hyers (Windy Deegan); Rags Ragland (Woozy Hogan); Phyllis Brooks (Leila Tree); Conchita (Mrs. Gonzalez); Eppy Pearson (Mac); Nadine Gray (Chiquita); Roger Gerry (Tim); Roy Blaine (Tom); Ted Daniels (Ted); Lipman Duckat (Ty); Elaine Shepard (Mildred Hunter); Ann Graham (Kitty Belle Randolph); Al Downing (Pete); Hal Conklin (1st Stranger); Frank DeRoss (2nd Stranger); Jack Donahue (Mike); James Kelso (Whitney Randolph); Linda Griffith (Fruit Peddler).

Just before she opened in *Panama Hattie*, Ethel Merman was featured on the cover of *Time* magazine and declared the "number-one musical-comedy songstress of these harassed times." *Panama Hattie* was the first of the starring vehicles in which her name alone was above the title. In *Anything Goes* (1934), William Gaxton and Victor Moore had been her co-stars. Her *Red, Hot and Blue* (1936) cohorts were Jimmy Durante and Bob Hope (in the show's billing, Merman and Durante's names crisscrossed each other, so neither was above the other.) In *DuBarry Was a Lady* (1939), she had shared center stage with Bert Lahr.

Ethel Merman as *Panama Hattie* is admired by sailors Rags Ragland, Frank Hyers, and Pat Harrington.

Like *DuBarry, Panama Hattie* was produced by B.G. De Sylva and was written by Cole Porter, De Sylva, and Herbert Fields. It was also the third hit in a row for De Sylva, after *DuBarry* and *Louisiana Purchase* (1940).

As in most of her previous Broadway outings, Merman played a nightclub chanteuse. She later said that Hattie was an expanded version of the title character in the song "Katie Went to Haiti" from *DuBarry*. Both Hattie and Katie are American singers struggling to make a living in a tropical setting. Hattie is the brassy belle of the Canal Zone and is in love with Philadelphia socialite Nick Bullet. In order to marry Nick, Hattie must win over his eight-year-old snob of a daughter. She does, in due course, and even foils a plot to blow up the Canal. In addition, Hattie has three sailor sidekicks who provide burlesque humor.

As if that weren't enough, future film star Betty Hutton bounced through two numbers. In fact, this cast was studded with soon-to-be film actresses. The chorus featured June Allyson (Hutton's understudy), Vera-Ellen, Betsy Blair, Lucille Bremer, Jane Ball, and Doris Dowling, all of whom subsequently appeared in Hollywood movies.

The highlight of the show was "Let's Be Buddies," a duet between Merman and Joan Carroll as the pint-sized aristocrat. Merman wore an outrageous hat and a gaudy dress covered with bows. During the course of the number, Carroll would snip the bows off the frock with a pair of scissors in order to simplify it. (She was actually removing specially fastened accessories.) Despite the humor, it drew tears from the audience.

David Grafton, the Cole Porter biographer, quotes the composer about his hit: "I took a tip from Buddy De Sylva's instinct for sentiment and agreed with him that a composition to diddle the public into tears would be useful at the box office. I wrote a tune called 'Let's Be Buddies' sung by Merman to a rather annoying brat; it was hogwash but it made the box office dizzy for a year."

Merman was having rather a dizzy time with her personal life during the run of the show. Less than three weeks into the run, she married actor's agent Bill Smith. The cast pelted her with rice at curtain calls on her wedding day. The following spring she divorced Smith. As the show continued, she courted and married Bob Leavitt, a newspaperman who disliked musical comedy. He had to have a few drinks to force himself to see his future wife's performance and as a result had a hard time staying awake. Unlike the Smith marriage, the Merman-Leavitt alliance outran *Panama Hattie.*

Red Skelton, Ann Sothern, and Lena Horne starred in the 1942 MGM movie version. A half-hour television condensation was broadcast in 1954 with Merman and Art Carney. Merman said that it was so condensed, "it evaporated."

MY SISTER EILEEN

by Joseph Fields and Jerome Chodorov, based on the stories of Ruth McKinney.

Opened December 26, 1940

864 Performances

The Biltmore Theatre

Directed by George S. Kaufman

Produced by Max Gordon

Cast: Shirley Booth (Ruth Sherwood); Jo Ann Sayers (Eileen Sherwood); Morris Carnovsky (Mr. Appopolous); Richard Quine (Frank Lippencott); Bruce MacFarlane (Chic Clark); William Post, Jr. (Robert Baker); Tom Dillon (Lonigan); Gordon Jones (The Wreck); Joan Tompkins (Helen Wade); Effie Afton (Violet Shelton); Charles Martin (Capt. Fletcher); Helen Ray (Mrs. Wade); Donald Foster (Walter Sherwood); George Cotton (Jensen); Joseph Kallini (The Consul); Benson Spring (Cossack); Eric Roberts (Street Arab); Robert White (Another Street Arab); Eda Heinemann (Prospective Tenant).

The whirlwind adventures of two sisters from Ohio coming to New York to seek their fortunes as writer and actress form the basis of *My Sister Eileen*. Eileen was the pretty but gullible sister, while Ruth was the not-so-pretty-but-wise-to-the-world one. This twosome began life in a series of sketches by Ruth McKinney published in *The New Yorker*.

The authors of the Broadway play were Joseph Fields and Jerome Chodorov. Fields was the son of Lew Fields, half of the famous vaudeville team Webber and Fields. The comic did not want any of his four children in show business. Even so, three of the four went into the theatre: In addition to Joseph, sister Dorothy and brother Herbert became writers for the stage, usually in collaboration. Dorothy was also a top lyricist (see *Blackbirds of 1928*). Joseph met Chodorov (who by coincidence also had a playwright for a brother) while the two were working at Republic Pictures. The pair didn't like working under the tyrannical sway of movie producers and decided to write a play together.

They saw the potential for a great comedy in McKinney's stories and asked her permission to dramatize them. It turned out the author had already done a play version with Leslie Reade, but it had failed to arouse any interest among producers. She gave Fields and Chodorov the go-ahead, though, and, in a rented beachhouse in Malibu, they turned out the script in a few months.

Moss Hart, a friend of Chodorov's playwright brother, took the script to producer Max Gordon, who was deeply in debt and suffering from chronic depression. For the first time in months, Gordon laughed. In the antics of the fictional Sherwood sisters he smelled a hit, but seeing that the play needed some work, he contacted one of the greatest play-doctors of them all, George S. Kaufman. Kaufman agreed to tighten up the play and direct it after a writing project with Edna Ferber failed to get off the ground.

Actually, Kaufman supervised the revision of the piece by the original authors while preparing the production of *George Washington Slept Here,* his last collaboration with Moss Hart.

After the initial rewrites of *My Sister Eileen* came the casting. Shirley Booth, later to win a Tony and an Oscar for *Come Back, Little Sheba* (as well as several Emmys for her *Hazel* TV series), was signed to play Ruth. Jo Anne Sayers, a newcomer, was engaged for Eileen. There was no out-of-town tryout; the producer and director were confident that the production didn't need any fine-tuning.

Just before the opening, misfortune struck the show. The real-life Eileen (McKinney's sister) died with her husband, the writer Nathaniel West (*Day of the Locust*), in an automobile accident. Everyone was pained by this news, but Kaufman pulled the company together. He extolled them to make the play a memorial for the late Eileen. The director's plea to his cast worked. Not only did the title heroine come beautifully alive on opening night, but she captivated audiences and critics.

Gordon sold the movie rights for $225,000 to Columbia Pictures, which filmed it twice. The first version was released in 1942, starring Rosalind Russell and Janet Blair, and made a hit. The 1955 remake added songs and featured Betty Garrett, Janet Leigh, Jack Lemmon, Dick York, and future choreographer-director Bob Fosse. Unlike its predecessor, it received a lukewarm reception.

Wonderful Town, with an entirely different score and libretto by Leonard Bernstein, Betty Comden, and Adolph Green, was another musical adaptation success that opened on Broadway in 1953. (See *Wonderful Town*, page 120).

McKinney's stories are one of the few properties to have been seen in four different media. After appearing in book form and in two different versions on both stage and screen, Eileen and her long-suffering sister became characters on a weekly CBS television series during the 1960–61 season.

ARSENIC AND OLD LACE

by Joseph Kesselring
Opened January 10, 1941
1,444 Performances
The Fulton Theatre
Directed by Bretaigne Windust
Produced by Howard Lindsay and Russel Crouse

Cast: Allyn Joslyn (Mortimer Brewster); Josephine Hull (Abby Brewster); Jean Adair (Martha Brewster); Boris Karloff (Jonathan Brewster); Edgar Stehli (Dr. Einstein); Helen Brooks (Elaine Harper); John Alexander (Teddy Brewster); Wyrley Birch (The Rev. Dr. Harper); John Quigg (Ofc. Brophy); Bruce Gordon (Ofc. Klein); Henry Herbert (Mr. Gibbs); Anthony Ross (Ofc. O'Hara); Victor Sutherland (Lt. Rooney); William Parke (Mr. Witherspoon).

Euthanasia is a controversial topic today or anytime, but in 1941 it was the subject of a hit comedy which became a standard in the American theatre. *Arsenic and Old Lace* concerns the Brewster family—primarily Abby and Martha, two spinster sisters who put lonely old gentlemen out of their misery with poisoned glasses of elderberry wine.

Sisters Josephine Hull and Jean Adair with nephew John Alexander who believes he is Teddy Roosevelt in *Arsenic and Old Lace*.

Their nephew Teddy thinks he's Theodore Roosevelt and conveniently buries the victims in the cellar, imagining them to have died of yellow fever during the digging of the Panama Canal. Nephew Jonathan is an escaped criminal, made to look like movie star Boris Karloff by a plastic surgeon; now home, he is looking for a hideout. It is left to nephew Mortimer, who has the relatively normal job of drama critic, to put everything right.

Under its original title, *Bodies in Our Cellar,* the play was sent to actress Dorothy Stickney, who was then playing opposite her husband Howard Lindsay in *Life with Father.* The playwright, Joseph Kesselring, was hoping she might be interested in playing one of the sisters. She showed it to her husband, saying nobody would ever be able to get away with a comedy about murder, but that the script was nonetheless very funny. Lindsay thought the concept could be gotten away with. He and his partner Russel Crouse bought the play, totally rewrote it, and produced it themselves.

Although they significantly altered Kesselring's script, sole credit for the play always went to him, and the producers denied that they had doctored it. None of Kesselring's previous or subsequent plays were up to *Arsenic*'s standard or were as successful. This bears out the theory that *Arsenic*'s longevity was due principally to Lindsay and Crouse.

Bretaigne Windust, who had staged *Life with Father,* was signed as director for *Arsenic.* Stickney elected not to play either of the Brewster sisters, who were eventually enacted by Josephine Hull and Jean Adair. Allyn Joslyn took the lead role of Mortimer, and John Alexander was Teddy.

For the frightening brother who resembles Boris Karloff, Lindsay and Crouse made the brilliant choice of casting Karloff himself for the role, though he was at first reluctant to accept the offer. In spite of his ghoulish cinema portrayals, including Frankenstein's monster and the Mummy, Karloff was a reclusive individual who was daunted by the prospect of acting without elaborate make-up in front of live audiences. Crouse made a special trek to Hollywood to win over the shy actor.

After a tryout in Baltimore, the show opened to rave notices at the Fulton Theatre on Broadway. Brooks Atkinson of the *New York Times* said "Kesselring has written a murder play as legitimate as farce-comedy. It is full of chuckles even when the scene is gruesome by nature. Swift, dry, satirical and exciting, it kept the first night audience roaring with laughter."

There was a sensation at the box office the next day, because not enough tickets had been printed to accommodate the demand. Within eleven days, the first profit check was sent out to the investors. Lindsay and Crouse wrote humorous letters accompanying subsequent checks. Many began with such satiric salutations as "Dear Little Cherub,"

"You Lucky Stiff," "You Money-Mad People," and "Dear Angie-Wangie" (for "angel," Broadway slang for a backer).

The London run, which began in 1942, reached 1,337 performances—almost as many as the American production. Numerous foreign-language versions prospered in European and South American countries.

Of course, any show this big would be coveted by Hollywood. In 1944 the movie of *Arsenic and Old Lace* was released. Directed by Frank Capra, it starred the hottest leading man of the day, Cary Grant, as Mortimer. Josephine Hull and Jean Adair repeated their stage roles. Raymond Massey appeared in the Karloff part, and Peter Lorre parodied his usual screen persona as the plastic surgeon.

A television adaptation with Helen Hayes and Lillian Gish was broadcast in the '60s. Jean Stapleton and Polly Holiday played the Brewster sisters in a 1986 Broadway revival with Tony Roberts, Abe Vigoda, and William Hickey co-starring. A clever touch of this production had all the poisoned old men emerge through the cellar door at curtain call to take a bow.

CLAUDIA

by Rose Franken
Opened February 12, 1941
722 Performances
The Booth Theatre
Directed by Rose Franken
Produced by John Golden

Cast: Dorothy McGuire (Claudia Naughton); Donald Cook (David Naughton); Frances Starr (Mrs. Brown); Adrienne Gessner (Bertha); Frank Tweddell (Fritz); John Williams (Jerry Seymoure); Olga Baclanova (Madame Daruschka); Audrey Ridgewell (Julia Naughton).

Rose Franken's *Claudia,* like *My Sister Eileen,* another of the season's comedy hits, was based on a series of magazine stories. Whereas the Sherwood sisters first came to life in *The New Yorker,* Claudia and her husband David sprang into being in the pages of *Redbook.* The author later collected her articles into two books—*Claudia* and *Claudia and David*—and directed her stage adaptation.

The title character is a newlywed of nineteen who lives with her husband David in a farmhouse. As the play begins we see her attempting to deal with income taxes, mortgages, and bank balances in a scatterbrained way. She doesn't realize, also, that the cow on the farm has to have a calf before it can give milk. During the course of the three acts, she innocently flirts with a neighbor, is glamourized by a visiting opera singer, and finally grows into womanhood. Even as she learns her mother is dying of cancer, Claudia discovers that she is going to have a baby.

The leading role was particularly demanding and difficult to cast. Claudia was onstage for all but two and a half minutes of the entire play. Thus she had to be an experienced actress, but not so mature that she couldn't convince an audience of her youthful naivete. Franken saw 209 actresses before choosing twenty-three-year-old Dorothy McGuire, whose only major credit was understudying Martha Scott in the original production of *Our Town*.

Several critics quipped about the implausiblity of a good play dealing with nice people, including a man who actually likes his mother-in-law. But they found the comedy-drama charming and warm-hearted. Louis Kronenberg of *PM* magazine called it "a nice play for the ladies." Willa Waldorf of the *New York Post* took exception to this remark; not all women were of the "matinee crowd." She pointed out that her male colleagues of the press were much more enthuiastic about *Claudia* than she was. And indeed they were. Richard Watts, Jr. of the *Daily News* called it "one of the best plays of the season." It played fifty-six weeks, went on tour, and returned to Broadway at reduced prices. Phyllis Thaxter succeeded McGuire in the New York company.

The film rights were sold for $187,000 to David O. Selznick. McGuire co-starred opposite Robert Young in the 1943 movie. A sequel entitled *Claudia and David* was released in 1946, again with McGuire and Young. The characters were also used in a recurring sketch on the Kate Smith radio show.

Claudia would probably not play well today, but during the early '40s, the heroine's slow journey from innocence to adulthood was closer to many people's experiences, and audiences, male and female, did identify with the play.

LET'S FACE IT

Book by Dorothy and Herbert Fields, based on *The Cradle Snatchers* by Russell Medcraft and Norma Mitchell.

Music by Cole Porter

Lyrics by Cole Porter, Sylvia Fine, and Max Liebman.

Opened October 29, 1941

547 Performances

The Imperial Theatre

Directed by Edgar MacGregor

Choreographed by Charles Walters

Produced by Vinton Freedley

Cast: Danny Kaye (Jerry Walker); Eve Arden (Maggie Watson); Benny Baker (Frankie Burns); Jack Williams (Eddie Hilliard); Vivian Vance (Nancy Collister); Edith Meiser (Cornelia Abigail Pigeon); Mary Jane Walsh (Winnie Potter); Nanette Fabray (Jean Blanchard); Betty Moran (Gloria Gunther); Houston Richards (Lt. Wiggins); James Todd (George Collister); Fred Irving Lewis (Judge Henry Clay Pidgeon); Joseph Macauley (Julian Watson); Marguerite Benton (Madge Hall); Helene Bliss (Helen Marcy); Helen Devlin (Dorothy Crowthers); Sunnie O'Dea (Muriel McGillicuddy); Mary Parker, Billy Daniel (Dance Team); Kalita Humphreys (Anna/Mrs. Wiggins); Lois Bolton (Mrs. Fink); Margie Evans (Mrs. Wigglesworth); Sally Bond (Another Maid); Marion Harvey (Molly Wincor); Beverly Whitney (Margaret Howard); Jane Ball (Ann Todd); Henry Austin (Philip); Tony Caridi (Jules); Miriam Franklin (Sigana Earle); William Lilling (Master of Ceremonies); Fred Nay (Private Walsh).

It was 1941, and although America had not yet entered the Second World War, the draft was in effect and its influence on daily life was on everyone's mind. Producer Vinton Freedley decided to take advantage of this situation by putting together a "service musical." He got the idea while reading a newspaper story of civilian women doing their patriotic duty by entertaining soldiers in their homes (no hanky-panky, though). He contracted three of Broadway's biggest talents to write the show: Cole Porter for the songs, and Dorothy and Herbert Fields for the book.

Porter had just had a hit the season before with *Panama Hattie*. *Let's Face It* would mark his return to the theatre after a brief sojourn in Hollywood, where he composed for a Fred Astaire film. Another distinction for the show was that it was to be the first that the two Fieldses worked on together. It's also one of the only three hit shows penned by a brother and sister team—the others being *Up in Central Park* and *Annie Get Your Gun*, a pair of later works of the Fieldses. Dorothy was a lyricist of note whose songs included "I Can't Give You Anything But Love," while Herbert had contributed the texts to such previous Cole Porter shows as *Fifty Million Frenchmen*, *DuBarry Was a Lady* and *Panama Hattie*.

The Fieldses based their book on the 1925 comedy *The Cradle Snatchers* (which had starred a young Humphrey Bogart), in which three wives discover their husbands have been stepping out on them. To get revenge and make their spouses jealous, they throw a party for three college boys. In the Fieldses' version, the college boys became new army recruits. The husbands, the husbands' mistresses, and the servicemen's girlfriends all show up at the party, complications ensue, and all ends happily. Porter's songs and the witty observations of the Fieldses on military life enlivened the plot even further.

The main soldier was played by a young comedian named Danny Kaye. After a string of successful nightclub appearances and his Broadway debut in *The Straw Hat Revue*, Kaye had made a tremendous impact in a supporting role in the Gertrude Lawrence vehicle *Lady in the Dark*. In that production, he stopped the show with the number "Tchaikovsky," in which he rattled off the names of Russian composers in a matter of seconds. *Let's Face It* gave him his first starring role on Broadway and the opportunity to perform similar tongue-twisting specialty material written for him by his wife Sylvia Fine and Max Liebman. The first, called "A Modern Fairy Tale" went over well, but it was the second, "Melody in 4F, or, Local Board Makes Good" that got the biggest hand. In ninety seconds, Kaye, with a kind of scat singing, unfolded the tale of a typical dogface recruit, from the opening of the letter containing his draft notice, to his medical inspection and boot camp, and finally to getting the Medal of Honor. Kaye used the material again in the film *Up in Arms*.

The supporting cast included such future stars as Eve Arden, Vivian Vance, and Nanette Fabray, who was just beginning her career as a musical comedy star. Arden's understudy was none other than Carol Channing.

José Ferrer replaced Danny Kaye late in the run. Since the specialty material had been tailored to the original star's talents, it was dropped, and a duet from *DuBarry Was a Lady* was substituted. Without Kaye headlining, the show was not as popular, and it closed a month after Ferrer took over.

Let's Face It launched Danny Kaye's career as a versatile musical comedian, especially in films. Apart from limited appearances, he did not return to Broadway until 1970, as Noah, in Richard Rodgers' musical *Two by Two*.

Bob Hope took Kaye's role in the 1943 Paramount film version of *Let's Face It*, but Betty Hutton delivered Kaye's rapid-fire numbers. Eve Arden re-created her original role. Only two of Porter's songs were used in the film. Jule Styne and Sammy Cahn wrote four new tunes for the movie score.

BLITHE SPIRIT

by Noël Coward

Opened November 5, 1941

657 Performances

The Morosco Theatre

Produced and directed by John C. Wilson

Cast: Clifton Webb (Charles); Leonora Corbett (Elvira); Peggy Wood (Ruth); Mildred Natwick (Madame Arcati); Philip Tonge (Dr. Bradman); Phyllis Joyce (Mrs. Bradman); Jacqueline Clarke (Edith).

While the American public was dealing with the peacetime draft (a theme in the musical hit *Let's Face It*), World War II had been going on for two years in Great Britain. Hitler's bombs were dropping on London and the rest of the country. Noël Coward, playwright, composer, actor, director, and celebrated wit, decided to give his country a light entertainment to take their minds off the destruction surrounding them. He called it *Blithe Spirit*, and it allowed British, and later, American theatregoers to laugh about death.

In the play, Charles Condomine is a novelist living with his second wife Ruth in the Kentish countryside. To gather metaphysical background detail for a book, he has invited Madame Arcati, a local medium, to dinner and to conduct a seance. Charles gets more than he bargained for when the ghost of his first wife Elvira is conjured up and plays havoc with his current marriage.

The spectral comedy was written in six days when Coward was vacationing in Wales with his friend Joyce Cary (who subsequently appeared in the film of the play). The only changes Coward made to his script were the correction of a few typographical errors and the cutting of two lines. It was finished on May 9 and had its pre-West End

(Left to right) Eve Arden, Edith Meiser, and Vivian Vance clean house in *Let's Face It*.

opening in Manchester on June 16. Cecil Parker, Kay Hammond, Faye Compton, and Margaret Rutherford headed the original British cast. The next month in London, the opening-night crowd had to walk across planks to avoid falling into a bomb crater. But once inside the theatre, they forgot the current dangers and obtained war relief in the form of laughter. *Blithe Spirit*'s London run extended through the war until 1946.

An American company, assembled by Coward's representative in the States, John C. Wilson, opened in November of 1941. It starred Clifton Webb, British actress Leonora Corbett, Peggy Wood, and Mildred Natwick. America welcomed this British import with open arms.

Ghostly Leonora Corbett (center) has a bit of supernatural fun with Clifton Webb and Peggy Wood in Noël Coward's *Blithe Spirit*.

Two other companies opened on the West Coast and in Chicago while the New York production was going strong.

There were several offers for the film rights and even a proposal for a radio series based on Elvira's spiritual adventures (Coward wired from London that they should try to get the rights to Shaw's *Saint Joan* instead). The playwright resisted, being disappointed by previous movie treatments of his work. *Blithe Spirit* finally reached the screen in 1945. David Lean, who had filmed Coward's patriotic paeans to Great Britain, *In Which We Serve* and *This Happy Breed*, cast Rex Harrison and Constance Cummings as Charles and Elvira. Kay Hammond and Margaret Rutherford repeated their stage roles as Ruth and Madame Arcati.

Coward himself played the male lead for two weeks on the London stage. Unfortunately, Prince George, the Duke of Kent and a close friend of Coward's, died in an auto-

mobile accident during this time. On the night of the tragedy, Coward found it difficult to get through the light comedy, especially since many of the jokes dealt with death. Coward later played Charles in a television version of the play on CBS in 1956 (an earlier telecast had been done in 1946). Coward edited the script down to seventy minutes to fit into the time slot. His co-stars were Lauren Bacall, Claudette Colbert, and Mildred Natwick, who again played Mme. Arcati.

In 1964, *High Spirits*, a musical version of the play by Hugh Martin and Timothy Gray, materialized. It featured Tammy Grimes, Edward Woodward, Louise Troy, and Beatrice Lillie. Coward himself directed this song-and-dance version of his play, and he quipped that it should have been called *An Evening With Beatrice Lillie*, since the comedienne was stealing the show as Madame Arcati. *High Spirits* ran for eight months on Broadway.

The last Broadway revival of *Blithe Spirit* materialized in 1987. Richard Chamberlain, Blythe Danner, Judith Ivey, and Geraldine Page starred. Page, who received a Tony nomination for her portrayal of Madame Arcati, made her last Broadway appearance in this role; she died during the run of this play about ghosts.

JUNIOR MISS

by Jerome Chodorov and Joseph Fields

Opened November 18, 1941

710 Performances

The Lyceum Theatre

Directed by Moss Hart

Produced by Max Gordon

Cast: Patricia Peardon (Judy Graves); Lenore Lonergan (Fuffy Adams); Philip Ober (Harry Graves); Barbara Robbins (Grace Graves); Joan Newton (Lois Graves); Matt Briggs (J.B. Curtis); Francesca Bruning (Ellen Curtis); Alexander Kirkland (Willis Reynolds); John Cushman (Barlow Adams); Peter Scott (Merrill Feurbach); Robert Willey (Sterling Brown); Jack Geer (Charles); John Hudson (Henry); Billy Redfield (Haskell Cummings); Kenneth Forbes (Joe); Paula Laurence (Hilda); James Elliott (Western Union Boy).

The trials of adolescence were treated in Broadway situation comedies such as Jerome Chodorov and Joseph Fields' *Junior Miss*. Judy Graves, the teenage heroine, has a fanciful infatuation with movies that causes all kinds of trouble for her middle-class New York family. After seeing her father innocently kiss his secretary on the cheek, she thinks of what happened to Clark Gable and Myrna Loy in *Wife Versus Secretary*. When her parents refuse to tell her about her mysterious visiting uncle, she immediately believes him to be an ex-con, just like Tyrone Power in *Criminal Code*. With the aid of her equally imaginative girlfriend, Fuffy Adams, Judy attempts to play matchmaker for her father's secretary and the mysterious uncle. Thus the teenagers make life miserable and lively for the grown-ups.

Like *My Sister Eileen*, Chodorov and Fields's previous hit, *Junior Miss* was based on a series of stories from the pages of *The New Yorker*. These were by Sally Benson, whose work was also adapted into the movie musical *Meet Me in St. Louis*. As with *Eileen*, Max Gordon was the producer. Moss Hart made his directing debut with *Junior Miss*.

As with the previous season's *Claudia*, the greatest problem in the casting of the show was finding an actress to play the lead. She had to be experienced enough to handle the demanding role, but not so mature as to be unconvincing as a fourteen-year-old. The problem was solved by the appearance in Gordon's office of sixteen-year-old Patricia Peardon, a sometime actress and the daughter of a navy admiral. She was not there to audition, but was waiting for a boyfriend who was trying out for one of the boys' roles. A stage manager inquired if she would be interested in auditioning, for she looked the right age. She replied

that of course she'd be interested, and the stage manager told her to return at 4 o'clock.

She immediately rushed home and put on makeup, a more grown-up dress, and high heels. At the audition, Hart, judging by her appearance, thought she would be better suited for the older sister, Lois, than for Judy. But once Patricia started reading, he sensed that her true personality belied her grown-up appearance. Hart had her read Judy, she was perfect, and he cast her immediately.

The play, an endearing piece of fluff, came along at just the right time. The harmless family situation took audiences' minds off the war in Europe, resulting in a two-year run.

Judy Graves and her teenage antics came to the screen in 1945 with Peggy Ann Garner in the title role of the 20th-Century Fox movie. *Junior Miss* was also adapted as a radio series for Shirley Temple.

SONS O' FUN

Sketches by Ole Olsen, Chic Johnson, and Hal Block

Songs by Jack Yellen and Sam E. Fain

Opened December 1, 1941

742 Performances

The Winter Garden Theatre

Directed by Edward Duryea Dowling

Choreographed by Robert Alton

Produced by the Shuberts

Cast: Ole Olsen, Chic Johnson, Carmen Miranda, Ella Logan, Frank Libuse, Joe Besser, Rosario Perez, Antonio Ruiz, Lionel Kaye, James Little, Ben Beri, Kitty Murray, Valentinoff, Ivan Kirov, Vilma Josey, Stanley Ross, Margaret Brander, Milton Charleston, Richard Craig, Martha Rawlins, Catherine Johnson, Eddie Davis, Moran & Wiser, Parker & Porthole, Watson & O'Rourke, Carter & Bowie, Statler Twins, Mullen Twins, The Crystal Twins, The Blackburn Twins, Al Ganz, Al Meyers, The Biltmorettes.

If Noël Coward's dry wit or the teenage antics of *Junior Miss* weren't enough to help audiences forget the war in Europe, Olsen and Johnson were back on Broadway with another dose of broad shenanigans as crazy as their first show *Hellzapoppin'*. The sequel, *Sons o' Fun*, used the same formula as the first show—comedy sketches onstage, punctuated by pranks played in the auditorium.

The fun began before the curtain went up. Actors posing as ushers sent patrons to the wrong seats and forced those with seats in the balcony and boxes to climb ladders to get to them. During the show, chorus girls would dance in the aisles and persuade audience members to join them. Invariably, a celebrity would be among the impromptu dancing partners, affording free publicity in the daily columns.

In addition to the masters of the revels Olsen and Johnson, the cast included Carmen Miranda, singer Ella Logan (who later starred in *Finian's Rainbow*), dancers Rosario and Antonio, and comic Joe Besser, a future member of the Three Stooges.

ANGEL STREET

by Patrick Hamilton

Opened December 5, 1941

1,295 Performances

The John Golden Theatre

Produced and directed by Shepard Traube

Cast: Judith Evelyn (Mrs. Manningham); Vincent Price (Mr. Manningham); Leo G. Carroll (Rough); Elizabeth Eustis (Nancy); Florence Edney (Elizabeth).

Thrillers and mysteries are the least represented genre among hit Broadway shows. Patrick Hamilton's *Angel Street* was the first mystery to surpass 500 performances since *The Bat* in 1920. The psychological suspense story premiered on the London stage under its better-known name *Gaslight* (which was also the title of the 1944 film version). British audiences were held spellbound as the deceptively charming husband attempted to systematically drive his young wife mad.

In the United States, the play was produced at several small, mostly summer stock theatres. This is how the script came to the attention of movie director–screenwriter Shepard Traube, who was in the market for a play so that he could return to the theatre. A friend who had seen the play sent the script to Traube, who immediately realized its chilling potential for Broadway.

The only problem was the title. Hamilton had already sold the rights to *Gaslight* to a British film company. Fearing that the movie could be released in competition with his production, Traube cabled Hamilton for permission to change the title. He suggested *5 Chelsea Square.* Hamilton's reply was "Wrong neighborhood, old man. The district is Pimlico." The playwright offered *Angel Street,* a thoroughfare in Pimlico, for an alternative. Traube accepted the suggestion.

Next came the matter of gathering angels for *Angel Street.* Traube went to several of his friends in the film community and gathered a consortium of thirteen investors, including the actresses Geraldine Fitzgerald and Rita Johnson and scenarists Dore Schary and George Seaton.

Rehearsals were kept fairly quiet, with Traube directing in the dining room of the Fifth Avenue Hotel. His small cast of five included Judith Evelyn, who was making her Broadway debut, Vincent Price, whose role as the husband

would be his first in a long line of villains, and reliable character actor Leo G. Carroll.

The show opened to enthusiastic notices. John Mason Brown of the *Evening Post* judged it superior to other recent suspense plays, *Kind Lady, Payment Deferred*, and *Night Must Fall.* Two days after this auspicious start, however, Japanese forces attacked Pearl Harbor. The box office was then in a slump for ten days, but business picked up thereafter and *Angel Street* had a phenomenally successful run of over three years, as well as two national tours.

What set this show apart from previous stage mysteries was the lack of violence. Unlike most thrillers, there were no on or offstage murders to be solved. The suspense was all in the interplay between the evil husband and his unsuspecting wife.

The popularity of *Angel Street* inspired a string of similiar thrillers: *The Walking Gentleman, Uncle Harry, Hand in Glove* and *Murder Without Crime* were all compared to *Angel Street* and found wanting. Only *The Two Mrs. Carrolls* was anywhere as well-received.

Curiously, the film version made by the British company went unreleased, and the rights for an American movie were acquired by Metro-Goldwyn-Mayer. The studio was

Vincent Price and Judith Evelyn appear to be a happily wedded couple in *Angel Street*. By the final curtain, the audience learned otherwise.

required to use the original title of *Gaslight*, which insured that no business would be drawn away from the play.

Ingrid Bergman won the first of her three Oscars for her performance in the 1944 MGM movie, and Charles Boyer, Joseph Cotten, and Angela Lansbury, who received a Best Supporting Actress nomination, were her co-stars.

The gaslights burned once more on Broadway in 1948 with Uta Hagen and José Ferrer, and again in 1975 with Dina Merrill and Michael Allinson. Traube staged and produced the second revival, which ran only 52 performances.

STAR AND GARTER

Assembled by Michael Todd

Songs by Irving Berlin, Al Dubin, Will Irwin, Harold Rome, Lester Lee, Irving Gordon, Alan Roberts, Harold Arlen, Frank McCue, Doris Tauber, Dorival Caymmi, Jerry Seelen, Jerome Brainin, John Mercer, Sis Wilner, and Al Stillman.

Opened June 24, 1942

609 Performances

The Music Box Theatre

Directed by Hassard Short

Choreographed by Al White, Jr.

Produced by Michael Todd

Cast: Bobby Clark, Gypsy Rose Lee, Prof. Lamberti, Georgia Sothern, Pat Harrington, Marjorie Knapp, Wayne and Martin, Lynn, Royce and Vanna, Gil Maison, La Verne Upton, Richard Robner, Eppy Pearson, Joe Lyons, Kate Friedlich, Bill Skipper, Carrie Finnall, Frank Price, Letitia, Juanita Rios, Frank and Jean Hubert, The Hudson Wonders.

Burlesque was dead. New York Mayor Fiorello La Guardia, elected as a reform candidate, closed down Minksy's and all the other burlesque houses on 42nd Street. The State Supreme Court denied Minsky's appeal to renew its theatre license. The court upheld La Guardia's decision, branding the girlie shows, which were quite tame by today's standards, "inartistic filth."

Flashy showman Michael Todd saw the shutting of the strip joints as a perfect opportunity to present a high-class burlesque show on Broadway. He figured he could get away with presenting baggy-pants comics and beautiful girls in expensive but skimpy costumes to carriage-trade audiences. Hassard Short, whose credits included such high-toned revues as *The Band Wagon* (1931) and *As Thousands Cheer* (1933), was hired as director to lend elegance to the low comedy and bumps and grinds. "But why should audiences pay four dollars to see the same old routines?" Short asked his producer.

"Because this is not the same audience that paid forty cents to see them on 42nd Street," replied Todd. It turned out he was right. Broadway theatregoers who had never seen a burlesque show paid the four dollars to see Todd's dressed-up version full of "low comics and tall dames," *Star and Garter*.

For his headliners he got Gypsy Rose Lee, the Queen of the Striptease, and Bobby Clark, the King of the Old-Time Gags. Lee was a stripper, but one with class—she accompanied her act with a sophisticated comedy monologue. Also, she had gained notoriety by authoring a best-selling murder mystery. (Her relationship with her domineering mother and her early years in vaudeville and burlesque later formed the basis of the musical *Gypsy*.) Clark had also come up in vaudeville and burlesque. He got laughs with his characteristic painted-on glasses and by growling like a dog whenever a pretty girl was in view.

Another highlight of the show was a classic routine featuring Professor Lamberti. He was discovered in front of the curtain with his xylophone. As he ineptly played a tune, a comely showgirl entered from the wings and began to strip. The audience applauded wildly. The Professor, thinking the reception was for him, would continue playing while the girl disrobed.

A particularly suggestive number had the girls of the chorus stroking furry objects on their costumes while singing about soft, furry bunnies. Innuendoes were the crudest thing about *Star and Garter*, and audiences loved them. Lee reported overhearing a woman leaving the theatre after a matinee telling a friend about the show. "Mabel," she said, "I have just seen without a doubt the dirtiest, filthiest show I've ever seen in all my life. Don't miss it."

Todd almost missed his chance to get the show on. Because of a lack of funds, he decided to open the show in New York with only one preview performance, and *sans* the customary out-of-town tryout. The preview performance was a disaster and a principal backer pulled out. Lee, who was a shrewd businesswoman and had considerable assets besides her stripping abilities, stepped in and contributed $30,000 of her own to meet expenses for an additional week of rehearsals.

When the time came to split up the profits and the lawyers were talking percentages, Lee asked Todd to draw a pie. "A pie?" asked Todd's lawyer.

"For chrissake," Todd exploded, "the dame wants a pie, give her a goddamn pie." The pie was drawn with the portion representing Lee's share shaded. She initialed her half, and Todd did the same for his. This was their contract.

Producer and star stripper spent long nights in Lee's apartment to work on the show, and there were rumors of an affair. Both denied this. They did work together again when Todd produced Lee's unsuccessful play *The Naked Genius*. He also later presented Cole Porter's *Mexican Hayride* in 1944, starring Bobby Clark and Lee's sister, June Havoc.

Broadway got another hit burlesque show nearly forty years later when *Sugar Babies* opened in 1979.

STARS ON ICE

Assembled by Sonja Henie and Arthur M. Wirtz

Music by Paul McGrane and Paul Van Loan

Lyrics by Al Stillman

Opened July 2, 1942

830 Performances

The Center Theatre

Directed by William M. Burke and Catherine Littlefield

Choreography by Catherine Littlefield

Produced by Sonart Productions

Cast: Carol Lynne, Skippy Baxter, Twinkle Watts, Dorothy Caley, Brandt Sisters, Paul Castle, Three Rookies, Freddie Trankler, The Four Bruises, A. Douglas Nelles, Vivienne Allen, Mary Jane Yeo, Paul Duke.

Soon after the opening of *Star and Garter*, a new kind of variety revue was being presented in the recently opened Center Theatre. *Stars on Ice* was the first hit ice revue. The Center, under the same management as Radio City Music Hall, had featured numerous attractions, including an annual ice show. This was the first presentation to run for over 500 performances.

Co-produced by Sonja Henie, America's skating sweetheart and star of a series of films which highlighted her skills on ice, the show combined eye-catching costumes with dazzling turns by champions. Numbers included a waltz, a foxhunt, and a glittery "Jack Frost Ballet," resplendent with sequins.

A later edition, *Hats Off to Ice*, opened two years later and had an even longer run.

JANIE

by Josephine Bentham and Herschel Williams, based on the novel by Herschel Williams.

Opened September 10, 1942

642 Performances

The Henry Miller Theatre

Directed by Antoinette Perry

Produced by Brock Pemberton

Cast: Gwen Anderson (Janie Colburn); Maurice Manson (Charles Coburn); Clare Foley (Elsbeth Colburn); John Marriott (Rodney); Howard St. John (John Van Brunt); Betty Breckenridge (Bernadine Dodd); Margaret Wallace (Paula Rainey); Frank Amy (Scooper Nolan); Linda Watkins (Thelma Lawrence); Herbert Evers (Dick Lawrence); Artiebell McGinty (Tina); Michael St. Angel (Andy); Franklin Kline (Frank); Paul Wilson (Oscar); Gertrude Beach (Hortense Bennington); Blaine Fillmore (Dead-Pan Hackett); J. Franklin Jones (Carl Loomis); Nicky Raymond (Joe Jerome); Kenneth Tobey (Mickey Malone); W.O. McWatters (Uncle Poodgie).

Hard on the heels of *Junior Miss*, a similar theatrical creampuff about an adolescent girl, *Janie*, opened to mildly appreciative notices and earned a respectable run. Unlike *Junior Miss*, the latter show did take into account that there was a war on—the heroine falls in love with a serviceman. While the grown-ups are away attending a country-club function, she invites her new boyfriend and all his pals from the nearby army base to a party. They eat all the food on the premises and drink all of Pop's liquor, leaving Janie to face her parents.

The team of Brock Pemberton (producer) and Antoinette Perry (director), whose past hits included *Strictly Dishonorable* and *Personal Appearance*, triumphed again with this simple, easy-going comedy. The long run was attributed to a two-for-one ticket policy. Michael Curtiz (*Casablanca*) directed the 1944 film version. *Janie Gets Married*, a sequel that detailed the heroine's newlywed days, followed in 1946.

ROSALINDA

Adapted from the Max Reinhardt version of Johann Strauss, Jr.'s *Die Fledermaus* by Gottfried Reinhardt and John Meehan, Jr.

Lyrics by Paul Kerby

Choreography by George Balanchine

Opened October 28, 1942

521 Performances

The 44th Street Theatre

Directed by Felix Brentano

Produced by Lodewick Vroom

Cast: Dorothy Sarnoff (Rosalinda Von Eisenstein); Oscar Karlweis (Prince Orlofsky); Gene Barry (Falke); Everett West (Alfredo Allevanto); Ernest McChesney (Gabriel Von Eisenstein); Virginia MacWatters (Adele); Paul West (Dr. Frank); Shelly Winter (Fifi); Edwin Fowler (Aide de Campe); Louis Sorin (Frosch); José Limon (Premier Danseur); Mary Ellen (Premiere Danseuse).

Operetta had been a popular genre on Broadway, with the works of Sigmund Romberg, Victor Herbert, and Gilbert and Sullivan achieving popular runs. These European-flavored valentines combined lilting melodies with spoken dialogue as an alternative to the esoteric world of grand opera, which was mostly sung in foreign languages. During the 1930s, the form faded from the scene, as musicals by the likes of Cole Porter, the Gershwins, and Rodgers and Hart emerged with a more distinctly American accent.

Operetta had a resurgence with the New Opera Company's Broadway mounting of *Rosalinda*, an adaptation of Johann Strauss, Jr.'s Viennese pastry, *Die Fledermaus*. The plot revolves around the efforts of a husband and wife to deceive each other at a masked ball. This whimsical work was first presented in New York in 1879 and had appeared under various titles since then. Its incarnations included *The Merry Countess* (1912), *A Wonderful Night* (1929)—featuring an unknown named Archie Leach, who went on to become Cary Grant—and *Champagne Sec* (1933) with Peggy Wood and Kitty Carlisle in the male role of Prince Orlovsky.

This fourth new version was based on a production by Max Reinhardt which had been a hit in Berlin and Paris. It was adapted for American audiences by Reinhardt's son Gottfried and John Meehan, Jr., with new lyrics by Paul Kirby. Dorothy Sarnoff, who later had a leading role in *The*

King and I, sang the title role. Oscar Karlweiss, a popular comedian in Europe, played Prince Orlovsky, a role usually sung by a woman. The role of Fifi, Orlovsky's paramour, was created by Reinhardt for a young actress who had impressed him at an audition. Her name was Shelly Winter. She later added an *e* and an *s* and achieved Hollywood stardom as Shelley Winters.

Two men who became major figures in ballet and modern dance, were involved in the show. George Balanchine, Broadway's leading choreographer at the time, did the dances. José Limon was the first male dancer.

The popularity of *Rosalinda* inspired producers to mount revivals of operettas like *Blossom Time*, *The Merry Widow*, and *The Vagabond King*. None were as successful. The Metropolitan Opera had been closed for the war, but afterwards mounted a version of *Fledermaus* with lyrics by Broadway playwright-director Garson Kanin. This version remains in its repertory. Another updated, translated opera appeared the season after *Rosalinda*, when Oscar Hammerstein's *Carmen Jones* opened. Operetta on Broadway got another boost with Mike Todd's production of *Up in Central Park*, featuring music by Romberg, the season after that.

THE DOUGHGIRLS

by Joseph Fields

Opened December 30, 1942

671 Performances

The Lyceum Theatre

Directed by George S. Kaufman

Produced by Max Gordon

Cast: Virginia Field (Edna); King Calder (Julian Cadman); Sydney Grant (Mr. Jordan); Reed Brown, Jr. (Col. Halsted); Arleen Whelan (Vivian); Doris Nolan (Nan); William J. Kelly (Brigadier Gen. Slade); Vinton Hayworth (Tom Dillon); Ethel Wilson (Judge Honoria Blake); Arlene Francis (Natalia Chodorov); Edward H. Robins (Warren Buckley); Natalie Schafer (Sylvia); Reynolds Evans (Chaplain Stevens); Thomas F. Tracey (Admiral Owens); James MacDonald (Timothy Walsh); Maurice Burke (Stephen Forbes); Maxim Pantelcieff (Father Nicholai); Harold Grau (Stranger).

Serious wartime dramas had not fared well on Broadway, even after Pearl Harbor, and the pattern held right through the end of 1942, when a farce called *The Doughgirls* dealt with the effects of the war. The plot concerned four young women forced to share a hotel suite in crowded wartime Washington, D.C. Like most farces, this one was chock-full of slamming doors, confused situations, and sexual innuendo. Three of the so-called doughgirls are living with men

(Left to right) Doris Nolan, Arlene Francis, Arleen Whelan, and Virginia Field share a hotel room in wartime Washington in *The Doughgirls*.

to whom they are not married. All branches of the service and various legislators are represented as complications arise. Naturally, the various plot twists are untwisted by the final curtain with a marriage ceremony conducted by a Russian priest, just in time for the newlywed couple to lunch at the White House.

This was playwright Joseph Fields's first show without his partner Jerome Chodorov, who had joined the Army. Fields got the idea for the play on a trip to Washington. His producer Max Gordon sent a note to the hotel manager to take care of his friend the writer. When Fields arrived, he learned that the manager had been drafted. There was no reservation. After searching the capital in vain for accommodations, the playwright went all the way to Baltimore to get a hotel room. He vowed to write a play about the difficulties of finding living space in D.C.

Gordon, the producer of Fields's two previous hits, *My Sister Eileen* and *Junior Miss*, and George S. Kaufman, the director of *Eileen*, were recovering from *Franklin Street*, a flop which closed out of town. But *The Doughgirls* was funny enough to act as a salve for their wounds.

The three leading women were played by Hollywood starlets Virginia Field, Arleen Whelen, and Doris Nolan. The fourth lead female role, that of Natalia Chodorov, a Russian army sharpshooter named for Fields's partner, was played by Arlene Francis, who was well known through her radio work on the quiz show *What's My Name?* (not to be confused with her later TV show *What's My Line?*). Also in the cast in a supporting role was Natalie Schaefer, Kaufman's love interest at the time. (Schaefer is best known for her role on television's *Gilligan's Island*.)

As with *My Sister Eileen*, Kaufman supervised Fields's rewrites and is believed to have contributed many funny lines. Kaufman was constantly badgering Fields to brighten up the script, particularly the exits, when every character, he believed, should get a laugh. At one rehearsal a backstage washerwoman crossed the stage doing her work. After she left, Fields turned to Kaufman and said "Jesus, George, she got off without a laugh."

Fields also got into constant arguments with producer Gordon over certain naughty lines. One particular exchange was between a female judge and one of the girls:

"I could have a baby at the drop of a hat," boasts the judge. "In fact, I'd be having one right now if my husband hadn't gone to Australia."

"And took the hat with him, I suppose," was the girl's rejoinder.

The opening did not contain that dialogue, but Fields insisted on its return once the play was running and, consistent with the Dramatists Guild contract, he got his way.

The reviews emphasized Kaufman's staging over Fields's script. The *New York Herald-Tribune* said Kaufman had

"taken a highly contrived lampoon and filled it with laughter." The *New York Sun* stated that the play "runs with the effortless precision of electric clockwork."

The playwright did quite well, too. With the success of *The Doughgirls*, Fields was the only author to have three hits running on Broadway simultaneously; *My Sister Eileen* and *Junior Miss* the two previous plays he had written with Chodorov, were still playing alongside of his new smash. In addition, *Let's Face It* and *Something for the Boys*, two Cole Porter musicals with books written by Fields's sister Dorothy and brother Herbert were on in the same season, making it quite a Fields day. This feat was not topped until 1967, when Neil Simon had four shows going at once.

The Doughgirls made it to the screen while the war was still on in 1944. Anne Sheridan, Alexis Smith, and Jane Wyman starred as the three girls, but, like Arlene Francis before her, Eve Arden was the standout as the Russian army officer.

KISS AND TELL

by F. Hugh Herbert

Opened March 17, 1943

956 Performances

The Biltmore Theatre

Produced and directed by George Abbott

Cast: Joan Caulfield (Corliss Archer); Tommy Lewis (Raymond Pringle); Judith Parrish (Mildred Pringle); Robert White (Dexter Franklin); Jessie Royce Landis (Janet Archer); Robert Keith (Harry Archer); John Harvey (Pvt. Earhart); Richard Widmark (Lt. Lenny Archer); Paula Trueman (Mary Franklin); Calvin Thomas (Bill Franklin); Lulu Mae Hubbard (Dorothy Pringle); Walter Davis (Uncle George); Robert Lynn (Robert Pringle); James Lane (Mr. Willard); Francis Bavier (Louise).

During his long career as a producer and director, George Abbott was a firm believer in the adage "Youth must be served." His productions of the comedies *What a Life* and *Brother Rat*, as well as the musicals *Too Many Girls* (1939) and *Best Foot Forward* (1941), were chiefly concerned with the foibles of adolescence. Abbott's hit production for the season, F. Hugh Herbert's *Kiss and Tell*, was a similar frolic. The heroine was Corliss Archer, a madcap teen always out for adventure.

Setting the plot in motion, Corliss falsely declares that she is pregnant; she does this in a scheme to cover up the secret marriage of a friend. Predictably, complications and misunderstanding keep things going for three acts. The rest of the family and the neighbors check in with comic bits: there's the obnoxious little boy with the big vocabulary; the bumbling, easily upset father; the wise, advice-dispensing mother; the nerdy boy next door, and so on.

Kiss and Tell drew mild reviews, but was able to sustain a 956-performance run. Joan Caulfield as Corliss was singled out for praise. George Jean Nathan in his annual

Theatre Book of the Year listed her among those who gave "especially interesting performances." Also featured in the cast were a pre–*film noir* Richard Widmark as a young Army lieutenant, and Francis Bavier, later known for her role on television's *The Andy Griffith Show*.

Former child star and future diplomat Shirley Temple played Corliss in the 1945 film of the play—one of her better roles as a bobbysoxer. She also appeared in the 1949 sequel, *A Kiss for Corliss*, her last film.

Playwright F. Hugh Herbert later wrote about more mature matters concerning sexuality in 1951 in *The Moon Is Blue*.

OKLAHOMA!

Book and lyrics by Oscar Hammerstein II, based on *Green Grow the Lilacs* by Lynn Riggs.

Music by Richard Rodgers

Opened March 31, 1943

2,212 Performances

The St. James Theatre

Directed by Rouben Mamoulian

Choreographed by Agnes de Mille

Produced by The Theatre Guild

Cast: Alfred Drake (Curly); Joan Roberts (Laury); Betty Garde (Aunt Eller); Lee Dixon (Will Parker); Celeste Holm (Ado Annie); Joseph Buloff (Ali Hakim); Howard da Silva (Jud Fry); Barry Kelley (Ike Skidmore); Ralph Riggs (Andrew Carnes); Jane Lawrence (Gertie Cummings); Edwin Clay (Fred); Herbert Rissman (Slim); Ellen Love (Ellen); Owen Martin (Cord Elam); Paul Schierz (Mike); George Irving (Joe); Jack Harwood (Cowboy); Hayes Gordon (Sam).

"No gags, no gals, no chance." That's how *Oklahoma!* was described during its out-of-town tryout. Some attribute this pithy critique to Mike Todd, others to Walter Winchell. Regardless of the source, the quote reflected the conventional show business thinking until the folksy musical broke all the rules. There was no big opening number with a line of gorgeous chorines, no stars in the cast, no elaborate scenery. The story was a simple variation on boy gets girl: cowboy Curly woos and wins farm girl Laurcy. How could audiences get excited about something as ordinary as that?

Aside from the high quality of the individual songs, dances, and cast members, what set *Oklahoma!* apart from the musicals of its day was the way these elements fit together. Rodgers's melodies, Hammerstein's libretto, Agnes de Mille's choreography, Rouben Mamoulian's direction—each complemented the others with no one segment dominating. Most musicals until then had been either vehicles tailored to individual talents (Ed Wynn's clowning, Ethel Merman's belting, or Fred Astaire's dancing) or showcases for the songwriters. The stories that framed Hammerstein's operettas or Rodgers's tunes (with his previous lyricist Lorenz Hart) had been eminently forgettable. *Oklahoma!* established the pattern of the actors, the writers, and the directors serving the story, rather than vice versa.

Alfred Drake and Joan Roberts contemplate their new marriage and statehood for *Oklahoma!*

The idea of song and dance expressing and developing the characters' feelings had begun with *Show Boat*. With *Oklahoma!* it fully bloomed. "People Will Say We're in Love" brought out the tentativeness of Curly and Laurey's romance, while de Mille's vibrant and earthy dream ballet exposed sexual fears. Humor was hardly forgotten, though; traditional comic leads were given extra dimensions with Ado Annie's "I Cain't Say No," Will Parker's "Kansas City," and their duet "All er Nuthin'."

The musical also established one of the most successful partnerships in the history of American theatre. Rodgers and Hammerstein collaborated on a total of ten musicals, including one for television (*Cinderella*, 1957), and they wrote a film score (*State Fair*, 1945). In addition, they produced Irving Berlin's *Annie Get Your Gun* as well as six straight plays.

Oklahoma! was based on *Green Grow the Lilacs*, a prairie love tale by Lynn Riggs. Presented by the Theatre Guild during the 1930–31 season and starring Franchot Tone and June Walker, this play had a limited run. Theresa Helburn of the Guild had always thought *Lilacs* should have been a musical. She approached Richard Rodgers about the project. When Rodgers asked Lorenz Hart if he were interested, the lyricist expressed no desire to depart from his cosmopolitan style. After years of alcoholism, Hart was in poor health and had become increasingly unreliable.

For this new show, Rodgers acquired a new partner, Oscar Hammerstein II. But this choice led insiders to doubt the project's prospects. Hammerstein had contributed a string of hits in the '20s, including the previous watershed work *Show Boat*. But he hadn't had a hit in many years.

Before their first collaboration opened in New Haven as *Away We Go!*, no one would credit it as having a chance. But to the surprise of Broadway's smart set, the out-of-town reception was tumultuous. In Boston, where the results were the same, it was decided to change the title to *Oklahoma!* Once it exploded onto the stage of the St. James in New York, tickets had become scarce. The national company toured for over ten years, then revisited New York for 100 performances.

The film of *Oklahoma!*, released in 1955, was filmed in the wide-screen Todd-AO process. Gordon MacRae and Shirley Jones (who later also co-starred in the film of Rodgers and Hammerstein's *Carousel*), played the leads. Charlotte Greenwood, Gloria Grahame, Gene Nelson, Eddie Albert, and a brooding Rod Steiger were the supporting cast.

Recent Broadway revivals have included a 1969 edition by the Music Theatre of Lincoln Center, with Bruce Yarnell, Leigh Berry, Margaret Hamilton, April Shawhan, and Lee Roy Reams. A well-received 1979 production was directed by Hammerstein's son William. The latter mounting featured Laurence Guittard, Christine Andreas,

Mary Wickes, Christine Ebersole, and Harry Groener.

A notable by-product of the triumph of *Oklahoma!* was the phonograph album. Although it was hardly the first of its kind (many other shows had been recorded), the 78-rpm recording by Decca Records, with the original ensemble, was a major seller. Thereafter, almost every Broadway musical has been preserved on a disc of some sort.

ZIEGFELD FOLLIES OF 1943

Sketches by Lester Lee, Jerry Seelen, Bud Pearson, Les White, Joseph Erens, Charles Sherman, Harry Young, Lester Lawrence, Baldwin Bergensen, Ray Golden, Sid Kuller, William Wells, and Harold Rome.

Music by Ray Henderson and Dan White

Lyrics by Jack Yellen and Buddy Burston

Opened April 1, 1943

553 Performances

The Winter Garden Theatre

Directed by John Murray Anderson

Choreographed by Robert Alton

Produced by the Shuberts, in assocaition with Alfred Bloomingdale and Lou Walters

Cast: Milton Berle, Ilona Massey, Arthur Treacher, Katerine Meskill, Jack Cole, Sue Ryan, Tommy Wonder, Nadine Gae, Dean Murphy, Christine Ayers, Jack McCauley, Imogene Carpenter, Jaye Martin, Mary Ganley, Manfred Hecht, Penny Edwards, Charles Senna, Patricia Hall, Ray Long, Dixie Roberts, Arthur Maxwell, Rebecca Lee, Virginia Miller, Ruth Rowan, Doris Brent, Marilyn Hightower, The Jansleys, Bil and Cora Baird, Yost's Vikings, The Rhythmaires, The Ziegfeld Show Girls.

The same week that Rodgers and Hammerstein were determining the future of American musical comedy with the opening of *Oklahoma!*, the Shuberts were looking back to the days when Broadway was a Great White Way of extravaganzas with a new edition of the *Ziegfeld Follies*.

From 1907 to 1931, Florenz Ziegfeld ruled Broadway. His annual revues featured sumptuous costumes, swelling music, satirical sketches and, of course, dozens of show-girls dressed to represent everything from the Allied nations during World War I to salad ingredients. Stars like Fanny Brice, Will Rogers, Eddie Cantor, W.C. Fields, Ray Bolger, Ed Wynn, Bert Williams, Marilyn Miller, and Ina Claire were first introduced to the public in Ziegfeld shows. The showman became a legend. He was portrayed in movies by William Powell in the mostly fictional *The Great Ziegfeld* and in two MGM fantasy-musicals, *Ziegfeld Girl* and *Ziegfeld Follies*.

After his death, the Shuberts put on four more editions of the *Ziegfeld Follies*. For the first two, in 1934 and 1936, Ziegfeld's widow Billie Burke was credited as sole producer to lend veracity to the projects. Fanny Brice headlined both productions and newcomers like Buddy Ebsen and his sister Vilma, Bob Hope, Eve Arden, Judy Canova, and Gypsy Rose Lee were featured. The third incarnation of the post-Ziegfeld Follies starred Milton Berle and had the longest run of any of the productions. The show opened with an elaborate chorus line of dancing boys in tuxedos. One dancer fell out of step and flat on his face. Naturally, this was Berle, who then chased the dancers off and launched into an opening monologue. "See what happens when the Shuberts try to put on a Follies?" he began. "This never would have happened if Ziggy were around today. How do you like the costumes? They're left over from *Blossom Time* and *The Student Prince*." This last joke referred to the Shuberts' reputation for cutting production costs.

In addition to Berle, the 1943 Follies featured singer Ilona Massey, future choreographer Jack Cole, who performed a Hindu dance, impressionist Dean Murphy, and puppeteers Bil and Cora Baird. Sketches parodied meat rationing (with Berle as a butcher keeping a steak in a safe), zoot suiters, and another popular show, *Hellzapoppin'*.

After years of performing in vaudeville, this was Berle's first show with his name above the title on the marquee. During the run, he also hosted a live radio program called *Let Yourself Go* from 7 to 7:30. Then, after the show, he would do a rebroadcast for the West Coast.

There were some worries that the new Follies would suffer from comparison with the new Rodgers and Hammerstein work. As Berle noted in his memoirs, "*Oklahoma!* was cheered because it got rid of the traditional chorus line, because it integrated ballet with the storyline, and God knows what else. And there we were opening the next night with chorus girls hoofing their brains out and big productions numbers." In spite of this competition, *Ziegfeld Follies* attracted wartime audiences eager for diversion.

The final *Follies* to reach Broadway was produced in 1957. Despite the presence of Beatrice Lillie, it failed to generate enough interest for a long run.

TOMORROW THE WORLD

by James Gow and Arnaud d'Usseau
Opened April 14, 1943
500 Performances
Ethel Barrymore Theatre
Directed by Elliott Nugent
Produced by Theron Bamberger

Cast: Ralph Bellamy (Michael Frame); Shirley Booth (Leona Richards); Skippy Homeier (Emil Bruckner); Joyce Van Patten (Patricia Frame); Dorothy Sands (Jessie Frame); Edit Angold (Frieda); Richard Taber (Fred Miller); Walter Kelly (Dennis); Richard Tyler (Butler); Paul Porter, Jr. (Tommy).

The only Broadway play to run over 500 performances and to deal seriously with the threat of Nazism was not set in a European capital or even in Washington, D.C. *Tomorrow the World*, by James Gow and Arnaud d'Usseau was set in a small college town in middle America. Michael Frame, a chemistry professor, is expecting his nephew to arrive from Europe. The boy is a war orphan, the son of Frame's sister and a German scientist who were killed in a concentration camp. Instead of a starved waif, young Emil turns out to be a full-fledged twelve-year-old Hitler Youth.

Brainwashed by his Nazi school, Emil believes Americans are soft and that his father was a traitor. He proudly shows the swatiska on his uniform. Michael is tempted to strangle the boy at one point, but Leona, Michael's fiancée, advises gentle persuasion. This despite the fact that the boy has called her a "Jewish whore."

Gow and d'Usseau, former Hollywood screenwriters, derived their story from an article in *Life* Magazine about three American youths returning to their native country after being educated in Hitler's Germany. Nazi indoctrination had rendered them unable to adapt, and they were sent back. The playwrights' version was more hopeful, with Emil slowly casting off fascist teachings.

Shirley Booth and Ralph Bellamy discuss the bad behavior of Nazi-in-training Skippy Homeier (seated) in *Tomorrow the World*.

Ralph Bellamy returned to the stage to play Michael Frame, the compassionate uncle. It was his first Broadway part after thirteen years and eighty-three films. He decided to trod the boards once again when he read a character description in a film script: "charming but naive fellow from the Southwest, a typical Ralph Bellamy part." Bellamy realized he had been typecast and decided to go back East.

Shirley Booth, who had made a hit with lighter roles in *My Sister Eileen* and *The Philadelphia Story,* played his Jewish fiancée. But both were upstaged by Skippy Homeier as the young Nazi. Critics called him the nastiest villain on Broadway, worse than José Ferrer's Iago.

Joyce Van Patten was another juvenile in the cast to receive rave reviews. She and her brother Dickie, who also appeared that season in *Decision,* were two of the busiest child actors in the business.

Homeier did not pursue acting after growing into long pants. He did repeat the role of Emil in the screen adaptation of *Tomorrow the World,* released in 1944, with Fredric March, Betty Field, and Agnes Moorehead in the leads.

The play was definitely a product of its time. Once the war ended, the question of what to do with Nazified children yielded to Allied concerns about rebuilding Europe. There were no major revivals of *Tomorrow the World* after hostilities had ceased. Lillian Hellman's *Watch on the Rhine* (1941), another drawing-room anti-Fascist play, is one of the few dramas of that era that has been seen by audiences in recent years.

THE TWO MRS. CARROLLS

by Martin Vale

Opened August 3, 1943

585 Performances

The Booth Theatre

Directed by Reginald Denham

Produced by Robert Reud and Paul Czinner

Cast: Elisabeth Bergner (Sally Carroll); Victor Jory (Geoffrey Carroll); Irene Worth (Cicely Harden); Michelette Burani (Clemence); Stiano Braggiotti (Pennington); Margery Maude (Mrs. Latham); Philip Tonge (Dr. Tuttle); Vera Allen (Harriet).

A happily married young woman is being victimized by her seemingly caring husband. The suspense builds as she discovers his true nature and valiantly tries to free herself from his evil clutches. Sound familiar? The plot just described is remarkably similiar to that of *Angel Street,* the smash hit from 1941. But this story is also the focus of *The Two Mrs. Carrolls,* another melodrama which chilled Broadway.

In *Angel Street,* the Victorian wife is slowly being driven insane by the husband so that he can gain control of a fortune. In *The Two Mrs. Carrolls,* the present lady of the title learns from a former Mrs. Carroll that her spouse has a history of marrying his models and then plotting their deaths. The two plays were full of suspense rather than onstage violence to thrill audiences.

The author's name, Martin Vale, was the *nom de plume* of Mrs. Bayard Veiller, who wrote the play in 1935. It ran for a year in London and was produced on three separate occasions in America, all unsuccessfully. For the third try, the playwright shifted the locale from the south of France to Long Island. On the fourth attempt, the producer used the original London script and had a hit.

Director Reginald Denham was an old hand at suspense thrillers. He had co-authored *Ladies in Retirement* (1940), and staged such mysteries as *Rope, Dial M for Murder, Bad Seed,* and *Hostile Witness.* Unfortunately, Mrs. Veiller died just before rehearsals for the 1943 New York production were to begin.

Reviews were decidedly mixed. Howard Barnes of the *New York Herald-Tribune* admitted that the play "packs quite a jolt in its final scenes, but it takes an unconscionable time in arriving at its climax, and the motivation for an attempted murder does not even have a base in credible insanity." Despite the critical quibbles, the play had a respectable run of over a year.

The drawing card was Elisabeth Bergner. A star on the stages of Vienna, Berlin, Paris, and London, the Austrian-born actress triumphed as the second Mrs. Carroll, moving from joyful innocence to sustained hysteria as she attempted to escape from her Bluebeard-like husband, enacted by veteran film actor Victor Jory. The cast also featured a young Irene Worth as Mr. Carroll's next intended victim. Worth went on to a distinguished career in New York and London.

Humphrey Bogart was cast against type to play the artist in the 1947 film version. Barbara Stanwyck played another of her smart women in trouble as the victimized wife.

ONE TOUCH OF VENUS

Book by S.J. Perelman and Ogden Nash, suggested by *The Tainted Venus,* by F. Anstey

Music by Kurt Weill

Lyrics by Ogden Nash

Opened October 7, 1943

567 Performances

The Imperial Theatre

Directed by Elia Kazan

Choreography by Agnes de Mille

Produced by Cheryl Crawford, in association with John Wildberg

Cast: Mary Martin (Venus); Kenny Baker (Rodney Hatch); John Boles (Whitelaw Savory); Paula Lawrence (Molly Grant); Teddy Hart (Taxi Black); Ruth Bond (Gloria Kramer); Sono Osato (Premiere Danseuse); Harry Clark (Stanley); Helen Raymond (Mrs. Kramer); Lou Willis, Jr. (Bus Starter); Florence Dunlop (Mrs. Moates); Sam Bonnell (Store Manager); Zachary A. Charles (Sam); Bert Freed (Police Lieutenant); Jane Hoffman (Rose); Harold J. Stone (Zuvetli); Johnny Stearns (Dr. Rook); Matthew Farrar (Anatolian); Allyn Ann McLerie and Pearl Lang appeared in the chorus.

the book. She asked Kurt Weill, the brilliant German composer of *The Threepenny Opera*, to compose the music, and Ogden Nash, the country's foremost writer of light verse, to try his hand at song lyrics.

When Spewack's adaptation did not meet with Crawford's approval, Nash collaborated on a new book with S.J. Perelman, best known for his humorous articles and stories. Dietrich, who preferred Spewack's version, backed out of the production after reading the new script, calling it "too racy and profane." After offering the role to Gertrude Lawrence and Lenora Corbett (*Blithe Spirit*) and being turned down again, Crawford took it to Mary Martin. She saw the possibilities of making Venus a serene beauty in a mad world—a perfect role for Martin—rather than a Dietrich-like siren.

The production would mark Martin's return to Broadway. After making a hit singing "My Heart Belongs to Daddy" in Cole Porter's *Leave It to Me* (1938), she had gone to Hollywood. Her film career proved disappointing, but she did find a consolation prize at Paramount Pictures: Richard Halliday, a story editor whom she married and who supported her stage career unstintingly. She came back to New York ready for the theatre. After turning down the lead in *Oklahoma!* (then known as *Away We Go!*), she starred in an undistinguished Vernon Duke show called *Dancing in the Streets*, which closed in Boston.

She almost turned down Venus as well, claiming she was unsure she could play a gorgeous heavenly being. In order to convince her she was capable of doing so, Halliday took her to the Metropolitan Museum of Art and showed her all the different intrepretations of the goddess, demonstrating that Venus was in the eye of the beholder. One trait that troubled Martin was her height. She felt her five-feet four-inch stature was insufficient for the statue. Lead dancer Sono Osato, herself rather diminutive, coached Martin to "think tall," so that she could seem so onstage. By wearing high heels, piling her hair on her head, and "thinking tall," the perky Martin created the illusion that she had grown several inches. Many friends remarked on being astonished at the difference when seeing her in her dressing room wearing flats.

To complete the illusion, the famous dress designer Mainbocher was sought to create Martin's wardrobe. At first, the celebrated couturier was reluctant; he had never designed for the theatre before. So Martin auditioned for him, sitting in a chair and singing "That's Him" from the score. He accepted with one condition, that Martin sing the song to the audience the same way she did to him. Mainbocher's creations cost $20,000, a record for costumes till then, but they caused a sensation. Venus had fourteen costume changes and each earned applause as well as fashion spreads in the major magazines.

Mary Martin and Kenny Baker in *One Touch of Venus*.

Mary Martin established herself as Broadway's eternal optimist with *One Touch of Venus*, a variation on the Pygmalion myth. Martin played the title goddess, a statue who is brought to life when a barber from Ozone Heights places a ring on her finger.

Surprisingly enough, the role was originally intended for the worldly Marlene Dietrich. Producer Cheryl Crawford thought of the screen diva when she came across an obscure 1884 novella entitled *The Tainted Venus*. The premise of the Roman goddess of love coming to life in the modern world appealed to her as the basis for a musical. She first approached Bella Spewack (*Boy Meets Girl,*) to do

Crawford hired director Elia Kazan, an associate from her Group Theatre days; the creators wanted it to be staged like a drama, so they hired the top drama man of the time. This was Kazan's first musical, and during out-of-town tryouts, he discovered the book scenes were simply not coming across. The humor of Nash and Perelman may have worked on the pages of *The New Yorker*, but for the stage the spoken dialogue had to be cut to an absolute minimum. Emphasis was placed upon the Weill–Nash score, which included such songs as "Speak Low" and "I'm a Stranger Here Myself," and on Agnes de Mille's dances, led by the stunning Osato.

The musical ran for 567 performances; the successful tour closed in Chicago when the pregnant Martin had a miscarriage.

The 1948 film version altered the story somewhat by changing the setting to a department store. Ava Gardner, Robert Walker, Dick Haymes, and Eve Arden starred.

CARMEN JONES

Book and lyrics by Oscar Hammerstein II

Music by Georges Bizet

Opened December 2, 1943

502 Performances

The Broadway Theatre

Directed by Hassard Short and Charles Friedman

Choreographed by Eugene Loring

Produced by Billy Rose

Cast: Muriel Smith/Muriel Rahn (Carmen Jones); Luther Saxon/Napoleon Reed (Joe); Glenn Bryant (Husky Miller); Carlotta Franzell/Elton J. Warren (Cindy Lou); Napoleon Reed (Corp. Morrell); Robert Clarke (Foreman); Jack Carr (Sgt. Brown); Sibol Cain (Sally); Edward Roche (T-Bone); William Jones (Tough Kid); Cosy Cole (Drummer); Melvin Howard (Bartender/Bullet Head); Edward Christopher (Waiter); June Hawkins (Frankie); Jessica Russell (Myrt); Edward Lee Tyler (Rum); Dick Montgomery (Dink); P. Jay Sidney (Mr. Higgins); Fredye Marshall (Miss Higgins); Alford Pierre (Photographer); Ruth Crumpton (Dancing Girl); William Dillard (Poncho); Tony Fleming, Jr. (Referee).

Muriel Smith as *Carmen Jones* is deaf to the pleading of Luther Saxon in Oscar Hammerstein's adaptation of the Bizet opera.

Lyricist Oscar Hammerstein II was listening to a concert version of Bizet's Carmen at the Hollywood Bowl when it occured to him that the opera would be more enjoyable if the words were easily understood. This was not the first time the idea had come to him. As a child he had been taken to see an opera and wondered why no one was singing in English. He asked his mother, who replied, "That's just the way it's done."

For his English rendition of *Carmen*, Hammerstein updated the story to the South of World War II. Bizet's Spanish gypsies became African-Americans. The cigarette factory where Carmen was employed became a parachute factory, the soldier Don José a military policeman, and the matador Escamillo, Don José's rival for Carmen's love, a prizefighter named Husky Miller.

Hammerstein wrote idiomatic lyrics to replace the original French ones. Carmen's sensuous "Habanera" was now "Dat's Love." "The Toreador Song," Escamillo's boastful hymn to his profession, was replaced with Husky Miller's "Stan' Up and Fight (Until You Hear de Bell)." The recitatives between arias were eliminated—which was actually in keeping with Bizet's intentions, for the music that accompanies the opera's dialogue was added after his death.

Max Gordon was originally set to produce *Carmen Jones*. But when he chose not to renew his option on the property, Billy Rose picked it up. Rose seemed an unusual choice for presenting an updated opera on Broadway. His previous productions ranged from night-club revues to aquacades to the circus extravaganza *Jumbo*. But he saw the show as good entertainment like any other.

Because of the demands of the score, two sets of leads were cast. One performed during the evenings, the other during the matinees. Most were, until now, nonprofessionals making their theatrical debuts. Muriel Smith, the evening Carmen, had been a film washer in a camera shop. Luther Saxon was a checker in the Brooklyn Navy Yard, and Glenn Bryant was a New York City policeman on an extended leave of absence.

When the show opened, there was much confusion as to what to label it. The Boston papers weren't sure if it should be covered as an opera by the music critics or as a musical by the theatre critics. There was also an outcry from opera purists over what they perceived as the desecration of a classic. Noted composer Virgil Thompson defended the adaptation, stating that it was no more unusual for Southern blacks to be singing Bizet's music than for Spanish gypsies to be singing in French. He also pointed out that several operas had changed locale during their composition. Verdi's *Rigoletto* (1851) had taken place in France until diplomatic necessity forced him to

move it to Mantua, and *Un ballo in maschera* (1859) had moved from Sweden to colonial Massachusetts. Despite the arguments, *Carmen Jones* ran for 502 performances and played Broadway two more times during a nationwide tour.

Hammerstein defended his choice of the use of a black cast with the explanation that the black man, like the gypsy, had "rhythm in his body and music in his heart"— a racially stereotyped characterization that many would shun today. The lyricist was pleased and excited with the finished adaptation and said in a newspaper interview that he might make updating classic opera his life's work. His next effort in this new genre would be a modernization of *La Boheme*, set among the artists of Greenwich Village. Of course, Hammerstein continued instead to collaborate with Richard Rodgers, and his career took an entirely different path.

Otto Preminger directed the 1954 film version, with Dorothy Dandridge (whose singing voice was dubbed by opera star Marilyn Horne), Harry Belafonte, Pearl Bailey, Diahann Carroll, and Brock Peters.

THE VOICE OF THE TURTLE

by John Van Druten
Opened December 8, 1943
1,557 Performances
The Morosco Theatre
Directed by John Van Druten
Produced by Alfred de Liagre, Jr.

Cast: Margaret Sullavan (Sally Middleton); Audrey Christie (Olive Lashbrooke); Elliott Nugent (Bill Page).

The Voice of the Turtle, John Van Druten's three-character comedy, has several elements in common with previous long-running comedies. Like Joseph Fields's *The Doughgirls*, it uses the wartime housing shortage as a source for its comic situation. Like *Strictly Dishonorable*, it concerns a one-night stand which becomes a serious romance. It's also similar to the Preston Sturges farce in that it takes promiscuity as its theme but comes out in favor of matrimony and fidelity, in that order. For its day the play was quite frank in its treatment of premarital sex; because of the war, the threat of death in combat imparted an urgency to romance for many men and tended to relax strict moral codes.

Actress Olive Lashbrooke has an engagement for the evening with soldier Bill Page, who has no place to stay in overcrowded Manhattan. But Olive wants to break off the date so she can go out with a hotter prospect. She foists Bill off on her friend and fellow thespian Sally Middleton. Sally agrees to entertain and put up the GI, who is about to be shipped to Europe.

Sally is no virgin and perfectly aware that something could develop between herself and her temporary roommate. Something indeed does, but neither expects the passionate embrace which ends the first act to develop into love or the subsequent proposal which concludes the comedy. The title comes from the biblical "Song of Solomon": "When the flowers appear on the earth, the time of the singing of birds is come and the voice of the turtle is heard in our land."

Van Druten explained his inspiration for the play in an article for the *New York Herald-Tribune*: "I had a hunch that an audience might find pleasure in watching two young and attractive people . . . go through all the domestic details of a weekend's housekeeping. It would be a vicarious pleasure, akin to that of children playing house."

He also wrote that he found the restrictions of a three-character play challenging. His next play, *I Remember Mama*, provided a challenge of a different kind with a cast of twenty-three. At the time a play with only three characters was thought to be a little strange, and some theatres wouldn't rent their stages to such a show. Producers, feeling that audiences would want their money's worth, thought that such a small ensemble would hardly be worth the price of a ticket. Today, with Broadway's high production costs, a one-set, three-actor play would be a producer's dream.

Margaret Sullavan returned to the stage as Sally after a stint in Hollywood, and director–actor Elliott Nugent played Bill. Howard Barnes of the *Herald-Tribune* called it "frankly escapist," and continued, "Whether Van Druten has been haunting young ladies' apartments, listening to conversations in the subway or merely drawing on his own fund of human experience, he has fashioned a comedy with a somewhat universal appeal."

The open treatment of sexuality raised a few eyebrows. One Brooklyn pastor called for the play to be closed because it was "rotten and indicative of immoral trends in the theatre." The police investigated but found no reason to close the play.

There was an all-male, military version performed by the American Army in occupied Germany, with the sexes reversed. Thus there was only one female impersonation required; the two actresses became two actors, and the soldier became a visiting Frenchwoman with no hotel reservation.

The Broadway run continued through World War II. After the war, the script had to be altered. Bill was no longer a soldier about to go off to battle, but one returning from the front. With no threat of a military death hanging over it, the urgency of the weekend affair was somewhat lessened.

Warner Brothers purchased the movie rights and Eleanor Parker, Eve Arden, and Ronald Reagan starred in the 1947 movie version.

FOLLOW THE GIRLS

Book by Guy Bolton, Eddie Davis, and Fred Thompson
Music by Phil Charig
Lyrics by Dan Shapiro and Milton Pascal
Opened April 8, 1944
882 Performances
The Century Theatre
Directed by Harry Delmar
Choreographed by Catherine Littlefield
Produced by David Wolper, in association with Albert Borde

Cast: Gertrude Niesen (Bubbles LaMarr); Jackie Gleason (Goofy Gale); Irina Baranova (Anna Viskinova); Bill Tabbert (Yokel Sailor); Frank Parker (Bob Monroe); Tim Herbert (Spud Doolittle); Buster West (Dinky Reily); Val Valentinoff (Sailor Val/Felix Charrel); Frank Kreig (Seaman Pennywhistle/Archie Smith); Geraldine Stroock (Catherine Pepburn); Dorothy Keller (Peggy Baker); Toni Gilman (Phyllis Brent); Robert Tower (Dan Daley); Lee Davis (Petty Ofc. Banner); Walter Long (Capt. Hawkins); George Spaulding (Ofc. Flanagan); The Di Gatanos (Dance Team); Ernest Goodheart (Doorman); Terry Kelly 1st Fan Girl); Rae MacGregor (2nd Fan Girl); Charles Conaway, Jr. (Marine); Kathryn Lazell (Cigarette Girl).

Follow the Girls was a burlesque show disguised as a book musical which managed to become one of the longest running hits of the decade. The plot—what there was of it—concerned a big-hearted stripper named Bubbles, who lends her talents to the war effort by entertaining at a stage door canteen. The laughs come in when her overweight fiancé, classified 4-f, attempts to get into the establishment. The canteen is off limits to civilians, so he makes numerous tries at gaining entry, including squeezing into a servicewoman's dress. Since the hapless boyfriend was played by Jackie Gleason, the comic shticks paid off big time.

As in Mike Todd's *Star and Garter,* the musical numbers were just an excuse for the chorus girls to prance across the stage wearing nothing but spangles and flowers. Bubbles was played by Gertrude Niesen, a popular radio songstress, who had one hit tune in the show called "I Wanna Get Married."

Why did this show for 882 performances? The answer lies in the time that it opened. World War II was on and servicemen on leave wanted to see pretty and skimpily clad women. The closing of the burlesque houses created a demand for legitimate "leg and ankle" shows. Both *Star and Garter* and *Follow the Girls* supplied these diversions. Gleason's expert clowning also drew in audiences.

Once the war was over and the public began to expect more of musicals than flashing thighs and low antics, this type of entertainment vanished from Broadway. A few

Follow the Girls authors (Bolton, Davis, and Shapiro) collaborated on a similar show called *Ankles Aweigh* in 1955. Since television was by then providing plenty of bad jokes and pretty faces for free, it closed after a summer's run.

Gleason went on to become one of America's top entertainers through his various variety television shows. His reputation for ad-libbing and minimal rehearsing started with *Follow the Girls*. Niesen wanted him fired for what she considered his unprofessional behavior. Besides, he was always cracking her up onstage with his surprise gags. Once the reviews came out praising the comic, Niesen stopped demanding that he be pink-slipped. Gleason returned to Broadway in 1959, playing the besotted uncle in *Take Me Along*, a musical version of Eugene O'Neill's only comedy *Ah, Wilderness!* He won a Tony Award as Best Actor in a Musical.

HATS OFF TO ICE

Music and lyrics by James Littlefield and John Fortis

Opened June 22, 1944

889 Performances

The Center Theatre

Directed by William H. Burke and Catherine Littlefield

Choreographed by Catherine and Dorothie Littlefield; skating directed by May Judels

Produced by Sonja Henie and Arthur M. Wirtz

Cast: Freddie Trenkler, Carol Lynne, the Brandt Sisters, Geoffe Stevens, Lucille Page, Rudy Richards, Claire Wilkins, Bob Ballard, Peggy Whight, Paul Castle, Jean Sturgeon, James Caesar, Elouise Christine, the Caley Sisters, Robert Uksila, Gretle Uksila, Pat Marshall, Andrei Kristopher, John Patterson, Everett Anderson, Don Loring Rogers.

Hats Off to Ice is the second example of an ice show in the annals of long-running Broadway productions. Like its predecessor, *Stars on Ice*, it was co-produced by skating star Sonja Henie and presented at Radio City's Center Theatre. Elaborate costumes, champion-style figure skating, and comedy acts were featured. Low ticket prices and the ongoing demand for light wartime entertainment kept the hats off for 889 performances.

Ice spectaculars came in vogue years later with a proliferation of Ice Capades and Ice Follies shows touring the country and airing as TV specials. Olympic medal winners like Peggy Fleming and Dorothy Hamill were grabbed for lucrative contracts as fast as they could complete a figure eight.

In the 1980s, gold-medalist John Curry had a brief career on Broadway. In addition to his own skating show, *Ice Dancing*, which had choreography by avant-gardist Twyla Tharp, he played Harry Beaton in a revival of *Brigadoon*. Today, Broadway's enthusiasm for ice seems to have cooled, but if the 1980s roller-skating show *Starlight Express* can pack them in, can another ice frolic be far behind?

SONG OF NORWAY

Book by Milton Lazarus, based on a play by Homer Curran.

Music by Edvard Grieg, adapted by Robert Wright and George Forrest

Lyrics by Robert Wright and George Forrest

Opened August 21, 1944

860 Performances

The Imperial Theatre

Directed by Edwin Lester and Charles K. Freeman

Choreographed by George Balanchine

Produced by Edwin Lester

Cast: Lawrence Brooks (Edvard Grieg); Helena Bliss (Nina Hagerup); Robert Shafer (Rikard Nordraak); Irra Petina (Louisa Giovanni); Sig Arno (Count Peppi Le Loup); Alexandra Danilova (Adelina); Walter Kingsford (Father Grieg); Ivy Scott (Mother Grieg); Philip White (Father Nordraak); Dudley Clements (Henrik Ibsen); Janet Hamer (Sigrid); Kent Edwards (Einar); Robert Antoine (Eric); William Carroll (Gunnar); Patti Brady (Grima); Jackie Lee (Helga); Frederic Franklin (Freddy/Tito); Lewis Bolvard (Innkeeper); Doreen Wilson (Frau Professor Norden); Sharon Randall (Elvera); Karen Lund (Hedwig); Gwen Jones (Greta); Ann Andre (Marghareta); Elizabeth Bockoven (Hilda); Sonia Orlova (Miss Anders); Robert Bernard (Maestro Pisoni); Nora White (Signora Eleanora).

Lawrence Brooks and Helena Bliss in *Song of Norway*.

Song of Norway follows the example of *Blossom Time* in borrowing the life and work of a popular classical composer for a musical. For *Blossom Time* it was Schubert; for *Song of Norway*, Edvard Grieg. In the romanticized book, covering the years 1860 to 1863, Grieg is torn between loyalty to his native Norway, as represented by the simple and loving Nina, and the temptations of the more glamorous world outside its borders, epitomized by a sensuous opera singer.

While in Rome cavorting with the diverting diva, Grieg learns of the death of his dear friend, the poet Rikard Nordraak. He realizes that he belongs in his homeland and rushes back to Nina. After a tearful reunion scene, Grieg reads the last poem written by his dead friend. Inspired by the poem's stirring tribute to their country, the grieving composer immediately sits at the piano and turns out his famous Concerto in A Minor. The walls of the set fall away to reveal majestic fjords. Members of the corps de ballet enter and perform a stunning dance, concluding the show.

It may sound a tad hokey today, but the sublime Grieg melodies, adapted and arranged by Robert Wright and George Forrest, and the choreography by the great George Balanchine—danced by members of the Ballets Russe de Monte Carlo—more than made up for the simplistic book.

The idea of using Grieg's music in a dramatic format began when movie mogul Sam Goldwyn approached operetta producer Edwin Lester. Goldwyn had a script about Danish storyteller Hans Christian Andersen. Lester suggested doing it as a stage show using the music of Andersen's fellow Scandinavian, Grieg. Negotiations were drawn out and complex, and finally the Andersen project was dropped. (A movie musical on the fablist was eventually filmed, with Danny Kaye in the lead and songs by Frank Loesser).

Despite the abandonment of the original idea, Lester still liked the notion of using some of Grieg's 200 compositions and decided to mount a production of his own. As producer of the Los Angeles Civic Light Opera and its sister organization in San Francisco, he had the theatres. For the show itself, Lester's partner in the venture, Homer Curran, wrote a basic outline. Milton Lazarus subsequently hammered out the final version of the book.

The production in Los Angeles drew plaudits from local reviewers, as well as national publications like *Variety*, which recommended *Song of Norway* for operetta fans who were tired of revivals, concertgoers who would enjoy hearing great symphonic music in a different context, and theatre lovers in favor of a change of pace.

Eight Broadway producers made the trip across the continent to California to make bids to bring the show back East with them. Lester and Curran wanted to retain a certain amount of control and sold fifty percent of the rights to Lee Shubert. This way they would maintain an active interest and be assured their production would play in one of the theatres owned by the Shuberts.

The land of the midnight sun came to Broadway during a midsummer heat wave. Reviewers carped about the inane book but praised everything else. Howard Barnes of the *Herald-Tribune* stated that the show "has superior music and dancing and a vibrant attack, which must certainly make its mark at the box office. It is a piece to be welcomed even with its flagrant deficiencies." Irra Petina of the Metropolitan Opera was singled out for her turn as the salacious and witty opera singer. At the end of the run, most of the original cast was still intact and went on an extensive tour.

Lester, Wright, and Forrest brought another musical of classical derivation to Broadway, in 1953, with *Kismet*, which used the themes of the Russian composer Alexander Borodin.

Song of Norway was not filmed until 1970. Norwegian leading man Toralv Maurstad, Florence Henderson, and Edward G. Robinson starred in this gorgeously filmed but dull adaptation.

ANNA LUCASTA

by Philip Yordan

Opened August 30, 1944

957 Performances

The Mansfield Theatre

Directed by Harry Wagstaff Gribble

Produced by John J. Wildberg

Cast: Hilda Simms (Anna); Frederick O'Neal (Frank); Alice Childress (Blanche); Theodora Smith (Katie); Rosetta LeNoire (Stella); Georgia Burke (Theresa); John Proctor (Stanley); George Randol (Joe); Hubert Henry (Eddie); Alvin Childress (Noah); Emory Richardson (Officer); Canada Lee (Danny); John Tate (Lester); Earle Hyman (Rudolf).

Anna Lucasta was the first nonmusical since *The Green Pastures* to feature an all-black cast to achieve a run of over 500 performances on Broadway. Like that earlier hit, it was not the original work of an African-American playwright, but an African-American did rewrite it. Philip Yordan's drama, originally called *Anna Lukaska*, told the story of a Polish-American prostitute seeking redemption and the forgiveness of her estranged family. Apart from the heroine's nationality, it bore more than a passing resemblance to Eugene O'Neill's *Anna Christie*, a Pulitzer Prize winner about a Swedish-American prostitute who wants to turn over a new leaf.

Commercial producers turned Yordan's play down, but it came to the attention of the American Negro Theatre. The ANT was co-founded by playwright Abram Hill and actors Frederick O'Neal and Austin Briggs-Hall in response to the lack of opportunity for black performers and writers. They presented original scripts at the 135th

Street branch of the New York Public Library. Hill saw potential for his company in Yordan's play, acquired it, and largely rewrote it.

In the new version, Anna is a black, down-at-heels streetwalker who is called back to her relatives in Pennsylvania. She later finds out that the only reason that they wanted her to return was to marry her off to an unsuspecting wealthy Southerner. Heartbroken, Anna runs back to her former haunts, the docks of New York. But she is followed by the Southerner, who has fallen in love with her. They are reunited in a happy ending.

The plot may sound dated, but it was to be the vehicle by which African-Americans would be seen by white audiences as other than servants or musical comedy performers.

The production in Harlem drew such raves that it was brought to Broadway by John J. Wildberg, who had been involved with recent hits like the revival of *Porgy and Bess* and *One Touch of Venus*. It was the first professional appearance for many of the actors.

Critics hailed its sensitive treatment of black characters. "Negroes Portrayed as Humans for First Time" read the headline of the review in the *New York World-Telegram*. Largely white Broadway audiences kept the show going for over 950 performances.

The second anniversary of the Broadway opening was celebrated by having three of the Annas, Isabelle Cooley, Yvonne Machen, and Ruby Dee play the role, alternating for each of the three acts.

Many of the orignal cast went on to distinguished careers on both sides of the footlights. Alice Childress, who garnered critical kudos for her performance as Anna's fellow streetwalker, later won an Obie Award for her play *Trouble in Mind* (1955), which dealt with a black actress working with a white director on a play by a white writer. Many believed the play was based on her experiences in *Anna Lucasta*. Rosetta LeNoire founded the AMAS Repertory Theatre, an off-off-Broadway interracial musical theatre. Frederick O'Neal became an executive officer and president of Actors Equity. Earle Hyman played numerous roles on the stage and was on TV's *The Cosby Show*.

The 1958 film version featured Eartha Kitt, Sammy Davis, Jr., and O'Neal repeating his stage role. An earlier edition with a white cast headed by Paulette Goddard was released in 1949.

It was not until 1959 that Broadway had a long-running play with both a black author and black cast. Lorraine Hansberry's *A Raisin in the Sun* was the first hit play to be written, performed, and directed by African-Americans on Broadway. Ntozake Shange's *for colored girls who have considered suicide/when the rainbow is enuf* (1976) and August Wilson's *Fences* (1987) are the only two other Broadway nonmusicals by black playwrights to run over 500 performances.

(Left to right) Isabelle Cooley, Yvonne Machen, and Ruby Dee all played *Anna Lucasta*.

BLOOMER GIRL

by Sig Herzig and Fred Saidy, based on a play by Dan and Lilith James.

Music by Harold Arlen

Lyrics by E.Y. Harburg

Opened October 5, 1944

654 Performances

The Shubert Theatre

Directed by E.Y. Harburg and William Schorr

Choreograped by Agnes de Mille

Produced by John C. Wilson and Nat Goldstone

Cast: Celeste Holm (Evelina Applegate); David Brooks (Jefferson Calhoun); Joan McCracken (Daisy); Margaret Douglass (Dolly Bloomer); Dooley Wilson (Pompey); Matt Briggs (Horatio Applegate); Richard Huey (Alexander); Mabel Taliaferro (Serena); Pamela Randell (Octavia); Claudia Jordan (Lydia); Toni Hart (Julia); Carol MacFarlane (Phoebe); Nancy Douglass (Delia); John Call (Gus); Robert Lyon (Joshua Dingle); William Bender (Herman Brasher); Joe E. Marks (Ebenezer Mimms); Vaughn Trinnier (Wilfred Thrush); Dan Gallagher (Hiram Crump); Lee Barrie (Paula); Eleanor Jones (Prudence); Arlene Anderson (Hetty); Eleanor Winter (Betty); Blaine Cordner (Hamilton Calhoun); Charles Howard (Sheriff Quimby); John Byrd (1st Deputy/State Official); Joseph Florestano (2nd Deputy); Ralph Sassano (3rd Deputy); Hubert Dilworth (Augustus); Butler Hixon (Govenor Newton).

Bloomer Girl is proof positive that a musical can be made from just about anything, including the struggle for comfortable women's underwear. The plot also drew on such larger themes as abolitionism and the Civil War, but the battle between bloomers and hoop skirts was the starting point. E.Y. Harburg drew his idea for the show from a play by Dan and Lilith James.

In the musical, Evelina Applegate is the daughter of a prosperous hoop-skirt manufacturer in 1865 Cicero Falls, New York. Each of her five sisters have married successful salesmen in their father's firm. Evelina is about to suffer the same fate. But she is inspired to rebel against her father's oppressive garments and choice of husband by her aunt, Dolly Bloomer, an advocate of the wearing of loose trousers which come to be known as bloomers.

The character of the aunt is somewhat historically accurate; there was an Amelia Bloomer, the wife of a Quaker postmaster who edited a radical newspaper called *The Lily* and fought alongside Lucretia Mott and Susan B. Anthony for women's rights and for temperance.

Aunt Dolly is also a champion of the abolitionist movement and, with Evelina's aid, helps runaway slaves escape to Canada through the Underground Railroad. One such slave, Pompey, is pursued by his master, Jefferson Calhoun. When he and Evelina meet, they fall in love, as people tend to do in musical comedies, and sing one of the show's hits, "Right as the Rain." Their political differences divide them at the end of the first act, but they are reunited after the Civil War. The great conflict was depicted by a stirring Agnes de Mille ballet of the women waiting for their men to return from the battlefield. This segment had a tremendous emotional impact, particularly on the many

female audience members who were reminded of their own husbands overseas fighting the Axis powers during World War II.

There was also a miniature version of *Uncle Tom's Cabin*, making it the first of two hit musicals to employ Harriet Beecher Stowe's novel: *The King and I* borrowed from the antislavery classic six seasons later.

Many saw *Bloomer Girl* as a follow-up to *Oklahoma!* Not only did it similarly deal with Americana in a rustic setting; it also had the same choreographer (de Mille), musical arranger (Robert Russell Bennett), set designer (Lemuel Ayers), costume designer (Miles White), and two members of the cast (Celeste Holm and Joan McCracken). Holm advanced from a supporting player in *Oklahoma!* (she was Ado Annie) to a lead role, while McCracken broke out of the chorus to featured comic as the hired girl Daisy. McCracken provided many of the evening's funniest moments including "Tomorra! Tomorra!," a satiric strip number in which she removed the heavy layers of 19th-century women's clothes. Holm also had costume tribulations. In one scene she was required to wear a sixty-pound hoop skirt, which had to be lowered onto her backstage by a crane-like contraption.

Dooley Wilson (famed for singing "As Time Goes By" in the film *Casablanca*), scored a hit as the runaway slave with a musical cry for freedom called "The Eagle and Me."

Unlike most long-running shows, *Bloomer Girl* was a success from the moment it opened out of town in Philadelphia. There were a few backstage battles. The producers and writers begged de Mille to cut the Civil War ballet because it was too depressing. But once it played to a cheering audience, the dance stayed. The New York run solidified Holm's star status and helped the career of Nanette Fabray, who replaced her, toured with the production, and brought it back to Broadway for a run at City Center in 1947.

I REMEMBER MAMA

by John Van Druten, adapted from *Mama's Bank Account,* by Kathryn Forbes.

Opened October 19, 1944

714 Performances

The Music Box Theatre

Directed by John Van Druten

Produced by Richard Rodgers and Oscar Hammerstein II

Cast: Mady Christians (Mama); Richard Bishop (Papa); Joan Tetzel (Katrin); Oscar Homolka (Uncle Chris); Marlon Brando (Nils); Carolyn Hummel (Dagmar); Frances Heflin (Christine); Oswald Marshall (Mr. Hyde); Adrienne Gessner (Aunt Trina); Ellen Mahar (Aunt Sigrid); Ruth Gates (Aunt Jenny); Bruno Wick (Mr. Thorkelson); Louise Lorimer (Woman); William Pringle (Dr. Johnson); Robert Antoine (Arne); Ottilie Kruger (Dorothy Schiller); Josephine Brown (Florence Dana Moorhead); Marie Gale (Nurse); Dorothy Elder (Antoher Nurse); Frank Babcock (Soda Clerk); Cora Smith (Madeline); Herbert Kenwith (Bellboy).

I Remember Mama was one of many Broadway comedies of the '40s based on magazine sketches about families. Like *Life with Father, Claudia, My Sister Eileen,* and *Junior Miss,* John Van Druten's play is adapted from an episodic book. Unlike the previously named plays, the play has no central plot either.

Based on *Mama's Bank Account,* Kathryn Forbes's fictionalized reminiscences of her Norwegian-American family and her girlhood in early 1900s San Francisco, the play opens with a spotlight on the adult Katrin Hansen sitting at a typewriter and reading from a manuscript not unlike Forbes's book. As she reads about memories, the lights come up center stage, and there is a kitchen of the 1910s. Katrin steps away from her desk and into the past. What follows is series of incidents of growing up. At the center of these vignettes is Mama, unlearned but wise, strict but tender.

The original book was purchased by RKO as a potential movie to star Greek actress Katina Paxinou. The studio dropped the project when they heard that Richard Rodgers and Oscar Hammerstein II were going to follow up *Oklahoma!* by producing a straight-play version of the book. The film studio's executives knew they would get more mileage out of the property if it were done on the stage first; they invested in the show and eventually filmed it.

Rodgers' wife Dorothy had read the book and thought it would make an excellent play. The two producers contracted

(Left to right) Joan Tetzel, Frances Heflin, Mady Christians, Richard Bishop, and a very young Marlon Brando in *I Remember Mama.*

John Van Druten, author of the last season's comedy smash *The Voice of the Turtle*, to do the adaptation and direct. Van Druten's back-to-back plays could not have been more different. While *Turtle* was worldly and sophisticated, *Mama* was folksy and simple. *Turtle* featured three characters and one set. *Mama* boasted a cast of twenty-three, three revolving stages, forty-three scenes, over a hundred light cues, and twenty-six stagehands.

Van Druten wanted Viennese-born Mady Christians, last seen on Broadway in Lillian Hellman's *Watch on the Rhine*, to play Mama, but was worried she would only be interested in heavy dramas. When Van Druten expressed his doubts to his producers, Rodgers immediately produced a letter from the actress expressing her desire to be considered for the role. The cast also featured a young actor named Marlon Brando, making his professional debut as the son Nils. The original press release misspelled his first name as Marion.

War-weary audiences found refuge in gentle Mama's warm kitchen of yesterday. The play ran for over two years. Christians, and later Charlotte Greenwood, starred in the national tour. The London production was staged by Christians, who continued to play Mama. As was the case with many sentimental Yankee comedies, the British found it "too American."

After the stage play became a hit, RKO finally did the film, in 1948, with Irene Dunne in the title role and Oscar Homolka, Barbara Bel Geddes, and Ellen Corby in support. All four were nominated for Academy Awards. The Hansens later became one of the first television families. *I Remember Mama* ran on CBS as a weekly half-hour series from 1949 to 1956. Peggy Wood starred as Mama and Dick Van Patten was Nils. Except for the final 13 episodes, the program was broadcast live. Few of the segments were preserved, so most of the series is gone forever.

Years after the original production, Richard Rodgers composed a musical version of *I Remember Mama*. The 1979 musical starred Swedish film actress Liv Ullman, not known for her singing talents. Martin Charnin directed, and wrote the lyrics. Thomas Meehan authored the book. Several members of the creative staff, including Charnin, were fired before the opening. The notices were almost all negative, but the singing *I Remember Mama* played for 108 performances. Charnin suffered a heart attack during the run and Rodgers died four months after the closing. While the health of the songwriters is not necessarily connected with the fate of their show, Charnin has stated that the stress caused by problems with *I Remember Mama* contributed to his attack.

An earlier musical adaptation entitled *Mama* was done in 1972 at the Studio Arena Theatre in Buffalo, with Celeste Holm in the lead.

HARVEY

by Mary Chase
Opened November 1, 1944
1,775 Performances
The 48th Street Theatre
Directed by Antoinette Perry
Produced by Brock Pemberton

Cast: Frank Fay (Elwood P. Dowd); Josephine Hull (Vita Louise Simmons); Janet Tyler (Ruth Kelly, R.N.); Tom Seidel (Lyman Sanderson, M.D.); Fred Irving Lewis (William R. Chumley, M.D.); Jesse White (Marvin Wilson); John Kirk (Judge Omar Gaffney); Jane Van Duser (Myrtle Mae Simmons); Dora Clement (Betty Chumley); Robert Gist (E.J. Lofgren); Eloise Sheldon (Miss Johnson); Frederica Going (Mrs. Ethel Chauvenet); Lawrence Hayes (Mr. Peeples).

Along with Bugs Bunny and Roger Rabbit, *Harvey* ranks as one of the best-known show business bunnies. Unlike his animated fellows, Harvey wore a hat, was six feet tall and invisible. This legendary hare was the creation of Mary Chase, of Denver, Colorado. Like many playwrights, Chase began as a newspaper reporter (for the *Rocky Mountain News*). After having one production to her credit (called *Now I've Done It*, presented by the Federal Theatre), she drew on her Irish background for her second work.

An uncle had told her as a child numerous Celtic folk tales of mysterious, oversized animals, called pookas, who could not be seen by ordinary mortals. Some advice her mother had given her was another source of her inspiration: "Never be unkind or indifferent to a person others say is crazy. Often they have a deep wisdom. We pay them a great respect in the old country, and we call them fairy people, and it could be they are sometimes."

Combining these two themes, Chase wrote a play of a lovable lush named Elwood P. Dowd, who has fought reality and won. His closest companion is the eponymous Harvey, seen only by Elwood. His sister Veta desperately wants to maintain respectability for the sake of her daughter, so she has Elwood committed. After several comic incidents at the local asylum, Veta decides she prefers her brother pixilated but happy, and they go home together.

Under various titles, including *The White Rabbit* and *The Pooka*, Chase rewrote the play fifty times, working with a four-foot miniature stage. The team of Brock Pemberton and Antoinette Perry, who were responsible as producer and director for such hits as *Strictly Dishonorable* and *Personal Appearance*, repeated these functions with *Harvey*, creating another long-running hit.

Frank Fay, a vaudeville song-and-dance man, went into the role of Elwood straight from an engagement at the Copacabana. Josephine Hull, one of the daffy, dear old poisoners from *Arsenic and Old Lace*, was signed on to play his put-upon sister.

One of the charms of the play was Harvey's invisibility; the audience had to use its imagination in order to see him.

Josephine Hull and Frank Fay in *Harvey*.

Producer Pemberton wanted the title character to appear on stage once during the course of the show. Over the playwright's objections, he paid for a $650 rabbit suit and had an actor dressed in it make an entrance at a Boston tryout for a group of servicemen. The play was going swimmingly, with plenty of laughs, until the fur-clad performer crossed the stage. The audience froze—and Harvey remained invisible from that day forward.

The play went on to win the Pulitzer Prize, over *The Glass Menagerie*. As with *You Can't Take It With You*, the Pulitzer judges were criticized in some quarters for bestowing the prize on a trivial comedy. A few called the play a justification for alcoholism. But, like many other wartime comedies, it took audiences' minds off the conflict overseas, and proved popular. It ran for seven years, toured successfully, and remains the longest running Pulitzer play with the exception of *A Chorus Line*.

Director Perry died at fifty-eight during the run of *Harvey*. She was immortalized in 1947 when the American Theatre Wing began presenting the Tony Awards, which were named for her.

James Stewart appeared in the lead on Broadway during the original run. Harvey's height had to be increased to six feet five and a half inches, so that he would tower over the six-foot Stewart. Stewart also played the role in the 1950 film version by Universal-International. Hull repeated her Veta and won an Oscar for Best Supporting Actress.

Stewart again played Elwood in a 1970 Broadway revival opposite Helen Hayes, which was subsequently broadcast on NBC's *Hallmark Hall of Fame*. Jesse White recreated his role of the asylum attendant for the Broadway and TV revivals. An earlier 1958 telecast starred Art Carney and Marion Lorne. An unsuccessful musicalization entitled *Say Hello to Harvey*, with songs by Leslie Bricusse, was attempted in Toronto in 1981. Donald O'Connor was Elwood and Patricia Routledge was Veta; it closed without reaching New York.

DEAR RUTH

by Norman Krasna

Opened December 13, 1944

683 Performances

Henry Miller's Theatre

Directed by Moss Hart

Produced by Joseph M. Hyman and Bernard Hart

Cast: Virginia Gilmore (Ruth); John Dall (Lt. William Seawright); Lenore Lonergan (Miriam Wilkins); Phyllis Povah (Edith Wilkins); Howard Smith (Judge Harry Wilkins); Barlett Robinson (Albert Kummer); Kay Coulter (Martha Seawright); Richard McCracken (Sgt. Chuck Vincent); Peter Dunn (Harold Kobbermeyer); Pauline Myers (Dora).

Miriam Wilkins of *Dear Ruth*—like Judy Graves of *Junior Miss*, Corliss Archer of *Kiss and Tell*, and the title character of *Janie*—is a spunky, fun-loving teenager whose attempts at acting grown-up result in mayhem for her parents and older siblings. In Norman Krasna's comedy, young Miriam demonstrates her concern for the state of the world by sending telegrams to cabinet members and calling her teachers fascists for assigning too much homework.

But the core of the comedy comes from attempts to do her bit for the soldiers overseas. She corresponds with one as part of her own morale-boosting crusade, called "Bundles for America," a response to "Bundles for Britain." She sends the Air Force lieutenant numerous love letters, quoting English poets and signing them with her older sister Ruth's name. She even mails him a picture of Ruth. Complications arise when the amorous lieutenant arrives on the family's Kew Gardens doorstep on a two-day pass, ready to propose marriage to Ruth—who is already engaged to a stuffy, sensible banker. She can't bring herself to break the poor guy's heart and so plays along with Miriam's fantasy romance until it becomes the real thing.

Like *Junior Miss*, this confection was directed by Moss Hart and featured Lenore Lonergan (who was the heroine's sidekick in the earlier play) as the intellectual adolescent who causes all the trouble. The new play was co-produced by Moss' brother Bernard. Movie juveniles Virginia Gilmore and John Dall (Bette Davis' co-star in *The Corn Is Green*) were the young lovers thrown together by Miriam's prank.

Critics found the plot a tired one. *The Saturday Review* said it was "so full of corn that it bears a closer resemblance to a silo than a play." But reviewers admitted that the story and jokes, albeit familiar, were funny, and the direction and performances expert. The situation combined concern for our men in uniform with amusement at the foibles of youth. During the Broadway run, two national tours were sent out and three USO groups performed it for servicemen.

The 1947 movie adaptation starred Joan Caulfield and William Holden. After its initial run, the play showed up on the summer stock circuit, but its World War II setting dated it and competition from television rendered its light, family comedy obsolete for the stage.

Krasna, also a screenwriter, had moderate success with later featherweight works like *John Loves Mary* (1947), produced by Rodgers and Hammerstein; *Kind Sir* (1953), with Mary Martin and Charles Boyer; *Who Was That Lady I Saw You With?* (1958) with husband and wife Peter Lind Hayes and Mary Healy; and *Sunday in New York* (1961) featuring a young Robert Redford.

UP IN CENTRAL PARK

by Herbert and Dorothy Fields

Music by Sigmund Romberg

Lyrics by Dorothy Fields

Opened January 27, 1945

504 Performances

The New Century Theatre

Directed by John Kennedy

Choreographed by Helen Tamiris

Produced by Michael Todd

Cast: Wilbur Evans (John Matthews); Maureen Canon (Rosie Moore); Noah Beery, Sr. (Boss Tweed); Maurice Burke (Thomas Nast); Betty Bruce (Bessie O'Cahane); Charles Irwin (Timothy Moore); Martha Burnett (Clara Manning); Watson White (James Fisk, Jr.); Daniel Nagrin (Daniel); Wally Coyle (Arthur Finch); Elaine Barry (Ellen Lawrence); Guy Standing, Jr. (George Jones); Walter Burke (Danny O'Cahane); John Quigg (William Dutton); Robert Field (Andrew Munroe); Paul Reed (Vincent Peters); Rowan Tudor (Mayor Hall); George Lane (Richard Connolly); Harry Meehan (Peter Sweeney); Lydia Fredericks (Mildred Wincor); Fred Barry (Joe Stewart); Delma Bryon (Lotta Stevens); Kay Griffith (Fanny Morris).

A musical about a park? There are two long-running entries that fall into this category, Stephen Sondheim and James Lapine's impressionistic *Sunday in the Park with George* (1984) and the more traditional operetta *Up in Central Park* (1945). Whereas the Sondheim–Lapine work really deals with the rarefied world of modern art, *Up in Central Park* detailed the corruption of Boss Tweed during the building of New York's giant backyard.

Impressario Mike Todd, whose last big hits had been the burlesque revue *Star and Garter* and the Cole Porter shows *Something for the Boys* and *Mexican Hayride*, conceived the show while reading *Boss Tweed and His Gang* by Dennis Lynch, a history of Tweed's enormous graft while undertaking the construction of the park. During his extraordinary career, Tweed bribed the governor, legislature, and mayor of New York, and it is estimated that he and his cronies bilked the city's taxpayers out of $200 million dollars in six years. His bill for park benches alone was over $800,000. From 1871 to '72, the *New York Times* printed a series of articles blasting Tweed, while political cartoonist Thomas Nast did the same with drawings in *Harper's Weekly*.

Todd discussed the idea of setting a musical during the period of the park's construction (1870–1880) with Dorothy and Herbert Fields, who had written the books for both *Something for the Boys* and *Mexican Hayride*. They added a romantic subplot to the Boss Tweed story. *Times* reporter John Matthews falls in love with Rosie Moore, aspiring singer and daughter of a Tweed underling.

For the music, Todd hired Sigmund Romberg, whose operettas had been extremely popular during the time of the show and into the early 1920s. (Romberg's Broadway output included such favorites as *Maytime* (1917), *Blossom Time* (1921), *The Student Prince* (1924), and *The New Moon* (1928).) The composer came out of retirement to collaborate with Dorothy Fields on the score, which included hit songs such as "Close as the Pages in a Book" and "When You Walk in the Room."

For the set, designer Howard Bay created a series of backdrops based on the nostalgic paintings of Currier and Ives. Each scene would begin with the cast frozen in place before the setting, resembling a period print.

For the opening night, Todd threw one of his legendary bashes. Outside the theatre, horse-drawn carriages waited to carry the audience, including the critics, to Tavern on the Green in Central Park. The ride through the snow-covered streets seemed like a continuation of the show. Once the partygoers arrived, they were greeted by overflowing champagne and two orchestras playing tunes from the score. Todd even arranged to have taxis waiting for his guests to take them home, all at his expense.

Todd need not have worried about the critics. "Just why Mr. Todd," wrote George Jean Nathan, "whose show was a sufficiently good and surefire one, should have deemed it necessary to ingratiate himself with the reviewers I cannot understand." The reviews were mostly positive. "*Central Park* is about as big as its namesake and just as pretty to look at," wrote Nichols in the *New York Times*.

During the same season, Todd was earning a substanial sum as owner of the 48th Street Theatre, where *Harvey* was playing. Though he continued to present shows on Broadway, he later focused his attentions on Hollywood. He produced the extravagant *Around the World in 80 Days* and married Elizabeth Taylor. His meteoric career was cut tragically short when he died in a plane crash in 1958.

Up in Central Park had a disappointing screen adaptation with many of the songs missing. It was released in 1948, with Deanna Durbin, Dick Haymes, and Vincent Price.

THE GLASS MENAGERIE

by Tennessee Williams

Opened March 31, 1945

561 Performances

The Playhouse Theatre

Directed by Eddie Dowling and Margo Jones

Produced by Eddie Dowling and Louis J. Singer

Cast: Laurette Taylor (Amanda Wingfield); Julie Haydon (Laura Wingfield); Eddie Dowling (Tom Wingfield); Anthony Ross (Jim O'Connor).

A shy young woman with a withered leg sits playing with her collection of glass animals. Her silly, domineering, but well-intentioned mother chatters on about the glories of her own girlhood in a fabled Southland populated by devoted "gentlemen callers." Her brother, who loves his sister dearly but resents having to work at a shoe factory in order to support the family, yearns to break out of their tenement apartment.

These are the Wingfields, who, along with a long-awaited gentleman caller for the shy daughter Laura, are the four characters of Tennessee Williams's delicate drama *The Glass Menagerie*. The playwright's only previously produced work was a florid melodrama, *Battle of Angels* (later rewritten as *Orpheus Descending*), which closed in Boston. The failure of *Battle* was to be followed by the spectacular success of *Menagerie*, a memory play which influenced later playwrights in its turning away from kitchen-sink realism in favor of a more lyrical, frankly theatrical style.

Williams originally wrote *Menagerie* as a film script entitled *The Gentleman Caller* while he was on salary at Metro-Goldwyn-Mayer. He worked on it while he was being paid to write a screenplay (or as the playwright put it, a "celluloid brassiere") for Lana Turner. He submitted it to the studio claiming it was another *Gone with the Wind*. The bigwigs rejected it, stating that they had already made *Gone with the Wind* and didn't need another. Thus MGM gave up any possible percentage of a play which turned out to be highly profitable.

After being fired by the studio, Williams rewrote his script as a stage play and renamed it *The Glass Menagerie*. With the help of his agent Audrey Wood, the play was taken on by actor-director-producer Eddie Dowling. Dowling cast himself as the son, Julie Haydon—whom he had directed in Saroyan's *The Time of Your Life*—as Laura, and Anthony Ross as Jim O'Connor, the gentleman caller.

For the role of the mother, Dowling made a bold choice. Laurette Taylor had been one of the great actresses of the 1910s and '20s, but she hadn't appeared onstage in ten years. She was living in relative seclusion in a midtown hotel and was an active alcoholic. Despite the risks, Dowling decided to take a chance and cast her as Amanda, the fanciful faded Southern belle.

Laurette Taylor is toasted by Eddie Dowling and Anthony Ross as Julie Haydon hides from reality by poring over her high school yearbook in Tennessee Williams's *The Glass Menagerie*.

An out-of-town tryout in Chicago's Civic Theatre was planned. Williams insisted that regional theatre director Margo Jones, nicknamed "the Texas Tornado," be brought in to assist Dowling with the staging. Rehearsals were nightmarish. Taylor was drinking and could barely remember her lines or even deliver them audibly. Williams wrote to a friend that the actress was giving her Southern accent such a broad reading that the play sounded like "The Aunt Jemima Pancake Hour." At one point, businessman Louis J. Singer, who was financing the project, attended a rehearsal and cried out to his co-producer Dowling: "Eddie! Eddie! What are you doing to me?"

But when a paying audience was in the house, Taylor came to blazing life. Her performance was illuminating and ranked alongside the best of Duse, according to *Chicago Daily Tribune* critic Claudia Cassidy, who also praised the play. Despite glowing notices, the war, a bitter snowstorm, and the Civic Theatre's inconvenient location kept audiences away. But Cassidy and Ashton Stevens of the *Herald American* actively supported *Menagerie* by returning several times and writing about the show in their daily columns. This unprecedented show of critical support had the desired effect, and the box office recovered from its handicaps.

Taylor's acting and the play were becoming hot news, and New York audiences eagerly awaited the Broadway premiere, which was an unqualified triumph. The enraptured opening night audience was unaware that Taylor was taking every offstage opportunity to vomit. In spite of her illness, she was letter-perfect. The cast received twenty-five curtain calls. Even though Taylor had contracted cancer, she remained with the play for a year and half, putting an extraordinary cap on a singular stage career. She died in December of 1946, soon after leaving the show.

Menagerie was produced in London in 1948, with Helen Hayes as Amanda under John Gielgud's direction. It was rather coolly received by the British press. Two years later, the Warner Brothers film version, featuring Gertrude Lawrence (by consensus woefully miscast) and a tacked-on happy ending, was released. This was Williams' least favorite screen adaptation of his work. But he needn't have worried about the play or subsequent screen treatments. A 1973 TV movie, starring Katharine Hepburn, and a 1987 film, with Joanne Woodward (directed by her husband Paul Newman) were acclaimed. The Wingfields have revisited Broadway a number of times, with revivals starring Helen Hayes, Shirley Booth, Maureen Stapleton, and Jessica Tandy. As if to pay her back for her contribution to the play, Williams gave half his royalties for *Menagerie* to his mother, Miss Edwina Dakin Williams, the model for Amanda.

CAROUSEL

Book and lyrics by Oscar Hammerstein II, based on the play *Liliom*, by Ferenc Molnar.

Music by Richard Rodgers

Opened April 19, 1945

890 Performances

The Majestic Theatre

Directed by Rouben Mamoulian

Choreographed by Agnes de Mille

Produced by The Theatre Guild

Cast: John Raitt (Billy Bigelow); Jan Clayton (Julie Jordan); Jean Darling (Carrie Pipperidge); Eric Mattson (Enoch Snow); Jean Casto (Mrs. Mullin); Christine Johnson (Nettie Fowler); Bambi Linn (Louise); Russell Collins (Starkeeper); Murvyn Vye (Jigger Craigin); Ralph Linn (Enoch Snow, Jr.); Franklyn Fox (David Bascome); Jay Velie (1st Heavenly Friend); Tom McDuffie (2nd Heavenly Friend); Annabelle Lyon (Hannah); Peter Birch (Boatswain); Connie Baxter (Arminy); Marilyn Merkt (Penny); Joan Keenan (Jennie); Ginna Moise (Virginia); Suzanne Tafel (Susan); Richard H. Jordan (Jonathan); Blake Ritter (Captain); Robert Byrn (1st Policeman); Larry Evers (2nd Policeman); Robert Pageant (Jimmy); Lester Freedman (Principal).

With *Carousel*, Rodgers and Hammerstein not only repeated the success of *Oklahoma!*, they went even further toward integrating songs into their story.

Whereas *Oklahoma!* eliminated the obligatory big opening number chockful of leggy chorines, *Carousel* got rid of the overture altogether and replaced it with a pantomimed scene accompanied by a single melody (the enchanting *Carousel Waltz*), rather than the usual medley of tunes. Music underscored the dialogue scenes, blended into the songs, and continued afterwards, almost as in an opera. Another operatic innovation was the hero's "Soliloquy," a long, aria-like solo, which allowed the gruff, inarticulate Billy Bigelow to give expression to his conflicting emotions and brought the curtain down on the first act.

The story was derived from the play *Liliom*, by Hungarian playwright Ferenc Molnar. The fantasy was first produced in America by the Theatre Guild in 1921, with Eva La Galliene and Joseph Schildkraut, and it was revived

Jan Clayton and John Raitt ride the *Carousel*.

in 1940 with Ingrid Bergman and Burgess Meredith. The plot concerned Liliom, a nasty carnival barker who has an affair with Julie, a shopgirl. When she becomes pregnant, he attempts a robbery in order to provide for his unborn child. When the robbery is thwarted, Liliom commits suicide. The fantasy element takes over at this point as Liliom is taken to purgatory by two celestial policemen. There he must remain for fifteen years. At the end of this period he is permitted to return to earth to perform a good deed in order to get into paradise. Back on earth, he attempts to give his daughter a star stolen from heaven. When she refuses to take it, he slaps her in frustration and leaves, returning to purgatory.

Theresa Helburn of The Theatre Guild, which had presented Oklahoma!, got the idea of making a musical of the play and took it to Rodgers and Hammerstein. They were ready to return to their collaboration, having separately worked on several projects. Molnar had previously rejected no less than Puccini and George Gershwin as adapters of his work. However, when the playwright saw Oklahoma!, he granted permission for Rodgers and Hammerstein to musicalize Liliom.

In their version, they changed the setting from 1920s Budapest to 1873 New England. The two lovers marry before Julie becomes pregnant, and the ending was altered to a more upbeat one. The hero, now called Billy Bigelow, encourages his unhappy daughter to have confidence in herself during the reprise of "You'll Never Walk Alone." For this good work, he is allowed past the Pearly Gates. During the show's tryout in Boston, a scene featuring a New Englandish Mr. and Mrs. God was eliminated and replaced by one with the Starkeeper, Billy's guardian angel and adviser.

Director Rouben Mamoulian, choreographer Agnes de Mille, and costume designer Miles White, all of whom had worked on Oklahoma!, were used again for Carousel. As with Oklahoma!, unknown performers were hired. John Raitt, a tall, strikingly handsome and well-built singer, was cast as Billy. He had played Curly in the Chicago company of Oklahoma! while Carousel was being written. Jan Clayton was chosen for Julie.

In addition to "You'll Never Walk Alone," the superlative score included "If I Loved You," a sort of "pre-love duet," the rousing "June Is Bustin' Out All Over," and the charming "When I Marry Mister Snow," a character number for Carrie, the second female lead. "It Was a Real Nice Hayride," dropped from Oklahoma!, became "It Was a Real Nice Clambake."

Carousel opened at the Majestic Theatre, across the street from the St. James, home of Oklahoma! The two shows ran together for more than two years. The parallel continued into the movies. The 1956 movie version of

Carousel starred Gordon MacRae and Shirley Jones, who also took the leads in the film of Oklahoma! John Raitt recreated his role in a 1965 Music Theatre of Lincoln Center revival. Also, a London revival by the National Theatre was transferred in 1994 to Lincoln Center's Vivian Beaumont Theatre.

THE RED MILL

Book and lyrics by Henry Blossom
Additional lyrics by Forman Brown
Music by Victor Herbert
Opened October 16, 1945
531 Performances
The Ziegfeld Theatre
Directed by Billy Gilbert
Choreographed by Aida Broadbent
Produced by Paula Stone and Hunt Stromberg, Jr.

Cast: Michael O'Shea (Con Kidder); Eddie Foy, Jr. (Kid Conner); Dorothy Stone (Tina); Odette Myrtil (Madame Le Fleur); Ann Andre (Gretchen); Charles Collins (Gaston); Lorna Byron (Juliana); Edward Dew (The Govenor); P.J. Kelly (Town Crier); Hal Prince (Willem); George Meador (Franz); Gordon Boelzner (Bill-Poster); Hope O'Brady (Flora); Lois Potter (Lena); Betty Galavan (Dora); Frank Jaquet (The Burgomaster); Robert Hughes (Capt. Hendrick Van Damm); Billy Griffith (Pennyfeather); Jean Walburn (Georgette); Nony Franklin (Suzette); Kathleen Ellis (Fleurette); Jacqueline Ellis (Nanette); Patricia Gardner (Lucette); Joan Johnston (Yvette).

The success of Rosalinda, Up in Central Park, and Song of Norway sparked renewed interest in operetta, a genre which had been gone from Broadway for almost two decades. In keeping with this trend, a revival of Victor Herbert's 1906 The Red Mill became the first hit of the 1945–46 season.

This new production originated at the Los Angeles Civic Light opera, home of Song of Norway. Milton Lazarus, author of the book for Norway, had contributed new dialogue, while Forman Brown wrote additional lyrics. Film comedian Billy Gilbert directed. The West Coast production was received with such enthusiasm that the producers moved it to Broadway for a limited six-week engagement. The intended brief stay quickly sold out, so the production was extended to an open commercial run.

The show had been written originally as a showcase for the talents of David Montgomery and Fred Stone, a popular comedy team. They first came to prominence playing the Tin Woodman and the Scarecrow in a stage version of The Wizard of Oz (1903). In The Red Mill, the duo played Kid Conner and Con Kidder, American tourists stuck without funds in the mythical Dutch town of Katwyk-aan-Zee. Kid and Con must work off their hotel bills at the Inn of the Red Mill. In the process, they become entangled with the love life of the innkeeper's daughter Gretchen, who is being forced to marry the much older governor of Zeeland. Gretchen is really in love with the handsome

(Left to right) Eddie Foy, Jr., Dorothy Stone, Charles Collins, and Jack Whiting in the hit revival of Victor Herbert's *The Red Mill.*

Captain Van Damm. Plots, chases, and rescues follow, including a daring escape on the blades of a windmill. In order to justify various schticks that Montgomery and Stone had perfected, their characters were made to put on a variety of disguises, such as those of Sherlock Holmes and Dr. Watson.

Dorothy Stone, Fred Stone's daughter, appeared in the 1945 revival. Her sister Paula was a co-producer.

Of the forty-one operettas that Herbert composed, *The Red Mill* was the most successful. The original 1906 engagement totaled 274 performances, and the new edition ran nearly twice as long.

Other popular Herbert shows include *The Fortune Teller* (1898), *Babes in Toyland* (1903), *Mlle. Modeste* (1905), and *Naughty Marietta* (1910).

STATE OF THE UNION

by Howard Lindsay and Russel Crouse

Opened Novemeber 14, 1945

765 Performances

The Hudson Theatre

Directed by Bretaigne Windust

Produced by Leland Hayward

Cast: Ralph Bellamy (Grant Matthews); Ruth Hussey (Mary Matthews); Minor Watson (Jim Conover); Myron McCormick (Spike McManus); Kay Johnson (Kay Thorndyke); Herbert Heyes (Sam Parrish); Fred Ayres Cotton (Swenson); G. Albert Smith (Judge Jefferson Davis Alexander); Maidel Turner (Mrs. Alexander); Aline McDermott (Mrs. Draper); Victor Sutherland (William Hardy); George Lessey (Senator Lauterback); Helen Ray (Norah); John Rowe (Stevens); Howard Graham (Bellboy); Robert Toms (Walter); Madeline King (Jennie).

A millionaire business executive runs for President on a platform of change from politics as usual. His personal integrity may be called into question because of an extra-marital affair. His strong-willed wife is brought in to present a happy front for the voters. No, these are not excerpts from the campaign diaries of real-life figures in American politics, but the plot of Lindsay and Crouse's 1945 Pulitzer Prize-winning comedy, *State of the Union.*

The authors' previous efforts were light comedies and musicals like *Anything Goes, Strip for Action,* and the long-running box office champion, *Life with Father.* Their foray into campaign comedy came at the suggestion of Helen Hayes, who remarked at a party that the two playwrights should write a show about the next Presidential election. The hero should be an idealist like Wendell Wilkie, who later lost to Roosevelt. Lindsay and Crouse agreed to fashion such a script, and Hayes consented to appear in it.

Although Hayes later declined to star in the finished *State of the Union* (she called it "*too* political"), the authors got the dynamic producer Leland Hayward to back the venture. They cast Ralph Bellamy and Ruth Hussey in the lead roles of maverick candidate Grant Matthews and his brutally frank wife Mary, who eventually wins her husband back from his mistress and political handlers.

In the climactic scene, Mary gets drunk and tells off a roomful of kingmakers in a stirring speech against compromise for political gain. "You're all thinking about the next election instead of the next generation," she rails at them. Finally, Grant gives up the quest for the Republican nomination and vows to make changes in society as a private citizen.

The production took the unusual out-of-town route of playing towns like Detroit and Pittsburgh, instead of the traditional New Haven and Boston. In Pittsburgh, after sitting through the show and taking notes on the performance, Crouse was approached by an angry member of the audience. "I've been watching you," she said. "What's the matter with you? You haven't laughed once. You're one of the reasons Pittsburgh doesn't get more good plays."

A stop in Washington, D.C., was also included, and the denizens of the capital laughed heartily at the topical references to then-current figures like Herbert Hoover, New York Governor Thomas Dewey, John L. Lewis, and others.

There were daily changes in the script in order to keep up with current events. In one scene, the candidate is reading a headline to his wife. At each performance, the headline was drawn from the day's newspapers. Once the play opened on Broadway, he could have been reading from the glowing reviews. The show ran for more than two years and launched two simultaneous tours.

Bellamy later graduated from portraying a presidential candidate to enacting a White House occupant when he was cast as Franklin D. Roosevelt, in both the stage and film versions of *Sunrise at Campobello.* (In real life, he served a term as President of Actors Equity.)

For the film version of *State of the Union,* Lindsay and Crouse stipulated that it be released in 1948, before the 1948 political conventions for the Presidential elections. Frank Capra directed Spencer Tracy and Katharine Hepburn in one of the best of their eight films together. Angela Lansbury, Adolphe Menjou, and Van Johnson co-starred.

Lindsay and Crouse tackled politics again with *The Prescott Proposals* (1953), with Katharine Cornell as a crusading delegate to the United Nations. It got respectable, but not enthusiastic, notices and ran only 125 performances.

BORN YESTERDAY

by Garson Kanin

Opened February 4, 1946

1,642 Performances

The Lyceum Theatre

Directed by Garson Kanin

Produced by Max Gordon

Cast: Judy Holliday (Billie Dawn); Paul Douglas (Harry Brock); Gary Merrill (Paul Verrall); Otto Hulett (Ed Devery); Larry Oliver (Senator Norval Hedges); Mona Bruns (Mrs. Hedges); Frank Otto (Ed Brock); Carroll Ashburn (Asst. Manager); Ellen Hall (Helen); William Henderson (Bellhop); Rex King (Another Bellhop); Ted Mayer (Barber); Mary Laslo (Manicurist); Paris Morgan (Bootblack); C.L. Burke (Waiter).

On the opening night of *Born Yesterday,* Ruth Gordon, married to the show's author, Garson Kanin, embraced the star Judy Holliday and exclaimed that show business clichés have a way of coming true. Gordon was referring to a theatrical adage about an unknown going onstage a youngster and coming back a star. This turn of events, a hackneyed plot device in the movies, was the offstage real-life drama of Kanin's comedy.

The play's plot centered on Billie Dawn, an ex-chorine being kept by tycoon Harry Brock. Both are in Washington, D.C., while Brock tries to win a large government contract by bribery. In order to make Billie fit in with the capital elite, Brock hires *New Republic* reporter Paul Verrall to smooth out her rough edges. Teacher and pupil fall in love and join forces to foil Brock's dishonest plans.

For the lead, Kanin had wanted Jean Arthur, the foghorn-voiced film star who had made her name playing tough, intelligent professional women in social comedies like *Mr. Smith Goes to Washington* and *Mr. Deeds Goes to Town.* But she had been absent from the stage for fifteen years, and it would be a stretch for her to play the brassy former showgirl. She also had a reputation for being difficult. But at Kanin's insistence, producer Max Gordon agreed to use Arthur.

Once rehearsals began, the actress demanded approval of the stage manager and press agent, a final say on billing and advertising, and a hairdresser, car, and chauffeur. These were not unusual perks for a big name, but the star also asked for line changes at every rehearsal.

Reviews for both the show and Arthur were weak for the tryout in Boston. Paul Douglas, a former sports announcer, drew the highest plaudits from the press for his performance as the tycoon. Arthur, perhaps jealous of the attention Douglas was getting, announced that she had a cold and bowed out of all the Boston performances—she would rejoin the company in Philadelphia. An understudy played Billie for the remainder of the Boston engagement. Arthur subsequently stated to the press that her cold had developed into a viral infection and hyperinsulinism, a lowering of the blood sugar. She would not be playing Philly either.

Kanin and Gordon were frantic. The understudy was not up to the demanding role, and an emergency replacement had to be found. The designer Mainbocher, a friend of Kanin's, suggested Judy Holliday, who had made a hit in the comedy group The Revuers and the short-lived show *Kiss Them for Me*. She was hurriedly called in and gave a sensational reading. The producer and author were delighted. Could she start right away? "Sure," the actress replied. "When do we open in Philadelphia?"

"Saturday." That meant only three days of rehearsal to learn the leading role in a major Broadway tryout. Holliday drilled lines with her friend John Houseman, the director, who was in Philadelphia with *Lute Song*, another pre-New York show. She later stated that the three days were a blur; she lived on coffee and dexedrine. On opening night, she was a nervous wreck offstage, but a revelation onstage. The *Philadelphia Inquirer* said the new star was "a new name of stellar potentialities in the theatre, romping off with comedy honors for her amazingly perfect performance."

Instead of going straight to Broadway, the show took a detour to Pittsburgh for another week of fine-tuning. Holliday was able to grow into the role and accomplished a believable growth of Billie from dumb blonde to informed crusader. She played her as bored and cynical but not stupid, so that her later enlightenment was credible. Holliday stayed with the show for most of its 1,642 performances.

For the film version, Columbia's Harry Cohn bought the rights for $1 million. But he did not want Holliday to repeat her Broadway success. Thinking the original star was an unknown who would not bring in customers, the mogul suggested Lucille Ball or Rita Hayworth instead. Kanin was determined to have Holliday triumph again as Billie. To prove that she had screen charisma, Kanin cast Holliday in *Adam's Rib*, a film comedy he co-authored with Ruth Gordon. Holliday stole her big scene with Katharine Hepburn. Cohn reluctantly gave Holliday the chance to recreate the loose-hipped, raspy-throated heroine. She went on to win a 1950 Oscar for the role, beating out such formidable competition as Bette Davis, Gloria Swanson, and Anne Baxter.

The sassy, dumb-but-smart Billie Dawn continues to fascinate the public. A 1989 Broadway revival starred Madeline Kahn and Ed Asner, and a 1993 film remake featured Melanie Griffith and Don Johnson.

Paul Douglas and Judy Holliday in *Born Yesterday*.

CALL ME MISTER

Sketches by Arnold Auerbach and Arnold B. Horwitt

Music and lyrics by Harold Rome

Opened April 18, 1946

734 Performances

The National Theatre

Directed by Robert H. Gordon

Choreographed by John Wray

Produced by Melvyn Douglas and Herman Levin

Cast: Betty Garrett, Jules Munshin, Harry Clark, Lawrence Winters, Bill Callahan, Betty Lou Holland, Maria Karnilova, David Nillo, Paula Bane, George S. Irving, George Hall, Alan Manson, Danny Scholl, Chandler Cowles, Glenn Turnbull, Ruth Feist, Kate Friedlich, Virginia Davis, Evelyn Shaw, Betty Gilpatrick, Joan Bartels, Marjorie Oldroyd.

World War II was over, and G.I. Joes were coming home. Just as wartime musicals like *This Is the Army* and *Let's Face It* reflected upon civilians becoming soldiers, *Call Me Mister* was a response to the reverse situation—the rank and file of the armed forces becoming part of the labor force again. The cast was composed of ex-servicemen and former USO entertainers. Betty Garrett, the only cast member to receive featured billing, had written and performed in numerous "G.I. Jane" shows in army bases and hospitals.

The producer, film star Melvyn Douglas, had directed the Army's Entertainment Production Unit in the China-Burma-India theatre of war. His duties involved mounting variety shows for soldiers near the front, usually in jungles. The material used was sent from Special Services Headquarters in New York. Douglas was particularly impressed with the songs of a Corporal Harold Rome and the sketches of a Sergeant Arnold Auerbach. In civilian life, Rome had done the tunes for such revues as *Pins and Needles*, *Sing Out the News*, and *Let Freedom Ring*. Auerbach had contributed sketches to Fred Allen's radio show.

After the war, Douglas was asked by the Army to put on one more show. He got together with Rome and Auerbach to assemble a revue. But the Army's plans fell though. The recently discharged producer and writers decided to put on their production anyway, with the aid of Herman Levin, a lawyer and Rome's financial manager.

The sketches and songs struck a chord with the new postwar audience. In one scene, the parents of a returning vet are anxious that their son is a psychotic basket case after the horrors of war. It turns out the son is fine and the parents are going nuts from worry. "Off We Go" showed how a typical infantryman imagined the easy life of the Air Corps after seeing too many Hollywood movies, in which the fantasized flyboys were shown continually drinking champagne and receiving medals. In "The Army Way," military red tape was satirized as Pvt. Paul Revere attempted to make his famous ride having to go through modern procedures of requisitions and signing in triplicate. "South Wind" portrayed Machiavellian Southern senators planning to exploit the new veterans for their votes.

The hit song of the show was "South America, Take It Away" sung by Betty Garrett as a canteen hostess tired of the samba craze. The humorous lyrics declared she had a "crack in the back of my sacroiliac." Controversial issues such as racial discrimination and housing shortages were dealt with in "The Red Ball Express" and "A Home of Our Own." "The Face on the Dime" was an emotional tribute to the late President Franklin D. Roosevelt. Maria Karnilova (later of *Gypsy* and *Fiddler on the Roof*) and David Nillo performed an intrepretive dance of a reunited couple. Bill Callahan and Betty Lou Holland were the energetic tap dancers in a contrasting number.

The run continued on Broadway while a successful touring edition crossed the country. Jane Kean replaced Betty Garrett in New York, while her sister Betty took the same role on tour. This is the first recorded instance of sisters having played the same part in the same production.

The 1951 movie version added the plot of soldier Dan Dailey leaving his post in Japan to be with his wife, USO entertainer Betty Grable. An unbilled Bobby Short also appeared.

ANNIE GET YOUR GUN

Book by Dorothy and Herbert Fields

Music and lyrics by Irving Berlin

Opened May 16, 1946

1,147 Performances

The Imperial Theatre

Directed by Joshua Logan

Choreographed by Helen Tamiris

Produced by Richard Rodgers and Oscar Hammerstein II

Cast: Ethel Merman (Annie Oakley); Ray Middleton (Frank Butler); William O'Neal (Buffalo Bill); George Lipton (Pawnee Bill); Harry Bellaver (Chief Sitting Bull); Marty May (Charlie Davenport); Lea Penman (Dolly Tate); Betty Anne Nyman (Winnie Tate); Kenny Bowers (Tommy Keeler); Lubov Roudenko (Riding Mistress); Nancy Jean Raab (Minnie); Camilla De Witt (Jessie); Marlene Cameron (Nellie); Bobby Hookey (Little Jake); Don Liberto (Harry); Ellen Hanley (Mary); Daniel Nagrin (Iron Tail/Wild Horse); Walter John (Yellow Foot); Cliff Dunstan (Mac); Art Barnett (Foster Wilson/Mr. Ernest Henderson); Beau Tilden (Coolie); Alma Ross (Mrs. Little Horse); Elizabeth Malone (Mrs. Black Tooth); Nellie Ranson (Mrs. Yellow Foot); Mary Woodley (Mabel); Ostrid Lind (Louise); Dorothy Richards (Nancy/Mrs. Adams); Earl Sauvain (Andy Turner); Victor Clarke (Clyde Smith); Rob Taylor (John/Mr. Clay); Robert Dixon (Freddie); Marjorie Crossland (Sylvia Potter-Porter); Don Liberto (Mr. Schuyler Adams); Bernard Griffin (Dr. Percy Ferguson); Marietta Vore (Mrs. Ferguson); Truly Barbara (Mrs. Henderson); Fred Rivett (Mr. Lockwood); Ruth Vrana (Debutante).

Thirty years before a red-headed orphan warbled "Tomorrow," the most famous Annie on Broadway was a sharpshooter named Oakley who got her gun, her man, and one of the longest runs of any musical of the 1940s. *Annie Get Your Gun* was a huge hit for both its star, Ethel Merman, and composer Irving Berlin. It was also the only hit musical produced by the team of Rodgers and Hammerstein that they themselves did not author.

Merman first heard of the show when she was in the hospital after the birth of her daughter. Her friend, the lyricist Dorothy Fields, paid a call and mentioned the idea of the star playing the legendary markswoman. Jerome Kern was to compose the music, and Fields would write the lyrics and co-author the book with her brother Herbert. The siblings took the idea to Rodgers and Hammerstein, who agreed to produce it though they were not interested in providing the score. *Annie Get Your Gun* called for pure, old-fashioned "entertainment-for-entertainment's-sake" tunes, the opposite of their own story-motivated songs. But they were eager to furnish the means for their idol, Jerome Kern (who had collaborated with Hammerstein on *Show*

Boat) to return to the stage. His last Broadway score had been for *Very Warm for May* (1939), a flop. Kern was all set to do the show, but died of a stroke the day after his arrival in New York from California.

Obviously, a replacement was needed right away. Berlin was not considered at first because he wrote his own lyrics. Rodgers and Hammerstein felt that since this was Dorothy Fields's idea she should be given the opportunity to write the words. But Fields agreed to using Berlin if he was available. At first, the composer of *As Thousands Cheer* (1933) and *This Is the Army* (1942) wasn't interested. Thanks to the success of the Rodgers and Hammerstein shows, the trend in musicals was to integrate the songs into the plot rather than making the plot work around the songs. Berlin had always worked the second way and wasn't sure he could learn new tricks.

Ethel Merman and the cast of *Annie Get Your Gun*.

The producers gave him the script and urged him to give it a try. In eight days, he wrote ten songs. Attesting to the composer's speed, the show's director, Josh Logan, related in his memoirs that Berlin wrote "Anything You Can Do, I Can Do Better" during a ride in a taxicab. One of the songs, the standard "There's No Business Like Show Business" was almost thrown out by Berlin when he felt that the production team wasn't sufficiently excited about it.

Tryout engagments in Boston and New Haven were well received. The musical was more than ready to open at Broadway's Imperial Theatre but, unfortunately, the Imperial wasn't ready for it or any other show. During a technical run-through, several pieces of overhanging scenery crashed to the stage, nearly killing Richard Rodgers. The Shuberts, who owned the theatre, quickly booked the show into their Philadelphia house while repairs were made. Rumors circulated that the falling scenery story was just that: a story, to cover the fact that the show was in trouble.

The opening-night audience expected this trouble and was polite but not effusive in its response during Act I. After intermission, they relaxed and laughed heartily. The notices ignored the book, dances, and songs (Atkinson of the *New York Times* called them "undistinguished"), but praised Merman. Over the years, many theatre companies have done *Annie Get Your Gun*, and many of the songs have become classics, including "They Say That Falling in Love Is Wonderful," "The Sun in the Morning" and the aforementioned "There's No Business Like Show Business." This track record proves that Merman alone was not the sole reason for *Annie*'s success.

Mary Martin did the tour and a televised version. Dolores Gray starred in the London production, which ran for four years.

The MGM film version of *Annie Get Your Gun* was beset with problems. Judy Garland was to have starred in the title role, but her advanced drug dependency necessitated her being replaced by Betty Hutton (who had appeared with Merman in *Panama Hattie*). The original director Busby Berkeley was dismissed, leading man Howard Keel sprained an ankle, and Frank Morgan, cast as Buffalo Bill, died during filming. The movie was finally released in 1950 to good box office returns.

In 1966 Merman returned to Broadway as Annie in a twentieth anniversary revival for the Music Theatre of Lincoln Center. Bruce Yarnell and Jerry Orbach co-starred. There was some criticism that Merman was too old to play love scenes with the much younger Yarnell, but the show received glowing reviews. Many felt that this production was better than the original. Berlin added a new song, "An Old-Fashioned Wedding," a contrapuntal duet for Annie and Frank Butler, her love interest.

HAPPY BIRTHDAY

by Anita Loos

Opened October 31, 1946

564 Performances

The Broadhurst Theatre

Directed by Joshua Logan

Produced by Richard Rodgers and Oscar Hammerstein II

Cast: Helen Hayes (Addie); Louis Jean Heydt (Paul); Margaret Irving (Gail); Musa Williams (Glorious); Thomas Heaphy (Dad Malone); Charles Gordon (Gabe); Florence Sundstrom (Bella); Jack Diamond (Herman); Jacqueline Paige (Myrtle); Jean Bellows (June); Lorraine Miller (Maude); Dort Clark (Don); Ralph Theadore (The Judge); Philip Dakin (Policeman); Enid Markey (Tot); Grace Valentine (Emma); Philip Gordon (Manuel); Eleanor Boleyn (Margot); James Livingston (Bert); Robert Burton (Mr. Bemis); Harry Kingston (Mr. Nanino).

"You want to hit the gutter, and by God, I'll get you there," said Anita Loos to her friend Helen Hayes. The encounter that prompted this remark was not a catfight, but Loos expressing her desire to see Hayes, dignified First Lady of the American Theatre, let her hair down on stage. Hayes was longing to get out of the hoop skirts and wimples associated with the roles she normally played.

Loos, whose credits included *Gentlemen Prefer Blondes*, obliged her friend by writing *Happy Birthday,* a confection about a repressed librarian , Addie, taking her first sip of alcohol and fun. The single set was the Jersey Mecca Cocktail Bar. The words "Through these portals pass the nicest people in Newark" are emblazoned over the entrance. Addie goes into the bar following the man she secretly loves. He, a bank clerk, has entered the establishment to meet his assignation, a flashy redhead.

Encouraged by the regulars, Addie drinks her first Pink Lady and lets her inhibitions fly out the window. She sings, dances a tango, recites poetry, and generally carries on. By the evening's end, the bank clerk has seen another side of Addie and lost interest in the redhead, whom he realizes is shallow. No role could have been further from Hayes's last appearance on Broadway, that of abolitionist crusader Harriet Beecher Stowe.

By this time, Richard Rodgers and Oscar Hammerstein II were developing a reputation for straight plays as well as musicals: in addition to *Oklahoma!* and *Carousel,* they had produced *I Remember Mama* and *Annie Get Your Gun.* The enterprising duo continued in this vein by presenting *Happy Birthday.* Josh Logan, director of *Annie Get Your Gun,* staged the Loos work.

In order to bolster this slight comedy, numerous stage effects were put in. When Addie takes her first drink, the bar suddenly becomes a wonderland. The bottles sprout flowers. The lighting shifts. The barstool upon which she is perched grows in size, like Alice's mushroom in Wonderland. Later in the play, a table similarly expands and becomes the canopy for a leafy glade. An orchestra was added and the songwriter-producers composed a

Encouraged by the regulars, Addie drinks her first Pink Lady and lets her inhibitions fly out the window. She sings, dances a tango, recites poetry, and generally carries on. By the evening's end, the bank clerk has seen another side of Addie and lost interest in the redhead, whom he realizes is shallow. No role could have been further from Hayes's last appearance on Broadway, that of abolitionist crusader Harriet Beecher Stowe.

By this time, Richard Rodgers and Oscar Hammerstein II were developing a reputation for straight plays as well as musicals: in addition to *Oklahoma!* and *Carousel,* they had produced *I Remember Mama* and *Annie Get Your Gun.* The enterprising duo continued in this vein by presenting *Happy Birthday.* Josh Logan, director of *Annie Get Your Gun,* staged the Loos work.

In order to bolster this slight comedy, numerous stage effects were put in. When Addie takes her first drink, the bar suddenly becomes a wonderland. The bottles sprout flowers. The lighting shifts. The barstool upon which she is perched grows in size, like Alice's mushroom in Wonderland. Later in the play, a table similarly expands and becomes the canopy for a leafy glade. An orchestra was added and the songwriter-producers composed a number called "I Haven't Got a Worry in the World" for Addie to warble.

Brooks Atkinson of the *New York Times* found the play a delightful change of pace for Hayes, but most of the other major critics gave the play a thumbs down, with a few compliments to the leading lady for her pluck. Despite the mixed notices, theatregoers were intrigued by the prospect of a clowning Helen Hayes and flocked to the show. At the end of the season, Hayes was honored with one of the first-ever Tony Awards for outstanding performance. She shared the distinction with Ingrid Bergman for *Joan of Lorraine,* José Ferrer for *Cyrano de Bergerac* and Fredric March for *Years Ago.* (Two years later, Tonys for acting began to be presented in individual categories.)

Happy Birthday would probably not go down well with contemporary audiences. Like *Harvey,* its comedy is based on the effects of alcohol; a lighthearted, romantic view of drinking might be seen as naive today. But it allowed audiences to see a different side to one of the great actresses of the theatre.

FINIAN'S RAINBOW

Book by E.Y. Harburg and Fred Saidy
Music by Burton Lane
Lyrics by E.Y. Harburg
Opened January 10, 1947
725 Performances
The 46th Street Theatre

Leprechaun David Wayne finds Anita Alvarez good enough to eat in *Finian's Rainbow.*

Directed by Bretaigne Windust
Choreographed by Michael Kidd
Produced by Lee Sabinson and William Katzell

Cast: Ella Logan (Sharon); Albert Sharpe (Finian McLonergan); Donald Richards (Woody Mahoney); David Wayne (Og); Anita Alvarez (Susan); Robert Pitkin (Senator Billboard Rawkins); Sonny Terry (Sunny); Eddie Bruce (Buzz Collins); Tom McElhany (Sheriff); Augustus Smith, Jr. (Henry); William Greaves (Howard); Roland Skinner (John the Preacher); Arthur Tell (Mr. Robust); Royal Dano (Mr. Shears); Diane Woods (Diane); Jane Earle (Jane).

tenor, this show required a reliable character actor who could handle a Gaelic dialect as well as sing. The first choice was Barry Fitzgerald, who had won an Oscar for his kindly Irish priest in the film *Going My Way*. Fitzgerald had so many film commitments that it was impossible for him to do the show. He wouldn't even read the script for fear of liking the project in which he would not be able to participate.

The producers then sent the script to Ria Mooney, former principal of the acting school of the Abbey Theatre in Dublin. She came up with several prospects, but none panned out. Mooney gave up on finding an authentic Irish Finian until she met Albert Sharpe on a British film in which they were both acting. Sharpe was flown to New York; he auditioned and promptly joined the cast, which included Ella Longan as Sharon, Finian's dreamy daughter, David Wayne as Og the leprechaun, and Anita Alvarez as Susan, the dancing mute girl who claims Og's heart and makes him mortal.

Finian marked the Broadway debut of choreographer Michael Kidd, who received one of the earliest Tony Awards for his energetic dances. They were performed by the first Broadway chorus to feature blacks and whites together. Kidd shared the Tony honor with Agnes de Mille for her work on *Brigadoon*, another fantasy-flavored musical with an accent from the British Isles.

Ironically, the London production of *Finian* did not fare well, closing after a short run. British critics found it too fantastic and cloyingly sentimental. But a Czechoslovakian version was presented in Prague: the title was changed to *The Magic Pot*, and Og became Cochtan, a legendary Bohemian water sprite.

There was the usual talk in show-biz circles of bringing *Finian* to the screen soon after it opened, but its left-leaning book became a liability in Hollywood as Senator Joseph McCarthy's anti-Communist crusade gathered strength. Fears of blacklisting and alienating Southern audiences prevented the major studios from taking on the musical's theme of harmony between the races, although award-winning animated-film producers John and Faith Hubley later attempted to make a cartoon version.

It was almost twenty years after the Broadway run that *Finian* was finally judged safe enough for the movies. In 1968, Francis Ford Coppola directed Fred Astaire in his last Hollywood musical, and Petula Clark, Tommy Steele, and Keenan Wynn also starred. The show's simple solutions for racial conflict seemed dated after the violent civil rights struggles of the 1960s. Movie audiences also seemed to be growing disenchanted with filmizations of Broadway musicals in general.

There was a revival of *Finian's Rainbow* on Broadway in 1960; it had only a brief run.

BRIGADOON

Book and lyrics by Alan Jay Lerner
Music by Frederick Loewe
Opened March 13, 1947
581 Performances
The Ziegfeld Theatre
Directed by Robert Lewis
Choreographed by Agnes de Mille
Produced by Cheryl Crawford

Cast: David Brooks (Tommy Albright); Marion Bell (Fiona MacLaren); George Keane (Jeff Douglas); Pamela Britton (Meg Brockie); Virginia Bosler (Jean MacLaren); Lee Sullivan (Charlie Dalrymple); James Mitchell (Harry Beaton); William Hansen (Mr. Lundie); Lidija Franklin (Maggie Anderson); Elliott Sullivan (Archie Beaton); Edward Cullen (Andrew MacLaren); Frances Charles (Jane Ashton); Walter Scheff (Angus MacGuffie); Hayes Gordon (Sandy Dean); Delbert Anderson (Stuart Dalrymple); Earl Redding (MacGregor); Bunty Kelley (Fishmonger); John Paul (Frank); Margaret Hunter (Kate McQueen).

Although they came from two different countries and generations, lyricist Alan Jay Lerner and composer Frederick Loewe fit together like a pair of scissors. Lerner's sharp, elegant lyrics complemented Loewe's rich, romantic music perfectly. Their first long-running show was *Brigadoon*, a charming fantasy of a Scottish town which emerges from the mists for one day every hundred years. Two modern young men happen onto the enchanted village. Naturally, one falls in love with a Brigadoon lass and sacrifices everything he knows to remain with her.

Viennese-born Loewe, who was forty-two, met the Harvard-educated Lerner, only twenty-four, at the Lambs Club in 1942. Their first collaboration, *Life of the Party*, died in Detroit. Their second attempt, *What's Up*, did make it to Broadway, but was up for only one week. The third time was not a charm for the duo: *The Day Before Spring* (1945), a musical about the then extremely unpopular subject of divorce, did only moderately well.

After the opening-night party for *The Day Before Spring*, Lerner and Loewe went to the Algonquin Hotel and began work on what was to become their first hit, *Brigadoon*. But producers right and left turned down the fantastic tale. Cheryl Crawford was sent a copy by her lawyer, who also happened to work for the authors. The script shared elements with her previous hit *One Touch of Venus* (mythical characters come to life, and love conquers all). Despite how busy she was helping to run the American Repertory Theatre, Crawford took up the producer's reins and hired *Venus* choreographer Agnes de Mille to stage the dances and Robert Lewis, her colleague from the Group Theatre, to direct.

Lewis and de Mille saw their major task as cutting down the show's sentimentality. "How do we set about killing Jeannette MacDonald?" the director asked of the choreographer. They did so by balancing love songs like "Waiting for My Dearie," "Almost Like Being in Love," and "The

Heather on the Hill" with a violent chase scene, a sword dance, and a solemn funeral. Several supporting characters, including the hero's nonbelieving friend Jeff, the brooding Harry Beaton, and the raucous Meg Brockie also offset the script's sweetness.

After the New York opening and a flood of love letters from the critics, there was a small controversy. Critic George Jean Nathan accused Lerner of stealing his story from a German legend called "Germelshausen," the tale of a similar hamlet which awoke once a century. Lerner reported in his memoirs that Nathan was in love with the leading lady Marion Bell, and when he found out that she was already engaged to Lerner, he struck back at his rival with a charge of plagiarism.

The inevitable film version was produced by MGM in 1954 with Vincente Minnelli directing. Since the film leads were Gene Kelly and Cyd Charisse, dance was emphasized. Van Johnson co-starred as Kelly's cynical comrade.

Brigadoon has always been a popular choice for revival. New York's City Center presented it a total of five times. A

(Left to right) George Keane, David Brooks, and William Hansen in *Brigadoon*.

1966 TV version aired on ABC. Robert Goulet, Sally Ann Howes, Marilyn Mason, ballet heart-throb Edward Villella, and Peter Falk headlined.

A 1980 Broadway production was staged by Tony winner Vivian Matalon, featuring Martin Vidnovic, Meg Bussert, and ice-skating champion John Curry. The New York City Opera chose *Brigadoon* to open a series of musical-comedy productions in 1986.

After *Brigadoon,* Lerner and Loewe split up for a while. Lerner wrote the highly unconventional *Love Life* (1948) with Kurt Weill, and the screenplay for *An American in Paris,* the Gershwin-flavored movie musical for which he received an Oscar. The pair reunited for *Paint Your Wagon* (1951), which had a middling run of 289 performances. They followed this disappointment with a show called *My Fair Lady,* in 1956.

HIGH BUTTON SHOES

Book by Stephen Longstreet, based on his book *The Sisters.*

Liked Them Handsome.

Music by Jule Styne

Lyrics by Sammy Cahn

Opened October 9, 1947

727 Performances

The New Century Theatre

Directed by George Abbott

Choreographed by Jerome Robbins

Produced by Monte Proser and Joseph Kipness

Cast: Phil Silvers (Harrison J. Floy); Nanette Fabray (Sara Longstreet); Jack McCauley (Henry Longstreet); Mark Dawson (Hubert Ogglethorpe); Helen Gallagher (Nancy); Joey Faye (Mr. Pontdue); Paul Godkin (Uncle Willie); Clay Clement (General Longstreet); Johnny Stewart (Stevie Longstreet); Lois Lee (Fran); Carole Coleman (Shirley Simkins); Nathaniel Frey (Elmer Simkins); Donald Harris (Elmer Simkins, Jr.); Tom Glennon (Coach); William David (Mr. Anderson).

In 1947, lyricist Sammy Cahn, glancing through the *New York Times Book Review* at his home in Hollywood, saw an ad for a book with a cover showing a family in 1910 out for a drive in their Model-T Ford. The image struck him as the perfect starting point for a musical. He took the ad to his collaborator, composer Jule Styne, who lived in nearby Beverly Hills, and told him, "This is our new musical."

The ad was for a novel entitled *The Sisters Liked Them Handsome* by Stephen Longstreet. "Would you like to meet the author?" Styne asked Cahn. The lyricist agreed. With his partner in tow, Styne then walked out of his house, went directly across the street, knocked on the door of the house there, and when it was answered, said, "Sammy, this is Stephen Longstreet."

This was how the authors of *High Button Shoes,* the only hit musical of the 1947–48 season, began their collaboration. Styne and Cahn were responsible for many hit movie

songs, but they had done only one stage show, *Glad to See Ya,* which closed in Boston before reaching Broadway. Longstreet, who had written movie scripts but never a play, adapted his nostalgic novel about his family's life in New Brunswick, New Jersey. Director George Abbott rewrote it with the aid of the show's star, Phil Silvers. This provided them with a hit, abetted by Silvers's clowning—he was playing his patented, rapid-fire con man character—and Nanette Fabray's fresh-faced appeal. Jerome Robbins' twenty-minute Mack Sennett ballet, mimicking the Keystone Kops silent films, was singled out for praise, and so were the songs "I Still Get Jealous" and "Papa, Won't You Dance with Me?" The slapstick and nostalgia of *High Button Shoes* lasted for 727 performances, as compared to Rodgers and Hammerstein's experimental *Allegro,* which opened the next night and played for only 315 performances.

Lew Parker played Silvers's role in the London version, while Eddie Foy, Jr. and Audrey Meadows took the show on a successful national tour. There was talk of a film version starring Milton Berle, but plans never came to fruition.

The show had numerous legal problems. Mack Sennett sued the producers for using his name in connection with the production's comedy ballet. His legendary name was later removed from the program. Mary Hunter won a suit claiming she had been contracted to stage the musical before Abbott became available, but was unfairly dropped when he became free. There was also a dispute between the producers and Cahn and Longstreet over royalties, but it was amicably settled.

Following *High Button Shoes,* Jule Styne composed numerous Broadway scores including *Gentlemen Prefer Blondes, Gypsy,* and *Funny Girl,* as well as more film tunes. Cahn returned to Hollywood to write more movie lyrics, for which he won four Academy Awards. He ventured onto Broadway in the '60s and '70s with three musicals of varying quality: *Walking Happy, Skyscraper, Look to the Lilies. Words and Music,* a backward glance at his career, featured Cahn and three singers.

A patchwork plot which depends on the star quality of an actor in the comic lead has prevented *High Button Shoes* from becoming a popular candidate for professional or amateur revival. There were two television versions. The first, in 1956, featured Silvers and Fabray. The second, in 1966, was an abbreviated edition starring Garry Moore, Jack Cassidy, Maureen O'Hara, and Carol Lawrence. Goodspeed Opera House, which specializes in seldom-performed musicals, mounted a production in 1982.

The high spot of the show, the manic Mack Sennett ballet, made an appearance on Broadway in 1989 as a part of *Jerome Robbins' Broadway,* the retrospective revue of the choreographer's career. "I Still Get Jealous" was also included.

A STREETCAR NAMED DESIRE

by Tennessee Williams

Opened December 3, 1947

855 Performances

Ethel Barrymore Theatre

Directed by Elia Kazan

Produced by Irene M. Selznick

Cast: Jessica Tandy (Blanche DuBois); Marlon Brando (Stanley Kowalski); Kim Hunter (Stella Kowalski); Karl Malden (Harold Mitchell); Peg Hillias (Eunice Hubbel); Rudy Bond (Steve Hubbel); Nick Dennis (Pablo Gonzales); Gee Gee James (Negro Woman); Edna Thomas (Mexican Woman); Vito Christi (Young Collector); Ann Dere (Nurse); Richard Garrick (Doctor).

When Blanche DuBois stepped off a streetcar named Desire into the shabby New Orleans apartment of her sister and brother-in-law, the Stanley Kowalskis, she entered theatre history as well. Blanche, the faded Southern belle who depends upon "the kindness of strangers," has become one of the most famous characters in American drama, along with her nemesis, the brutal, but attractive, Stanley. Through the clash between Blanche and Stanley, polar opposites sexually drawn to each other, playwright Tennessee Williams explores the conflict between the romantic and the utilitarian, the wounded and the insensitive. Following his breakthrough Broadway debut with *The Glass Menagerie* (1945), *Streetcar* established Williams as a major American dramatist.

Under its original title, *The Poker Night,* the script for *Streetcar* was submitted by Audrey Wood, Williams's agent, to a novice producer, Irene Selznick, the estranged wife of David O. Selznick and daughter of Louis B. Mayer. After a lengthy meeting with Wood and Williams in Charleston, South Carolina, Selznick was confirmed as the project's producer. She wired her office the following cable: "Blanche has come to live with us." Elia Kazan, hot from the triumph of staging Arthur Miller's *All My Sons,* was signed on to direct and began a string of collaborations with Williams.

Marlon Brando and Jessica Tandy as enemies Stanley Kowalski and Blanche DuBois in Tennessee Williams's *A Streetcar Named Desire.*

When stars Margaret Sullavan and John Garfield were judged unsuitable or unavailable to play the leads, two relative unknowns were found to be perfect. Jessica Tandy had been laboring in unrewarding parts in undistinguished Hollywood films. Her husband Hume Cronyn directed her in a well-received Los Angeles production of a Williams one-act entitled "Portrait of a Madonna." The playwright made a special trip to the West Coast to see it, and Tandy was offered Blanche, the role of a lifetime.

Twenty-year-old Marlon Brando had four Broadway credits on his resumé but little reputation. Kazan advanced him carfare to Provincetown, Massachusetts, where Williams was staying for the summer. The charismatic young actor arrived at Williams' cottage, fixed the broken plumbing and faulty electricity, and then gave a sensational reading of Stanley.

With Kim Hunter as Stella, Blanche's sister, and Karl Malden as Mitch, Stanley's friend and Blanche's suitor, the principal roles were set. *Streetcar*'s raw sensuality captivated critics and audiences, causing a major sensation. The play went on to win both the Pulitzer Prize and New York Drama Critics Award. The Broadway run lasted over two years. Uta Hagen and Anthony Quinn replaced Tandy and Brando on Broadway and headed the national tour.

Despite its tremendous stage success, *Streetcar*'s road to the screen was a rough one. Producer Charles Feldman bought the rights for $350,000. But he had difficulty in interesting any of the major studios in taking the project on, for surely its strong adult themes would have to be toned down to meet stringent Production Code standards for motion pictures. Finally, Warner Brothers accepted Feldman's package, and the film was produced with most of the original New York cast. The significant exception was Vivien Leigh, who had played Blanche on the London stage under the direction of her husband, Laurence Olivier. The Production Code's guidelines were relaxed somewhat in order for the film to recreate some of the play's power. The result was that rare occurence—a faithful cinematic record of a great theatre piece. Leigh, Malden, and Hunter won Oscars. Brando (in only his second film role) became the country's hottest sex symbol and actor—and he never returned to the Broadway stage.

Every few years, a major production of *Streetcar* is mounted in New York, in America's regional theatres, or abroad. Some of the later Blanches have included Tallulah Bankhead, Claire Bloome, Rosemary Harris, Lois Nettleton, Faye Dunaway, Ann-Margaret (on television), and Blythe Danner. Stanley is an equally irresistible role. Movie star Alec Baldwin turned down several million dollars for a film role in order to fill Kowalski's T-shirt, opposite Jessica Lange's Blanche, in a 1992 Broadway revival.

MISTER ROBERTS

by Thomas Heggen and Joshua Logan, based upon the novel by Heggen.

Opened February 18, 1948

1,157 Performances

The Alvin Theatre

Directed by Joshua Logan

Produced by Leland Hayward

Cast: Henry Fonda (Lt. Doug Roberts); David Wayne (Ensign Pulver); Robert Keith (Doc); William Harrigan (The Captain); Jocelyn Brando (Lt. Ann Girard); Rusty Lane (Chief Johnson); Joe Marr (Dowdy); Harvey Lembeck (Insigna); Ralph Meeker (Mannion); Karl Lukas (Lindstrom); Steven Hill (Stefanowski); Lee Krieger (Schlemmer); John Campbell (Reber); Casey Walters (Dolan); Fred Barton (Gerhart); James Sherwood (Payne); John Jordan (Shore Patrolman); Marshall Jamison (Military Policeman); Murray Hamilton (Shore Patrol Officer).

One of the great war heroes presented on Broadway never saw combat, at least not onstage. Lieutenant Douglas Roberts (junior grade), the noble protagonist of Thomas Heggen's novel and of Joshua Logan's stage adaptation, serves aboard the cargo ship *Reluctant* in a quiet part of the

Casey Walters and Henry Fonda pipe aboard an important visitor in *Mister Roberts*.

South Pacific during World War II. Roberts is itching for action and constantly applies for a transfer to an active theatre of war. He eventually gets his wish, but the play is devoted to Roberts's relationship with his crew, who voyage "from Apathy to Tedium with occasional sidetrips to Monotony and Ennui."

While serving active wartime duty in the navy, Heggen wrote *Night Watch*, the first of a series of stories which formed the basis of his novel, a bestseller optioned for the stage by Leland Hayward.

Logan, who had served in the army during the war, received an early version of the script by Heggen and Max Schulman, sent by Hayward. There was no dramatic conflict or suspense except for a scene in which the tyrannical captain agrees to give the crew liberty only if Roberts stops requesting to be transferred, which would darken the captain's record.

Logan rewrote the first act so that it led up to this scene and planned the second to resolve the basic conflict between Roberts and the captain. Logan also strengthened Roberts's character, for he hardly spoke in the book. After reading the new version, Heggen agreed to collaborate with Logan on finishing the play. They hired a male secretary so that their language would not be inhibited—the salty Navy dialogue had to sound realistic.

Both authors wanted Henry Fonda for the title role, but worried that the star was only interested in making movies. They decided to have Fonda read for the part, but called in David Wayne, who was appearing in *Finian's Rainbow*, as a back-up. Contrary to the playwrights' fears, Fonda leaped at the role and got out of a movie contract to play it. Wayne agreed that Fonda was the best actor for Roberts; he was given the supporting role of Ensign Pulver.

Logan's brother-in-law, Bill Harrigan, was cast as the captain. Eva Marie Saint was hired to play the sole female in the cast, but she was considered so charming and pretty that the audience would keep wanting her to come back after her one scene. She was replaced by Marlon Brando's sister, Jocelyn.

Mister Roberts sailed onto Broadway in triumph. Returning veterans recognized the plight of the average Navy recruit battling boredom, and civilians cheered for the gallant Roberts fighting bureaucracy and lifting morale. At the end of the season, the show won the Tony Award for Best Play over *A Streetcar Named Desire*. It ran for 1,154 performances, with Fonda remaining with the production through most of the run. Tyrone Power headed the London company. Fonda, and later John Forsythe, took the lead in the national touring version.

Fonda recreated Roberts in the 1955 Warner Brothers screen adaptation. The studio had wanted a younger, bigger star for the part, but director John Ford insisted on Fonda. Once filming started, Fonda and Ford could not get along, and the director was replaced by Mervyn LeRoy. The two directors received joint credit. The cast also featured James Cagney as the captain, William Powell as the ship's doctor, and newcomer Jack Lemmon, who won a Supporting Actor Oscar for his Ensign Pulver. There was also a short-lived NBC television series, during the 1965–66 season; it featured Roger Smith in the title role. A televised production of the original play, starring Robert Hays, Charles Durning, Howard Hesseman, and Marilu Henner, was broadcast during the 1980s.

Unfortunately, Thomas Heggen never saw any of the later adaptations of his book and play. Unable to cope with the huge success of his first effort, and fearing he'd never be able to duplicate it, Heggen spiraled into numerous periods of depression. He attempted two other writing projects with Logan which were not completed. In 1949, just a year after *Mister Roberts* opened, Heggen was found dead in his apartment, drowned in a bathtub, at the age of twenty-nine.

WHERE'S CHARLEY?

Book by George Abbott, based upon *Charley's Aunt*, by Brandon Thomas.
Music and lyrics by Frank Loesser
Opened October 11, 1948
792 Performances
The St. James Theatre
Directed by George Abbott
Produced by Cy Feuer and Ernest Martin

Cast: Ray Bolger (Charley Wykeham); Allyn Ann McLerie (Amy Spettigue); Doretta Morrow (Kitty Verdun); Bryon Palmer (Jack Chesney); Paul England (Sir Francis Chesney); Jane Lawrence (Donna Lucia D'Alvadorez); Horace Cooper (Mr. Spettigue); John Lynds (Brassett); Edgar Kent (Wilkinson); Jack Friend (Professor); James Lane (Photographer); Marie Foster (Patricia); Douglas Deane (Reggie).

Transvestism has been a source of comedy from Shakespeare to *La Cage Aux Folles*. But the champion of crossdressing is the play *Charley's Aunt* (1892), which was transformed into *Where's Charley?* a musical for Ray Bolger in 1948. The original London farce by Brandon Thomas deals with an Oxford undergraduate who agrees to disguise himself as the aunt of one of his chums so that the lads will have a proper chaperone when their lady friends come to call.

This frivolous romp proved incredibly popular with the British and with the rest of the world. Productions sprang up everywhere, from summer stock to the Old Vic. After the author's death, his children changed their surnames to Brandon-Thomas and hired a full-time legal staff to control the worldwide rights to their father's moneymaker. Some of the more famous actors to don petticoats in the thousands of productions of this farce were John Gielgud,

Ray Bolger (center) in
Where's Charley?

Leslie Howard, Laurence Olivier, Rex Harrison, Robert Donat, John Mills, Emylyn Williams, and José Ferrer. Jack Benny starred in one of seven film versions.

For the musical, producers Cy Feuer and Ernest Martin negotiated with the Brandon Thomas office for the rights. They acquired the services of Ray Bolger (best known today for his Scarecrow in *The Wizard of Oz*) in the lead, and his wife, Gwen Rickard, as co-producer. Bolger had turned down the idea of doing a revival of the original in 1939, but the musical appealed to him. George Abbott, with *High Button Shoes* a fresh hit, was hired to direct and write the adaptation. Frank Loesser made his Broadway debut with the score. The songwriter's reputation had been made with his World War II morale-booster, "Praise the Lord and Pass the Ammunition," and his film tunes.

In Abbott's book, the characters of Charley and the roommate who agrees to impersonate the aunt ("from Brazil, where the nuts come from") were combined. This meant that Bolger, playing Charley, would have to sing, dance, and go through eleven costume changes during the course of the show.

Two of Loesser's songs broke out of the score to become hit material. "My Darling, My Darling" was a lilting love duet sung by two secondary characters. It got a boost when comedienne Beatrice Lillie, starring in the revue *Inside USA*, hummed the melody during one of the show's sketches. The other hit song, "Once in Love with Amy," was sung, tapped, and clowned through by Bolger as a delirious declaration of infatuation with the ingénue. He heightened the audience's appreciation of the number by having them sing along with him during the encore. One critic correctly predicted that the number would be identified with the star for the rest of his life.

While most of the reviewers loved the star, they panned the production itself. Howard Barnes of the *Herald-Tribune* called it "heavy-handed and witless entertainment." Without Bolger, the show would have been "exceedingly trying," according to Barnes. Robert Coleman of the *Mirror* echoed these sentiments, declaring the proceedings "mediocre." Allyn Ann McLerie as Amy, the object of Bolger's show-stopping revelry, drew enthusiastic notices and went on to star in Irving Berlin's *Miss Liberty* less than a year later.

Despite the drubbing from the critics, Bolger's star turn promoted enough word of mouth to keep the show running after the large advance sale had been used up.

Bolger starred in the touring edition, which played Broadway again in 1951, and in the 1952 film of the musical. Unfortunately, his following Broadway vehicles, *All-American* (1962) and *Come Summer* (1968), were flops.

Since *Where's Charley?* depends so heavily upon the talent and charm of the lead, it is not revived often. The only Broadway production without Bolger was presented in 1974 at Circle in the Square, with Raul Julia as Charley and Tom Aldredge as his unwitting older suitor.

KISS ME, KATE

Book by Samuel and Bella Spewack
Music and lyrics by Cole Porter
Opened December 30, 1948
1,070 Performances
The New Century Theatre
Directed by John C. Wilson
Choreographed by Hanya Holm
Produced by Saint Subber and Lemuel Ayers

Cast: Alfred Drake (Fred Graham/Petruchio); Patricia Morison (Lilli Vanessi/Katharine); Lisa Kirk (Lois Lane/Bianca); Harold Lang (Bill Calhoun/Lucentio); Harry Clark (First Man); Jack Diamond (Second Man); Thomas Hoier (Harry Trevor/Baptista); Noel Gordon (Gremio); Charles Wood (Hortensio); Annabelle Hill (Hattie); Don Mayo (Ralph); Lorenzo Fuller (Paul); Denis Green (Harrison Howell); Dan Brennan (Stage Doorman); Fred Davis, Eddie Sledge (Specialty Dancers); John Castello (Haberdasher).

> Another openin', another show,
>
> In Philly, Boston, or Baltimo',
>
> A chance for show folk to say "Hello,"
>
> Another openin' of another show.

These lyrics, which open Cole Porter's *Kiss Me, Kate,* serve as a tribute to the composer and to the theatre itself. After a long period of failure and of suffering from the effects of a crippling riding accident in 1937, Porter emerged triumphant with "another openin' of another show." The song has also become, like "There's No Business Like Show Business," an unofficial anthem of Broadway.

The concept for *Kate* originated with fledgling producer Arnold Saint Subber. During his tenure as a stagehand for the Alfred Lunt and Lynn Fontanne revival of Shakespeare's *The Taming of the Shrew,* Subber noticed that the glamorous acting couple quarreled offstage almost as much as their characters did onstage. He came up with the idea of a play-within-a-play about a warring husband-and-wife team enacting Shakespeare's comedy. After dropping the Arnold from his name, Subber pooled his resources with costume designer Lemuel Ayers, a top Broadway figure, to produce the show. They hired Bella and Sam Spewack to write the adaptation.

The first choice for a composer was Burton Lane, who had struck it rich with *Finian's Rainbow.* When Lane declined the project, Bella Spewack pushed for Cole Porter, with whom she and her husband had collaborated on *Leave It to Me.* Porter's last two musicals, *The Seven Lively Arts* and the Orson Welles-directed *Around the World in Eighty Days* had had brief runs. His score for the MGM movie *The Pirate* had been less than warmly received. So he was reluctant to tackle another show, especially one based on Shakespeare, in which the songwriter's words would be compared with those of the Bard of Avon's. He was also worried that the material would be too sophisticated for Broadway audiences.

But Bella Spewack convinced him otherwise, pointing out that the story was basically about theatre folk putting on a show—a tried-and-true formula. Once he accepted the assignment, Porter turned out a score full of hits. He turned his worry over comparison to Shakespeare to his advantage by taking inspiration from him. Several of the songs in the *Shrew* section were derived from the original text. These include "I've Come to Wive It Wealthily in Padua," "Were Thine That Special Face," and "Where Is the Life That Late I Led?" For the modern scenes, he produced jazzy, rhythmic riffs like "Too Darn Hot," the operetta parody "Wunderbar," and the urgent "So in Love."

Despite the songs, it took one year to raise the capital, perhaps because Porter's recent track record was spotty. Another reason for doubt was the cast. Alfred Drake had been the original Curley in *Oklahoma!,* but his last four shows had bombed. Patricia Morison had never headlined a Broadway musical before and was known only for a few Hollywood B-pictures.

But the show was hailed as witty and supremely entertaining from the first tryout performance in Philadelphia. The reception for *Kate* was a vindication for Porter—prematurely written off as washed up. He became "the top" once again, appearing on the cover of *Time* magazine soon after the opening. *Kate* had the longest New York run of any of Porter's musicals. The tour played for almost two years, and in London it racked up 400 performances.

Howard Keel, Kathryn Grayson, Ann Miller, Tommy Rall, James Whitmore, Keenan Wynn, and future choreographer-director Bob Fosse starred in the 1953 Metro-Goldwyn-Mayer film, which was originally shot in 3-D. The entire score was kept, with the addition of "From This Moment on," the only hit from Porter's next Broadway show *Out of This World.* On television, *Hallmark Hall of Fame* offered a 1958 revival with most of the original cast.

Other Shakespeare-inspired musicals include *The Boys from Syracuse* (1938), from *The Comedy of Errors; West Side Story* (1957), from *Romeo and Juliet; Your Own Thing* (1968), from *Twelfth Night;* and *Two Gentlemen of Verona* (1971).

DEATH OF A SALESMAN

by Arthur Miller
Opened February 10, 1949
742 Performances
The Morosco Theatre
Directed by Elia Kazan
Produced by Kermit Bloomgarden and Walter Fried

Cast: Lee J. Cobb (Willy Loman); Mildred Dunnock (Linda); Arthur Kennedy (Biff); Cameron Mitchell (Happy); Don Keefer (Bernard); Winnifred Cushing (The Woman); Howard Smith (Charley); Thomas Chalmers (Uncle Ben); Alan Hewitt (Howard Wagner); Ann Driscoll (Jenny); Tom Pedi (Stanley); Constance Ford (Miss Forsythe); Hope Cameron (Letta).

Willy Loman (Lee J. Cobb) is comforted by his wife Linda (Mildred Dunnock) as his sons Biff (Arthur Kennedy) and Happy (Cameron Mitchell) eavesdrop in Arthur Miller's *Death of a Salesman*.

The closest thing to a classic tragedy among Broadway hits is Arthur Miller's heart-rending *Death of a Salesman*. Willy Loman, the title character, has his American Dream: Opportunity and riches abound for the man who is well-liked. But Willy is reaching the end of his career, and the dream is fading. With no financial security to show for his years on the road, and with his firm about to sack him, he pins his hopes on his two sons—especially the elder, Biff, a shining star in high school, but like his sibling Happy, a mediocrity as an adult. Willy's tragedy is his misplaced faith in the false promise of quick wealth, a promise which ultimately destroys him. In one of the most affecting speeches in American drama, Willy's long-suffering wife Linda pleads: "Attention must be paid to such a person."

Miller initially took his script to Elia Kazan, who had directed his *All My Sons* (1947). Kazan recognized his own father in the protagonist, and he was sure millions of men would see theirs, too. The director later reported that this was the first production of his in which he had heard grown men in the audience crying. He ascribed this phenomenon to the play's ability to invoke memories of their fathers.

After being turned down by producer Cheryl Crawford, Kazan and Miller brought the script to Kermit Bloomgarden, who believed as deeply in the work as the playwright and director did. But Bloomgarden was afraid a depressing title like *Death of a Salesman* would mean death at the box office and wanted it changed. He suggested the more upbeat *Free and Clear*, after a phrase Linda uses in her final speech. Both Miller and Kazan refused to alter the title, and Bloomgarden conceded to their wishes.

Lee J. Cobb, a fellow actor with Kazan in the Group Theatre, was cast as Willy, with Mildred Dunnock as Linda. Arthur Kennedy, who was to appear in many of Miller's later plays, was the disillusioned son Biff. Their simple, direct acting made the Lomans as real as the family next door.

At the first performance in Philadelphia, there was no applause after the play ended, but stunned silence. Many could be heard weeping. Finally, a few tentative hands clapped, and the sound grew into an ovation that never stopped as the tragedy swept into New York, collecting all the major awards and a place in world literature.

Frederic March played Willy in the 1951 screen adaptation. He received an Oscar nomination, as did Mildred Dunnock and Kevin McCarthy. A 1966 telecast captured the classic performances of Cobb and Dunnock. George Segal, James Farentino, and Gene Wilder were in the supporting cast.

Thirty-five years after the Broadway opening, *Death of a Salesman* was the first Western play directed by an American (the playwright) in the People's Republic of China. Miller wrote of the experience in the book *Salesman in Beijing*.

In 1984, Dustin Hoffman took on the lead in an acclaimed Broadway production with John Malkovich, Kate Reid, and Stephen Lang. Many skeptics thought the casting of Hoffman was ludricous, for he was too young for the role and so unlike Lee J. Cobb. In fact, Hoffman was older than Cobb was when the latter originated the role. Miller had first intended Willy to be a short man like Hoffman, rather than a large one like Cobb. The new production was filmed for television a year later.

Death of a Salesman is Arthur Miller's only play to run over 500 performances on Broadway. His other works, while not long runs in their original New York productions, have had numerous productions on Broadway and regional, university, and community stages. Most deal with the individual at odds with a repressive society. These include *The Crucible* (1953), Miller's most frequently produced play; *A View from the Bridge* (1955); the autobiographical *After the Fall* (1964); *Incident at Vichy* (1964); and *The Price* (1968). Interestingly, his later plays, as well as revivals of his earlier pieces, have been best received in London.

DETECTIVE STORY

by Sidney Kingsley
Opened March 23, 1949
581 Performances
The Hudson Theatre
Directed by Sidney Kingsley
Produced by Howard Lindsay and Russel Crouse

Cast: Ralph Bellamy (Detective McLeod); Meg Mundy (Mary McLeod); Edward Binns (Detective Gallagher); Patrick McVey (Detective Callahan); Horace McMahon (Lt. Monoghan); Robert Strauss (Detective Dakin); John Boyd (Detective O'Brien); James Westerfield (Detective Brody); Lou Gilbert (Joe Feinson); Warren Stevens (Arthur Kindred); Joan Copeland (Susan Carmichael); Les Tremayne (Mr. Sims); Alexander Scourby (Tami Giacoppetti); Lee Grant (Shoplifter); Joseph Wiseman (1st Burglar); Michael Strong (2nd Burglar); Michelette Burani (Mrs. Bagatelle); Harry Worth (Dr. Schneider); Joseph Ancona (Mr. Bagatelle); Jean Adair (Mrs. Farragut); Earl Snydor (Patrolman Barnes); Byron C. Halstead (Patrolman Keogh); Joe Roberts (Patrolman Baker); Carl Griscom (Willy); Maureeen Stapleton (Miss Hatch); Sarah Gable (Mrs. Feeney); Jim Flynn (Mr. Feeney); Archie Benson (Crumb-Bum); Garney Wilson (Mr. Gallantz); James Maloney (Mr. Pritchard); Michael Levin (Photographer); Ruth Storm (Lady); John Alberts (Gentleman); Jacqueline Paige (Indignant Citizen).

Police procedurals, a familiar genre in television today, owe a considerable debt to Sidney Kingsley's stage play *Detective Story*. The gripping drama of a single night in a New York City squad room was the prototype for the many law-enforcement stories which would follow.

As he had with such previous works as *Men in White*, *Dead End*, and *The Patriots*, Kingsley meticulously researched his subject before beginning to write *Detective Story*. He interviewed police, judges, and district attorneys. Once the play was written, he was just as detailed in his direction. The playwright plotted out each actor's movement on a model of Boris Aronson's set.

There were changes in personnel from the original concept to the finished product. Early press releases stated that Kingsley's wife, actress Madge Evans, was a co author and would play the leading female role. However, once the production was mounted, Kingsley received sole credit, and Meg Mundy was starred. Leland Hayward was to have been producer, but when he became tied up with *South Pacific*, producer–authors Howard Lindsay and Russel Crouse took the reins.

Leading man Ralph Bellamy was equally dedicated in his research. For his role of Detective McLeod, the self-righteous cop whose overzealous devotion to duty costs him everything, Bellamy spent six weeks visiting station houses and riding in patrol cars. He later took Chester Morris, who was assuming his part in the road company, and William Wyler, the director of the film version, to the same police hangouts he had frequented.

Bellamy was playing a law enforcer on the infant medium of television while enacting one on Broadway. On Friday nights, he was private investigator Mike Barnett on CBS's *Man Against Crime*, the first live, half-hour dramatic show on the air. The program was broadcast from the third floor of Grand Central Station's remodeled radio studios. After the episode was aired, Bellamy then raced to a waiting elevator and into a squad car, which rushed him to the theatre where the curtain went up at 9 PM.

One of the drawing points of the play was its never-ending parade of perpetrators, patrolmen, parasites, and pedestrians in and out of the squad room. Each of the thirty-two characters afforded a juicy acting opportunity for the cast. The original ensemble was a vibrant mix of established and new talent, including Maureen Stapleton, Joseph Wiseman, Joan Copeland (the sister of Arthur Miller), Alexander Scourby, Lee Grant, and others. Many were singled out in the reviews for their performances, no matter what the size of their roles.

Alan Ladd and Ray Milland had been mentioned for the lead in the 1951 Paramount film version. Kirk Douglas got it, with Eleanor Parker and William Bendix in support. Lee Grant, Joseph Wiseman, and Horace McMahon recreated their Broadway roles.

Grant was nominated for a Best Supporting Actress Oscar for her hapless shoplifter. It was her first film, at age seventeen. She showed great promise, but her career was almost immediately halted by the Hollywood blacklist of those suspected of Communist leanings. Her professional life was not revived until seventeen years later in the '60s and '70s, when she won two Emmys and an Oscar.

There was a star-studded revival of *Detective Story* in 1984 starring Charlton Heston, Mariette Hartley, and Keith Carradine at Los Angeles' Ahmanson Theatre.

SOUTH PACIFIC

Book by Oscar Hammerstein II and Joshua Logan, based on James A. Michener's *Tales of the South Pacific.*

Music by Richard Rodgers

Lyrics by Oscar Hammerstein II

Opened April 7, 1949

1,925 Performances

The Majestic Theatre

Directed and choreographed by Joshua Logan

Produced by Rodgers and Hammerstein, in association with Leland Hayward and Joshua Logan

Cast: Ezio Pinza (Emile de Becque); Mary Martin (Nellie Forbush); Myron MacCormick (Luther Billis); Juanita Hall (Bloody Mary); William Tabbert (Lt. Cable); Betta St. John (Liat); Martin Wolfson (Capt. Brackett); Harvey Stephens (Cmdr. Harbison); Archie Savage (Abner); Henry Slate (Stewpot); Fred Sadoff (Professor); Richard Silvera (Henry); Barbara Luna (Ngana); Michael or Noel De Leon (Jerome); Alan Gilbert (Yeoman Quale); Thomas Gleason (Sgt. Thomas); Dickinson Eastham (Seabee West); Henry Michel (Seabee Wise); Bill Dwyer (Seaman O'Brien); Biff McGuire (Radio Operator McCafferty); Jim Hawthorne (Marine Cpl. Steeves); Jack Fontan (Staff Sgt. Hassinger); Beau Tilden (Seaman Hayes); Jacqueline Fisher (Lt. Marshall); Roslyn Lowe (Ensign Murphy); Sandra Deel (Ensign MacGregor); Bernice Saunders (Ensign MacRae); Pat Northrop (Ensign Yaeger); Gloria Meli (Ensign Minelli); Mardi Bayne (Ensign Walewska); Evelyn Colby (Ensign Whitmore); Helena Schurgot (Ensign Noonan); Richard Loo (Marcel); Don Fellows (Lt. Buzz Adams); Musa Williams (Bloody Mary's Asst.).

As with the earlier *Finian's Rainbow,* Rodgers and Hammerstein's *South Pacific* made its case for racial tolerance in the escapist world of musical comedy. *South Pacific* was the third hit written by Rodgers and Hammerstein, the reigning kings of Broadway. After the smashing successes of *Oklahoma!,* and *Carousel,* and a middling run with *Allegro,* they produced Irving Berlin's *Annie Get Your Gun* and the straight plays *Happy Birthday* and *John Loves Mary.* Their next musical, *South Pacific,* was not their longest running hit, but many believe it to be their best.

The idea originated with Joshua Logan, who had staged *Annie Get Your Gun.* He had read James Michener's Pulitzer Prize–winning book, *Tales of the South Pacific,* a collection of short stories that take place on some South Sea islands during World War II. It struck Logan that the subject would make a great musical. "Fo' Dolla'," the story of Lt. Joe Cable, who falls in love with Liat, a Polynesian woman, seemed to be the strongest and served as his starting point. The character of Bloody Mary, a wily island trader and Liat's mother would add color. He took the idea to producer Leland Hayward, who cautioned him not to let anyone know about it until they had acquired the rights. Against Hayward's advice, Logan suggested the concept to Richard Rodgers at a party. The team of Rodgers and Hammerstein bought up fifty-one percent and controlling interest of the rights, leaving the remainder to Logan and Hayward.

Once work on *South Pacific* began in earnest, it was decided that the "Fo' Dolla" story was too similar to the David Belasco play and the Puccini opera based on it, *Madama Butterfly,* so "Our Heroine," another story from the collection, was adapted as the main plot. This was another romance, involving Nellie Forbush, an army nurse, and Emil de Becque, a French planter who has had two children by an island woman now dead. The nurse cannot accept this interracial relationship and leaves him. "Our Heroine" was linked with "Fo' Dolla" by having the Navy lieutenant and the planter go on a dangerous mission behind Japanese lines. The lieutenant dies, but Nellie and de Becque are reunited.

Hammerstein was supposed to do the book, but he found the wartime Navy situations too distant from his experience. Logan, familar with military jargon from his tenure in the service and from working on *Mister Roberts,* went to Hammerstein's farm in Doylestown, Pennsylvania, to help out. Although Logan wrote at least half the book, there was a big brouhaha over billing and royalties. Since Rodgers and Hammerstein owned over fifty percent of the rights, they called the shots. Logan only received his royalties as director and did not share in any royalties as a co-author.

Mary Martin, who had played in *Annie Get Your Gun* on tour, was a natural choice for Nellie Forbush from Little Rock, Arkansas. For de Becque, Rodgers and Hammerstein bought out the opera contract of bass singer Ezio Pinza. Martin worried that she wouldn't be able to hold her own on the stage with the great opera singer. To placate her fears, Rodgers and Hammerstein wrote no duets for them.

As with most classic musicals, the score was created by trial and error. There needed to be a number in the second act to establish the relationship between Lt. Cable and Liat. The initial song was judged totally useless by Logan, the second too light. Then Rodgers played a song that was cut from *Allegro*. Logan knew it would work and, with new lyrics, it became "Younger than Springtime." The discarded song judged too light later become "Getting to Know You" in *The King and I*.

The song "I'm Going to Wash That Man Right out of My Hair" came about because Mary Martin had cut her hair short and realized it now dried in about three minutes. She thought it would be a great idea to wash her hair onstage. Hence the song and Logan's inventive staging of her shampooing.

These songs, along with "Some Enchanted Evening," "This Nearly Was Mine," "Honey Bun," and many others, combined with the strong book and Logan's expert staging to form what *Life* magazine called "a landmark musical." It became the second-longest-running musical of the decade and the only show to win Tonys in all the acting categories.

But not all of the creative team were totally pleased. Logan felt slighted by the billing and the lesser royalties. This was compounded when the Pulitzer committee awarded their prize for drama to *South Pacific* making no mention of Logan. The committee was quickly called and their error was pointed out. Amends were made to Logan and he received the proper Pulitzer recognition, but the damage had been done. Rodgers and Hammerstein offered Logan the chance to direct their next musical, *The King and I*, but he turned them down.

The touring company, featuring Janet Blair, Richard Eastham, Ray Walston, and future opera star Julia Migenes as one of de Becque's children, ran for over five years. The London company, with Martin repeating her role, ran for two years at the Drury Lane Theatre. The film rights were purchased by 20th-Century Fox for $6 million. The movie starred Mitzi Gaynor and Rossano Brazzi (whose songs were dubbed by Giorgio Tozzi), was directed by Logan, and became the top grossing film of 1958.

Revivals included a 1967 production at the Music Theatre of Lincoln Center with Florence Henderson and Giorgio Tozzi, and a 1987 mounting by the New York City Opera.

Mary Martin and Ezio Pinza are having "Some Enchanted Evening" in *South Pacific*.

GENTLEMEN PREFER BLONDES

Book by Joseph Stein and Anita Loos, based on the book by Anita Loos.

Music by Jule Styne

Lyrics by Leo Robin

Opened December 8, 1949

740 Performances

The Ziegfeld Theatre

Directed by John C. Wilson

Choreographed by Agnes de Mille

Produced by Herman Levin and Oliver Smith

Cast: Carol Channing (Lorelei Lee); Yvonne Adair (Dorothy Shaw); Jack McCauley (Gus Esmond), Eric Brotherson (Henry Spofford); Rex Evans (Sir Francis Beekman); Alice Pearce (Mrs. Spofford); Reta Shaw (Lady Phyllis Beekman); George S. Irving (Josephus Gage); Anita Alvarez (Gloria Stark); Howard Morris (Louis Lemanteur); Mort Marshall (Robert Lemanteur); Charles "Honi" Coles and Cholly Atkins (Dance Team); Irving Mitchell (Mr. Esmond, Sr.); Judy Sinclair (Zizi); Hope Zee (Fifi); Robert Cooper (Frank); Eddie Weston (George); Peter Birch (Bill); Bob Neukum (Pierre); Peter Holmes (Leon); Kazimir Kokic (Taxi Driver/Headwaiter); William Krach (Tenor).

Carol Channing was not the typical Broadway leading lady. Most musical-comedy heroines were either sweet sopranos like Jan Clayton, perky personalities like Mary

Martin or brassy belters like Ethel Merman. Channing was tall and had a voice that could drop down nearly to a bass or shift to a squeaky croak. Her unique style and delivery first drew attention in the revue *Lend an Ear* (1948). One of its sketches was a parody of a typical 1920s show, replete with flappers, bathtub gin, and ridiculous dance crazes.

Channing revisited the '20s in her next Broadway appearance, *Gentlemen Prefer Blondes,* a musical version of Anita Loos' slim volume of sketches about the golddigger Lorelei Lee. The book was originally a series of articles in *Harper's Bazaar* detailing the adventures of the shrewd flapper in New York, London, and Paris. The stories became a bestseller, inspiring a straight stage version by Loos and her husband John Emerson, a silent movie, also by Loos, who was a screenwriter for D.W. Griffith, and a sequel, *But They Marry Brunettes.*

The musical came about when producer Herman Levin was searching for a project. He had great luck with the postwar revue *Call Me Mister,* but failed with Jean-Paul Sartre's existential vision of hell, *No Exit,* his revival of Shakespeare's *Richard III,* and *Bonanza Bound,* which closed in Philadelphia. During a return cruise from Europe, music publisher Jack Robbins suggested to Levin a musical retelling of *Gentlemen.* Back in New York, Levin promptly bought the rights. For the score, he hired Jule Styne, who had just split with his partner Sammy Cahn. Leo Robin provided the catchy lyrics for such hits as "Diamonds Are a Girl's Best Friend" and "A Little Girl from Little Rock." Anita Loos adapted her book, in collaboration with Joseph Fields (*The Doughgirls*).

Channing's success in *Lend an Ear* won her the lead role, one of the most coveted in many years. Ethel Merman, June Havoc, Betty Hutton, Celeste Holm, Doris Day, Dolores Gray, Janet Blair, Gertrude Niesen, and Vivian Blaine had all been mentioned as possibilities for Lorelei. It was a triumph for Channing and elevated her to star status during the two-year run. Yvonne Adair, another *Lend an Ear* vet, was cast as Dorothy Shaw, the heroine's friend.

The show cashed in on a wave of nostalgia for the '20s. Choreographer Agnes de Mille eschewed her usual ballet sequences for razzmatazz period steps. Costume designer Miles White studied '20s fashion magazines and recreated the short skirts and spangled show gowns of the era.

Marilyn Monroe took over the role in the 1953 movie version, which had some new songs by Hoagy Carmichael. Using her legendary combination of innocence and sensuality, which was quite different from Channing's, she made Lorelei a modern girl intelligent enough to play dumb when it suited her purposes. Jack Cole's staging of "Diamonds Are a Girl's Best Friend" became identified with Monroe. Jane Russell toiled thanklessly as the movie Dorothy alongside the mesmerizing blonde bombshell.

Channing reclaimed the jewel-loving showgirl with a revised version of *Gentlemen* called *Lorelei,* in 1974, during another period of nostalgia. The revamping featured the original score augmented with new songs by Styne and Betty Comden and Adolph Green. Kenny Solms and Gail Parent were the authors of the updated book, in which Channing played Lorelei as a widow looking back on her husband-hunting follies. The flashback segments were mostly excerpts from the original *Gentlemen.* Channing received a Tony nomination for her performance. The show ran for 320 performances after an eleven-month national tour.

Between Loreleis, Channing appeared in a little something called *Hello, Dolly!*

THE 1950s

Broadway attendance declined somewhat as television's glaring eye hypnotized audiences and kept them at home. The infant medium fostered playwrights like Paddy Chayefsky, Gore Vidal, Horton Foote, Tad Mosel, and J.P. Miller, who wrote more video dramas than stage plays. With the exception of these writers and William Inge (*Picnic, Bus Stop*), few significant dramatists surfaced during the 1950s. Tennessee Williams and Arthur Miller continued to hold dramatic sway throughout the decade. The former produced *The Rose Tattoo, Camino Real, Cat on a Hot Tin Roof,* and *Sweet Bird of Youth,* while the latter penned *The Crucible, A Memory of Two Mondays, A View from the Bridge,* and an adaptation of Henrik Ibsen's *An Enemy of the People.* ✪ Lee Strasberg, one of the founders of the Group Theatre, became the principal teacher of the Actors Studio and instructed new actors in his interpretation of the techniques set down by Constantin Stanislavski. Strasberg's dictums became popularly known as Method acting. Many Studio students, such as Marlon Brando, James Dean, Montgomery Clift, Paul Newman, and Joanne Woodward left the theatre for film stardom. But there were quite a few who remained loyal to the stage: Maureen Stapleton, Eli Wallach, Anne Jackson, Geraldine Page, Kim Stanley, and Julie Harris were among them. ✪ Many regarded this period as the Golden Age of the Broadway Musical. The list of tuneful hits produced during the decade reads like a musical buff's dream. Lerner and Loewe set new standards for adapting difficult material with flair and professionalism when they made *My Fair Lady* out of Bernard Shaw's *Pygmalion.* Rodgers and Hammerstein checked in with *The King and I, Flower Drum Song* and *The Sound of Music.* Frank Loesser gave us *Guys and Dolls* and *The Most Happy Fella.* Bob Fosse and Harold Prince ignited successful Broadway careers as choreographer and producer with *The Pajama Game* and *Damn Yankees.* Both shows were directed by George Abbott, continuing his Midas-like reign over the world of musical comedy. ✪ Most nonmusical hits were either light comedies (including *The Moon Is Blue, The Seven-Year Itch, Teahouse of the August Moon, The Fifth Season, Anniversary Waltz, Auntie Mame*); murder mysteries (*Dial M for Murder, Witness for the Prosecution*); or melodramas (*The World of Suzie Wong*). Broadway also had its fair share of long-running serious dramas, such as *Tea and Sympathy, Inherit the Wind, The Diary of Anne Frank, Sunrise at Campobello, Look Homeward, Angel,* and *The Miracle Worker.*

THE MEMBER OF THE WEDDING

by Carson McCullers, based on her novel.

Opened January 5, 1950

501 Performances

The Empire Theatre

Directed by Harold Clurman

Produced by Robert Whitehead, Oliver Rea, and Stanley Martineau

Cast: Julie Harris (Frankie Addams); Ethel Waters (Berenice Sadie Brown); Brandon De Wilde (John Henry West); James Holden (Jarvis); Janet De Gore (Janice); William Hansen (Mr. Addams); Margaret Barker (Mrs. West); Mitzie Blake (Helen Fletcher); Joan Shepard (Doris); Phyllis Walker (Sis Laura); Harry Bolden (T.T. Williams); Henry Scott (Honey Camden Brown); Jimmy Dutton (Barney MacKean); Phyllis Love (Muriel).

A kitchen in a Georgia household provides the setting for Carson McCullers' *The Member of the Wedding*, a sensitive drama she based upon her novel. The main characters are a trio of unlikely friends: Frankie, a motherless girl on the brink of adolescence; Berenice, the black cook and housekeeper who watches over her; and John Henry, Frankie's seven-year-old cousin.

There is no plot in the usual sense. The action concerns Frankie's desperate attempt to run off with her brother and his new wife after their wedding. She describes the young couple as "the we of me," making the newlyweds the cure for her isolation. Frankie finally finds her identity as she outgrows the world of the kitchen, leaving Berenice behind. John Henry has died of meningitis, and the play ends with the cook seated alone in the kitchen hugging an abandoned doll.

Some critics said *Wedding* was so loosely structured that it wasn't even a play. But the majority of the press and the public praised the drama for its aching portrayal of the transition from childhood to maturity.

McCullers's career as a novelist began with *The Heart Is a Lonely Hunter*, when she was twenty-two. She followed the well-received debut with *Reflections in a Golden Eye* and *The Member of the Wedding*. The touching novel became a prize-winning play at the urging of Tennessee Williams. He invited his fellow Southerner McCullers to spend the summer with him in Nantucket for the purpose of collaborating on a stage version of *Wedding*. They began writing together, and one day Williams told his guest, "Now you're on your own." He had begun the collaboration to get McCullers started, and he saw to it that she did most of the work. For the rest of that summer, the two sat across from each other at a kitchen table, McCullers making her novel into a play while Williams labored on his latest drama *Summer and Smoke*.

McCullers' finished product closely resembled the novel, with a few scenes and extra characters, which were later deleted. The production was directed by Harold Clurman, a veteran of the Group Theatre. Twenty-four-year-old Julie Harris left the cast of Lillian Hellman's *Montserrat* to play twelve-year-old Frankie. Ethel Waters, who had last appeared in a nonmusical play in 1939 (*Mamba's Daughters*), was cast as Berenice.

There was a nationwide search to find the right boy to enact John Henry. Casting director Terry Fay found Brandon De Wilde, whose parents were both actors. Mr. and Mrs. De Wilde were cast as understudies in the show. On the night of the first public performance in Philadelphia, young

Julie Harris (seated) is heartbroken that she cannot go away with the newlywed couple in *The Member of the Wedding*. Brandon De Wilde, Janet de Gore, James Holden, Ethel Waters, and William Hansen console her.

Brandon developed stage fright and asked to be taken home. After his parents calmed him down, he was letter-perfect. It was Ethel Waters who flubbed a line that night.

Harris, Waters, and De Wilde repeated their roles in the 1952 film version, directed by Fred Zinnemann. Harris, in her film debut, was nominated for an Oscar as Best Actress.

The play is not done often, because it does require special casting. The leading actress must be mature enough to carry the show, but must plausibly appear to be twelve years old. The role of John Henry calls for a brilliantly talented little boy of seven. The play was revived on Broadway in 1975 as a part of the New Phoenix Repertory season, with Mary Beth Hurt as Frankie and Glenn Close as Janice, the bride. A 1989 production at off-Broadway's Roundabout Theatre starred Esther Rolle as Berenice. An unsuccessful musical version, with songs by G. Wood, ran briefly off-Broadway in 1971. A 1982 television broadcast featured Pearl Bailey and Dana Hill.

McCullers suffered from a series of strokes and from alcoholism, which prevented her producing a large body of work. Her only other writing for the theatre was *The Square Root of Wonderful* (1957). Edward Albee adapted her novella *The Ballad of the Sad Cafe* for the stage in 1963. She died of a massive brain hemmorhage in 1967.

THE HAPPY TIME

by Samuel Taylor, based on the book by Robert Fontaine.

Opened January 24, 1950

614 Performances

The Plymouth Theatre

Directed by Robert Lewis

Produced by Richard Rodgers and Oscar Hammerstein II

Cast: Claude Dauphin (Papa); Leora Dana (Maman); Johnny Stewart (Bibi); Edgar Stehli (Grandpere); Richard Hart (Uncle Desmond); Kurt Kasznar (Uncle Louis); Mary Aurelius (Aunt Felice); Eva Gabor (Mignonette); Marlene Cameron (Sally); Gage Clarke (Dr. Gagnon); James O'Rear (Alfred); Oliver Cliff (Mr. Frye).

Broadway comedies disprove Leo Tolstoy's dictum that all happy families are alike. The clans depicted in *You Can't Take It With You, Life with Father,* and *I Remember Mama* all had their own ways of dealing with the common crises of everyday life. The same can be said for the French-Canadian Bonnards of *The Happy Time,* Samuel Taylor's dramatization of Robert Fontaine's novel.

Numerous attempts had been made to bring Fontaine's episodic stories to the stage. Taylor wrote his version after several producers and playwrights, including Fontaine himself, had given up. The main problem of adaptation was stitching together the loosely related segments of the book with a common theme. Taylor made the focus of the play the maturation of the young son Bibi as his strict Scottish mother tries to get her fun-loving

French husband and male relatives to set a good example.

Taylor's play had gone through several revisions, and it also went through many producers' offices. They liked Taylor's treatment but were busy with other projects. Leland Hayward had his hands full with *Anne of a Thousand Days,* Alfred de Liagre, Jr. with *The Madwoman of Chaillot,* and Saint Subber and Lemuel Ayers with *Kiss Me, Kate.* Rodgers and Hammerstein finally agreed to back the production after they finished with *South Pacific.* But they still had to wait for director Robert Lewis to get *Regina,* the operatic version of *The Little Foxes,* on its feet.

Taylor wrote in his introduction to the script: "No accents necessary." But there was a smorgasbord of dialects amid a cast supposedly all playing French-Canadians. Claude Dauphin as Papa spoke with a Parisian French lilt. Edgar Stehli, the grandfather, was also French, but articulated in rather British English. Kurt Kasznar, who enacted a tippling uncle, was Viennese, and Eva Gabor, as Mignonette, the destitute young girl staying with the family, was unable to alter her Hungarian inflections—whenever she said "Oui," it came out as "Vee." After numerous attempts to get the actress to pronounce it correctly, a change was made in the dialogue to explain her peculiar way of speaking; when Papa introduces her to the clan, he says, "She is a Hungarian acrobat."

Despite the clash of accents, the cast got along beautifully. Lewis and Gabor both stated in their autobiographies that rehearsals and performances were a regular love fest. On matinee days the company took turns hosting teas and parties between the afternoon and evening shows. There was so much affection going around that two of the ensemble, Leora Dana and Kurt Kasznar got married.

Warm feelings came from the public as well. The show became known as a "quiet hit." It had no star names, no Pulitzer Prize, no smash reviews; most critics labelled it pleasant and cozy entertainment. Box office returns were steady enough to keep the show running for 614 performances.

Rodgers and Hammerstein were not as lucky with their other straight-play ventures. A month before *Happy Time* opened in New York, their production of *The Heart of the Matter,* an adaptation of a Graham Greene novel, closed in Boston. Later that year, they presented *Burning Bright,* a rare play by literary giant John Steinbeck, which closed after a short run on Broadway. That was the last work that Rodgers and Hammerstein backed that was not written by themselves.

The Happy Time had a second life eighteen years later. The basic story went through further revisions when it was musicalized in 1968. To make the original material fit into a pre-existing play by N. Richard Nash (author of *The Rainmaker*), an additional uncle was made the focus of the plot. He was a world-weary photographer who appears glamorous to Bibi but is in fact a lonely failure. John Kander and Fred Ebb provided beautiful songs, and director Gower Champion used photographs projected on a screen to set the mood. But with mixed reviews, the show ran 286 performances. Robert Goulet did win a Tony Award as the photographer, as did Champion for staging.

AFFAIRS OF STATE

by Louis Verneuil

Opened September 25, 1950

610 Performances

The Royale Theatre

Directed by Louis Verneuil

Produced by Richard W. Krakeur and Fred F. Finklehoff

Cast: Celeste Holm (Irene Elliott); Shepperd Strudwick (George Henderson); Reginald Owen (Philip Russell); Barbara O'Neil (Constance Russell); Harry Bannister (Byron Winkler); Elmer Brown (Lawrence).

Politics made strange bedfellows of breezy Broadway comedy and French bedroom farce in *Affairs of State*, the first English-language work by veteran Parisian playwright Louis Verneuil. The play starred Celeste Holm (of *Oklahoma!* and *Bloomer Girl*) as Irene Elliott, a shy midwestern schoolteacher who marries George Henderson, a rising young Senator, in a union of convenience. The alliance is based on the premise that married politicians have a more wholesome image than bachelors. The whole union has been arranged by Irene's influential uncle. But it seems that Irene's Aunt Constance is attracted to George, yet cannot get a divorce from her husband, a distinguished elder statesman.

Constance figures that her current hubby, being much older, will die before her. Her niece will dutifully leave the field clear when her spouse expires. The only problem is that Irene blossoms into a brilliant Washington hostess and George truly falls in love with her.

The contrived plot strained the credulity of reviewers, but the accomplished Verneuil provided enough witty dialogue in his second language to keep the play running for 610 performances.

Verneuil was the author of sixty plays and, on two separate occasions, seven of his works were playing in Paris simultaneously. He came to America in 1940 because he could get none of his works produced in Nazi-occupied France. While in Hollywood, he met Holm, who was looking for a play after spending some years in films. (Her Oscar-nominated performance in *All About Eve* came out at the same time as *Affairs of State*). She asked him to write a vehicle for her, so the author penned the political comedy. Verneuil still had trouble with his English, and Holm assisted him in making the dialogue more idiomatic and less stilted.

A cast was assembled and rehearsed on the West Coast before opening on Broadway. The biggest name was veteran film character actor Reginald Owen (*A Tale of Two Cities, A Christmas Carol*), who was loaned out by MGM to play the heroine's uncle.

June Havoc replaced Holm during the Broadway run and headlined the national tour.

CALL ME MADAM

Book by Howard Lindsay and Russel Crouse

Music and lyrics by Irving Berlin

Opened October 12, 1950

644 Performances

Imperial Theatre

Directed by George Abbott

Choreographed by Jerome Robbins

Produced by Leland Hayward

Cast: Ethel Merman (Sally Adams); Paul Lukas (Cosmo Constantine); Russell Nype (Kenneth Gibson); Galina Talva (Princess Maria); Pat Harrington (Congressman Wilkins); Alan Hewitt (Pemberton Maxwell); Geoffrey Lumb (Secretary of State); Owen Coll (Supreme Court Justice/Grand Duke Otto); William David (Henry Gibson); Ralph Chambers (Sen. Gallagher); Jeanne Bal (Secretary); Jay Velie (Sen. Brockbank); E.A. Krumschmidt (Hugo Tantinnin); Henry Lascoe (Sebastian Sebastian); Lilia Skala (Grand Duchess Sophie); William Hail (Butler); Stowe Phelps (Clerk); William David (Court Chamberlain); Lily Paget (Maid).

The program for *Call Me Madam* stated that "the play is laid in two mythical countries. One is called Lichtenburg. The other is the United States." It further announced that "neither the character of Mrs. Sally Adams nor Miss Ethel Merman resemble any person living or dead." The reason for this amusing disclaimer was that Merman's character, Sally Adams, was indeed based on Perle Mesta, a prominent millionairess and Washington hostess recently appointed by President Harry Truman as ambassador to Luxembourg.

Howard Lindsay (co-author of *Life with Father*) came up with the idea of Merman playing a Mesta-like diplomat when vacationing in Colorado Springs at the same time as the famous belter. He spied her sunning herself poolside and, remembering the news about Ms. Mesta, got the idea of turning this quintessentially American songstress loose in a mythical European country. To compose the score, Lindsay and his collaborator, Russel Crouse, approached Irving Berlin. The songwriter had had a flop with *Miss Liberty* the previous season and was growing tired of the Broadway game. But, of course, he also wanted one last hit, and this new show could be it.

The production was bankrolled by RCA, which, like more and more record companies, was getting into producing. George Abbott directed with his customary single-minded authority. At one rehearsal, Lindsay and Crouse arrived late to find that some of their lines had been

Ethel Merman advises Russell Nype that he's "Just in Love" in *Call Me Madam*.

changed by Abbott. Lindsay remarked "Well, I hope we have the same title." Abbott summarily dismissed the company and explained to the playwrights that whatever changes he made would be for the good of the show and that (contrary to the dramatists' contract) he would brook no interference, not even from them.

Paul Lukas was playing Merman's romantic interest, an aristocratic nobleman. Despite his Oscar for the film version of *Watch on the Rhine*, he was insecure about his singing voice and wanted to drop out. The discovery of the show was young Russell Nype, as the embassy's press agent who falls in love with a princess. He couldn't see without his glasses, so Lindsay and Crouse told him to keep them on and to wear his hair in a crewcut to give him an Ivy League look. Once the show opened, glasses and crewcuts became all the rage for young men desiring an intellectual profile.

There were the usual problems out of town. Two of the numbers in Act II simply were not working: "Mister Monotony," which had been salvaged from two other Berlin shows, and "Free" were cut to be replaced by "Something to Dance About" and "You're Just in Love," the hit of the show that became a standard. The latter melody, a contrapuntal duet for Merman and Nype, was given seven encores at its first performance in Boston. In keeping with Berlin's practice of never throwing a song away, "Free" later turned up in the film "White Christmas" with new lyrics as "Snow." "Mister Monotony" finally resurfaced almost forty years later as a number in *Jerome Robbins' Broadway*.

There were other minor changes and additions, but once the show came into New York, Merman demanded a halt to them. "Boys, as of right now," she told the authors, "I am Miss Bird's-Eye of 1950. I am frozen. Not a new comma."

No new commas were necessary. Berlin had his hit to make up for the failure of *Miss Liberty*. In addition to "You're Just in Love," "They Like Ike" was well received and became Eisenhower's official campaign song for the 1952 presidential election. Unfortunately, Merman did not get to sing any of the songs from the score on the original cast album. RCA had produced the show, but Merman was signed to an exclusive contract with a rival, Decca Records. So the album featured Dinah Shore's voice. Decca released a competing record with Merman singing opposite Dick Haymes.

Merman did appear in the movie. After having been passed over for the film versions of *DuBarry Was a Lady*, *Panama Hattie*, and *Annie Get Your Gun*, she finally got to preserve one of her Broadway performances on celluloid. (Merman had previously done the truncated movie version of *Anything Goes*.) The 20th-Century Fox feature opened in 1953 with Donald O'Connor and George Sanders co-starring.

Call Me Madam was Berlin's last successful Broadway score. His next show, *Mister President* (1962), also had a political theme. It ran for only eight months.

GUYS AND DOLLS

Book by Abe Burrows and Jo Swerling, based on characters created by Damon Runyon.

Music and lyrics by Frank Loesser

Opened November 24, 1950

1,200 Performances

The 46th Street Theatre

Directed by George S. Kaufman

Choreographed by Michael Kidd

Produced by Cy Feuer and Ernest Martin

Cast: Robert Alda (Sky Masterson); Isabel Bigley (Sarah Brown); Sam Levene (Nathan Detroit); Vivian Blaine (Adelaide); Stubby Kaye (Nicely-Nicely Johnson); Pat Rooney, Sr. (Arvide Abernathy); B.S. Pully (Big Jule); Johnny Silver (Benny Southstreet); Douglas Deane (Rusty Charlie); Paul Migan (Calvin); Margery Oldroyd (Agatha); Christine Matsios (Priscilla); Tom Pedi (Harry the Horse); Paul Reed (Lt. Brannigan); Tony Gardell (Angie the Ox); Bern Hoffman (Joey Biltmore); Beverly Tassoni (Mimi); Netta Packer (Gen. Matilda B. Carstairs); Eddie Philips (Drunk); Joe Milan (Waiter). Future choreographers Onna White and Peter Gennaro were in the chorus.

When it was revived on Broadway in 1992, *Guys and Dolls* became the hottest show of the season. Forty years earlier, the original production caused a similar sensation, and the show was almost immediately regarded as a truly American, classic musical comedy. When it was first conceived, producers Cy Feuer and Ernest Martin didn't want a comedy at all. The two envisioned a serious love story based on the Damon Runyon short story, "The Idyll of Miss Sarah Brown," which was inspired by a former showgirl who joined the Salvation Army and preached to Times Square low-lifes. In Runyon's story, she falls in love with an inveterate gambler and attempts to reform him.

Film scenarist Jo Swerling and composer-lyricist Frank Loesser (*Where's Charley?*) were recruited to write the show. After they submitted a first draft, Loesser's score was kept, but Swerling's book rejected. Although Swerling's script was not used, his name was on the program; a clause in his contract stipulated that no matter what version of the musical was produced, he had to receive at least partial acknowledgement. Thus the book is credited to Swerling and Abe Burrows, even though the two never collaborated.

The producers had eventually decided to make the show funnier and acquired the services of Burrows, a radio and television writer. Burrows started from scratch, writing a libretto around Loesser's songs, and the songwriter provided additional new numbers to fit what Burrows wrote. (Swerling's son claims that Burrows only did a polishing job on his father's work.)

In Burrows' version, the romantic pairing of Sarah Brown and gambler Sky Masterson is contrasted with the fourteen-year engagement of the comic leads, Nathan Detroit and Miss Adelaide. Characters from other Runyon works, such as Nicely-Nicely Johnson—who was given the show-stopping number "Sit Down, You're Rocking the Boat"—were also added.

Burrows' joining the creative team caused some anxiety among investors, for he had never had a hit in the theatre before. Broadway showman Billy Rose withdrew his money from the show for that reason. To make up for Burrows' newness, veteran director and play-doctor George S. Kaufman was called in to stage the show. Burrows and Kaufman knew each other from their stints as fellow panelists on the TV game show *This Is Show Business*.

Vivian Blaine as Miss Adelaide in *Guys and Dolls*.

The four leads were something of a risk as well. Only Sam Levene (Nathan) had a successful Broadway track record. Robert Alda (Sky) and Vivian Blaine (Adelaide) had appeared in films, but not in musicals. Isabel Bigley (Sarah) was totally new to the spotlight and making her Broadway debut also. Levene had played a gambler before in *Three Men on a Horse*, but couldn't sing a note. He was given only one song, "Sue Me," a duet with Adelaide. During group numbers, he would mouth the words. When Frank Sinatra played Nathan in the movie version, extra songs were added for him.

In spite of the lack of stage experience on the part of the leading players and the bookwriter, *Guys and Dolls* became one of the few Broadway productions of the decade to exceed 1,000 performances. In addition, many of Loesser's tunes joined the Hit Parade, including "If I Were a Bell," and "A Bushel and a Peck."

Allan Jones and Jan Clayton headed the national touring company. Sam Goldwyn paid $1 million for the film rights, the highest ever up until that time. Marlon Brando made his musical debut in the 1955 movie adaptation; also starring were Frank Sinatra, Jean Simmons, and, in their original stage roles, Vivian Blaine and Stubby Kaye.

A 1976 production featured an all-black cast, lead by James Randolph, Ernestine Jackson, Robert Guillaume, Norma Donaldson, and Ken Page. It ran 239 performances. The smash 1992 revival starred Peter Gallagher, Josie de Guzman, Nathan Lane, and Faith Prince and won Tony Awards for Best Revival, Actress (Prince), and Director (Jerry Zaks).

THE MOON IS BLUE

by F. Hugh Herbert
Opened March 8, 1951
924 Performances
Henry Miller's Theatre
Directed by Otto Preminger
Produced by Richard Aldrich and Richard Myers, with Julius Fleischman
Cast: Barbara Bel Geddes (Patty O'Neill); Barry Nelson (Donald Gresham); Donald Cook (David Slater); Ralph Dunn (Michael O'Neill).

F. Hugh Herbert graduated from the wartime adolescence of *Kiss and Tell* (1943) to adult sexuality in the slightly risqué comedy *The Moon Is Blue*. The action begins at the Empire State Building, where pert actress Patty O'Neill meets sincere young architect Donald Gresham. Patty is frank about her virginity and the possibility of losing it to Donald. They retire to Donald's apartment where aging roué David Slater, the father of Donald's ex-girlfriend, barges in and becomes the third side of a romantic triangle. The humor came from the idea of a young girl openly and objectively discussing her sexual status—pretty heady stuff for 1951.

While in Hollywood, author Herbert took the play to the autocratic Prussian director, Otto Preminger. At the time, Preminger wanted out of his restrictive contract with mogul Darryl Zanuck of 20th-Century Fox. The director demanded half a year off from his exclusive agreement with Zanuck so that he could stage his own projects for theatre and film. The movie executive had no use for the stage and felt the director would wind up broke trying to produce films independently, so he agreed to Preminger's wishes.

During tryouts in New Haven, Preminger insisted that Herbert rewrite the third act, despite the laughs it was getting. The playwright agreed, eliminating the character of Patty's roommate (played by Neva Patterson) and generally tightening the action.

The producers were simultaneously engaged in mounting another Broadway play, *Four Twelves Are Forty-Eight* by Joseph Kesselring (*Arsenic and Old Lace*). The Kesselring play flopped miserably, while *Moon* was an immediate hit.

The simple set and small cast of four made the play ideal for revival. (The fourth player was Patty's father, who walks on in one scene, belts Donald because he believes the young man has dishonored his daughter, and then walks out.) Within two weeks of the New York opening, the Chicago company was in rehearsals. The production there ran for over a year. A third company toured the country, including the West Coast. Eventually, a total of eight companies were touring the U.S. and Canada.

When Preminger brought the comedy to the screen, he met with the opposition of the Catholic Legion of Decency and the Breen Office, which enforced the strict Motion Picture Code. Both groups objected to the use of the words "virgin," "seduction," and "pregnant." Preminger cried censorship and went ahead without the approval of either organization. William Holden enacted the architect, David Niven, who had appeared in the Los Angeles company, was Slater, and Maggie McNamara of the Chicago production was Patty. The director simultaneously shot a German-language version entitled *Die Jungfrau auf dem Duch (The Virgin on the Roof)*.

The American edition of the film, released in 1953, did reasonably well despite the condemnation of the Catholic Church and absence of the motion picture community's seal of approval. Today the supposedly racy dialogue and carnal innuendoes seem tame. But by 1950s standards, the play's open discussion of sex was considered scandalous.

McNamara became a star overnight. Her performance garnered her an Oscar nomination, but quick fame proved difficult to handle for the young actress. After starring in *Three Coins in the Fountain*, another light film comedy, her marriage broke up and she suffered a nervous breakdown. The Oscar nominee left show business to work in an insurance firm.

THE KING AND I

Book and lyrics by Oscar Hammerstein II, based on *Anna and the King of Siam*, by Margaret Landon.

Music by Richard Rodgers

Opened March 29, 1951

1,246 Performances

St. James Theatre

Directed by John Van Druten

Choreographed by Jerome Robbins

Produced by Rodgers and Hammerstein

Cast: Gertrude Lawrence (Anna Leonowens); Yul Brynner (The King); Dorothy Sarnoff (Lady Thiang); Doretta Morrow (Tuptim); Larry Douglas (Lun Tha); Sandy Kennedy (Louis Leonowens); Johnny Stewart (Prince Chulalongkorn); John Juliano (The Kralahome); Charles Francis (Capt. Orton); Leonard Graves (The Interpreter); Len Mence (Phra Alack); Baayork Lee (Princess Ying Yaowalak); Robin Craven (Sir Edward Ramsey).

The King and I, the tender-hearted account of the relationship between a domineering 19th-century Asian monarch and the widowed English governess he hires to tutor his children, was Rodgers and Hammerstein's first show written expressly for a star. However, Yul Brynner, who originated the role of the Siamese king and has become forever identified with it through numerous revivals, was not the instigator of the project.

The star who wanted a vehicle was Gertrude Lawrence, a veteran of London and New York stages in search of a follow-up musical after her triumph in *Lady in the Dark*

(1940). She had read Margaret Landon's book *Anna and the King of Siam* and seen the 1946 film with Irene Dunne and Rex Harrison. She suggested the idea to Cole Porter, who turned her down. Rodgers and Hammerstein, despite trepidations about the star's limited vocal ability, took up the creative reins.

The movie's king, Rex Harrison, *Oklahoma*'s Alfred Drake, and even the erudite Noël Coward, Lawrence's favorite stage partner, were approached to play the monarch. But they were either unavailable or uninterested. Mary Martin recommended Brynner, who had appeared with her in *Lute Song* (1946). The young Russian-born actor had been a circus acrobat and nightclub entertainer. He was working at CBS as a director at the time. Rodgers described his audition in his memoirs: "[Brynner] scowled in our direction, sat down on the stage, and crossed his legs, tailor-fashion, then plunked one whacking chord on his guitar and began to howl in a strange language that no one could understand. He looked savage, he sounded savage,

Gertrude Lawrence and Yul Brynner get to know each other in *The King and I*.

and there was no denying that he projected a feeling of controlled ferocity." They had found their king.

John Van Druten, author of the Rodgers and Hammerstein–produced *I Remember Mama*, was the director of record, but the actual staging was a conglomerate of the efforts of Hammerstein, Brynner, and the choreographer Jerome Robbins, whose ballet "The Small House of Uncle Thomas" (the Harriet Beecher Stowe classic seen through the eyes of the King's concubine Tuptim) was a highlight of the show.

Lawrence was highly insecure about her singing voice, which tended to go flat. Several heavy ballads were dropped in New Haven, and the bouncy "Getting to Know You," which was reworked from a rejected song in *South Pacific*, was added.

Producer Leland Heyward, also an investor in the show, suggested that they close before reaching Broadway. He was later thankful that Rodgers and Hammerstein did not listen to his advice, for *The King and I* went on to have the fourth-longest run of any Broadway show of the 1950s.

Lawrence died in September of 1952, to be succeeded by Constance Carpenter, Annamary Dickey, Celeste Holm, and Patricia Morison, respectively. Alfred Drake assumed the King's role briefly while Brynner was on vacation. The national tour starred Morrison and Brynner. Valerie Hobson and Herbert Lom headed the London company. Revivals would feature Farley Granger and Barbara Cook (City Center, 1960); Darren McGavin and Risâ Stevens (Music Theatre of Lincoln Center, 1964); and Michael Kermoyan and Constance Towers (City Center, 1968).

Though Brynner was originally billed below the title and received a Tony Award as Outstanding Featured Actor, he was elevated to star status during the run of the show. For the 20th-Century Fox movie version, he won the 1956 leading, rather than supporting, Oscar. Deborah Kerr was Anna, and Marni Nixon dubbed in her singing voice. (Nixon was to perform similar off-screen vocalizing for Audrey Hepburn in *My Fair Lady* and Natalie Wood in *West Side Story*).

Brynner would return again and again to the role that made him a star. A national revival tour, in which he played opposite Constance Towers, hit Broadway in 1977 and ran 696 performances. While Brynner took a two-week vacation, Angela Lansbury was brought in as Anna to lend lustre to the marquee, but ticket sales plummeted. Another tour brought Brynner back to Broadway in 1984. This time, Mary Beth Peil played Anna and received a Tony nomination. Brynner was the recipient of a special 1985 Tony Award for playing the King 4,525 times. He even appeared in the role for a short-lived CBS series entitled *Anna and the King* which ran for thirteen episodes in 1972. Samantha Eggar was the TV Anna. Not surprisingly, the actor died while on tour with the show in 1985.

THE FOURPOSTER

by Jan de Hartog
Opened October 24, 1951
632 Performances
Ethel Barrymore Theatre
Directed by José Ferrer
Produced by The Playwrights' Company
Cast: Jessica Tandy (Agnes); Hume Cronyn (Michael).

The Fourposter is the first instance of a play with a cast of two achieving a long run on Broadway. The characters: Agnes and Michael, a married couple. The setting: their bedroom with the titular bed occupying center stage. The time: thirty-five years of matrimony, from the wedding night through pregnancies, quarrels, and extramarital infatuations to the couple's last day in the house as they leave for a smaller place once the children have grown up.

The play was written by Dutch author Jan de Hartog, who had two previous Broadway credits, *This Time Tomorrow* (1947) and *The Skipper Next to God* (1948). In a *New York Times* article, the author claimed that he wrote the play while in hiding from the Nazis during World War II. His novels had invoked "nationalist pride" and the wrath of the occupying Germans. He hid in a ladies' retirement home, under the name of "Mrs. Flyingheart," an invalid woman whose lumbago prevented her from leaving her room. During his confinement, he worked on the manuscript, only to leave it behind when he was smuggled to England. The script was later recovered and produced on the London stage.

Hume Cronyn had been looking for just such a play to appear in with his wife Jessica Tandy. Their separate acting careers were keeping them apart, and this two-seated vehicle was perfect. Cronyn first heard of *The Fourposter* when he read a newspaper item about a screen version being made of the play, which had been a hit in London. Cronyn had never heard of the play before and later found out that it had failed on the West End stage.

Undeterred by this news, the actor obtained the American stage rights to the play and sought a producer. None of the legitimate entrepreneurs were interested, so Cronyn booked the show into a ten-week tour of summer-stock stages, many of which were in his native Canada.

During the strenuous stretch of playing dates, the original director was fired and replaced by José Ferrer. The script also needed extensive rewrites, but de Hartog was difficult to locate. He lived on a barge which travelled between Amsterdam and Paris. But when the Cronyns were playing their final week of the tour in Skowhegan, Maine, de Hartog was found and a visa was arranged. The author could get from Europe to New York, but there were no commercial flights to the Maine village. Cronyn booked a charter plane and de Hartog barely made it for the final two performances of his play.

After a week of revising the script, the playwright returned to Europe to winterize his floating home. Meanwhile, the Playwrights' Company agreed to sponsor a Broadway run of *The Fourposter*, which became a hit. During its summer-stock stint, *Variety* called the play "a two-character trick and . . . a parlor charade. The Cronyns, being wise theatre people, will probably discover it is not for them and will leave it in the sticks after their tour." The couple had the last laugh when, after the play opened in New York, a *Variety* headline reported "*Fourposter* Paying Off in 6 1/2 Weeks; Quickest in Recent Legit History."

Cronyn persuaded Columbia Pictures not to release their movie edition of *The Fourposter* for several months, so as not to compete with the stage version. Another husband and wife, Rex Harrison and Lilli Palmer, starred on screen.

The Cronyns went on a national tour with the play, while Burgess Meredith and Betty Field took over their roles on Broadway. Romney Brent and Sylvia Sydney succeeded Meredith and Field.

Tandy and Cronyn later appeared in such two-handers as *The Gin Game* (1977) and *The Petition* (1986). The play later became a hit musical *I Do! I Do!* (1966), starring Robert Preston and Mary Martin.

PAL JOEY

Book by John O'Hara

Music by Richard Rodgers

Lyrics by Lorenz Hart

Opened January 3, 1952

540 Performances

Broadhurst Theatre

Directed by Robert Alton and David Alexander

Choreographed by Robert Alton

Produced by Jule Styne and Leonard Key

Cast: Harold Lang (Joey); Pat Northrop (Linda); Vivienne Segal (Vera); Helen Gallagher (Gladys); Lionel Stander (Ludlow Lowell); Elaine Stritch (Melba); Helen Wood (Kid); Robert Fortier (Victor); Jack Waldron (Mike); Barbara Nichols (Valerie); Janyce Ann Wagner (Agnes); Phyllis Dorne (Mickey); Frances Krell (Diane); Lynn Joelson (Dottie); Eleanor Boleyn (Sandra); Rita Tanno (Adele); Gloria O'Malley (Francine); Ina Learner (Janet); Ethel Martin (Fraser); Thelma Tadlock (Amarilla); Gordon Peters (Ernest); Lewis Bolyard (Louis the Tenor); T.J. Halligan (O'Brien).

Revivals are rarely as successful as the original production. But sometimes a second production can give audiences a new perspective on an overlooked play or musical and cause them to appreciate what they missed the first time around. Richard Rodgers and Lorenz Hart's *Pal Joey* (1940) went through such a process when the revival had a longer run than the premiere outing and enhanced the show's reputation.

Jessica Tandy and Hume Cronyn prepare to spend a night in *The Fourposter*.

Pal Joey was somewhat unappreciated in its initial mounting. The title character, Joey, was an ambitious, amoral entertainer who would do anything to get his name in lights. The "anything" includes dumping the faithful Linda for Vera, a tough but rich older lady who sets up Joey in his own bistro. Vera soon becomes bored with Joey and he is out on the street at the final curtain.

Like many other hits (*Life with Father, My Sister Eileen, Junior Miss*), the show was based on a series of short stories first published in *The New Yorker*. They were written by novelist John O'Hara in the form of letters sent by Joey to a famous band leader. The author wrote to Rodgers suggesting that the pieces would make a good show.

The musical was unconventional in portraying a realistic but unseemly situation. Its heel of a hero, avaricious supporting characters, frank sexuality, and nightclub netherworld setting put some theatre patrons off. The authors wanted to do a musical in which not everything was sweetness and light and the ending wasn't happy. Director George Abbott was sure the unsympathetic story would cause the show to fail. While the press and public loved Gene Kelly in the title role, Vivienne Segal as the flinty Vera, and the sumptuous score (including "Bewitched, Bothered, and Bewildered," and "I Could Write a Book"), some found the story heavy going. Brooks Atkinson of the *New York Times* found it hard to imagine the authors "drawing sweet water from such a foul well." The musical did have its supporters, though, and Gene Kelly became a star because of the show. It had a moderately successful run of 374 performances. That was in 1940.

Twelve years later, Jule Styne and Leonard Key produced a revival starring ballet dancer Harold Lang in the lead and Vivienne Segal recreating her original role. Helen Gallagher, Lionel Stander, and Elaine Stritch had prominent roles. While the show was trying out in New Haven, Stritch had a commitment to understudy Ethel Merman in *Call Me Madam*. This forced the actress to check in before curtain at the Imperial in New York, where *Madam* was playing, then race to catch a train to New Haven in order to sing her number in *Joey*, which fortunately came near the end of the show.

In the interval between the two productions, theatregoers became more receptive to adult themes in their musicals. This was largely because of the influence of the shows Rodgers wrote with Hammerstein after his partnership with Lorenz Hart ended. *Oklahoma!, Carousel,* and *South Pacific* paved the way for *Joey*'s greater acceptance in its second Broadway incarnation.

The modest run of the original failed to spark interest among the major movie studios. The success of the revival

prompted a film version in 1957. Frank Sinatra was a nicer Joey, and Rita Hayworth and Kim Novak were the women vying for his affections. The score was truncated for the film and other Rodgers and Hart songs were interpolated.

Bob Fosse and Viveca Lindfors starred in a 1963 production at City Center. Joan Copeland and Chris Chadman starred in a 1976 version at Circle in the Square.

Other revivals which out-ran the original productions include *The Red Mill* (1906, 1945); *Dracula* (1927, 1977); *Anything Goes* (1934, 1987); *On Your Toes* (1936, 1983); *The Boys from Syracuse* (1938, 1963); *The Iceman Cometh* (1946, 1956); *The Boy Friend* (1954, 1958); *Peter Pan* (1954, 1979); and *Candide* (1956, 1974).

WISH YOU WERE HERE

Book by Arthur Kober and Joshua Logan, based on Kober's play *Having Wonderful Time*.

Music and lyrics by Harold Rome

Opened June 25, 1952

598 Performances

Imperial Theatre

Directed and choreographed by Joshua Logan

Produced by Leland Hayward and Joshua Logan

Cast: Patricia Marand (Teddy Stern); Jack Cassidy (Chick Miller); Sheila Bond (Fay Fromkin); Sidney Armus (Itchy Flexner); Paul Valentine (Pinky Harris); John Perkins (Harry "Muscles" Green); Sammy Smith (Lou Kandel); Harry Clark (Herman Fabricant); Fred Sadoff (Marvin); Elaine Gordon (Sonja); Larry Blyden (Schmutz); Frank Aletter (Eli); Ray Hyson (Barney); Robert Dixon (Sid); Richard France (Lenny); Joe Milan (Sam); Tom Ayre (Monty); Mardi Bayne (Henrietta); Leila Martin (Gussie), Roslynd Lowe (Irma); Sybil Lamb (Shirley); Denise Griffith (Lena); Shirley Anne Prior (Judy); Nancy Franklin (Miriam); Florence Henderson (The New Girl); Beverly Weston (The Girl Diver); Steve Wiland (The Acrobat); Joseph Thomas (Eccentric Diver). Reid Shelton, Tom Tryon, and Phyllis Newman were in the chorus.

Long before *Miss Saigon*'s helicopter, *Wish You Were Here* sported an enormous stage prop, a full-sized swimming pool onstage. The musical took place at Camp Karefree, a Catskills summer camp where attractive singles search for romance, so a pool was a logical addition to the set.

And the Catskills was a logical setting for a musical. These upstate New York mountains contained numerous resorts which were popular with middle-class, mostly Jewish, New Yorkers. Based on Arthur Kober's 1937 comedy *Having Wonderful Time*, the story focused on a young secretary from Brooklyn who breaks off her engagement with an older man and falls in love with a law student who is working as a waiter by day and a dance partner by night.

For the musical version, Kober eliminated the heavy Borscht Belt accents and older characters of his straight play. Joshua Logan, his collaborator on the book as well as the director and co-producer, had a difficult time casting the show, for all the lead characters were now under thirty. At the time, there were no musical stars who could believably play youngsters in their twenties (especially in bathing suits), so Logan went with unknowns Patricia Marand and Jack Cassidy for the romantic leads. The chorus featured such soon-to-be stars as Phyllis Newman, Larry Blyden, Florence Henderson, and Tom Tryon.

The pool, which had to be dug into the stage of the Imperial Theatre at a cost of $20,000, prevented the producers from taking the show on the traditional out-of-town tryout route. A series of paid previews was instituted instead. Today's expenses being several times higher than those of 1952, paid previews in lieu of Boston and New Haven performances have become common practice .

Opening night was on June 25, in the middle of the most brutal heat wave in recent memory. This was in the days before air-conditioned theatres. Even the cast, attired only in bathing suits, was sweating profusely. Some would have called it "flop sweat," for almost all the reviews were negative. Only John Chapman of the *Daily News* filed an enthusiastic notice.

Co-producer Leland Hayward was all for cutting his losses and closing. Logan wanted to go on. The first two weeks of the run had been booked by Jewish groups. Logan thought that would be enough time to improve the production. The director rewrote eight scenes to make the heroine more sympathetic. In the opening-night version, she returns her engagement ring to her elderly fiancé early in Act I, thereby eliminating any suspense. In the rewritten scenes, the engagement was not broken off until closer to the final curtain. Composer Harold Rome wrote two new songs as well. The changes worked, and good word of mouth spread; the box office went into the black. *Wish You Were Here* was called the musical miracle of the decade.

The show received an additional boost when Eddie Fisher recorded the title song. It mentioned the musical's name several times in each chorus, providing free advertising every time it was played on the radio. Even after the show was established as a hit, Logan continued to rewrite and restage. When *Wonderful Town* opened later in the season to raves, the director made more use of the pool, in order to compete with the new show.

It would be impossible for producers to risk extending the run of a poorly received show on the Broadway of today. With production costs so high, negative reviews almost always ensure a short run.

The pool made touring an expensive proposition, but a Chicago production did well. The London staging was not a hit. In Britain, summer camps are strictly for families, so the audiences were confused by the romantic goings-on in Camp Karefree.

DIAL M FOR MURDER

by Frederick Knott
Opened October 29, 1952
552 Performances
Plymouth Theatre
Directed by Reginald Denham
Produced by James P. Sherwood

Cast: Maurice Evans (Tony Wendice); Gusti Huber (Margot Wendice); Richard Derr (Max Halliday); Anthony Dawson (Captain Lesgate); John Williams (Inspector Hubbard); Porter Van Zandt (Thompson).

Most murder mysteries revolve around finding the perpetrator of a homicide among a gallery of likely suspects. *Dial M for Murder* had a decided twist. In Frederick Knott's thriller, the audience knows the identity of the killer. Tennis player Tony Wendice plans to have his wealthy wife,

Maurice Evans gets a grip on his intended victim Gusti Huber in *Dial M for Murder*.

Margot, extinguished in order to inherit her money. He blackmails a former college chum to do the job. But when Margot stabs and kills her attacker, the mystery becomes not whodunnit, but how will whodunnit get away with it.

Dial M has the distinction of being the first hit Broadway play which was first seen as a TV show. British author Knott had no success in peddling his well-crafted script to producers in London. He adapted it for television, and that shorter version was broadcast on the BBC. It was an immediate sensation with viewers. Producer James P. Sherwood presented the stage edition in the West End, opening on June 19, 1952.

Classical actor Maurice Evans saw the play and wanted to take it to Broadway, but there was a slight impediment to the transatlantic transfer. Movie mogul Alexander Korda had acquired the film rights and stipulated that no stage production of *Dial M* could run during exhibition of the cinema version. This prevented most producers from gambling on it. Evans, who had appeared in Korda's film *Gilbert and Sullivan*, persuaded the moviemaker to withhold release of the film until the fall of 1954, allowing plenty of time for a successful New York run. Evans was scheduled to produce John Patrick's *Teahouse of the August Moon* for the 1952–53 season, but he pushed it back by a year in order to star in *Dial M*.

American reviewers agreed with their British colleagues in assessing the tight plot and rivetting direction. The cast was also highly praised. John Williams, as a caustic police inspector, received a Tony Award for Outstanding Featured Actor in a Play.

Although the national American tour closed after only a few months, international productions proliferated, with engagements in twenty-seven countries in eighteen languages. These included stagings in Paris, where it was known as *Crime Parfait (Perfect Crime)*; Copenhagen, under the title *Mord Pa Bestilling (Murder to Order)*; Stockholm, *Sla Nollan Till Polisen (Dial Zero for Police)*; and Moscow—where it was denounced by *Pravda* as a "low-level bourgeois gutter play."

Korda sold the film rights for $75,000 to Warner Brothers. He had paid only $2,800, so he made a profit of over $70,000. The 1954 picture was directed by the master of suspense, Alfred Hitchcock. Ray Milland, Grace Kelly, Robert Cummings, and John Williams (from the stage play) were the principals. The story was retold as a TV movie in 1981 with Angie Dickinson, Christopher Plummer, and Anthony Quayle.

Knott did not have another play produced until 1966, when *Wait Until Dark*, another thriller, creeped up on Broadway. Lee Remick and Robert Duvall starred in this play about a blind woman tangling with drug smugglers. It ran 373 performances.

THE SEVEN-YEAR ITCH

by George Axelrod

Opened November 20, 1952

1,141 Performances

The Fulton Theatre

Directed by John Gerstad

Produced by Courtney Burr and Elliott Nugent

Cast: Tom Ewell (Richard Sherman); Vanessa Brown (The Girl); Neva Patterson (Helen Sherman); Johnny Klein (Ricky); Marilyn Clark (Miss Morris); Joan Donovan (Elaine); Irene Moore (Marie Whatever-Her-Name-Was); Robert Emhardt (Dr. Brubaker); George Keane (Tom MacKenzie); George Ives (Richard's Voice); Pat Fowler (The Girl's Voice).

Most people remember *The Seven-Year Itch* as a 1955 film that firmly established Marilyn Monroe as the nation's reigning sex symbol. What is not generally recalled is that it was first a hit Broadway comedy with the emphasis placed on Tom Ewell in the male lead. Vanessa Brown, a former child actress (she appeared as one of the refugee children in Lillian Hellman's *Watch on the Rhine*) and Hollywood starlet, originated the role later to be immortalized by Monroe.

Ewell starred as Richard Sherman, an average fellow with an apartment in New York's Gramercy Park section whose wife and son are vacationing in the country. Temporarily cut loose from family ties and chafing at the constraints of a seven year marriage, he gives in to temptation in the form of his young female neighbor, referred to simply as "The Girl." After a one-night fling, both parties realize that parting would be the right thing to do and they break off the relationship. Playwright George Axelrod shook up this fairly standard plot with extended fantasy sequences, long monologues, and dialogues with an off-stage voice representing the conscience of his straying hero.

This was Axelrod's first stage play. In addition to writing several TV and radio scripts, the thirty-year-old author had contributed to two musical revues called *Small Wonder* and *Curtain Going Up*. During the run of the latter show, which closed in Philadelphia, he met producer Courtney Burr, who suggested that he write a play. *Itch* was the result. Burr agreed to present the show with his partner, actor–producer Elliott Nugent (*The Voice of the Turtle*).

Nugent was simultaneously acting in a revival of *The Male Animal*, a comedy he had co-authored with James Thurber. During out-of-town tryouts, Nugent would catch the last train on Saturday night to Boston after performing in *Animal*, confer with his partner Burr about the production all day Sunday, and then return to New York in time for the evening show on Monday night.

Nugent kept the *Itch* in the family. His son-in-law John Gerstad directed, while his father-in-law Charles Washburn handled press relations for the national tour. Nugent himself starred in the lead role for a time in the Chicago company. Eddie Bracken and Eddie Albert also assumed the lead, both on Broadway and on tour.

For the film rights, 20th-Century Fox paid $225,000, plus an additional $175,000 to release the movie during the run of the Broadway show. Billy Wilder (who also directed another Monroe classic, *Some Like It Hot*), directed Axelrod's screenplay. A London edition opened in 1953, with Brian Reece as Richard and Rosemary Harris making her West End debut as The Girl.

The play is not revived often; the central female role is closely identified with Monroe, and the play's attitude towards women is dated. Although she does have her share of interior monologues, The Girl exists almost exclusively as a screen upon which Richard projects his fantasies—she doesn't even have a name.

Axelrod wrote two other lightweight comedies, which were also filmed: *Will Success Spoil Rock Hunter?* (1955) and *Goodbye, Charlie* (1959).

THE FIFTH SEASON

by Sylvia Regan

Opened January 23, 1953

654 Performances

Cort Theatre

Directed by Gregory Ratoff

Produced by George Kondolf

Cast: Menasha Skulnik (Max Pincus); Richard Whorf (Johnny Goodwin); Augusta Roeland (Frances Goodwin); John Kullers (Ruby D. Prince); Nita Talbot (Shelly); Phyllis Hill (Lorraine McKay); Norman Rose (Ferelli); Dick Kallman (Marty Goodwin); Lois Wheeler (Miriam Oppenheim); Dorian Leigh (Dolores); Midge Ware (Redhead Model); Carolyn Block (Brunette Model); John Griggs (Miles Lewis).

The joke in the title of Sylvia Regan's *The Fifth Season* refers to the garment industry. One character explains: "In this business, there are five seasons: spring, summer, winter, fall, and slack." The play follows the ups and downs of two partners in the fashion trade. One chases women, and the other is constantly bailing him out of trouble.

Playwright Regan's husband had written a musical for Menasha Skulnik, a diminutive comic who was a great favorite of the Yiddish-speaking theatre, centered on Second Avenue in Manhattan, but who had yet to reach a broader public. Regan decided to write a vehicle for Skulnik for his English-language and Broadway debut.

After the opening of *The Fifth Season*, she wrote in *Theatre Arts*, "Hollywood had Chaplin, France had Raimu and Fernandel, Mexico had Cantinflas—those exquisite, eternal little men—and Second Avenue had Skulnik." She had worked in a garment factory at age seventeen and knew it was a logical setting for Skulnik's Jewish-flavored humor.

In several different drafts, and under various titles, including *Mind Your Business* and *Business Is Business*, the play was rejected. Once producer George Kondolf had taken a chance and acquired the rights, it took eighteen months to assemble the necessary backers. But only two months were required to earn back the initial investment.

The show was popular with audiences, but critics were cool, calling the play well-constructed but corny. *Variety* stated that it was "another of those theatrical productions with which a play-catcher can't find too much fault, nor can he find too much to shout about."

Since the action centered on ladies' fashions, the women in the cast got a completely new wardrobe a year into the run to reflect the changes in current tastes.

The original company included an assistant stage manager named John Cassavettes, who went on to become a highly-regarded actor and independent filmmaker. Joseph Buloff, another great figure of the Yiddish stage, starred in the London production. The British press gave him kudos and agreed that he outshone the play.

WONDERFUL TOWN

Book by Joseph Fields and Jerome Chodorov, based on their play *My Sister Eileen*.

Music by Leonard Bernstein

Lyrics by Betty Comden and Adolph Green

Opened February 25, 1953

559 Performances

Winter Garden Theatre

Directed by George Abbott

Choreographed by Donald Saddler

Produced by Robert Fryer

Cast: Rosalind Russell (Ruth Sherwood); Edith Adams (Eileen Sherwood); George Gaynes (Robert Baker); Henry Lascoe (Appopolous); Chris Alexander (Frank Lippencott); Michele Burke (Helen); Jordan Bentley (Wreck); Walter Kelvin (Lonigan); Dody Goodman (Violet); Ted Beniades (Valenti); Dort Clark (Chick Clark); Isabella Hoopes (Mrs. Wade); Nathaniel Frey (Strange Man/Chef); Warren Galjour (Guide/Associate Editor); Delbert Anderson (Drunk/Waiter); Lee Papell (Drunk/Shore Patrolman); Albert Linville (Associate Editor); Alvin Bean (Delivery Boy); David Lober (1st Cadet); Ray Dorian (2nd Cadet); Chris Robinson (Ruth's Escort).

Plans for a musical version of *My Sister Eileen*, Joseph Fields and Jerome Chodorov's dramatization of Ruth McKinney's *New Yorker* stories, had gone awry three times before *Wonderful Town* burst onto Broadway. The tale of two sisters on the loose in New York, struggling for separate careers as a writer and an actress, had been a hit as both a play and a film. A retelling with songs seemed like the natural next step.

First, Max Gordon asked Herbert and Dorothy Fields to write the book and lyrics, Burton Lane the music, and George S. Kaufman to direct. Then Leland Hayward planned to mount his own adaptation with libretto by the Fields brother-and-sister team in collaboration with their brother Joseph and a score by either Irving Berlin or Cole Porter. A third attempt had Ella Logan of *Finian's Rainbow*

Edith (later Edie) Adams, Dody Goodman, and Rosalind Russell in *Wonderful Town*.

in the lead. Each of these tries was confounded by the negotiations of Harry Cohn, who had owned the rights to the material ever since his Columbia Pictures had filmed the nonmusical version in 1942 with Rosalind Russell.

The fourth time was the charm. Producer Robert Fryer managed to acquire the rights. He also convinced George Abbott to stage the show and Chodorov and Fields to adapt their original work. The songs were to be written by the team of Leroy Anderson and Arnold Horwitt. Rosalind Russell, who had not appeared on a Broadway stage since *Garrick Gaieties* in 1930, and who was insecure about her nonexistent singing voice, was persuaded to re-create her film role.

Five weeks before rehearsals were to begin, Anderson and Horwitt were dismissed over a disagreement with Fields and Chodorov. Betty Comden and Adolph Green were called in to write the lyrics. They, in turn, called in their collaborator from *On the Town* (1944), Leonard Bernstein.

Fields and Chodorov still had problems with their collaborators. The playwrights felt that Comden and Green were ruining the original sentimental comedy by giving it a hard, satirical edge and inserting a series of revue-like sketches into the book. The conflict over interpretation led to several shouting matches during rehearsals and previews, but Abbott sided with the lyricists and their sharp, parodistic view won out.

For Russell's sister Eileen, Abbott hired Edie (then known as Edith) Adams, who was co-starring with her future husband, comic Ernie Kovacs, on a CBS morning program, *Kovacs Unlimited*.

The show opened to rave reviews in New Haven, but that did not prevent the usual out-of-town calamities. Jerome Robbins was called in to tighten up the dance numbers. Russell, not a natural singer, had been damaging her vocal chords during her comedy number "A Hundred Easy Ways to Lose a Man." She came down with the flu, and her understudy had to go on for several performances. With advice from trained singer Adams, Russell played the remainder of the run without losing her voice. She even managed the difficult harmonies of "Ohio," a duet with Adams, so long as Adams was there to give the star her first note. Then, in Boston, a chorus boy dropped Russell during the "Conga" number, spraining her back.

In New York, the reviews were once again laudatory. Brooks Atkinson cheered that Russell should be elected President, even though her voice sounded like "the Ambrose Lightship calling to its mate." The show ran for a year and a half, with Carol Channing succeeding Russell.

CBS telecast a special edition of the show in 1958. Rosalind Russell returned to her role as Ruth, and Jacqueline McKeever was Eileen.

Because of contract disputes, Columbia produced its own musical film version of *My Sister Eileen* with a different score in 1955. Betty Garrett, Janet Leigh, Jack Lemmon, and Bob Fosse starred.

CAN-CAN

Book by Abe Burrows

Music and lyrics by Cole Porter

Opened May 7, 1953

892 Performances

Shubert Theatre

Directed by Abe Burrows

Choreographed by Michael Kidd

Produced by Cy Feuer and Ernest Martin

Cast: Lilo (La Mome Pistache); Peter Cookson (Aristide Forestier); Gwen Verdon (Claudine); Hans Conried (Boris Adzinidzinadze); Erik Rhodes (Hilaire Jussac); Robert Penn (Hercule); Phil Leeds (Theophile); Richard Purdy (Etienne); C. K. Alexander (Judge Paul Barriere); David Thomas (Court President/Customer); Mary Anne Cohan (Gabrielle); Beverly Purvin (Marie); Jean Kraemer (Celestine); Deedee Wood (Jailer); Clarence Hoffman (Waiter); Ferdinand Hilt (2nd Waiter/Customer/Prosecutor); Jon SIlo (Cafe Waiter); Joe Cusanelli (Cafe Customer); Pat Turner (Model); Dania Krupska (Mimi); Sheila Arnold (Customer); Michael Cavallaro (Doctor); Arthur Rubin (Second).

When producers Cy Feuer and Ernest Martin asked Abe Burrows (librettist for *Guys and Dolls*) to write and direct their next musical, the only storyline they gave him was the locale, the time, and the title: Paris, the late 1890s, *Can-Can*. That Cole Porter would be doing the score encouraged Burrows greatly, but he still had worries about making up a whole show with so little to go on.

Feuer and Martin supplied their author with more raw material by hiring a researcher to dig up as much about the City of Light near the turn of the century as possible. The findings revealed that the can-can, in which the chorus girls would bare their panties and then some, was considered the 1890s version of "dirty dancing." Irate citizens' groups with names like the League Against Licentiousness of the Streets were lobbying for its prohibition. Burrows came up with the plot of a puritannical magistrate out to ban the can-can yet falling in love with the sexy owner of a nightclub where it is performed.

At first, the production team tried to interest Carol Channing in starring, but she was set to appear in the London version of *Gentlemen Prefer Blondes*. During a trip to Paris, Martin had heard a French musical comedy star named Lilo. It was decided to sign the single-named singer, which the producers and author did while on another sojourn to the French capital to soak up atmosphere for the show. Peter Cookson, who had scored a hit in the dramatic play *The Heiress*, was chosen for the male lead. He would be making his musical debut.

But the show was stolen by a new star named Gwen Verdon in the ingénue role. On opening night, Verdon received such a tremendous ovation performing Michael Kidd's choreography that she stopped the show twice. At the conclusion of one number, Verdon left the stage, went to her dressing room and changed into her bathrobe. The audience was still applauding and would not let the per-formance continue until Verdon took another bow, which she did dressed in her bathrobe.

While the critics wrote love letters to Verdon and Kidd, they were less kind to Burrows and Porter. The book was dismissed as contrived, and Porter's melodies were classified as "not up to his usual standard." In spite of the reviewers' disdain, five of the songs made the Hit Parade in versions by popular singers: "I Love Paris," "It's All Right with Me," "C'est Magnifique," "Allez-Vous-En," and "I Am in Love."

Can-Can went on to become Porter's second-longest running musical after *Kiss Me, Kate*. The composer was going through several personal crises during this show. The death of his mother, the failing health of his wife Linda, and his own constant pain from a riding accident were taking their toll. His next Broadway score, *Silk Stockings* (1955), was his last.

The 1960 film version of *Can-Can* altered the story somewhat, with Frank Sinatra, as a new character, rivaling Louis Jourdan, as the official, for the affections of Shirley MacLaine. Maurice Chevalier and Juliet Prowse co-starred. Additional tunes from the Porter canon augmented the original Broadway score.

A 1981 revival starred Zizi Jeanmarie and Ron Husmann and received a Tony nomination for Roland Petite's choreography. Chita Rivera headlined a 1988 touring edition.

TEA AND SYMPATHY

by Robert Anderson

Opened September 30, 1953

712 Performances

Ethel Barrymore Theatre

Directed by Elia Kazan

Produced by The Playwrights Company

Cast: Deborah Kerr (Laura Reynolds); John Kerr (Tom Lee); Leif Erickson (Bill Reynolds); Florida Friebus (Lilly Sears); Richard Midgley (David Harris); Alan Sues (Ralph); Dick York (Al); Arthur Steuer (Steve); Richard Franchot (Phil); John McGovern (Herbert Lee); Yale Wexler (Paul).

Like Lillian Hellman's *The Children's Hour*, Robert Anderson's *Tea and Sympathy* is set in a private school and centers on a false accusation of homosexuality. The hero, Tom Lee, does not fit in with his fellow students. He doesn't play football, wears his hair too long, and likes to stay in his room playing folk music on his guitar. When Tom is caught swimming in the nude with a teacher who is suspected of being gay, his classmates and the faculty members immediately condemn him as a "pervert." Only Laura Reynolds, the unappreciated wife of Tom's housemaster, understands that Tom's nonconformity is not "deviant." The title refers to Laura's habit of counseling troubled boys by offering them "tea and sympathy."

After confronting her hypermasculine husband with doubts about his own sexuality, Laura decides to prove to Tom the allegations against him are untrue. She goes into the boy's room and utters the now classic line "Years from now when you talk about this—and you will—be kind." The lights fade as she unbuttons her blouse.

Like Hellman's play, Anderson's work does not directly confront the issue of homosexuality as an acceptable way of living. *Children's Hour* is about the power of libel to destroy lives. *Tea and Sympathy* concerns tolerance for those who do not join the herd, who are are slightly "off-center."

The play was Anderson's first produced stage work. It had impressed the Playwrights' Company, which agreed to produce it and admitted the young dramatist into its membership. Elia Kazan was enthusiastic about the script. Realizing the play was an intimate piece which required a light touch, he directed with a delicacy absent from the high-voltage dramas he had previously staged—*Death of a Salesman* and *A Streetcar Named Desire*.

Kazan had objected to Anderson's choice of the British film actress Deborah Kerr for the lead. The director resisted working with movie stars in the theatre; he believed their demands tended to undermine stage productions. Once he met Kerr, he admitted that she was the right choice. Kerr triumphed in her American stage debut, while

three of her movies, *From Here to Eternity*, *Dream Wife* and *Julius Caesar*, were in release. John Kerr, son of actress June Walker, played Tom and won a Tony Award as Best Featured Actor in a Play.

Deborah Kerr took the play on an extensive road tour, while another Hollywood star, Joan Fontaine, took over the lead in the New York company. Anthony Perkins replaced John Kerr.

The play was not presented in London until 1957, when it was mounted in a private club production. The Lord Chamberlain's office, which acted as a censor for commercial theatre, forbade its performance because of the subject matter. Unencumbered by such censorship, European productions flourished, including a Paris edition starring Ingrid Bergman.

Both Kerrs and Leif Erickson recreated their stage roles for the 1956 Metro-Goldwyn-Mayer film version, directed by Vincente Minnelli. The studio censored any direct reference to homosexuality. Tom was knitting with the faculty wives rather than sunbathing with a teacher in the milder film script. In order to please the powerful Catholic Legion of Decency, Anderson tacked on an epilogue in which Tom attends a reunion at the school. He is handed a letter from Laura in which she declares that their affair was "wrong."

It would not be until fifteen years after the Broadway opening of *Tea* that homosexuality would be directly examined on a New York stage, in Mart Crowley's *The Boys in the Band*; even then it would be viewed as an illness rather than another style of sexuality.

Deborah Kerr and John Kerr share *Tea and Sympathy*.

COMEDY IN MUSIC

by Victor Borge
Opened October 2, 1953
849 Performances
John Golden Theatre
Produced by Harry D. Squires

Numerous variety artists have played on Broadway in solo presentations, often to display their musical comedy talents. Beatrice Lillie, Danny Kaye, Judy Garland, Diana Ross, Bette Midler, and Shirley MacLaine are just a few such performers to take on Broadway alone. But these were mostly limited engagements. Victor Borge, the Danish classical pianist who specializes in comic antics at the keyboard, is the only one to achieve a run of over 500 performances in a one-person show with his *Comedy in Music.*

Using audiences' apprehensions about "long-hair, high-brow" music, Borge educated and amused by shattering myths about the classics. While playing "Clair de Lune," for example, he encouraged the audience to cough.

In addition to his musical hijinks, Borge's schtick included a now famous routine on audible punctuation. While reading from a book, he made exaggerated sounds for each comma, period, exclamation point, and so on.

Borge brought new editions of *Comedy in Music* to Broadway in 1964 and in 1977.

There have been many popular one-person Broadway shows that were nonmusical; these have included Hal Holbrook in *Mark Twain Tonight!* (1965); Henry Fonda as *Clarence Darrow for the Defense* (1974); Julie Harris as Emily Dickinson in *The Belle of Amherst* (1977); Lily Tomlin in *The Search for Signs of Intelligent Life in the Universe* (1985); Robert Morse as Truman Capote in *Tru* (1989); and Lynn Redgrave in *Shakespeare for My Father* (1993).

THE TEAHOUSE OF THE AUGUST MOON

by John Patrick, based on the novel by Vern Sneider.
Opened October 15, 1953
1,027 Performances
Martin Beck Theatre
Directed by Robert Lewis
Produced by Maurice Evans

Cast: David Wayne (Sakini); John Forsythe (Capt. Fisby); Paul Ford (Col. Wainwright Purdy III); Mariko Nikki (Lotus Blossom); Harry Jackson (Sgt. Gregovich); Larry Gates (Capt. MacLean); Naoe Kondo (Old Woman); Mara Kim (Old Woman's Daughter); Kame Ishikawa (Ancient Man); Chuck Morgan (Mr. Hokaida); Kuraji Seida (Mr. Omura); Kaie Deei (Mr. Sumata); Kikuo Hiromura (Mr. Sumata's Father); Haim Winant (Mr. Seiko); Shizu Moriya (Miss Higa Jiga); Yuki Shimoda (Mr. Keora); William Hansen (Mr. Oshira).

Just as Broadway comedy helped America deal with World War II, postwar relations were gently chided in one of the biggest hits of the early '50s, *The Teahouse of the August Moon.* The gradual orientalizing of American forces in occupied Okinawa was the theme of *Teahouse,* John Patrick's adaptation of Vern Sneider's novel. Both the original author and the playwright drew on wartime experiences; Sneider had been military government supervisor of Tobaru, Japan, and Patrick had served in India and Burma.

The casting of Sakini, the narrator, was most difficult. There were no Asian actors who could carry a show at that

David Wayne (center) offers John Forsythe the kind attentions of Mariko Nikki in *The Teahouse of the August Moon.*

time, according to director Robert Lewis. "There were so few opportunities for them then that none had the experience to do it. The crowd in the play were a whole mixture of Asians. We had Japanese, Chinese, even blacks. But Sakini was a starring part where he had to not only act in all the scenes but had to step out of the play and talk to the audience all evening and be an emcee. To do that, you have to have a certain charm and the ability to make the audience laugh." He auditioned every possible Asian actor, and, with producer Maurice Evans, even went to Chinese and Japanese restaurants trying to find a Sakini. "We really wanted an Asian in the role," Lewis said. "We actually found a man named Sho Onedera. He was a Japanese journalist working in America. He was personable and spoke English beautifully. We thought, 'My God, we have found him.' We brought him to the theatre and started to work with him . . . and he just couldn't do it." Sho Onedera did stay on as an adviser and translated all the lines into Japanese that the crowd had to say.

The role went to David Wayne, who had excelled in character parts in *Finian's Rainbow* and *Mister Roberts*.

Despite feuds between the playwright and the producer, the show came together and was a hit; five companies of *Teahouse* played to great success, in New York, Chicago, London, and in tours of the United States and England. Eli Wallach starred as Sakini in London and later replaced Wayne on Broadway, while Burgess Meredith headed the national company. There were subsequent productions from Israel to Mexico, where Sakini was played by a woman. The play was presented in Japan with Americans playing themselves and Japanese playing the Okinawan roles, each in their native language. An unsuccessful musical version of the play entitled *Lovely Ladies, Kind Gentlemen* opened on Broadway in 1970. It closed after a run of 16 performances.

The 1956 film version of *Teahouse* starred Marlon Brando as Sakini. Glenn Ford was Fisby, and Paul Ford repeated his blustering Colonel Purdy.

THE SOLID GOLD CADILLAC

by Howard Teichmann and George S. Kaufman

Opened November 5, 1953

526 Performances

The Belasco Theatre

Directed by George S. Kaufman

Produced by Max Gordon

Cast: Josephine Hull (Mrs. Laura Partridge); Loring Smith (Edward L. McKeever); Geoffrey Lumb (T. John Blessington); Wendell K. Philips (Alfred Metcalfe); Reynolds Evans (Warren Gille); Henry Jones (Clifford Snell); Mary Welch (Miss Amelia Shotgraven); Jack Ruth (Mark Jenkins); Charlotte Van Lein (Miss L'Arriere); Vera Fuller Mellish (Miss Logan); Carl Judd (A.P.); Al McGranary (U.P.); Howard Adelman (I.N.S.); Henry Norell (Bill Parker); Mark Allen (Dwight Brookfield); Lorraine MacMartin (Estelle Evans); Gloria Maitland (Woman).

The Solid Gold Cadillac, George S. Kaufman and Howard Teichmann's satire on big business, follows the fairy-tale-like story of a little old lady with ten shares in a huge corporation who eventually wrests control from the corrupt board of directors and becomes chairwoman. At the final curtain, she is awarded the titular vehicle as a reward for her services to the company.

Teichmann had worked as Orson Welles's stage manager and later wrote for Welles's radio program, *The Mercury Theatre on the Air*. Producer Max Gordon had read a television script of Teichmann's and, recognizing the writer's potential, suggested that he and George S. Kaufman work together. The collaboration resulted in a comedy about the United Nations. Gordon, who was to have produced it, dropped the project, fearing it would be too controversial.

Teichmann came up with the idea of a play on wicked ways in executive suites. Although Kaufman had three operations during the six weeks after the rejection of the U.N. play, the script for *Cadillac* was completed soon after he returned home from the hospital. He originally insisted that the finished product not bear his name, for his last few works had been disasters. Teichmann wouldn't hear of it, and Kaufman finally settled for second billing.

Gordon agreed to produce this second attempt. Josephine Hull, who had made a hit in three previous long-running shows—*You Can't Take It With You, Arsenic and Old Lace,* and *Harvey*—was signed for the lead.

When the play arrived in Washington, D.C., for a tryout, the play was too long and there were several technical problems. The capital critics were not kind. One said Hull had "the shape of a battered coal barge and the face of an amiable bulldog." The playwrights worked feverishly to revise the script, and in New Haven the notices were better. By the time the company reached New York, the engine had been fine-tuned, and Broadway critics gave *The Solid Gold Cadillac* the green light for a run of a year and a half.

Columbia released the film version in 1956 with certain adjustments to the script by Abe Burrows. Instead of having an adorably naive elderly woman in the lead, the movie starred Judy Holliday, playing an adorably naive young woman.

The Solid Gold Cadillac was Kaufman's last hit as a writer. He collaborated with Teichmann on two more plays, which were never produced. The final produced work to bear his name was the book of the musical *Silk Stockings* (1955), which he wrote with his wife Leueen MacGrath. Kaufman's last directing credit was Peter Ustinov's *Romanoff and Juliet* (1957), but Ustinov himself did most of the directing as Kaufman's age and illness advanced. Kaufman died in 1961.

KISMET

Book by Charles Lederer and Luther Davis, based on the play by Edward Knoblock.

Music by Alexander Borodin

Musical adaptation and lyrics by Robert Wright and George Forrest

Opened December 3, 1953

583 Performances

Ziegfeld Theatre

Directed by Albert Marre

Choreographed by Jack Cole

Produced by Charles Lederer

Cast: Alfred Drake (Hajj); Doretta Morrow (Marsinah); Joan Diener (Lalume); Henry Calvin (Wazir); Richard Kiley (Caliph); Philip Coolidge (Omar); Truman Gaige (Jawan); Jack Dodds (Akbar); Marc Wilder (Assiz); Florence Lessing (Street Dancer/Princess Zubbediya); Beatrice Kraft (Princess Sumaris); Lucy Andonian (Ayah to Zubbediya); Thelma Dare (Ayah to Sumaris); Patricia Dunn, Bonnie Evans, Reiko Sato (Princesses of Ababu); Tom Charlesworth (Chief Policeman); Hal Hackett (Hassan-Ben/2nd Policeman); Earle MacVeigh (Prosecutor/Peddler/1st Beggar); Richard Oneto (Imam/Bangle Man); Jack Mei Ling (Doorman); Robert Lamont (2nd Beggar); Rodolfo Silva (3rd Beggar); Kirby Smith (Merchant); Richard Vine (Servant); Barbara Slate (The Widow Yussef); Steve Reeves, Stephen Ferry (Wazir's Guards).

When reviewing *Kismet*, *New York Times* critic Brooks Atkinson stated: "it has not been written. It has been assembled from a storehouse of spare parts." The "parts" were a somewhat creaky drama and the lush themes of a 19th-century Russian composer. Despite the unoriginality of *Kismet*, the musical proved popular with audiences and remains a favorite in the Broadway canon to this day.

The idea for the show began with Edwin Lester, director of the Los Angeles and San Francisco Civic Light Operas, who had a hit in 1944 by adapting Edvard Grieg's music for *Song of Norway*. Now Lester decided to popularize another classical composer, Alexander Borodin.

The story was taken from a 1911 play by Edward Knoblock that had provided a personal triumph for matinee idol Otis Skinner. An adventure tale, it followed the exploits of Hajj, a street beggar, over the course of twenty-four eventful hours in legendary Baghdad. Hajj's daughter falls in love with a mighty Caliph, and the beggar foils a dastardly Wizar and makes off with his attractive wife.

Alfred Drake finds himself a stranger in paradise in *Kismet*.

The story was filmed on three separate occasions, in 1920, 1933, and 1944. The last film starred Ronald Coleman and Marlene Dietrich as the Wizar's wife.

In the musical version, Hajj was transformed into a poet, which facilitated his bursting into song. As with *Norway*, the score was adapted and the lyrics written by Robert Wright and George Forrest. *Kismet* played at both the Los Angeles and San Francisco Civic Light Operas just as their earlier collaboration had. Before the show reached New York, Lester bowed out as producer and co-author Charles Lederer took his place.

Alfred Drake, a star from *Oklahoma!* and *Kiss Me, Kate*, Doretta Morrow, of *The King and I*, and newcomers Joan Diener and Richard Kiley starred. Albert Marre, artistic director of the New York City Drama Company, staged the show. Choreographer Jack Cole gave the dances his trademark Oriental flavor. Future film muscleman Steve Reeves appeared as a beefy palace guard. (Kiley and Diener would later appear together in *Man of La Mancha* (1965).)

The show had the misfortune to open in New York during a newspaper strike. When the reviews did come out, they ran the gamut from damning to ecstatic. The acerbic George Jean Nathan of the *Journal-American* stated "*Kismet* has most of the attributes of the old-fashioned musical comedy save only the latter's occasional novelty." *Cue*'s Emory Lewis called it "a gala Christmas present, an opulent, melody-drenched Arabian nights musical."

Good word of mouth about Lemuel Ayers's lavish sets and costumes and the gorgeous melodies kept audiences coming during the strike and before the mixed notices were printed. Another factor contributing to the show's box office was the Hit Parade status of several of the tunes from the score, including "Stranger in Paradise," "And This Is My Beloved," and "Baubles, Bangles, and Beads."

Coincidentally, the London production with Broadway stars Drake, Morrow, and Diener, opened in the midst of another newspaper strike. The English edition went on to a successful run in spite of, or perhaps because of, this setback. As in New York, the British *Kismet* built up a following before the press could express its views.

Metro-Goldwyn-Mayer owned the film rights to the original story, and since the Borodin music was in the public domain, the studio could have filmed their own story of *Kismet* without paying a penny to the authors of the stage show (as long as they did not use the arrangements or lyrics by Wright and Forrest). But MGM did buy the stage version and used the Broadway score. Howard Keel played the role originated by Alfred Drake. Ann Blyth, Dolores Gray, Monty Woolley, Sebastian Cabot, and Vic Damone were also in the 1955 release.

Drake returned to the role of Hajj in the 1965 Lincoln Center revival. New York City Opera presented a produc-

tion in 1985. In 1978, *Timbuktu*, a revised version featuring an all-black cast, ran 221 performances. Eartha Kitt and Gilbert Price were nominated for Tonys, as was Geoffrey Holder for his costumes.

ANNIVERSARY WALTZ

by Jerome Chodorov and Joseph Fields
Opened April 7, 1954
615 Performances
Broadhurst Theatre
Directed by Moss Hart
Produced by Joseph M. Hyman and Bernard Hart

Cast: Kitty Carlisle (Alice Walters); Macdonald Carey (Bud Walters); Phyllis Povah (Mrs. Gans); Howard Smith (Mr. Gans); Warren Berlinger (Okkie Walters); Mary Lee Dearring (Debbie Walters); Pauline Myers (Millie); Andrew Duggan (Chris Steelman); Jean Carson (Janice Revere); Don Grusso (Harry); Donald Hylan (Sam); Kermit Kegley (Handyman).

Broadway hit back at its chief rival, television, in the marital comedy *Anniversary Waltz*. Bud and Alice Walters, a middle-class family with two kids, comic maid, and East Side Manhattan apartment, are celebrating their fifteenth wedding anniversary. Alice's parents have bought them a television set. The only problem is that Bud hates the box and, after numerous arguments, smashes the picture tube in—not once but twice. The only thing that stops him a third time is the news that Alice is pregnant.

The other plot point which kept the couple's conflicts going for three acts was the revelation that they had enjoyed premarital sex—not big news to today's audiences, but scandalous enough in 1954 to prevent Ed Sullivan from inviting the cast onto his TV variety show.

Authors Joseph Fields and Jerome Chodorov were responsible for many previous long-running comedies. The writing team had three shows running simultaneously on Broadway. In addition to *Anniversary Waltz*, *Wonderful Town* and *The Girl in Pink Tights*, two musicals for which they had written the librettos, were playing. At this point, Fields was the only playwright to have this triple play on Broadway twice. During the 1942–43 season his *The Doughgirls* was running alongside *My Sister Eileen* and *Junior Miss*, the latter two being collaborations with Chodorov.

Fields got his good friend Moss Hart to direct *Anniversary Waltz*. Hart's wife, Kitty Carlisle, a musical star, made her straight-play debut as Alice. Macdonald Carey, who was last seen on stage in Hart's musical *Lady in the Dark*, played Bud.

The reviews were mixed. Brooks Atkinson of the *New York Times* declared the plot was so hackneyed, "the playwrights had become mechanics." John McClain of the *Journal-American* said the television should have been given a bow at the curtain calls, since it played such an important part. But positive word of mouth kept the show running through almost two full seasons.

Kitty Carlisle was replaced by Marjorie Lord, later prominent on television's *Make Room for Daddy*. In fact, most of the stars of this TV-hating play went on to become household names by appearing on the small screen: Carlisle as a panelist on the popular game show *To Tell the Truth*, and Carey on the soap opera *Days of Our Lives*.

David Niven, Mitzi Gaynor, and Patty Duke appeared in the 1959 movie adaptation, which was titled *Happy Anniversary*.

THE PAJAMA GAME

Book by George Abbott and Richard Bissell, based on Bissell's novel *7½ Cents*.

Music and lyrics by Richard Adler and Jerry Ross

Opened May 13, 1954

1,063 Performances

St. James Theatre

Directed by George Abbott and Jerome Robbins

Choreographed by Bob Fosse

Produced by Frederick Brisson, Robert Griffith, and Harold Prince

Cast: John Raitt (Sid Sorokin); Janis Paige (Babe Williams); Eddie Foy, Jr. (Hines); Carol Haney (Gladys); Reta Shaw (Mabel); Ralph Dunn (Hasler); Stanley Prager (Pres); Ralph Farnworth (Joe); Ralph Chambers (Charlie); Thelma Pelish (Mae); Marion Colby (Brenda); Rae Allen (Poopsie); Jim Hutchinson (Eddie); William David (Pop); Jack Drummond (1st Helper); Buzz Miller (2nd Helper); Jack Waldron (Salesman); Peter Gennaro (Worker). Shirley MacLaine and Peter Gennaro were also in the chorus.

The Pajama Game, the musical love story of a pajama-factory union organizer and her supervisor, is set during a strike. When the neophyte producers, Harold Prince and Robert Griffith, went searching for backers for the show, its labor-versus-management theme was considered risky and the usual investors were scared off.

In later backers' auditions, held in Edie Adams's living room, the strike angle was downplayed in favor of the romance, and capital was raised—but not quite enough to get things rolling. George Abbott, the director, advanced the remaining funds to Prince and Griffith, who had worked for him on *Wonderful Town* as stage managers. The show's third producer, Frederick Brisson, raised the money to pay back Abbott. The budget was so tight that Prince and Griffith served as their own stage managers.

Pajama Game was to be a first for many others involved. In addition to the producers, the book writer, songwriters, and the choreographer were all making their Broadway debuts in their respective capacities. The show was based on Richard Bissell's novel "7½ Cents" about his family's pajama factory in Dubuque, Iowa. According to Prince, it took Bissell only four days to pack his family and belongings and move to Connecticut to work on the show.

Carol Haney models some sleepwear for Eddie Foy, Jr., in *The Pajama Game.*

Frank Loesser was approached to do the score. He wasn't interested, but recommended Richard Adler and Jerry Ross, whose previous credits included only a few published songs (one of which was the Tony Bennett hit "Rags to Riches"). Jerome Robbins had racked up quite a few Broadway hits as a choreographer, but *Pajama Game* marked his first billing as a director, a credit he shared with Abbott. Robbins had been brought in to back up Bob Fosse, who was making his choreographic debut on Broadway. One of Fosse's dancers was a very young Shirley MacLaine. During the run MacLaine went on for star Carol Haney, got spotted by Hollywood producer Hal Wallis, and was signed for a lead role in Alfred Hitchcock's *The Trouble with Harry*.

The show's two big showstoppers were the ballad "Hey There" and Fosse's inventive dance number "Steam Heat." Abbott wanted to cut both because they slowed the progress of the story. "Steam Heat" featured Carol Haney, who had danced with Fosse in the film version of *Kiss Me, Kate.* Haney, Buzz Miller, and Peter Gennaro, dressed in derbies, white gloves, and black suits, popped through the steam-whistle-punctuated number. Haney (and later MacLaine) stole the show, and Fosse established his sexy, hip-thrusting style.

Although the musical opened in May of 1954, at the end of the season, it managed to survive the doldrums of summer and pick up three Tony Awards at the conclusion of the following season.

The film version came out in 1957, co-directed by Abbott and Stanley Donen, with Raitt, Haney, and Foy re-creating their roles. Doris Day had the female lead. A 1973 Broadway revival had Hal Linden, Barbara McNair, and Cab Calloway heading a racially mixed cast.

Richard Bissell subsequently wrote *Say, Darling,* a novel based on his experiences with *The Pajama Game.* This book about the making of a musical was made into a musical in 1958, with Robert Morse playing a character supposedly based on producer Prince.

FANNY

Book by S.N. Behrman and Joshua Logan, based on Marcel Pagnol's trilogy *Marius, Fanny,* and *Cesar.*

Music and lyrics by Harold Rome

Opened November 4, 1954

888 Performances

Majestic Theatre

Directed by Joshua Logan

Choreographed by Helen Tamiris

Produced by Joshua Logan and David Merrick

Cast: Walter Slezak (Panisse); Ezio Pinza (Cesar); Florence Henderson (Fanny); William Tabbert (Marius); Gerald Price (The Admiral); Alan Carney (Escartifique); Nejla Ates (Arab Dancing Girl); Edna Preston (Honorine); Don McHenry (M. Brun); Lloyd Reese (Cesario); Wally Strauss (Charles); Tani Seitz (Claudine); Dran Seitz (Claudette); Norma Doggett (Nanette); Carolyn Maye (Mimi); Ellen Matthews (Marie); Jane House (Michellette); Mohammed el Bakkar (Arab Rug Seller); Katherine Grave (Maori Vendor); Betty Carr (Lace Vendor); Herb Banke (Sailor); Charles Blackwell (Moroccan Drummer); Henry Michel (Second Mate); Steve Wiland (Fisherman); Jack Washburn (Sailmaker); Florence Dunlap (Fish-stall Woman); Michael Scrittorale (Arab); Ruth Schumacher (Nun); Mike Mason (Butler); Pat Finch (Maid); Tom Gleason (Garage Owner); Ray Dorian (Priest).

Fanny was the first of over ninety Broadway shows produced by a former St. Louis lawyer named David Merrick, whose later work would include such hits as *Oliver!, Hello, Dolly!, Promises, Promises,* and *42nd Street.* Merrick had acquired the rights to Marcel Pagnol's trilogy of plays about life on the Marseilles waterfront, *Marius, Fanny,* and *Cesar.* He took many trips to France to persuade Pagnol to allow him to make a musical of the plays, which also inspired a series of popular films.

Merrick hired Joshua Logan to write the book, direct, and to interest Rodgers and Hammerstein in doing the songs. That famous team, however, demanded sole producing credit. Merrick was willing to have the programs and posters read "Rodgers and Hammerstein, in association with David Merrick, present *Fanny*". But Rodgers and Hammerstein balked at this and withdrew altogether. Merrick wanted Alan Jay Lerner and Burton Lane to replace them, but they were unavailable. Logan suggested Harold Rome, who wrote the songs for *Wish You Were Here,* Logan's last hit.

For the book, Logan found the job of translating from the French all three plays and then condensing them into one show, while leaving room for the musical numbers, too enormous a task for a solo effort. For a partner, he chose S.N. Behrman, the distinguished playwright whose output included such light comedies as *The Second Man* (1927), *Biography* (1934), and *No Time for Comedy* (1939). *Fanny* was to be Behrman's only musical.

As *Fanny* was being written, Logan was simultaneously directing the pre-Broadway tryout of Norman Krasna's *Kind Sir,* with Mary Martin and Charles Boyer, as well as negotiating for the rights to make a musical of James Michener's new novel, *Sayonara.* (Logan was later to direct the film version, but the stage musical never got beyond the planning stages.) The pressures of three different projects, plus a tendency toward manic depression, combined to send Logan to a mental hospital.

Once he had recovered, the director was sure *Fanny* was kaput. But Merrick insisted that the work continue and, in true Broadway fashion, the show went on.

The story followed the complicated lives of Panisse, Cesare, Fanny, and Marius. Panisse and Cesare are two old waterfront cronies. Cesare's son Marius is in love with Fanny, but the call of the sea takes him away from Marseilles and the pregnant Fanny. In order to save her honor, Panisse weds the girl and acts as father to her son. When Marius returns, the sailor gives up his claim on the child. A few years later, Panisse dictates a letter on his deathbed, asking Marius to marry Fanny.

Ezio Pinza (*South Pacific*) and Walter Slezak played the old friends, while Florence Henderson (from the chorus of *Wish You Were Here*) and William Tabbert (Lt. Cable in *South Pacific*) were the young lovers.

The 1961 Warner Brothers film version was shot on location in Marseilles, with Logan directing and Leslie Caron, Maurice Chevalier, Charles Boyer, and Horst Buchholz in the leads. There were no songs in the movie, for studio head Jack Warner had decided to make fewer film musicals; they were losing money. This was a portent of the decline of Hollywood musicals in the decades ahead.

WITNESS FOR THE PROSECUTION

by Agatha Christie

Opened December 16, 1954

645 Performances

Henry Miller's Theatre

Directed by Robert Lewis

Produced by Gilbert Miller and Peter Saunders

Cast: Francis L. Sullivan (Sir Wilfrid Robarts, Q.C.); Patricia Jessel (Romaine); Gene Lyons (Leonard Vole); Ernest Clark (Mr. Myers, Q.C.); Horace Braham (Mr. Justice Wainwright); Una O'Connor (Janet MacKenzie); Gordon Nelson (Carter); Mary Barclay (Greta); Robin Craven (Mr. Mayhew); Claude Horton (Inspector Hearne); Guy Spaull (Dr. Wyatt); Michael McAloney (Mr. Clegg); Dawn Steinkamp (The Other Woman).

Agatha Christie wrote the world's longest running play, *The Mousetrap*, which opened in 1952 in London's West End and is still racking up performances. Although its record is not as impressive, *Witness for the Prosecution*, her second most popular play, was a resounding hit on both sides of the Atlantic.

Based on her short story of the same name, *Witness* is a spine-tingling courtroom drama in which handsome Leonard Vole is on trial for the murder of an elderly spinster. Despite the best efforts of wily barrister Sir Wilfrid Robarts, Leonard appears fit to be hanged. His wife, an enigmatic German emigrant named Romaine, testifies against him as a witness for the prosecution. Two surprise twists at the final curtain dash the audience's expectations and take its collective breath away.

When the New York production opened, the London company was in its second year. The Broadway edition was delayed until a suitable actress could be found to play the demanding role of Romaine Vole. No American actress was found to have the special quality necessary for the part. (To reveal any more about the demands of the role would spoil the surprise ending for those who have not yet read or seen the play.) Thus the original British actress, Patricia Jessel, recreated the role. For her nemesis, Sir Wilfrid, the

One of the dramatic courtroom scenes from *Witness for the Prosecution*.

heavy-set British film character actor Francis L. Sullivan was brought in. His association with Christie went back to 1928 when he played her immortal detective Hercule Poirot in *Alibi*, a stage adaptation of Christie's novel *The Murder of Roger Ackroyd*. Both Sullivan and Jessel won Tonys for their performances in the featured categories, for their names were billed below the show's title. Also, *Witness* copped the New York Drama Critics Circle Award for Best Foreign Play (the only mystery to be so honored), and the Edgar Allan Poe Award from the Mystery Writers of America, a distinction usually bestowed upon novels.

It was the director Robert Lewis's first experience in the mystery genre. "I told the cast," Lewis recalled, "that I was so poor at solving mysteries that I didn't know who did it until the third week of rehearsal."

In a case of life imitating art, several members of the company mysteriously died. Beginning with the suicide of one of the actors and the death of the wardrobe mistress, over half a dozen people connected with the production met their end during or soon after the show's run.

Witness was filmed twice. In its first celluloid incarnation, Billy Wilder wrote and directed a screenplay which emphasized humor. Charles Laughton, Marlene Dietrich,

and Tyrone Power starred in the 1957 release. Laughton's wife, Elsa Lanchester, played a new character, an officious nurse attending to Laughton's Sir Wilfrid. The mystery was remade in 1982 as a TV movie with Ralph Richardson, Diana Rigg, Beau Bridges, and Deborah Kerr.

CAT ON A HOT TIN ROOF

by Tennessee Williams

Opened March 24, 1955

694 Performances

Morosco Theatre

Directed by Elia Kazan

Produced by The Playwrights' Company

Cast: Barbara Bel Geddes (Margaret); Ben Gazzara (Brick) Burl Ives (Big Daddy); Mildred Dunnock (Big Mama); Madeleine Sherwood (Mae); Pat Hingle (Gooper); Fred Stewart (Rev. Tooker); R. G. Armstrong (Dr. Baugh); Maxwell Glanville (Lacey); Musa Williams (Sookey); Darryl Richards (Buster); Pauline Hahn (Dixie); Seth Edwards (Sonny); Janice Dunn (Trixie); Eva Vaughn Smith (Daisy); Brownie McGhee (Brightie); Sonny Terry (Small).

A shapely young woman enters a bedroom, screaming at a bunch of offstage children, calling them "no-neck monsters." She proceeds to take off her soiled dress and, attired only in her slip, begins to deliver a monologue to her sex-

Burl Ives as Big Daddy declares that Maggie the Cat (Barbara Bel Geddes) "has life in her" in *Cat on a Hot Tin Roof*. Ben Gazzara as Brick looks on.

ually uninterested husband. Nowadays this opening of Tennessee Williams' *Cat on a Hot Tin Roof* is not especially risqué, but at its 1955 opening, it was theatrical dynamite. So was what followed: a brutally frank drama of a rich Southern family dealing with greed, repressed heterosexuality, latent homosexuality, and rampant lying, or as the colorful patriarch Big Daddy calls it, "mendacity."

Critics and audiences responded to Williams' adult treatment of these hard subjects. Like his previous *Streetcar Named Desire, Cat* won both the Pulitzer Prize and the New York Drama Critics Circle Award for best play. It opened too late in the season to be considered for the Tony Awards, because of their earlier deadline, and lost in 1956 to *The Diary of Anne Frank*.

Cat on a Hot Tin Roof refers to the sexually frustrated and determined Margaret, wife of a former athlete, the currently alcoholic Brick. The play is loosely based on a Williams short story "Players of a Summer Game." The playwright developed the piece into a full-length play in Rome, New Orleans, and Key West. The finished manuscript was delivered to *Streetcar* director, Elia Kazan, who liked it, but suggested revising the third act. Kazan believed that Big Daddy, Brick's father, was too important a character to not reappear in the third act. He also thought that Brick should go through a character change as a result of his confrontation with his father and that Maggie should be made more sympathetic. Williams acquiesced and made the revisions. When the play was published, the printed version contained both the original and the performed third acts.

Williams had some reservations about Kazan's interesting choices for the casting of cool, blonde, non-Southern Barbara Bel Geddes as Maggie, and folk-singer Burl Ives as Big Daddy. But both were lauded for their performances, along with Ben Gazzara as Brick and Mildred Dunnock (Linda Loman from *Death of a Salesman*) as Big Mama.

Kim Stanley played Maggie in the London *Cat*, which received a tepid reception. Stanley later played Big Mama in a telecast of the play and won an Emmy for best supporting actress.

The film rights for *Cat* were purchased for $750,000 by MGM (the same studio that had fired Williams and rejected his early screenplay—which eventually became *The Glass Menagerie*). The principal roles were played by Elizabeth Taylor, Paul Newman, Burl Ives, and Judith Anderson. As with *Streetcar*, the screen adaptation was watered down to appeal to broader tastes and conform to the Production Code standards, but it retained the play's basic strengths.

Maggie the Cat has since proved an irresistible lure to top actresses to test their mettle. Among those who have bared their claws in this role are Elizabeth Ashley and Kathleen

Turner, on Broadway, and Natalie Wood (opposite Laurence Olivier's Big Daddy), and Jessica Lange, on television.

After *Cat*, none of Tennessee Williams' plays achieved a Broadway run of over 500 performances. Some, like *Sweet Bird of Youth* (1959) and *Night of the Iguana* (1961), were met with critical praise and became well-regarded films, but none matched the commercial and popular success of his earlier work.

INHERIT THE WIND

by Jerome Lawrence and Robert E. Lee

Opened April 21, 1955

806 Performances

The National Theatre

Produced and directed by Herman Shumlin

Cast: Paul Muni (Henry Drummond); Ed Begley (Matthew Harrison Brady); Tony Randall (E.K. Hornbeck); Karl Light (Bertram Cates); Bethel Leslie (Rachel Brown); Muriel Kirkland (Mrs. Brady); Staats Cotsworth (Rev. Jeremiah Brown); Louis Hector (Judge); James Maloney (Mayor); Willaim Darrid (Tom Davenport); Robert P. Lieb (Meeker); Salem Ludwig (Mr. Goodfellow); Sara Floyd (Mrs. Krebs); Fred Herrick (Corkin/Sillers); Donald Elson (Bollinger); Fred Miller (Platt); Charles Thompson (Mr. Bannister); Mary Kevin Kelly (Melinda); Eric Berne (Howard); Rita Newton (Mrs. Loomis); Howard Caine (Hot Dog Man); Margherita Sargent (Mrs. McClain); Ruth Newton (Mrs. Blair); Charles Brin (Elijah); Harry Shaw (Hurdy Gurdy Man); Jack Banning (Timmy); Fred Miller (Dunlap); Edmund Williams (Reuter's Man); Perry Fiske (Harry Y. Esterbrook).

The oppressive atmosphere of the blacklisting period of the early '50s delayed the production of *Inherit the Wind*, the searing courtroom drama by Jerome Lawrence and Robert E. Lee, based on the 1925 Scopes "monkey" trial. In that infamous case, Paul Scopes was tried for teaching Darwin's theory of evolution in Dayton, Tennessee, where such lessons were illegal. The subsequent trial received unprecedented press coverage as former presidential candidate William Jennings Bryant argued for the prosecution and celebrated criminal lawyer Clarence Darrow stood for the defense.

Wind intended to show that the threats to academic freedom in 1925 were pertinent to the McCarthyite 1950s, but both playwrights felt the restrictive atmosphere in the arts frightened many producers away from their play.

Lawrence and Lee, whose previous credits included several radio and television scripts and the book for the musical *Look Ma, I'm Dancing* (1948), were turned down by every producer in town. One Hollywood agent even suggested they burn the script. The partners had given up hope until Margo Jones, artistic director of Theatre '55 in Dallas, Texas, expressed interest. Unafraid of potential controversy, Jones staged the play in the round and drew praise from both the local and national press.

Producer-director Herman Shumlin staged and presented the show on Broadway. This was one of the first instances of a successful mounting of a new play in a regional theatre leading to a production in New York. As the costs of traditional Boston–New Haven tryouts soared, institutional theatres such as Theatre '55 would increasingly become the source for Broadway plays. (In the '70s, New York versions of regional hits became the rule rather than the exception.)

For the Broadway production, the producer and playwrights wanted a star to play the Bryant character, Matthew Harrison Brady. They offered the role to Orson Welles and Lee J. Cobb. But both felt Drummond, the Darrow stand-in, was the juicier part and asked to play him. Lawrence and Lee judged both actors wrong for Drummond, but decided to cast a "name" actor for that role rather than for Brady. They picked Oscar-winner Paul Muni, who had publicly stated he was retired from the stage. A search of Hollywood and Europe turned up nothing until it was discovered that the actor was in New York, staying at a hotel not three blocks from Shumlin's offices.

The producer hand-delivered a copy of the script to Muni, who accepted the assignment the next morning. At first, the actor was concerned about not physically resembling Darrow. He went through several experiments with elaborate makeup, including a headpiece which gave him an all-new forehead. He finally settled on only whitening his hair and affecting Darrow's slouched posture. His resultant performance was considered the high point of a long career. Ed Begley as Brady and Tony Randall as E.K. Hornbeck (based on *Baltimore Sun* reporter H.L. Mencken) were also praised.

Muni had to leave the play in August of 1955, when he developed a cataract. His wife vowed that he would be back in the part by Christmas. Shumlin closed the play for two weeks and reopened with Melvyn Douglas playing Drummond. Refitted with a prosthetic eye, Muni returned to the stage of the National on December 1, three weeks before Christmas. Douglas went on to head the national touring company. Later in the run, Begley made the switch from enacting Brady to Drummond, earning the distinction of playing both leading roles in a long-running hit.

Stanley Kramer purchased the film rights and directed the 1960 movie version. Spencer Tracy and Frederic March starred as Drummond and Brady, with song-and-dance man Gene Kelly cast against type as the cynical Hornbeck.

Inherit the Wind has been adapted for television twice. It appeared first on the *Hallmark Hall of Fame*, during the 1965–66 season, with Melvyn Douglas and Ed Begley re-creating their stage roles. There was an NBC TV-movie remake in 1988, with Jason Robards and Kirk Douglas as the legal adversaries. The presentation won an Emmy, and Robards was named Best Actor.

DAMN YANKEES

Book by George Abbott and Douglass Wallop, based on Wallop's novel *The Year the Yankees Lost the Pennant*.

Opened May 5, 1955

1,019 Performances

The 46th Street Theatre

Music and lyrics by Richard Adler and Jerry Ross

Directed by George Abbott

Choreographed by Bob Fosse

Produced by Frederick Brisson, Robert Griffith, and Harold Prince

Cast: Gwen Verdon (Lola); Stephen Douglass (Joe Hardy); Ray Walston (Applegate); Russ Brown (Van Buren); Rae Allen (Gloria); Nathaniel Frey (Smokey); Shannon Bolin (Meg); Robert Shafer (Joe Boyd); Jean Stapleton (Sister); Elizabeth Howell (Doris); Al Lanti (Henry); Eddie Philips (Sohovik); Albert Linville (Vernon/Postmaster); Jimmie Komack (Rockie); Del Horstmann (Lynch/Commissioner); Richard Bishop (Welch); Janie Janvier (Miss Weston); George Marcy (Guard); Cherry Davis (Teenager).

Only a few weeks after *The Pajama Game* began its long run, the same creative team began work on a second project which was just as popular and profitable. *Damn Yankees* had the same director (George Abbott), songwriters (Richard Adler and Jerry Ross), producers (Frederick Brisson, Robert Griffith, and Harold Prince), choreographer (Bob Fosse), music director (Hal Hastings), and orchestrator (Don Walker) as *Pajama Game*. It opened almost exactly one year later and ran approximately as many performances—*Pajama* played 1,063, while the final score for *Yankees* was 1,019.

Like *Pajama Game*, *Yankees* was derived from a popular comic novel. *The Year the Yankees Lost the Pennant* was Douglass Wallop's fantastic takeoff on the Faust legend, in which a disgruntled baseball fan agrees to sell his soul to the devil in order to pitch for his beloved Washington Senators. He takes them on to the World Series, defeating the accursed New York Yankees.

Abbott co-authored the libretto with Wallop, with an uncredited assist from *Pajama Game*'s Richard Bissell. There were numerous changes in both the book and score during out-of-town tryouts. One third of the numbers were excised, including a bizarre musical-chairs dance led by a baseball player dressed as a gorilla. This was replaced with a simple mambo duet called "Who's Got the Pain?". Gwen Verdon, an audience favorite as the seductress Lola, who assists the devil in snaring the hero's soul, was given an earlier entrance and more songs.

Damn Yankees marked the ending of one theatrical relationship and the beginning of another. Soon after the show opened, songwriter Jerry Ross died of respiratory illness. His partner Richard Adler did not have another hit after that. The show was also the first joint effort of choreographer Bob Fosse and Gwen Verdon. This was the second Broadway venture for both. Fosse had won the Tony for *Pajama Game*, as did Verdon for *Can-Can*. Long-legged, sexy Verdon was the perfect instrument for Fosse's razzle-dazzle, hip-popping style. The baseball musical firmly established the two as stars in their respective positions, and five years later, they merged both personal and professional lives. Their marriage did not last as long as their collaboration as choreographer and dancer. The shows they worked together on included *New Girl in Town* (1957), *Redhead* (1959), *Sweet Charity* (1966), and *Chicago* (1975).

Although critics hailed Verdon as a new star in *Yankees*, opening-night audiences were dissatisfied with how she was treated in the story. In the original script, Lola is transformed into an old hag at the final curtain. Sensing that theatregoers were unhappy with seeing the luscious temptress suffer after they had fallen in love with her, the creative team reworked the ending and on the second night Lola remained as gorgeous as ever.

The success of *Yankees* defied the conventional wisdom that all shows with a sports theme would be failures.

The producers encountered the public's resistance to sports in theatre the first few weeks after the opening. Despite the enthusiastic notices, the box office was not raking in advance orders. The blame for the public's lack of excitement was placed on the advertising. The poster for the show displayed Gwen Verdon posing impishly in a baseball uniform, looking like a mischievous little girl. A new design was created with Verdon in the provocative tight corset that she wore while belting out "Whatever Lola Wants, Lola Gets." The color was changed from pastoral green to a sexy red. As a result of these shifts, lines began to form at the box office.

Gwen Verdon demonstrates to Stephen Douglass that "Whatever Lola Wants, Lola Gets" in *Damn Yankees*.

In the touring version, burlesque comedian Bobby Clark starred. The spotlight moved from Lola (played by Sherry O'Neill) to Clark's role, the Devil. The London edition was also a hit despite the British ignorance of baseball and an inept performance by a former ice-skater, known only as Belita, in the Verdon role. Belita was soon replaced by Elizabeth Seal, who drew more favorable reviews.

Following *The Pajama Game* pattern, the 1958 film of *Yankees* was co-directed by Abbott and Stanley Donner and featured most of the original Broadway cast, including Verdon, Ray Walston, Russ Brown, and Jean Stapleton. Then-heartthrob Tab Hunter replaced Stephen Douglass as the athletic hero. A 1994 Broadway revival starred Victor Garber and Bebe Neuwirth.

No other baseball musical or straight play has been a hit on or off Broadway. In 1984, Prince directed *Diamonds*, an off-Broadway revue about the "national pastime" which ran only a few months. *The First*, a musical treatment of the life of Jackie Robinson, the first black baseball player in the major leagues, was a failure in 1982.

THE DIARY OF ANNE FRANK

by Frances Goodrich and Albert Hackett, based on the book *Anne Frank: The Diary of a Young Girl*.

Opened October 5, 1955

717 Performances

The Cort Theatre

Directed by Garson Kanin

Produced by Kermit Bloomgarden

Cast: Susan Strasberg (Anne Frank); Joseph Schildkraut (Mr. Frank); Gusti Huber (Mrs. Frank); Jack Gilford (Mr. Dussel); Dennie Moore (Mrs. Van Daan); Lou Jacobi (Mr. Van Daan); David Levin (Peter Van Daan); Eva Rubinstein (Margot Frank); Gloria Jones (Miep); Clinton Sunberg (Mr. Kraaler).

On July 6, 1942, a thirteen-year-old Dutch Jewish girl named Anne Frank went into hiding from the occupying Nazi forces. For two years, Anne, her family, and some friends remained in the attic annex of her father's Amsterdam spice company. They attempted to live as normal a life as possible, as a few cohorts smuggled in food and supplies. On August 4, 1944, the inhabitants of the attic were discovered by German police and transported to the concentration camp, Auschwitz, in Poland. All of the hideaways except for Anne's father Otto, perished.

The difference between Anne and millions of other victims of the Holocaust was that she kept of a diary of her experiences. It was found after World War II ended and subsequently published under the title *Anne Frank: The Diary of a Young Girl*. This record of an adolescent girl's impressions of a world gone mad was translated into more than fifty languages. The total number of copies sold is now estimated at over thirteen million.

The diary was a natural for the stage. It had one set (the attic), a small cast, and a pre-sold audience based on the popularity of the book. But some theatrical insiders were skeptical about the potential of a play dealing with such a painful subject. Despite this, several producers bid to acquire the rights, and Cheryl Crawford gained the first option. Meyer Levin, who had extensively covered the Holocaust as a reporter, wrote the first stage version. Crawford was not satisfied with it and asked Carson McCullers (*Member of the Wedding*) to do a new adaptation. McCullers was not interested, and Crawford eventually dropped the project.

Kermit Bloomgarden then picked up the rights. He hired the screenwriting husband-and-wife team of Albert Hackett and Frances Goodrich, whose credits included several of *The Thin Man* films. The Hacketts spent two years writing their version. The playwrights and director Garson Kanin also visited Anne's father in Switzerland to research the story.

The role of Otto Frank was to be played by Joseph Schildkraut, a handsome leading man of the '20s and '30s. The plum role of Anne went to sixteen-year-old Susan Strasberg, daughter of Lee Strasberg, the legendary acting teacher at the Actors Studio. During the run of the play, Strasberg was elevated to star status, making her the youngest actor in Broadway history to be so billed. (Twelve-year-old Patty Duke of *The Miracle Worker* would later break Strasberg's record).

Most of the rest of the cast were unknowns, including night-club comedian Jack Gilford; David Levin, just out of London's Royal Academy of Dramatic Arts; and Eva Rubinstein, daughter of pianist Arthur Rubinstein.

The Diary of Anne Frank received an overwhelming response not only on Broadway, where it won every award possible, but in twenty-two other countries as well. In Germany and Holland, where the events depicted on stage hit closest to home, audiences did not even applaud after the final curtain, but sat in stunned silence.

One who was not so enthusiastic over the play was Meyer Levin. The author of the abandoned first adaptation sued Kermit Bloomgarden, Cheryl Crawford, and Otto Frank, who owned the rights to the original diary. Levin claimed Crawford was guilty of breach of contract. He further charged that the Goodrich–Hackett version used characters, plots, and situations from his play that were not in the diary. The case against Crawford was dismissed, but the jury did award Levin $50,000 in damages on the other claim. However, the Supreme Court later set aside the award.

Millie Perkins played Anne in the 1959 20th-Century Fox film version. Schildkraut and Lou Jacobi repeated their Broadway roles. Shelley Winters won an Oscar as Best Supporting Actress and later donated the statuette to the Anne Frank Museum in Amsterdam.

Melissa Gilbert headlined in a 1980 television movie in which Maximilian Schell, Joan Plowright, and James Coco were also featured.

Husband-and-wife team Eli Wallach and Anne Jackson co-starred with their daughters Roberta and Katherine Wallach as the Frank family in a 1979 off-Broadway revival. There was also a musical version of the diary, entitled *Yours, Anne* with libretto by Enid Futterman and music by Michael Cohen, which briefly played off-Broadway in 1985.

NO TIME FOR SERGEANTS

by Ira Levin, based on the novel by Mac Hyman.

Opened October 20, 1955

796 Performances

The Alvin Theatre

Directed by Morton Da Costa

Produced by Maurice Evans

Cast: Andy Griffith (Will Stockdale); Myron McCormick (Sgt. King); Roddy McDowall (Ben Whitledge); Robert Webber (Irvin Blanchard); Don Knotts (Preacher/2nd Classification Corp.); Floyd Buckley (Pa Stockdale); O. Tolbert-Hewitt (Draft Man/Senator); Michael Thoma (Bus Driver); Maree Dow (Rosabelle/Nurse/Cigarette Girl); Ed Peck (Captain); Ray Johnson (1st Classification Corp.); Earle Hyman (Lieutenant); James Millhollin (Psychiatrist); Arthur P. Keegan (Infantryman); Jules Racine (Air Force Policeman); Rex Everhart (Colonel/Lt. Abel); Hazen Gifford (Lt. Bridges); Carl Albertson (Lt. Gardella); Cecil Rutherford (Lt. Kendall); Bill Hinant (Lt. Cover); Howard Freeman (Gen. Bush); Royal Beal (Gen. Pollard); Edmund Johnson (Lt. Baker); Wynn Pearce (Capt. Charles)

No Time for Sargeants, the third long-running hit to feature the services of Maurice Evans either as actor (*Dial M for Murder*) or producer (*The Teahouse of the August Moon*), had much in common with the previous two projects. Both *Teahouse* and *Sergeants* were based on novels and dealt with nonconformity in the peacetime military. Like *Murder*, *Sergeants* was broadcast as a television special before reaching the stage. The service comedy, based on Mac Hyman's novel, first appeared in a one-hour version on ABC's *U.S. Steel Hour*, on March 15, 1955.

Hyman's novel was a satirical look at the Armed Forces through the eyes of a country boy who is drafted and drives his superiors crazy with his naiveté and overeagerness to please. The TV version starred a young unknown named Andy Griffith. It was written by another unknown, Ira Levin. Aside from TV work, Levin's major credit was a mystery novel called *A Kiss Before Dying*, which had won the Edgar Allan Poe Award. He was later to write the hit play *Deathtrap* and several bestselling suspense novels.

Evans had previously announced he would employ the services of Edmund Trzcinski and Donald Bevan, authors of the dramatization of *Stalag 17*. But he decided to hire Levin to do the adaptation for his stage edition after seeing the author's *U.S. Steel Hour*. The telecast which also convinced Evans to hire Griffith to repeat his performance as Will Stockdale, the endearingly ingenuous rural recruit.

Levin's script was loose and episodic. Stockdale narrated the many scenes, much as David Wayne, as Sakini, had done in *Teahouse of the August Moon*. Jack Gaver, a reviewer for United Press International, summed up the critical reaction by stating, "A strong case could be made that *Sergeants* isn't a very good play by the usual standards—or that it isn't a play at all. But it certainly is a funny, funny show."

Barry Nelson headed the 1956 London company, while James Holden played the lead in the road version.

Mervyn LeRoy directed the 1958 film, with Griffith and McCormick repeating their roles. Nick Adams appeared as Griffith's sidekick and Don Knotts, who had been in the Broadway cast, also had a small part. (Griffith and Knotts were famously reunited, of course, on the CBS-TV series *The Andy Griffith Show*.)

A television series was based on *Sergeants*, with Sammy Jackson as Will and Harry Hickox as Sgt. King; it ran only one season (1964–65).

Andy Griffith shares a joke with cigarette girl Maree Dow in *No Time for Sargeants*.

Rex Harrison makes note of Julie Andrews' speech patterns in *My Fair Lady*.

MY FAIR LADY

Book and lyrics by Alan Jay Lerner, based on the play *Pygmalion*, by Bernard Shaw.

Music by Frederick Loewe

Opened March 15, 1956

2,717 Performances

Mark Hellinger Theatre

Directed by Moss Hart

Choreographed by Hanya Holm

Produced by Herman Levin

Cast. Rex Harrison (Prof. Henry Higgins); Julie Andrews (Eliza Doolittle); Stanley Holloway (Alfred P. Doolittle); Robert Coote (Col. Pickering); Cathleen Nesbitt (Mrs. Higgins); John Michael King (Freddy Eynsford-Hill); Philippa Bevans (Mrs. Pearce); Viola Roache (Mrs. Eynsford-Hill); Gordon Dilworth (Harry/Lord Boxington); Ron McLennon (Jamie/Ambassador); Olive Reeves-Smith (Mrs. Hopkins/Lady Boxington); Christopher Hewett (Bystander/Zoltan Karpathy); David Thomas (Bartender); Reid Shelton (1st Cockney/Butler); Glenn Kezer (2nd Cockney); James Morris (3rd Cockney); Herb Surface (4th Cockney); Barton Mumaw (Chauffeur/Constable); Cathy Conklin (Flower Girl); Paul Brown (Flunkey); Maribel Hammer (Queen of Transylvania); Judith Williams (Mrs. Higgins' Maid).

Like so many other smash hits, *My Fair Lady* was not given a ghost of a chance by most Broadway professionals when it was first conceived. Many talents, such as Rodgers and Hammerstein and Noël Coward, had essayed musicalizing Bernard Shaw's *Pygmalion*. But it was Alan Jay Lerner and Frederick Loewe who, with a little bit of luck and lots of hard work, finally made Professor Henry Higgins and Eliza Doolittle dance all night—and for six and a half years on Broadway and for almost forty around the world.

Film producer Gabriel Pascal owned the rights to Shaw's plays and had made successful movies of many of them. He felt a musical version of *Pygmalion*—Shaw's story of an arrogant phonetics expert transforming a Cockney flower-seller into a lady by changing her speech—would be a natural. The producer encountered Lerner while the lyricist was in Hollywood and hired him and Loewe to do the transformation. The team were later to find out why Rodgers and Hammerstein and Coward had given up on the project. The play is a non-love story.

Eliza leaves Higgins at the final curtain, and in an epilogue, Shaw made it clear that the former flower girl marries the foppish Freddy Eynsford-Hill. They also found it difficult to cut any of Shaw's brilliant dialogue and to move the action out of Higgins' study.

Lerner and Loewe dropped the project in 1952, and their partnership was temporarily severed. The death of Pascal brought the two together again. As a result of the producer's passing, the rights to *Pygmalion* were in question, and the pair were eventually able to acquire them. They met to recommence work on the musical version, solved the problems encountered during their first attempt by following the screenplay, rather than the play, and altered the ending to have Eliza come back to Higgins.

For the role of the misogynist linguist, Lerner wanted Rex Harrison, an experienced Shavian actor. Mary Martin had initially expressed interest in playing Eliza, but when she heard what the team had written so far, she immediately concluded that they had lost their talent.

Harrison was more pleased about the production, but he still had to be persuaded. The actor had little confidence in his singing voice. After promising to tailor the material to his talent, Lerner and Loewe finally got the actor to accept the role. For Eliza, they chose a new young star, eighteen-year-old Julie Andrews, who had made a hit in *The Boy Friend*, a parody of '20s musicals, in London and New York.

Moss Hart, co-author of many hits with George S. Kaufman and director of several smashes by others, as well as his own musical *Lady in the Dark*, was hired to stage the work, which was still titleless as the company was leaving for New Haven for tryouts. After rejecting *Liza* and *The Lady Liza*, the authors settled on the title they hated least: *My Fair Lady*.

In New Haven, Harrison's fear of singing resulted in his near refusal to go on for the opening night, but the star reluctantly did. *My Fair Lady* became an immediate success and went on to break *Oklahoma*'s record as the longest-running musical on Broadway (a distinction which it held for over nine years). Like the New York edition, the touring company, originally with Brian Aherne and Anne Rogers, played for more than six years.

The reason for the show's longevity is the perfect marriage between the brilliant libretto and the sparkling score. Loewe's music was lush and romantic. Lerner's clever lyrics seemed to be an extension of Shaw's dialogue, and Harrison's caustic speak-singing of them established a new style of performing. Andrews was transformed from a dirt-smudged guttersnipe to an independent young woman—and from an unknown to a Broadway star.

For the 1964 film version, producer Jack L. Warner insisted on internationally known performers, since movie musicals were becoming harder to sell. Cary Grant was his choice for Higgins and Audrey Hepburn for Eliza. Grant refused the role, stating he could never follow Rex Harrison, who did play the role on screen. Andrews was not considered a large enough draw, so Hepburn was the movie Eliza (with vocals supplied by Marni Nixon). (As if to compensate for the loss, Andrews was immediately cast in the title role of Walt Disney's film musical *Mary Poppins*. While the Academy Awards that year graced *Lady* with eight Oscars, including Best Picture and Best Actor for Harrison, Andrews got her revenge by winning Best Actress for *Poppins*.)

In addition to thousands of productions all over the world, *My Fair Lady* has had three Broadway revivals. Ian Richardson and Christine Andreas starred in the 1976 production, for which George Rose won a Tony as Eliza's father, Alfred P. Doolittle. Harrison returned to play Henry Higgins in 1981, with Nancy Ringham as Eliza and Milo O'Shea as Doolittle. Richard Chamberlain headlined a touring version which played Broadway in 1993–94.

THE MOST HAPPY FELLA

Book, music, and lyrics by Frank Loesser, based on the play *They Knew What They Wanted*, by Sidney Howard.

Opened May 3, 1956

676 Performances

Imperial Theatre

Directed by Joseph Anthony

Choreographed by Dania Krupska

Produced by Kermit Bloomgarden and Lynn Loesser

Cast: Robert Weede (Tony); Jo Sullivan (Rosabella); Art Lund (Joe); Susan Johnson (Cleo); Shorty Long (Herman); Mona Paulee (Marie); Keith Kaldenberg (The Doctor); Lee Cass (Cashier/Postman); Arthur Rubin (Giuseppe); Rico Froehlich (Pasquale); John Henson (Ciccio); Louis Polacek (Max); Alan Gilbert (Clem); Roy Lazarus (Al); Meri Miller (Country Girl); John Sharpe (City Boy); Russell Goodwin (Priest); Zina Bethune (Tessie); Christopher Snell (Gussie); Norris Greer (Brakeman); Ralph Farnworth (Bus Driver).

When Frank Loesser was asked by the *New York Tribune* what musical category his new show *The Most Happy Fella* should be placed in, he replied, "Whatta ya mean what is it? It's a musical . . . with a lot of music." In fact, the show had a record of thirty-three numbers. Many reviewers and theatregoers didn't know what to make of so many tunes. The aim was to seamlessly blend the songs with the dialogue. In the original program, the musical numbers were not listed so that they would not seem like isolated segments but rather a natural overflowing of the spoken scenes. Some critics started to call the show a folk opera. Knowing that the words "folk" and "opera" would mean death at the box office, Loesser attempted to disparage the term: "Folk? What's folk?" he said in the same *Tribune* interview.

The story was based on Sidney Howard's 1924 Pulitzer Prize–winning play, *They Knew What They Wanted*.

Loesser began his adaptation at the suggestion of playwright Samuel Taylor (*The Happy Time*). "I thought it was crazy," said Loesser. "But when I reread the play, I knew he was right. I figured 'Take out all the political talk, the labor talk, the religious talk. Get rid of all that stuff and you got a good love story.'"

The "good love story" was between Tony, an aging Napa Valley vintner and a much younger San Francisco waitress he calls Rosabella (her real name, Amy, is not revealed until the musical's conclusion). The two have never met, but conduct a romance via the mail. When asked for his picture, Tony sends Rosabella a photograph of his handsome, young foreman, Joe.

The waitress comes to Tony's ranch intending to marry him, but when she learns the truth, she is heartbroken. She goes through with the wedding. Confused and disappointed, Rosabella spends the night with Joe while Tony recovers from an automobile accident.

The new bride gradually falls in love with her older husband, realizing she was attracted to the kind gentleman who wrote the letters more than to the young hunk in the photo. Just as the marriage appears to be working out, Rosabella learns that she is pregnant by Joe. At first, Tony is shocked and ashamed, but overcomes his pride and agrees to raise the child as his own. The curtain falls as the winegrower declares himself "the most happy fella."

Loesser wrote the book as well as the music and lyrics. The songs varied from Italian folk melodies to operatic arias to jazz to the more standard Broadway tunes, "Standing on the Corner" and "Big D." Just as the score was bigger than the usual Broadway fare, the orchestra was larger—thirty-six instruments, including twenty-four strings, a harp, and no piano.

The broad range of the score called for a variety of voices. The cast was drawn from different worlds in show business. Co-producer Lynn Loesser (the author's wife) and conductor Herbert Greene auditioned over a thousand singers. No established stars were cast. Robert Weede and Mona Paulee were drawn from the world of opera, Jo Sullivan from the off-Broadway hit *The Threepenny Opera*, and Art Lund from the big-band circuit and the recording studios.

Out-of-town changes involved cutting down the score because there was so much music. The choreographer and one of the leading actors were also changed. The pre-Broadway and New York reviews were favorable, but the operatic comparisons continued. Critics didn't know what to make of the music-heavy show, but appreciated its ambitions and touching story. Robert Coleman of the *Daily Mirror* said, "Frank Loesser has taken an aging play and turned it into a timeless musical. A masterpiece of our time." The huge score prompted the release of a three-record album set, which included both the songs and dialogue.

During the run of the show, Loesser separated from his wife and co-producer and later married the leading lady Jo Sullivan.

Two major New York revivals were presented: in 1979, with Giorgio Tozzi, and in 1991, with Spiro Malas and Sophie Hayden. The latter was a surprise—a well-received and intimate production that utilized a duo-piano reduction instead of Loesser's ambitious orchestral score.

AUNTIE MAME

by Jerome Lawrence and Robert E. Lee

Opened October 31, 1956

639 Performances

The Broadhurst Theatre

Directed by Morton Da Costa

Produced by Robert Fryer and Lawrence Carr

Cast: Rosalind Russell (Auntie Mame); Polly Rowles (Vera Charles); Robert Allen (Babcock); Jan Handzlik (Patrick Dennis as a boy/Michael); Robert Higgins (Patrick Dennis as a young man); Peggy Cass (Agnes Gooch); Robert Smith (Beauregard Burnside); Beulah Garrick (Norah); Yuki Shimoda (Ito); Grant Sullivan (Ralph Devine); John O'Hare (Lindsay Woolsey); Marian Winters (Sally Cato); Ethel Cody (Mother Burnside); William Martel (Cousin Jeff/Theatre Manager/Bishop); Nan McFarland (Cousin Fan); Frank Roberts (Cousin Moultrie); Barry Blake (Emory MacDougal); James Monks (Brian O'Bannion); Joyce Lear (Gloria Upson); Dorothy Blackburn (Doris Upson); Walter Klavun (Claude Upson); Patricia Jenkins (Pegeen Ryan); Geoffrey Bryant (Dr. Shurr); Walter Riemer (Lord Dudley); Cris Alexander (Mr. Loomis).

Auntie Mame, the gorgeously eccentric madcap who has been holding forth at cocktail parties on the stages of Broadway, summer stock, and community theatres since her premiere in 1956, was originally the creation of Edward Everett Tanner III, scion of a wealthy Chicago family. Under the *nom de plume* Patrick Dennis, Tanner wrote a hilarious novel of the misadventures of the nonconformist Mame and her wide-eyed nephew. The manuscript was rejected twenty times before Vanguard finally published it in 1955. The work subsequently topped bestseller lists for 112 weeks. A sequel, *Around the World with Auntie Mame* was equally successful. Tanner stated that Mame was a totally fictional character, although a relative of his did claim to be the model for the character.

The stage rights were acquired by Robert Fryer and Lawrence Carr, who asked Rosalind Russell to do the title role. For the script, Sumner Locke Elliot and then Tanner himself were considered. But Fryer and Carr finally hired Jerome Lawrence and Robert E. Lee, a writing team who had a hit with *Inherit the Wind* and a failure with *Shangri-La*, a musical version of *Lost Horizon* which Fryer and Carr had produced. For the director, Morton Da Costa was chosen because of his work on *No Time for Sergeants*, another novel-based play that the director had successfully brought to the stage. Like *Sergeants*, *Auntie Mame* resembled a series of episodic revue sketches, which Da Costa staged with rapid pacing. In her memoirs, Russell claimed that she and Da Costa wrote a great deal of the script. The director would then submit the results to Lawrence and Lee.

The production was big, with a cast of thirty, twenty-six sets, and Russell going through sixteen costume changes. Yet Russell didn't totally dominate the action. In order to get a second wind and to keep the audience wanting more of her, the star "gave" the second act to Agnes Gooch, her mousy secretary who learns the facts of life while on a bender with an Irish poet. Peggy Cass was hilarious in the role and won a Tony Award as Best Featured Actress in a Play.

Even though the second act spotlight was shared with Gooch, Mame was a plum role actresses would give their beaded gowns to play. Russell was followed on Broadway by Greer Garson. Beatrice Lillie was next. Lillie also took the show to London, where the British critics were flum-moxed by the broad American humor; still, audiences loved it. There were four separate road companies, headed by Constance Bennett, Sylvia Sidney, Eve Arden, and Shirl Conway. Sidney's production played New York's City Center for a brief engagement in 1958.

There were also several foreign productions, including one in Norway called *Min Fantasticke Tante* which starred a granddaughter of the great dramatist Henrik Ibsen.

Russell headlined the 1958 Warner Brothers film version, with her husband Frederick Brisson producing, Da Costa directing, and Betty Comden and Adolph Green adapting the script. Both Russell and Peggy Cass were nominated for Oscars. After appearing as a book, a play, and a film, *Auntie Mame* was tapped for a musical—one in which another star delivered a tour de force performance as the nutty, lovable aunt—Angela Lansbury (see *Mame*, page 194).

Jan Handzlik offers his arm to his *Auntie Mame* played by the elegant Rosalind Russell.

L'IL ABNER

Book by Norman Panama and Melvin Frank, based on the comic-strip characters created by Al Capp.

Music by Gene de Paul

Lyrics by Johnny Mercer

Opened November 15, 1956

693 Performances

St. James Theatre

Directed and choreographed by Michael Kidd

Produced by Norman Panama, Melvin Frank, and Michael Kidd

Cast: Peter Palmer (L'il Abner); Edith Adams (Daisy Mae); Stubby Kaye (Marryin' Sam); Charlotte Rae (Mammy Yokum); Joe E. Marks (Pappy Yokum); Howard St. John (Gen. Bullmoose); Tina Louise (Appassionata Von Climax); Bern Hoffman (Earthquake McGoon); Carmen Alvarez (Moonbeam McSwine); Julie Newmar (Stupefyin' Jones); William Lanteau (Available Jones); Ted Thurston (Senator Phogbound); Stanley Simmonds (Dr. Finsdale); Al Nesor (Evil Eye Fleagle); Anthony Mordente (Lonesome Polecat); Chad Block (Hairless Joe); Marc Breaux (Romeo Scragg/Dr. Schleifitz); James Hurst (Clem Scragg); Anthony Saverino (Alf Scragg); Oran Osburn (Mayor Dawgmeat); Richard Maitland (Government Man); George Reeder (Colonel/Dr. Smithborn); Lanier Davis (President/State Dept. Man/Colonel); Ralph Linn (Dr. Krogmeyer); James J. Jeffries (Butler). Future choreographers Deedee Wood and Grover Dale were in the chorus.

Many songwriting teams, including Rodgers and Hammerstein and Alan Jay Lerner and Burton Lane, considered turning Al Capp's long-running comic strip *L'il Abner* into a Broadway musical. The satiric cartoon, which first appeared in 1934, was set in the mythical hillbilly community of Dogpatch and took potshots at numerous sacred cows of American society. The extremely popular denizens of Dogpatch included muscular, innocent L'il Abner; luscious Daisy Mae, who is always after him to marry her; and indomitable Mammy Yokum. At its peak, the strip appeared in 700 publications and had served as the inspiration for both an animated and live-action series of short films.

The strip was a hot property, but circumstances prevented a Broadway adaptation on the first two tries. Rodgers and Hammerstein were too busy producing *John Loves Mary* and writing *Allegro*. Lerner and Lane got as far as starting work on a script and even announcing which of Capp's bizarre pen-and-ink creations would be brought to flesh-and-blood onstage. But Lerner went off to write *My Fair Lady* and that version of *Abner* was abandoned before it reached the rehearsal stage.

It fell to filmmakers Norman Panama and Melvin Frank to bring Dogpatch to New York. The duo had written, directed, and/or produced such Hollywood comedies as *Mr. Blandings Builds His Dream House*, for Cary Grant; *Knock on Wood* and *The Court Jester*, with Danny Kaye in the lead; and *That Certain Feeling*, starring Bob Hope. Paramount Studios bankrolled the production with an eye towards gaining the film rights.

Michael Kidd lent his energetic and athletic style to the staging and choreography, having won Tonys for his dances in *Guys and Dolls* and *Can-Can*; he was also a co-

producer. The score was by Gene de Paul and Johnny Mercer, collaborators with Kidd on the original MGM movie musical *Seven Brides for Seven Brothers*.

Casting the show proved difficult. Since the characters were so well known to the public, the actors had to bear at least some resemblance to Capp's creations. Dick Shawn, Andy Griffith, and even Elvis Presley were considered for Abner. But the role went to unknown Peter Palmer who had been spotted by the producers on *The Ed Sullivan Show*. The 6'4", former University of Illinois football tackle was appearing as part of an Army talent search. He began rehearsals just as his tour of duty as a private was ending. Daisy Mae was played by Edie (then known as Edith) Adams, fresh from *Wonderful Town*. She was also offered the role of Cunegonde in Leonard Bernstein's musical version of Voltaire's *Candide*. Her *Wonderful Town* director George Abbott advised her that while the Bernstein show would be popular among college students, it would not be a long-running hit like *Abner*. She took Abbott's advice and went with the sure thing.

Highlights of the show included Stubby Kaye as Marryin' Sam, delivering the show stopper "Jubilation T. Cornpone," a mock tribute to Dogpatch's incompetent Civil War hero, and Kidd's "Sadie Hawkins Day" ballet, in which women of the chorus chased prospective husbands.

Also appearing were Tina Louise and Julie Newmar, beauties who later captivated television audiences on *Gilligan's Isle* and *Batman*. Naturally, the cast included a whole barnyard of animals: the original company included six geese, six chickens (the geese's understudies), three pigs, two dogs, and a mule.

Peter Palmer recreated his Abner in the 1959 movie. Capp's comic strip continued until 1977.

BELLS ARE RINGING

Book and lyrics by Betty Comden and Adolph Green

Music by Jule Styne

Opened November 29, 1956

924 Performances

Shubert Theatre

Directed by Jerome Robbins

Produced by The Theatre Guild

Choreographed by Jerome Robbins and Bob Fosse

Cast: Judy Holliday (Ella Peterson); Sydney Chaplin (Jeff Moss); Jean Stapleton (Sue); Eddie Lawrence (Sandor); Dort Clark (Inspector Barnes); George S. Irving (Larry Hastings); Jack Weston (Francis); Peter Gennaro (Carl); Bernie West (Dr. Kitchell); Frank Aletter (Blake Barton); Pat Wilkes (Gwynne); Frank Milton (Ludwig Smiley); Frank Green (Charles Bessemer/Actor/Singer at Nightclub); Tom O'Steen (Joey); Norma Doggett (Olga); Ellen Ray (Carol); Michelle Reiner (Michelle); Steve Roland (Paul Arnold); Eddie Heim (Telephone Man/Master of Ceremonies); Ed Thompson (Waiter); David McDaniel (Maitre d'Hotel); Gordon Woodburn (Police Officer); Donna Sanders (Madame Grimaldi); Jeannine Masterson (Mrs. Mallet); John Perkins (Man from Corvello Mob); Kasimir Kokich (Other Man).

Sydney Chaplin removes Judy Holliday's disguise in *Bells Are Ringing*.

Librettists Betty Comden and Adolph Green had been working on an idea for a musical to star their friend Judy Holliday. The three had appeared in a nightclub act called the Revuers before they went on to separate show business triumphs—Holliday to the stage and screen versions of *Born Yesterday*, Comden and Green to writing *On the Town*, *Wonderful Town*, and numerous movie musicals.

"We sat for weeks and weeks and tried to think of an idea," Green told *Playbill* magazine, "until one day one of us looked at the back of a phone book, where there was a picture of a lady with all sorts of wires coming out of her head. Wow! It was an ad for an answering service. . . . So we went to look at Adolph's answering service, because neither of us had ever been to such a place. We imagined a big office full of people, and what it turned out to be was one lonely fat lady in a dingy little room with a dog peeing in the corner."

Comden and Green called their show *Bells Are Ringing* and fashioned a story about Ella Peterson, a big-hearted answering service operator who gets involved in the lives of her clients. (This trait paralleled Holliday's tendency to

offer constant advice to friends.) One of the service's customers is a handsome young playwright. Naturally, Ella falls in love with him, but he only knows her as a voice on the phone. Numerous subplots involve such clients as a bookie, a songwriting dentist, and a would-be actor with a Marlon Brando fixation. Each of these customers, as well as the two leads, wind up happily ever after.

Comden and Green's collaborators on the musical were director-choreographer Jerome Robbins and composer Jule Styne. The four had previously worked together on *Peter Pan*. This was Robbins's second assignment as a director, so Bob Fosse was brought in to assist with the dances.

Holliday was enthusiastic about the project, but not about singing. During her Revuer days, she had only vocalized in comedy numbers and was insecure about performing musically. "I'll do all the patter stuff. Leave the love songs for the male lead," she told Comden and Green. Unfortunately, the male lead was not a great singer either. Holliday insisted on casting her current beau, handsome Sydney Chaplin (son of Charlie), as her co-star. Robbins agreed that he had the right look for the part, but not the voice. Holliday stubbornly stood her ground and offered a compromise. If Chaplin was not giving a satisfactory performance by the first week of tryouts in New Haven, he would be replaced.

Chaplin did more than satisfactorily. His laid-back charm wowed the out-of-town critics and threatened to steal the show from Holliday. To bring the spotlight back to their star, Comden, Green, and Styne gave her a "ten o'clock number," a socko song that would bring the audience to Ella's side just before the final curtain dropped. Previously, her final number had been "The Party's Over," a slow ballad. "I'm Going Back" was added. In this showstopper, Ella belts out her frustrations and announces her intention to return to her prior position at the Bonjour Tristesse Brassiere Factory, where there is no possibility of interfering in the customers' affairs.

The new number reshifted the focus back to Holliday. At the end of the season, she and Chaplin won Tony Awards as outstanding leading actress and featured actor.

Holliday recreated her role in the 1960 Metro-Goldwyn-Mayer version directed by Vincente Minnelli. Dean Martin was just as "laid-back" as Chaplin in the part of her love interest. The comedienne headlined another Broadway musical, the short-lived *Hot Spot*, in 1963. She died of cancer at forty-two years of age, two years later.

WEST SIDE STORY

Book by Arthur Laurents

Music by Leonard Bernstein

Lyrics by Stephen Sondheim

Opened September 26, 1957

732 Performances

Winter Garden Theatre

Directed and choreographed by Jerome Robbins

Produced by Robert Griffith and Harold Prince

Cast: Carol Lawrence (Maria); Larry Kert (Tony); Ken Le Roy (Bernardo); Chita Rivera (Anita); Mickey Calin (Riff); Art Smith (Doc); Arch Johnson (Schrank); William Bramley (Krupke); John Harkins (Glad Hand); Lee Becker (Anybodys); Jamie Sanchez (Chino); Wilma Curley (Graziella); Carole D'Andrea (Velma); Eddie Roll (Action); Tony Mordente (A-Rab); David Winters (Baby John); Grover Dale (Snowboy); Martin Charnin (Big Deal); Hank Brunjes (Diesel); Tommy Abbott (Gee-Tar); Frank Green (Mouthpiece); Lowell Harris (Tiger); Nanette Rosen (Minnie); Marilyn D'Honau (Clarice); Julie Oser (Pauline); George Marcy (Pepe); Noel Schwartz (Indio); Al De Sio (Luis); Gene Gavin (Anxious); Ronnie Lee (Nibbles); Jay Norman (Juano); Erne Castaldo (Toro); Jack Murray (Moose); Marilyn Cooper (Rosalia); Reri Grist (Consuelo); Carmen Gutierrez (Teresita); Elizabeth Taylor (Francisca); Lynn Ross (Estella); Liane Plane (Margarita).

Exploding across the footlights, *West Side Story* brought the reality of gang violence to Broadway. Based on Shakespeare's *Romeo and Juliet*, the tragedy of warring aristocratic families, *West Side Story* depicted the Jets and the Sharks, rival street gangs warring over control of a small stretch of

"turf" in a dangerous Manhattan neighborhood. Shakespeare's star-crossed lovers became Polish-American Tony and Puerto Rican–born Maria, whose romance sets off a deadly confrontation between the two bands of youths.

In addition to telling a riveting story, the show was a watershed in the development of musical theatre. Director–choreographer Jerome Robbins furthered the use of dance as both an expression of character and as a way to tell a story. His dances utilized the main characters, not just the chorus, to physicalize all the relationships among the inarticulate gang members. Unlike the chorus members of previous musicals, all of the *West Side* youths were individual characters with names and histories. Add to this Robbins's direction of all the book scenes as well as choreographing the show, and the result is that music, dance, and story became all of a piece rather than a blending of still-separate elements.

Robbins was also credited with "conceiving" the show. The idea came to him in 1949, when an actor friend asked how Romeo could be played in a relevant way. The choreographer came up with an outline, recasting Shakespeare's tragedy in contemporary terms, with a Lower East Side Jewish girl falling in love with a Catholic-Italian boy. He decided to develop this idea and called it *East Side Story*. Leonard Bernstein, who had collaborated with Robbins on *On the Town*, was to write the songs, and Arthur Laurents the book. Scheduling conflicts, including an unproduced musical version of James M. Cain's *Serenade*—involving all three—prevented *East Side* from reaching fruition, so eventually the project fizzled out.

Then, in 1954, Bernstein met Laurents in Hollywood, where both were working on films. As the two were reminiscing about *East Side Story*, the composer glanced at a newspaper headline about recent Hispanic gang warfare in Los Angeles. "Why don't we make it about the Puerto Ricans in New York?" suggested Bernstein. Robbins was contacted, and the project was reborn.

Bernstein was originally to write both music and lyrics. But as the show, now called *West Side Story*, developed, the amount of music in the score increased and a collaborating lyricist was needed to lighten Bernstein's burden. Betty Comden and Adolph Green were considered, but they were busy in Hollywood. Stephen Sondheim, who had auditioned his songs for the unproduced *Serenade*, was hired. In the end he was given sole credit for the lyrics. The writing of the show took two years, during which Bernstein took a six-month break to complete his score for *Candide*. Another delay was caused by the number of producers who rejected the project. It was finally optioned by Cheryl Crawford and Roger Stevens. Crawford went so far as to begin production, but withdrew; she was replaced by Harold Prince and Robert Griffith.

Along with every other aspect of the show, the casting took longer than usual: six months. There were no stars, for the cast had to be young enough to be convincing as teenagers. In addition, they all had to sing, dance, and act well. Rehearsals took an unprecedented eight weeks, as the green Broadway youngsters were transformed into believable street gangs.

West Side Story's breakthroughs were acknowledged by the press, but with reservations as to the rawness of the cast. At awards time, its innovations went largely unappreciated. Both the Tony and New York Drama Critics Circle Awards for best musical went to the more conventional hit, *The Music Man*.

The show ran a respectable 732 performances, had a successful national tour, and then returned to Broadway for another six months.

When United Artists brought the show to the screen, the awards poured in. The film, co-directed by Robbins and Robert Wise, won a record eleven Oscars, including Best Picture.

The musical has been revived at the Music Theatre of Lincoln Center, in 1968, and on Broadway, in 1980.

JAMAICA

by E.Y. Harburg and Fred Saidy

Music by Harold Arlen

Lyrics by E.Y. Harburg

Opened October 31, 1957

558 Performances

Imperial Theatre

Directed by Robert Lewis

Choreographed by Jack Cole

Produced by David Merrick

Cast: Lena Horne (Savannah); Ricardo Montalban (Koli); Josephine Premice (Ginger); Ossie Davis (Cicero); Adelaide Hall (Grandma Obeah); Augustine Rios (Quico); Roy Thompson (Snodgrass); Hugh Dilworth (Hucklebuck); Erik Rhodes (The Governor); James E. Wall (Lancaster); Ethel Ayler, Adelaide Boatner (Island Women); Tony Martinez (1st Ship's Officer); Michael Wright (2nd Ship's Officer); Joe Adams (Joe Nashua); Allen Richards (Dock Worker); Alan Shayne (Radio Announcer); Alvin Ailey, Christyne Lawson (Lead Dancers).

Lena Horne in *Jamaica*.

A mediocre book did not prevent *Jamaica* from a year-and-a-half run on Broadway. The reason for this show's success was its star, Lena Horne. Written by E.Y. Harburg and Fred Saidy, with music by Harold Arlen, the simple story takes place on mythical Pigeon Island. In order to capitalize on the Calypso music craze of the time, the authors wanted to cast singing sensation Harry Belafonte as Koli, a fisherman content with the idyllic island life. Lena Horne was the choice for Savannah, his starry-eyed seamstress girlfriend, who yearns for the high life in New York City. Because of his heavy schedule, Belafonte fell away from the project.

"Lena had been asked to be in it when Harry Belafonte was going to do it," director Robert Lewis explained. "Arlen, Harburg, and Saidy said that if Lena would still do it, they would shift the emphasis of the story towards her and make it a star part. She was a very big star, but not on the stage. She had never even spoken in public."

Horne's only previous stage appearance was in the chorus of *Blackbirds of 1939*. Her fame derived from club appearances and film musicals, in which she sang isolated "specialty numbers" which could be cut from the picture in Southern markets where the appearance of a black singer would hurt box office returns. Only in two all-black films (*Cabin in the Sky* and *Stormy Weather*) did Horne play a character integral to the story.

Finding a good replacement for Belafonte was an important factor. Not only would he have to sing and dance; he had to be a strong enough actor to support Horne. Mexican-born Ricardo Montalban was finally chosen to play the Jamaican fisherman.

Jack Cole was hired to stage the musical numbers, and top-notch black dancers, including future choreographers Alvin Ailey and Billy Wilson, filled the chorus.

Despite the well-staged musical numbers, the book was weak enough for producer David Merrick to threaten to close the show in Boston unless a play doctor was brought in. Harburg and Saidy weren't happy with the ultimatum, but Joseph Stein (author of the Sammy Davis, Jr. vehicle, *Mister Wonderful*, and of *Plain and Fancy*) did some patchwork.

"The book never got any better," Lewis admitted, "but everything else did, and we had a chance to be a hit. I got together with Merrick and Lena. We decided the only thing to do was cut the book right down to the bone. This way we could get very quickly from number to number." The leading lady stayed with the production during its entire New York run.

Horne returned to Broadway during the 1980–81 season with a one-woman show entitled *Lena Horne: The Lady and Her Music* and won a special Tony Award and a citation from the New York Drama Critics Circle.

LOOK HOMEWARD, ANGEL

by Ketti Frings, based on the novel by Thomas Wolfe.

Opened November 28, 1957

564 Performances

Ethel Barrymore Theatre

Directed by George Roy Hill

Produced by Kermit Bloomgarden and Theatre 200, Inc.

Cast: Anthony Perkins (Eugene Gant); Jo Van Fleet (Eliza Gant); Hugh Griffith (W.O. Gant); Arthur Hill (Ben Gant); Frances Hyland (Laura James); Rosemary Murphy (Helen Gant Barton); Leonard Stone (Hugh Barton); Bibi Osterwald (Madame Elizabeth); Arthur Storch (Luke Gant); Florence Sundstrom (Mrs. Marie "Fatty" Pert); Tom Flatley Reynolds (Will Pentland); Joseph Bernard (Jake Clatt); Mary Farrell (Mrs. Clatt); Elizabeth Lawrence (Florry Mangle); Julia Johnston (Mrs. Snowden); Dwight Marfield (Mr. Farrell); Susan Torrey (Miss Brown); Victor Kilian (Dr. McGuire); Jack Sheehan (Tarkinton).

"I shall never express myself dramatically," wrote Thomas Wolfe to his drama instructor. Wolfe, one of America's great novelists, had always wanted to see a play of his produced. But it was not until after his death of cancer in 1938, at the age of thirty-seven, that a play based on a work of his would reach the stage.

The stage adaptation of his autobiographical novel *Look Homeward, Angel* was a dramatic success beyond what Wolfe had yearned for. The author had studied playwriting with such eminent instructors as Frederick Koch of the University of North Carolina and George Pierce Baker of Harvard. Given to florid and eloquent writing, he felt constrained by the stage, which calls for suggestion and conciseness. Despite dropping out of Baker's English 47 Workshop at Harvard, Wolfe later submitted a play, *Welcome to Our City,* to the Theatre Guild. The Guild insisted on cuts and changes in the lengthy script, but the would-be playwright's changes made the work even longer.

In its original form, *Look Homeward, Angel,* published in 1930, had enough material for several evenings in the theatre. The novel, originally titled *O, Lost,* was 1,113 typed pages in its submitted form. The hefty manuscript was pared down through the patient efforts of editor Maxwell Perkins, working with Wolfe. Ketti Frings, who had previously adapted the plays *Come Back, Little Sheba* and *The Shrike* to the screen, took the final third of the novel as the basis for her stage version.

The central conflict is between a domineering mother and a sensitive son with ambitions of becoming a writer. Parsimonious Eliza Gant runs a boarding house with the eccentric name of "Dixieland" in Altamont (based on Wolfe's hometown of Asheville, in North Carolina). The year is 1916. Eliza keeps the Gant family working at "Dixieland," and constantly searches for ways to attain financial security. Youngest son Eugene (Wolfe's fictional self-portrait) is champing at the bit to escape and enter college at Chapel Hill.

Eliza attempts to persuade her alcoholic husband to sell his stonecutting yard and use the money to purchase more real estate. The yard contains a perfectly carved Carrara Angel, symbolizing his dashed artistic dreams. Also under Eliza's thumb are older son Ben, longing to join the Canadian Air Force but dying of tuberculosis, and daughter Helen, resentful of the household drudgery imposed upon her.

Angel went on to win both the Pulitzer Prize and the Drama Critics Circle Award, but lost all seven of its Tony nominations. (The Best Play Tony Award went to the Franklin Roosevelt bio *Sunrise at Campobello*.)

A television production with Geraldine Page, Lee J. Cobb, and Timothy Bottoms, was broadcast by CBS in 1972. *Angel*, an unsuccessful musical version of the play, landed on Broadway in 1978. Frings co-authored the book with Peter Udell, who also wrote the lyrics. Gary Geld composed the music for this five-performance flop.

THE MUSIC MAN

Book, music and lyrics by Meredith Willson, based on a story by Willson and Franklin Lacey.

Opened December 19, 1957

1,375 Performances

Majestic Theatre

Directed by Morton Da Costa

Choreographed by Onna White

Produced by Kermit Bloomgarden

Cast: Robert Preston (Harold Hill); Barbara Cook (Marian Paroo); David Burns (Mayor Shinn); Iggie Wolfington (Marcellus Washburn); Helen Raymond (Eulalie Mackecknie Shinn); Pert Kelton (Mrs. Paroo); Danny Carroll (Tommy Djilas); Dusty Worrall (Zaneeta Shinn); Eddie Hodges (Winthrop Paroo); Marilyn Siegel (Amaryllis); Paul Reed (Charlie Cowell); Al Shea, Wayne Ward, Vern Reed, Bill Spangenberg (The Buffalo Bills); Barbara Travis (Gracie Shinn); Adnia Rice (Alma Hix); Elaine Swann (Maud Dunlop); Peggy Mondo (Ethel Toffelmier); Martha Flynn (Mrs. Squires); Carl Nicholas (Conductor/Constable Locke).

Robert Preston as *The Music Man*.

The Music Man, the exuberant celebration of small-town America that gave us "Seventy-Six Trombones" went through almost as many drafts and song changes during its long road to Broadway. This valentine to Fourth of July picnics and church socials was the brainchild of Meredith Willson, an author and radio personality. In a rare accomplishment, Willson wrote both the book and the score. The seed for *The Music Man* was planted soon after he had published a volume about his childhood in Mason City, Iowa, and his experiences playing in John Philip Sousa's band. His friend Frank Loesser (*Where's Charley?*, *Guys and Dolls*) suggested that he write a musical derived from the work.

The title character is "Professor" Harold Hill, a charming charlatan out to dupe the townsfolk of River City into buying band uniforms and instruments for the children of the town. Naturally, the wily fellow falls in love with a local miss (the straitlaced librarian Marian) and remains in town to face the music. That music turns out to be awful, as the River City youth squeak and groan through a passage with their new instruments. But their parents beam, and all ends happily.

Willson used the innovative device of rhythmic spoken dialogue to bridge the nonmusical scenes to the songs. In fact, the entire opening sequence, set on board a train's smoking car full of travelling salesmen, had no opening song, only rhythmic unrhymed patter. There was also "The Piano Lesson," which was sung to exercise scales, and "Pick-a-Little" featuring the neighborhood gossips clucking like hens, while a barbershop quartet sang "Good Night Ladies" in counterpoint. Another clever use of melody was giving Hill and Marian the same tune but with different emphasis and tempi: Hill's "Seventy-Six Trombones" was an exhilarating march, while Marian's "Goodnight, My Someone" was a tender ballad.

Originally titled *The Silver Triangle*, the script was taken by Willson and his wife Rini to producers' offices and apartments, where they sang all the parts. After several such auditions, Cy Feuer and Ernest Martin (producers of *Guys and Dolls*, *Can-Can*, etc.) expressed interest. However, they were busy mounting *The Boy Friend* and *Silk Stockings*. They promised to put on the show as soon as their other projects were on Broadway. They advised Willson to use the time to fix the book.

After numerous rewrites, and delays by Feuer and Martin, Willson took the play to Kermit Bloomgarden, who promptly set the wheels in motion to get the show on. Morton Da Costa, who had staged such large-ensemble pieces as *No Time for Sergeants* and *Auntie Mame*, was hired to direct.

Casting Harold Hill was the biggest obstacle to starting production. Danny Kaye, Dan Dailey, Gene Kelly, and Phil Harris all turned the part down. Hill was finally cast in a way similar to that of another musical professor: Henry Higgins. Both were played by an actor making his debut in musicals who mostly spoke the songs. Robert Preston, known principally for playing either cowboys or Mounties in "B" movies, landed the lead and scored a personal triumph.

Preston took the lead in the 1962 movie version with Shirley Jones, Paul Ford, and Hermione Gingold as the citizens of River City.

Forrest Tucker headed the national touring company, while Van Johnson starred in the London edition. Michael Kidd directed a 1980 revival with Dick Van Dyke and Meg Bussert.

TWO FOR THE SEESAW

by William Gibson
Opened January 16, 1958
750 Performances
Booth Theatre
Directed by Arthur Penn
Produced by Fred Coe
Cast: Henry Fonda (Jerry Ryan); Anne Bancroft (Gittel Mosca).

Two for the Seesaw, a charming two-character study of a pair of lonely souls who come together briefly in Manhattan, marked the Broadway debut of almost all the personnel involved: the playwright (William Gibson), director (Arthur Penn), producer (Fred Coe), and leading lady (Anne Bancroft). Male star Henry Fonda had more professional theatrical experience than all the other parties combined.

The seesawing duo are Jerry Ryan, a lawyer from Nebraska escaping a failing marriage, and Gittel Mosca, a pert woman from the Bronx who fancies herself a modern dancer. They have a brief affair which ends with Jerry

Anne Bancroft is getting an ulcer from her love for Henry Fonda in *Two for the Seesaw*.

returning to his home state to patch things up with his wife, and Gittel promising to grow up and piece together her tattered personal life.

The production team had little trouble casting the female half of the cast. Anne Bancroft, who had appeared in a few television shows and undistinguished films, showed up at the audition sporting a thick Bronx dialect and attitude. She asked to use the john and removed one of her shoes during the reading. Gibson thought he was seeing the character he had created step right off the page.

Finding an actor for Jerry was another story. With the unknown Bancroft cast, it was necessary to hire a "name" for the other half of the seesaw in order to get backing. Van Heflin, Paul Newman, Jack Lemmon, Jack Palance, Barry Nelson, Eli Wallach, Don Murray, Robert Preston, and Fritz Weaver were all approached, but each turned the role down. At first, Henry Fonda was reluctant to take on the part, feeling that the role was two-dimensional compared to the vibrant Gittel. Gibson rewrote his script and sent the new version to Fonda who was vacationing in Europe. The star still wasn't satisfied with the character's development but finally reasoned that any playwright who could write Gittel would do all right by Jerry after revisions. He sent a cablegram to producer Coe: "Start it rolling. I am yours."

Gibson recorded the play's progress through rehearsals and tryout engagements in Washington, D.C., and Philadelphia. His production diary, later published as *The Seesaw Log*, revealed conflicts between Fonda and Gibson over the lack of depth in the male character, and the psychological approach to acting, favored by Bancroft and Penn, versus Fonda's more traditional methods.

The script was rewritten right up until opening night, when Fonda yelled at the playwright to stay out of his dressing room. Despite the backstage battles, Bancroft became a star for her vital performance, and Fonda received glowing notices for making his character more than Gittel's straight man.

Fonda left the play at the end of his six-month contract, and was replaced by Dana Andrews. Lee Grant took over for Bancroft when she withdrew to begin rehearsals for another Gibson play, *The Miracle Worker*, which was also directed by Penn. Jeffrey Lyon and Ruth Roman, and later Hal March (host of *The $64,000 Question)* and Sheila Copeland, were the national touring company. The London cast consisted of American Gerry Jedd and Australian Peter Finch.

Shirley MacLaine and Robert Mitchum rode the seesaw in the 1962 United Artists big-screen version. A musical reworking of the script called *Seesaw*, with a score by Cy Coleman and Dorothy Fields (her last Broadway show), opened late in the 1972–73 season. Despite Michael Bennett's well-received direction, it closed after ten months, at the loss of its investment.

SUNRISE AT CAMPOBELLO

by Dore Schary

Opened January 30, 1958

556 Performances

The Cort Theatre

Directed by Vincent J. Donehue

Produced by The Theatre Guild and Dore Schary

Cast: Ralph Bellamy (Franklin Delano Roosevelt); Mary Fickett (Eleanor Roosevelt); Henry Jones (Louis McHenry Howe); Anne Seymour (Sara Delano Roosevelt); Mary Welch (Missy LeHand); Alan Bunce (Gov. Alfred E. Smith); Roni Dengel (Anna Roosevelt); Kenneth Kakos (Franklin D. Roosevelt, Jr.); James Bonnet (James Roosevelt); Perry Skaar (Elliott Roosevelt); James Earl Jones (Edward); Jeffrey Rowland (John Roosevelt); Ethel Everett (Marie); James Reese (Dr. Bennet); William Fort (Franklin Calder); Clifford Carpenter (Mr. Brimmer); Richard Robbins (Mr. Lassiter); Jerry Crews (Daly); Floyd Curtis (Policeman); Vincent Dowling (Senator Walsh); Edwin Philips (Speaker).

Franklin Delano Roosevelt's struggle with polio provided the inspiration for Dore Schary's *Sunrise at Campobello*, named for FDR's summer home in Nova Scotia. It was at the Canadian lodge, in 1921, that Roosevelt was first struck with the illness which rendered his legs paralyzed. With his domineering mother urging him to give up politics and his wife supporting his return to public life, the future President learns to live with the physical limitations of the paralysis. The play ends with FDR standing at the podium of the 1924 Democratic National Convention about to deliver the nominating speech for the party's candidate for President, Alfred E. Smith. That moment marked Roosevelt's return to the political arena and the start of his rise to the White House.

Dore Schary had begun his career as an actor and was returning to the theatre after a sojourn as head of film production at RKO and MGM, during which he served as executive producer on over 300 films. He co-produced his play with the Theatre Guild. The most vital element of the production was the casting of the lead role. They needed an actor tall and powerful enough to resemble the 32nd President, but not one who would stoop to imitation. Lawrence Langner of the Theatre Guild suggested Anthony Quayle. Schary balked at an having an Englishman play an American head of state, and then Schary's wife remembered Ralph Bellamy, who had previously played a Presidential candidate in *State of the Union* and seemed perfect for the part.

Bellamy accepted and went on to play the role of his career. The actor made several trips to the Institute for the Crippled and Disabled to study the effects of the disease which had afflicted FDR. Edward R. Murrow lent him tape recordings of Roosevelt's speeches.

Pre-Broadway engagements for *Sunrise* in New Haven and Boston went over well. Schary overheard one audience member say to his wife at the play's beginning, "If I'd known it was about this fellow, I don't think I'd have come. I had enough of that son of a bitch when he was alive." After the final curtain, the same man was heard to say, "You know, if I'd known all this a few years ago, I might have voted for him . . . once."

Another patron whose opinion had changed was Eleanor Roosevelt. Upon first reading the play, the former First Lady told the playwright, "It's quite remarkable. It sounds exactly like Franklin." After the opening night on Broadway, she was quoted as saying, "A good play, but as much like the Roosevelt family as some people from Mars."

Schary adapted, produced and directed the 1960 film version, with Bellamy repeating his stage role, Greer Garson as Eleanor, and Hume Cronyn as FDR's right-hand man Louis Howe. On television, Bellamy later played Roosevelt on *The Winds of War* and *War and Remembrance*.

FDR also appeared as a character in the musicals *I'd Rather Be Right* (1937), *Annie* (1977), and *Annie Warbucks* (1993). Other Presidents in Broadway plays have included George Washington (*Valley Forge*, 1934); John Adams and Thomas Jefferson (*1776*, 1969); Washington, Jefferson, James Madison, and James Monroe (*The Patriots*, 1943); Abraham Lincoln (*Abraham Lincoln*, 1919, and *Abe Lincoln in Illinois*, 1938); Theodore Roosevelt (*Teddy and Alice*, 1987); Woodrow Wilson (*In Time to Come*, 1941); Richard Nixon (*An Evening with Richard Nixon*, 1972); James Garfield and Gerald Ford (*Assassins*, off-Broadway, 1991).

THE WORLD OF SUZIE WONG

by Paul Osborn, based on the novel by Richard Mason.

Opened October 14, 1958

508 Performances

Broadhurst Theatre

Directed by Joshua Logan

Produced by David Merrick, Seven Arts Productions, Inc., and Mansfield Productions

Cast: William Shatner (Robert Lomax); France Nuyen (Suzie Wong); Ron Randell (Ben Jeffcoat); Sarah Marshall (Kay Fletcher); Noel Leslie (George O'Neill); Stephen C. Cheng (Ah Tong); Sirat (Typhoo); Takayo (Gwenny); Flavia Hsu Kingman (Wednesday Lulu); Mary Mon Toy (Minnie Ho); Vie Von Thom (Fifi); Ellen Davalos (Lily); Clifford Arashi (Chinese Officer); David Hill (Chinese Policeman); Viraj Amonsin (Waiter/Bystander); David Kitchen (British Sailor); Warren Robertson (Drunken Sailor).

France Nuyen, William Shatner, and Ron Randell in *The World of Suzie Wong*.

The Broadway season of 1958–59 featured an unusual number of productions with Asian characters and themes. Rodgers and Hammerstein took a trip to San Francisco's Chinatown with *Flower Drum Song*. *A Majority of One* followed the unlikely romance of a Brooklyn housewife and a Japanese businessman. Two others, *Kataki* and *Rashomon* had brief runs.

The first of these Oriental excursions was *The World of Suzie Wong*, a sentimental play with a plot reminiscent of David Belasco's early 1910s *Madama Butterfly*. The world that Suzie Wong inhabited was the *demi-monde* of exotic Hong Kong, where she works as a prostitute. Of course, she has a heart of gold and is only plying her trade in order to support her illegitimate baby. Canadian painter Robert Lomax rents a room in the bordello where Suzy is employed, unaware of the nature of the establishment. The two meet, but do not fall immediately in love. First Suzy has an affair with a British married man. After he returns to his wife, leaving her without a source of income, a deluge strikes Hong Kong, levelling Suzy's house and killing her baby. After this tragedy, Lomax and Suzy finally realize their true feelings for each other. She resolves to quit the world's oldest profession and the two plan to marry.

Lomax was played by a young actor from the Canadian Shakespeare Festival named William Shatner, who would later soar to fame on the television series *Star Trek*. Suzy was portrayed by Eurasian actress France Nuyen, who had appeared as Liat in the film version of *South Pacific*.

The response of the *Daily News*'s John Chapman was typical. He labelled the show "the corniest tearjerker imaginable." Despite these negative reviews, *Suzie Wong* had a respectable run of 508 performances. The show's longevity can be attributed to Joshua Logan's imaginative staging (his more spectacular scenes included a realistic rainstorm and a boat scene in which the actors slightly shifted their weight to suggest being on the water), Jo Mielziner's colorful settings, and a two-for-one ticket-sale policy.

Producer David Merrick's genius for publicity also helped prolong the run. When Rodgers and Hammerstein's *Flower Drum Song* began to sell more tickets than *Suzie Wong*, Merrick had protesters carry placards with slogans like "*The World of Suzie Wong* is the only authentic Oriental show on Broadway" outside the theatre where the musical was playing.

The 1960 movie version, scripted by John Patrick (*Teahouse of the August Moon*) was filmed on location in Hong Kong. William Holden was starred as Lomax, and Nancy Kwan was a much more wholesome Suzie. All the play's explicit sexual references were washed away, rendering the story even sudsier.

LA PLUME DE MA TANTE

Written and devised by Robert Dhery
Music by Gerald Calvi
English lyrics by Ross Parker
Opened November 11, 1958
835 Performances
Royale Theatre
Directed by Robert Dhery
Choreographed by Colette Brosset
Staged by Alec Shanks
Produced by David Merrick, Joseph Kipness, and Jack Hylton

Cast: Robert Dhery, Colette Brosset, Pierre Olaf, Jacques Legras, Roger Caccia, Jean Lefevre, Ross Parker, Nicole Parent, Pamela Austin, Michael Kent, Henri Pennec, Michel Modo, Yvonne Constant, Genevieve Coulombel.

During the run of *La Plume de Ma Tante*, at the Royale Theatre, a sign reading "English Spoken Here" was hung from the marquee. The legend was meant to convince theatregoers that despite the musical revue's Gallic title, the gags would be perfectly understandable to an American audience. The script contained some fragmentary English, but the show emphasized the international language of pantomime. Created by the husband and wife team of Robert Dhery and Colette Brosset, *La Plume* was a hit in three theatre capitals. Like the 1922 revue *Chauve-Souris*, it played in Paris and London before coming to Broadway. The title, derived from a sample sentence seen in most French phrasebooks, means "The pen of my aunt." While the show had nothing to do with the writing implements of female relatives, it was meant as a satire on all things French: French cuisine, French air travel, French entertainment, French lovers.

Sketches included a tardy musician trying to find his way into the orchestra pit; Pierre Olaf as an agitated waiter dealing with his last customer of the evening; Brosset as a stripper with a stuck zipper; a soprano growing taller with every high note she hits, until she's twenty feet tall; a chorus girl kicking out of step; a delayed airline passenger whose bowtie starts spinning like a propeller and causes him to fly. In one elaborate ballroom section, costumes changed color and couples changed partners in the time it took to step behind a pillar. The most popular scene, and the one most cited by the reviewers, was the bell-pulling sketch. Four tired monks begin their duties of pulling the bell ropes of their monastery. Carried away by the rhythm, they erupt into a frenzied dance, leaping off the ground and twisting their ropes around each other.

Producer David Merrick, along with Joseph Kipness, brought the production of the revue across the Atlantic from London, where it was presented by Jack Hylton. Merrick's other hits that season were *The World of Suzie Wong* and *Gypsy*.

The entire cast of the show was nominated as a group for Tony Awards under the category of Featured Actor and Actress in a Musical. Though they lost the individual awards to Pat Stanley and Russell Nype of *Goldilocks*, the company was honored with a Special Tony. The revue also won the New York Drama Critics Award for Best Musical.

Dhery and Bossert returned to Broadway in 1965 with another revue, *La Grosse Valise*, which had an unsuccessful run of seven performances.

La Plume was one of the last revues combining music and comedy to achieve hit proportions. Competition from TV variety series proved too tough for shows like *Angels in the Wings, Two on the Aisle, Catch a Star, Phoenix '55* and *Two's Company* to proliferate. *Beyond the Fringe*, a sketch-oriented show, featuring political and social humor written and performed by four British comedians, brought the form back to popularity in 1962.

FLOWER DRUM SONG

Book by Oscar Hammerstein II and Joseph Fields, based on the novel by C.Y. Lee.

Music by Richard Rodgers

Lyrics by Oscar Hammerstein II

Opened December 1, 1958

600 Performances

St. James Theatre

Directed by Gene Kelly

Choreographed by Carol Haney

Produced by Rodgers and Hammerstein, in association with Joseph Fields

Cast: Miyoshi Umeki (Mei Li); Pat Suzuki (Linda Low); Larry Blyden (Sammy Fong); Ed Kenney (Wang Ta); Keye Luke (Wang Chi Yang); Juanita Hall (Madame Liang); Arabella Hong (Helen Chao); Conrad Yama (Dr. Li); Jack Soo (Frankie Wing); Rose Quong (Liu Ma); Patrick Adiarte (Wang San); Harry Shaw Lowe (Mr. Lung); Jon Lee (Mr. Huan); Peter Chan (Professor Chen); Anita Ellis (Night Club Singer); Chao Li (Dr. Lu Fong); Eileen Nakamura (Madam Fong); George Young (Headwaiter).

In a season of Asian-flavored plays, Rodgers and Hammerstein's *Flower Drum Song*, set in San Francisco's Chinatown, was the longest-running book musical.

Joseph Fields (co-author of *My Sister Eileen, Junior Miss, Wonderful Town*, etc.) had read *The Flower Drum Song*, C.Y. Lee's novel about conflicts between first- and second-generation Chinese-American families, and brought it to Rodgers and Hammerstein as a possible source for a new musical. This Fields was the only member of the theatrical family that Rodgers had not worked with. Father Lew, the comedian, produced the first Rodgers and Hart show. The composer had worked with Fields's siblings, Dorothy and Herbert, on numerous projects, including *Annie Get Your Gun*.

Fields collaborated with Hammerstein on the book. They trimmed several of the novel's episodes and shifted the focus from patriarch Wang Chi-yang to a romantic triangle involving his eldest son Wang Ta, picture-bride Mei

Miyoshi Umeki is a picture-bride in *Flower Drum Song*.

Li, and brassy nightclub entertainer Linda Low. They also added the character of Sammy Fong, the nightclub owner. As in *The King and I*, Rodgers didn't employ authentic Eastern music but used influences to suggest an Asian flavor. Likewise, Hammerstein's lyrics were a mix of Asian and Broadway styles, depending on which characters were singing them. For instance, in Mei Li's song "I Am Going to Like It Here," which she sings after arriving in San Francisco, Hammerstein used a Malaysian form of poetry called "pantoum," in which the second and fourth lines of each stanza became the first and third of the next. The score also included the very Western "I Enjoy Being a Girl" for the assimilated Linda Low.

Gene Kelly, who became a star in the original production of Rodgers' *Pal Joey*, was hired as director. Although he directed many film musicals, this proved to be Kelly's only theatrical staging assignment. Carol Haney, who dazzled Broadway as Gladys in *The Pajama Game*, made her debut as a choreographer.

Finding an all-Chinese cast proved impossible. So few opportunities existed for Asian performers that there were not many Chinese actors in the business. Most roles were cast on the West Coast. Miyoshi Umeki (an Oscar winner for *Sayonara*) and Pat Suzuki were Japanese-American. Ed Kenney was Hawaiian. Juanita Hall, the original Bloody Mary of *South Pacific*, was black. Keye Luke, best-known as Charlie Chan's Number One Son in numerous films, was the only Chinese among the principals. Larry Storch, a Caucasian actor, was slated to play Sammy Fong.

Problems cropped up in the Boston tryout. Storch was replaced by Larry Blyden, Haney's husband. He agreed to take on the role only if he could have a big number. This resulted in the hot comedy song *Don't Marry Me*, in which Sammy gives Mei Li hundreds of reasons why they shouldn't wed.

After the moderate run of *Me and Juliet* (1953) and the out-and-out failure of *Pipe Dream* (1955), *Flower Drum Song* was Rodgers and Hammerstein's first solid hit after *The King and I* (1951).

Flower Drum Song enjoyed a long run, toured for a year and a half, and was made into a 1961 film. Umeki and Hall were retained from the Broadway cast for the film, with James Shigata, Nancy Kwan, Benson Fong, and Jack Soo in the other leads.

The show has never had a major revival, probably due to the difficulties in casting. Later musicals featuring Asian casts include *Pacific Overtures* (1976) and *Miss Saigon* (1991).

A MAJORITY OF ONE

by Leonard Spigelgass

Opened February 16, 1959

556 Performances

Shubert Theatre

Directed by Dore Schary

Produced by Dore Schary and The Theatre Guild

Cast: Gertrude Berg (Mrs. Jacoby); Cedric Hardwicke (Koichi Asano); Ina Balin (Alice Black); Michael Tolan (Jerome Black); Mae Questel (Mrs. Rubin); Kanna Ishii (Ayako Asano); Marc Marno (Eddie); Tsuruko Kobayashi (Tateshi); Sahomi Tachibana (Noketi); Yasuko Adachi (Servant Girl); Barnard Hughes (Capt. Norcross); Selma Halpern (Lady Passenger); Arsenio Trinidad (House Boy/Chauffeur).

The third Broadway hit of the season to feature an Asian theme and setting was Leonard Spigelgass's *A Majority of One*. A sort of middle-aged, East–West *Romeo and Juliet* story, the comedy detailed the budding romance between Jewish widow Mrs. Jacoby and Japanese business tycoon Koichi Asano.

They meet on a cruise ship bound for Tokyo, where Mrs. Jacoby's son-in-law Jerome Black is to embark on a diplomatic mission. At first, they do not get along. Mrs. Jacoby's son was killed by the Japanese during World War II. Mr. Asano's daughter perished in the atom bomb attack on Hiroshima. Gradually, this odd couple forgets their wounds and spends time together in the Japanese capital. It turns out that Jerome's mission involves acquiring a trade agreement with Asano's company. Jerome suspects that the businessman is courting his mother-in-law merely to gain an advantage in the talks. When the widow's daughter and son-in-law object to the relationship, she agrees to stop seeing Asano. This in turn causes Asano to break off talks with the American delegation. Mrs. Jacoby visits Asano again and convinces him to resume negotiations. The play ends with the middle-aged heroine returning to Brooklyn, and Asano following as a delegate to the United Nations. The question of their marrying is left open to speculation.

While not a masterpiece, the gentle comedy provided warm humor and a touching plea for interracial harmony. Despite the improbale plot and a cool critical reception, *A Majority of One* ran for 556 performances.

One of the reasons for the show's long run was the presence of Gertrude Berg in the female lead. Berg was an audience favorite, having come into American living rooms on a weekly basis, first on radio and then on television, as Molly Goldberg, the lovable matriarch of *The Goldbergs* series. She won a Tony Award as Best Actress for *Majority*. Her suitor was played by the English character actor Sir Cedric Hardwicke. Molly Picon and Robert Morley were in the leads in the London edition.

In a stroke of bizarre casting, elegant comedienne Rosalind Russell played the earthy Mrs. Jacoby in the 1961 film version. Another Englishman, the great character actor Alec Guinness was her Japanese love interest.

A musical version of *Majority* called *Hot Sake with a Pinch of Salt* was produced off-Broadway in 1986 in a showcase presentation.

The 1958–59 season was a rarity in the number of Asian plays and musicals and the opportunities for Asian actors they produced. Even with the relatively large number of Asian roles available, many leading ones were filled by Caucasians.

The situation has improved somewhat on Broadway today, and off-Broadway the Pan Asian Repertory Theatre, founded in 1977, provides a creative home for Asian performers, dramatists, and directors.

A RAISIN IN THE SUN

by Lorraine Hansberry

Opened March 11, 1959

530 Performances

Ethel Barrymore Theatre

Directed by Lloyd Richards

Produced by Philip Rose and David J. Cogan

Cast: Sidney Poitier (Walter Lee Younger); Claudia MacNeil (Lena Younger); Ruby Dee (Ruth Younger); Diana Sands (Beneatha Younger); Louis Gossett (George Murchison); Ivan Dixon (Joseph Asagai); Glynn Turman (Travis Younger); John Fiedler (Karl Linder); Lonne Elder III (Bobo); Ed Hall, Douglas Turner (Moving Men).

The Broadway production of *A Raisin in the Sun* boasted many firsts. It was the first play written, directed, and acted by African-Americans to have a run of over 500 performances. It was also the first play by an African-American to win the New York Drama Critics Circle Award. The playwright Lorraine Hansberry, at age twenty-nine, was the youngest recipient of the citation. It was her first play. Born in Chicago, Hansberry was writing for the New York newspaper *Freedom* when she came up with the idea for the drama.

The title was derived from a poem by Langston Hughes: "What happens to a dream deferred?/Does it dry up/Like a raisin in the sun? . . . /*Or does it explode?*" Each of the Youngers of the play has a dream. Lena, the matriarch, envisions the family leaving their tenement apartment to move into a cozy house. Son Walter Lee has plans to buy partnership in a liquor store and become a well-heeled businessman. Sister Beneatha is studying for a career in medicine.

An insurance check from Lena's late husband can make all their ambitions a reality. But when Walter's prospective partner absconds with most of the money, the family's future seems shattered.

Supporting characters represent other facets of the black experience. Joseph Asagai, an African emigré studying at Beneatha's university, serves as a reminder of the family's roots. George Murchison, another of Beneatha's beaus, is a scion of the new black upper middle class. Karl Linder, the only white character and an emissary from the neighborhood the family wishes to move into, symbolizes the forces of prejudice as he makes the Youngers a cash offer not to enter his community. The family rejects Linder's proposal in order to realize a part of their dream by living in their own home.

Sidney Poitier confronts his mother, played by Claudia MacNeil, in *A Raisin in the Sun*.

A Raisin in the Sun came along at a time when white middle-class America witnessed the heightened struggles of blacks to gain equal recognition under the law. The Civil Rights movement was provoking backlashes, and families like the Youngers were being bombed out of their houses. Protestors against segregation were brutalized in front of news cameras. *Raisin* showed the faces behind the disturbing headlines.

Sidney Poitier and Ruby Dee were already well-known names, but the rest of the original cast all went on to bright futures in show business as well. Louis Gossett later won the Oscar for *An Officer and a Gentleman.* Ivan Dixon and Glynn Turnman became regulars on television series. Lonne Elder III wrote the play *Ceremonies in Dark Old Men.* Douglas Turner (he later added Ward to his surname) became artistic director of the Negro Ensemble Company and wrote *Happy Ending* and *Day of Absence,* two one-acts which had a long run off-Broadway.

Ossie Davis, Ruby Dee's husband, replaced Poitier during the Broadway run of *Raisin.* Most of the original cast re-created their roles in the 1961 Columbia film version.

Tragically, Lorraine Hansberry's career did not extend far beyond her initial success. Her next play was *The Sign in Sidney Brustein's Window* (1965). It ran for 101 performances, closing the day after its author died of cancer at the age of thirty-four.

The playwright's husband, Robert Nemiroff, later co-wrote the book of the musical version of Hansberry's first play; entitled *Raisin,* it opened on Broadway in 1973.

The twenty-fifth anniversary of the original production was marked by numerous revivals in regional theatres during the 1983–84 season. The Roundabout Theatre Company's mounting ran off-Broadway and starred Olivia Cole. It was televised by PBS's *American Playhouse* series in 1989, with Esther Rolle and Danny Glover in the leads.

GYPSY

by Arthur Laurents, suggested by the memoirs of Gypsy Rose Lee.

Music by Jule Styne

Lyrics by Stephen Sondheim

Opened May 21, 1959

702 Performances

Broadway Theatre

Directed and choreographed by Jerome Robbins

Produced by David Merrick and Leland Hayward

Cast: Ethel Merman (Rose); Jack Klugman (Herbie); Sandra Church (Louise); Lane Bradbury (June); Paul Wallace (Tulsa); Maria Karnilova (Tessie Tura); Faith Dane (Mazeppa); Chotzi Foley (Electra); Marilyn Cooper (Agnes); Karen Moore (Baby Louise); Jacqueline Mayro (Baby June); Peg Murray (Miss Crachit); Mort Marshall (Uncle Jocko/Mr. Goldstone); Erv Harmon (Pop); Joe Silver (Weber/Phil); David Winters (Yonkers); Ian Tucker (Angie); Michael Parks (L.A.); Loney Lewis (Kringlein/Cigar).

Mama Rose in *Gypsy* was the role of a lifetime for Ethel Merman. Usually her assignments required little more than standing center stage and belting out song after song to the balcony. This time she showed she could act as well as project her voice to New Jersey.

Another aspect of the show that set it apart from other Merman vehicles was the nature of the leading role. Rose was not the friendly, overzealous good old gal the star normally portrayed. She was a bossy, domineering "stage mother" who drives almost everyone she loves away from her. Based on the autobiography of the stripper Gypsy Rose Lee (star of a long-running hit, *Star and Garter*), the musical follows the careers of Rose and her two daughters, June and Louise, as they trudge through every two-bit vaudeville house in the country. Eventually the talented June runs away, and the pitiful remains of the act winds up on the bill of a burlesque joint. The shy Louise finds her nitch as a stripper and becomes the fabulous Gypsy Rose Lee. In the final number, "Rose's Turn," Rose takes to the empty burlesque stage to prove that she's a bigger star than either of her offspring. Tearing through reprises of almost every song in the show, including the show-stopping "Everything's Coming up Roses," the flinty mother reveals that she's just an insecure child craving to be noticed.

Both Irving Berlin and Cole Porter were approached to write the songs, but turned the offer down. Director Jerome Robbins had been contracted to stage an upcoming musical based on ancient Roman farces by Plautus, *A Funny Thing Happened on the Way to the Forum* (1962), with a score by his *West Side Story* collaborator, Stephen Sondheim. The director loved the two songs Sondheim had written for *Forum,* so he recommended that the young man do the *Gypsy* score. Merman did not want a novice to provide her with songs. It was fine with her if Sondheim wrote the lyrics, but she required an experienced professional for the music. Sondheim was resistant to a "words-only" job, but his mentor Oscar Hammerstein advised him that writing for a star of Merman's caliber would be a valuable lesson. Veteran tunesmith Jule Styne signed on to compose the music.

For the role of Herbie, Rose's love interest and manager of the act, it was decided to choose an actor rather than a singer. Jack Klugman had never been in a musical before, but he had the right combination of rough intensity and sincerity to play opposite Merman. Despite Klugman's lack of vocal ability, he and Merman clicked. *Gypsy* was lauded by the critics, ran for a year and a half, and toured successfully with Merman. Given the quality of the reviews and the star's once-in-a-lifetime acting, the producers and authors were disappointed that it did not have the run of *Oklahoma!* or *My Fair Lady.* The show's respectable but less-than-smash run can be attributed to the unlikability of the characters.

with a regular supply of chairs, since at least three were broken every week. The actresses had to wear special padding to avoid injury.

During the run of the play, Duke's name was elevated above the title, making her the youngest performer on Broadway to receive star billing.

Bancroft and Duke recreated their roles in the 1962 screen version, winning Oscars as Best Actress and Supporting Actress. At fourteen, Duke was the youngest person ever to win an Academy Award. (Her record was later beaten by ten-year-old Tatum O'Neal for *Paper Moon* in 1973.) Duke returned to *The Miracle Worker* in a 1979 TV-movie remake. This time she played Annie Sullivan and won an Emmy. Melissa Gilbert was Helen.

Gibson wrote a sequel to the play entitled *Monday After the Miracle*, which opened on Broadway in 1982 with Jane Alexander and Karen Allen as the older Annie and Helen. It received lukewarm notices and closed after seven performances. Allen later played Sullivan in a 1987 revival of *The Miracle Worker* at off-Broadway's Roundabout Theatre.

THE TENTH MAN

by Paddy Chayefsky
Opened November 5, 1959
623 Performances
Booth Theatre
Directed by Tyrone Guthrie
Produced by Saint Subber and Arthur Cantor

Cast: Donald Harron (Arthur Brooks); Risa Schwartz (Evelyn Foreman); Arnold Marle (Hirschmann); David Vardi (Sexton); Lou Jacobi (Schlissel); Jack Gilford (Zitorsky); George Voskovec (Alper); Jacob Ben-Ami (Foreman); Martin Garner (Harris); Gene Saks (Rabbi); Alan Manson, Paul Marin (Kessler Boys); Tim Callaghan (Policeman).

Paddy Chayefsky's *The Tenth Man*, his longest-running theatrical work, was neither strictly naturalistic like his famous television dramas (*Marty*) nor darkly comic like his screenplays (*Network*), but a serious examination of religious faith in a skeptical world.

The setting is a ramshackle synagogue in Mineola, Long Island. The principal worshippers are a group of old men who come to temple more out of habit and the desire to gossip than piety. They are short of the necessary ten men, called a minyan, for a proper service. The sexton grabs Arthur Brooks, a young man off the street, to fulfill the quorum. Arthur is a spiritually aimless lawyer, ambling along the streets after suffering numerous emotional crises. Then one of the regular congregation enters with his disturbed granddaughter. He believes the girl is possessed by a dybbuk, a wandering spirit caught between this world and the next.

The young man is in the grip of a spirit as well, that of discontent and lovelessness. The old men decide to perform an exorcism, but it is not the girl who is relieved of her affliction, but Arthur. He pledges to love the girl and cure her of her sickness, whether it be psychological or supernatural.

There were some contrivances in Chayefsky's script, but audiences and reviewers hailed its thought-provoking questions and touches of humor. "My daughter-in-law, may she grow rich and buy a hotel with a thousand rooms and be found dead in every one," is one of the many homey imprecations used by the congregants.

The Irish director Tyrone Guthrie, known mostly for his productions of the classics, mounted this Jewish-themed play. The cast included many names associated with the Yiddish-language theatre: Jacob Ben-Ami was a star on the Yiddish stage, while Risa Schwartz, who played his possessed granddaughter, was the daughter of Maurice Schwartz, another veteran of that theatrical subculture.

There was some confusion for theatregoers between *The Tenth Man* and *The Best Man*, Gore Vidal's political drama, which had several characters supposedly based on real officeholders. There were several stories of customers ordering tickets for the wrong show. One anecdote told of a lady who went to *The Tenth Man* and remarked afterward "Which one was supposed to be Nixon?"

There were revivals of the play: in 1967, at City Center; in 1980, at the American Jewish Theatre; and in 1989, at Lincoln Center Theatre, with Bob Dishy, Phoebe Cates, Joseph Wiseman, and Jack Weston.

THE SOUND OF MUSIC

Book by Howard Lindsay and Russel Crouse, based on *The Von Trapp Family Singers* by Maria von Trapp.
Lyrics by Oscar Hammerstein II
Music by Richard Rodgers
Opened November 16, 1959
1,443 Performances
Lunt–Fontanne Theatre
Directed by Vincent J. Donehue
Choreographed by Joe Layton
Produced by Leland Hayward, Richard Halliday, Richard Rodgers, and Oscar Hammerstein II.

Cast: Mary Martin (Maria); Theodore Bikel (Capt. Von Trapp); Patricia Neway (Mother Abbess); Kurt Kasznar (Max Detweiler); Marion Marlowe (Elsa Schraeder); Brian Davies (Rolf Gruber); Laurie Peters (Liesl); William Snowden (Friedrich); Kathy Dunn (Louisa); Joseph Stewart (Kurt); Marilyn Rogers (Brigitta); Mary Susan Locke (Marta); Evanna Lien (Gretl); John Randolph (Franz); Nan McFarland (Frau Schmidt); Elizabeth Howell (Sister Berthe); Muriel O'Malley (Sister Margaretta); Karen Shepard (Sister Sophia); Luce Ennis (Ursula); Stefan Gierasch (Herr Zeller); Kirby Smith (Baron Elberfeld); Sue Yeager (Postulant); Michael Gorrin (Admiral Von Schreiber).

The Sound of Music marked the end and near-end of two of Broadway's most prolific and successful partnerships. It would be the last show for songwriter-producers

Richard Rodgers and Oscar Hammerstein and the penultimate production for playwrights Howard Lindsay and Russel Crouse.

Set in 1938 Austria, the musical tells the true story of Maria, a postulant at Nonnberg Abbey, who becomes a governess to the lonely children of Captain Von Trapp, a gruff widower. As Maria gradually reawakens the spirit of the Von Trapp offspring through music lessons, she finds herself falling in love with their father. They marry, the new family becomes a singing ensemble and, with the aid of the Nonnberg nuns, they escape the persecution of the Nazis by climbing over the mountains to Switzerland.

Director Vincent J. Donehue had screened a German-language film about the Von Trapps and immediately recognized its potential for the stage, with Mary Martin in the lead. With Leland Hayward and Martin's husband Richard Halliday as producers, the project began to take shape. The original concept was to stage it as a straight play by Lindsay and Crouse, with authentic Tyrolean folk songs and perhaps one original tune by Rodgers and Hammerstein.

The duo balked at a mixed-score show; such shows never worked. It should be all-new or all-old, not a hybrid. Martin agreed to having Rodgers and Hammerstein write an original score, thrilled to be reunited with the men responsible for *South Pacific*'s songs. The duo also signed on as producers, bringing the total to four. Since the songwriting team was busy with *Flower Drum Song*, *Sound of Music* would be their only production in which Hammerstein did not contribute to the book. The score would be completed after Lindsay and Crouse had done their work and *Flower Drum Song* had blossomed on Broadway.

The songs included such evergreen standards as "My Favorite Things," "Do-Re-Mi," "Climb Every Mountain," and "Edelweiss," Hammerstein's final lyric.

Like *The Music Man*, *The Sound of Music* was assailed by a few reviewers as being overly sentimental. But like the Meredith Willson show, it was an audience favorite. The Tony Awards that year were dominated by *The Sound of Music* and the totally different *Fiorello!*, a sharp musical biography of a popular New York mayor. The two shows shared the Best Musical award in a tie. *The Sound of Music* was up for a total of nine Tonys, and won four. The Tony nominating committee considered all the Von Trapp children as a unit and nominated them for Best Featured Actress in a Musical—despite the fact that two of them were boys!

Martha Wright, Jeannie Carson, and Nancy Dussault played Maria during the Broadway run. Florence Henderson headed the touring company.

Hammerstein died of cancer nine months after the opening. Rodgers provided his own lyrics for his next project, *No Strings (1962)*. Lindsay and Crouse went on to write the libretto for one more musical, the mediocre *Mister President* (1962).

Theodore Bikel and Mary Martin harmonize in *The Sound of Music*.

The 1965 film of *The Sound of Music* from 20th-Century Fox was much more successful and became one of the highest-grossing films ever. The cast included Julie Andrews, Christopher Plummer, Eleanor Parker, Richard Haydn, Peggy Wood, and Marni Nixon (a veteran voice-dubber for stars, but this time playing an actual part). Three songs were dropped, and replaced by two new ones ("I Have Confidence" and "Something Good") with both words and music by Rodgers.

The 1990 revival at New York City Opera, directed by Hammerstein's son James, starred Debbie Boone and Laurence Guittard.

FIORELLO!

Book by Jerome Weidman and George Abbott

Music by Jerry Bock

Lyrics by Sheldon Harnick

Opened November 23, 1959

796 Performances

Broadhurst Theatre

Directed by George Abbott

Choreographed by Peter Gennaro

Produced by Robert Griffith and Harold Prince

Cast: Tom Bosley (Fiorello); Patricia Wilson (Marie); Ellen Hanley (Thea); Howard da Silva (Ben); Mark Dawson (Floyd); Nathaniel Frey (Morris); Pat Stanley (Dora); Eileen Rodgers (Mitzi); Bob Holiday (Neil); Michael Scrittorale (Frankie Scarpini/Heckler/2nd Man); Helen Verbit (Mrs. Pomerantz); H.F. Green (Mr. Lopez); David Collyer (Mr. Zappatella); Del Horstmann (Ed Peterson); Pat Turner (Nina); Lynn Ross (Sophie); Mara Landi (Secretary); Deedy Irwin (Florence); Stanley Simmonds (2nd Player); Michael Quinn (3rd Player/Commissioner); Ron Husman (4th Player); David London (5th Player/Tough Man); Julian Patrick (6th Player/Reporter); Joseph Toner (Seedy Man/Heckler/Judge Carter); Frederic Downs (Senator); Bob Bernard (Heckler/Derby); Scott Hunter (1st Man); Jim Maher (Heckler).

As the curtain rose on opening night for the musical *Fiorello!* at the Broadhurst Theatre, the audience burst into spontaneous applause. They were not clapping in recognition of any big stars in the cast, since there were none. Nor were they showing appreciation for the scenery, for the only piece of furniture onstage was a small desk. The object of their affection was the character sitting behind that desk: a short, rotund man narrating the funny papers into a radio microphone.

That little man was Tom Bosley, in the role of Fiorello La Guardia, beloved mayor of New York City from 1934 to 1946. The scene recreated La Guardia's famous reading of "Dick Tracy" and "Little Orphan Annie" to the children of the city during a newspaper strike. Known as "The Little Flower," a literal translation of his first name, La Guardia was an extremely popular mayor, ending the reign of corrupt Tammany Hall politics with his twelve years in office. The musical covered the period of 1914 to 1933, from La Guardia's beginnings as a Greenwich Village lawyer,

through his election to Congress, his service as an airman in World War I, his first unsuccessful mayoral bid against Tammany hack Jimmy Walker, and his second run to defeat Walker, this one resulting in his election. Interspersed with the political scenes were romantic interludes depicting La Guardia's love life. He meets his first wife, Thea, while she is arrested during a strike. She later becomes ill and dies. The politician's second campaign coincides with a second marriage to his faithful secretary, Marie.

The idea for the show originated with director Arthur Penn, who sold producers Robert Griffith and Harold Prince on the notion of a musical on the Little Flower. Jerome Weidman, a friend of Griffith and author of the novel *I Can Get It for You Wholesale*, was contracted for the book. Penn did not like Weidman's efforts, judging his libretto was too light and sentimental. The producers disagreed, stating that a heavier psychological treatment would be wrong for the bouncy La Guardia. Penn left the project but maintained a one-percent interest in the box office. Griffith and Prince then asked their old mentor George Abbott to come aboard as director and co-author. Once he began work on the book, Abbott shifted the emphasis from first wife Thea to second wife Marie and her lifelong devotion to Fiorello.

A composer–lyricist team was then signed on, but not together. The first to be hired was Jerry Bock, composer of the Sammy Davis, Jr. vehicle, *Mr. Wonderful*, and *The Body Beautiful*. Sheldon Harnick was the final choice for wordsmith after Stephen Sondheim turned down the position. Harnick began a partnership with Bock that continued with *Tenderloin* (1960), *She Loves Me* (1963), *Fiddler on the Roof* (1964), *The Apple Tree,* (1966) and *The Rothschilds* (1970).

Eli Wallach and Mickey Rooney were discussed as possible candidates for the lead, but a large talent search turned up Tom Bosley, a little-known actor with off-Broadway and TV credits. Standing at 5'7" and weighing 170 pounds, the thirty-two-year-old actor bore a striking physical resemblance to the mayor. Bosley strove for an impression of boundless energy and enthusiasm, rather than imitating La Guardia's voice and manner.

At the end of the season, *Fiorello!* won both the Drama Critics Circle and Tony Award (in a tie with *The Sound of Music* for the latter). It was also the third musical after *Of Thee I Sing* and *South Pacific* to win the Pulitzer Prize.

There have been two other musicals about New York mayors: *Jimmy*, with Frank Gorshin as La Guardia's opponent Jimmy Walker, had a brief run in 1969. The off-Broadway revue *Mayor* poked gentle fun at Edward Koch, then City Hall's occupant, in 1985. Also, Tony LoBianco played the Little Flower in a 1989 nonmusical one-man show entitled *Hizzoner*.

THE 1960s

The social upheavals of the '60s were not apparent in most long-running Broadway shows, which, even after the trail-blazing of Tennessee Williams and Arthur Miller, still catered to audiences that were considered comfortable, middle-class, and inclined to escapist diversions. The revolutionary rock musical *Hair* was one of the few hits to indicate that sweeping changes were going on outside the theatre doors. But the theatre was far more daring than movies or television. Nudity and coarse language became elements in many productions towards the end of the decade. ✮ After a series of sharp one-acts, Edward Albee burst onto Broadway with his marital witches' brew, *Who's Afraid of Virginia Woolf?*. Veterans Williams and Miller were not as successful; with few exceptions, their newer works were not able to sustain sufficient audience interest for profitable runs. Off-Broadway and its younger cousin off-off-Broadway became a force for alternative theatre. Sam Shepard, Lanford Wilson, Leroi Jones, Ed Bullins, Israel Horovitz, Leonard Melfi, and Charles Ludlum were among its diverse, startlingly new writing talents. ✮ Neil Simon, a brilliantly funny playwright who appealed to more conventional tastes, first made the Broadway scene with *Come Blow Your Horn* and hasn't stopped writing hit shows since. His tally sheet for the decade included the plays *Barefoot in the Park, The Odd Couple, Plaza Suite*, and *Last of the Red Hot Lovers*, and the musicals *Sweet Charity* and *Promises, Promises.* ✮ *Fiddler on the Roof* and *Hello, Dolly!* broke musical comedy records for long runs. *Dolly*'s producer David Merrick became the dominant showman on Broadway, presenting ten of the decade's hits. ✮ With production costs rising, single-set, small-cast productions became popular and profitable. Most of these more intimate presentations were comedies which dealt with sexual matters: *Mary, Mary, Any Wednesday, Luv, The Impossible Years, Cactus Flower, You Know I Can't Hear You When the Water's Running*, and *Forty Carats.* ✮ Long-running serious plays were in short supply. *A Man for All Seasons, Virginia Woolf, The Subject Was Roses* and *The Great White Hope* were the only dramas to play over 500 Broadway performances.

TOYS IN THE ATTIC

by Lillian Hellman

Opened February 25, 1960

556 Performances

The Hudson Theatre

Directed by Arthur Penn

Produced by Kermit Bloomgarden

Cast: Maureen Stapleton (Carrie Berniers); Anne Revere (Anna Berniers); Jason Robards (Julian Berniers); Irene Worth (Albertine Prine); Rochelle Oliver (Lily Berniers); Percy Rodriguez (Henry Simpson); Charles McRae (Gus).

At the end of the 1950s, Lillian Hellman was experiencing writer's block. Her last work, *Candide* (1956), an operetta with music by Leonard Bernstein, based on Voltaire's 18th-century satire, was regarded as a failure. Her unfriendly testimony before the House Un-American Activities Committee had almost completely blacklisted her from working in the movie industry.

It was her companion Dashiell Hammett who suggested the idea that broke the block and became *Toys in the Attic*, her second-longest running play after *The Children's Hour*. In order to put a stop to her creative dry spell, Hammett gave the playwright the premise of a man who makes good at the insistence of his family. But his relatives don't like him as a success, preferring that he remain weak and dependent on them. So he destroys his good fortune and becomes a worse failure than before. Hellman took this simple concept and, adding elements from her own childhood, expanded it into a powerful Southern drama heavy with detailed plot and Freudian psychology.

Julian Berniers returns with his young bride Lily to the New Orleans boarding house of his two sisters, Carrie and Anna. The sisters have bailed him out of many failed financial schemes, including a shoe business in which Lily's wealthy mother, Mrs. Albertine Prine, invested. But this time Julian is rich, no longer requiring his siblings' largesse or that of Lily's mother. Carrie, Anna, and Lily find that they must have Julian dependent on them. Now that he no longer needs them for money, they fear he will

Jason Robards attempts to buy the affections of his sisters Maureen Stapleton and Anne Revere in *Toys in the Attic*.

stop needing them emotionally. With Carrie's compliance, Lily ruins her husband's new-found wealth and future plans.

Like Hellman's earlier *Little Foxes, Toys'* central theme is that of the power of money to control and destroy lives. Each of the characters seeks to buy and sell love through material gain and security. All, that is, except for Albertine, the only truly mature and self-possessed person on stage. The character was based on the author's Aunt Lilly who, like Albertine, had a black male servant for a lover. The sensational topic of incest was also employed: Anna accuses Carrie of wanting to sleep with their brother.

Anne Revere, an original cast member of Hellman's first play, *The Children's Hour,* and a fellow victim of blacklisting, played Carrie. Jason Robards and Maureen Stapleton were her siblings. Four of the cast were nominated for Tonys (Revere won a Best Featured Actress award), and the play was voted Best American Play by the New York Drama Critics Circle. The touring company starred Scott McKay, Patricia Jessel, Constance Bennett, and Revere. *Toys* was not as well-received in London (where critics blasted it) or on screen.

The 1963 movie version starred a miscast Dean Martin as Julian; Wendy Hiller and Geraldine Page contributed their considerable skills as the smothering sisters.

THE BEST MAN

by Gore Vidal

Opened March 31, 1960

520 Performances

Morosco Theatre

Directed by Joseph Anthony

Produced by The Playwrights Company

Cast: Melvyn Douglas (William Russell); Frank Lovejoy (Joe Cantwell); Lee Tracy (Art Hockstader); Leora Dana (Alice Russell); Kathleen Maguire (Mabel Cantwell); Karl Weber (Dick Jensen); Ruth McDevitt (Mrs. Gamadge); Joseph Sullivan (Bill Blades); Graham Jarvis (Sheldon Marcus); Gordon B. Clarke (Senator Carlin); Hugh Franklin (Dr. Artinian); Martin Fried (Mike); Howard Fischer (1st Reporter); Tony Bickley (2nd Reporter); Barbara Berjer (3rd Reporter); Tom McDermott (4th Reporter); Ruth Maynard (Asst. to Dick Jensen).

At the age of thirty-four, the witty and erudite Gore Vidal had written eight novels, almost thirty television plays, six screenplays, including *Ben-Hur* and *Suddenly, Last Summer,* and a Broadway play, *Visit to a Small Planet,* a clever comedy combining the flying saucer craze with political satire. In 1960, the prolific author landed with *The Best Man,* a hit comedy-drama chronicling the rivalry for the Presidential nomination at a national party convention. Life imitated art during the run of the play, as Vidal launched his own campaign to represent Dutchess County, his New York district, in Congress. "You'll get more with Gore" was his campaign slogan.

As Vidal waged his real campaign, *The Best Man*'s candidates were entertaining theatregoers with their fictitious one. William Russell, a former Secretary of State and liberal, has sound ideals, but a personal life which spells political poison. His troubles include a break-up with his wife and regular visits to a psychiatrist (a shocking weakness in 1960). His main opponent, Senator Joseph Cantwell, is a ruthless opportunist who gauges his stands on the issues by consulting the latest polls. Both are seeking the blessing of former President Art Hockstader, a popular "man of the people." Deals, blackmail, and careers are made and broken during the course of the convention. Russell finally realizes that he can't win, but that he can't allow the shallow Cantwell to triumph either. In the last scene, Russell proves himself "the best man" by throwing his support behind a dark-horse candidate who gets the nomination.

There was great speculation as to whom the fictional candidates were meant to represent. Many thought Russell was based on two-time Democratic presidential hopeful Adlai Stevenson, while an equal number figured Cantwell was a stand-in for Vice President Richard Nixon. Harry S Truman was thought to be the model for Art Hockstader.

Vidal denied any intention of copying real-life pols. He told the *New York Tribune,* "To put it in hideously simple terms, there are three archetypes in American politics: the great hick, the smooth opportunist, and the man of conscience. These were the people I tried to show."

Melvyn Douglas went from playing a character based on President Warren G. Harding in *The Gang's All Here* to candidate Russell. Ironically, Douglas's wife Helen Gahagen Douglas ran against, and lost to, Richard Nixon in the 1950 California senatorial race. For Cantwell, handsome movie star and TV-tough guy Frank Lovejoy was chosen. Art Hockstader was played by Lee Tracy, veteran of such '20s Broadway hits as *The Show-Off* and *Broadway.*

While the play was a hit, the playwright's real-life campaign was not. Democrat Vidal lost the mostly Republican district.

The author wrote the screenplay for the 1964 filmization, with Henry Fonda as Russell running against Cliff Robertson's Cantwell. Lee Tracy was in for another term as the former President. Edie Adams, Margaret Leighton, Kevin McCarthy, Ann Sothern, and Shelly Berman played assorted wives, aides, and delegates.

The Best Man was too relevant to its time to be revived. The methods of campaigning depicted are out of date. Today, each party's nominee for President is usually chosen in the primaries rather than in the smoke-filled rooms of conventions. Political dramas are evidently outmoded as well. Aside from *State of the Union* (1945) and *Affairs of State* (1950), Vidal's work is the only play of its genre to win a term of over 500 performances.

BYE, BYE, BIRDIE

Book by Michael Stewart

Music by Charles Strouse

Lyrics by Lee Adams

Opened April 14, 1960

607 Performances

Martin Beck Theatre

Directed by Gower Champion

Choreographed by Gower Champion

Produced by Edward Padula

Cast: Dick Van Dyke (Albert Peterson); Chita Rivera (Rose Grant); Kay Medford (Mae Peterson); Dick Gautier (Conrad Birdie); Susan Watson (Kim MacAfee); Paul Lynde (Mr. MacAfee); Michael J. Pollard (Hugo Peabody); Barbara Doherty (Ursula Merkle); Marijane Maricle (Mrs. MacAfee); Johnny Borden (Randolph MacAfee); Norma Richardson (Gloria Rasputin); Will Jordan (Ed Sullivan's Voice); Charles Nelson Reilly (Mr. Henkle); Allen Knowles (Mayor); Amelia Haas (Mayor's Wife); George Blackwell (Charles F. Maude); Sharon Lerit (Sad Girl); Karin Wolfe (Another Sad Girl); Kenny Burrell (Guitar Man); Kasimir Kokich (Conductor); Pat McEnnis (Mrs. Merkle); Dori Davis (Old Woman); Tony Mordente (TV Stage Manager).

The rock 'n' roll phenomenon belatedly reached Broadway just after the decade in which it started was over. *Bye, Bye, Birdie* satirized the music craze with its screaming teenagers. Conrad Birdie, the show's hip-swiveling singing idol, was based on Elvis Presley.

Everything is rosy for Dick Van Dyke and Chita Rivera in *Bye, Bye, Birdie.*

Birdie was the brainchild of Edward Padula, a stage manager with ambitions of becoming a producer. He wanted to put together a musical employing the "new sound" of rock 'n' roll and featuring a cast of mostly teenagers. Composer Charles Strouse and lyricist Lee Adams, whose credits included *The Shoestring Revue*, were hired for the songs. Several librettists were tried before Michael Stewart, a writer on the Sid Caesar television show, was given the job.

Under the title *Let's Go Steady*, the show went through many rewrites without a main focus. Then reality gave the writers and producer a cue. In 1958, Elvis Presley was drafted into the Army and his legion of fans were horrified. Padula and company decided to incorporate this story into their show. A new character, singing sensation Ellsworth Birdie (later changed to Conrad), was created. The teenage theme was supplanted by the story of Birdie's managers, Albert and Rose, scheming to create one last hit song so they can afford to lead a normal life together.

Padula explained his concept of the show to the *Philadelphia Inquirer* during out-of-town tryouts: "I wanted a contemporary spoof with a legitimate theatre score that had a dynamic beat in a broader and more popular vein." He saw the production as a comment on the youth of our times, but an upbeat one. He called *Birdie* "the antithesis of *West Side Story*," with its gangs and violence.

Chita Rivera, just back from the London production of *West Side*, was cast as Rose. Dick Van Dyke, a comedian seen on TV shows and in an unsuccessful revue, *The Boys Against the Girls*, earlier in the season, played Albert.

Gower Champion was making his debut as a director–choreographer of a book musical. His previous credits were for two revues. Among his inventive *Birdie* stagings were "The Telephone Hour," with teenagers in various pretzel-like positions chatting on the phone; Van Dyke cheering up two sad chorus girls in "Put on a Happy Face"; and Rivera breaking up a stuffy lodge meeting in "The Shriners' Ballet."

Dick Patterson and Gretchen Wyler toured the country in the road version, while Rivera and Peter Marshall bid Birdie bye-bye in London. The 1963 film version featured Van Dyke and Paul Lynde re-creating their original roles. Janet Leigh, Maureen Stapleton, Ann-Margaret, and Bobby Rydell completed the cast.

A 1981 sequel entitled *Bring Back Birdie,* with Donald O'Connor as Albert and Chita Rivera again as Rose, failed.

Despite its many dated references, *Birdie* is still popular. A 1991 touring production featuring Tommy Tune, Ann Reinking, and two new songs, was a smash hit.

Birdie was not, strictly speaking, a "rock" musical; most of the score was in the conventional Broadway mode. "Rock" would not totally dominate the music of a Broadway hit show until *Hair* opened eight years later.

IRMA LA DOUCE

Book and lyrics by Alexandre Breffort

English book and lyrics by Julian More, David Heneker, and Monty Norman

Music by Marguerite Monnot

Opened September 29, 1960

Plymouth Theatre

524 Performances

Directed by Peter Brook

Choreographed by Onna White

Produced by David Merrick

Cast: Elizabeth Seal (Irma La Douce); Clive Revill (Bob Le Hotu); Keith Michell (Nestor Le Fripe); Stuart Damon (Frangipane); George S. Irving (Police Inspector); Fred Gwynne (Polyte Le Mou); George Del Monte (M. Bougne/2nd Warder); Zack Matalon (Jojo Les Yeux Sales); Aric Lavie (Roberto Les Diams); Osborne Smith (Persil Le Noir); Rico Froehlich (Counsel for the Prosecution/3rd Warder); Rudy Tronto (Counsel for the Defense/Tax Inspector); Elliott Gould (Usher/1st Warder/Priest); Eddie Gasper (Client); Joe Rocco (Honest Man); Byron Mitchell (Court Gendarme).

Irma La Douce was the first Broadway book-musical hit to have originated in Paris (*Chauve-Souris* and *La Plume de Ma Tante* were plotless revues.) This ribald story was told with music by Marguerite Monnot and book and lyrics by former Parisian taxi driver Alexandre Breffort. It opened in 1956 in Paris and ran for four years. British director Peter Brook saw it and persuaded Julian More, David Heneker and Monty Norman to do an English rendering for the London stage, where it also proved popular.

David Merrick brought the British version across the Atlantic, along with leads Elizabeth Seal, Keith Michell, and Clive Revill. Seal, the only woman in the cast, played the title character, a hooker with the obligatory heart of gold. Michell was Nestor, a poor student in love with her. In order to keep her affections, he disguises himself as a rich aristocrat and buys all her time. When Irma begins to fall for his alter-ego, Nestor plots his "murder." Through laws of logic which only apply in musical comedy, Nestor is convicted of the imaginary wealthy man's death and sentenced to Devil's Island. Of course, he gets out, clears his name, and gets the girl. Revill was the sage narrator and acted various characters also. Elliott Gould and Fred Gwynne were in the cast, too, playing small roles.

For the busy Merrick, the show was the first hit of the season and of the '60s. In 1960–61 alone, he also produced the hit *Carnival,* the moderately successful *Do Re Mi,* two British imports, *A Taste of Honey* and *Becket,* and a flop revue, *Vintage 60.*

Aside from its Parisian origin, *Irma La Douce* can also boast being one of the few Broadway musicals to be composed by a woman. (There are several female lyricists, but not many composers.) It was also one of the few musical productions staged by Peter Brook, whose credits include *The Visit* (1958) with Alfred Lunt and Lynn Fontanne; the strikingly staged *Marat/Sade* (1965); and a famous, eye-

opening *Midsummer Night's Dream,* which conquered Broadway in 1970. His only other American musical was *House of Flowers* (1954), a short-lived show by Truman Capote and Harold Arlen.

The 1963 film version of *Irma La Douce* reunited *The Apartment* director-scenarist Billy Wilder and his stars Jack Lemmon and Shirley MacLaine. All the songs were removed, indicating the decrease in popularity of movie musicals, but André Previn adapted Monnot's score for the background music and won an Oscar.

Other Broadway shows about the world's oldest profession include *Anna Christie* (1921); *Anna Lucasta* (1944); and *The World of Suzie Wong* (1958). *Les Misérables* (1987) and *Miss Saigon* (1991) were the next Broadway musical hits by French authors.

Elizabeth Seal is about to burst Clive Revill's balloon as Keith Michell prepares for the explosion in *Irma La Douce.*

THE UNSINKABLE MOLLY BROWN

Book by Richard Morris

Music and lyrics by Meredith Willson

Opened November 3, 1960

Winter Garden Theatre

532 Performances

Directed by Dore Schary

Choreographed by Peter Gennaro

Produced by The Theatre Guild and Dore Schary

Cast: Tammy Grimes (Molly Tobin); Harve Presnell (Johnny Brown); Cameron Prud'homme (Shamus Tobin); Edith Meiser (Mrs. McGlone); Mony Dalmes (Princess De Long); Mitchell Gregg (Prince De Long); Christopher Hewett (Roberts); Patricia Kelly (Grand Duchess Marie Nicholaiovna); Sterling Clark (Michael Tobin); Bill Starr (Aloysius Tobin); Bob Daley (Patrick Tobin/Baron of Auld); Norman Fredericks (Father Flynn/Mr. Waldington); Woody Hurst (Charlie); Joseph Sirola (Christmas Morgan); Tom Larson (Burt); Billy Faier (Banjo); Joe Pronto (Gitter); Paul Floyd (Boy); Terry Violino (Sherriff); Jack Harrold (Monsignor Ryan); Dale Malone (Professor Gardella); Wanda Saxon (Countess); June Carol (Germaine); Michael Davis (Count Feranti); Barbara Newman (Duchess of Burlingame); Ted Adkins (Duke of Burlingame); Barney Johnston (Malcolm Broderick); Lynne Osborne (Mrs. Wadlington); Michael Davis (Young Waiter); Bobby Brownell (Page); Marvin Goodis (Male Passenger); Nada Rowand (Mother); Bill Starr (Wounded Sailor).

Meredith Willson followed up *The Music Man* with another folk-flavored piece of Americana. For *The Unsinkable Molly Brown*, however, he wrote only the songs, not the book.

The musical originated with television writer Richard Morris and producer-director Dore Schary, who wanted to do a show based on the real-life heroine Molly Toban Brown, a survivor of the Titanic. (That's where the "unsinkable" part comes in.) The story had previously been adapted as a television play starring Cloris Leachman, in 1955.

Morris and Schary hired Willson to provide the score. "I saw in it the things I believe fit my kind of interest," Willson told the *New York Times*. "Period Americana and the love story of two characters I could like. I said, 'If you'll take the cussin' out of there and be mindful of beautifyin' the love story, I'm your boy.'"

Molly rises from poverty in Hannibal, Missouri, to marry "Leadville" Johnny Brown, a prospector who strikes it rich during the Colorado Silver Strike at the turn of the century. Her one ambition is to be accepted by the upper crust. Snubbed by Denver society, the Browns voyage to Europe and become the toast of the Continent. Molly returns to the States with an entourage of royalty in tow, only to find herself still an outcast. The couple separate, as the determined Molly returns to Europe over Johnny's objections. She almost loses her husband, but gets him back after nearly drowning on the Titanic.

Like his songs for *Music Man*, Willson's *Molly* score had a distinctly American feel to it. The rousing march "I Ain't Down Yet" recalled "Seventy-Six Trombones," and rhythmic numbers like "Chick-a Pen" resembled "Pick-a-Little."

Waifish Tammy Grimes floated to stardom as the unsinkable title character. The actress had previously appeared on Broadway in Noël Coward's Feydeau adaptation, *Look After Lulu*, and off-Broadway in the revue *Phoenix '55*. Neither role compared to the workout she would receive in this show. She was onstage almost constantly, made sixteen costume changes requiring three dressers, and missed four Philadelphia tryout performances because of laryngitis. She even got splinters during a barefoot dance number. Choreographer Peter Gennaro would wait backstage with a pair of tweezers to remove them from Grimes's feet.

There were rumors that the creative team was not satisfied with her, but they were dispelled once the show opened in New York. Critics outdid themselves to describe the gamine Grimes's offbeat appeal and raspy voice. Walter Kerr of the *Herald-Tribune* went so far as to call her a genius.

She went on to win the Tony Award. Since her name was billed below the title she was considered a supporting actress, even though she was unquestionably playing the lead part.

The reviewers were not so laudatory about the production itself, calling the book weak and the leading lady the only strong point of the show. Despite the critical coolness, *Molly* kept her head above water for 532 performances, with Grimes remaining in the role during the entire run. Whether the show would have continued without its highly-touted star is doubtful.

Metro-Goldwyn-Mayer announced plans to film their own version of the same story entitled *The Unsinkable Mrs. Brown*. The authors of the Broadway musical strongly objected, protesting that the similar titles would ruin their business. Eventually, in 1964, 20th-Century Fox brought the Morris–Willson version to the screen, with Debbie Reynolds as Molly and Harve Presnell repeating his Broadway performance as Johnny. The MGM rendition was never made.

CAMELOT

Book and lyrics by Alan Jay Lerner, based on *The Once and Future King* by T.H. White.

Music by Frederick Loewe

Opened December 3, 1960

873 Performances

Majestic Theatre

Directed by Moss Hart

Choreographed by Hanya Holm

Produced by Alan Jay Lerner, Frederick Loewe, and Moss Hart

Cast: Richard Burton (Arthur); Julie Andrews (Guinevere); Robert Goulet (Lancelot); Robert Coote (King Pellinore); Roddy McDowall (Mordred); M'el Dowd (Morgan Le Fay); John Cullum (Sir Dinadan); Bruce Yarnell (Sir Lionel); David Hurst (Merlyn); Marjorie Smith (Nimue); Leland Mayforth (Page); Michael Clarke-Laurence (Dap); Richard Kuch (Clarius); Christina Gillespie (Lady Anne); Leesa Troy (Lady); James Gannon (Sir Sagramore); Peter De Vise (Page); John Starkweather (Herald); Virginia Allen (Lady Catherine); Michael Kermoyan (Sir Ozanna); Jack Dabdoub (Sir Gwilliam); Robin Stewart (Tom).

Alan Jay Lerner and Frederick Loewe recaptured some of their *My Fair Lady* success with *Camelot.* They utilized the services of the same director, Moss Hart, and once again, Julie Andrews was the leading lady, Robert Coote a comic supporting character, and an actor not known for his musical ability took the lead: Richard Burton did the speak-singing this time, rather than Rex Harrison.

Based on T.H. White's book *The Once and Future King,* the musical, set during the reign of King Arthur, focused on the illicit love between Arthur's queen, Guinevere, and his best friend and knight of the Round Table, Lancelot, played by handsome baritone Robert Goulet.

At first, too much of White's tome was crammed into the show. The running time was four and half hours when it opened in Toronto. "Only *Tristan and Isolde* equalled it as a bladder contest," Lerner quipped in his memoirs.

Robert Goulet, Julie Andrews, and Richard Burton form a medieval romantic triangle in *Camelot.*

The stress of the out-of-town tryout took its toll, as members of the creative team succumbed to illness. In Toronto, Lerner suffered a severe hemmorhage, which kept him out of commission for two weeks. On the day of his release from the hospital, Hart checked in with a heart attack. Broadway wags began to call the show a "medical" rather than a musical.

Loewe, who had already had his own heart attack after the songwriting team finished the film *Gigi*, urged Lerner to find a new director as soon as possible. But Lerner had promised Hart that he would not hire a successor. The lyricist carried on staging the show without receiving credit in the program. The disagreement over Hart drove a wedge between Lerner and Loewe. Although they did write four new songs for a 1973 stage version of *Gigi* and the score for the 1974 film *The Little Prince*, *Camelot* was their last full stage show together.

Despite conflicts between the authors, *Camelot* opened on Broadway in good shape. Yet the critics were divided. Most loved the score (which included the uplifting title song and Lancelot's gorgeous ballad "If Ever I Would Leave You"), but they came down hard on the uneven book. There was a huge advance sale because of the names involved, and then fewer orders were placed after the mixed notices appeared. Prospects for a long run appeared bleak until Ed Sullivan came to the rescue. A twenty-minute excerpt from the show on Sullivan's immensely popular TV variety show resulted in lines at the box office. A touring version, featuring William Squire, Kathryn Grayson, Robert Peterson, and Arthur Treacher went on to do well across the country.

The 1967 film, directed by Joshua Logan, featured Richard Harris, Vanessa Redgrave, and Franco Nero as the three sides of the medieval triangle.

Richard Burton returned to the show in a 1980 national tour, making a stop in New York. Illness struck the star, forcing Burton to be succeeded by Richard Harris, who also played Broadway in 1981. Robert Goulet switched to playing Arthur in a 1993 national tour that also briefly appeared on Broadway.

COME BLOW YOUR HORN

by Neil Simon

Opened February 22, 1961

677 Performances

Brooks Atkinson Theatre

Directed by Stanley Prager

Produced by William Hammerstein and Michael Ellis

Cast: Hal March (Alan Baker); Arlene Golonka (Peggy Evans); Warren Berlinger (Buddy Baker); Lou Jacobi (Mr. Baker); Sarah Marshall (Connie Dayton); Pert Kelton (Mrs. Baker); Carolyn Brenner (A Visitor).

Neil Simon began his reign as Broadway's top playwright with *Come Blow Your Horn*, which focuses on the Baker brothers. Older sibling Alan takes it upon himself to introduce his kid brother Buddy to the world of women. Constant interference from their Old-World parents and mix-ups as to whose girl is whose provided the comic conflicts.

The situation in the play paralleled Simon's relationship with his own older brother, Danny. The two had started out as comedy writers in radio and television. Among the top-name comics they supplied with material were Jerry Lewis, Red Buttons, Jackie Gleason, Phil Silvers, and Sid Caesar. They also contributed sketches to the Broadway revues *Catch a Star* (1955) and *New Faces of 1956*. Eventually, Danny migrated to California, where most of the television industry had moved. Neil, or "Doc" as his friends called him, remained in New York, writing for *The Garry Moore Show*, one of the few variety hours still telecast from the Big Apple. But Simon was not happy.

Some years later, he told *Newsweek*, "I knew I had to get out of television; I'd run into so many aging television writers who complained that their agents never got them the right job—a picture, a Broadway show. I knew if I wanted to do anything I'd have to do it myself. So I started writing *Come Blow Your Horn* during the evenings and on weekends, partly as an exercise, but partly in the hope that it would really work. I didn't want to start writing plays in my forties."

After fruitlessly peddling his script, Simon finally got an offer by Michael Ellis to have it presented at the Bucks County Playhouse in New Hope, Pennsylvania. After a successful tryout, it was brought to New York.

In a different interview for radio, Simon continued the story: "When *Come Blow Your Horn* went into rehearsal in the fall of 1961, I gave up my job on *The Garry Moore Show*. I burned bridges behind me, in a way, because if it failed I had given up a job on the only important comedy show which comes out of New York. To get into TV again I'd have to go to the Coast. That meant losing contact with New York and theatre."

The comedy's two-year run enabled Simon to quit television to concentrate on playwriting. His next effort was the book of a musical, *Little Me* (1962), which starred his old boss Sid Caesar in seven roles. His next play, *Barefoot in the Park*, opened and there began a nearly unbroken string of hits. Simon's output so far has included twenty-eight Broadway shows, of which sixteen have run over 500 performances.

Frank Sinatra and Tony Bill were the brothers in the 1963 film of the play, with Lee J. Cobb and Molly Picon as the parents.

MARY, MARY

by Jean Kerr

Opened March 8, 1961

1,572 performances

Helen Hayes Theatre

Directed by Joseph Anthony

Produced by Roger L. Stevens

Cast: Barbara Bel Geddes (Mary McKellaway); Barry Nelson (Bob McKellaway); Michael Rennie (Dirk Winston); Betsy von Furstenberg (Tiffany Richards); John Cromwell (Oscar Nelson).

Jean Kerr's *Mary, Mary* was one of the first and most successful of the long-running sex comedies which proliferated on Broadway during the '60s.

Mary of the title is indeed quite contrary, always ready with a sharp quip or retort. She and her ex-husband Bob are reunited to go over their taxes and tie up all the loose ends of their divorce. In the process of reviewing the paraphernalia of their marriage, they fall in love again. Despite the presence of Bob's young fiancée and advances toward Mary from a handsome movie star, the couple get back together. The slim plot was peppered with witty remarks on marriage, sex, taxes, Hollywood, food, and health fads.

Kerr was best known for her humorous articles on mostly domestic matters which were collected in two bestselling books, *Please Don't Eat the Daisies* and *The Snake Has All the Lines*. The former had been adapted into a film and would later become a television series. *Mary* was her first try at Broadway without a collaborator. Previous efforts included *King of Hearts* (1954), co-authored with Eleanor Brooks; sketches for revues; and the musical *Goldilocks* (1958), written with her husband Walter Kerr, the drama critic of the *New York Herald-Tribune*. The Kerrs were thought to be the models for the lead characters in Ira Levin's *Critic's Choice*, a comedy about a theatre reviewer and his playwright-wife, which opened the same season as *Mary, Mary*.

Barbara Bel Geddes and Barry Nelson were the reconciling couple; the film star was played by Michael Rennie, making his American stage debut.

"I wrote the part for Barbara," Kerr told her husband's newspaper. "I had seen her in *The Moon Is Blue*, and I thought she was adorable. I saw her later in some serious plays, and I kept wondering why nobody ever wrote a comedy for her. So I wrote one for her myself. At first I was a little reluctant about having Barry Nelson in the play, since he had also been in *The Moon Is Blue*, and I was afraid it might make my play seem like *Son of The Moon Is Blue*. But Barry is a fine actor and that seemed to be the most important consideration."

The play's single setting and small cast kept production costs down. This contributed to its phenomenal

Barbara Bel Geddes is driven crazy by ex-husband Barry Nelson in *Mary, Mary*.

1,572-performance run and its many productions on tour nationally and abroad. The leads were later played in New York by Diana Lynn, Tom Poston, and Edward Mulhare. Maggie Smith starred in the London production. Mervyn LeRoy directed the stagebound 1963 film adaptation, with Debbie Reynolds in the title role and Nelson and Rennie from the Broadway cast.

Kerr's later plays, *Poor Richard* (1964), starring Alan Bates and Gene Hackman, *Finishing Touches* (1973), again with Barbara Bel Geddes, and *Lunch Hour* (1980), with Gilda Radner, followed *Mary* in concept: small cast, one set, well-structured but light plot, heavy on the laughs.

CARNIVAL

Book by Michael Stewart, based on material by Helen Deutsch

Music and lyrics by Bob Merrill

Opened April 13, 1961

719 Performances

Imperial Theatre

Directed and choreographed by Gower Champion

Produced by David Merrick

Cast: Anna Maria Alberghetti (Lili); Jerry Orbach (Paul Berthalet); Pierre Olaf (Jacquot); James Mitchell (Marco the Magnificent); Kaye Ballard (The Incomparable Rosalie); Henry Lascoe (Mr. Schlegal); Will Lee (Grobert); June Meshonek (Greta Schlegal); Bob Murray (Cyclist); George Marcy (Miguelito); Paul Sydell (Dog Trainer); Carvel Carter (Wardrobe Mistress); Jennifer Billingsley (Bear Girl/Blue Bird); Luba Lisa (Princess Olga); Dean Crane (Stilt Walker/Aerialist); Bob Dixon, Harry Lee Rogers (Clowns); C.B. Bernard, Peter Lombard (Band); The Martin Brothers (Jugglers); Pat Tolson (Strongman); Mary Ann Niles (Gladys Zuwicki); Christine Bartel (Gloria Zuwicki); Anita Gillette (Gypsy); Igors Gavin (Dr. Glass); Nicole Barth, Iva March, Beti Seay (Harem Girls/Blue Birds); George Marcy, Tony Gomez, Johnny Nola, Buff Shurr (Roustabouts).

Broadway began to turn to the movies for its musicals with *Carnival*, a theatrical version of *Lili*, the 1953 film which starred Leslie Caron as an orphan who joins a European sideshow and finds love with a disabled puppeteer. Like *Carousel*, the show begins without an overture. The audience entered the theatre to find the curtain up and the stage empty except for a simple backdrop of a country setting.

As the lights dimmed, the carnival roustabouts and performers came out, setting up their tents and wagons as the main theme played. Songwriter Bob Merrill had to come up with a main theme distinctively different from the one used in the movie, "Hi-Lili, Hi-Lili, Hi-Lo," which had been a tremendous hit. His solution, "Love Makes the World Go Round," proved equally popular. The simple, captivating opening was suggested by Helen Deutsch, author of the screenplay for *Lili* and the original librettist

Pierre Olaf and Anna Maria Alberghetti meet as bitter puppeteer Jerry Orbach looks on in *Carnival*.

for *Carnival*. The director and choreographer was Gower Champion. Merrill, whose previous Broadway credits included *New Girl in Town* (1957) and *Take Me Along* (1959), told *Back Stage*'s Ira J. Bilowit: "I brought Helen and Gower together. They worked for about three days, and she, who was a very strong-willed woman, said she could not work with Gower. And Gower said that he couldn't work with her. So they parted company. Michael Stewart came in when Helen walked out—he had just done *Bye, Bye, Birdie* with Gower and was Gower's choice for the book writer."

Jerry Orbach, of the off-Broadway triumphs *The Threepenny Opera* and *The Fantasticks*, was cast as Paul, the bitter puppeteer. Pierre Olaf, a *Plume de Ma Tante* comic, was his partner. Kaye Ballard turned down the lead in the touring production of *Gypsy* in order to play the featured role of the magician's assistant. The curtain had to be held for her so she could make her regular appearances on TV's *The Perry Como Show*, which was taped at a Brooklyn studio. James Mitchell, a dancer, was cast as the magician, and learned to do professional magic tricks. Carnival acts like clowns, jugglers, tumblers, dog acts, and belly dancers were added for authentic atmosphere.

Finding a leading lady who could sing, dance, and obliterate the memory of Leslie Caron seemed a daunting task, but the perfect candidate was found singing in a New Jersey nightclub: Anna Maria Alberghetti made Lili her own and later won a Tony Award, tying with Diahann Carroll for *No Strings*. She played in the touring version and was replaced by Anita Gillette, Susan Watson, and Anna Maria's sister, Carla Alberghetti, during the remainder of the New York run.

The London production of the musical was decried as overly sentimental by the press. *The London Daily Mail* reviewer stated he was so revolted by the overwhelming sweetness, his first instinct was to "flee from the theatre and kick a cat."

Metro-Goldwyn-Mayer had put up most of the money with an eye towards gaining the record and film rights. The film studio did record the original cast album, but due to a contract dispute with producer David Merrick, the movie was never made. The litigation also prevented any major New York revival from being staged until 1993, when the off-Broadway York Theatre Company mounted a production.

Later musicals to rely on films for their source material included *Sweet Charity* (1966); *Promises, Promises* (1968); *Applause* (1970); *Sugar* (1972); *A Little Night Music* (1973); *Shenandoah* (1975); *42nd Street* (1980); *Nine* (1982); and *The Goodbye Girl* (1993).

MILK AND HONEY

Book by Don Appell

Music and lyrics by Jerry Herman

Opened October 10, 1961

541 Performances

Martin Beck Theatre

Directed by Albert Marre

Choreographed by Donald Saddler

Produced by Gerald Oestreicher

Cast: Robert Weede (Phil); Mimi Benzell (Ruth); Molly Picon (Clara Weiss); Lanna Saunders (Barbara); Tommy Rall (David); Juki Arkin (Adi); Ellen Madison (Zipporah); Addi Negri (Mrs. Weinstein); Dorothy Richardson (Mrs. Strauss); Rose Lischner (Mrs. Breslin); Diane Goldberg (Mrs. Segal); Ceil Delli (Mrs. Kessler); Thelma Pelish (Mrs. Perlman); Reuben Singer (Mr. Horowitz); Ellen Berse (The Guide); Lou Polacek, David London (Cantors); José Gutierres, Linda Howe, Michael Nestor, Jane Zachary (Wedding Couples); Matt Turney (Maid of Honor); Burt Bier (Porter); Johnny Borden (Shepherd Boy); Ronald Holgate (Policeman); Renato Cibelli (Cafe Arab); Art Tookoyan (Man of the Moshav).

Originally titled *Shalom*, *Milk and Honey* was the first (and so far only) hit musical set in the young country of Israel. Robert Weede, of *The Most Happy Fella*, was again cast as an older gentlemen smitten with a younger woman. He played Phil, a retired contractor living with his daughter and son-in-law on a kibbutz. He is separated from his wife, who refuses to give him a divorce.

The younger woman, Ruth, was played by Mimi Benzell. She is a recent widow on a tour of the nation with six other women. The two are attracted, but Ruth's middle-class morality prevents her from going any further than holding hands with Phil. She goes through much musical anguishing before deciding to embark on an affair. Phil wants to live with Ruth without benefit of a marriage license, but for that to be the show's resolution would have been a bit much for 1961 audiences to take. The two finally split up, but with Phil returning to his wife to make a final plea for a divorce.

Both Weede and Benzell had operatic backgrounds and sang their numbers with admirable precision and technique. But the real star was Molly Picon, leading light of the Yiddish theatre (she was referred to as the Yiddish Helen Hayes), as the wisecracking Clara Weiss, leader of the tour group. Her expert comic timing enlivened the book scenes. In her show-stopping song to her late husband, "Hymn to Hymie," she even worked in a somersault. It was hard to believe she was making her Broadway musical debut.

Also making his debut was songwriter Jerry Herman. Producer Gerald Oestreicher selected him after seeing his material in an off-Broadway revue called *Parade*. Herman and book writer Don Appell journeyed to Israel to soak up atmosphere.

The resulting libretto was weak, but Donald Saddler's lively musical numbers and Picon's performance held the show together. Picon said in her autobiography that she suspected the producer didn't want her to be "too Jewish." She was told not to use her hands too much. It was briefly suggested that she not speak the dialogue with inflections. "But it's written that way" was her defense. The suggestion was discarded. After the show opened and drew raves, the producer soon learned that his "too Jewish" star was the cause of the show's success.

When Picon left the cast to appear in the film version of Neil Simon's *Come Blow Your Horn*, she was replaced with the miscast and definitely Gentile Hermione Gingold. Ticket sales dropped dramatically. Picon returned to the role after her film stint, but it was too late. The show closed with a deficit of $70,000. Picon later starred in a *Milk and Honey* national tour.

HOW TO SUCCEED IN BUSINESS WITHOUT REALLY TRYING

Book by Abe Burrows, Jack Weinstock, and Willie Gilbert, based on Shepard Mead's book.

Music and lyrics by Frank Loesser

Opened October 16, 1961

1,417 Performances

46th Street Theatre

Directed by Abe Burrows

Choreographed by Bob Fosse and Hugh Lambert

Produced by Cy Feuer and Ernest Martin

Cast: Robert Morse (J. Pierpont Finch); Rudy Vallee (J.B. Biggley); Charles Nelson Reilly (Bud Frump); Bonnie Scott (Rosemary); Virginia Martin (Hedy LaRue); Ruth Kobart (Miss Jones); Claudette Sutherland (Smitty); Sammy Smith (Mr. Twimble/Womper); Ray Mason (Gatch/Toynbee); Robert Kaliban (Jenkins); David Collyer (Tackaberry); Casper Roos (Peterson); Paul Reed (Bratt); Mara Landi (Miss Krumholtz/Scrubwoman); Lanier Davis (Ovington); Bob Murdock (Policeman); Silver Saunders (Scrubwoman); Donna McKechnie was in the chorus.

Rudy Vallee (left) and Robert Morse inspect pirate girl Virginia Martin in *How to Succeed in Business Without Really Trying*.

How to Succeed in Business Without Really Trying was the long and attention-grabbing title of Shepard Mead's satiric book on America's postwar business ethics (and lack thereof) which served as the basis for one of Broadway's most successful musicals. Subtitled *A Dastard's Guide to Fame and Fortune*, the book mercilessly skewers the backstabbing, nepotism, and soulless ladder-climbing in corporate America. The moniker was catchy and the volume was funny, but could this parody of "how-to" primers be made into a play? This was the task comedy writers Willie Gilbert and Jack Weinstock set for themselves. They purchased the rights to Mead's book with the intention of making it into a nonmusical.

Producers Cy Feuer and Ernest Martin (*Guys and Dolls, Can-Can*, etc.) were interested but saw it as a musical. Enter Abe Burrows, director and play doctor. He transformed Gilbert and Weinstock's script into the musical's book. Though the team received program credit on the book, they did not collaborate with Burrows, who brought his *Guys and Dolls* colleague Frank Loesser in to compose the score.

Loesser had trouble envisioning singing and dancing businessmen in gray-flannel suits, but Burrows persuaded him to take on the assignment. "I convinced Frank that if he could put a crap game to music in *Guys and Dolls*," Burrows later related, "he certainly could put a big corporation to music."

While Loesser musicalized capitalists, Burrows was giving Mead's sharp observations a shape and a storyline. He focused on one J. Pierpont Finch, who uses the *How to Succeed* book as his Bible during his meteoric rise through the ranks at World Wide Wicket Company. Following the book's instructions, Finch ascends by means of deception, flattery, manipulation, and (as the title indicates) very little real work.

The boyish Robert Morse was cast as the Machiavellian Finch. Morse was so ingratiating, charming, and downright lovable that audiences cheered his machinations. The remainder of the cast amiably spoofed stereotypical businessmen. Rudy Vallee came out of semi-retirement (his last Broadway appearance had been in *George White Scandals of 1935*) to portray J.B. Biggley, the company's pompous president. Charles Nelson Reilly launched his career of portraying nervous, neurotic types as Biggley's scheming nephew, Bud Frump.

Putting the chorus through its paces was Broadway's dance master of the moment, Bob Fosse. During the show's Philadelphia tryout, Fosse was brought in to replace Hugh Lambert, the previously hired young choreographer who was proving unequal to the task of creating dances for his first Broadway effort. Fosse generously allowed the young man to keep his credit as choreographer while he, the more experienced and talented of the two, was listed as being responsible for "musical staging."

The unique, stylized Fosse movement changed a daily office routine into a frenetic conga line in the "Coffee Break" number and underscored sexual tension with a typewriter-driven soft shoe in "A Secretary Is Not a Toy."

How to Succeed went on to win the triple crown of Tony, Drama Critics Circle, and Pulitzer awards. It sent out a profitable national tour, and ran for almost four years on Broadway. The film version was released in 1967, with Morse and Vallee repeating their original roles.

This was to be Loesser's last Broadway score. His next show, *Pleasures and Palaces* (1965), a musical about Catherine the Great, closed in Detroit before reaching Broadway.

A MAN FOR ALL SEASONS

by Robert Bolt
Opened November 22, 1961
637 Performances
ANTA Theatre
Directed by Noel Willman
Produced by Robert Whitehead and Roger L. Stevens

Cast: Paul Scofield (Sir Thomas More); George Rose (The Common Man); Keith Baxter (King Henry VIII); William Redfield (Richard Rich); Albert Dekker (Duke of Norfolk); Carol Goodner (Alice More); Olga Bellin (Margaret More); Jack Creley (Cardinal Wolsey); Thomas Gomez (Thomas Cromwell); David J. Stewart (Chapuys); John Colenback (Attendant); Peter Brandon (William Roper); Sarah Burton (The Woman); Lester Rawlins (Cranmer).

"More is a man of an angel's wit and singular learning; I know not his fellow. For where is the man of that gentleness, lowliness, and affability? And as time requireth a man of marvelous mirth and pastimes; and sometimes of as sad gravity: a man for all seasons." This quote is from Robert Whittinton, a Tudor-era schoolteacher, describing Sir Thomas More, the Lord Chancellor to King Henry VIII. *A Man for All Seasons* is Robert Bolt's play about More and his conflict with Henry over the latter's divorce from Catherine of Aragon, which the King wanted in order to marry Anne Boleyn. In so breaking with Catherine, Henry was breaking with the Catholic Church. More came to oppose Henry's actions and, as a result, was beheaded.

The play charts More's fall from his position at the King's right hand to a cell in the Tower of London, never wavering in his beliefs. Presiding over the action and acting as narrator is an omniscient figure referred to as The Common Man. With the aide of a basketful of props, he plays servant, innkeeper, jury, jailer, and finally, executioner.

A Man for All Seasons opened in London in 1960 at the same time as another work of Bolt's called *The Tiger and the Horse*. While *Tiger* failed, the historical drama, with Paul Scofield's intelligent and powerful performance in the lead role, was an immediate hit.

There was talk of bringing the show to New York. *Variety*'s review predicted, "It's a doubtful bet for popular appeal and despite the name of Paul Scofield as marquee bait, is unlikely for Broadway." Bolt's first play, *The Flowering Cherry,* had been successful in the West End but withered on the Great White Way. Scofield, an unknown to Americans, would be making his United States debut (he had played in Canada).

In spite of these misgivings, New York rehearsals began. Bolt missed them because he was in jail for taking the More-like stand of protesting nuclear weapons in a British sit-down strike. *Variety*'s forecast proved false. "It is not only about a man for all seasons but also about an inspiration for all times," trumpeted the *New York Times.* The show won a total of five Tony Awards, the most for any straight play up to that point. This record was later tied by *Who's Afraid of Virginia Woolf?, Amadeus,* and *The Real Thing.*

Two national touring companies were sent out. Emlyn Williams succeeded Scofield on Broadway and a pre-*Bonnie and Clyde* Faye Dunaway played More's daughter in the replacement company.

The 1966 Columbia film, directed by Fred Zinneman from a screenplay by Bolt, proved equally as popular. Scofield, who had only three films to his credit, was billed sixth after Wendy Hiller, Leo McKern, Robert Shaw, Orson Welles, and Susannah York, and he won the Oscar as Best Actor. The picture took a total of six Academy Awards including Best Picture, making it one of the few plays to have won both the Tony and Oscar.

An off-Broadway revival of *A Man for All Seasons,* starring Philip Bosco, was presented at the Roundabout Theatre in 1987. Charlton Heston starred in and directed a

Diahann Carroll and Richard Kiley have a Parisian romance with *No Strings.*

1988 cable-television version with Vanessa Redgrave and John Gielgud in support.

Additional historical dramas to hit Broadway include *Elizabeth the Queen* (1930); *Mary of Scotland* (1933); *Anne of the Thousand Days* (1948); *The Lion in Winter* (1966); *Becket* (1960); and Bolt's own *Vivat! Vivat! Regina!* (1972). *Victoria Regina* (1935) was the only other historical play to run over 500 performances.

NO STRINGS

Book by Samuel Taylor

Music and lyrics by Richard Rodgers

Opened March 15, 1962

580 Performances

54th Street Theatre

Directed by Joe Layton

Choreographed by Joe Layton

Produced by Richard Rodgers

Cast: Diahann Carroll (Barbara Woodruff); Richard Kiley (David Jordan); Noelle Adam (Jeanette Valmy); Alvin Epstein (Luc Delbert); Polly Rowles (Mollie Plummer); Don Chastain (Mike Robinson); Mitchell Gregg (Louis dePourtal); Bernice Massi (Comfort O'Connell); Ann Hodges (Gabrielle Bertin); Paul Cambeilh (Marcello Agnolotti).

Richard Rodgers was watching TV's *The Tonight Show* when he found the inspiration for his first musical after the death of his partner Oscar Hammerstein. Diahann Carroll, a young black performer, was singing an old standard, "Goody, Goody," as if it had been written yesterday just for her. Rodgers decided to write a show for Carroll in which she would play a sophisticated, entrancing woman, totally in control of her world and singing beautiful songs.

The story devised between Rodgers and his book writer Samuel Taylor took place in Paris, where Barbara Woodruff (Carroll) is an international success as a model. She meets and falls in love with expatriate American author David Jordan (Richard Kiley). The script makes no mention of the interracial aspect of David and Barbara's romance, or of Barbara's color. The composer felt that casting Carroll in a commanding, dignified role would do more for promoting racial understanding than any blatant political statement. (Carroll, however, was the only African-American in the cast of forty-one.)

This was the first show for which Rodgers wrote both the music and the lyrics. He told Jack Gaver of UPI that this was "the first time it's ever happened in all the years and all the shows—having a complete score before rehearsals. The reason is that the lyric writer wasn't late with any of his material."

The show contained many innovations. The orchestra was freed from the pit and integrated into the action. In keeping with the title, there were no strings, only brass and woodwinds. The chorus moved the scenery in full view of the audience. The plot was also unconventional, with the romantic leads separating but agreeing to keep their options open with "no strings." The implication was that David and Barbara would never be accepted as a couple in America, where David was returning.

After winning the Tony Award as Best Actress in a Musical (in a tie with Anna Maria Alberghetti for *Carnival*), Carroll was distressed to read in the news that her role would be played in the Warner Brothers–Seven Arts movie version by Nancy Kwan (star of the filmizations of *Flower Drum Song* and *The World of Suzie Wong*). Ironically, Carroll had auditioned for *Flower Drum Song*, but the heavy Asian makeup created for her didn't work. Apparently it was acceptable to depict a black-white romance on Broadway, but not on screen. Columnist Earl Wilson printed the unhappy star's views, which lead to a controversy. Perhaps because of this sticky situation, the film project was shelved.

The musical did tour, with Howard Keel and Barbara McNair. *No Strings* was Rodgers' last long-running hit (not including a 1983 revival of *On Your Toes*). His later works were *Do I Hear a Waltz?* (1965), *Two by Two* (1970), *Rex* (1976), and *I Remember Mama* (1979).

A FUNNY THING HAPPENED ON THE WAY TO THE FORUM

Book by Burt Shevelove and Larry Gelbart, based on the plays of Plautus.
Music and lyrics by Stephen Sondheim
Opened May 8, 1962
964 Performances
Alvin Theatre
Directed by George Abbott
Choreographed by Jack Cole
Produced by Harold Prince

Cast: Zero Mostel (Pseudolus/Prologus); Jack Gilford (Hysterium); David Burns (Senex); Ruth Kobart (Dominia); Brian Davies (Hero); Preshy Marker (Philia); John Carradine (Lycus); Ron Holgate (Miles Gloriosus); Raymond Walburn (Erronius); Roberta Keith (Tintinnabula); Lucienne Bridou (Panacea); Lisa James, Judy Alexander (The Geminae); Myrna White (Vibrata); Gloria Kristy (Gymnasia); Eddie Phillips, George Reeder, David Evans (Proteans).

A Funny Thing Happened on the Way to the Forum proved the adage that everything old is new again. The broadly comic musical was based on the ancient Roman comedies of Plautus, but seemed fresh and funny.

Forum marked Stephen Sondheim's debut as both composer and lyricist after writing the lyrics for *West Side Story* and *Gypsy*, and it was Harold Prince's first solo production after the death of his partner Robert Griffith.

David Burns and Zero Mostel in *A Funny Thing Happened on the Way to the Forum.*

Sondheim and librettists Burt Shevelove and Larry Gel-bart originally intended for Phil Silvers to play the lead role of Pseudolus, the clever slave who wins his freedom through a series of comic machinations. After Silvers, and then Milton Berle, rejected the script, Prince suggested Zero Mostel, an actor rather than a comic. The authors were reluctant to hire Mostel, whose only musical experi-ence was in *Beggar's Holiday* (1946). Mostel was also hesi-tant; he had an offer to play Falstaff in Stratford, Con-necticut. His wife had to persuade him to take the more lucrative offer of a Broadway musical over Shakespeare in the regions.

Jerome Robbins was the original choice to stage the show, but he backed out. Prince's old mentor George Abbott was called in and immediately made cuts in the script, eliminating many subplots. The altered book didn't work during tryouts in New Haven. The secondary stories were restored to add a sense of organized madness.

In Washington, D.C., the response was poor and get-ting worse with a large percentage of the audience walking out at many performances. Robbins was called in to take a look. This step was taken despite possible friction with the cast. The director-choreographer had given friendly testi-mony to the House Un-American Activities Committee, naming several performers as Communists. Both Mostel and his friend and co-star Jack Gilford had been victims of an unofficial blacklist. In fact, one of the actors Robbins had named to the Committee was Gilford's wife Madeline. "I asked Zero if he would have any trouble with Robbins coming in," Prince said. "And he said, 'Well, as long as you're not asking me to have lunch with him.'" Gilford's wife persuaded him to stay with the show.

The major change Robbins made was to alter the open-ing number, "Love Is in the Air," a pleasant little number that set up the audience for a light romance. They were dis-appointed when they got a farce. Over the course of a weekend, Sondheim wrote "Comedy Tonight" to prepare the crowd for the boisterous fun ahead. Robbins staged it inside of a week, and theatregoers started laughing rather than leaving.

During the New York run, Mostel got impatient with his role and ad-libbed shamelessly. Despite his shenani-gans, Mostel won a Tony as Best Actor in a musical, one of six Tonys for *Forum*, awarded during the 1962–63 season since the show opened late in the 1961–62 season.

Mostel also starred in the 1966 film version, along with Gilford. Phil Silvers, who turned down the lead on Broad-way, was given the supporting role of Marcus Lycus, the local pimp. The story was somewhat overshadowed by the frenetic, jump-cut-happy direction of Richard Lester. Sil-vers appeared in a 1972 Broadway revival of *Forum* and won his own Tony, as did Larry Blyden for his interpreta-

tion of Jack Gilford's original role. The new production was directed by co-author Burt Shevelove and featured two new songs by Sondheim.

STOP THE WORLD—I WANT TO GET OFF

Book, music, and lyrics by Leslie Bricusse and Anthony Newley
Opened October 3, 1962
555 Performances
Shubert Theatre
Directed by Anthony Newley
Choreographed by John Broome and Virginia Mason
Produced by David Merrick

Cast: Anthony Newley (Littlechap); Anna Quayle (Evie/Anya/Ilse/Ginnie); Jennifer Baker (Jane); Susan Baker (Susan).

Stop the World—I Want to Get Off, the metaphorical musi-cal with the long, funny title was the collaboration of Eng-lishmen Anthony Newley and Leslie Bricusse. The partners wrote the entire show, book as well as score. In addition, Newley directed and played the lead role. Newley's only rival in number of hats worn is George M. Cohan, who also wrote, composed, staged, and performed his own shows in the early part of the century.

Subtitled "A New-Style Musical," the show traces the life of Littlechap (Newley), a Chaplinesque clown, as he goes through school, marriage, business, politics, and finally death. The only other major characters are the four women in his life: British Evie, Russian Anya, German Ilsa, and American Ginny (all were played by Anna Quayle in a Tony-winning performance); and his two daughters (played by real-life twins Jennifer and Susan Baker). The authors used pantomime, sketches, and jokes in a combi-nation of British music hall and circus sideshow to spin their tale of an average man's obsession with material suc-cess and his failure to relate to his wife and family.

The circus theme was reinforced by Sean Kenny's tent-like set and the clown makeup and costumes worn by the performers.

The score included such hits as "What Kind of Fool Am I?," which became Newley's signature tune in his nightclub and concert appearances, "Gonna Build a Mountain," and "Once in a Lifetime." Another highlight was Quayle's ren-dition of the four songs that introduced her international characters. The melody was always the same, but the arrangements and lyrics were altered to fit the nationality she was playing: a bright, cheery tune for Evie; a Slavic folk dance for Anya; an insistent military march for Ilsa; and a slow Gershwin-style ballad for Ginny.

Most of the script was written in a New York apartment lent to the authors by the British comedienne Beatrice Lil-lie, for whom Bricusse was writing special material. David Merrick saw the production during its pre-London tryout

(Left to right) Uta Hagen, Arthur Hill, and George Grizzard in Edward Albee's intense *Who's Afraid of Virginia Woolf?*

in Nottingham and immediately acquired the rights for an American production.

Joel Grey and Julie Newmar took over for the leads on Broadway. Tony Tanner and Millicent Martin starred in the 1966 film version, which closely imitated the original production. A revival rewritten to suit the talents of Sammy Davis, Jr. was presented on Broadway in 1978. Marian Mercer played the female leads. It was retitled *Sammy Stops the World* and was filmed a year later.

David Merrick produced a similar show by Newley and Bricusse with another playful title in 1965: *The Roar of the Greasepaint, the Smell of the Crowd* again featured Newley, who co-authored, directed, and played a clownish Everyman figure. (This time the central metaphor was "Life Is a Game" rather than "Life Is a Circus.") It had a moderate run of 232 performances.

WHO'S AFRAID OF VIRGINIA WOOLF?

by Edward Albee

Opened October 13, 1962

664 Performances

Billy Rose Theatre

Directed by Alan Schneider

Produced by Theatre 1963, Richard Barr, and Clinton Wilder

Cast: Uta Hagen (Martha); Arthur Hill (George); George Grizzard (Nick); Melinda Dillon (Honey).

Edward Albee was a relatively new playwright with a short string of successful off-Broadway one-acts (*The Zoo Story,*

The American Dream, The Death of Bessie Smith) to his credit. This hardly prepared the theatre world for his Broadway debut, *Who's Afraid of Virginia Woolf?*, a three-and-a-half-hour living-room war between a bitter professor and his shrewish wife who happens to be the daughter of the college's president.

Returning home late from a faculty party, George and Martha prepare to entertain the new biology instructor and his giggly wife. What ensues is a devastating night-long encounter as the older couple draws the younger into their deadly games and domestic skirmishes. Albee was indicting the entire American middle-class through George and Martha. Intelligent and educated, they still attack and claw at each other like unthinking beasts. Their unfulfilled hopes and dashed expectations are symbolized by an imaginary child. As dawn breaks, the embattled duo are left to begin again with no illusions.

Albee got the title from an epithet scrawled on the walls of a Greenwich Village toilet. He first wrote the play as a brief scene for a public television series called "Playwright at Work." Over the course of a year, he expanded it to more than full-length. The play was originally going to be produced by the Actors Studio. Geraldine Page and Eli Wallach were slated for the leads. But Roger Stevens and Cheryl Crawford, the Studio's producers, disliked the play's strong language. The script then passed to producer Richard Barr.

"I first read the script, all three acts, in Richard Barr's kitchen," recalled the play's director Alan Schneider during a Dramatists Guild symposium. "I felt as though I'd been hit over the head with a great big granite boulder—not because of the length of the script, but because of the size of the emotions." The three-act battle proved so exhausting for the cast that a second company was hired to play the matinees.

Some gentlemen of the press were shocked by the play's brutality. "For Dirty-Minded Females Only," said the headline of John Chapman's review in the *Daily News.* "No red-blooded American would bring his wife to this shocking play," huffed Robert Coleman in the *Daily Mirror.* But the majority of notices were more in agreement with Richard Watts, Jr. of the *New York Post,* who called the play "the most shattering drama I have seen since O'Neill's *Long Day's Journey into Night.*"

The play won five out of six possible Tony Awards, but did not take the Pulitzer Prize. Although *Virginia Woolf* was recommended for the Prize by a three-man jury of theatre critics, the committee of judges who made the final decision elected to give no Pulitzer in drama that season because they found the play's frankness distasteful. The jury resigned in protest.

The 1966 film version, which marked Mike Nichols' debut as a film director, caused a sensation, as Elizabeth Taylor discarded her glamour and beauty to play the frumpy Martha opposite Richard Burton's George. The film also broke barriers in adult language and subject matter. The movie won six Oscars, including one for Taylor as Best Actress and another for Sandy Dennis as Best Supporting Actress.

Albee later won the Pulitzer that was denied him for *Virginia Woolf* for *A Delicate Balance* (1967) and again for *Seascape* (1975). Despite this double honor, *Virginia Woolf* remains Albee's only commercial Broadway success. His succeeding dramas, such as *Tiny Alice* (1964), *Everything in the Garden* (1967), and *All Over* (1971), fared poorly at the box office. More recently, his new work has been produced in Europe, off-Broadway, and in regional theatres.

Virginia Woolf was revived on Broadway in 1977 with Colleen Dewhurst and Ben Gazzara as the battling couple. The playwright directed.

BEYOND THE FRINGE

by Alan Bennett, Peter Cook, Jonathan Miller, and Dudley Moore

Opened October 27, 1962

667 Performances

John Golden Theatre

Produced and directed by Alexander H. Cohen

Cast: Alan Bennett, Peter Cook, Jonathan Miller, and Dudley Moore

"Satire is what closes on Saturday night," according to George S. Kaufman. *Beyond the Fringe,* an intimate revue lampooning British and American social and political issues, proved Kaufman wrong by running almost two years.

The show was a collaboration of four young British entertainers recently out of college. From Oxford came history scholar and lecturer Alan Bennett and musician Dudley Moore. Physician Jonathan Miller and writer Peter Cook had graduated from Cambridge. Each had written and acted in separate university shows.

The quartet was assembled by John Bassett, assistant to the artistic director of the Edinburgh Festival, the annual event which brings theatre companies from around the globe to the Scottish capital. Bassett needed to fill a hole in the Festival's schedule and decided the perfect plug would be a comedy revue similar to undergraduate hijinks which had proved popular at previous Festivals. He contacted the four comedians, none of whom had met before. They would confer in various pubs and restaurants, brainstorming ideas for their show. They even met with Miller while he was on duty at a hospital.

The result was an hour-long razzing of such stuffy British institutions as the Anglican Church, the press, English literature, and the political system. The revue was an official part of the Festival program, while previous college shows were part of the unofficial, peripheral goings-on, known as the Fringe. Thus the title *Beyond the Fringe.* Offers poured in to present the show in London and New York.

In an expanded version, *Fringe* played London's West End and later Broadway as a part of Alexander Cohen's Nine O'Clock Theatre series, which presented similar offbeat comics like Mort Sahl and the team of Mike Nichols and Elaine May.

Sketches included "Aftermyth of War," a caricature of World War II documentaries, mocking the conventions of the genre ("Then, unfortunately, peace broke out," intones the narrator); Cook's impersonation of a miner who never got to be a judge; Moore's musical madness, in which he desperately searches for a final chord to the piano piece he was playing; Bennett as a long-winded minister; Miller poking fun at philosophical conundrums; and the highly praised "So That's the Way You Like It," a wicked parody of Shakespeare. *Fringe* was the last long-running Broadway sketch show, although off-Broadway has had numerous successes with the genre.

The original cast went on to separate distinguished careers. Miller became a stage and opera director. Bennett emerged as a playwright. His works include *Habeas Corpus, Single Spies,* and *Talking Heads,* and *The Madness of George III.* Peter Cook and Dudley Moore remained together after *Fringe,* appearing in their own British TV series. They returned to Broadway in 1973 in a two-man show called *Good Evening,* which featured mostly new material with a few sketches from *Fringe.* The show won a special Tony Award. Moore later pursued a film career, while Cook continued to work in television.

NEVER TOO LATE

by Sumner Arthur Long
Opened November 27, 1962
1,007 Performances
Playhouse Theatre
Directed by George Abbott
Produced by Elliott Martin and Daniel Hollywood

Cast: Paul Ford (Harry Lambert); Maureen O'Sullivan (Edith Lambert); Orson Bean (Charlie); Fran Sharon (Kate); Leona Maricle (Grace Kimborough); House Jameson (Dr. James Kimborough); Wallace Engelhardt (Mr. Foley); John Alexander (Mayor Crane); Ed Griffith (Policeman).

George Abbott's 84th production as director was, appropriately, a slight comedy celebrating late middle age, *Never Too Late*. Sumner Arthur Long's Broadway bauble concerned the impact of an unexpected pregnancy on a couple in their 50s who already have a married daughter. Comic situations arise as the wife—until now treated little better than a servant by her domineering husband—uses her condition to get whatever she wants, including a new wing added onto the house.

Long stated that he got the idea from seeing an expectant middle-aged woman and wondering how her husband felt about the situation. Originally titled *Cradle and All*, the comedy tried out in summer stock. Abbott saw it in Westport, Connecticut, and felt it had the makings of a funny show. Although he claimed no co-authorship credit, Abbott probably doctored the script for New York.

Long's storyline hung on the single joke of the unlikely pregnancy. But Abbott staged it with the slam-bang velocity of one of his '30s farces. Paul Ford, the pompous general from *Teahouse of the August Moon*, drew raves from the critics as the flustered expectant father. His bassett hound face perfectly expressed his sorrow as his comfortable near-retirement is destroyed by the coming little stranger. Maureen O'Sullivan graced the stage as the expectant mother, joyfully exercising her new-found power over her spouse. Orson Bean was also applauded for his comic performance as the put-upon son-in-law.

In addition to *Never Too Late*, Abbott had two other hits on the boards the same season: the musical *A Funny Thing Happened on the Way to the Forum* and the comedy *Take Her, She's Mine*. He was nominated for Tony Awards as Best Director for both a play and musical, making him the first director to be nominated in both categories in the same year.

At 1,007 performances, *Never Too Late* was Abbott's longest-running nonmusical. There followed such short-lived Abbott-directed shows as *Fade In, Fade Out* (1964), *Flora, the Red Menace* (1965), *Anya* (1965), *How Now, Dow Jones?* (1967), *The Fig Leaves Are Falling* (1969), and *Norman, Is That You?* (1970). Abbott did not have another hit until the 1983 revival of *On Your Toes*.

Maureen O'Sullivan's pregnancy is too much for Paul Ford to take in *Never Too Late*

Ford and O'Sullivan re-created their Broadway roles in the 1965 film version, with Connie Stevens and Jim Hutton as their daughter and son-in-law.

OLIVER!

Book, music, and lyrics by Lionel Bart, based on *Oliver Twist*, by Charles Dickens.
Opened January 6, 1963
774 Performances
Imperial Theatre
Directed by Peter Coe
Produced by David Merrick and Donald Albery

Cast: Bruce Prochnik (Oliver Twist); Clive Revill (Fagin); Georgia Brown (Nancy); David Jones (The Artful Dodger); Danny Sewell (Bill Sikes); Willoughby Goddard (Mr. Bumble); Hope Jackman (Mrs. Corney); Ruth Maynard (Old Sally); Barry Humphries (Mr. Sowerberry); Helena Carroll (Mrs. Sowerberry); Cherry Davis (Charlotte); Terry Lomax (Noah Claypole); Alice Playten (Bet); Geoffrey Lumb (Mr. Brownlow); John Call (Dr. Grimwig); Dortha Duckworth (Mrs. Bedwin).

After *Irma La Douce* and *Stop the World*, David Merrick brought another British hit musical to Broadway, Lionel Bart's adaptation of Charles Dickens' *Oliver Twist*. The longest-running musical to play London's West End in the 1960s, it ran 2,618 performances. While its American incarnation had a much shorter run (774 performances), it remained the longest-running British musical on Broadway until *Evita* surpassed it nearly twenty years later.

Dickens's dark story of the orphan Oliver Twist painted a bleak portrait of lower-class life in Victorian England. Bart brightened it up with such cheery songs as "Food, Glorious Food," "Consider Yourself," and "I'd Do Anything." There were also tender ballads like "Where Is Love?" and "As Long as He Needs Me," which became standards. The character of Fagin, leader of a gang of 19th-century juvenile delinquents which Oliver joins, was altered from Dickens's blunt Jewish caricature to a lovable rascal.

Young Bruce Prochnik, as the title character, and Georgia Brown, as the doomed Nancy, were among those retained from the London cast. There was some trouble with thirteen-year-old Prochnik's playing the lead in America. After he had come to the States, accompanied by his mother, an obscure British law was invoked which forbade minors under fourteen from working outside the U.K. Prochnik's father was given a five-pound fine. The matter was largely academic since the lad had his fourteenth birthday before the musical opened on Broadway. Clive Revill, from Merrick's production of *Irma La Douce*, was brought in for the juicy role of Fagin. David Jones, later of the pop group The Monkees, was the Artful Dodger, one of Fagin's prize protégés.

Because of a newspaper strike, Merrick put the show on an extensive road tour in hopes that the dispute would be settled by the time the musical reached New York. *Oliver!* went the unusual out-of-town route of Los Angeles, San Francisco, Detroit, and Toronto. It appeared that a labor settlement was still elusive, but the producer brought the show to the Imperial Theatre (home of such Merrick hits as *Jamaica*, *Gypsy*, and *Carnival*).

During the two-year run, Prochnik outgrew the title role and was replaced by Paul O'Keefe, who was simultaneously appearing on Patty Duke's TV series. A succession of Olivers followed. After a successful national tour, the company returned to Broadway in 1966 for a brief stay.

The 1968 film version won a total of six Oscars, including Best Picture. Onna White was awarded a special Oscar for her choreography.

A 1984 revival, featuring Patti LuPone and Ron Moody, the London and film Fagin, had a short run.

Other Dickens works to become Broadway material include *The Pickwick Papers*, as the musicals *Mr. Pickwick* (1903) and *Pickwick* (1965); *David Copperfield*, as the musical *Copperfield* (1981); *The Life and Adventures of Nicholas Nickelby*, as the Royal Shakespeare Company's eight-hour adaptation by David Edgar (1981); *A Christmas Carol*, as the musical *Comin' Uptown* (1979), which relocated the story to Harlem, and as Patrick Stewart's one-man show (1991); and *The Mystery of Edwin Drood*, as a hit musical (1985).

BAREFOOT IN THE PARK

by Neil Simon
Opened October 23, 1963
1,530 Performances
Biltmore Theatre
Directed by Mike Nichols
Produced by Saint Subber

Cast: Elizabeth Ashley (Corie Bratter); Robert Redford (Paul Bratter); Mildred Natwick (Mrs. Banks); Kurt Kasznar (Victor Velasco); Herb Edelman (Telephone Man); Joseph Keating (Delivery Man).

Neil Simon's reputation as writer of long-running comedies was cemented with *Barefoot in the Park*. His previous hit, *Come Blow Your Horn*, had a successful run of 677 performances, while *Barefoot* more than doubled that with 1,530.

This play is a lighthearted lark about a pair of newlyweds in their first apartment (a fifth-floor East Side walk-up) coming to terms with their differences. The husband, Paul Bratter, is a somewhat stuffy lawyer, while his wife, Corie, is the epitome of a free spirit, ready for any adventure, including going barefoot in the park in sub-zero weather. After a disastrous dinner party with Corie's mother and an eccentric writer from upstairs, the young couple fight and Paul stomps out. Naturally, they are reunited once the husband drops his inhibitions and the wife grows up a little.

The plot bears a surface resemblance to Frank Craven's 1920 *The First Year*, in which a newlywed couple argue after a dinner party, split up, and then get back together.

With *Barefoot*, Simon's writing moved away from his TV-sketch origins into more fully developed characterizations and situations. He compared the play with his previous hit *Come Blow Your Horn* for the *New York Herald-Tribune*: "*Come Blow Your Horn* was farce. Every entrance was a crisis. This play isn't more serious . . . it's 'realer.' The characters in *Come Blow Your Horn* were caricatures. These are not. This play is truer to life." Simon later stated at a Dramatists Guild symposium that the play started out being autobiographical. The first apartment he had with his first wife Joan closely resembled Oliver Smith's set for the play, with a tiny living room, leaky sklight, and cramped bedroom.

Mike Nichols, known till then as half a comedy team with Elaine May, began his phenomenal directing career with this production. The young marrieds were played by two bright newcomers named Robert Redford and Elizabeth Ashley who had recently starred in similar light comedies, Redford in *Sunday in New York* and Ashley in *Take Her, She's Mine*, for which she won a Tony Award.

Barefoot first played at the Bucks County Playhouse in New Hope, Pennsylvania, under the title *Nobody Loves Me*. The cast remained the same for the play's pre-Broadway tour with the exception of Kurt Kasznar, who replaced George Voskovec as the upstairs neighbor. Major changes

(left to right) Mildred Natwick, Elizabeth Ashley, Kurt Kasznar, and Robert Redford in Neil Simon's *Barefoot in the Park*.

in the script included returning the character of the telephone man for the third act, and having the mother spend the night (although platonically) with the upstairs neighbor. The latter was suggested to Nichols by Lillian Hellman.

Richard Benjamin, Joan Van Ark, and Myrna Loy starred in the national tour, while Robert Reed and Penny Fuller were among those who continued as the Bratters on Broadway. Robert Redford starred opposite Jane Fonda in the 1967 screen version. Mildred Natwick recreated her stage role as the mother. A TV sitcom version ran for twelve episodes during the 1970–71 season.

HELLO, DOLLY!

Book by Michael Stewart, based upon *The Matchmaker,* by Thornton Wilder.

Music and lyrics by Jerry Herman

Opened January 16, 1964

2,844 Performances

St. James Theatre

Directed and choreographed by Gower Champion

Produced by David Merrick

Cast: Carol Channing (Mrs. Dolly Gallagher Levi); David Burns (Horace Vandergelder); Eileen Brennan (Irene Molloy); Charles Nelson Reilly (Cornelius Hackl); Sondra Lee (Minnie Fay); Jerry Dodge (Barnaby Tucker); Igors Gavin (Ambrose Kemper); Alice Playten (Ermengarde); Mary Jo Catlett (Ernestina); Amelia Haas (Mrs. Rose); David Hartman (Rudolph); Gordon Connell (Judge); Ken Ayers (Court Clerk).

As the title character glides down the stairs of the Harmonia Gardens Restaurant to be serenaded by the adoring staff of waiters, *Hello, Dolly!* makes audiences exultant.

The infectious chorus of greeting for the heroine is one of the most familiar in all musical comedy. The show itself is among the longest-running in Broadway history. It's also the first of two star vehicles for women (the second being *Mame*) featuring brassy scores by Jerry Herman. In both *Dolly* and *Mame*, the leading woman is serenaded with the title song by a male chorus.

The lady being welcomed back is Dolly Gallagher Levi, a take-charge, all-purpose busybody, efficiently making her way in a man's world, in Yonkers, New York, near the turn of the century. After mourning her late husband, she decides not to let the parade pass her by. She returns to life, engineering matches between several couples and even snagging a new husband for herself.

The story has been seen in many forms. First it was a British play, *A Day Well Spent*, by John Oxenford, produced in 1835. Viennese playwright Johann Nestroy lifted it for his *Einen Jux Will er Sich Machen (He Wants to Have a Lark)*, which was presented in Vienna in 1842. Nearly a century later, American Thornton Wilder picked up the story again and changed the locale; his version, *The Merchant of Yonkers*, was produced by the Theatre Guild in 1938.

Unsatisfied with *Merchant*, Wilder rewrote his work as *The Matchmaker*, shifting the emphasis from the previous title character to a new one, Dolly. The new version, starring Ruth Gordon and directed by Tyrone Guthrie, played Scotland's Edinburgh Festival and London in 1954, and then Broadway in 1955. This edition was also filmed in 1958, with Shirley Booth in the lead.

David Merrick produced the New York *Matchmaker*, and it was his idea to make it into a musical. He hired Herman to write the songs and approached Ethel Merman for the lead. But she was too exhausted from performing in the road company of *Gypsy* and turned it down. Carol Channing was not the next, logical choice for Merrick and his director, Gower Champion. The wide-eyed, childlike demeanor Channing had developed for Lorelei Lee, of *Gentlemen Prefer Blondes*, was wrong for the forthright, aggressive Dolly. But after working with Champion on the role, she convinced him she could make Dolly different from Lorelei and won the part.

Channing later told the *New York Times*: "We were a terrible flop out of town with *Hello, Dolly!*. We kept changing and changing right up until opening night . . . to swing it over from being the story of Horace Vandergelder (the merchant Dolly woos), to make it Dolly's story. David Merrick poured in $50,000 worth of new costumes and scenery and the show turned out all right."

A bit more than all right. *Hello, Dolly!* went on to win a record ten Tony Awards and to gross $60 million, with a profit of $9 million. The show's record-breaking run can be attributed to Champion's artful staging, a succession of big-name Dollys, and Merrick's highly developed sense of publicity.

When box office receipts were falling, the producer hired Pearl Bailey and Cab Calloway to head an African-American cast. This move drew new audiences. After Bailey left, the production was slipping financially again. Merrick didn't want to close the show until it had beaten out *My Fair Lady* for longest run. He finally persuaded Ethel Merman, the star for whom the show was written, to play Dolly for three months until it outran *Lady*. *Dolly* became the longest-running Broadway musical ever when it closed in 1970. Ten months later, *Fiddler on the Roof* broke that record.

Ginger Rogers, Martha Raye, Betty Grable, Bibi Osterwald, and Phyllis Diller also donned Dolly's feathered hats in the Broadway production. Mary Martin and Loring Smith (who played the merchant in Wilder's *Matchmaker*) were the stars of the first touring company, which included London, Tokyo, and even Vietnam (to entertain American troops) on its itinerary. Two subsequent tours starred Channing, Eve Arden, Dorothy Lamour, and Grable. Broadway revivals have played in 1974 (with Bailey) and 1978 (with Channing). Barbra Streisand was the screen Dolly in 1969.

Carol Channing displays the practical side of the title character of *Hello, Dolly!*

ANY WEDNESDAY

by Muriel Resnick

Opened February 18, 1964

Music Box Theatre

982 Performances

Directed by Henry Kaplan

Produced by George W. George, Frank Granat, Howard Erskine, Edward Specter Productions, and Peter S. Katz.

Cast: Sandy Dennis (Ellen Gordon); Don Porter (John Cleeves); Gene Hackman (Cass Henderson); Rosemary Murphy (Dorothy Cleeves).

Like *Mary, Mary, Any Wednesday* dealt with sex and taxes. In Muriel Resnick's comedy, a high-powered industrialist keeps his kooky young mistress in a tax-exempt apartment, claiming it as a business deduction and visiting her every Wednesday. As with numerous other sex comedies of the period, the play turns on a simple plot twist. A new secretary mistakenly sends the businessman's wife and a visiting manufacturer from Akron, Ohio, to the apartment. Before the final curtain, the mistress is successfully wooed by the out-of-town manufacturer, and the tycoon returns to his wife.

This fluffy piece offered the offbeat charm of Sandy Dennis, a quirky actress given to highly individual line readings and mannerisms, as the childlike kept woman. She had won a Tony for a supporting role in *A Thousand Clowns* the season before.

The team of George W. George and Frank Granat produced the comedy. For contrast they also did a "prestige piece," a biographical drama on the Welsh poet Dylan Thomas called *Dylan*, starring Alec Guinness. They also put on a musical, *Ben Franklin in Paris*, starring Robert Preston the following fall.

Any Wednesday had more production complications than a business merger. By the time the show was in tryouts in New Haven, three more producers were added to the ranks and four directors had come and gone. Michael Rennie, who was playing the adulterous businessman, quit when the show moved to Boston because Gene Hackman, as his romantic rival, was getting too many laughs. Television actor Don Porter took over Rennie's role.

In New York, the show was a hit; Walter Kerr of the *Herald-Tribune* rapturously declared, "Let me tell you about Sandy Dennis. There should be one in every home."

Dennis won a second Tony. Guinness also won for his performance as Dylan Thomas. Despite this, *Dylan*, which had received mixed notices, ran only 153 performances. *Ben Franklin in Paris* played for a disappointing seven months. But *Any Wednesday* racked up 982 performances. Barbara Cook played her first nonmusical role when she replaced Sandy Dennis.

Jane Fonda and Jason Robards played in the 1966 movie version. Dean Jones enacted the young man from Akron, and Rosemary Murphy was retained from the Broadway show as the industrialist's waspish wife.

WHAT MAKES SAMMY RUN?

Book by Budd and Stuart Schulberg, based on the novel by Budd Schulberg.

Music and lyrics by Ervin Drake

Opened February 27, 1964

540 Performances

54th Street Theatre

Directed by Abe Burrows

Choreographed by Matt Mattox

Produced by Joseph Cates

Cast: Steve Lawrence (Sammy Glick); Robert Alda (Al Manheim); Sally Anne Howes (Kit Sargeant); Bernice Massi (Laurette Harrington); Barry Newman (Sheik Orsini); Walter Klavun (H.L. Harrington); John Dorrin (Osborn); George Coe (Julian Blumberg); Graciela Daniele (Rita Rio); Richard France (Tracy Clark); Edward McNally (O'Brien/Lucky Dugan); Arny Freeman (Sidney Fineman); Mace Barrett (Seymour Glick); Ralph Vucci (Bartender); Bob Maxwell (Technical Adviser); Lynn Gremmler, Doug Spingler (Swing Couple).

Budd Schulberg's bestselling novel about a ruthless Hollywood producer formed the basis of the Broadway musical *What Makes Sammy Run?* Collaborating with his brother Stuart, Schulberg co-wrote the book, while Ervin Drake provided the songs. (A nonmusical adaptation of the novel had appeared as a television drama in 1959, with Larry Blyden in the lead).

Like *Pal Joey* and J. Pierpont Finch, of *How to Succeed*, Sammy Glick (Steve Lawrence) is an opportunist clawing his way to the top. Whereas Joey and Finch had a certain charm, Sammy was an out-and-out scoundrel. As he advances from copyboy to scriptwriter to studio mogul, Sammy betrays friends and lovers left and right. One of his former comrades even commits suicide.

The reviews were mixed, but the box office was strong because of Lawrence's draw; he was popular through his recordings and television and nightclub appearances. The performer's recording of one of the songs from the score ("A Room Without Windows") became a hit.

The show continued to run while Lawrence's name was above the marquee, but there was friction between him and the producers as he began to ad-lib dialogue and miss performances. Ticket sales dropped, since the public could not be assured that the star they had paid to see would be onstage. Unable to find another headliner with equal appeal, the producers kept the show running with the unreliable Lawrence. *Sammy* closed after 540 performances, losing more than $285,000.

Lawrence returned to Broadway in *Golden Rainbow* (1968) co-starring with his wife Eydie Gorme. Again, the show received a tepid reception and ran for a few months on the strength of the stars' reputations.

Barbra Streisand as Fanny Brice in *Funny Girl.*

FUNNY GIRL

Book by Isobel Lennart

Music by Jule Styne

Lyrics by Bob Merrill

Opened March 26, 1964

1,348 Performances

Winter Garden Theatre

Directed by Garson Kanin and Jerome Robbins

Choreographed by Carol Haney

Produced by Ray Stark

Cast: Barbra Streisand (Fanny Brice); Sydney Chaplin (Nick Arnstein); Kay Medford (Mrs. Brice); Danny Meehan (Eddie Ryan); Roger De Koven (Florenz Ziegfeld, Jr.); Jean Stapleton (Mrs. Strakosh); Lydia S. Fredericks (Mrs. Meeker); Joyce O'Neal (Mrs. O'Malley); Joseph Macaulay (Tom Keeney); Royce Wallace (Emma); Robert Howard (John/Mike Halsey); Victor R. Helon (Heckie); Buzz Miller (Snub Taylor/Ben); Blair Hammond (Trombone Smitty); Alan E. Weeks (Five Finger Finney); Dick Perry (Trumpet Soloist); Shellie Farrell (Bubbles); Joan Lowe (Polly); Ellen Halpin (Maude); Marc Jordan (Stage Director/Mr. Renaldi); Sharon Vaughn (Mimsey/Showgirl); Diana Lee Nielsen (Showgirl); John Lankston (Ziegfeld Tenor/Adolph); George Reeder (Ziegfeld Lead Dancer); Rose Randolf (Mrs. Nadler); Larry Fuller (Paul); Joan Cory (Cathy); Lainie Kazan (Vera); Diane Coupe (Jenny).

After Carol Channing conquered in *Hello, Dolly!,* a second show highlighting the special talents of another leading lady opened in the same season. Whereas *Dolly* thrived in Channing's incarnation and in that of the many actresses who succeeded her, the funny girl of the musical bio of comedienne Fanny Brice will always indelibly be Barbra Streisand.

The twenty-one-year-old actress and singer had already established herself as a exceptional talent. Having stolen the show in a supporting role in *I Can Get It for You Wholesale* (1962), Streisand went on to numerous nightclub and television appearances before landing the role of Brice.

Funny Girl's story was a weak and conventional one of the homely Brice rising to stardom and surviving a heartbreaking marriage to gambler Nicky Arnstein. *Funny Girl*'s chief distinction was its incandescent star and vibrant score, especially when Streisand stopped the show cold with "People," "Don't Rain on My Parade," and "I'm the Greatest Star."

Independent film producer Ray Stark, who was married to Brice's daughter Frances, originally intended his mother-in-law's life story to be told on the screen. The producer made several attempts to record the Brice bio on celluloid. After Brice's death in 1951, Stark paid $50,000 to a publisher to have her autobiography destroyed so that his would be the only version. Then, in 1960, Isobel Lennart wrote another screen adaptation called *My Man.* This time, when Stark could not sell it to the Hollywood studios, he decided to take it to Broadway.

The rest of the creative personnel changed many times in a game of Broadway musical chairs. For the score, Jule Styne and Stephen Sondheim, his collaborator on *Gypsy,* were contacted. Styne was gung-ho, but Sondheim was not interested in another "lyrics-only" job. Bob Merrill eventually came on as wordsmith.

Jerome Robbins was the initial stager, and David Merrick was to co-produce with Stark. Both Merrick and Robbins eventually pulled out, but not before Merrick came up with *Funny Girl* as the title and Robbins insisted on Streisand for the lead. Mary Martin, Anne Bancroft, Carol Burnett, and Eydie Gorme had been considered. After Robbins and Styne saw Streisand at the Bon Soir nightclub, there was no other choice for them. The singer had stage presence, an exciting voice, comic timing, and even the same kind of unconventional appearance that Brice had used to her advantage in her act. The Starks were resistant, wanting someone a bit more glamorous, but the director and composer stood firm and eventually got their way.

Evidently Robbins did not get his way often enough and quit in a dispute with Stark. Bob Fosse, Sidney Lumet, and finally Garson Kanin replaced him. The script went through endless rewrites during a strenuous fifteen-week out-of-town tryout. As he did with *A Funny Thing Happened on the Way to the Forum*, Robbins came back to the show to fix it after having walked off. Kanin was still billed as the official director, but Robbins got a special box in the program with the words "Production Supervised by" above his name.

After five postponements and still more rewrites, opening night in New York finally came. Streisand was hailed and the musical praised for showcasing her. "Actress, songstress, dancer, comedienne, mimic, clown—she is the theatre's new girl for all seasons," declared *Time*. Streisand made her film debut in the 1968 movie version. She won an Oscar in a tie with Katharine Hepburn for *The Lion in Winter*, and she did a 1975 movie sequel, *Funny Lady*.

Mimi Hines also played the lead on Broadway and Marilyn Michaels toured in the road company.

Unfortunately, Streisand's performance in the London company of the show was her last legitimate stage appearance. A dynamic stage performer had been lost to Hollywood, as would happen increasingly in succeeding years.

Jack Albertson (standing) is left out of the joke between Irene Daily and Martin Sheen in *The Subject Was Roses*.

THE SUBJECT WAS ROSES

by Frank D. Gilroy
Opened May 25, 1964
832 Performances
Royale Theatre
Directed by Ulu Grosbard
Produced by Edgar Lansbury
Cast: Jack Albertson (John Cleary); Irene Daily (Nettie Cleary); Martin Sheen (Timmy Cleary).

Sheer determination turned *The Subject Was Roses*, a small-scale kitchen-sink drama with a shoestring budget and no apparent prospects, into a long-running hit. Frank D. Gilroy's semi-autobiographical play focuses on the dysfunctional relationships in an Irish-American family of

three, just when the son returns home from World War II and finds his parents bitterly divided.

Gilroy had had a success off-Broadway with *Who'll Save the Plowboy?*, winner of the off-Broadway Obie Award for Best Play of 1962, and was making a living writing for films and television. He was determined to bring his new play *Roses* to Broadway.

He was also insistent on casting Jack Albertson, a former vaudevillian who had played second banana to the likes of Bert Lahr and Phil Silvers, for the role of the father. The playwright told *Playbill* magazine, "I wanted Jack Albertson for a key part, but since he wasn't a Big Name it took a year and a half to raise the money. I wanted Ulu Grosbard to direct, and he had no Broadway credits either. Ed Lansbury, whom I'd known when he was a set designer for [the TV series] *Studio One*, raised the money and produced the play—very well—for less than $40,000."

As with William Gibson's *Two for the Seesaw*, almost everyone involved was new to Broadway. The author, producer, director, and general manager would all be making their debuts. Like Gibson, Gilroy kept a production diary and published it with the script of the play. In it he voiced his frustration about dredging up backers for his project: "*Roses* is like a diamond lying in plain view on the street: no one picks it up because each assumes that if it were of real value, someone would have grabbed it before this."

The advance sale for *Roses* was a paltry $165. An out-of-town tryout was judged too costly, so there was no breaking-in of the script before live audiences, except for a brief preview period. The opening was toward the end of the season after the awards had been given out. The public was unfamiliar with Albertson and his co-stars Irene Dailey and newcomer Martin Sheen. Everything spelled a short run.

But the reviews were encouraging. "From this day forth, Frank D. Gilroy is a major playwright," cheered the *World-Telegram*. The producer borrowed money in order to keep the play running and slowly build an audience. There was not a full house until the 136th performance. *Roses* finally blossomed when the play won the triple crown of the Tony, Pulitzer, and Drama Critics Circle Awards at the end of the following season. Albertson also copped a Tony as Best Featured Actor.

Keeping a marginal play going on the prohibitively expensive Broadway of today would be a gamble that few, if any, contemporary producers would risk.

Gilroy adapted his play to the screen in 1968. Albertson and Sheen repeated their roles, with Patricia Neal as the mother. Albertson won an Oscar as Best Supporting Actor, making him one of the few performers to win an Oscar and a Tony for playing the same role.

Gilroy's next four Broadway offerings *That Summer—That Fall* (1967); *The Only Game in Town* (1968); *Last*

Licks (1979); and *Any Given Day* (1993) were not as well received and closed after brief runs.

A 1991 off-Broadway revival of *Roses* at the Roundabout Theatre featured John Mahoney, Dana Ivey, and Patrick Dempsey.

FIDDLER ON THE ROOF

Book by Joseph Stein, based on the stories by Sholom Aleichem.

Music by Jerry Bock

Lyrics by Sheldon Harnick

Opened September 22, 1964

3,242 Performances

Imperial Theatre

Directed by Jerome Robbins

Choreographed by Jerome Robbins

Produced by Harold Prince

Cast: Zero Mostel (Tevye); Maria Karnilova (Golde); Beatrice Arthur (Yente); Austin Pendelton (Motel Kamzoil); Joanna Merlin (Tzeitel); Julia Migenes (Hodel); Tanya Everett (Chava); Marilyn Rogers (Shprintze); Linda Ross (Bielke); Bert Convy (Perchik); Michael Granger (Lazar Wolf); Joe Ponazecki (Fyedka); Helen Verbit (Shandel); Zvee Scooler (Mordcha); Gluck Sandor (Rabbi); Leonard Frey (Mendel); Paul Lipson (Avram); Maurice Edwards (Nahum); Sue Babel (Grandma Tzeitel); Carol Sawyer (Fruma-Sarah); Mitch Thomas (Yussel); Joseph Sullivan (Constable); Robert Berdeen (Sasha); Gino Conforti (The Fiddler).

Zero Mostel as Tevye the milkman wishes he were a rich man in *Fiddler on the Roof*.

Zero Mostel followed his side-splitting Pseudolus in *A Funny Thing Happened on the Way to the Forum* with the long-suffering Tevye in *Fiddler on the Roof*. The musical retelling of Yiddish writer Sholom Aleichem's stories about the trials of Tevye the milkman in Tsarist Russia ran for almost eight years. It was Broadway's longest-running show until 1979, when *Grease* slid by *Fiddler*'s record. Mostel explained *Fiddler*'s longevity in a *New York Times* interview: "Tevye is universal. He has no nationality really, because he symbolizes the underpriviledged in every country—no matter what adversity he meets, he just puffs up his chest and goes on."

The show opens with the cast extolling the importance of "Tradition" in their little Jewish Orthodox community of Anatevka. But as the tale unfolds, Tevye, his family, and the entire village are bereft of their way of life. Three of Tevye's five daughters marry against Orthodox customs. At one of the weddings, tradition is broken as men dance with women. Near the final curtain, a government official announces that the town will be destroyed in a pogrom and that every Jew must leave the country. As the townspeople are scattered, Tevye and his family hope for a new life in America.

Mostel lightened the dark mood with comic conservations with God ("With your help, I'm starving to death," he complains to the deity). The songs "If I Were a Rich Man," "Matchmaker, Matchmaker," "Sunrise, Sunset," and "Do You Love Me?" proved hits. Jerome Robbins's staging of a hilarious dream sequence and a bottle dance were highlights.

The idea for the show was born with composer Jerry Bock, lyricist Sheldon Harnick, and librettist Joseph Stein, who had collaborated on *The Body Beautiful* (1958), a boxing musical. The songwriters wanted to work with Stein again and suggested that they adapt *Wandering Star*, a novel by Aleichem.

Stein told the *New York World-Telegram*, "I didn't like it for a musical. But it joggled my memory. When I was a child in the Bronx, my father used to read to me Sholom Aleichem's short stories about Tevye and his daughters. I suggested the stories, and Jerry and Sheldon were intrigued. We decided not to approach a producer until we were finished. We were in love with it, but weren't sure it would work. It was pure speculation and pure affection."

This would not be the first time Tevye had appeared in theatrical form. A Yiddish theatre production entitled *Tevye the Dairyman* had opened in 1935 and was filmed in 1939. *Tevye and His Daughters* had appeared in 1957.

Once a script was finished, producer Fred Coe optioned the show, but had trouble raising the necessary capital. Then Harold Prince, director and producer of Bock and Harnick's *She Loves Me*, stepped in as co-pro-

ducer. When the partnership didn't work out, Prince bought out Coe's interest and became sole producer.

Before rehearsals began, the title was changed from *Tevye and His Daughters* to *Fiddler on the Roof*, inspired by Marc Chagall's surrealist painting in which a fiddler soars over a small Eastern European town. Boris Aronson's stylized set also reflected Chagall's influence.

For the vital role of Tevye, stars such as Danny Kaye, Danny Thomas, Tom Bosley, and Howard Da Silva were considered. Prince wanted Mostel. Despite the actor's hijinks during the run of *Forum*, the producer was sure Mostel was the right candidate. Mostel drew critical raves and won another Tony Award, but continued to mug and ad-lib during his nine-month tenure. When his contract was up, he was followed by six Tevyes: Luther Adler, Herschel Bernardi, Harry Goz, Jerry Jarrett, Jan Peerce, and Paul Lipson, with no slackening at the box-office. Bette Midler and Pia Zadora appeared as two of Tevye's daughters during the Broadway run. The national tour was headlined by Luther Adler.

Mostel returned to the role in a national tour which stopped in New York in 1976. Topol, the London and the 1971 film Tevye, starred in a 1990 revival.

GOLDEN BOY

Book by Clifford Odets and William Gibson, based on the play by Clifford Odets.

Music by Charles Strouse

Lyrics by Lee Adams

Opened October 20, 1964

569 Performances

Majestic Theatre

Directed by Arthur Penn

Choreographed by Donald McKayle

Produced by Hillard Elkins

Cast: Sammy Davis, Jr. (Joe Wellington); Billy Daniels (Eddie Satin); Paula Wayne (Lorna Moon); Johnny Brown (Ronnie); Kenneth Tobey (Tom Moody); Ted Beniades (Roxy Gottlieb); Louis Gossett (Frank); Charles Welch (Tokio); Roy Glenn (Mr. Wellington); Jeannette DuBois (Anna); Terrin Miles (Terry); Stephen Taylor (Stevie); Benny Payne (Benny); Albert Popwell (Al); Lola Falana (Lola); Jaime Rogers (Lopez); Mabel Robinson (Mabel); Lester Wilson (Les); Don Crabtree (Drake); Theresa Merritt (Theresa); Maxwell Glanville (Fight Announcer); Bob Daley (Reporter); Ralph Vucci (Driscoll); Buck Heller (Hoodlum).

Diminutive, dynamic Sammy Davis, Jr. was one of the most versatile talents in all of show business, eventually conquering all media. After films, television, and nightclubs, the next logical step was Broadway. His first venture there, *Mister Wonderful* (1956), was a virtual re-creation of his nightclub act. Although it gave him the opportunity to wow the folks with his singing, dancing, and impressions, it was not very demanding of his abilities as an actor. His next show would make use of all his considerable skills.

It was producer Hillard Elkins's idea to star Davis in an updated musical version of *Golden Boy*, Clifford Odets' 1937 drama of a young man torn between his true calling as a violinist and the fast fame and money of becoming a boxer. Davis was cast in the lead role of Joe Wellington (punnily changed from Joe Bonaparte in the play) and the emphasis was shifted from commerce versus art to racial conflict.

Unlike the Diahann Carroll vehicle, *No Strings*, Davis's show was a serious attempt to integrate the cast beyond its star and to directly address issues of concern to African-American audiences. A production number, "Don't Forget 127th Street," was set in Harlem, while Diahann Carroll only sang about coming from "north of Central Park" in *No Strings*.

British director Peter Coe (*Oliver!*) was hired to stage the show. Clifford Odets began the rewrite of his original play, but died of cancer before he finished. As a result, everyone connected with the production made some contribution to the book, even Davis. The script went through numerous changes during its twenty-two-week pre-New York tryout. First Joe was a violinist, then a pianist, finally a medical student.

The long out-of-town tour began in Philadelphia. The press was not loving in the City of Brotherly Love, and the reaction was the same in Boston. Elkins asked Elliott Norton, the dean of the Boston critics, for his advice on what didn't glisten in *Golden Boy*. As a result, a new librettist and director were hired.

Peter Coe was fired and replaced by Arthur Penn. Playwright William Gibson, who had worked with Penn on *Two for the Seesaw* and *The Miracle Worker*, came aboard to fix the book. The new personnel still didn't have it ready after a stint in New Haven. Elkins booked the production into Detroit's Fisher Theatre—a classic case of bad timing, since the motor city was troubled with a race riot. The onstage interracial romance between Joe and his manager's white mistress Lorna Moon (Paula Wayne) paralleled Davis's real-life marriage to Swedish film actress May Britt. Numerous death threats were received and necessitated bodyguards for the two leads.

When the musical finally opened on Broadway, it was in good shape for the big bout with the critics. Most praised Davis's powerhouse performance and choreographer Donald McKayle's brilliant staging of the climactic fight scene. But they clobbered the weak script. "At the same time Sammy Davis is winning one fight, the musical is losing another to the book" was Walter Kerr's jab in the *Herald-Tribune*. Audiences flocked to see Davis, but once he left after a two-year run, the show closed without having earned back its initial investment.

LUV

by Murray Schisgal
Opened November 11, 1964
901 Performances
Booth Theatre
Directed by Mike Nichols
Produced by Claire Nichtern
Cast: Alan Arkin (Harry Berlin); Eli Wallach (Milt Manville); Anne Jackson (Ellen Manville).

Like many other hit comedies of the decade, *Luv* had a small cast and a single set. But it differed from shows like *Mary, Mary, Barefoot in the Park*, and *Any Wednesday*, in that the setting was not a Manhattan living room, but a bridge from which one of the characters was attempting to jump. Ironically, another show about leaping from bridges, the musical *Kelly* opened the same season. *Kelly* sank on its opening night, while *Luv* played 901 performances.

In slightly exaggerated style, playwright Murray Schisgal satirized neurotic New Yorkers and psychoanalysis. The characters were three highly educated, deeply troubled sides of a romantic triangle. Each was striving after his or her own ideal of love. Real-life husband and wife Eli Wallach and Anne Jackson were the comically co-dependent Manvilles. Alan Arkin, fresh from a splashy triumph in another comedy, *Enter Laughing*, was Harry Berlin, the failed suicide who crashes into their marriage.

Schisgal explained the spelling of the title to the *New York Post*. "Love properly spelled is a word that has lost its meaning for most of us. The emotion we feel should be described by a cliché or should be described by another word or redefined."

Luv was the playwright's Broadway debut. He had worked at various odd jobs to support himself, including setting up pins in a bowling alley, hanging up dresses at Klein's Department Store, and unsuccessfully being a teacher and a lawyer. After turning out three novels and sixty short stories (all unpublished), he went to Spain to write. On the way, he left five of his one-acts in London with the British Drama League. Two of them *The Typists* and *The Tiger* were produced there in 1960. Then a British production of *Luv* was mounted in 1963.

That same year, Clare Nichtern, a former production coordinator with the Phoenix Theatre and one of New York's few female producers, presented *The Typists* and *The Tiger* off-Broadway with the Wallachs. The double bill had a moderately profitable run and gave Nichtern the clout to get *Luv* on Broadway. She acquired the services of the hottest young director on the street, Mike Nichols, who went right from *Luv* to *The Odd Couple* and won a Tony for his direction of both shows.

Larry Blyden, Gabriel Dell, and Barbara Bel Geddes were the New York replacement company, while Tom Bosley, Herb Edelman, and Dorothy Loudon toured the country.

Peter Falk, Jack Lemmon, and Nichols' comedy partner Elaine May formed the trio in the 1967 movie, which attempted to expand the play beyond the bridge setting. A musical version entitled *Love* played off-Broadway for a brief run in 1984. A revised musical version, *What About Love?* was presented off-Broadway in 1991.

THE ODD COUPLE

by Neil Simon

Opened March 10, 1965

964 Performances

Plymouth Theatre

Directed by Mike Nichols

Produced by Saint Subber

Cast: Walter Matthau (Oscar Madison); Art Carney (Felix Ungar); Paul Dooley (Speed); Nathaniel Frey (Murray); Sidney Armus (Roy); John Fiedler (Vinnie); Carole Shelley (Gwendolyn Pidgeon); Monica Evans (Cecily Pidqeon).

In *Barefoot in the Park*, Neil Simon chronicled the first week of marriage. In his next play, *The Odd Couple*, he examined the wreckage left in the wake of divorce.

Newswriter Felix Ungar, recently estranged from his wife, shares quarters with his divorced pal, sportswriter Oscar Madison. The problem is that Felix is an obsessive neatnik, Oscar a compulsive slob. The mismatched roommates soon find themselves engaged in the same battles and conflicts which caused their marriages to end.

Simon explained the origin for the now-classic comedy to the *Manchester Guardian*: "The idea came to me when I was at a party in California. There were twenty-four people there; and do you know every one of them was a divorcee? The men were either on their second marriage or recently divorced, and the women were in the process of getting divorced. All the men shared apartments because they had to be able to keep up their payments and this was the cheapest method of living. And I noticed that two friends of mine were going through the same problems that they'd had in their marriage and I thought it was a good idea for a play." At the time, Simon's brother Danny was going through a separation and setting up housekeeping with a friend who was divorced.

Director Mike Nichols won a Tony Award for his staging of both *Luv* and Simon's new hit. Walter Matthau also won a Tony for his portrayal of the sloppy sportswriter. Art Carney did an about-face from his loose-limbed Ed

The eternal battle of slob versus neatnik rages as Oscar Madison (Walter Matthau) confronts Felix Ungar (Art Carney) in *The Odd Couple*.

Norton character on TV's *The Honeymooners* to play the buttoned-down Felix.

Simon won a Tony for this, his third long-running hit, as well. That year there were separate categories for Best Play and Best Author of a Play. Simon triumphed as outstanding playwright, but *The Subject Was Roses*, which opened late the previous season, was named Best Play.

Matthau played Oscar in the 1968 Paramount movie version, with Jack Lemmon as the persnickety Felix.

Simon later reversed the sexes of the characters and came up with a female *Odd Couple*. Rita Moreno and Sally Struthers were Olive Madison and Florence Ungar for a moderate Broadway run in 1985.

Jack Klugman and Tony Randall are the most famous Oscar and Felix, having played them for five years on the ABC series based on the play (1970–75).

ABC brought back the series in 1982 with two black actors, Ron Glass and Demond Wilson, as the mismatched pair; it ran for only 13 episodes. There was even a 1975 animated cartoon version (called *The Oddball Couple*) with Fleabag, a slobby dog, and Spiffy, a fussy cat, as the two leads.

HALF A SIXPENCE

Book by Beverly Cross, based on the novel *Kipps*, by H.G. Wells.

Music and lyrics by David Heneker

Opened April 25, 1965

512 Performances

Broadhurst Theatre

Directed by Gene Saks

Choreographed by Onna White

Produced by Allen-Hodgdon, Stevens Productions, and Harold Fielding

Cast: Tommy Steele (Arthur Kipps); Polly James (Ann Pornick); Carrie Nye (Helen Walsingham); Ann Shoemaker (Mrs. Walsingham); John Cleese (Young Walsingham); Will Mackenzie (Sid Pornick); Norman Allen (Buggins); Grover Dale (Pearce); James Grout (Chitterlow); William Larsen (Carshot); Michele Hardy (Flo); Reby Howells (Emma); Louise Quick (Kate); Sally Lee (Victoria); Mercer McLeod (Mr. Shalford); Trescott Ripley (Mrs. Botting); Eleonore Treiber (Laura); Rosanna Huffman (Girl Student); Sterling Clark (Boy Student); Sean Allen (Photographer); Robert Gorman (Photographer's Asst.); Reid Klein (1st Reporter); Fred Cline (2nd Reporter); Ann Rachel (Gwendolin).

With little fanfare and no big names in the cast, *Half a Sixpence*, a British import, opened toward the end of the 1964–65 season and became a sleeper hit. Based on H.G. Wells's 1905 novel *Kipps*, the show focused on the up-and-down career of one Arthur Kipps, a lively young Cockney who inherits a fortune, woos two women, loses his money, and winds up happily ever after running a small bookstore.

The slender plot was a diversion to mark time between the numbers. As the *Saturday Review* noted in its review, "Like many an old-fashioned musical comedy, the story of *Half a Sixpence* is not much more than a plausible excuse for its songs, dances, and slightly corny jokes. But very for-

tunately, the new British import is also an excuse for presenting Tommy Steele."

Steele, formerly one of Britain's top rock stars, had made a tremendous hit with *Sixpence* in London, playing it for eighteen months. His boyish charm and boundless energy gave life to the thin offering. Harold Hobson of the *London Times* was moved to say, "Mr. Steele's performance is the best I have ever seen in a musical. It is the most varied and the most penetrating."

There was very little dancing in the original British staging. For the Broadway edition, choreographer Onna White was hired to add kicks to *Sixpence*'s step. Steele did not know how to dance. "But I was determined to learn," he told *Life* magazine. "I came to the States six weeks early and did barre work from ten in the morning until six every night. I'd go home and soak in a soda bath for hours every night."

The cast also included Carrie Nye as Kipps' snobbish fiancée, and John Cleese, who left an off-Broadway revue, *Cambridge Circus*, for the role; Cleese would later become famous as one of the zanies of TV's *Monty Python's Flying Circus*. Word Baker, director of the long-running off-Broadway hit *The Fantasticks*, was hired to stage the show. He was later fired and replaced by Gene Saks in his musical debut—just three days before out-of-town tryouts began in Boston.

Steele put over a total of twelve numbers, even playing the banjo in one ("Money to Burn"). *Sixpence* overshadowed the other British shows that season (*Oh What a Lovely War* and *The Roar of the Greasepaint, the Smell of the Crowd*), running over a year.

Tony Tanner, Joel Grey, and Dick Kalman replaced Steele on Broadway, while Kalman and Kenneth Nelson played the leads in separate tours. The Broadway production closed at a loss, as Steele's absence led to a weaker box office. But the touring version earned back the loss and the entire enterprise showed a profit.

Steele repeated his role in the mediocre 1967 film version

THE IMPOSSIBLE YEARS

by Bob Fisher and Arthur Marx

Opened October 13, 1965

670 Performances

Playhouse Theatre

Directed by Arthur Storch

Produced by David Black and Walter A. Hyman

Cast: Alan King (Dr. John Kingsley); Jane Elliot (Linda Kingsley); Neva Small (Abbey Kingsley); Janet Ward (Alice Kingsley); Terrence Logan (Ricky Fleisher); Bert Convy (Richard Merrick); Sudie Bond (Miss Hammer); Donna Baccala (Francine); Kenneth Carr (Wally); Jeff Siggins (Dennis); Scott Glenn (Andy); Michael Hadge (Bartholomew Smuts); Michael Vale (Dr. Harold Fleischer); Jack Hollander (Arnold Brecher); Kenneth Kealey (Irwin Kniberg).

The generation gap hit Broadway with *The Impossible Years*, a leering comedy in which comedian Alan King played a psychiatrist and bestselling author of a book on how to control teenagers. The central joke was, of course, that King's character proved unable to cope with his own children, an eighteen-year-old daughter and her thirteen-year-old sister.

Although most critics dismissed the comedy as television without the commercials, the play by Bob Fisher and Arthur Marx (son of Groucho) was a big hit with theatre parties and ran for 670 performances. Norman Nadel of the *World-Telegram* sneered, "A few honest laughs are scattered across *The Impossible Years*, but they certainly aren't worth sitting through two hours of television pap. . . . Bob Fisher and Arthur Marx . . . must have drawn their inspiration from every movie, play, and television show dealing with parents and teenagers over the past forty years." The authors were indeed from the world of sitcoms, having worked together on scripts for such TV series as *My Three Sons* and *McHale's Navy*.

During their work sessions, Marx would constantly regale his partner Fisher with tales of his troublesome daughter Linda. It was Fisher's suggestion that they write a play about parents and their terrible teens. They incorporated several of Marx's own experiences into the show, even naming the daughter Linda.

Their collaboration was similiar to the featherweight adolescent comedies of the '40s (*Junior Miss, Dear Ruth, Kiss and Tell*), except that Linda Kingsley was more sexually advanced than her bobby-soxer predecessors. By the final curtain, she has lost her virginity and subsequently married. Luckily, the groom is not any of the boyfriends who were her parents' worst nightmares, but a perfectly respectable young man, played by Bert Convy.

After playing Nathan Detroit in a City Center revival of *Guys and Dolls*, Borscht-Belt comic King took on the unlikely role of an intellectual head shrinker—one who knew how to deliver punchlines. Sample joke: "If I ever meet the man who invented the portable transistor radio, I'll kick him in the Watusi." The play's humor totally ignored the social conflicts of the day, concentrating instead on family squabbles. Most of the gags were at the expense of the younger generation, depicting them as sloppy, promiscuous, and drug-crazed. (Three years later, *Hair* opened, and rebellious youngsters got to tell their side of the generational battle.)

Sam Levene replaced King on Broadway and also played the father on a national tour. When Metro-Goldwyn-Mayer made the film version in 1968, the very elegant and British David Niven (about as far away from Alan King as you could get) was cast in the lead.

MAN OF LA MANCHA

Book by Dale Wasserman
Music by Mitch Leigh
Lyrics by Joe Darion
Opened November 22, 1965
2,328 Performances
ANTA Washington Square Theatre
Directed by Albert Marre
Choreographed by Jack Cole
Produced by Albert W. Selden and Hal James

Cast: Richard Kiley (Cervantes/Quixote); Irving Jacobson (Sancho); Joan Diener (Aldonza); Ray Middleton (The Innkeeper); Robert Rounseville (The Padre); Jon Cypher (Dr. Carrasco); Mimi Turque (Antonia); Gino Conforti (The Barber); Shev Rodgers (Pedro, Head Muleteer); Eleanore Knapp (The Housekeeper); Marceline Decker (Maria, The Innkeeper's Wife); Gerianne Raphael (Fermina); Renato Gibelli (Capt. of the Inquisition); David Serva (Guitarist); Harry Theyard, Eddie Roll, John Aristedes, Antony De Vecchi, Fernando Grahal (Muleteers).

Man of La Mancha came into being because of a mistake in a newspaper column. Television and film writer Dale Wasserman was in Madrid doing research for a movie when he read an erroneous press report that the reason for his visit was to write a play about Don Quixote, the windmill-tilting hero of Miguel Cervantes' 16th-century classic. The mistake prompted Wasserman to read the two-volume opus and retrace both Quixote's and Cervantes' travels throughout Spain. He became fascinated with the delusional hero and the author who created him. Wasserman compiled a list of the more than 200 productions about the knight—operas, ballets, plays, films, and TV shows.

As a result of his extensive research, Wasserman wrote a television drama *I, Don Quixote*, which was broadcast on CBS in 1959, starring Lee J. Cobb. The author was going to make it into a straight play, but director Albert Marre suggested that it should be a musical. It would not be a show just about Quixote, but about his creator as well. As Wasserman explained to the *Herald-Tribune*, "It is not a play about Don Quixote. It is a play about Miguel Cervantes and his relationship to his fictional hero, Don Quixote."

Man of La Mancha takes place in a prison cell, where Cervantes is awaiting trial before the Spanish Inquisition. His fellow prisoners hold a mock trial to pass their own judgment. By way of explaining his idealistic philosophy, the writer acts out the story of Quixote, the eccentric old man who ventures forth in search of adventure, believing himself to be a chivalrous knight. Beset by cutthroats, bandits, and even his own relatives, Quixote remains true to his quest, which he articulates in the hit song "The Impossible Dream."

The production first played at the Goodspeed Opera House, in East Haddam, Connecticut. Richard Kiley, who had played opposite Gwen Verdon in *Redhead* and *New*

Girl in Town and Diahann Carroll in *No Strings*, now had a leading role in which he was not secondary to a female star. Marre's wife, Joan Diener (Kiley's co-star in *Kismet*) was Aldonza, the slovenly tavern wench who serves as Quixote's inspiration. Irving Jacobson, a veteran of Yiddish theatre, played Sancho Panza, the knight's trusty squire.

After the Goodspeed engagment, there were no suitable theatres available in the Broadway theatre district because of a booking jam. *La Mancha* found a home at the ANTA Washington Square Theatre in Greenwich Village. Some critics therefore referred to the show as being off-Broadway, but it was considered Broadway by the Tony Award Committee and made eligible for nomination. It won five Tonys, including Best Musical.

Then the ANTA Washington Square was torn down. The show moved to Broadway. The Martin Beck, the Eden, and the Mark Hellinger theatres, respectively, all played home to the dreaming knight.

José Ferrer was Quixote in the national tour. The Broadway Quixotes included Ferrer, John Cullum, David Atkinson, Hal Holbrook, and Bob Wright. During the New York run, there was an "international festival" in which actors who had played the lead in various foreign capitals would step into the role. These included Claudio Brook (Mexico), Keith Michell (England), Somegoro Ichikawa (Japan), Charles West (Australia), and Gideon Singer (Israel). Composer Jacques Brel played the role in Paris as well as translating the show into French.

Kiley returned to Broadway twice as Don Quixote. In 1972, Diener and Jacobson joined him. In 1977, Emily Yancy and Tony Martinez were his co-stars. The 1972 film version, starring Peter O'Toole, Sophia Loren, and James Coco was not well received. A 1992 revival starred Raul Julia and pop singer Sheena Easton as a very Scottish Aldonza.

Richard Kiley as Don Quixote explains his quest to innkeeper Robert Middleton in *Man of La Mancha*.

CACTUS FLOWER

by Abe Burrows, based on a play by Pierre Barillet and Jean Pierre Gredy.

Opened December 8, 1965

1,234 Performances

Royale Theatre

Directed by Abe Burrows.

Produced by David Merrick

Cast: Lauren Bacall (Stephanie); Barry Nelson (Julian); Brenda Vaccaro (Toni); Burt Brinckerhoff (Igor); Eileen Letchworth (Mrs. Durant); Robert Moore (Harvey); Arny Freeman (Senor Sanchez); Will Gregory (Customer); Michael Fairman (Waiter); Marjorie Battles (Botticelli's Springtime); Michael Fairman (Music Lover).

The Parisian playwriting team of Pierre Barillet and Jean Pierre Gredy were popular imports on Broadway in the '60s. American adaptations of two of the Barillet–Gredy comedies were presented during the decade and both were tremendous hits.

The first was *Cactus Flower*, followed by *Forty Carats* two seasons later. The first hit had a simple plot about Julian, a philandering bachelor dentist who claims to be married in order to avoid making a commitment to Toni, his much younger girlfriend. When the girl attempts suicide, the dentist agrees to divorce his "wife" and marry Toni. The girl demands to hear the news straight from the wife. So Julian is forced to produce his imaginary spouse. Stephanie, his starchy nurse, reluctantly poses as the wife. As Stephanie takes on daring and flamboyant traits in order to play her "role," she blooms like the cactus flower of the title. The dentist realizes he really loves his nurse, and Toni winds up with a young man who lives in her apartment building.

Originally titled *Fleur de Cactus*, the play was translated literally by Lee Stevens of the William Morris Agency and sent to play doctor and director Abe Burrows, who Americanized the setting and humor.

Lauren Bacall was enlisted for the starring role of the blossoming nurse. Gunshy after her last stage appearance in *Goodbye, Charlie* (1959), which closed after three months, she was nevertheless willing to try the stage again. In her autobiography, Bacall states that she was one of the few actors to get along with tempestuous producer David Merrick. That is, until she asked for a raise for her dresser. Merrick exploded upon hearing the request and did not come backstage for the remainder of the run.

When then-unknown Brenda Vaccaro auditioned for the second female lead with her characteristic raspy voice, she was asked if she had a cold. "No, this is the way I talk," she replied. Joseph Campanella got the male lead, but when his performance was not up to par during out-of-town tryouts, Merrick replaced him with comedy veteran Barry Nelson (*The Moon Is Blue, Mary, Mary*).

While reviewers called the plot contrived, they admitted to laughing. The response of Howard Taubman of the *Times* was typical: "If you are willing to leave your mind parked outside, you will find the jokes fast and funny."

Betsy Palmer succeeded Bacall, and Kevin McCarthy and later Lloyd Bridges took over Nelson's role. Burrows again revamped the script for a London edition, which was also a hit.

Cactus Flower bloomed on the screen in 1969, starring Walter Matthau and Ingrid Bergman. Goldie Hawn made her film debut as Toni and won an Oscar for Best Supporting Actress for this role.

SWEET CHARITY

Book by Neil Simon, based on the film *Nights of Cabiria* by Federico Fellini, Tunio Pinelli, and Ennio Flaiano.

Music by Cy Coleman

Lyrics by Dorothy Fields

Opened January 29, 1966

608 Performances

Palace Theatre

Directed and choreographed by Bob Fosse

Produced by Robert Fryer, Lawrence Carr, and Sylvia and Joseph Harris

Cast: Gwen Verdon (Charity); John McMartin (Oscar); Helen Gallagher (Nickie); Thelma Oliver (Helene); James Luisi (Vittorio Vidal); Barbara Sharma (Career Girl/Rosie); John Wheeler (Herman/1st Cop); David Gold (Barney/2nd Cop); Arnold Soboloff (Daddy Johann Sebastian Brubeck); Sharon Ritchie (Ursula); Carmen Morales (Carmen); Michael Davis (Dark Glasses/Mike); John Stratton (Bystander/Waiter); Ruth Buzzi (Woman with Hat/Receptionist/Good Fairy); Gene Foote (Ice Cream Vendor); John Sharpe (Football Player); Lee Roy Reams (Young Spanish Man); Bud Vest (Manfred/Husband); Elaine Cancilla (Old Maid/Wife); I. W. Klein (Doorman); Harold Pierson (Brother Harold/Policeman); Eddie Gasper (Brother Eddie).

Gwen Verdon, Broadway's top dancing actress and the winner of four Tony Awards, had not been in a show since *Redhead* in 1959. Her husband Bob Fosse brought her back with *Sweet Charity*, a dazzling showcase for her talents.

The show was based on *Nights of Cabiria*, Federico Fellini's 1957 Italian film about a soft-hearted prostitute. Coincidentally, that movie also featured the director's wife (Giulietta Masina) in the starring role.

Cabiria became Charity Hope Valentine and was changed from a hooker to the more musical occupation of dance-hall hostess. At that time, the Times Square area adjacent to the Broadway theatre district was filled with sleazy "dance palaces," remnants of the '20s and '30s, when lonely guys would pay "ten cents a dance." In the '60s, the "hostesses" would charge male customers $6.50 for a half-hour of their time to dance, talk, or grope a little. (During the '70s, the dance halls finally vanished, to be replaced by porno theatres.)

Verdon explained the show's genesis to the *New York Journal-American*, "Ever since *Redhead*, the producers of that show were looking for the right script. One day we all saw a film, *Nights of Cabiria*. . . . Bob Fosse came up with the idea of taking it out of Italy, putting it in the strange world of dance-hall palaces and keeping the girl as the same warm-hearted, comical charmer, but having her work as a dance-hall hostess. . . . I worked for two nights in a dance palace on Broadway and I visited all of them as an observer."

Fosse himself would do even more research in the dance halls. As a result, he came up with the "Hey, Big Spender" number, in which the taxi dancers gyrate together like one huge octopus enticing prospective clients. "The Rich Man's Frug" cleverly parodied a current dance craze. Verdon was given numerous kicky star turns, including "If They Could See Me Now" and "I'm a Brass Band."

In addition to directing and choreographing, Fosse had started the libretto, but it needed work. His friend and neighbor Neil Simon largely rewrote the book, but demanded sole credit.

The production reopened the Palace Theatre, once a mecca for vaudeville performers; *Sweet Charity* was the first legitimate musical to play the refurbished theatre. Some critics were annoyed by the story's sleazy atmosphere, but all hailed Verdon, who remained with the show for most of its run. "In less skillful hands," said John Chapman of the *News*, "the story of *Sweet Charity* could be rather shoddy and its unhappy ending an emotional letdown. But with the fabulous Gwen Verdon in the number-one spot, the musical is out of the ordinary. Miss Verdon, an appealing comedienne and an incomparable dancer, seems to be onstage most of the time, working at a whirlwind pace."

Juliet Prowse played the title role in the London edition. Fosse made his film directorial debut with the 1969 film version starring Shirley MacLaine. Verdon was not considered a big enough box office draw to repeat her Broadway triumph on screen. She did coach MacLaine in the role.

Fosse also directed and Verdon coached Debbie Allen (and later Anne Reinking) in a well-received 1986 revival that received four Tony Awards, including two for featured performers Michael Rupert and Bebe Neuwirth. During the 1987 national tour of the *Charity* revival, which starred Donna McKechnie, Fosse suffered a heart attack and died.

Two other Fellini-inspired musicals were the flop *La Strada* (1969) and the hit *Nine* (1982), derived from the director's autobiographical film *8½*.

MAME

Book by Jerome Lawrence and Robert E. Lee, based on their play *Auntie Mame* and the novel by Patrick Dennis.

Music and lyrics by Jerry Herman

Opened May 24, 1966

1,508 Performances

The Winter Garden Theatre

Directed by Gene Saks

Choreographed by Onna White

Produced by Robert Fryer, Lawrence Carr, and Sylvia and Joseph Harris

Cast: Angela Lansbury (Mame Dennis); Beatrice Arthur (Vera Charles); Jane Connell (Agnes Gooch); Frankie Michaels (Patrick Dennis, age 10); Charles Braswell (Beauregard Burnside); Jerry Lanning (Patrick Dennis, age 19-29); Willard Waterman (Dwight Babcock); Charlotte Jones (Mme. Branislowski/Mother Burnside); George Coe (M. Lindsay Woolsey); Ron Young (Ralph Devine); Sab Shimono (Ito); Randy Kirby (Junior Babcock); Diana Walker (Gloria Upson); Johanna Douglas (Mrs. Upson/Dance Teacher); John C. Becher (Mr. Upson); Diane Coupe (Pegeen Ryan); Michael Maitland (Peter Dennis); Margaret Hall (Sally Cato); Ruth Ramsey (Cousin Fan); Clifford Fearl (Uncle Jeff); Jack Davison (Bishop/Leading Man); Art Matthews (Doorman/Stage Manager); Stan Page (Elevator Boy); Bill Stanton (Messenger); Jo Tract (Art Model); John Taliaferro (Gregor).

Five months after Gwen Verdon dazzled theatregoers as *Sweet Charity*, the same producers brought another flashy musical lady to Broadway: Angela Lansbury. As *Mame*, the latest incarnation of Patrick Dennis's outlandish aunt, Lansbury sang Jerry Herman's bouncy songs. Audiences fell in love with the unconventional madcap all over again and Lansbury became a major star. Yet she had been far from the first choice for this plum role.

Since Carol Channing had been such a hit in Herman's previous *Hello, Dolly!*, she was at the top of the list of potential Mames. But Channing turned it down, as did Ethel Merman, Mary Martin, and the original Mame, Rosalind Russell. Lucille Ball, Judy Garland, and even Elizabeth Taylor were also in the running.

Lansbury waited a year while forty actresses auditioned for the part. The creative team was reluctant to hire Lansbury because she was thought a secondary Hollywood character actress with little musical experience. Her only other musical stints were singing "Goodbye, Little Yellow Bird" in the film *The Picture of Dorian Gray* and playing the lead in *Anyone Can Whistle*, the Stephen Sondheim show which ran for a week on Broadway in 1964.

But she proved she could handle the singing and dancing chores expertly. The demanding role required Lansbury to sing seven songs, dance in numerous styles— including the tango, cakewalk, Charleston, shag and Lindy hop—as well as act. Her performance emphasized Mame's sentimental side, while Rosalind Russell had called attention to the character's eccentricities.

Lansbury told Rex Reed in a *New York Times* interview after the opening, "Let's face it. I've finally arrived. I'd

Jane Connell, Beatrice Arthur, and Angela Lansbury make a bold fashion statement in *Mame*.

always known I would hit on something that would unlock all the doors and hit all those people between the eyes. . . . I'm out to get the taxi drivers, shop ladies, and people on the street. Even teenagers are paying $9.50 a seat to see Mame. They love this dame."

They loved Lansbury, who won the first of her four Tonys for this role. The second was for *Dear World* (1969), a short-lived show by the same authors, in which she played a similar eccentric, the Countess Aurelia in this adaptation of *The Madwoman of Chaillot*. Her next two Tonys were for a revival of *Gypsy* (1974) and *Sweeney Todd* (1979).

While Lansbury went on to other shows, numerous other stars were only too happy to play Mame. There were almost as many Mames as there were Dollys. On Broadway, Lansbury was succeeded by Janis Paige, Celeste Holm, Jane Morgan, Ann Miller, and understudy Sheila Smith, who stepped into the role several times. Four road companies starred Holm, Lansbury, Susan Hayward, and Janet

Blair, respectively. Mames on the summer stock circuit included Edie Adams, Giselle McKenzie, Elaine Stritch, Juliet Prowse, Gretchen Wyler, and Patrice Munsel. Ginger Rogers toplined the London version. Just as in the case of the straight play, the British critics just didn't get the musical's humor. ("*Mame*, You're Just Not That Sensational" ran the sarcastic headline of the *London Daily Express* review.) And just as they did with the straight play, the British public took *Mame* to their hearts and the show was a popular success, if not a critical one.

The same could not be said of the 1974 screen edition of the show. Television's leading comedienne, Lucille Ball, was out of her element as the sophisticated Mame. Despite the presence of Beatrice Arthur reprising her stage role as actress Vera Charles, Mame's boozy best friend, the film quickly failed.

Lansbury did return in *Mame* on Broadway for a brief run in 1983.

DON'T DRINK THE WATER

by Woody Allen

Opened November 17, 1966

598 Performances

Morosco Theatre

Directed by Stanley Prager

Produced by David Merrick

Cast: Lou Jacobi (Walter Hollander); Kay Medford (Marion Hollander); Anita Gillette (Susan Hollander); Anthony Roberts (Axel Magee); Dick Libertini (Father Drobney); James Dukas (Krojack); House Jameson (Ambassador James F. Magee); Gerry Matthews (Kilroy); Curtis Wheeler (Burns); Gene Varrone (Chef); Oliver Clark (Sultan of Bashir); Donna Mills (Sultan's 1st Wife); John Hallow (Kaznar); Sharon Talbot (Countess Bordoni); Luke Andreas (Novotny); Jonathan Bolt (Waiter).

Before he blossomed into America's premier film director–writer–actor, Woody Allen was one of the country's top stand-up comedians and a fledging playwright. Aside from a few sketches he contributed to a revue called *From A to Z*, his first work for the stage was the gag-filled farce *Don't Drink the Water*. The plot concerned a typical American family on vacation in a mythical European country. They are mistakenly accused of being spies by the local Communist government. After a wild chase they take refuge at the American embassy, which is populated with such bizarre types as a priest who does magic tricks.

Tony Roberts, who later showed up in numerous Allen films as Woody's sidekick, played an Allen-like figure as the ambassador's klutzy son.

The play was originally going to be presented by Max Gordon, but the retired showman decided it wasn't ready. Broadway's busiest producer, David Merrick, took over; Allen's managers Charles Joffe and Jack Rollins were associate producers. Robert Sinclair was the director, but he hadn't staged in a play in thirty years. The production was a mess in Philadelphia, but a mess that got laughs. Still, the houses were not even half-filled, while *Breakfast at Tiffany's*, another Merrick-produced show trying out in Philly, was doing a boffo business. (Ironically, *Tiffany's* closed during previews in New York, while *Water* went on to a profitable run and a national tour). Sinclair was fired and Allen briefly filled in as director. Stanley Prager took over as permanent director and greatly improved the blocking and pacing. Business was better in the second tryout town, Boston, where Allen came down with the flu and did rewrites in his hotel bed.

There were thirteen cast changes on the road. Merrick had hired Vivian Vance (Ethel from *I Love Lucy*) to play the tourist mother because of her name value. Allen wanted a more Jewish type, and eventually Kay Medford, who had played Barbra Streisand's mother in *Funny Girl*, replaced Vance.

When the show finally opened in New York, critics found it lacking in structure, but plentiful in chuckles. Not minding the weak craftsmanship, and loving the jokes, audiences supported the show for eighteen months. Changing theatres twice prevented a longer run.

Vivian Blaine and Phil Foster starred in the national tour. The 1969 movie version was directed by Howard Morris and was declared a flop; Jackie Gleason, Estelle Parsons, and Ted Bessel muddled through an uninspired screen adaptation.

Allen wrote two more pieces for the theatre. *Play It Again, Sam* (1969), starring the author and Diane Keaton, was a variation on his nightclub routine about a young neurotic who is inept with women. *The Floating Light Bulb* (1981) was a Brooklyn variation on *The Glass Menagerie*.

CABARET

Book by Joe Masteroff, based on *Berlin Stories,* by Christopher Isherwood, and on *I Am a Camera,* by John Van Druten.

Music by John Kander

Lyrics by Fred Ebb

Opened November 20, 1966

1,165 Performances

Broadhurst Theatre

Produced and directed by Harold Prince

Choreographed by Ron Field

Cast: Lotte Lenya (Fraulein Schneider); Jack Gilford (Herr Schultz); Jill Haworth (Sally Bowles); Bert Convy (Clifford Bradshaw); Joel Grey (Master of Ceremonies); Peg Murray (Fraulein Kost); Edward Winter (Ernst Ludwig); John Herbert (Max); Howard Kahl (Custom Official); Tresha Kelly (Telephone Girl); Frank Bouley (Maitre D'); Ray Baron (Bartender); Mary Ehara, Rita O'Connor (Two Ladies); Mara Landi (Frau Wendel); Eugene Morgan (Herr Wendel); Miriam Lehmann-Haupt (Frau Kruger); Sol Frieder (Herr Erdmann); Jere Admire (Bobby); Bert Michaels (Victor); Jayme Mylroie (Greta); Robert Sharp (Felix).

The audience enters the theatre to be faced not with the traditional curtain but a huge mirror. Then a bizarre little figure in a clown's white makeup, with rouged cheeks and slicked-back hair, jauntily struts onto the stage and welcomes everyone. This was the opening of the dark-hued musical *Cabaret*, set in Berlin during the rise of the Nazi movement.

Fun-loving, amoral chanteuse Sally Bowles has a brief affair with American writer Clifford Bradshaw but breaks it off when she becomes pregnant. She has an abortion. Their relationship is paralleled by that of Cliff's landlady, Fraulein Schneider, and Herr Schultz, a Jewish fruit vendor. As anti-Semitic forces come to power, Schneider realizes she may lose her license to rent rooms if she marries a Jew. It was not your typical musical comedy plot with plenty of laughs. Even the chorus girls were made to look unattractive.

Not only was the subject matter more serious and sinister; the way in which the show was staged was startlingly different. Several of the numbers featuring the androgynous emcee took place in a "limbo" setting and ironically commented on the book scenes that preceded them. There were also conventionally directed numbers and scenes. Despite the grim storyline, theatregoers were fascinated by this bizarre but powerful mesh of traditional and ground-breaking musical styles.

Cabaret was based on Christopher Isherwood's *Berlin Stories* and John Van Druten's 1951 stage adapatation *I Am a Camera*, which had starred Julie Harris as Sally Bowles. After making his directorial debut with *She Loves Me* (1963), Harold Prince recruited Joe Masteroff, librettist for that show's book, and Fred Ebb and John Kander, from another Prince show *Flora, the Red Menace* (1965), for the songs. Prince wanted to show that the conditions in Weimar Germany which led to Nazism could be, and indeed were, developing again in America.

Casting Schneider, Schultz, and the Master of Ceremonies was not difficult, for the roles were written for Lotte Lenya, Jack Gilford, and Joel Grey. Lenya lent versimilitude to her role; she was a veteran of the German cabaret scene of the '20s and '30s, where she sang the songs of her husband Kurt Weill. The roles of Sally and Cliff were harder to cast. Liza Minnelli, the star of *Flora*, was consid-ered for Sally, but Prince and Masteroff didn't think she could handle a British accent, and she sang too well. (Sally is supposed to be only a so-so performer.) Jill Haworth got the part (opposite Bert Convy's Cliff). Melissa Hart played it on tour, while Judi Dench essayed the role in London.

The 1972 screenplay of *Cabaret,* by Jay Presson Allen and directed by Bob Fosse, went back to Van Druten's original stage adaptation and downplayed the characters of Fraulein Schneider and Herr Schultz. The film starred Minnelli as Sally, with Michael York as the writer infatuat-ed with her; he was changed from American to English, as in the original stories. Sally switched nationalities in reverse, from Brit to Yank. One element remained con-stant: Joel Grey as the smirking Master of Ceremonies. Songs were added to beef up Sally's part, including "Maybe This Time" and "Mein Herr." Minnelli, Grey, and Fosse won Oscars.

Prince directed the 1987 Broadway revival in which Grey was given star billing and Cliff was made bisexual, as had been originally intended. Regina Resnick, Werner Klemperer, and Alyson Reed were nominated for Tonys.

Joel Grey serves as the ominous Emcee in *Cabaret.*

I DO! I DO!

Book and lyrics by Tom Jones, based on *The Fourposter*, by Jan de Hartog.
Music by Harvey Schmidt
Opened December 5, 1966
560 Performances
46th Street Theatre
Directed by Gower Champion
Produced by David Merrick
Cast: Mary Martin (Agnes); Robert Preston (Michael).

Mary Martin—the innocent exotic of *One Touch of Venus*, cockeyed optimist of *South Pacific*, and governess of *The Sound of Music*—joined forces with Robert Preston—the huggable humbug of *The Music Man*—to make up the entire cast of *I Do! I Do!*, Broadway's first two-character musical. Harvey Schmidt and Tom Jones's adaptation of Jan de Hartog's 1951 *The Fourposter* had a run of 632 performances. Like de Hartog's play, *I Do! I Do!* covered fifty years of a marriage and took place entirely in the couple's bedroom. Only this time, the bed was moved and twirled in some of the musical numbers.

Preston and Martin were seldom gone from the stage in Gower Champion's clever staging. Both stars carried on props to eliminate scene breaks. While one was delivering a solo number, the other would be offstage making a costume change. Before the final scene, small makeup tables were wheeled on and the actors aged their faces in full view of the audience.

It was all stops out for both stars. The couple Michael and Agnes go through honeymoon, childbirth, near-divorce, comfortable middle-age, and golden anniversary. They even played musical instruments (Preston on the saxophone and Martin at the fiddle) to express joy at their offspring's leaving the nest in "When the Kids Get Married."

A musical *Fourposter* had been attempted before. *No Bed of Roses*, with songs by Martin Kalmanoff had been tried out in summer stock, but it never got any further.

For this incarnation, Preston came right from *The Lion in Winter*. Martin had just completed a London version of *Hello, Dolly!*. At the beginning of the run, there were no understudies or standbys. Due to the strenuousness of the roles, the performers could only play them once a day. Saturday or Wednesday matinees were eliminated, leaving only evening performances. A few performances had to be cancelled when Martin had a cold. Then Carol Lawrence and Gordon MacRae became a matinee company as a warm-up for replacing Martin and Preston, who were going on the national tour. Ian Carmichael and Anne Rogers made up the cast in London.

This was Martin's last Broadway musical. Her next New York stage appearance was in another two-character play, but it had no songs or dances. She co-starred with Anthony Quayle in *Do You Turn Somersaults?*, an adaptation of a Russian play about a retired circus performer, in 1978.

Preston's next musical was as silent-film pioneer Mack Sennett in the short-lived *Mack and Mabel* (1974). His last musical cast him in the unlikely role of a star of the Yiddish theatre in *The Prince of Grand Street*, which closed out of town in 1978.

Robert Preston and Mary Martin are newlyweds in *I Do! I Do!*

YOU KNOW I CAN'T HEAR YOU WHEN THE WATER'S RUNNING

by Robert Anderson

Opened March 13, 1967

755 Performances

Ambassador Theatre

Directed by Alan Schneider

Produced by Jack Farren and Gilbert Cates

Cast: Martin Balsam (Richard Pawling/George/Chuck); Eileen Heckart (Harriet/Edith/Muriel); George Grizzard (Jack Barnstable/Salesman/Herbert); Joe Silver (Herb Miller); Melinda Dillon (Dorothy/Jill/Clarice).

Martin Balsam (left) will do anything to get an audition for George Grizzard's new play in *You Know I Can't Hear You When the Water's Running.*

After exploring adolescent sexuality in his drama *Tea and Sympathy*, Robert Anderson examined the carnal urges of adults with a comic perspective in four one-act plays collectively entitled *You Know I Can't Hear You When the Water's Running.*

The quadruple bill was a field report from the sexual revolution, with each piece documenting a different bedroom skirmish. Unlike the lighthearted sex comedies of the *Any Wednesday* variety, *Water's Running* attempted to offer some serious commentary on the confusing nature of relationships and on attitudes towards sex.

The Shock of Recognition dealt with nudity in the theatre. An Anderson-like playwright wants to change his boy-scout image by having the lead character in his new play appear naked on stage. Although no one appeared without their drawers, the playlet anticipated the full disclosures of *Hair* and *Oh! Calcutta!* which would disrobe on Broadway only a few years later.

The Footsteps of Doves was a sketch about a couple arguing over purchasing two single beds and getting rid of their old reliable double. In *I'll Be Home for Christmas*, two parents are in conflict over how much they should tell their teenagers about the facts of life. The middle-aged suburban couple hardly know their children or what to say to them, reflecting the ever-widening generation gap of the '60s. The program ended with *I'm Herbert*, a "Who's-on-First" roundelay between two oldsters getting confused about their respective marital pasts.

Anderson had not had a hit since *Tea and Sympathy*. His *All Summer Long* (1954), and *Silent Night, Lonely Night* (1959) had brief stays on Broadway. Not unlike the author in *The Shock of Recognition*, he decided to change his image from polite gentleman to naughty satirist. Under the title of *Plays for a Saturday Night*, he wrote the four sketches for an off-Broadway company called The Paperback Theatre.

When the off-Broadway production never came about, the four-in-one script was peddled to Broadway. "The fact is, the play was turned down by a good many Broadway producers," the dramatist told the *Morning Telegraph*. "For one thing, they were wary of one-act plays. I have to say in justice that the history of success of

one-act plays has not been great. They have a way of not attracting audiences."

The script was picked up by two newcomers to the theatre, Jack Farren and Gilbert Cates, who had credits in television. Walter Matthau and Teresa Wright, Anderson's wife, were originally up for the leads. The roles eventually went to Martin Balsam and Eileen Heckart.

The advance sale was only slightly over $200, but positive reviews caused lines to form outside the box office.

Larry Blyden, Irene Dailey, and William Redfield replaced the leads on Broadway, while Eddie Bracken and Ruth Manning headed the national tour. Husband and wife King Donovan and Imogene Coca were starred in another traveling company. The London production, with Tom Ewell, Rosemary Murphy, and Mason Adams drew mixed notices and closed after 36 performances.

Water's Running and Neil Simon's *Plaza Suite* are the only evenings of one-acts to achieve a run of over 500 performances on Broadway.

PLAZA SUITE

by Neil Simon

Opened February 14, 1968

1,097 Performances

Plymouth Theatre

Directed by Mike Nichols

Produced by Saint Subber

Cast: George C. Scott (Sam/Jesse/Roy); Maureen Stapleton (Karen/Muriel/Norma); Claudette Nevins (Jean/Mimsey); Bob Balaban (Bellhop/Borden); José Ocasio (Waiter).

With *Plaza Suite*, Neil Simon continued his winning streak. Although his previous play, *The Star-Spangled Girl* (1966), had only a modest run of eight months, it was playing while three other Simon shows, *Barefoot in the Park, The Odd Couple,* and *Sweet Charity,* were still on the boards, giving the playwright four simultaneous productions on Broadway. The only other dramatists to achieve the same feat were Clyde Fitch, in 1901, and Avery Hopwood, in 1916. *Plaza Suite* began another Simon dynasty. It was still running when *Promises, Promises* (1968) and *Last of the Red Hot Lovers* (1969) opened.

The play is actually three one-acts, each of which concerns the romantic foibles of a middle-aged couple, and all the action is set in the same Plaza Hotel room. The first piece, *Visitor from Mamaroneck*, was Simon's first play with an unhappy ending and a serious bent. Karen and Sam Nash have been married twenty-four years (or twenty-three, depending on which of the two is correct). By booking them into the same suite they occupied during their honeymoon, Karen is hoping for a romantic anniversary celebration together, but Sam is absorbed by his business. As they argue over the correct date of their wedding and which floor their bridal suite was on, it comes out that Sam is trying recapture his lost youth by having an affair with his secretary. The play ends with Karen left alone and the future of her marriage in doubt.

In *Visitor from Hollywood*, a jaded movie producer comically seduces his former high school sweetheart, now a bored housewife. He slowly leads her into the bedroom as she quizzes him on the life-styles of his rich and famous friends. After the semi-serious *Mamaroneck* and the sex comedy *Hollywood*, the evening ends with *Visitor from Forest Hills*, an out-and-out farce in which a frustrated father attempts to get his reluctant daughter out of the bathroom where she has locked herself on her wedding day.

A fourth sketch, *Visitor from Toledo*, originally intended to open the show, was cut during rehearsals. "The first was about a man who came to New York from out of town and had lost his luggage," Simon told the *Newark Evening News.* "He got there in the middle of a transit strike. It was snowing. So after he had checked into the Plaza he had this monologue. We put *Plaza Suite* into rehearsal, and after about the fifth day [director] Mike Nichols said 'We just have too much show here. If we include that monologue, the curtain will be coming down at midnight.'" Simon later adapted this material into an original screenplay, *The Out-of-Towners* (1970), with Jack Lemmon and Sandy Dennis.

Maureen Stapleton and George C. Scott were acclaimed for their versatile acting of all three couples, and Mike Nichols won his third Tony Award for directing.

Dan Dailey and Lee Grant headed one national touring company, while Forrest Tucker and Betty Garrett toplined another.

Walter Matthau played all the male roles in the 1971 film, with Maureen Stapleton, Barbara Harris, and Lee Grant as the women. Simon returned to the hotel-room theme, setting the action on the West Coast in his 1976 comedy *California Suite,* which starred Tammy Grimes, George Grizzard, Jack Weston, and Barbara Barrie.

HAIR

Book and lyrics by Gerome Ragni and James Rado

Music by Galt MacDermot

Opened April 29, 1968

1,750 Performances

Biltmore Theatre

Directed by Tom O'Horgan

Choreographed by Julie Arenal

Produced by Michael Butler

Cast: James Rado (Claude); Gerome Ragni (Berger); Ronald Dyson (Ron); Steve Curry (Woof); Lamont Washington (Hud/Father/Principal); Lynn Kellogg (Sheila); Sally Eaton (Jeannie/Mother); Melba Moore (Dionne); Shelley Plimpton (Crissy); Jonathan Kramer (Tourist Lady/Mother/Young Recruit); Diane Keaton (Waitress/Parent); Robert I. Rubinsky (Tourist/Parent); Paul Jabara (Mother/General Grant); Lorri Davis (Abraham Lincoln); Donnie Burks (Sergeant); Suzannah Norstrand (Mother/Principal).

"Long, straight, curly, fuzzy, snaggy, shaggy, ratty, matty, oily, greasy, fleecy, shining, gleaming, streaming" were some of the adjectives used in the title song of *Hair* to describe—that's right—the hair of the cast. They could also be applied to the production itself. Subtitled "The American Tribal Love Rock Musical," this practically plotless and phenomenally profitable show was a free-form celebration of a youth culture that was in rebellion against mainstream society.

The loose staging and high-decible score were hailed as fresh and frank, but many were offended by the liberal use of four-letter words and "adult" subject matter. Even the song titles, such as "Sodomy," "Hashish," and "Colored Spade" were inflammatory. Virtually every hot button of the day was pressed: the Vietnam War, air pollution, interracial love, promiscuous sex (both gay and straight), and drugs. The most controversial scene took place at the end

This protest march scene from *Hair* reflected what was going on outside the theatre in 1968.

of the first act, when most of the ensemble stripped naked and stood facing the audience.

Public opinion was sharply divided. Letters to the *New York Times* called it both "the insidious undermining of every symbol and tradition held sacred in the history of Western culture" and "a manifestation and a contribution to social and mental health."

It was also Broadway's first hit rock musical. *Bye, Bye, Birdie* had satirized rock 'n' roll from a middle-aged parent's point of view, but *Hair* was the real thing. It offered staid suburbanites a chance to see what the hippies were up to.

Written by two actors with Broadway credits, Gerome Ragni and James Rado, and composer Galt MacDermot, the show was the premiere offering of Joseph Papp's New York Shakespeare Fetsival in its new quarters in the refurbished Astor Place Library. Michael Butler, a wealthy Chicago entrepreneur with no theatrical experience, attended a performance and decided that *Hair* should not be cut short; it needed to grow in other surroundings.

The production was moved to a Broadway-area discotheque called Cheetah. Then Butler bought the production rights from Papp and hired a new director, Tom O'Horgan, who had staged many imaginative productions at off-off-Broadway's La MaMa Theatre. The script was revised, certain cast members were replaced, and *Hair* was transplanted to the Biltmore Theatre. Butler had rushed the Broadway opening in order to qualify for the Tony Awards, only to be told that it was ineligible because it had originated off-Broadway. The rules were changed the following season and *Hair* was nominated in one category, Best Musical. It lost to a show about another American revolution, the original one that took place almost 200 years earlier, *1776.*

Road companies of *Hair* were banned not only in Boston but in Acapulco. For the London production, Butler waited until the office of the Lord Chamberlain, England's official censor, was abolished, before opening. Back in New York, Rado and Ragni were barred from performing in their own show when they began inserting new material without consulting Butler. The matter was later settled amicably.

The author-actors never had another smash, though MacDermot did have a success with a rock adaptation of Shakespeare's *Two Gentlemen of Verona* (1971), produced by Papp. But Ragni's *Dude* (with music by MacDermot) failed in 1972. Rado's *Rainbow* faded quickly off-Broadway the same year.

There was a revival of *Hair* mounted in 1977, but tastes had changed radically and the production closed after a month's run.

Milos Forman's 1979 film treatment (with screenplay by Michael Weller) added a strong plot and dazzling cinematography. The cast included Treat Williams, John Savage, Beverly D'Angelo, and Annie Golden.

THE GREAT WHITE HOPE

by Howard Sackler
Opened October 3, 1968
556 Performances
Alvin Theatre
Directed by Edwin Sherin
Produced by Herman Levin

Cast: James Earl Jones (Jack Jefferson); Jane Alexander (Eleanor Bachman); Lou Gilbert (Goldie); Jimmy Pelham (Tick); George Matthews (Cap'n Dan); Marlene Warfield (Clara); Jon Cypher (D.A./Klossowski); George Ebeling (Fred); Peter Masterson (Smitty); Hilda Haynes (Mrs. Jefferson); Eugene R. Wood (Pop Weaver); Gil Rogers (Brady); Edward McNally (Roller); Joseph Hamer (Bettor); Hector Elizondo (Blackface/El Jafe); Dan Priest (Col. Cox); Garwood Perkins (Deacon); Woodie King (Young Negro); David Cannell (Barker); Michael Prince (Mr. Donnelly); Ruth Gregory (Mrs. Bachman); Brooks Rogers (Mr. Dixon); Antonio Fargas (Scipio); L. Errol Jaye (Pastor); Mel Winkler (Rudy); Larry Swanson (Mr. Eubanks); David Thomas (Mr. Treacher); Lance Cunard (Porter); Thomas Barbour (Sir William Griswold); Max Wright (Mr. Coates); Sheila Coonan (Mrs. Kimball); George Curley (Mr. Farlow); Bob Horen (Official); Marshall Efron (Ragosy); Don Blakely (African Student); Lou Meyer (Juggler); Donald Girard (Paco); Edd K. Gasper (Gov't Agent); Yvonne Southerland (Signature Recorder); Sean J. Walsh (The Kid); Luis Espinosa (Cuban Boy).

The regional theatre movement came into its own with the Broadway production of *The Great White Hope*, Howard Sackler's sprawling epic loosely based on the life of Jack Johnson, the first African-American heavyweight boxing champion of the world. *Hope* was the first major new play from the resident theatres to achieve a long run on Broadway since *Inherit the Wind,* in 1955, and it started the trend for other shows developed outside New York to transfer there.

Although the playwright changed the champ's name from Johnson to Jefferson, the drama parallels the real-life boxer's oppression by a racist society just before and during World War I. He is hounded into exile in Europe. His white mistress commits suicide. Finally, he gives up his title to a "great white hope," in return for which trumped-up charges are dropped against him and he is permitted to return to the States.

Sackler told the *Chicago Tribune* about the differences between his drama and the actual events, "My play is not supposed to be historically accurate. That's one reason I changed the fighter's name to Jack Jefferson. I used story elements of Jack Johnson's career and created new characters, especially the girl." Johnson had married three white women. In the play there is only one, Eleanor Bachman.

The drama had its world premiere at the Arena Stage in Washington, D.C. The huge, three-hour production required twenty-three scenes and a cast of sixty-three actors playing 250 roles. Despite a grant from the National Foundation for the Arts, Arena Stage lost $50,000. But the event drew national attention. Since most regional theatres were performing revivals of the classics, the production of a major new play outside of New York was news.

Producer Herman Levin had not seen the Washington premiere but had read the reviews and wanted to bring *Hope* to New York. Levin, producer of *My Fair Lady*, had not had a show on the boards since his 1963 flop, *The Girl Who Came to Supper*. Sackler made a deal with Levin: The playwright was the sole backer of the production, putting up $220,000. But Arena Stage was left out of the deal entirely. Arena's artistic director, Zelda Fichandler, who had worked with the author on the script, filed suit for a share of the profits for her theatre. Sackler and Levin claimed that they had offered the Washington company five percent of the royalties up to $50,000, but were refused. Arena lost their case.

Nowadays most resident regional theatres have some financial as well as artistic interest in their productions which go to Broadway.

James Earl Jones leads a jubilant cakewalk in *The Great White Hope.*

The Great White Hope won the triple crown of the Pulitzer, Tony, and New York Drama Critics Circle Award, and made stars out of the leads James Earl Jones and Jane Alexander.

20th-Century Fox bought the film rights. The movie, with a screenplay by Sackler, was released in 1970 and featured Jones and Alexander repeating their roles. Both received Oscar nominations. Brock Peters and Claudette Nevins played Johnson and his lover in the national touring company.

In the decades to follow, most of Broadway's nonmusical attractions would trace their lineage to the regional theatres. They include *The Gin Game* (1977), *Crimes of the Heart* (1981), and *Agnes of God* (1982) from Actors Theatre of Louisville; *I'm Not Rappaport* (1985) and *The Heidi Chronicles* (1988) from Seattle Repertory Theatre; and *Fences* (1987) from Yale Repertory Theatre.

PROMISES, PROMISES

Book by Neil Simon, based on the film *The Apartment,* by Billy Wilder and I.A.L. Diamond.

Music by Burt Bacharach

Lyrics by Hal David

Opened December 1, 1968

1,281 Performances

Shubert Theatre

Directed by Robert Moore

Choreographed by Michael Bennett

Produced by David Merrick

Cast: Jerry Orbach (Chuck Baxter); Jill O'Hara (Fran Kubelik); Edward Winter (J.D. Sheldrake); A. Larry Haines (Dr. Dreyfuss); Marian Mercer (Marge MacDougall); Dick O'Neill (Jesse Vanderhoff); Paul Reed (Mr. Dobitch); Norman Shelly (Mr. Kirkeby); Vince O'Brien (Mr. Eichelberger); Adrienne Angel (Sylvia Gilhooley); Ken Howard (Bartender Eddie/Karl Kubelik); Millie Slavin (Peggy Olson); Donna MacKechnie (Vivien Della Hoya); Baayork Lee (Miss Wong/Lum Ding Hostess); Margo Sappington (Miss Polansky); Kay Oslin (Helen Sheldrake); Carole Bishop (Company Nurse); Graciela Daniele (Clancy's Employee/Date); Gerry O'Hara (Company Doctor); Rita O'Connor (Dentist's Nurse); Michael Vita (Attendant/Bartender Eugene); Scott Pearson (Waiter); Betsy Haug (Dining Room Hostess); Rod Barry (New Young Executive).

Promises, Promises was a huge hit in the traditional mold. The plot focused on a love story which ends happily. The insurance company setting was a familiar one to the "tired-businessman" crowd. Based on Billy Wilder's 1960 Oscar-winning film *The Apartment,* starring Jack Lemmon and Shirley MacLaine, the show told the same story of junior executive Chuck Baxter (played by Jerry Orbach), who curries favor with the higher-ups by lending them the keys to his flat for their clandestine liaisons. This arrangement is blown apart when one of the big execs' playthings, Fran Kubelik (played by Jill O'Hara), attempts suicide in Chuck's apartment. After nursing her back to health, Chuck quits, and the two remain together.

Marian Mercer and Jerry Orbach won Tony Awards for *Promises, Promises.*

Despite its familiar elements, the show also contained many innovations and portents of the future changes for the American musical.

By the late '60s, Broadway was no longer the prime source of popular songs. The more driving, less lilting rock music had largely replaced Broadway's pronouncedly melodic fare on the radio airwaves. But while its score was far from that of *Hair, Promises, Promises* did boast music by a pop songwriting team whose work straddled both worlds, Burt Bacharach and Hal David. Their hits had been performed by such recording artists as Dionne Warwicke and Herb Albert. ("I'll Never Fall in Love Again" and the title song were later recorded by Warwicke and were big successes.) The *Promises* score had a "now" sound which most musicals had not yet captured. In the next decade, more shows would be using rock and contemporary idioms (though Bacharach and David found the high-pressure world of Broadway too stressful and returned to the more relaxing employment of turning out hit records.)

Neil Simon's book had its usual quotient of on-target gags, but it also employed an unusual stage device. The lead character would often step out of the action to directly address the audience. Scenes would be replayed the way he wanted them to come out rather than the way they did "in reality." This foreshadowed later shows such as *Company, Follies, Pippin* and *Nine,* which also relied on highly theatrical approaches.

The musical also indicated the growing importance of the off-Broadway theatre. Leading man Orbach had made his name starring as the Narrator in the original cast of off-Broadway's longest running show, *The Fantasticks,* and had just appeared in another downtown hit *Scuba Duba,* Bruce Jay Friedman's comedy. Director Robert Moore had previously staged the explosive off-Broadway play, *The Boys in the Band.* (Moore replaced Bob Fosse, who dropped out of *Promises* to direct the movie version of *Sweet Charity.*) It was now routine for actors and directors to work both on and off Broadway.

Promises also showed the beginnings of innovations in musical staging. Choreographer Michael Bennett gave each member of the dancing chorus a distinct personality and staged the scene changes as self-contained numbers. This broke away from the traditional faceless chorus and blackouts common to most musicals and anticipated the seamless action of such Bennett shows as *A Chorus Line* (1975) and *Dreamgirls* (1981).

In another innovation, back-up vocalists were placed in the orchestra pit, a practice later used in *Company* (1970).

Tony Roberts and Jenny O'Hara (Jill's sister) replaced the leads in the New York company. Roberts and Melissa Hart played them in the touring version.

FORTY CARATS

by Jay Presson Allen, adapted from a play by Pierre Barillet and Jean-Pierre Gredy.

Opened December 26, 1968

780 Performances

Morosco Theatre

Directed by Abe Burrows

Produced by David Merrick

Cast: Julie Harris (Ann Stanley); Marco St. John (Peter Latham); Iva Withers (Mrs. Adams); Polly Rowles (Mrs. Margolin); Murray Hamilton (Billy Boylan); Franklin Cover (Eddy Edwards); Glenda Farrell (Maud Haynes); Gretchen Corbett (Trina Stanley); Nancy Marchand (Mrs. Latham); John Cecil Holm (Mr. Latham); Michael Nouri (Pat).

After his success with *Cactus Flower,* Abe Burrows, as a director this time, brought another hit comedy from France to these shores. *Forty Carats* was also by the Parisian playwrighting team of Pierre Barillet and Jean-Pierre Gredy. The play involved a forty-year-old divorced businesswoman falling for a twenty-two-year-old lad whom she meets through the convenient plot device of a broken-down auto. Her friends and family are shocked and matters are complicated when her daughter starts dating a man in his forties. The script was adapted by Jay Presson Allen, who had dramatized Muriel Spark's novel *The Prime of Miss Jean Brodie* the season before.

Julie Harris, known for her serious roles, pleasantly surprised audiences with her light comedy turn as the smitten divorcee. She won the third of her five Tony Awards for this performance. Former film starlet Glenda Farrell played Harris's elegant mother, and the reliable Polly Rowles (*Auntie Mame, No Strings*) was the wisecracking secretary. Marco St. John from the APA–Phoenix Repertory was the youthful fiancée. John Cecil Holm, co-author of the '30s hit *Three Men on a Horse,* and Nancy Marchand, were his sophisticated parents.

Clive Barnes of the *New York Times* gave the show a negative review. Producer David Merrick was ready to close it, but Walter Kerr in the *Times* Sunday edition loved it, calling it "easy, breezy, and beguiling." Merrick, a genius at publicity, reprinted the rave notice word for word in a large newspaper advertisement and *Forty Carats* glittered for two seasons.

Harris was replaced by June Allyson and Zsa Zsa Gabor. Barbara Rush took the production on tour. But like *Cactus Flower, Forty Carats* is not done much these days, since sexual attitudes have changed.

Burrows attempted one more Americanization of a Barillet-Gredy farce. It was four one-acts all taking place in the same apartment. Although it starred popular comics Sid Caesar and Carol Channing, *Four on a Garden* (1970) was a flop, as was the film of *Forty Carats.* During her Hollywood period, Swedish dramatic actress Liv Ullmann was miscast in the film version of this light comedy. Gene Kelly, Binnie Barnes, and Nancy Walker attempted to liven up the 1973 feature.

1776

Book by Peter Stone

Music and lyrics by Sherman Edwards

Opened March 16, 1969

1,217 Performances

46th Street Theatre

Directed by Peter Hunt

Choreographed by Onna White

Produced by Stuart Ostrow

Cast: William Daniels (John Adams); Howard Da Silva (Benjamin Franklin); Paul Hecht (John Dickinson); Ken Howard (Thomas Jefferson); Ron Holgate (Richard Henry Lee); David Ford (John Hancock); Virginia Vestoff (Abigail Adams); Betty Buckley (Martha Jefferson); Clifford David (Edward Rutledge); Paul-David Richards (Dr. Josiah Bartlett); Roy Poole (Stephen Hopkins); David Vosburgh (Roger Sherman); Ronald Krass (Lewis Morris); Henry Le Clair (Robert Livingston); Edmund Lyndeck (Rev. John Witherspoon); Emory Bass (James Wilson); Robert Gaus (Caesar Rodney); Bruce MacKay (Col. Thomas McKean); Duane Bodin (George Read); Philip Polito (Samuel Chase); Charles Rule (Joseph Hewes); Jonathan Moore (Dr. Lyman Hall); Ralston Hill (Charles Thomson); William Duell (Andrew McNair); B.J. Slater (Leather Apron); Scott Jarvis (Courier).

A musical about the Declaration of Independence? It would never work, declared Broadway insiders when news of *1776,* the musical depiction of America's birth pangs, was announced.

It was unconventional in every way. It had a mostly male cast, with only two women. There was no singing and dancing chorus. It was cast without stars and performed without an intermission.

The show was conceived by Sherman Edwards, a songwriter who had provided tunes for many pop bands and singers, such as Elvis Presley. "This really started while I was teaching history and discovered how very little most Americans know about their past," Edwards explained to the *Washington Post* during the show's out-of-town tryout in the nation's capital. "Actually I began the real work six years ago—book, music, and lyrics. My basic story was okay, but the outline and lines were terrible, and I was delightfully relieved when our producer, Stuart Ostrow, suggested Peter Stone to do the book and let me concentrate on the music and lyrics."

Stone, an Oscar-winner for his screenplay for *Father Goose*, largely rewrote Edwards' book. The final result was mostly historically accurate. Some events were condensed, such as the actual signing of the Declaration, which took place over a period of months, rather than on one day (July 4) as depicted on stage. One of the book's strengths was its portrayals of the Founding Fathers as flawed humans rather than as cardboard Olympian-sized heroes.

"But we're not thinking of them as heroes," said Edwards in the same *Post* interview. "And that's our point. They were live, very human people once, struggling in the early summer heat of Philadelphia, coping with little money and cooperation."

1776 was the sleeper hit of the season, taking audiences and reviewers by surprise with its warmth, ingenuity, intelligent dialogue, and memorable songs. It won both the Tony and Drama Critics Award for Best Musical. William Daniels was nominated for a Featured Actor Tony, since his name was placed below the show's title. Daniels refused the nomination, claiming that his role of John Adams was a leading one. Indeed, Daniels was seldom offstage, and his character is the prime figure in the action. The award went instead to Ron Holgate, in the much smaller part of Richard Henry Lee, who had only one major number, the lively march "The Lees of Old Virginia."

There was a national tour, and a London production as well. The Broadway company also played the Nixon White House in 1970 in a command performance. Presidential aide William Safire suggested that such potentially controversial songs as the antiwar "Mama, Look Sharp" and anticonservative "Cool, Cool, Considerate Men" be cut. But the show remained intact, making it the first Broadway musical to play in its entirety at 1600 Pennsylvania Avenue.

"May it run until 1976," cheered WCBS-TV. In fact, it ran until 1972, the same year that the film version was released. The feature retained almost all the original Broadway cast. Appropriately, it is shown on many local TV stations on the Fourth of July.

William Daniels as John Adams and Howard Da Silva as Ben Franklin ponder the newly written Declaration of Independence in *1776*.

BUTTERFLIES ARE FREE

by Leonard Gershe

Opened October 21, 1969

1,128 Performances

Booth Theatre

Directed by Milton Katselas

Produced by Arthur Whitelaw, Max J. Brown, and Byron Goldman

Cast: Keir Dullea (Don Baker); Blythe Danner (Jill Tanner); Eileen Heckart (Mrs. Baker); Michael Glaser (Ralph Austin).

A blind man's struggle for independence seems an unlikely subject for a hit comedy. But *Butterflies Are Free* shattered expectations by becoming one of the longest running plays of the '70s.

Don Baker, the protagonist of *Butterflies*, was based on Harold Kreats, a blind Harvard law student who had been drafted in 1967 at the height of the Vietnam War. He wrote back to his draft board, applying for exemption because of his sightlessness. The board didn't believe him and gave him an A-1 rating. Kreats then wrote a satiric song about

Keir Dullea and Blythe Danner in *Butterflies Are Free.*

the situation, in which said he would gladly serve as long as the recruiting officers joined him in Vietnam "just to help me point my gun."

Kreats appeared on several talk shows, singing his ballad. Playwright Leonard Gershe heard the young man on the radio and was inspired by the law student's sense of humor to write a play about a blind boy who deals with his infirmity with laughter and courage. Gershe had been known primarily as a writer of Hollywood film musicals like *Funny Face* and *Silk Stockings*.

He told the *New York Times* that he wrote the play "because I wanted to change my image as a writer of musicals, and besides, I couldn't get a movie to write at that time." Gershe used Kreats as a model for his hero and his Hollywood neighbor Mia Farrow as the prototype for the offbeat girl next door.

The production was optioned for Broadway, but, according to Gershe, "the options were dropped because the producers felt, in effect, that a funny play about blindness would not be commercial."

Shunned by New York producers, the play was tried out on the summer-stock circuit. Keir Dullea was the blind young man, and Blythe Danner his love interest. Dullea was ready for a comedy after such serious film roles as a mentally disturbed youngster in *David and Lisa*, the male intruder in a lesbian relationship in *The Fox*, and second fiddle to a computer in *2001: A Space Odyssey*. Newcomer Danner grabbed most of the attention and later a Tony Award.

Reaction was positive enough to bring the play to Broadway. There were two cast changes from the summer production. Eileen Heckart replaced Maureen O'Sullivan as Don's domineering mother, and Michael Glaser took over for Michael Zaslow in the brief role of an off-off-Broadway director.

A few of the New York reviewers criticized the sentimentality of the play, but most praised its warm and funny treatment of a sensitive subject. Clive Barnes of the *Times*, the city's most powerful critic, grudingly admired the playwright's workmanship and the performances but compared the show to a soap opera. He later recanted and had praises for *Butterflies*.

After Kreats attended a performance, he stated, "It means a lot to me to hear how their tin-cup stereotype of a blind person is being changed. I feel I am in some way responsible."

Former silent-movie star Gloria Swanson was given top billing in the national tour and later played the mother on Broadway. Edward Albert and Goldie Hawn played the leads in the 1972 filming of *Butterflies*. Heckart reprised her stage role and won an Oscar for Best Supporting Actress.

LAST OF THE RED HOT LOVERS

by Neil Simon

Opened December 28, 1969

706 Performances

Eugene O'Neill Theatre

Directed by Robert Moore

Produced by Saint Subber

Cast: James Coco (Barney Cashman); Linda Lavin (Elaine Navazio); Marcia Rodd (Bobbi Michele); Doris Roberts (Jeanette Fisher).

Neil Simon, Broadway's most successful playwright, closed the '60s and examined the impact of the sexual revolution with *Last of the Red Hot Lovers*.

The playwright told the *New York Times* that he drew his inspiration from *Oh! Calcutta!*, the controversial erotic musical revue which was playing off-Broadway at the time. He said he wanted to write about those average, middle-class theatregoers who see *Oh! Calcutta!* in their mid-forties. "They're not part of the sexual revolution, but want to be. They're trying to conform to a whole way of life they're not really geared to."

The ironically named "red hot lover" is Barney Cashman, the middle-aged, somewhat overweight owner of a seafood restaurant who wants to spice up his ordinary existence with a little of the sexual excitement he sees all around him. In three successive acts, he invites three different women (a bored socialite, a ditzy young actress, and the wife of a friend) to his mother's vacant apartment for attempts at illicit trysts. Each fails miserably. While there were plenty of laughs, Simon treated his characters as human beings with phobias and flaws.

Writing the first act, the playwright had Martin Balsam in mind for the lead. Then he went to see Terrence McNally's one-act play *Next* off-Broadway with James Coco as a heavy, forty-ish draftee going through a humiliating physical examination. It was one of those times when the author sees his character alive in front of him. Coco was signed for *Red Hot Lovers*, and Simon wrote the remaining two acts to suit the actor's talents.

For the three female roles, the author made a list of his first choices, auditioned 300 actresses and then cast his initial selections: Linda Lavin, Marcia Rodd, and Doris Roberts.

Robert Moore, the director of the Simon musical *Promises, Promises*, staged the play. Simon's previous regular director, Mike Nichols, was engaged in filming *Catch-22*.

The only problem with the play during out-of-town tryouts was one of excess. The final curtain at the New Haven opening rang down at 11:30. There were changes in the second act to make Rodd's character funnier and younger. Simon revealed in the same *Times* interview that rewriting was his favorite part of a production. "I love it sometimes when we're out of town and someone says 'That scene doesn't work' and I have to go home and rewrite it. I can't wait to put in new stuff."

The show was booked into the Eugene O'Neill Theatre, of which Simon was the owner. Both *Plaza Suite* and *Promises, Promises* were still running as *Lovers* opened, giving the playwright three shows on Broadway simultaneously.

Last of the Red Hot Lovers did not translate well to the screen in the 1972 movie, which starred Alan Arkin as the would-be Romeo.

THE 1970s

The theatre of off-Broadway, of London, and of the past became the lifeblood of Broadway during the 1970s. It was becoming too risky to mount new productions directly in the town's most expensive theatres, so producers began to look for already tested "product." They cast their glances downtown, across the Atlantic to England, or in the trunk for a good old show that might work again. ✫ Joseph Papp, head of the New York Shakespeare Festival and nurturer of much of the young playwriting talent in America, became the top purveyor of theatrical fare on and off Broadway. *Two Gentlemen of Verona, Sticks and Bones, That Championship Season, Streamers*, and *A Chorus Line* were some of the notable shows that made the trip uptown from the Shakespeare Festival's Public Theatre to Broadway. ✫ The British provided Broadway with the majority of its serious drama for the decade. Six of the ten Tony Awards for Best Play went to British authors or to plays by Americans that were first produced in Britain. These included *Borstal Boy, Sleuth, Equus, Travesties, Da*, and *The Elephant Man*. The New York Drama Critics Circle agreed with the Tony voters on these plays (except for *Sleuth*) and, in addition, gave English imports like *Home, The Changing Room, The Contractor* and *Otherwise Engaged* their top prize. ✫ The nostalgia craze contributed to the success of revivals of *No, No, Nanette*, and *Irene*, and a new tribute to the '50s called *Grease*. Plays which got a deserved second viewing included O'Neill's *A Moon for the Misbegotten* and *Anna Christie*, Williams's *Cat on a Hot Tin Roof* and *Sweet Bird of Youth*, Albee's *Who's Afraid of Virginia Woolf?*, and even a stylish remounting of *Dracula*. ✫ Of course, not all Broadway musicals and plays were echoes of the past. Songwriter Stephen Sondheim and producer-director Harold Prince threw out the standard boy-meets-girl formula and created startlingly original musicals: *Company, Follies, A Little Night Music* and *Pacific Overtures*. A new crop of American playwrights, such as Lanford Wilson and David Mamet, emerged to explore fresh dramatic topics and challenge audience complacency. Still, during the "me" decade, light entertainment tended to get the box office bucks on Broadway. ✫ Emerging stars Kevin Kline, William Hurt, Swoosie Kurtz, Edward Herrmann, Glenn Close, and Patti LuPone were getting exposure on the New York stage, but most would abandon Broadway for the more lucrative fields of film and television. ✫ As the number of New York's daily newspapers dwindled, Clive Barnes, the drama critic for the *New York Times* became increasingly powerful. A positive review from the paper could make a show a hit, and a negative one could close it.

PURLIE

Book by Ossie Davis, Philip Rose, and Peter Udell, based on the play *Purlie Victorious*, by Ossie Davis.

Music by Gary Geld

Lyrics by Peter Udell

Opened March 15, 1970

688 Performances

Choreographed by Louis Johnson

Produced and directed by Philip Rose

Cast: Cleavon Little (Purlie); Melba Moore (Lutiebelle); Novella Nelson (Missy); Sherman Hemsley (Gitlow); C. David Colson (Charlie); Helen Martin (Idella); John Heffernan (Ol' Cap'n); Linda Hopkins (Church Soloist). Future choreographers Hope Clarke and George Faison were in the chorus.

Purlie was the first 500-performance-plus African-American musical written by a black author since *Shuffle Along* in 1921. (The sketches for *Blackbirds of 1928* may have been by black authors but they were uncredited.) Previous musicals like *Carmen Jones, Jamaica, Golden Boy,* and *Hallelujah, Baby!* were white writers' visions of the black experience.

When composer Gary Geld, lyricist Peter Udell, and director-producer Philip Rose (all white) decided to musicalize the 1961 comedy *Purlie Victorious*, which Rose had produced, they asked its author Ossie Davis to collaborate on the book. Davis, a black actor, had written the play as vehicle for himself and his wife Ruby Dee. He was motivated to write the play while acting as stage manager for the Broadway production of *The World of Sholom Aleichem* (1953), a stage adaptation of several of the Yiddish writer's stories. Davis wanted to write a play which would dramatize the African-American experience as Aleichem had done with the Jewish experience.

Davis's play used humor to disarm racism. The title character Purlie Victorious Judson is a self-styled preacher who returns to his little Southern hometown in order to start his own church. He runs afoul of the segregationist plantation owner Ol' Cap'n. Through various schemes and tricks, Purlie gains control of the church, and Ol' Cap'n dies of a heart attack. In the musical version, the show opens with a rousing funeral service for the departed bigot and the story is told in flashback.

Cleavon Little gave a career-making performance in the title role. Melba Moore as his love interest, Lutiebelle, stopped the show with her dynamic delivery of the song "I've Got Love," added just days before opening.

Despite generally favorable reviews, the show was in danger of closing due to lack of a strong box office. Rose then attained the services of publicity director Sylvester Leaks, who launched a campaign to attract black church and social groups, including the NAACP. The strategy paid off in the form of higher ticket sales.

Little and Moore both won Tony Awards for their performances. Cast member Sherman Hemsley later appeared on the long-running TV series *The Jeffersons*. Another future television star, Robert Guillaume (*Soap, Benson,*) headed the national touring company, which returned to New York for a brief engagement in 1972.

Purlie heralded a new era of African-American musicals. It proved that such shows could have popular appeal for all audiences. Musicals with predominantly or entirely black casts which played Broadway during the 1970s included *Ain't Supposed to Die a Natural Death* (1971); *Don't Play Us Cheap* (1972); *Don't Bother Me, I Can't Cope* (1972); *Raisin* (1973); *The Wiz* (1975); *Bubbling Brown Sugar* (1976) and *Ain't Misbehavin'* (1978).

APPLAUSE

Book by Betty Comden and Adolph Green, based on the Joseph L. Mankiewicz screenplay *All About Eve* and the original story by Mary Orr.

Music by Charles Strouse

Lyrics by Lee Adams

Opened March 30, 1970

896 Performances

Directed and choreographed by Ron Field

Produced by Joseph Kipness and Lawrence Kasha

Cast: Lauren Bacall (Margo Channing); Penny Fuller (Eve Harrington); Len Cariou (Bill Sampson); Robert Mandan (Howard Benedict); Brandon Maggart (Buzz Richards); Ann Williams (Karen Richards); Lee Roy Reams (Duane Fox); Bonnie Franklin (Bonnie); Alan King (Tony Host); Tom Urich (Bert); Jerry Wyatt (Bartender); John Anania (Peter); Howard Kahl (Bob); Orrin Reiley (Piano Player/TV Director); Ray Becker (Stan Harding); Bill Allsbrook (Danny); Carol Petri (Carol/Autograph Seeker); Mike Misita (Joey). Renee Baughman, Sammy Williams, and Nicholas Dante (later of *A Chorus Line*) were in the chorus.

Lauren Bacall joined the ranks of Broadway's musical comedy divas when she played Margo Channing, the electric stage star in *Applause*, the musicalization of the 1950 film *All About Eve*.

Eve Harrington, a spiritual sister to Joey of *Pal Joey* or Sammy Glick of *What Makes Sammy Run?*, plots to take over Margo's roles and her lover, director Bill Sampson. The movie and the show both ended with Eve becoming a star, but destined for a loveless life, and with Margo getting her man.

The story originated in 1946 when Mary Orr published a short story called "The Wisdom of Eve." Orr stated that she got the idea for her tale of an ambitious, unscrupulous actress from Elisabeth Bergner, who had had an experience with just such a pretty, young schemer. It was made into a radio play in 1949. The following year, 20th-Century Fox released Joseph L. Mankiewicz's screen adaptation. Titled *All About Eve*, the film was nominated for a record fourteen Oscars and won six, including Best Picture. The film provided a comeback opportunity for Bette Davis, who triumphed as Margo. The musical afforded a similar chance for Bacall. After headlining in one Broadway flop (*Goodbye, Charlie*) and one hit (*Cactus Flower*), the actress, dissatisfied with her mediocre film career, became a star in her own right in *Applause*. Despite her throaty, near-baritone voice, she dominated the show, gamely dancing through eight musical numbers and conveying Margo's glamorous, dynamic, yet insecure personality.

Charles Strouse and Lee Adams (*Bye, Bye, Birdie*) were signed to compose the score and Sydney Michaels (*Dylan, Ben Franklin in Paris*) to write the book. Michaels did not work out and was replaced by the team of Betty Comden and Adolph Green, who were accustomed to collaborating with stars not known for their singing abilities (Rosalind Russell in *Wonderful Town*, Judy Holliday in *Bells Are Ringing*).

Comden and Green updated the story to 1970s Broadway and made a few changes among the characters (the acidic drama critic played by George Sanders was eliminated, and Thelma Ritter's wisecracking maid was replaced by Lee Roy Reams's wisecracking gay hairdresser), but the basic plot remained the same.

As Bacall told *Newsday*, "The story and the characters are as true today as they were when the movie was made. There's a woman's insecurity and God knows that's timeless enough, the fear of aging, of losing out to the young people who are always coming along. There are too many parallels between my life and Margo's. It gives me the chills thinking about it. There's an awful lot of me in Margo Channing and there's an awful lot of Margo Channing in me." Comden and Green gave Margo a former Hollywood career, just like Bacall's.

There were rough periods during the out-of-town tryouts. Diane MacAfee was judged too sweet for the cunning Eve and was replaced by Penny Fuller. Ron Field, making his debut as a director, was almost axed in Baltimore, but Bacall demanded that he stay. Once his position was secure, Field tightened the show and had it running like a sleek steam engine.

Anne Baxter, the original Eve from the movie, replaced Bacall during the Broadway run; she was followed by another former film star, Arlene Dahl. Bacall played Margo on the road, in London and on television (receiving an Emmy nomination in 1973). She later starred in *Woman of the Year* (1981), another musical based on a Hollywood film.

Lauren Bacall and Lee Roy Reams whoop it up in a Village bar in *Applause*.

COMPANY

Book by George Furth

Music and lyrics by Stephen Sondheim

Opened April 26, 1970

690 Performances

Alvin Theatre

Choreographed by Michael Bennett

Produced and directed by Harold Prince

Cast: Dean Jones (Robert); Barbara Barrie (Sarah); Charles Kimbrough (Harry); Merle Louise (Susan); John Cunningham (Peter); Teri Ralston (Jenny); George Coe (David); Beth Howland (Amy); Steve Elmore (Paul); Elaine Stritch (Joanne); Charles Braswell (Larry); Pamela Myers (Marta); Donna McKechnie (Kathy); Susan Browning (April).

With *Company*, songwriter Stephen Sondheim and producer-director Harold Prince began their productive partnership and broke all the rules of musical comedy. There was no plot, no pair of principal lovers, no duo of secondary comedy lovers, no singing and dancing chorus. In place of these conventions, the authors offered a series of loosely related vignettes about the state of contemporary marriage and relationships in general.

Larry Kert (center) as eternal bachelor Robert blows out the candles on his birthday cake, as his married friends urge him on, in *Company*.

Five married couples are waiting for their best friend, the bachelor Robert, so that they can surprise him on his birthday. This opening scene serves as a springboard for a revue-like evening of Robert's ruminations on matrimony, sparked by his observations on his married friends and on the singles scenes, symbolized by Robert's relations with three very different women.

Company began in the mind of George Furth, an actor with writing ambitions who had penned eleven one-acts and wanted to get them on the stage with Kim Stanley playing all the female leads. When Furth was unable to get then produced, he brought them to Sondheim, who in turn took them to Prince. "I read them and said 'Let's make a musical of them,'" Prince recalled. "They all said, 'You're crazy.' But then we all got together and made a musical of them. We used three and a half of the plays and George wrote one and a half brand-new." Some of the unused one-acters wound up in *Twigs*, Furth's collection of short plays, which later won a Tony for Sada Thompson and was directed by *Company* choreographer Michael Bennett.

Anthony Perkins was the original choice for Robert, but he wanted to direct and so begged out of the show to take on the job of staging *Steambath,* off-Broadway. Dean

Jones, known principally for his roles in Disney film comedies, took over the part.

There were many changes during the tryout in Boston, the biggest of which was dropping Robert's penultimate musical statement "Happily Ever After," a bitter indictment of the compromises of marriage. Audiences were not responding to this downbeat ending. Sondheim substituted the soaring and somewhat more optimistic "Being Alive," giving the show an "up" ending. Like most of the later Prince–Sondheim shows, it received mixed notices in Boston.

In New York, the reviews were mostly good, except for the most important one of all, that of Clive Barnes, of the *New York Times,* who regarded Sondheim as a brilliant songwriter but the people onstage as "trivial, shallow, worthless, and horrid"—not the kind of folks you would want to spend an evening with, let alone pay for tickets to see.

Dean Jones left after a month of performances, to be replaced by his standby Larry Kert (the orignal Tony in *West Side Story*). The official press release stated that Jones was withdrawing because he had contracted hepatitis. But the truth was that the actor was having troubles going through his own divorce, and he considered playing the role too emotionally draining.

In spite of Barnes' negative response, *Company* had a modestly successful run of twenty months, launched a year-long national tour with George Chakiris and Elaine Stritch, was nominated for thirteen Tonys (a record), and won six, as well as the New York Drama Critics Circle Award for Best Musical. The London production, in which most of the Broadway cast repeated their roles, ran for six months and then two more with British replacements.

Company has never been filmed for TV or the movies. There is a film documentary on the recording of the original cast album. In 1981, the same creative team (Furth, Sondheim, and Prince) reunited for *Merrily We Roll Along*, which opened at the same theatre as *Company* but was closed after a short run.

THE ROTHSCHILDS

Book by Sherman Yellen, based on the book by Frederic Morton.

Music by Jerry Bock

Lyrics by Sheldon Harnick

Opened October 19, 1970

507 Performances

Lunt–Fontanne Theatre

Directed and choreographed by Michael Kidd

Produced by Lester Osterman and Hillard Elkins

Cast: Hal Linden (Mayer Rothschild); Keene Curtis (Prince William/Joseph Fouche/Herries/Metternich); Paul Hecht (Nathan Rothschild); Leila Martin (Gutele (Mama) Rothschild); Jill Clayburgh (Hannah Cohen); Timothy Jerome (Amshel Rothschild); David Garfield (Solomon Rothschild); Chris Sarandon (Jacob Rothschild); Allan Gruet (Kalman Rothschild); Leo Leyden (Budurus); Howard Honing (Blum); Nina Dova (Mrs. Kaufman); Peggy Cooper (Mrs. Segal); Michael Maitland (1st Urchin/Young Nathan); Kim Michels (2nd Urchin); Robby Benson (3rd Urchin/Young Solomon); Lee Franklin (Young Amshel); Mitchell Spers (Young Jacob); Roger Hamilton (Guard/Banker); Thomas Trelfa (1st Vendor); Kenneth Bridges (2nd Vendor); Jon Peck (3rd Vendor); Paul Tracey (General/Skeptic); Elliott Savage (1st Banker); Carl Nicholas (2nd Banker); Christopher Chadman (Peasant).

The Rothschilds is a richer cousin to *Fiddler on the Roof.* Both feature songs by Jerry Bock and Sheldon Harnick and deal with European Jews struggling against anti-Semitism. But Tevye and his family were poverty-stricken, while Mayer Rothschild and his brood rose to become one of the most powerful banking dynasties on the Continent. Perhaps because more audience members could identify with Tevye's plights than those of the banking family, *Fiddler* continued after *The Rothschilds* closed.

Producer Hillard Elkins came up with the idea of musicalizing Frederic Morton's bestselling book on the influential clan and hired British writer Wolf Mankiewicz to do the adaptation. Bock and Harnick were offered the show while they working on *Fiddler*. Harnick told the *New York Times*, "The funny thing is, there may not have been a *Fiddler* had we agreed to do *The Rothschilds* when Hilly first offered it to us in 1963. Our *She Loves Me* was running and, completely on our own, on spec, we had been working on the

Sholom Aleichem stories, focusing on Tevye. But we didn't take *The Rothschilds* then because we didn't care for Wolf Mankiewicz's treatment for Frederic Morton's book."

After Elkins had gone through four other writers and Bock and Harnick had provided the score for another Broadway show, *The Apple Tree* (1966), a new treatment by Sherman Yellen caught the songwriters' interest and they began work on the new project. While *Fiddler*'s score reflects its Russian-Jewish setting, the music for *The Rothschilds* was influenced by classical music from the 18th and 19th centuries, the time of the show's action.

At first Yellen's book lacked a clear focus. Act I was definitely about Mayer raising his five boys to become prosperous businessmen, but Act II meandered all over Europe as the grown sons set out to fulfill their father's instructions. To pull the two acts together Mayer's role was expanded, keeping him alive longer than historical fact would have it. He was also given an "Impossible Dream"-like ballad called "In My Own Lifetime." To tighten the action of the second act, the romance of son Nathan and Hannah Cohen was now the central theme.

Reviews were mixed, ranging from "overproduced" and "shallow" to "warm" and "ingratiating." Despite Tony Awards for Hal Linden as Mayer and Keene Curtis as four separate villains, the production returned only 25 percent of its original investment.

In 1990, the American Jewish Theatre mounted a revival in their off-Broadway space. Lonnie Price, who had played one of the young Rothschilds on the national tour, directed the show and scaled it down to fit in the small theatre. The cast was reduced from forty to sixteen, with all the actors doubling and tripling roles. Israeli actor Mike Burstyn played Meyer. The production received better reviews than the original and transferred to Circle in the Square Downtown for a commercial run of close to a year.

SLEUTH

by Anthony Shaffer

Opened November 12, 1970

1,222 Performances

Music Box Theatre

Directed by Clifford Williams

Produced by Helen Bonfils, Morton Gottlieb, and Michael White

Cast: Anthony Quayle (Andrew Wyke); Keith Baxter (Milo Tindle).

Sleuth was one of two mystery plays to achieve hit proportions on Broadway during the 1970s (the other being 1978's *Deathtrap*). The '40s had *Angel Street* and *The Two Mrs. Carrolls. Dial M for Murder* and *Witness for the Prosecution* chilled the '50s. No thrillers had long runs in the '60s, but *Sleuth* proved to be one of the biggest hits of the following decade.

Anthony Quayle and Keith
Baxter in *Sleuth*.

British dramatist Anthony Shaffer, twin brother of playwright Peter Shaffer, who had written *Five Finger Exercise* (1959), *The Royal Hunt of the Sun* (1965), and *Black Comedy* (1967), had made his mark as a television dramatist and collaborated with his twin on two mystery novels. He stepped out from his sibling's shadow when *Sleuth* opened at London's St. Martin's Theatre in February of 1970. The English critics and audience loved the show, and a transatlantic transfer of the original production and cast (Anthony Quayle and Keith Baxter) was accomplished by November.

Clive Barnes in the *New York Times* called it "clever . . . and as intricate as the Hampton Court maze." The plot is a series of cat-and-mouse games between Andrew Wyke, a snobbish writer of detective novels, and Milo Tindle, a handsome young travel agent and the lover of Wyke's wife. Set in Wyke's puzzle-filled country house, the two rivals don disguises, trap, trick, and outwit each other in an increasingly deadly round of one-upmanship.

The small cast and single set contributed to the play's longevity. The production also demonstrated the dominance of British plays on Broadway. As costs mounted, fewer Main Stem producers were taking chances with unknown American authors, so they presented plays which had been hits on London stages. *Sleuth* was one of three British dramas nominated for the Tony Award for Best Play for the 1970–71 season. It won over David Storey's *Home* and Christopher Hampton's *The Philanthropist*. The only American show nominated was Paul

Sills' *Story Theatre*, a revue based on the fairy tales of Aesop and the Brothers Grimm.

During *Sleuth*'s Broadway run, Paul Rogers, Patrick MacNee, and George Rose succeeded Quayle while Donal Donnelly, Brian Murray, and Jordan Christopher took Baxter's role. Michael Allinson and Donnelly took the play on a national tour. Laurence Olivier and Michael Caine comprised the cast of the 1973 film version.

Shaffer later had another mystery, *Whodunnit,* on Broadway for a short run in 1982.

THE ME NOBODY KNOWS

Book by Robert H. Livingston and Herb Schapiro, based on the book by Stephen M. Joseph.

Music by Gary William Friedman

Lyrics by Will Holt

Opened December 18, 1970

587 Performances, including 208 performances off-Broadway.

Helen Hayes Theatre

Directed by Robert H. Livingston

Choreographed by Patricia Birch

Produced by Jeff Britton

Cast: Melanie Henderson (Rhoda); Laura Michaels (Lillian); José Fernandez (Carlos); Irene Cara (Lillie Mae); Douglas Grant (Benjamin); Beverly Ann Bremers (Catherine); Gerri Dean (Melba); Paul Mace (Donald); Northern J. Calloway (Lloyd); Carl Thoma (Clorox); Kevin Lindsay (William); Hattie Winston (Nell).

The Me Nobody Knows was a best-selling book of writings by New York City school children, gathered by teacher

Stephen Joseph. Subtitled "Children's Voices from the Ghetto," the anthology's pieces were written by mostly African-American and Latino kids from seven to eighteen who went to school in such neighborhoods as Bedford–Stuyvesant, in Brooklyn, and Harlem, in Manhattan. The writings included those of a thirteen-year-old boy trying heroin for the first time; another boy witnessing an alcoholic black man being picked up by an ambulance; a youngster feeling glad that there will be more food in the house because his baby brother has died; and others dealing with the hardships of everyday ghetto life.

Director Herb Schapiro had the idea of making the anthology into a musical. After a tryout at a small theatre in Trenton, New Jersey, the show opened in May of 1970 at off-Broadway's Orpheum Theatre with a cast of twelve kids. The ensemble was a mix of professional and nonprofessional performers.

It was greeted enthusiastically by the press and audiences. John Simon, the toughest critic in town, wrote in *New York* magazine, "We have the best rock score in years in the one provided by Gary William Friedman for *The Me Nobody Knows*, a musical about ghetto children that is so good that if every legislator and slum landlord were to see it . . . it might put an end to ghettos."

After a run of 208 performances, a labor dispute between Actors Equity and off-Broadway theatre managers resulted in a strike, closing the show and sixteen others. The producers moved the production to Broadway (where the strike was not in effect), and it continued to run for a total of 587 performances.

The next season another musical dealing with ghetto life, *Don't Bother Me, I Can't Cope*, began a long run. Elizabeth Swados covered similar themes of youth and deprivation in a loosely structured musical, *Runaways* (1978).

NO, NO, NANETTE

Book by Burt Shevelove, based on the original book by Otto Harbach and Frank Mandel.

Music by Vincent Youmans

Lyrics by Irving Caesar and Otto Harbach

Opened January 19, 1971

861 Performances

46th Street Theatre

Directed by Burt Shevelove

Choreographed by Donald Saddler

Produced by Pyxidium Ltd. (Cyma Rubin)

Cast: Ruby Keeler (Sue Smith); Jack Gilford (Jimmy Smith); Bobby Van (Billy Early); Helen Gallagher (Lucille Early); Patsy Kelly (Pauline); Susan Watson (Nanette); Roger Rathburn (Tom Trainor); K.C. Townsend (Flora Latham); Loni Zoe Ackerman (Betty Brown); Pat Lysinger (Winnie Winslow).

Nothing could be further from the ghetto of *The Me Nobody Knows* than the 1920s Atlantic City of *No, No, Nanette*. Billed as "The New 1925 Musical," the revival of *No, No, Nanette* rode the crest of a wave of nostalgia. For the first part of the 1970s, anything to do with the 1920s, '30s and '40s was all the rage. Fashion, music, movies, television, and theatre all reflected a presumably golden bygone age.

The frivolous plot dealt with a Bible publisher who is supporting three different flappers in three different cities. Comedy ensues when all three of the publisher's protégés, his lawyer and the lawyer's wife, his young ward Nanette, her boyfriend, and a comedy maid converge on a weekend cottage in Atlantic City. But the story was merely a springboard for spritely

Bobby Van and Helen Gallagher stopped the show with "You Can Dance with Any Girl," in *No, No, Nanette*.

production numbers. The highpoint of the show was provided by Ruby Keeler, star of many '30s Hollywood musicals, tap-dancing faster and faster to "I Want to Be Happy." Another was Bobby Van and Helen Gallagher as the attorney and his spouse demonstrating the castle walk, turkey trot, polka, bunny hug and Peabody in "You Can Dance with Any Girl." As the sarcastic maid, Patsy Kelly (another '30s star), won a Tony; so did Gallagher.

Nanette onstage contrasted sharply with the backbiting backstage. The principal battle was between co-producers Harry Rigby and Cyma Rubin. Both claimed to have come up with the idea of cashing in on the recent on-campus interest in Busby Berkeley movie musicals by bringing Berkeley himself out of retirement to stage an extravagant Broadway show in the style of his elaborate Warner Brothers productions. *Nanette* was chosen because it had more plot than most shows of the era (which isn't saying much).

Rigby told the *New York Times* on the first day of rehearsal, "Unlike a lot of shows these days, there is no message in *No, No, Nanette*. There is just entertainment with beautiful girls, great songs, and fun. And when you have that kind of property, who better than Busby Berkeley could you call on to help get it onstage?" In fact, the 75-year-old Berkeley did little with the production except lend his name to the credits and pose with some of the chorus girls for publicity pictures. Donald Saddler staged the dances and Burt Shevelove directed and rewrote the creaky book.

While Berkeley remained nominally with the show, Rigby disappeared after a successful Boston tryout. Rubin had bought him out and was now sole producer. Keeler later told Rex Reed of the *Sunday News*: "When I signed on to do the show, I thought Harry Rigby was the producer and Cyma Rubin was just the woman who put up the money. In the old days, the investors didn't try to run things. They left that up to the talent. But Mrs. Rubin started firing people the minute we started rehearsals."

Aside from Rigby, both Hiram Sherman, who was hired to play the Bible publisher, and Carol Demas, as Nanette, were fired. Jack Gilford and Susan Watson ultimately took over the parts. Despite out-of-town cast changes, *Nanette* was a solid hit on Broadway. Several stars of Keeler's age were cast in replacement and road companies. June Allyson played her role in the first national touring company, while Evelyn Keyes enacted it in the second. On Broadway, Penny Singleton replaced Keeler, and Martha Raye took over for Kelly.

Nanette had been filmed in 1930 and 1940. Rigby later mounted his own "nostalgia" production with a revival of *Irene*, starring Debbie Reynolds.

OH! CALCUTTA!

Devised by Kenneth Tynan

Sketches by Samuel Beckett, Jules Feiffer, Dan Greenberg, John Lennon, Jacques Levy, Leonard Melfi, David Newman and Robert Benton, Sam Shepard, Clovis Trouille, Kenneth Tynan, and Sherman Yellen

Music and lyrics by The Open Window (Robert Dennis, Peter Schickele, and Stanley Walden)

Opened February 26, 1971

610 Performances, after a run of 704 performances off-Broadway

Belasco Theatre

Directed by Jacques Levy

Choreographed by Margo Sappington

Produced by Hillard Elkins

Cast: Mel Auston, Raina Barrett, Ray Edelstein, Samantha Harper, Patricia Hawkins, William Knight, Mitchell McGuire, Pamela Pilkenton, Gary Rethmeier, Nancy Tribush.

"Some time ago," wrote the British theatre critic Kenneth Tynan in the *Village Voice*, "it occured to me that there was no place for a civilized man to take a civilized woman to spend an evening of civilized erotic stimulation. At one end, there's burlesque, at the other an expensive nightclub, but no place in between. We're trying to fill the gap with this show." The show Tynan was referring to is *Oh! Calcutta!*, the world's longest-running erotic musical. For the sexually explicit revue, Tynan solicted contributors from such diverse writers as the Nobel Prize–winning Samuel Beckett, former Beatle John Lennon, cartoonist Jules Feiffer, and playwright Sam Shepard.

"He said that we could write about anything in the world within the realm of sexuality," David Newman, one of the contributors, told *Time* magazine. "The only other caveat was that our piece should have absolutely no redeeming social value." The songs were by a group called The Open Window (Robert Dennis, Peter Schickele, and Stanley Walden); Schickele had achieved fame by spoofing classical music in his P.D.Q. Bach concerts.

Not only did the skits deal frankly with such sexual matters as masturbation, wife-swapping, and fetishes, but the production also featured frontal nudity. The cast of *Hair* had briefly flashed their birthday suits for a few dimly lit moments at the end of the first act. *Calcutta* opened with the eight-member cast standing downstage in full lighting and in bathrobes, then stripping down so that their only costumes were dimples and freckles.

The show opened off-Broadway on June 17, 1969, at the Eden Theatre, with a cast that included Bill Macy, Alan Rachins, and the choreographer Margo Sappington.

The critics found the revue tasteless and gratuitous. Clive Barnes of the *Times* sneered, "Voyeurs of the city unite. You have nothing to lose but your brains." But audiences were attracted by the enormous publicity surrounding this first-ever legitimate production featuring extensive nudity. After a run of 704 performances, *Oh! Calcutta!* moved to Broadway's Belasco Theatre, where it continued for 610 performances.

Then, in September of 1976, Norman Kean, general manager for the original production, revived the show. Kean's strategy was to attract tourists visiting New York for the nation's bicentennial celebrations. The new *Calcutta!* opened at the Edison Theatre, a converted ballroom in the Edison Hotel, playing in repertory with *Me and Bessie*, a revue starring Linda Hopkins as blues singer Bessie Smith. *Me and Bessie* closed that December, but *Calcutta!* continued 5,959 times for the second-longest run in Broadway history. Because it was sometimes performed ten or eleven times a week, as opposed to the traditional eight common to most shows, for a while *Calcutta!* had more performances racked up than any other show on the Main Stem, including *A Chorus Line*. (*Chorus Line* closed after the nudie revue to claim the title of longest run.)

Tourists, mainly those from Japan where onstage nudity is forbidden, became the main audience for *Calcutta!* during its phenomenally long life. Kean played to this market by advertising in Japanese publications, offering a simultaneous Japanese translation, and by providing translations of the sketches in nine languages.

Business began to fall off in the late '80s. For one thing, the spectre of AIDS dampened the fun of the show's licentious humor. There were also waves of negative publicity, understandably, when producer Kean murdered his wife, actress Gwyda DonHowe, and then leaped to his death from their apartment. The final blow came when the

Japanese tourist trade slowed. The cast threw in the towel for the last time on August 6, 1989. It was estimated that *Oh! Calcutta!* had grossed more than $350 million and been seen by 85 million people around the world.

FOLLIES

Book by James Goldman
Music and lyrics by Stephen Sondheim
Opened April 4, 1971
522 Performances
Winter Garden Theatre
Directed by Harold Prince and Michael Bennett
Choreographed by Michael Bennett
Produced by Harold Prince

Cast: Alexis Smith (Phyllis Rogers Stone); Dorothy Collins (Sally Durant Plummer); John McMartin (Benjamin Stone); Gene Nelson (Buddy Plummer); Yvonne De Carlo (Carlotta Campion); Mary McCarty (Stella Deems); John J. Martin (Max Deems); Fifi D'Orsay (Solange LaFitte); Ethel Shutta (Hattie Walker); Justine Johnson (Heidi Schiller); Ethel Barrymore Colt (Christine Donovan); Arnold Moss (Dimitri Weismann); Virginia Sandifur (Young Phyllis); Marti Rolph (Young Sally); Kurt Peterson (Young Ben); Harvey Evans (Young Buddy); Michael Bartlett (Roscoe); Victoria Mallory (Young Heidi); Fred Kelly (Willy Wheeler); Sheila Smith (Meredith Lane); Helon Blount (Deedee West); Marcie Stringer (Emily Whitman); Charles Welch (Theodore Whitman); Victor Griffin (Victor); Jayne Turner (Vanessa); Michael Misita (Young Vincent); Graciela Daniele (Young Vanessa); Ralph Nelson (Kevin); Julie Pars (Young Stella); Dick Latessa (Major-Domo); John Grigas (Chauffeur).

Although *Follies* ran on Broadway for over 500 performances, won seven Tonys, and is regarded by many as one of the finest musicals of the '70s, it was a costly financial failure, losing its entire initial investment of $800,000. The show, a Proustian evocation of a reunion of former show-

Dorothy Collins and Alexis Smith reminisce in *Follies*.

girls, achieved its most lasting success as a cult favorite after the end of its original run.

Follies, originally titled *The Girls Upstairs*, was the brainchild of James Goldman (*The Lion in Winter*) and Stephen Sondheim. They conceived the show as a realistic whodunnit in which the two principal couples spent most of the reunion evening bitching at each other á la *Who's Afraid of Virginia Woolf?* and building suspense towards a murder.

Harold Prince, Sondheim's collaborator on *Company* and the new show's director, was inspired to change the concept by a photograph he saw in *Life* magazine. It featured an elderly but elegant Gloria Swanson, posing amid the rubble of the demolished Roxy Theatre, a cinema that had opened with one of her movies during the silent era. Prince suggested that the focus should shift from a naturalistic depiction of marital squabbling to a metaphoric merging of the past and the present by having younger versions of the characters, ghosts of their former selves, onstage with them.

Company choreographer Michael Bennett was asked to repeat his dance duties for *Follies*, but Bennett felt he was ready to go beyond creating just dance routines; he wanted to direct an entire production. In order to keep Bennett, Prince gave him co-director status with himself.

The past was brought into the present in every aspect of the production, from Sondheim's pastiche songs (which were affectionate tributes to Berlin, Porter, De Sylva, Henderson, and Brown) to the casting. Leading roles were played by Alexis Smith, Dorothy Collins, Gene Nelson, and Yvonne De Carlo, all minor stars from the '40s and '50s. Only John McMartin, who played Smith's estranged husband, had no such background.

With nostalgia a selling point at the time of the show's opening, one would think *Follies* would have been an immediate hit. No jokey song-and-dance romp with leggy chorines, the show was instead a hard-edged examination of the old-timers' shattered illusions and, by extension, those of the country itself. When the show premiered in Boston, the press was divided. Michael Bennett wanted to bring in Neil Simon to lighten up the show. "With all respect to Michael, I thought it was a ridiculous idea," Prince says. "I love Doc [Simon], but that was not the show we were doing. We were not doing a show where we needed more laugh lines."

Despite Bennett's reservations, *Follies* moved to New York for the Broadway opening. The New York critics were divided also. Most acknowledged the brilliant work of Sondheim, Prince, and Bennett but found Goldman's book lacking and the characters unsympathetic. A lavish production like *Follies* requires a huge budget and capacity audiences to keep it running. The show developed a modest following, but the downbeat theme and a mixed press kept sellout crowds away. It opened too late in the

1970–71 season to qualify for the Tonys. By the time it triumphed with seven wins at the following year's ceremonies, the awards were too late to help at the box office, and the ghostly reunion was held for the last time on Broadway that July.

In 1985 an all-star concert version of the complete, twenty-two song *Follies* was produced. Lee Remick, George Hearn, Barbara Cook, Mandy Patinkin, and Carol Burnett were among the performers. Diana Rigg, Millicent Martin, Daniel Massey, and Dolores Gray starred in a hit 1987 London revival, directed by Bennett's former assistant Bob Avian, which featured one new song. Both projects enhanced the show's reputation as an unappreciated gem, containing one of Sondheim's most inspired scores.

JESUS CHRIST SUPERSTAR

Music by Andrew Lloyd Webber

Lyrics by Tim Rice

Opened October 12, 1971

720 Performances

Mark Hellinger Theatre

Directed by Tom O'Horgan

Produced by Robert Stigwood

Cast: Jeff Fenholt (Jesus of Nazareth); Ben Vereen (Judas Iscariot); Yvonne Elliman (Mary Magdalene); Barry Dennen (Pontius Pilate); Bob Bingham (Caiaphas); Phil Jethro (Annas); Alan Braunstein (First Preist); Michael Meadows (Second Priest); Steven Bell (Third Priest); Dennis Buckley (Simon Zelotes/Merchant/Leper); Michael Jason (Peter/Merchant/Leper); Paul Ainsely (King Herod/Merchant/ Leper). Anita Morris, Ted Neeley, and Kay Cole were in the chorus.

Probably the most controversial musical of the decade was *Jesus Christ Superstar* by a pair of English songwriters, twenty-three-year-old Andrew Lloyd Webber and twenty-seven-year-old Tim Rice. Set during the last seven days of the life of Christ, the rock opera portrayed Jesus as a mortal figure with human weaknesses.

In a press release, the authors stated "basically, the idea of our whole opera was to have Christ seen through the eyes of Judas, with Christ as a man, not a god. Our intention was to take no religious stand on the subject, but rather to ask questions. We purposely avoided any reference to Christ's divinity, choosing to end our story with his death rather than resurrection."

This humanistic view of the gospels incensed various Catholic and Protestant groups, as well as Jewish organizations, which objected to the portrayal of the Hebrew priests as the principal cause of Christ's crucifixion. Picketers carried signs outside the Mark Hellinger Theatre, where *Superstar* was playing. Yet there were also clergymen who commended the production for making the story appealing to young people.

The score was originally released as a recording. A single 45-rpm of Mary Magdalene's ballad "I Don't Know How to Love Him" on one side and the title song on the other, became a hit in Britain. This prompted entrepreneur Robert Stigwood, who was also Lloyd Webber and Rice's manager, to produce the entire score on a two-disk album, which was released in 1970. With backing from MCA, *Jesus Christ Superstar* became the first Broadway hit musical to originate this way. (*Tommy,* by the rock group The Who, was recorded a year earlier but did not reach Broadway until 1993.) Other album-to-stage transfers include the Lloyd Webber–Rice *Evita* (1979) and *Joseph and the Amazing Technicolor Dreamcoat* (1981), and Rice's *Chess* (1988).

The *Superstar* album was a golden seller in America but failed in the UK, and it launched a series of unauthorized live "concert versions." In order to prevent further copyright infringements, Stigwood produced a series of authorized concerts of the score across the United States.

The Broadway production was staged and conceived by Tom O'Horgan, whose credits included the imaginative renderings of *Hair* on Broadway and *Futz* and *Tom Paine* at off-off-Broadway's La MaMa Theatre. His version of *Superstar* was equally flamboyant. Judas descended on a "butterfly bridge" accompanied by three chorus girls. Caiaphas and the priests were suspensed from a platform made of dinosaur bones. The palms in the palm Sunday procession were replaced by weird symbols including protozoan molecules. Many critics felt O'Horgan's circus-like production overwhelmed the score, but most reviewers praised

the show for giving the Christ story immediacy. Despite (or because of) the religious controversy, the show ran for 720 performances in New York, and the London production surpassed *Oliver!* as the longest-running musical on the British stage. It was later surpassed by Lloyd Webber's *Cats* and *Phantom of the Opera.*

Meanwhile, Stephen Schwartz's *Godspell* was telling the story of Christ's passion in somewhat more whimsical fashion as a clown show off-Broadway.

The 1973 Universal film version made *Jesus Christ Superstar*'s media blitz complete.

One of the more spectacular scenes from *Jesus Christ Superstar.*

THE PRISONER OF SECOND AVENUE

by Neil Simon

Opened November 11, 1971

780 Performances

Eugene O'Neill Theatre

Directed by Mike Nichols

Produced by Saint Subber

Cast: Peter Falk (Mel Edison); Lee Grant (Edna Edison); Vincent Gardenia (Harry Edison); Florence Stanley (Pearl); Tresa Hughes (Jessie); Dena Dietrich (Pauline).

Neil Simon's humor got darker with his eighth long-running production, *The Prisoner of Second Avenue*, a comedy about urban crises not unlike his original screenplay for *The Out-of-Towners*. Executive Mel Edison loses his job and is beset by faulty appliances, noisy neighbors, robbers, and strikes, and he finally has a nervous breakdown. His wife Edna gets a job to keep them afloat, but her company goes bankrupt. The conclusion is both funny and unhappy at the same time, as Mel and Edna sit in their freezing apartment and snow begins to fall.

Simon's previous Broadway outing, *The Gingerbread Lady,* had been even weightier, telling the story of a self-destructive, alcoholic ex-singer. Although Maureen Stapleton won a Tony Award for her portrayal of the demanding lead role, the play closed after a run of only five months, the shortest of any Simon play up to that point.

"I don't think audiences expect or want me to write serious plays," the playwright told the *Chicago Tribune.* "Maybe I was a little more successful with *Prisoner*. It's a serious play that's very funny." Audiences identified with and laughed at the numerous disasters associated with living in New York or any modern metropolis.

The playwright was accused of hating his city because of the bad image *Prisoner* was supposedly giving it. He replied in a *New York Daily News* interview, "Who hates it? I love it. I'm writing about big city life. The problems in *Prisoner* are not exclusive to New York. People are robbed everywhere. There are major strikes in London, Paris, every major city. I only single out New York because I happen to live there."

Mike Nichols, director of such Simon hits as *Barefoot in the Park* and *The Odd Couple*, took time off from making movies to stage the show. Peter Falk and Lee Grant were the beseiged couple. Vincent Gardenia won a Tony for his supporting role as Mel's brother.

Art Carney (the original Felix Ungar) and Barbara Barrie played the Edisons on tour. Hector Elizondo and Gabriel Dell played Mel on Broadway; Barrie, Phyllis Newman, and Rosemary Prinz filled in as Edna.

Jack Lemmon, who played a similar Simon role in *The Out-of-Towners*, and Anne Bancroft were the leads in the 1975 film version.

TWO GENTLEMEN OF VERONA

Book by Mel Shapiro and John Guare, based on the play by William Shakespeare.

Music by Galt MacDermot

Lyrics by John Guare

Opened December 1, 1971, after an off-Broadway run at the Delacorte Theatre

627 Performances

St. James Theatre

Directed by Mel Shapiro

Choreographed by Jean Erdman

Produced by Joseph Papp, The New York Shakespeare Festival

Cast: Clifton Davis (Valentine); Raul Julia (Proteus); Jonelle Allen (Sylvia); Diane Davila (Julia); Alix Elias (Lucetta); Frank O'Brian (Thurio); José Perez (Speed); John Bottoms (Launce); Frederic Warriner (Antonio/Tavern Host); Norman Matlock (Duke of Milan); Alvin Lum (Eglamour). Stockard Channing and Jeff Goldblum were in the chorus.

Two Gentlemen of Verona was the first of the New York Shakespeare Festival's several Broadway transfers from off-Broadway. Founded in 1954 by Joseph Papp, the Festival began as a workshop in a church basement on the Lower East Side. In 1956, the company began giving free performances of Shakespeare in city parks. A permanent outdoor theatre, the Delacorte, was erected in Central Park, in 1962, for the Festival's annual free summer season. A year-round theatre (The Public) was opened in 1967, when the Festival presented the first production of *Hair*. (Michael Butler, not Joseph Papp, moved the latter to Broadway.)

Two Gentlemen first appeared on the stage of the Delacorte as a part of the 1971 summer season. The first production of that year had been a dull rendition of the obscure *Timon of Athens. Two Gentlemen*, another lesser-known play by the Bard, was anything but dull or routine. With music by *Hair*'s Galt MacDermot and lyrics by John Guare (author of the well-received off-Broadway comedy *The House of Blue Leaves*), the musical mixed Shakespeare's original text with driving rock rhythms. The adaptation by Guare and director Mel Shapiro sprinkled in contemporary references to psychoanalysis and Vietnam in iambic pentameter. Shakespeare's locale of Milan and Verona were symbolically transferred to modern Puerto Rico and New York City. The story concerned the romantic rivalry between two friends, Valentine and Proteus, and the ladies Sylvia and Julia. The cast was ethnically mixed, featuring black performers Jonelle Allen and Clifton Davis and Latin-Americans Raul Julia and Carla Pinza as the two pairs of lovers.

A week before the Delacorte opening, Papp attended a rehearsal and declared it "a disaster." Under his energetic supervision, the show was pulled apart and put back together, opening to the cheers of the nonpaying audiences and critics. The musical reopened at the St. James Theatre in December, with Diana Davila replacing Carla Pinza and

John Bottoms taking over Jerry Stiller's role as the servant Launce. At first theatregoers were reluctant to plunk down cash to see what had been a free show, but good word of mouth soon built up the box office.

Later that season, David Rabe's *Sticks and Bones* made the journey from the Festival's Public Theatre to Broadway. The controversial antiwar play was a hit with critics but was losing money. The profits from *Gentlemen* were plowed into *Sticks* to keep the drama running for 245 performances. Papp would later employ this same tactic by using the proceeds from the immensely popular Festival production of *A Chorus Line* to support less popular plays and musicals. At the end of the season, *Gentlemen* and *Sticks and Bones* took the Tonys for Best Musical and Play.

Larry Kert and Stockard Channing headed a national company of *Gentlemen*.

So far, a total of seventeen New York Shakespeare productions, either from the Delacorte or the Public, have played Broadway. Subsequent transfers from the Central Park stage include a revival of *The Pirates of Penzance* (1981) and *The Mystery of Edwin Drood* (1985).

Like *Hair*, this musical *Two Gentlemen* was very much a product of its time; the 1970s references now date the script.

GREASE

Book, music, and lyrics by Jim Jacobs and Warren Casey

Opened February 14, 1972

3,388 Performances

Eden Theatre

Directed by Tom Moore

Choreographed by Patricia Birch

Produced by Kenneth Waissman and Maxine Fox

Cast: Barry Bostwick (Danny Zuko); Carole Demas (Sandy Dumbrowski); Adrienne Barbeau (Betty Rizzo); Timothy Meyers (Kenickie); James Canning (Doody); Walter Bobbie (Roger); Garn Stephens (Jan); Katie Hanley (Marty); Jim Borrelli (Sonny LaTierri); Marya Small (Frenchy); Dorothy Leon (Miss Lynch); Ilene Kristen (Patty Simcox); Tom Harris (Eugene Florcyzk); Don Billett (Vince Fontaine); Alan Paul (Johnny Casino/Teen Angel); Kathi Moss (Cha-Cha Di Gregorio).

As the '70s began, the American public, numbed by the political turmoil of the previous decade, looked back to earlier times. Popular culture followed suit in turning back the clock to the Eisenhower era. *No, No, Nanette* invoked nostalgia for the '20s and '30s, while *Grease* paid tribute to the '50s and became the longest-running musical on Broadway (that is, until *A Chorus Line* came along).

The rock 'n' roll musical was the creation of Jim Jacobs and Warren Casey, two amateur actor-writers who met at the Kingston Mines, a community theatre in Chicago. *Grease* was first performed at Kingston Mines' theatre, a converted trolley barn. "At that point," said the show's future producer, Kenneth Waissman, to the *New York Times*, "it was five hours long and the book was the size of the Manhattan phone directory." Waissman and Maxine Fox, his wife and co-producer, acquired the rights to the marathon musical. Jacobs and Casey trimmed it to a more acceptable length, and the production opened at the Eden Theatre in New York's Lower East Side, where it received mixed notices. "Mildly amusing" was the best they got.

Technically, the Eden was an off-Broadway theatre since it was not in the Times Square theatre district, but the cast was paid on a Broadway contract. The producers persuaded the Tony Award Committee to consider *Grease* eligible for the Broadway-only prizes. Although the show did not win in any of its seven Tony categories, good word of mouth prompted a move to the Broadway area's Broadhurst Theatre, and later the Royale, where it spent most of its long run.

Baby boomers who grew up during the '50s and youngsters who enjoyed the rock music flocked to the show. Warren Casey explained to *Women's Wear Daily*: "*Grease* is not really a spoof of the '50s, but rather a spoof of the sentiments of that period. You know, when the biggest tragedies in your life would have been to have rain on prom night or to be alone at a drive-in."

The show served as a springboard for numerous Hollywood careers, particularly those of young leading men. Barry Bostwick, Richard Gere, John Travolta, Jeff Conway, Ted Wass, Treat Williams, Patrick Swayze, Adrian Zmed, Greg Evigan, Peter Gallagher, and Rex Smith appeared either in the Broadway, touring or London companies. Adrienne Barbeau, Marilu Henner, and Judy Kaye were also *Greasers*.

The 1978 Paramount movie version was the number-one box office attraction that year. Travolta and Conway starred, along with Olivia Newton-John, Stockard Channing, and veterans of the '50s such as Eve Arden, Sid Caesar, and Frankie Avalon.

SUGAR

Book by Peter Stone, based on the film *Some Like It Hot,* by Billy Wilder and I.A.L. Diamond.

Music by Jule Styne

Lyrics by Bob Merrill

Opened April 9, 1972

505 Performances

Majestic Theatre

Directed and choreographed by Gower Champion

Produced by David Merrick

Cast: Robert Morse (Jerry); Tony Roberts (Joe); Elaine Joyce (Sugar Kane); Cyril Ritchard (Osgood Fielding, Jr.); Sheila Smith (Sweet Sue); Alan Kass (Bienstock); Steve Condos (Spats Palazzo); Dick Bonelle (Knuckles Norton); Eileen Casey (Olga); Gerard Brentte (Dude); Igors Gavon (Poker Player); Ken Ayers (Cabdriver); George Blackwell (Train Conductor); Andy Bew (Bellboy).

Just as he had gathered top talent to make a musical version of the Billy Wilder comedy *The Apartment* and come up with the hit *Promises, Promises*, producer David Merrick once again attempted to mine another Wilder comedy for Broadway gold. This time it was the movie *Some Like It Hot*, about two musicians who witness the St. Valentine's Day Massacre and escape the mob by disguising themselves as members of an all-girl band. The 1959 film starred Marilyn Monroe as the sexy Sugar Kane, lead singer with the all-girl band, and Tony Curtis and Jack Lemmon as the cross-dressed musicians.

Merrick aimed high, hiring Jule Styne and Bob Merrill (*Funny Girl*) to write the songs, Gower Champion (*Bye, Bye, Birdie, I Do!, I Do!*) to direct and choreograph, and Michael Stewart (*Hello, Dolly!*) to write the book. Tony Roberts and Robert Morse were signed to play the Curtis and Lemmon roles. Elaine Joyce, wife of Bobby Van (*No, No, Nanette*) took up the challenge of the Monroe part. Cyril Ritchard was to play the Joe E. Brown character, a wealthy fop who begins to woo Jack Lemmon. With a cast and creative team like that, the forecast was for smooth sailing. But the resulting musical, called *Sugar*, was nothing but trouble on the road.

Changes were rife in Washington, Toronto, Philadelphia, and Boston. Sugar's three songs were cut and then put back in. Peter Stone was finally credited with the libretto, after Michael Stewart and George Axelrod withdrew. Rumors of new scenes by Neil Simon and new songs by Jerry Herman crept into the Broadway columns.

When the show finally opened at New York's Majestic Theatre, reviews were mixed, but audiences loved Champion's dances and the men-in-dresses gags. Robert Morse was nominated for a Tony.

DON'T BOTHER ME, I CAN'T COPE

Conceived by Vinette Carroll
Music and lyrics by Micki Grant
Opened April 19, 1972
Playhouse Theatre
1,065 Performances
Directed by Vinette Carroll
Choreographed by George Faison
Produced by Edward Padula and Arch Lustberg
Cast: Alex Bradford, Hope Clarke, Micki Grant, Bobby Hill, Arnold Wilkerson.

Actress and songwriter Micki Grant addressed the dilemmas of contemporary African-American life with her song-filled revue *Don't Bother Me, I Can't Cope*. Mixing rock, gospel, calypso, folk and West Indian elements, the score optimistically examined the problems and celebrated the achievements and pride of black people. The show won the Grammy Award for Best Original Cast Album.

I Can't Cope was first presented in workshop form at the off-off-Broadway Urban Arts Corps. It then played Washington, D.C., Philadelphia, Detroit, and opened on Broadway at the Playhouse Theatre. Two other musicals delineating the black experience opened on Broadway that season. Both, *Ain't Supposed to Die a Natural Death* and *Don't Play Us Cheap*, were by Melvin Van Peebles and took a more militant, angry stance. While the Van Peebles shows had moderately successful runs of several months each, *I Can't Cope* played for over two years.

Another Urban Arts Corps production to transfer to Broadway was *Your Arms Too Short to Box with God* (1976) with music and lyrics by *I Can't Cope* cast member Alex Bradford and additional songs by Grant.

THAT CHAMPIONSHIP SEASON

by Jason Miller
Opened September 14, 1972
700 Performances
Booth Theatre, after an Off-Broadway run at the Public Theatre
Directed by A.J. Antoon
Produced by Joseph Papp, New York Shakespeare Festival
Cast: Walter McGinn (Tom Daley); Charles Durning (George Sikowski); Michael McGuire (James Daley); Paul Sorvino (Phil Romano); Richard A. Dysart (Coach).

Alex Bradford, Arnold Wilkerson, Bobby Hill, and Hope Clarke surround composer and lyricist Micki Grant in *Don't Bother Me, I Can't Cope.*

(Left to right) Michael McGuire, Paul Sorvino, Richard A. Dysart, Charles Durning, and Walter McGinn in *That Championship Season.*

Joseph Papp's New York Shakespeare Festival followed up its award-winning productions of *Two Gentlemen of Verona* and *Sticks and Bones* with another prize-winning play, Jason Miller's *That Championship Season,* a gritty study of four former high-school basketball stars and their coach. They gather to celebrate a reunion during which their illusions of adolescent glory and middle-class respectability are shattered.

Each of the ex-athletes is now in his late 30s and a respected citizen, but hiding a shameful secret. George, now the local mayor, is a petty crook. Industrialist Phil is destroying the environment and sleeping with George's wife. School principal James is dissatisfied with his career, and his brother Tom is a sneering alcoholic. Only the coach still believes in the platitudes about sportsmanship and fair play he used to spout at the "boys" when they were playing ball for him. Even their championship trophy was won through deceit.

The play reflected the country's cynical Vietnam-and-Watergate-era mentality. This searing comedy-drama recalled the work of another playwright named Miller (Arthur) in its living room confrontations among brothers and male friends.

The playwright and his director A.J. Antoon brought the play to Joseph Papp after it had been turned down by a commercial Broadway producer. Papp was unsure of the work's quality, but gave the go-ahead for a staged reading at the Shakespeare Festival's home base, the Public Theatre. Seeing the play "on its feet" with live actors convinced Papp to fully mount the play.

Charles Durning, Walter McGinn, and Michael McGuire, veterans of previous Festival productions, participated in the reading and were cast in the final production. Richard Dysart and Paul Sorvino joined the ensemble later. The play opened at the Public on May 2, 1972, and moved to the Booth Theatre on Broadway in September. "Wow!" exclaimed the powerful Clive Barnes, of the *New York Times,* "Here at last is the perfect Broadway play of the season, perfectly acted and perfectly staged."

That Championship Season was the theatre season's championship play, winning the New York Drama Critics Circle Award for 1972 and the Pulitzer and Tony for 1973.

Later that season, Antoon's staging of *Much Ado About Nothing,* set in the early 1900s, moved from the Delacorte Theatre to Broadway's Winter Garden. With *Two Gentlemen, Sticks and Bones,* and *Championship Season,* this made a total of four New York Shakespeare Festival productions playing on Broadway simultaneously. Papp expanded his influence over Broadway even further when the Festival took over Lincoln Center's Vivian Beaumont and Newhouse Theatres in 1973.

As for *Season,* it continued for 700 performances at the Booth, played on tour and in London. Forrest Tucker played the coach on tour, while Broderick Crawford took on the role in London. An all-star squad was assembled for the 1982 movie (Robert Mitchum, Stacey Keach, Martin Sheen, Bruce Dern, and Paul Sorvino), but they failed to score points at the box office.

Miller later achieved temporary stardom as an actor by playing a leading role in the horror film *The Exorcist* (1973). He was nominated for a Supporting Actor Oscar. So far, he has not written another play of *That Championship Season*'s caliber.

PIPPIN

Book by Roger O. Hirson

Music and lyrics by Stephen Schwartz

Opened October 23, 1972

1,944 Performances

Imperial Theatre

Directed and choreographed by Bob Fosse

Produced by Stuart Ostrow

Cast: Ben Vereen (Leading Player); John Rubinstein (Pippin); Jill Clayburgh (Catherine); Eric Berry (Charles); Leland Palmer (Fastrada); Christopher Chadman (Lewis); Irene Ryan (Berthe); Shane Nickerson (Theo); John Mineo (Musician); Richard Korthaze (Beggar); Paul Solen (Peasant); Gene Foote (Nobleman); Roger Hamilton (The Head/Field Marshall); Candy Brown, Ann Reinking, Jennifer Nairn-Smith, Kathryn Doby, Pamela Sousa (Players).

In the opening number of *Pippin*, Ben Vereen, as the dazzling Leading Player, and his troupe sing "Magic to Do." Amid swirling stage fog, white-gloved hands, seemingly suspended in mid-air, performed various feats of legerdemain. Director-choreographer Bob Fosse used some magic of his own to cover up a weak script and kept the show running for almost 2,000 performances.

Although *Pippin* was the creation of composer-lyricist Stephen Schwartz, it was Fosse who shaped it. Schwartz wrote *Pippin* as a college show while he was a student at Carnegie Tech in Pittsburgh. After the success of Schwartz's *Godspell* off-Broadway, producer Stuart Ostrow optioned *Pippin* for Broadway. The musical related the *Candide*-like journey of the title character, the son of the medieval Frankish ruler Charles Martel, as he attempts to find fulfillment as a warrior, lover, king, and finally, family man. Fosse felt the material was treated too sentimentally and gave it a hard, glitzy edge. Dance numbers were interjected freely into the simple story, which was rewritten by Roger O. Hirson, with additional contributions by Fosse.

Schwartz's score included such fine tunes as "Corner of the Sky," "No Time at All," and "Kind of Woman." But all anyone remembered was Fosse's inventive staging. *Pippin* was "unmistakenly and triumphantly the director's show," said Douglas Watt in his *Daily News* review. And the director used every trick in the book, from the magical opening number to a sing-along with Irene Ryan (formerly of TV's *The Beverly Hillbillies*), from flaming hoops to a near-orgy sequence which Fosse later parodied in his autobiographical film *All That Jazz*.

The young composer and the veteran director did not get along. Schwartz felt Fosse was perverting his work, and during rehearsals he raised his objections. Fosse eventually had the songwriter barred from all rehearsals. (Schwartz restored his script to its original concept when *Pippin* was staged in Mexico and Australia, but those productions were not hits.)

Although John Rubinstein was playing Pippin, the show was stolen by Ben Vereen in his Mephistophelian role, a character similar to the Emcee in *Cabaret*, who presides over and comments on the action. Vereen's performance won him a Tony Award, and he was highlighted in the television commercial for *Pippin*, the first one ever to show scenes from a Broadway show. The effectiveness of the ad, directed by Fosse, contributed to the show's four-year run. Two national touring companies widened its success, and a cable television version was later produced starring Vereen, William Katt, and Chita Rivera.

Fosse won Tonys for his direction and choreography.

THE SUNSHINE BOYS

by Neil Simon

Opened December 20, 1972

538 Performances

Broadhurst Theatre

Directed by Alan Arkin

Produced by Emanuel Azenberg and Eugene V. Wolsk

Cast: Jack Albertson (Willie Clark); Sam Levene (Al Lewis); Lewis J. Stadlen (Ben Silverman); Joe Young (Patient); John Batiste (Eddie); Lee Meredith (Sketch Nurse); Minnie Gentry (Nurse).

It was a busy year for Neil Simon. In 1972, in addition to a film (*The Heartbreak Kid*) and a television special (*The Trouble with People*), he wrote his annual Broadway comedy, *The Sunshine Boys*, which became his ninth long-running hit. After the dark urban crisis of his last show, *The Prisoner of Second Avenue*, he penned an entertaining comedy about two former vaudevillians reuniting for a television special. Like an older Oscar and Felix, Willie Clark and Al Lewis simply cannot get along. "As an actor, no one could touch him," Willie says about Al. "As a human being, no one would want to touch him."

The playwright commented to the *Long Island Press*: "The most welcome compliments I've had about *The Sunshine Boys* came from recognition, not the recognition that this old vaudeville team could make people think of [the team of] Smith and Dale and their 'Dr. Kronkite' sketch, which would be perfectly accurate, but the recognition that Willie and Al are the viewers' own fathers or uncles or someone they know well."

The Sunshine Boys of the original cast, Jack Albertson and Sam Levene, were eventually replaced by Jack Gilford and Lou Jacobi. The 1975 movie version starred Walter Matthau and George Burns, who won an Oscar as Best Supporting Actor.

Simon's next two productions broke his nearly uninterrupted streak of hits. *The Good Doctor* (1973), based on the short stories of Anton Chekhov, may have been too esoteric for the usual Simon audience; it ran a disappointing seven months and 208 performances. *God's Favorite* (1974) parodied the Book of Job. The jokes about pestilence con-

Lewis J. Stadlen mediates between former vaudeville partners Jack Albertson (left) and Sam Levene (right) in *The Sunshine Boys.*

tributed to its shutdown after 119 performances. The following year, Simon moved to California to be closer to the film community. His next play was *California Suite* (1976), a quartet of one-acts. As in his earlier *Plaza Suite*, all the playlets took place in the same hotel, but this one was on the West Coast. It ran for 445 performances.

A LITTLE NIGHT MUSIC

Book by Hugh Wheeler, suggested by the film *Smiles of a Summer Night,* by Ingmar Bergman.

Music and lyrics by Stephen Sondheim

Opened February 25, 1973

601 Performances

Shubert Theatre

Choreographed by Patricia Birch

Produced and directed by Harold Prince

Cast: Glynis Johns (Desiree Armfeldt); Len Cariou (Frederik Egerman); Hermione Gingold (Mme. Armfeldt); Victoria Mallory (Anne Egerman); Mark Lambert (Henrik Egerman); Laurence Guittard (Count Carl-Magnus Malcolm); Patricia Elliott (Countess Charlotte Malcolm); Judy Kahan (Fredrika Armfeldt); D. Jamin-Bartlett (Petra); George Lee Andrews (Frid); Benjamin Rayson (Mr. Lindquist); Teri Ralston (Mrs. Nordstrom); Barbara Lang (Mrs. Anderssen); Gene Varrone (Mr. Erlanson); Beth Fowler (Mrs. Segstrom); Despo (Malla); Sherry Mathis (Osa).

Although Stephen Sondheim has attained cult status among musical comedy fans, his only Top 40 hit has been "Send in the Clowns," from his sophisticated valentine to adult sex and romance, *A Little Night Music.* Based on Ingmar Bergman's bittersweet 1955 film comedy *Smiles of a Summer Night, Night Music* follows the intersecting amours of a group of lovers in turn-of-the-century Sweden.

Actress Desiree Armfeldt wants to retire from the stage and settle down with lawyer Frederik Egerman, the father of her thirteen-year-old daughter. Unfortunately, Frederik is newly married to a child bride of eighteen, and Desiree is engaged in an affair with a jealous dragoon. To further complicate matters, Frederik's son is in love with his young stepmother. All these love-knots are untangled during a country weekend party at the mansion of Desiree's mother, a former courtesan.

Prince and Sondheim were looking for a romantic musical that would be elegant, mature, and appealing. Prince explained, "Steve and I had talked about making a musical of either Jean Renoir's film *Rules of the Game* or the Jean Anouilh play *Ring Round the Moon.* We couldn't get the rights. But we did get them to *Smiles of a Summer Night* and did that instead."

Hugh Wheeler, who had written the screenplay of Prince's film *Something for Everyone,* was brought in to do the book. Prince told Wheeler to write the book as if it were a film script, and the director staged all the scenes on designer Boris Aronson's rolling green lawn in a forest of birch trees.

Sondheim composed his unique score all in three-quarter time. But only about half of the thirteen waltzes, scherzos, minuets, polonaises, and barcaroles were ready when rehearsals started. "Send in the Clowns" wasn't added to the show until two weeks before the company left New York for the Boston tryout.

Another unique feature of Sondheim's score was the use of five lieder singers to comment musically on the action, rather than a conventional singing and dancing chorus. Actors Equity ruled that these singers should be employed under chorus, rather than principal, contracts, since they had no spoken dialogue. The singers refused to sign the lower-paying contracts and Prince backed them up, stating that their roles were just as important as those of the main characters. The union threatened to bring the matter to arbitration as rehearsals began, but Equity eventually relented.

There was more trouble once the show went into its tryout in Boston. Garn Stephens in the role of the saucy maid was having vocal problems with her solo, "The Miller's Son," one of the show's biggest songs. She was let go and replaced by D. Jamin-Bartlett.

Once the production moved to New York, there was a minor crisis. During previews leading lady Glynis Johns got sick with intestinal flu. Prince recalled: "She was taken to the hospital, almost didn't make opening night. She almost didn't make the show. But she pulled herself together in time." Tammy Grimes was briefly considered as a replacement, but Johns recovered.

The all-important *New York Times* review by Clive Barnes, who had disliked *Company* and *Follies,* was an unqualified rave. "Good God, an adult musical," he joyously declared. The other reviewers followed suit, with only a few caveats, such as Kevin Kelly's in the *Boston Globe,* that the show was too specialized in its appeal. At the end of the season, *Night Music* split the spoils at the Tony Awards with *Pippin.* Each show won five prizes.

With the exception of *Hair,* Broadway music had not been the main source for pop music hits in two decades. But when Judy Collins recorded "Send in the Clowns," it topped the charts and won the Grammy for Best Song in 1975. Frank Sinatra and Barbra Streisand also cut their own versions.

Jean Simmons and Margaret Hamilton headlined the national tour. Prince directed the movie of *Night Music* with the vocally limited Elizabeth Taylor as Desiree and Len Cariou recreating his Frederik. The film had a small and critically panned release in 1978. However, Jonathan Tunick did win an Oscar for his score adaptation. The summer nights smiled more broadly in 1990 when the New York City Opera added *Night Music* to its repertoire. Sally Anne Howes and George Lee Andrews (who originated the role of the butler Frid on Broadway) played the leads in this well-received revival.

Hermione Gingold offers sage advice to Glynis Johns in *A Little Night Music.*

IRENE

Book by Hugh Wheeler and Joseph Stein, from an adaptation by Harry Rigby, based on the original play by James Montgomery.

Music by Harry Tierney

Lyrics by Joseph McCarthy

Additional music and lyrics by Charles Gaynor, Otis Clements, Fred Fisher, and James Monaco

Opened March 13, 1973

604 Performances

Minskoff Theatre

Directed by Gower Champion

Choreographed by Peter Gennaro

Produced by Harry Rigby, Albert W. Selden, and Jerome Minskoff

Cast: Debbie Reynolds (Irene O'Dare); Monte Markham (Donald Marshall); Patsy Kelly (Mrs. O'Dare); George S. Irving (Madame Lucy); Ruth Warrick (Emmeline Marshall); Janie Sell (Jane Burke); Carmen Alvarez (Helen McFudd); Bruce Lea (Jimmy O'Flaherty); Bob Freschi (Clarkson); Ted Pugh (Ozzie Babson); Kate O'Brady (Arabella Thornsworthy); Carrie Fisher was in the chorus.

Hoping to cash in on the success of the revival of *No, No, Nanette*, producer Harry Rigby, who had been fired from *Nanette* by his co-producer and chief backer Cyma Rubin, mounted a revival of *Irene*, another musical from the same era. As with *Nanette*, the book was totally rewritten, a star of yesteryear (Debbie Reynolds, making her Broadway debut) was hired to headline, and there were numerous problems on the road to Broadway.

The basic *My Fair Lady*-like story of the 1919 original was retained with Irene as a poor but plucky Irish girl rising to the top of society by modeling clothes at a swank Long Island party. Her occupation was changed from upholsterer to piano tuner so that Reynolds could have a tap number with the boys of the chorus on top of a series of upright pianos. Rigby had done the first adaptation, but further revisions were written by Joseph Stein and Hugh Wheeler (also represented that same season on Broadway by his libretto for *A Little Night Music*). Only five of the songs from the original score were retained. Other popular tunes of the period like "You Made Me Love You" and "They Go Wild, Simply Wild Over Me" were added.

Rigby contracted British classical actor Sir John Gielgud to stage the show. Billy de Wolfe signed on to play the fussy male courtier known as Madame Lucy, and Patsy Kelly, the comic maid from *Nanette*, was Irene's earthy mother. De Wolfe left the production due to illness and was replaced by George S. Irving, who later won a Featured Actor Tony Award. Reynolds was struck with laryngitis in Toronto, and at one particularly memorable performance she silently acted out her part while Gielgud read a synopsis of the scenes. In response to some disgruntled booing from the audience, Reynolds hoarsely said, "I don't have to be here. I could be home with my seven maids."

Gielgud was replaced by Gower Champion, who got the show in shape by the time it reached Washington, D.C.

There, President Richard Nixon gave *Irene* a favorable review, calling it "a great show, a good family show, a lot of fun." He added that jaded New Yorkers probably wouldn't appreciate its simple pleasures. The President's comments provided plenty of free publicity.

When the show opened in New York at the new Minksoff Theatre, the critics disagreed with Nixon. They found Reynolds hard-working but uninspired and Champion's production and Peter Gennaro's choreography proficient but routine. But the nostalgia craze was still going strong. The revival ran for a year and a half. Jane Powell succeeded Reynolds, who went out on the national tour.

RAISIN

Book by Robert Nemiroff and Charlotte Zaltzberg, based on the play *A Raisin in the Sun* by Lorraine Hansberry.

Music by Judd Woldin

Lyrics by Robert Brittan

Opened October 18, 1973

847 Performances

46th Street Theatre

Directed and choreographed by Donald McKayle

Produced by Robert Nemiroff

Cast: Virginia Capers (Lena Younger); Joe Morton (Walter Lee Younger); Ernestine Jackson (Ruth Younger); Debbie Allen (Beneatha Younger); Ralph Carter (Travis Younger); Robert Jackson (Joseph Asagai); Helen Martin (Mrs. Johnson); Ted Ross (Bobo Jones); Walter P. Brown (Willie Harris); Richard Sanders (Karl Linder); Chief Bey (African Drummer).

Lorraine Hansberry's drama *A Raisin in the Sun* had a second life on Broadway when the late playwright's husband Robert Nemiroff produced and adapted the play as a musical called *Raisin*. The story of an African-American family remained essentially the same. The Youngers are living in a crowded Chicago tenement. An insurance check could buy a college education for the daughter, a partnership in a liquor store for the son, and a new home for the whole family. But the son's prospective partner absconds with the money and all that is left is the down payment on a house in an all-white neighborhood. The Youngers decide to move into their dream home despite opposition from their new neighbors.

Nemiroff and his co-librettist Charlotte Zaltzberg adapted Hansberry's script. To expand upon the play's single setting, the story was opened up to include scenes at a Sunday-morning church service, a bar, and a fantasy sequence with a full chorus of dancers in African garb. The kitchen-sink realism of the play gave way to evocative scenery and imaginary props.

The production was first presented at Washington D.C.'s Arena Theatre, where it drew favorable notices. The New York reaction was mixed, but mostly positive. Many critics felt that Hansberry's drama was dated and even soap

Virginia Capers, Joe Morton, and Ernestine Jackson in *Raisin*, the musical version of *A Raisin in the Sun*.

opera-ish but still admired Donald McKayle's lively staging. Others opined that the musical didn't match the original but was still enjoyable. Edwin Wilson of the *Wall Street Journal* stated, "Unlike [Hansberry's] play on which it based, the musical is not a landmark, but it is a strong, stimulating piece of work." At awards time, *Raisin*'s chief competition was the revised version of Leonard Bernstein's *Candide*. The New York Drama Critics Circle voted *Candide* the best musical, but the Tony Award Committee considered it a revival, leaving the way clear for *Raisin* to take its top musical prize.

Many of the unknown cast members went on to star in film and TV projects. Joe Morton went on to do classical theatre for a while, and he played the title role in John Sayles's film *The Brother from Another Planet* and was a regular on the ABC series *Equal Justice*. Debbie Allen headlined the 1986 Broadway revival of *Sweet Charity*. Ralph

Carter played the youngest son on the CBS series *Good Times*. Ted Ross later won a Tony for playing the Cowardly Lion in *The Wiz*. Virginia Capers, who won a Tony Award for her performance as the matriarch, stayed with the show for the entire Broadway run and headed the national tour.

CANDIDE

Book by Hugh Wheeler, based on Voltaire's *Candide*.

Music by Leonard Bernstein

Lyrics by Richard Wilbur, with additional lyrics by Stephen Sondheim and John Latouche

Opened March 10, 1974

740 Performances

Broadway Theatre, after an off-Broadway run at the Brooklyn Academy of Music.

Choreographed by Patricia Birch

Directed by Harold Prince

Produced by the Chelsea Theatre Center of Brooklyn, with Harold Prince and Ruth Mitchell

Cast: Lewis J. Stadlen (Voltaire/Pangloss/Spanish Governor, etc.); Mark Baker (Candide); Maureen Brennan (Cunegonde); Sam Freed (Maximillian); Deborah St. Darr (Paquette); June Gable (Old Lady); Mary-Pat Green (Baroness, etc.); Joe Palmieri (Baron/ Grand Inquisitor, etc.); Jeff Keller (Rich Jew/Judge, etc.); Jim Corti (Chinese Coolie/Westphalian Soldier/Lion, etc.); David Horwitz (Huntsman, 1st Recruiting Officer, etc.); Robert Henderson (Servant/Agent of the Inquisition, etc.); Peter Vogt (2nd Recruiting Officer, etc.); Gail Boggs (Penitente/Whore, etc.); Lynne Gannaway (Penitente, etc.); Carolann Page (Aristocrat, etc.); Chip Garnett (Westphalian Soldier/Agent, etc.); Carlos Gorbea (Bulgarian Soldier, etc.); Kelly Walters (Bulgarian Soldier, etc.); Becky McSpadden (Aristocrat, etc.); Kathryn Ritter (Aristocrat/Whore, etc.); Renee Semes (Lady with Knitting/1st Sheep, etc.); Rhoda Butler (Swing Girl).

Voltaire's *Candide*, a wicked 18th-century satire on the then-prevailing philosophy of optimism, follows the young titular hero's adventures through a world of conniving and injustice. The history of the theatrical version of Voltaire's story is almost as complicated and involved.

The work was first brought to Broadway in musical form in 1956 with music by Leonard Bernstein, lyrics by Richard Wilbur, John Latouche and Dorothy Parker, and a book by Lillian Hellman (her first and last musical). Everyone agreed that the score was lovely, but the overall tone and production values were too heavy-handed for the satire. Although the show closed after only a three-month run, its legend grew as the original cast album became more and more popular.

There were numerous attempts to bring *Candide* back to the stage with the same enchanting songs but a different libretto. A 1959 London production and a 1971 mounting by the Kennedy Center of Washington, D.C., failed to ignite a spark of interest among Broadway producers.

Robert Kalfin, artistic director of the Chelsea Theatre Center at the Brooklyn Academy of Music, believed that Harold Prince was the man to give this potential classic the production it deserved. Prince hit upon the concept of cutting the show down to less than two hours and staging it in the manner of a triptych, with various small stages depicting the numerous locations of the story.

Lillian Hellman was contacted about rewriting her original work, but she declined. She did grant Prince the right to do a new book as long as none of her original dialogue was used. Hugh Wheeler, librettist for Prince's production of *A Little Night Music*, was hired to write a new version. The author returned to the original source, Voltaire, and emphasized the work's comic elements.

Wheeler told *After Dark* magazine, "We opted for a free-form staging and I began to make a series of short scenes. Although I used only about a third of the material in Voltaire's book, it was still rather long. Then Hal cut it down to size. I had to figure out how I could get in as many of the original songs as possible and yet I had to retain the quality, the tone of Voltaire. This meant that certain songs had to be rearranged." Stephen Sondheim supplied new lyrics for the tunes which were placed in different contexts.

To realize Prince's concept, set designer Eugene Lee remodeled the Chelsea's 180-seat theatre to accommodate a multilevel environmental playing space replete with ramps, catwalks, platforms, drawbridges, and trapdoors. The audience sat on bleachers and stools interspersed throughout the set. The clever set, hilarious new book, slightly revamped score, and rapid pacing gave *Candide* a new lease on life. Clive Barnes of the *New York Times* wrote, "This is a doll of a show. I loved it and loved it. I think Voltaire would have loved it too. If he didn't—to hell with him."

The limited six-week engagement in Brooklyn quickly sold out and a move to the Broadway Theatre, which was renovated for the flexible staging, was accomplished. The production was praised again and won the Drama Critics Circle Award for Best Musical. However, *Candide* lost $310,000 of its $450,000 initial investment after 740 Broadway performances. Various factors contributed to the shortfall. The theatre's renovations cut down on the seating capacity. The musicians' union demanded that twenty-five of their members be hired when the score only required twelve. The complicated set prevented a national tour which might have helped recoup the loss.

Candide has since appeared in opera houses and on concert stages throughout the world. Prince directed a 1982 production for the New York City Opera. Nonmusical *Candides* included a 1971 production by the Organic Theatre Company at the New York Shakespeare Festival's Public Theatre and an adaptation by Len Jenkin presented by the Classic Stage Company in 1992.

Lewis J. Stadlen (center) as Dr. Pangloss declares that this is "The Best of All Possible Worlds" in the revival of *Candide*. (left to right) Students Mark Baker, Deborah St. Darr, Sam Freed, and Maureen Brennan soon learn otherwise.

THE MAGIC SHOW

Book by Bob Randall

Music and lyrics by Stephen Schwartz

Opened May 28, 1974

1,920 Performances

Cort Theatre

Directed and choreographed by Grover Dale

Produced by Edgar Lansbury, Joseph Beruh, and Ivan Reitman

Cast: Doug Henning (Doug); Robert LuPone (Manny); David Ogden Stiers (Feldman); Annie McGreevey (Donna); Cheryl Barnes (Dina); Dale Soules (Cal); Ronald Stafford (Mike); Loyd Sannes (Steve); Anita Morris (Charmin); Sam Schacht (Goldfarb).

Magicians had long been popular on vaudeville bills and occasionally Broadway, but none had sustained a long run there. That is, until Doug Henning took *The Magic Show*, a rickety book musical, and transformed it into a hit.

Henning hardly fit the typical image of a magician. Rather than a dashing figure in white tie, tails, top hat, and cape, he was a reed-thin, toothy young man with shoulder-length hair, usually dressed in jeans and a T-shirt. But his repertoire of magic went beyond the rabbit-out-of-the-hat tricks.

Henning's illusions in the show included burning a woman to a skeleton; sawing another one in half and then separating the sections; topping that by cutting a woman into three segments and then rearranging her parts so the feet were above her head; and transforming the lovely Anita Morris into a cougar. Of course, *The Magic Show*'s plot was a merely an excuse for these spectacles. Henning played a conjurer named Doug, a rising star at a low-rent nightclub in Passaic, New Jersey. David Ogden Stiers provided comedy turns as a hammy older magician whom Doug overshadows, and Stephen Schwartz wrote some pleasant songs, but the main attraction was Henning's magic.

Clive Barnes of the *New York Times* summed up the critical reaction by calling Henning "the greatest illusionist I have ever seen and, particularly as a child, I have seen plenty. He is amazing. On the other hand, the show is awful." Despite the weakness of the story, Henning's truly astonishing feats sustained audience interest and kept the show running for 1,920 performances. This was the third hit in a row for Schwartz after *Godspell* and *Pippin*.

Jospeh Abaldo continued the prestidigitation on Broadway and Peter De Paula performed the lead on tour.

Henning later attempted the same trick of turning a mediocre musical into a smash hit, but with *Merlin* (1983), in which he played a young version of the legendary wizard, he ran out of magic. Another pair of unconventional magicians, Penn and Teller, had a long run off-Broadway in 1985 (see page 349) and a Broadway stint in 1991.

ABSURD PERSON SINGULAR

by Alan Ayckbourn

Opened October 8, 1974

592 Performances

Music Box Theatre

Directed by Eric Thompson

Produced by the Theatre Guild and the Kennedy Center for the Performing Arts

Cast: Carole Shelley (Jane); Larry Blyden (Sidney); Richard Kiley (Ronald); Geraldine Page (Marion); Sandy Dennis (Eva); Tony Roberts (Geoffrey).

Playwright Alan Ayckbourn, sometimes called the British Neil Simon, has had numerous hits in his native Britain. Over twenty of his comedies, mostly about middle-class married people dealing with various midlife crises, have played in London's commercial West End and at the non-profit National Theatre. But only one, *Absurd Person Singular*, has had a long run on Broadway.

The comedy contrasts the relations of three disparate English couples. Jane and Sidney are a pair of rather crass social climbers. Ronald is a patrician banker, while his wife Marion is a bitchy alcoholic. Architect Geoffrey has a roving eye, and his spouse Eva is chronically depressed. There's also a fourth offstage couple, Dick and Lottie, who seem to have a perfect union.

Unlike Simon's, Ayckbourn's humor derives mainly from situation rather than clever dialogue. Ayckbourn compared himself to America's top comic playwright in a *New York Times* interview: "His characters are often very funny verbally. None of my characters ever made a good joke in his life." Accordingly, there are no "jokes" in *Absurd Person*, but plenty of comic situations. The play takes place on three successive Christmases in the kitchens of the three couples. In each act, something goes terribly wrong with a festive Yuletide gathering. The comedy is often laced with bitter irony. Fastidious housekeeper Jane is locked out of her own house. Depressed Eva attempts to commit suicide in hers, as the others blithely clean up and make repairs. At Marion's place, the hostess has slid into an booze-induced haze and cannot cope with visitors.

As the play progresses, Ayckbourn offers pointed observations on marriage and class as the relationships among the couples shift. Jane and Sidney are seen at first as annoying pests, but eventually they control the fates of all the others. Ronald and Marion are the best off of the three in Act I, but have slid into financial and emotional despair in Act III. By the end of the play, the formerly smug Geoffrey is unemployed, and Eva emerges as the stronger of the two. The curtain descends on the entire company playing a mad Christmas game with Sidney calling the shots.

The American staging was presented by the Theatre Guild, which had not mounted a stage production since 1968's flop musical *Darling of the Day*. The Guild's Philip

Geraldine Page is alarmed by Larry Blyden's Christmas cheer in *Absurd Person Singular*.

Langer happened to see *Absurd Person* in London, where it was in its second year and had won the *Evening Standard* Award as Best Comedy. For the Broadway production, the Guild took no chances and assembled a first-rate star cast: Carole Shelley, Larry Blyden, Richard Kiley, Geraldine Page, Sandy Dennis, and Tony Roberts.

Ayckbourn's only previous New York production was *How the Other Half Loves*, in which Phil Silvers and Sandy Dennis had starred in 1971. The script had been Americanized, and the show failed. For *Absurd Person Singular*, the dialogue remained as it had been in the West End, and Ayckbourn had a hit.

The touring edition featured Betsy von Furstenberg, Judy Carne, Sheila MacRae, Patrick MacNee, Michael Callen, and David Watson. Among those who appeared in the Broadway replacement company were Fritz Weaver, Carol Lynley, Scott McKay, Paul Shyre, and Marilyn Clark. Ayckbourn's later New York productions were critically well-received but failed to draw big enough audiences for a sustained run. These plays included *The Norman Conquests* (1975), a trio of full-length comedies; *Bedroom Farce* (1979); and *A Small Family Business* (1992) on Broadway. *Woman in Mind* (1988) and *Absent Friends* (1991) played limited engagements off-Broadway.

EQUUS

by Peter Shaffer
Opened October 24, 1974
1,209 Performances
Plymouth Theatre
Directed by John Dexter
Produced by Kermit Bloomgarden and Doris Cole Abrahams
Cast: Anthony Hopkins (Dr. Martin Dysart); Peter Firth (Alan Strang); Marian Seldes (Hesther Salomon); Frances Sternhagen (Dora Strang); Michael Higgins (Frank Strang); Roberta Maxwell (Jill); Walter Matthews (Harry Dalton); Everett McGill (Horseman/Nugget); Mary Doyle (Nurse).

When a friend told English playwright Peter Shaffer the horrific true story of a young stable boy who had blinded the horses in his care, the image fired the writer's imagination. He took this seed of a story and, using his considerable dramatic skills, made it grow into *Equus*, the taut psychological thriller that became a triumph on both sides of the Atlantic.

While writing the play, Shaffer decided not to research the actual facts behind the gruesome anecdote, but provided characters and motivations of his own. He placed two antagonists at the center of his drama: Alan Strang, his version of the stable boy, and Dr. Martin Dysart, the self-doubting child psychologist assigned to discover the trauma that caused Alan to commit the crime.

The biggest problem in staging *Equus* was representing the horses. "You can't just have actors pretending to be horses," Shaffer said. The solution was masks, a device employed in his earlier play *The Royal Hunt of the Sun*. Designer John Napier constructed imposing steel-wired helmets and six-inch "hooves" for six black-clad actors playing the horses. Director John Dexter wanted the set to be as simple as possible in order to highlight the masks and to emphasize Shaffer's polished dialogue. A square on top of a circle was used, with audience members seated around it onstage to suggest an operating theatre in which Dysart would present his conflicted views on the case.

Equus opened in July of 1973, at London's Old Vic Theatre, as part of the National Theatre's repertory. Alec McCowen was Dysart and twenty-year-old Peter Firth played the tormented Alan. The stark theatricality of the production caused a sensation with both the London critics and their colleagues in New York. Walter Kerr of the *New York Times* called it "a psychological detective story of infinite skill."

When the show was scheduled to move to Broadway, Dexter wanted Anthony Hopkins, his original choice for Dysart, to play the role. Hopkins had declined performing in *Equus* after walking out of an argument-ridden National Theatre production of *Macbeth*. Dexter flew to Vienna, where Hopkins was making a film with Goldie Hawn, in order to secure his services. After much persuasion and promises of a harmonious atmosphere, Hopkins agreed to the New York engagement.

All seemed to bode well for the highly anticipated American transfer. There was some concern about a five-minute, well-lit nude scene between Alan and Jill, a stable girl. Roberta Maxwell, the actress hired to play Jill, was quoted in the *New York Post* as saying "I'm used to baring my soul, but this is the first time I'll be baring my all. [Producer] Kermit Bloomgarden asked me after the reading, 'How are your breasts?' I said, 'Firm and flawless, except for the mosquito bites.'" Broadway audiences that had been exposed to *Oh! Calcutta!* and *Hair* hardly batted an eye at *Equus*' brief skin scene.

But they more than batted an eye at its dramatic power. The opening night crowd gave playwright Shaffer (who was seated in a box) a five-minute standing ovation. *Equus* galloped onto Broadway at a time of few solid, nonmusical hits and quickly established itself as the play to see. In the course of a three-year run, it made over $10 million.

Hopkins and Firth left at the end of their nine-month contracts to be replaced by Anthony Perkins and Tom Hulce.

Perkins was succeeded by Richard Burton. The word on the street was that he was auditioning for the movie version by doing the play. (Jack Nicholson and Marlon Brando were also rumored to be under consideration).

Burton's appearance drew tremendous publicity. Not only was he making his first Broadway appearance in twelve years, but he had also recently embarked on a second try at marriage with Elizabeth Taylor. His twelve-week engagement quickly sold out, as did the two-week extension.

Although his stint was a comeback victory, the new marriage was not. In spite of Taylor's note of congratulation, written in lipstick on his dressing-room mirror ("You were fantastic, love"), the Burtons were separated before Richard's *Equus* contract expired.

Perkins returned to the role, to be followed by Leonard Nimoy. Burton did star with Firth in the movie version, directed by Sidney Lumet and released by United Artists in 1977. Stripped of its theatricality, the film did not fare as well as the play at the box office. However, Oscar nominations went to Burton and to Shaffer, who did the screenplay.

THE WIZ

Book by William F. Brown, based on *The Wonderful Wizard of Oz*, by L. Frank Baum.

Music and lyrics by Charlie Smalls

Opened January 5, 1975

1,672 Performances

Majestic Theatre

Directed by Geoffrey Holder

Choreographed by George Faison

Produced by Ken Harper

Cast: Stephanie Mills (Dorothy); Hinton Battle (Scarecrow); Tiger Haynes (Tinman); Ted Ross (Lion); Dee Dee Bridgewater (Glinda); Mabel King (Evillene); Andre De Shields (The Wiz); Clarice Taylor (Addaperle); Tasha Thomas (Aunt Em); Ralph Wilcox (Uncle Henry/Lord High Underling); Evelyn Thomas (Tornado); Danny Beard (Gatekeeper); Carl Weaver (Soldier Messenger); Andy Torres (Winged Monkey). Phylicia Ayers-Allen (later Phylicia Rashad) was in the chorus as a Munchkin and a mouse.

The familiar story of *The Wonderful Wizard of Oz*, L. Frank Baum's 1900 American fairy tale, was retold in contemporary terms in *The Wiz*. Bookwriter William F. Brown explained the differences in the two productions in an interview: "The show is in many ways faithful to the original story. It takes Dorothy from Kansas to Oz and back again; she meets all the familiar characters and problems; but there the similarity ends."

The idea of redoing the tale with an African-American cast originated with producer Ken Harper. As program affairs director at a New York radio station, Harper was an expert on trends in popular music. He figured the time was right for a black family musical. At first, he thought of using Baum's story for a television special, but after the success of *Purlie* and *Raisin*, Broadway seemed the perfect venue. Together with songwriter Charlie Smalls, Harper persuaded 20th-Century Fox to invest $650,000 in the production.

The Wiz was less than wonderfully received during its tryout. Friends advised Harper to close it in Baltimore.

Stephanie Mills (center) and friends "Ease on Down the Road" on their way to see the Wiz.

Director Gilbert Moses left in Detroit to be replaced by Geoffrey Holder, who had been contracted to design the costumes. Holder made several changes, including restoring the Tornado Ballet (in which a dancer twirled around the stage trailing a long piece of gauzy fabric which grew longer and longer as the tornado whisks Dorothy to Oz); advancing eighteen-year-old Hinton Battle from the chorus to take over for an ailing Stu Gilliam as the Scarecrow; and changing Dorothy's costume from boyish jeans to a frilly white dress. The role of the Queen of the Mice, played by Butterfly McQueen, was eliminated.

After more successful performances in Detroit and Philadelphia, the production opened in New York to mixed notices from the mostly white press. Rather than judging the show on its own merits, many of the critics compared it unfavorably to the classic 1939 MGM movie with Judy Garland. A closing notice was posted on opening night, but Harper convinced 20th-Century Fox to spend money on an advertising campaign. Following the lead of *Pippin*, a television commercial was made which drew audiences. There was also an active effort to attract black audiences, especially groups, to the show.

Ticket sales mounted, as word of George Faison's dazzling choreography and Holder's imaginative staging and costumes spread. Among the more clever combinations of Faison and Holder's work was the "Ease on Down the Road" number. Dorothy and her three companions (Scarecrow, Tin Man, and Cowardly Lion) are surrounded by four dancers in blond Afros, representing the Yellow Brick Road. As the quartet advances on their journey, the dancers guide them on the way. At the end of the season, *The Wiz* won seven Tonys, including Best Musical. Holder was honored for both his direction and costumes. On the occasion of the production's first anniversary, Harper stated,"Fortunately, I realized very soon on the road that the show had tremendous appeal, especially among people who had never been to the theatre before. Once they found us and discovered what we were about, we inevitably built to capacity. Word of mouth was what made us."

Two touring companies, one of which starred Ren Woods and Ben Harney (future Tony winner for *Dreamgirls*), played for three years.

Sidney Lumet directed the 1978 film version, which was filmed on location in New York City and replaced Kansas with Harlem and the Emerald City with midtown Manhattan. Diana Ross was a mature Dorothy, with Michael Jackson, Nipsey Russell, and Ted Ross (repeating his Tony-winning performance) as her three friends. Lena Horne (Lumet's mother-in-law) played Glinda.

Touring revivals of *The Wiz* paid visits to New York in 1984 and 1993, both starring Stephanie Mills.

An earlier stage version of *The Wonderful Wizard of Oz*, adapted by Baum himself, had played Broadway in 1903. The combined success of the book and the play led to thirteen other Oz books by Baum and three silent films before the MGM version was made.

SHENANDOAH

Book by James Lee Barrett, Peter Udell and Philip Rose, based on Barrett's original screenplay.

Music by Gary Geld

Lyrics by Peter Udell

Opened January 7, 1975

1,050 Performances

Alvin Theatre

Directed by Philip Rose

Choreographed by Robert Tucker

Produced by Philip Rose, Gloria and Louis K. Sher

Cast: John Cullum (Charlie Anderson); Ted Agress (Jacob); Joel Higgins (James); Jordan Suffin (Nathan); David Russell (John); Penelope Milford (Jenny); Robert Rosen (Henry); Joseph Shapiro (Robert/The Boy); Donna Theodore (Anne); Chip Ford (Gabriel); Charles Welch (Rev. Byrd/Tinkham); Gordon Halliday (Sam); Edward Penn (Sgt. Johnson); Marshall Thomas (Lieutenant); Casper Roos (Carol); Gary Harger (Corporal); Gene Masoner (Marauder); Ed Preble (Engineer); Craig Lucas (Confederate Sniper).

Two days after a rock-inspired *The Wiz* opened, a musical recalling a different era appeared on Broadway. *Shenandoah* was a return to musical theatre's Rodgers-and-Hammerstein–style show. Based on the 1965 film of the same name, the Civil War story celebrated American individualism and the importance of family. In the age of Watergate cynicism, several pundits dismissed the production as naive. Despite this, it racked up 1,050 performances.

The score was by Gary Geld and Peter Udell, who had had a hit with *Purlie.* James Lee Barrett, author of the original screenplay, collaborated with Udell and producer-director Philip Rose (another *Purlie* veteran) on the libretto. The story concerned Virginia farmer Charlie Anderson, who wants no part of the conflict between the North and the South. But the war soon tears his family apart as two sons and a daughter-in-law are killed and a third son is kidnapped by Union soldiers.

Like *Man of La Mancha*, *Shenandoah* started out at the Goodspeed Opera House in East Haddam, Connecticut, during its summer season. Response was so positive that a Broadway run was planned. During the out-of-town tryout in Boston, Kevin Kelly of the *Boston Globe* hailed the show, but overall the critics were split on its merits.

The press was divided in New York as well. Some critics disliked the show's sentimentality. Walter Kerr of the

New York Times led the chorus of supporters by hailing its simplicity and honesty. The show built a modest following and won two Tonys at the end of the season. John Cullum triumphed for his performance as the pacifist father, and Barrett, Geld, and Rose won for Best Book. In an unusual acceptance speech, the authors thanked reviewers Kelly and Kerr for their support. The awards helped draw audiences and continue the show's long run. William Chapman replaced Cullum, and John Raitt played the lead on tour.

Cullum also headlined a 1989 revival, which briefly played Broadway. Geld and Udell later collaborated on the musicals *Angel* (1978), *Comin' Uptown* (1979), and *The Amen Corner* (1983), all of which had brief runs.

SAME TIME, NEXT YEAR

by Bernard Slade

Opened March 13, 1975

1,453 Performances

Brooks Atkinson Theatre

Directed by Gene Saks

Produced by Morton Gottlieb, Dasha Epstein, Edward L. Schuman, and Palladium Productions

Cast: Ellen Burstyn (Doris); Charles Grodin (George).

Same Time, Next Year is sort of an adulterous version of *The Fourposter*, covering twenty-four years of an illicit liaison rather than fifty of a marriage, as the latter play did. Doris and George first meet at a seaside motel in 1951. Both are away from their respective spouses and very much attracted to each other. After an initial encounter, they embark on a semi-affair. Using the excuse of an annual religious retreat (for Doris) and regular business trips (for George), the lovers meet on an annual basis at the same motel for the next quarter-century.

Through six scenes, Canadian-born playwright Bernard Slade charts the development of each character and the changing social mores of America. Doris's transformation parallels the growing women's movement as she changes from dutiful, shy housewife to capable businesswoman. George becomes increasingly conservative, loses a son in the Vietnam war, and finally gives up his lucrative accounting concern to play piano in a cocktail bar and pursue various '70s social philosophies like EST and encounter groups. Ellen Burstyn and Charles Grodin skillfully and warmly enacted the clandestine couple going through their metamorphoses.

As with the sex comedies of the '60s, *Same Time, Next Year* gently mocked the sexual attitudes of its middle-class audience, but the sexual revolution allowed the play to be franker in its language and depiction of the subject matter than would have been possible a decade before. Of course, the thrilling danger of adultery was kept at a safe remove by being available only once a year.

Slade's credits included several plays written for Canadian repertory companies and innumerable TV scripts for such shows as *Bewitched*. He left these TV credits out of his bio in the program, so that the reviewers wouldn't categorize him as a sitcom hack. The critics enjoyed the comedy, as did audiences, which kept it running for 1,453 performances.

Ellen Burstyn won the Tony Award for Best Actress the same week she was awarded an Oscar for her film performance in *Alice Doesn't Live Here Anymore*. Grodin was overlooked by most of the award committees, except for the Outer Critics Circle Awards, which honored both actors.

Burstyn starred in the 1978 film version with Alan Alda. The touring cast consisted of Joyce Van Patten and Conrad Janis, who were succeeded by Barbara Rush and Thomas Troupe. On Broadway, Doris was played by Loretta Swit, Sandy Dennis, Hope Lange, and Betsy Palmer, and George by Ted Bessell, Don Murray, and Monte Markham. The single set and small cast made the play an economical choice for production; it has been seen in thirty-three countries, including Canada, where the playwright co-starred with his wife.

Slade's next Broadway plays were *Tribute* (1978), with Jack Lemmon, and *Romantic Comedy*, (1979) with Anthony Perkins and Mia Farrow. Both enjoyed moderately successful runs.

CHICAGO

Book by Fred Ebb and Bob Fosse, based on the play by Maurine Watkins.

Music by John Kander

Lyrics by Fred Ebb

Opened June 3, 1975

898 Performances

46th Street Theatre

Directed and choreographed by Bob Fosse

Produced by Robert Fryer and James Cresson

Cast: Gwen Verdon (Roxie Hart); Jerry Orbach (Billy Flynn); Chita Rivera (Velma Kelly); Mary McCarty (Matron); Barney Martin (Amos Hart); M. O'Haughey (Mary Sunshine); Gary Gendell (Fred Casely); Richard Korthaze (Sgt. Fogarty); Cheryl Clark (Liz); Michon Peacock (Annie); Candy Brown (June); Graciela Daniele (Hunyak); Pamela Sousa (Mona); Michael Vita (Martin Harrison); Charlene Ryan (Go-to-Hell Kitty); Paul Solen (Harry); Gene Foote (Aaron); Ron Schwinn (Judge); Ross Miles (Court Clerk).

Despite its being one of the darkest Broadway musicals ever, *Chicago* was a hit with audiences. The show took a Brechtian view of the corrupt 1920s Windy City, where evil is rewarded and, as one of the characters states, "murder is a form of entertainment." The production was staged like a vaudeville show with each of the scenes announced and performed like an individual act, including stripping, ventriloquism, and female impersonation. Some reviewers were put off by the cold, brutal tone. But, as he did with *Sweet Charity*, director and choreographer Bob Fosse razzle-dazzled and made an unpleasant subject palatable, even enjoyable.

Chita Rivera and Gwen Verdon strut their stuff in *Chicago*.

The musical is based on Maurine Watkins's 1926 play about a showgirl who murders her lover and, thanks to the wiles of her attorney, gets off. In the musical, she becomes a vaudeville headliner. Watkins's play was drawn from her experiences as a cub reporter for the *Chicago Tribune*, when she was granted exclusive interviews with a stripper who had shot her boyfriend. The newspaper stories gained public sympathy for the murderess, and she was acquitted. The play was first produced in 1926 by Sam H. Harris, with George Abbott directing. It was filmed twice, first as a silent, in 1927, with Phyllis Haver, and later under the title of *Roxie Hart*, the lead character, played by Ginger Rogers.

The musical version took almost two decades to get onstage. Pursuit of the rights began in 1956, when producer Robert Fryer and his partner Lawrence Carr attempted to acquire them, in order to create a vehicle in which Gwen Verdon would be directed by Fosse. Watkins had since retired from the newspaper business and was living as a virtual recluse with her mother in Florida. The two were making a living writing greeting cards for Hallmark. Consulting astrology charts, Miss Watkins refused to release the rights to her play, stating that it was a frivolous work that should not be reproduced.

When the playwright died in 1969, her mother sold the rights to Verdon. Another six years passed as Fosse fulfilled numerous commitments, the latest of which was the direction of the film *Lenny*. As that movie was being edited, rehearsals finally began on *Chicago*. In the interim, Verdon and Fosse had married and separated; a second leading role had been created for Chita Rivera; and Carr had died (he was replaced by James Cresson).

Another delay occured when Fosse suffered a heart attack and underwent bypass surgery. Despite a second heart attack in the hospital, he recovered and brought *Chicago* into Philadelphia. (These events were later dramatized in Fosse's autobiographical movie *All That Jazz*—except in the film the director dies.) All three of the Philly papers panned the show. Fosse subsequently told *Cue* magazine, "At that point, the show was half traditional and half offbeat. It was straddling two separate lines, without accomplishing either. It could have gone either way. The problem was, I wasn't sure which direction to take it. So I gambled."

The director took the nontraditional road, and the gamble paid off. Although *Chicago* was too late for awards at the end of the 1974–75 season and opened during the dog days of summer—always a slow time for Broadway—good word of mouth kept the show running.

Liza Minnelli substituted for Verdon early in the run when the latter was having throat surgery. Anne Reinking later took over the role, and Lenore Nemetz succeeded Chita Rivera. There was talk of a film version with Minnelli and Goldie Hawn, but nothing came of it.

A CHORUS LINE

Conceived by Michael Bennett

Book by James Kirkwood and Nicholas Dante

Music by Marvin Hamlisch

Lyrics by Ed Kleban

Opened October 19, 1975

6,137 Performances, after an off-Broadway run at the Public Theatre.

Shubert Theatre

Directed by Michael Bennett

Choreographed by Michael Bennett and Bob Avian

Produced by Joseph Papp, New York Shakespeare Festival

Cast: Donna McKechnie (Cassie); Robert LuPone (Zach); Sammy Williams (Paul); Carole Bishop (Sheila); Priscilla Lopez (Diana); Pamela Blair (Val); Wayne Cilento (Mike); Scott Allen (Roy); Renee Baughman (Kristine); Chuck Cissel (Butch); Clive Clerk (Larry); Kay Cole (Maggie); Ronald Dennis (Richie); Donna Drake (Tricia); Brandt Edwards (Tom); Patricia Garland (Judy); Carolyn Kirsch (Lois); Ron Kuhlman (Don); Nancy Lane (Bebe); Baayork Lee (Connie); Cameron Mason (Mark); Don Percassi (Al); Michael Serrecchia (Frank); Michel Stuart (Greg); Thomas J. Walsh (Bobby); Crissy Wilzak (Vicki).

Along with *Show Boat, Oklahoma!*, and *West Side Story*, *A Chorus Line* is acknowledged as a milestone in American musical theatre history and holds the record for longest running show of any kind—play or musical—on Broadway. Using the framework of an audition for an unnamed musical, the show exposes the souls, dreams, and desires of a group of dancers. Eschewing the traditional plot-oriented book, *Chorus Line* offers brief glimpses into the lives of the auditioners so that they are seen as individuals. In the dazzling finale, "One," they don identical golden top hats and tails and their uniqueness vanishes as they form a perfect, uniform line. More than an inside "show-biz" story, the musical is about anyone who's ever had to prove themselves in order to get a job.

Director Michael Bennett, who was credited with conceiving the show, stated to *Playbill* magazine that he wanted to do a show "for my people—Broadway's beautiful, brilliant chorus dancers. . . . Every single one of them is very special, and I wanted them and audiences to know it."

No less than four books detail the creation of this production (two biographies of Bennett and two histories of *Chorus Line*). The seed for the show was sown in 1974, when dancers Michon Peacock and Tony Stevens were depressed after appearing in a flop musical (*Rachel Lily Rosenbloom*) and determined to do something to improve the lot of the Broadway chorus performer. They contacted Bennett with the desire to create a show or repertory company of their own. As a result, twenty-four veteran chorus dancers gathered in a rehearsal studio and stayed up all night talking about their experiences on the chorus line; Bennett conducted the session and taped the talks. Using the tapes as raw material, Bennett and Nicholas Dante, one of the dancers who was also a writer, began to fashion a script.

(Left to right) Sammy Williams, Pamela Blair, Donna McKechnie, Robert LuPone, Carole (later Kelly) Bishop, and Pricilla Lopez in *A Chorus Line*.

A nonprofit off-Broadway theatre provided the birthplace for Broadway's biggest hit. Joseph Papp of the New York Shakespeare Festival had wanted Bennett to direct a revival of *The Threepenny Opera*. Bennett was not interested in revivals, but asked Papp to sponsor a workshop to develop his musical about dancers. Papp agreed to foot the bill. This led to a whole new way of writing musicals. Material could be written, tried out, and staged, without the pressure of performing it for paying audiences. As out-of-town tryouts in Boston, New Haven, and Philadephia became too costly, workshops became the new wave of creating musicals.

During the resultant two *Chorus Line* workshops, Bennett and Dante were joined by composer Marvin Hamlisch, lyricist Ed Kleban, playwright James Kirkwood, who would collaborate with Dante, and Bennett's fellow choreographer, Bob Avian. The final product was four hours and twenty minutes long. As Kirkwood wrote in *Playbill* magazine, "Had we been going the usual route (Boston, Philly, etc.) we could have achieved nothing more from night to night, what with paying customers to please, than cosmetic surgery, applying a Band-Aid here, taking a snip or tuck

there. Knowing we were only returning to West 19th Street with no audience to please but ourselves, we could perform major surgery without benefit of press or public scrutiny."

When the revised, two-hour-long production began previews at the Newman Theatre, one of the stages at the Festival's Public Theatre, in April of 1975, it took off. The Broadway transfer took place in July, where the show previewed until October. *A Chorus Line* won every award imaginable, including the Tony, New York Drama Critics Circle, Drama Desk, Outer Critics Circle, Pulitzer Prize, and even an Obie for its off-Broadway run.

Many of the characters' lives that the original cast were enacting paralleled their own. Donna McKechnie's unhappy sojourn in Hollywood was repeated in her character Cassie, and her personal relationship with future husband Bennett was mirrored by Cassie's ties to the character of Zach, a director who is auditioning the dancers. Several original cast members returned to the Broadway and two national touring companies.

On the night of September 29, 1983, *A Chorus Line* broke the record held by *Grease* to become the longest running show in Broadway history. In a gala performance, 332 cast members from the Broadway, touring, and international companies joined for a once-in-a-lifetime celebration. The final showing on April 28, 1990, was anticlimactic after the spectacular 1983 performance. Many of the show's creators, including Michael Bennett, James Kirkwood, and Ed Kleban, had died.

Richard Attenborough directed the 1985 movie version, which was unable to recreate the dynamism of the stage show.

BUBBLING BROWN SUGAR

Book by Loften Mitchell, based on a concept by Rosetta LeNoire.

Music and lyrics by various authors

New songs by Danny Holgate, Emme Kemp, and Lillian Lopez.

Opened March 2, 1976

766 Performances

ANTA Theatre

Directed by Robert M. Cooper

Choreographed by Billy Wilson

Produced by J. Lloyd Grant, Richard Bell, Robert M. Cooper and Ashton Springer.

Cast: Vivian Reed (Marsha/Young Irene); Josephine Premice (Irene Paige); Avon Long (John Sage/Rusty); Joseph Attles (Checkers/Dusty); Chip Garnett (Jim/Male Nightclub Singer); Ethel Beatty (Ella); Anthony Whitehouse (Tony/Waiter/Dutch); Barbara Rubenstein (Judy/Dutch's Girl); Lonnie McNeil (Skip/Young Checkers); Carolyn Byrd (Carolyn/Gospel Lady/Female Nightclub Singer); Vernon Washington (Bill/Time Man/Bumpy/Emcee); Newton Winters (Ray/Young Sage); Karen Grannum (Norma); Alton Lathrop (Gene/Gospel Lady's Son); Dyann Robinson (Helen); Charlisse Harris (Laura); Barry Preston (Charlie/Count).

The cast of *Bubbling Brown Sugar.*

Harlem nightlife from the 1920s to the '40s was the subject of *Bubbling Brown Sugar,* a revue that began life at the AMAS Repertory Theatre, an off-off-Broadway musical theatre company located in uptown Manhattan. *Brown Sugar* eventually strutted downtown to Broadway and launched two national touring companies and a production in London.

Rosetta LeNoire, artistic director of AMAS, first came up with the idea of presenting a show using the songs of Eubie Blake and Noble Sissle, whose works included "I'm Just Wild About Harry." The revue, entitled *Reminiscing with Sissle and Blake,* was a hit at AMAS, but legal complications over the rights to the tunes prevented it from moving on to Broadway. (Another show employing the Blake–Sissle songbook, entitled *Eubie,* opened on Broadway in 1979.)

Loren Mitchell, African-American historian and author of *Voices of the Black Theatre,* was brought in to reshape the show into an overview of the work of many black entertainers of the past. A thin plotline was added: a group of older black performers take two young couples (one black and one white) on a trip back through time to the heyday of Harlem nightspots like the Cotton Club, the Savoy Ballroom, and Small's Paradise. This provided an excuse for the musical numbers.

LeNoire explained her original concept for the new version: "All my life in show business I was called 'Brown Sugar.' When I started doing nightclub work, the man who wrote my act for me called me 'Bubbling Brown Sugar' because he said I was so bubbly and full of energy. When it came time to put the show together, I wanted to do something that brings all people together and call it *Bubbling Brown Sugar,* because for brown sugar, you've got to have white sugar as well as the dark sugar." Moreover, the show aimed to reveal Harlem as a place of glamour and excitement, rather than as the ghetto prevalent in media images. Mitchell told *Ebony* magazine that the show would portray Harlem as a place "that engendered pride and built hope."

The cast included such veterans as Avon Long, who appeared in *Shuffle Along* (1921), the first successful black musical; Joseph Attles, a cast member of *Blackbirds of 1928*; and Thelma Carpenter, an experienced actress and cabaret singer whose credits included a stint on television's *Barefoot in the Park* series. There was a nine-month out-of-town tour covering such cities as Washington, D.C., Chicago, and Philadephia. *Brown Sugar* grossed over $3 million on the tour. Chip Garnett replaced Chris Beard, who left the show to become part of the pop singing group The Fifth Dimension, and Josephine Premice took over for Thelma Carpenter just before the New York opening.

There was some critical carping about the weakness of Mitchell's book, but the reviews were otherwise excellent. Two national companies were crisscrossing the country while the show played on Broadway, and a London version opened in September of 1977.

Bubbling Brown Sugar was the first in a group of revues in the '70s and '80s that focused on music written or made famous by African-American performers and composers. After *Sugar* was through bubbling, there was *Ain't Misbehavin'* (1978), *Eubie* (1979), *Sophisticated Ladies* (1981), *Uptown . . . It's Hot* (1985), and *Black and Blue* (1989).

GODSPELL

Book by John-Michael Tebelak

Music and lyrics by Stephen Schwartz

Opened June 22, 1976

527 Performances, after an off-Broadway run of 2,124 performances at the Cherry Lane and Promenade Theatres

Broadhurst Theatre

Directed by John-Michael Tebelak

Produced by Edgar Lansbury, Stuart Duncan, Joseph Beruh, and the Shubert Organization.

Cast: Lamar Alford, Laurie Faso, Lois Foraker, Robin Lamont, Elizabeth Lathram, Bobby Lee, Tom Rolfing, Don Scardino, Marley Sims, Valerie Williams.

The passion of Christ was retold as a clown show in *Godspell*, a bouncy rendition of the Gospel of St. Matthew (godspell is an archaic version of the word gospel). Unlike the flamboyant, elaborate production of *Jesus Christ Superstar*, the staging of *Godspell* had a light touch, as did its score and libretto.

The show opens with the cast dressed as various philosophers, arguing dictums in a "Tower of Babel" number. Then John the Baptist advises them to "Prepare Ye the Way of the Lord." They remove their drab clothes and emerge as colorful hippies in bright face paint and outlandish costumes. Christ enters wearing a Superman T-shirt and an exaggerated, bright-red clown smile on his face. The cast acts out the parables in story-theatre style, with different members of the ten-person ensemble trading roles as narrators and participants. The infectious energy of the direction, cast, and score made the Sunday school lessons into joyful entertainment.

Like *Pippin*, *Godspell* originated as a student show at Carnegie Tech in Pittsburgh. Long-haired theatre student John-Michael Tebelak was inspired to write a positive show about the persecution of Christ when, after attending early Easter services, he was stopped by a policeman and searched for drugs. Tebelak wrote and directed *Godspell* as part of his master's thesis project. Once the young man graduated, a theatre professor suggested he take the show to Ellen Stewart's off-off-Broadway theatre, Café La MaMa.

Stewart presented a workshop production, which featured only a few tunes written by cast members. Producers Edgar Lansbury, Stuart Duncan, and Joseph Beruh

enjoyed the show and wanted to mount it off-Broadway, but they thought it needed a fuller score. Stephen Schwartz, another Carnegie Tech alumnus who had graduated two years ahead of Tebelak, was commissioned to write new songs. Among them were "Day by Day," which became a Top 40 hit.

After a sensational response at the Cherry Lane Theatre in New York's Greenwich Village, *Godspell* transferred to the Promenade Theatre on the Upper West Side, where it remained for the rest of its off-Broadway run. The producers wanted to move the show to Broadway's Ethel Barrymore Theatre on its fourth anniversary and attract new audiences, but a dispute with the authors prevented it. An agreement was worked out for a Broadway transfer one year later, and *Godspell* arrived there after 2,651 off-Broadway performances. It joined two other Schwartz hits, *Pippin* and *The Magic Show*, which were still running.

At one point, *Godspell* companies were playing in Boston, Washington, D.C., Los Angeles, San Francisco, Toronto, Chicago, and Miami, and there were national tours and a traveling company playing other cities. Among the many foreign companies was the British edition, in which Jeremy Irons played John the Baptist.

The 1973 movie featured Victor Garber and David Haskell and was shot in various New York City locations. Don Scardino, the Jesus of the Broadway company, directed a 1988 revival which played off-Broadway.

Schwartz returned to religious themes when he co-wrote the performance piece *Mass* with Leonard Bernstein.

FOR COLORED GIRLS WHO HAVE CONSIDERED SUICIDE / WHEN THE RAINBOW IS ENUF

by Ntozake Shange

Opened September 15, 1976

742 Performances, after an off-Broadway run at the New Federal Theatre and the Public Theatre

Booth Theatre

Directed by Oz Scott

Choreographed by Paula Moss

Produced by Joseph Papp, the New York Shakespeare Festival, and Woodie King, Jr.

Cast: Janet League (Lady in Brown); Aku Kadogo (Lady in Yellow); Trazana Beverly (Lady in Red); Paula Moss (Lady in Green); Risë Collins (Lady in Purple); Laurie Carlos (Lady in Blue); Ntozake Shange (Lady in Orange).

One of the few long-running plays written by a black woman, Ntozake Shange's *for colored girls who have considered suicide / when the rainbow is enuf* journeyed from the cafes and bars of San Francisco and Berkeley to off-Broadway and finally to Broadway. Called a "choreopoem," this unique piece combined dance and dialogue in a series of vignettes depicting the lives of young African-American women. These ranged from a little girl in Louisiana in her first encounter with boys, to a 19th-century octoroon dancing at a carnival, to a new high school graduate about to lose her virginity.

The cast consisted of seven actresses, including the author, dancing and singing on a nearly bare stage; the only scenery was a huge flower. Each of the women tells her stories of pain and loss, concluding with the shattering monologue of the Lady in Red, whose lover, a crazed Vietnam veteran, drops her children from a tenement window. (Trazana Beverly won a Tony for this role.) The women then cling together and sing triumphantly, "I found God in myself and loved her fiercely."

The playwright, Ntozake Shange, was born Paulette Williams, the daughter of upper-middle-class parents. At twenty-two, she changed her name in observance of her African heritage. She began reading her poems in bars in the San Francisco Bay area. She was soon joined by dancer Paula Moss, who added choreography to Shange's readings.

They came to New York and presented the pieces at various East Village bars, the first being Studio Rivbea.

Shange recalled the opening evening in a *New York Times* interview: "The first night—I remember it was July 7 —there were maybe fifteen people who came to see the show, but among them was Oz Scott. Oz liked what we were doing but thought we could use some help with the staging. What did I know about staging? I'd never had more than five feet at the end of the bar to work with."

As Scott refined the presentation, more actresses were added to the ensemble. It began to become a full-fledged theatre piece, and *for colored girls . . .* was picked up by Woodie King, Jr., who presented it in an off-off-Broadway showcase production at the Henry Street Settlement's New Federal Theatre.

Trazana Beverly (center) with the cast of *for colored girls who have considered suicide/when the rainbow is enuf.*

Joseph Papp, who had presented the works of numerous other African-American playwrights, including Charles Gordone (the first black playwright to win the Pulitzer Prize), Ed Bullins, Richard Wesley, and Alice Childress, moved the production to the Anspacher Theatre in the New York Shakespeare Festival's complex, the Public Theatre, and eventually to Broadway's Booth Theatre. A national tour and a London production followed.

The play stirred controversy when several black leaders accused Shange of too harshly judging black men, for all her portrayals of them were negative.

Later in the Broadway run, the choreopoem played in repertory with James Earl Jones in a one-man show about Paul Robeson.

Additional Shange works presented by the New York Shakespeare Festival include *A Photograph* (1977); *Spell #7* (1979), and an adaptation of Brecht's *Mother Courage* (1980). In 1982, *for colored girls . . .* was adapted for television and presented on the PBS series, *American Playhouse*.

OH! CALCUTTA!

Devised by Kenneth Tynan

Sketches by Jules Feiffer, Dan Greenberg, Lenore Kandel, John Lennon, Jacques Levy, Leonard Melfi, David Newman and Robert Benton, Sam Shepard, Clovis Trouille, Kenneth Tynan, and Sherman Yellen.

Music and lyrics by Robert Dennis, Peter Schickele, and Stanley Walden; additional music and lyrics by Jacques Levy.

Opened September 24, 1976

5,959 Performances

The Edison Theatre

Directed by Jacques Levy

Produced by Hillard Elkins, Norman Kean, and Robert S. Fisko

Cast: Haru Aki, Jean Andalman, Bill Bass, Dorothy Chansky, Cress Darwin, John Hammil, William Knight, Cy Moore, Pamela Pilkenton, Peggy Jean Walker.

This production, at the Edison Theatre, was a revival of the erotic revue that had previously been a hit in its original Broadway production during the 1970–71 season. See the history of the show on page 216.

MUMMENSCHANZ

Opened March 30, 1977

1,326 Performances

Bijou Theatre

Production supervised by Christopher Dunlap

Produced by Arthur Shafman Ltd.

Cast: Andrés Bossard, Floriana Frassatoetto, Bernie Schürch

Mummenschanz, the three-person, Swiss–Italian mime and mask troupe, astonished Broadway by opening for a three-week run at the Bijou Theatre and continuing for 1,326 performances. Their bizarre show consisted of silent sketches depicting the evolution of the human race in the

Two of the bizarre masks of *Mummenschanz*.

first act and that of modern relationships in the second. The main attraction was the outlandish and clever masks worn by the small cast. During the evolution part of the program, the ensemble wore large costumes to play various amoebas, insects, and animals. In another part, two of the players wore masks made up of twenty cubes, and they played chess with portions of the masks. In another, the masks were made of pastry to be eaten during the sketch. In other scenes, the masks featured rolls of toilet paper which are unravelled to simulate rambling conversation. Other skits had the performers' faces covered with slide puzzles and huge note pads. The expressions of the characters were altered as the puzzles were shifted and different looks were drawn on the pads.

The group originated when Andrés Bossard and Bernie Schürch met at the Jacques Lecoq Mime School in Paris. The two mime students wanted to break away from the white-faced Marcel Marceau tradition and began experimenting with masks and body wrappings. They were joined by Italian Floriana Frassatoetto when she saw them perform in Rome.

Cast member Bernie Schürch explained the group's name to the *New York Times*: "It means, literally, 'chance of the game' and goes back to the medieval Swiss mercenaries who, before they went into battle, would play at dice or cards or some other game of chance. While they were playing they would put on these poker-face masks, in order to hide their expressions and reactions. Such a mask came to be called Mummenschanz."

Mummenschanz made its first North American tour in 1973 and was an immediate hit. They made subsequent appearances with the Muppets and on the TV's Tonight Show. Producer Arthur Shafman booked the troupe into the Bijou for what he thought would be a limited engagement. Reaction was so overwhelming, he extended the run four times before finally making it open-ended. During the Broadway run, the cast was replaced while the original three went on tour.

Another unusual feature of the production was the cast album. Since the show was in pantomime, the record consisted of applause and laughter.

I LOVE MY WIFE

Book and lyrics by Michael Stewart, based on a play by Luis Rego.
Music by Cy Coleman
Opened April 17, 1977
872 Performances
Ethel Barrymore Theatre
Directed by Gene Saks
Choreographed by Onna White
Produced by Terry Allen Kramer and Harry Rigby

Cast: Lenny Baker (Alvin); Ilene Graff (Cleo); James Naughton (Wally); Joanna Gleason (Monica); Michael Mark (Stanley); Joe Saulter (Quentin); John Miller (Harvey); Ken Bichel (Norman).

Hair and *Oh! Calcutta!* had introduced Broadway audiences to the sexual revolution. *I Love My Wife* domesticated it for them. The Cy Coleman–Michael Stewart musical gently satirized the changing morales of America as two New Jersey couples experiment with wife-swapping on Christmas Eve. As in the film *Bob & Ted & Carol & Alice*, the four-way tryst results in embarrassment rather than gratification, and everyone remains monogamous.

Michael Stewart (*Bye, Bye, Birdie, Hello, Dolly!*) based his book on a French farce by Luis Rego. In addition, he wrote the lyrics to Cy Coleman's music, which ran the gamut from country and western to blues to traditional Broadway. Director Gene Saks intregrated four musicians into the action. Like the orchestra in *No Strings*, the band became another character, dressing in overalls, devil costumes, pajamas, and togas and musically commenting on the action. They stopped the show with their upbeat Act II curtain raiser, "Hey There, Good Times."

Lenny Baker won a Tony for Best Featured Actor and garnered the best reviews for his performance as Alvin, the shyer of the two husbands. He drew several minutes of laughter during his pantomime of slowly undressing and

carefully folding his clothes in order to avoid joining the others in an overcrowded bed. A promising future was predicted for the young actor. Clive Barnes of the *Times* said, "Mr. Baker, with his look of heroic idiocy, his good nature and baffled mind, is a total joy. As an actor he has always been one of a kind, and this is just the chance he has deserved." Tragically, he died of cancer in 1982 at the age of thirty-seven.

The male leads were later played by Tom and Dick Smothers. Late in the run, the entire company was replaced by an all-black cast (Lawrence Hilton-Jacobs, Larry Riley, Hattie Winston, and Marjorie Barnes). A London edition featured a young Ben Cross.

ANNIE

Book by Thomas Meehan
Music by Charles Strouse
Lyrics by Martin Charnin
Opened April 21, 1977
2,377 Performances
Alvin Theatre
Directed by Martin Charnin
Choreographed by Peter Gennaro
Produced by Mike Nichols and Lewis Allen

Cast: Andrea McArdle (Annie); Dorothy Loudon (Miss Hannigan); Reid Shelton (Daddy Warbucks); Sandy Faison (Grace Farrell); Robert Fitch (Rooster); Barbara Erwin (Lily); Raymond Thorne (FDR/Harry); Laurie Beechman (Sophie/Star-to-Be, etc.); Danielle Brisbois (Molly); Robyn Finn (Pepper); Donna Graham (Duffy); Janine Ruane (July); Diana Barrows (Tessie); Shelley Bruce (Kate); James Hosbein (Bundles, etc.); Steven Boockvor (Dog Catcher, etc.); Donald Craig (Dog Catcher, etc.); Richard Ensslen (Lt. Ward/Morganthau); Edwin Bordo (Drake); Edie Cowan (Mrs. Pugh/Connie Boylan); Penny Worth (Annette/Ronnie Boylan); Bob Freschi (Fred McCracken/Hopkins); Mari McMinn (NBC Page).

There is a show-biz adage that advises never to perform with children or dogs. Perhaps that was the reason *Annie*, the musicalization of Harold Gray's famous comic strip "Little Orphan Annie," had such trouble getting produced. "I don't think there was a producer in New York we didn't see," relates Martin Charnin, *Annie*'s director and lyricist. The money men were convinced that a show about the frizzy-haired little girl in the red dress with the pupilless eyes would be a campy flop on the order of *Superman* (1966). But Charnin detected deeper meanings in the time-worn strip. "I saw it as the story of two orphans," he said, referring to Annie and her millionaire guardian, Daddy Warbucks. "One happened to be eleven, the other fifty-five. I wanted to know how they met and fell in love with one another."

Charnin got his inspiration for *Annie* in a bookstore. "I was doing some last-minute Christmas shopping, and I bought this book called *Arf: The Life and Hard Times of Little Orphan Annie*. I had no other intention than wrapping it and giving it away to a friend. But that night I read it and became absorbed. I saw a potential musical there."

He obtained the rights from the *Chicago Tribune* syndicate and shared his idea with writer Thomas Meehan, with whom he had collaborated on an Emmy-winning television special for Anne Bancroft, and composer Charles Strouse (*Bye, Bye, Birdie, Applause*). "They had to be talked into it," Charnin remembers.

Following "endless" backers' auditions before potential investors, *Annie* was finally presented in East Haddam, Connecticut, at the Goodspeed Opera House (birthplace of *Man of La Mancha* and *Shenandoah*) as a part of their 1976 summer season. Toward the end of a critically panned run, Mike Nichols, who had just started producing films and television, attended a performance, loved it, and decided to produce it on Broadway.

During the Goodspeed run there were two important cast changes. The original Annie was judged to be too sweet and not spunky enough. Charnin replaced her with Andrea McArdle, one of the other orphans. "It was a real Ruby Keeler story. She learned the role in three days, went on, and the show got a standing ovation for the first time," Charnin recalled. For the pivotal role of Miss Hannigan,

the wicked head of the orphanage, the Goodspeed actress was not enough of a comedienne. Dorothy Loudon, for whom Charnin had written nightclub material, was hired to take over. She had a huge personal success with it, her first after a string of Broadway disasters.

From the Goodspeed, Annie, Sandy, and the orphans moved on to the Kennedy Center in Washington, D.C., where the show became a favorite of the Carter White House. The show's message of optimism tied in with the new Democratic regime's theme of national unity after the disillusion of Watergate. "Tomorrow," Annie's theme song, became Jimmy Carter's "Camelot."

Annie not only bolstered the Carter administration; it also lit up a darkened Broadway. After the D.C. engagement, Little Orphan Annie found a home in the Big Apple. The show paid back its initial investment of $800,000 in only eight months.

The list of little girls who have appeared as Annie or one of the orphans reads like a Who's Who of juvenile talent. Many have landed television roles: Danielle Brisbois (*All in the Family*), Allison Smith (*Kate and Allie*), and

Reid Shelton as Daddy Warbucks and Andrea McArdle as Little Orphan Annie with Sandy in *Annie*.

Alyssa Milano (*Who's the Boss?*); Sarah Jessica Parker and Molly Ringwald also were former Annies and orphans who have gone on to successful acting careers.

The film rights for *Annie* were purchased by Ray Stark for Columbia at $9.5 million, the highest ever paid for a Broadway musical. Albert Finney, Carol Burnett, Bernadette Peters, Tim Curry, and Anne Reinking starred, with Aileen Quinn as Annie. John Huston, who had never done a musical before, directed. The 1982 film was thought overblown by many critics and did not recoup its $40 million cost. The movie's failure fatally damaged the stage show's box office, causing it to close the day after New Year's in 1983.

But the creators of *Annie* went on to another tomorrow. *Annie II*, a sequel by the same team, played in Washington in 1989 and closed before reaching Broadway. ("We went over like a wet doughnut," according to Charnin). The second *Annie* was reworked as *Annie Warbucks*, performed at several regional theatres and opened to acclaim off-Broadway in the summer of 1993.

THE KING AND I

Book and lyrics by Oscar Hammerstein II

Music by Richard Rodgers

Opened May 2, 1977

696 Performances

Uris Theatre

Directed and choreographed by Yuriko (re-creating Jerome Robbins' original choreography)

Produced by Lee Guber and Shelly Gross

Cast: Yul Brynner (King); Constance Towers (Anna Leonowens); Michael Kermoyan (Kralahome); June Angela (Tuptim); Martin Vidnovic (Lun Tha); Hye-Young Choi (Lady Thiang); Alan Amick (Louis Leonowens); Gene Profanato (Prince Chulalongkorn); Julie Woo (Princess Ying); John Michael King (Sir Edward Ramsey); Larry Swansen (Capt. Orton); Jae Woo Lee (Interpreter).

This revival was a hit like its original Broadway production during the 1950–51 season. See page 114 for a history of the show.

GEMINI

by Albert Innaurato

Opened May 21, 1977

1,788 Performances, after an off-Broadway run at Circle Repertory Company

Little Theatre

Directed by Peter Mark Schiffer

Produced by Jerry Arrow, Jay Broad, Circle Repertory Company, and PAF Playhouse

Cast: Robert Picardo (Francis Geminiani); Jessica James (Bunny Weinberger); Danny Aiello (Fran Geminiani); Reed Birney (Randy Hastings); Carol Potter (Judith Hastings); Jonathan Hadary (Herschel Weinberger); Anne DeSalvo (Lucille Pompi).

The circuitous route taken by *Gemini* was typical of many productions from the mid-70s to the present. The comedy traveled from an off-off-Broadway showcase to a Long Island regional theatre to off-Broadway and finally to a long run on Broadway itself.

Albert Innaurato's slice of Italian–American life was first produced at Playwrights Horizons in December of 1976, with a young Sigourney Weaver in the cast. Audiences responded warmly to the twenty-eight-year-old playwright's tale of an Ivy League undergraduate's sexual confusion. Francis Geminiani, a scholarship student at Harvard, is spending his twenty-first birthday with his coarse but loving father in South Philadelphia. The visit becomes a farcical free-for-all when Francis's WASP girlfriend Judith and her brother Randy drop by. It seems Francis is attracted to both siblings. Add the father's fussy mistress, Lucille, the blowsy neighbor, Bunny, and her overweight son, Herschel, to the simmering sexual tension and you get an explosive feast of hilarity.

Innaurato does not resolve Francis's dilemma but maintains the balancing of the opposites of gay and straight; chubby and thin; WASP and Italian.

After a few cast changes and script revisions, there followed a production at the PAF (Performing Arts Foundation) Playhouse in Huntington, Long Island, the following January, and another at the off-Broadway Circle Repertory Company in March. Critics were divided on the Circle version. Alan Rich of *New York* magazine called it "a rambunctious, hilarious, touching, quite beautiful play." Mel Gussow of the *New York Times* found it less cartoonish than the Playwrights Horizons edition, where he felt Jessica James's outlandish portrayal of the Phyllis Diller–like Bunny had dominated the evening. But Martin Gottfried of the *Post* called it "bland," and Douglas Watt of the *News* gave it the left-handed compliment, "boisterous but uneven." Several reviewers argued over the homosexual overtones of the play, some claiming Innaurato was too "pro-gay," while others felt he was homophobic for not going far enough.

Three days prior to *Gemini*'s opening at Circle Rep, another Innaurato work, *The Transfiguration of Benno Blimpie*, began off-Broadway performances at the Astor Place Theatre. The plays share a South Philadelphia setting and Italian background, but there the similarity ends. *Gemini* is a touchy-feely bear hug of a show which reaffirms the strength and love of friends and family. *Benno* was an expressionist nightmare in which James Coco gave a stunning performance as a monstrously obese young man eating himself to death.

Gemini was the second Circle Rep production to move to Broadway. (Two earlier Circle shows, *The Hot L Baltimore* and *When You Comin' Back, Red Ryder?* had transferred to off-Broadway commercial engagements.) The company's first foray on Broadway was Jules Feiffer's fantasy *Knock, Knock* (1976), which was recast with stars when it made the trip uptown, but folded within two weeks.

(Left to right) Reed Birney, Jessica James, Danny Aiello, Robert Picardo, Anne DeSalvo, and Carol Potter in *Gemini*.

Innaurato's play retained the same ensemble it had had off-Broadway and ran for over 1,700 performances.

A film version, retitled *Happy Birthday, Gemini* was released in 1980. Madeline Kahn and Rita Moreno starred. Innaurato's later works include *Passione* (1980), *Coming of Age in SoHo* (1985), and *Gus and Al* (1989).

BEATLEMANIA

Conceived by Steven Leber, David Krebs, and Jules Fisher

Editorial conception by Robert Rabinowitz, Bob Gill, and Lynda Obst

Music and lyrics by the Beatles

Opened May 31, 1977

920 Performances

Winter Garden Theatre

Production supervised by Jules Fisher

Produced by David Krebs and Steven Leber

Cast: Joe Pecorino, Mitch Weissman, Leslie Fradkin, and Justin McNeill

A strange hybrid of Broadway musical, rock concert, and social documentary, *Beatlemania* bypassed the critics and went straight to its young audience for a long run. A multimedia assault on the eyes and ears, the show featured four Beatles look-and-sound-alikes singing and playing the top hits of rock's most famous foursome, from "I Wanna Hold Your Hand" to "Let It Be." At the same time, hundreds of slide projections of popular figures like Marilyn Monroe, Doris Day, John F. Kennedy, and Martin Luther King, Jr. were flashed between and during the songs, and a ticker-tape neon sign would spew headlines from the Beatles era.

The cumulative effect was the re-creation of the mood of the 1960s pop-music scene, as the show traced the evolution of the Liverpudlians from mop-topped teen idols to long-haired social critics. The images and headlines documented the turbulent decade from the Twist to the end of the Vietnam war.

Beatlemania producers Steve Leber and David Krebs had managed rock groups and the touring version of *Jesus Christ Superstar*. They secured the rights to the Beatles songs and went to producer and lighting designer Jules Fisher, whose credits included tours of the Rolling Stones, as well as of numerous Broadway shows. The producers then hired a staff of thirty-six writers, researchers, photographers, graphic designers, and film editors to assemble the 2,000 images used in the production.

After an out-of-town tryout, the "rockumentary" began playing previews at the Winter Garden Theatre but never officially opened. Critics began to trickle in and filed mostly positive reviews, although a few objected to the show's form and stated it wasn't really theatre. But that didn't matter: *Beatlemania* had already started a mania among an audience too young to have seen the group firsthand and old enough to want to relive their experiences of the Beatles' heyday.

In addition to the Broadway version, four successful touring companies were launched, and a 1981 film version was released.

THE GIN GAME

by D. L. Coburn
Opened October 6, 1977
517 Performances
John Golden Theatre
Directed by Mike Nichols
Produced by the Shubert Organization
Cast: Jessica Tandy (Fonsia Dorsey); Hume Cronyn (Weller Martin)

With *The Gin Game*, a newly discovered playwright, a veteran acting couple, and a successful director came together to create a Broadway hit. D.L. Coburn's two-character comedy-drama, as directed by Mike Nichols, provided the vehicle for Jessica Tandy and Hume Cronyn to recapture the triumph of *The Fourposter* (1951).

Cronyn described the play to the *New York Times*: "It deals with . . . two elderly people living in a rather shabby retirement home. They meet over a game of gin rummy. The play is their discovery of themselves, of what they were and what brought them to this moment. It's a play about mutual dependence, people's need for one another, the end of loneliness."

Tandy added, "It doesn't sound like a load of laughs." But there were laughs aplenty as the two retirees play hand after hand of gin, with Fonsia Dorsey (Tandy) constantly beating Weller Martin (Cronyn). The competition over cards gives way to painful revelation and both characters realize they have nothing left after a lifetime of emotional stinginess.

Coburn had worked as an advertising copywriter in Baltimore and Dallas. At age thirty, he started writing short stories. Soon thereafter, he saw *Diary of a Madman*, a one-man piece acted by Thomas Troupe, at the Dallas Theatre Center. He attended the play several times and mustered up the courage to go backstage and meet Troupe, stating that he was a playwright. The actor asked to see some of Coburn's work. This forced the young author to actually write a play. After several months, he penned *The Gin Game*, basing it on an aunt's experience in a nursing home and his own love of the game.

Coburn was unable to find Troupe, who had since left Dallas, but he located the director of *Madman*, Don Eitner. The director agreed to stage Coburn's play on the tiny American Theatre Arts stage in Los Angeles if the fledgling dramatist would rewrite the second act. Coburn did so, *Variety* reviewed the production, and Jon Jory, artistic director of the Actors Theatre of Louisville, seeing the review, called Coburn for a copy of the script. Just before the production was presented in Louisville, Jory showed the script to Cronyn, who wanted to present it on Broadway. The entire chain of events, from Los Angeles to Louisville to New York, all took place within a year. After the rewrite of Act II, only three lines of dialogue were changed.

The novice playwright won the Pulitzer Prize for drama, and Tandy copped a Tony Award for her performance.

The leads were later played by Maureen Stapleton and E.G. Marshall while Tandy and Cronyn went on tour. The Broadway run would have continued beyond its 517 performances, but a suitable star-caliber replacement could not be found for Stapleton, who had another commitment.

Tandy and Cronyn subsequently videotaped *The Gin Game*, and later starred together in *Foxfire* (1982) and *The Petition* (1986).

Hume Cronyn and Jessica Tandy play *The Gin Game*.

DRACULA

by Hamilton Deane and John L. Balderston, based on Bram Stoker's novel.

Opened October 20, 1977

925 Performances

Martin Beck Theatre

Directed by Dennis Rosa

Produced by Jujamcyn Theatres, Elizabeth I. McCann, Nelle Nugent, John Wulp, Victor Lurie, and Max Weitzenhoffer

Cast: Frank Langella (Count Dracula); Ann Sachs (Lucy Seward); Jerome Dempsey (Abraham Van Helsing); Dillon Evans (Dr. Seward); Alan Coates (Jonathan Harker); Richard Kavanaugh (Renfield); Gretchen Oehler (Miss Wells); Baxter Harris (Butterworth).

Rarely has a production had a designer as its star, but such was the case with the 1977 revival of the immortal (or should we say "undead") vampire play, *Dracula*. Edward Gorey, famous for macabre cartoons, was given prominent billing for his sets and costumes. Gorey's eerie production scheme was covered with bats. From the wallpaper to the buttons on a pair of pajamas, the winged rodents were everywhere. Apart from a single stab of red in each scene, everything was in shades of black and gray. The solitary startling blots of scarlet were provided by such telling details as a glass of red wine, a rose on the heroine's bed, and, naturally, the lining of Count Dracula's cape.

Frank Langella made the count a romantic figure, irresistibly drawing his female victims into his clutches. Director Dennis Rosa avoided campiness and staged the melodrama seriously. This successful revival was only part of a vampiric theatrical season, which also saw the off-Broadway *The Passion of Dracula*, at the Cherry Lane Theatre (see separate entry), and *Count Dracula*, at the Equity Library Theatre.

While known today principally through the movies, *Dracula* actually started in the theatre, for Bram Stoker wrote his classic horror novel while working in the box office at London's Lyceum Theatre as business manager for the British actor Sir Henry Irving. The

Frank Langella makes a magnetic vampire in *Dracula*.

novel, published in 1897, was brought to the West End stage on February 14, 1927, by Hamilton Deane, the son of a friend of Stoker's. Deane directed and played the vampire hunter, Dr. Van Helsing. Uniformed nurses were hired by the theatre to tend to those of faint heart.

When the Count made the transatlantic crossing to Broadway, the play received a collaborator, John L. Balderston, but according to records of both performances, there were only slight modifications. One big change in the American production was the actor playing the lead: Bela Lugosi, a Hungarian who would become forever identified with the vampire by playing him in the 1931 film version.

In the 1977 revival, Raul Julia succeeded Langella and also played the bloodthirsty Count on tour, as did Jeremy Brett and Jean LeClerc. Terence Stamp sank his teeth into the part in London.

Langella appeared again in the 1979 film version, with Kate Nelligan as his victim, and Laurence Olivier and Donald Pleasance as his pursuers. In countless film, stage, and television productions, the role has been played by a variety of stars, including Jack Palance, Louis Jourdan, Christopher Lee, Peter Cushing, Klaus Kinski, William Marshall (as Blacula), George Hamilton (in a comic film version), and Gary Oldman.

CHAPTER TWO

by Neil Simon

Opened December 4, 1977

57 Performances

Imperial Theatre

Directed by Herbert Ross

Produced by Emanuel Azenberg

Cast: Judd Hirsch (George Schneider); Anita Gillette (Jennie Malone); Cliff Gorman (Leo Schneider); Ann Wedgeworth (Faye Medwick).

Neil Simon continued to draw from his own life for his plays with *Chapter Two*. While *Barefoot in the Park* was based on the early weeks of his first marriage, *Chapter Two* chronicled the difficult early stages of his second. Just four years before the play opened, Joan Simon, the playwright's wife of twenty years, died of cancer. Four months after her death, Simon met actress Marsha Mason while she was auditioning for his play *The Good Doctor*. She was going through a divorce at the time. Three weeks later, they were married. But Simon felt incredible guilt for having remarried so quickly. He told the *New York Times*, "Here I'd married this incredible new girl, and I was still successful in my work, in everything, and I was finding all sorts of ways to destroy it if I could." After a bumpy few months, Simon managed to overcome his guilt and, a bit later, dramatize the situation.

"I wrote it about two years after finally letting go of a lot of ghosts," he said in an interview with the *Daily News*. "It took that long for me to be able to deal with things." In his new play, Simon cast himself as spy novelist George Schneider and Mason as actress Jennie Malone. A second couple, consisting of George's brother Leo and Jennie's friend and fellow thespian Faye Medwick, provide comic contrast as they embark on an adulterous affair and illustrate the darker side of marriage by not being able to grow or change.

Simon wrote the role of George with Judd Hirsch in mind. The playwright sent Hirsch a copy of the script, then called *George Feiffer Meets Annie Malone*. The actor dropped out of a TV pilot in order to do the play, which had been retitled *Chapter Two* to indicate new beginnings for the characters. The names were changed when it was discovered there actually was a George Feiffer who wrote spy novels and after *Annie* opened, with its heroine of the same name.

Cliff Gorman was cast as Leo, and Anita Gillette joined the show as Jennie after another actress dropped out. Simon thought Anne Wedgeworth was an unlikely choice for Faye, for the actress's Texas twang seemed out of place with his fast-paced New York dialogue. But after an initial reading she won the part and later a Tony Award.

Herbert Ross, a Broadway choreographer (*The Apple Tree*) and the director of many films of Simon's work (including *The Goodbye Girl* and *The Sunshine Boys*), made his debut as a stage director with *Chapter Two*. The production tried out in Los Angeles, where *Variety* called it an "almost perfect blend of comedy and drama, perhaps the best and most complete play [Simon] has written." New York critics agreed when the show opened at the Imperial Theatre.

George was later played on Broadway by David Groh and Laurence Luckinbill and Jennie by Robin Strasser and Marilyn Redfield. The tour was headed by Jerry Orbach and Redfield.

Marsha Mason played the character based on herself in the 1979 film version. James Caan, Valerie Harper, and Joseph Bologna co-starred.

DEATHTRAP

by Ira Levin

Opened February 26, 1978

1,793 Performances

The Music Box Theatre

Directed by Robert Moore

Produced by Alfred de Liagre, Jr. and Roger L. Stevens

Cast: John Wood (Sydney Bruhl); Marian Seldes (Myra Bruhl); Victor Garber (Clifford Anderson); Marian Winters (Helga ten Dorp); Richard Woods (Porter Milgrim).

"Two acts, one set, five characters, a juicy murder in Act I, unexpected developments in Act II, sound construction, good dialogue, laughs in the right places, highly commercial." This is how one of the characters in Ira Levin's *Deathtrap* describes the ideal mystery play. He could be talking about the play itself, for Levin's thriller contains all those desired elements: a tricky plot, a small cast, intrigue, comedy, and a little blood.

And it was certainly "highly commercial," achieving the longest run of the decade for a straight play and the fourth-longest nonmusical run in Broadway history (preceded by *Life with Father, Tobacco Road*, and *Abie's Irish Rose*). It was also Broadway's longest-running mystery play, topping *Angel Street, Sleuth, The Bat, Witness for the Prosecution, The Two Mrs. Carrolls* and *Dial M for Murder*. (However, off-Broadway's *Perfect Crime* is still running as of this writing, at over 2,000 performances.)

Deathtrap's hero (or villain, depending on how you look at it) is playwright Sydney Bruhl, who has not had a success in eighteen years. His one hit suspense play was followed by four flops. He's reduced to leaning on his wife for financial support and teaching a seminar in order to make ends meet. One of his students has written the perfect mystery vehicle and is bringing the only copy to Sydney's isolated Connecticut home. What's to stop Sydney from killing the student and taking credit for the play? Would the desperate dramatist commit murder for a hit on Broadway? Will Sydney's emotional wife, Myra, prevent him?

The answers are not as obvious as they seem, as Levin weaves a web of suspense. Sydney's psychic next-door neighbor, Helga, provides the "laughs in the right places" and Porter Milgrim, Sydney's lawyer, completes the cast of five.

Levin loosely based his protagonist on himself. Though the real-life author had been more succesful than the fictional Bruhl, Levin's record with Broadway mysteries paralleled that of his creation. Levin had had one hit Broadway show and one moderate success, the comedies *No Time for Sargeants* (1955) and *Critic's Choice* (1960), but his suspense plays *Dr. Cook's Garden* (1967) and *Veronica's Room* (1975) had played barely two weeks between them. (He did have more success with thrillers in the novel form: *A Kiss Before Dying, Rosemary's Baby, The Stepford Wives*, and *The Boys from Brazil*.)

During the play's five-year run, the lead was played by John Wood, Stacy Keach, John Cullum, Robert Reed, and Farley Granger; Brian Bedford starred on tour. Marian Seldes, who played Myra, remained with the thriller through its entire Broadway engagement. For a while, she was in the Guinness Book of World Records for giving the most performances in the same role.

The 1982 movie version starred Michael Caine as Sydney, Dyan Cannon as Myra, Christopher Reeve as the student, Clifford, and Irene Worth as Helga.

Deathtrap was Broadway's last hit mystery. Subsequent attempts such as *Sleight of Hand* (1987), *Whodunnit* (1982), *Accomplice* (1990), and *Solitary Confinement* (1992) failed to grab audiences for very long.

DANCIN'

Opened March 27, 1978

1,744 Performances

Broadhurst Theatre

Directed and choreographed by Bob Fosse

Produced by Jules Fisher, the Shubert Organization, and Columbia Pictures

Cast: Gail Benedict, Sandahl Bergman, Karen G. Burke, René Ceballos, Christopher Chadman, Wayne Cliento, Jill Cook, Gregory B. Dartar, Vicki Frederick, Linda Haberman, Richard Korthaze, Edward Love, John Mineo, Ann Reinking, Blaine Savage, Charles Ward.

In *Dancin'*, Bob Fosse was able to dispense with any collaborators and concentrate on his choreography. He eliminated the book and used existing songs to create an evening of pure Broadway show dance. He tossed in jazz, rock, pop, ballet, and even a salute to the flag in a rousing finale.

Ann Reinking was featured in several numbers and drew the most attention, but the entire company of sixteen dancers, many of whom went on to become choreographers, were praised. In "Mr. Bojangles," Christopher Chadman played an old hoofer, and Gregory B. Dartar was his youthful spirit. "Fourteen Feet" featured seven dancers stepping into nailed-down shoes and swaying and swinging without moving their pedal extremities. "I Wanna Be a Dancin' Man" was a tribute to Fred Astaire, with the company in white suits and straw hats. "Swing, Swing, Swing," a jazzy, zoot-suited number set to Benny Goodman's "Sing, Sing, Sing," and was dedicated to Fosse's mentor, Jack Cole. "Percussion" employed only rhythm instruments like bongos, drums, and bells for accompaniment.

Fosse created the show partially in response to Michael Bennett's *A Chorus Line*, in order to pay his own tribute to dancers. The Shubert Organization, which also had money in *A Chorus Line*, provided the principal financing (along with Columbia Pictures). There was difficulty getting insurance for Fosse, however; since his heart attack during the rehearsals of *Chicago*, Fosse was still smoking four packs of cigarettes a day. The Shuberts finally did acquire a policy from Lloyds of London, but it only extended to the show's opening in New York.

Before that, two numbers caused much trouble in Boston during the tryout period. As with many other Fosse shows, the problematic dances were sexually explicit. One, "Welcome to the City" depicted the pornographic blandishments a tourist is bombarded with upon arriving in New York. In "The Dream Barre," a male dance student elaborately fantasizes about a young woman in his class (Reinking). The Shuberts were worried that the numbers would offend the audience. Fosse reluctantly cut the tourist sequence but stubbornly kept "The Dream Barre," which was excised from the show's national touring version.

Despite a mixed press in New York, the show was a tremendous hit. The production received a boost from attendance by foreign tourists. Since the emphasis was on dance and the show contained little spoken dialogue, there was no language barrier. Gwen Verdon was listed as Fosse's assistant and acted as "production supervisor" when the show toured.

DA

by Hugh Leonard

Opened May 1, 1978

697 Performances, after an Off-Broadway run at the Hudson Guild Theatre

Morosco Theatre

Directed by Melvin Bernhardt

Produced by Lester Osterman, Marilyn Strauss, Marc Howard, and Craig Anderson (for the Hudson Guild)

Cast: Barnard Hughes (Da); Brian Murray (Charlie Now); Richard Seer (Young Charlie); Sylvia O'Brien (Mother); Ralph Williams (Oliver); Lester Rawlins (Drumm); Mia Dillon (Mary Tate); Lois de Banzie (Mrs. Prynne).

Irish playwrights have long charmed Broadway audiences. The longest running work by a Gaelic author was *Da*, Hugh Leonard's autobiographical play about an estranged son attempting to come to terms with the memory of his father.

The play takes place during the course of a single day, as Charlie, a stand-in for the author, returns to his boyhood home in Dublin after the death of his father, or "da," as the Irish abbreviate it. But Charlie's feelings for the old man are anything but affectionate as his father refuses to stay dead, walking through his son's mind. Shifting through time and various locations, Leonard illuminated the tentative and awkward relationships between sons and fathers who cannot express their emotions.

Like *Da*, Leonard's father was a poor gardener continually taken advantage of by his wealthy employers. He was pensioned off with a pittance and a weird gift, thirty pairs of eyeglasses fused together in the San Francisco earthquake. Leonard's father was also known to take strange political positions—such as the time he was all for Hitler because the Fuerher was attacking the hated English. While spinning his "da" stories around a table with a group of actors at the Olney Theatre in Maryland (they were playing in his farce *The Patrick Pearce Motel*), Leonard was asked by actor John McGiver, "Is there a play in this?"

Indeed there was. The resulting work was given its world premiere at the Olney in 1973, with McGiver in the title role. Most of Leonard's plays were produced in Dublin and in America, at the Olney; only occasionally were there productions in London and New York. But *Da* proved to be the exception.

After an American production in Chicago, again with McGiver, the play was mounted in the Irish capital and then in London's West End. At one point, it was under option to David Merrick for Broadway. It was finally presented by off-Broadway's Hudson Guild Theatre.

McGiver had died since the Olney and Chicago engagements. The plum lead role was played at the Hudson Guild

Brian Murray and Richard Seer as Charley at different ages, Barnard Hughes as Da and Sylvia O'Brien as Ma in *Da*.

by veteran character actor Barnard Hughes. After a sellout run off-Broadway, the production moved to the Morosco Theatre. It won the Tony and New York Drama Critics Circle Award for Best Play. Hughes was named Best Actor by the Tony voters.

Brian Keith replaced Hughes during the Broadway run. Hughes played the role on tour with his wife, Helen Stenborg, and daughter Laura. The author later wrote a play about Drumm, Charlie's irascible first employer, played on Broadway by Lester Rawlins, who won a Featured Actor Tony for the role. The Drumm play, called *A Life*, ran in New York in 1980 for 72 performances.

Hughes repeated his Broadway role in the 1988 film version of *Da*, which was shot on location in Ireland. Martin Sheen played Charlie.

AIN'T MISBEHAVIN'

Conceived by Richard Maltby, Jr. and Murray Horwitz

Music by Fats Waller (and others)

Opened May 9, 1978

1,604 Performances, after an off-Broadway run at Manhattan Theatre Club

Longacre Theatre

Directed by Richard Maltby, Jr.

Choreographed by Arthur Faria

Produced by Emanuel Azenberg, Dasha Epstein, the Shubert Organization, Jane Gaynor, and Ron Dante

Cast: Nell Carter, André De Shields, Armelia McQueen, Ken Page, Charlaine Woodard, Luther Henderson (pianist).

The spirit of jovial, rotund jazz pianist and composer Fats Waller was evoked in *Ain't Misbehavin'*, a revue of thirty songs which were written or performed by Waller. While there was no performer playing the composer and no biography of him was imparted, the show did convey his satirical, sexually suggestive, self-parodying style of performing in such sizzling numbers as "Honeysuckle Rose," "T'Ain't Nobody's Biz-ness If I Do," and "The Joint Is Jumpin'." Toward the end of the revue, the hilarity and hijinks stopped as the cast sat face-front and sang "Black and Blue"—a 1929 plaintive lament about being black in a racist society—adding poignancy to the fun.

The revue was conceived when director Richard Maltby, Jr., heard the recordings of Waller for the first time at the apartment of his friend Murray Horwitz. Maltby told the *New York Times*, "What I thought was that it was the wittiest music I had ever heard. Not the jokes and the asides, not Fats Waller the performer, but the piano music itself was so elegant, so funny. I knew that if I could have performers on stage doing what was so witty in the music, we would have something that would deserve to be onstage. That was all I started with. That was the premise of the show."

With Horwitz signed on as associate director, Maltby then went to Lynne Meadow, artistic director of Manhattan Theatre Club, and obtained the use of that off-Broadway theatre's 65-seat cabaret space.

Arthur Faria was hired to choreograph. Maltby had not seen his work, but had heard of

The entire company of *Ain't Misbehavin'*

Faria's show *The All-Night Strut,* which re-created dances of the '30s and '40s and had a run in Washington, D.C.

The five young singers who made up the cast were not familiar with Waller, so Maltby screened clips from the films the pianist had appeared in, including *Stormy Weather.* He instructed the ensemble not to imitate him, but to find what was like Waller in themselves.

Digging up the songs required an enormous amount of research; most of Waller's work had fallen into obscurity, and there was not much sheet music available. In addition to the songs, Maltby and Horwitz wrote lyrics for several nonvocal Waller piano compositions.

After a sellout engagement at the Manhattan Theatre Club, the show transferred to the Longacre, with Charlaine Woodard taking over for Irene Cara.

Although the five members of the ensemble were given equal billing and time onstage, Nell Carter won a Tony Award as Best Featured Actress and went on to a prominent career in television. When *Misbehavin'* was revived in 1988, Carter was given top billing and an extra song.

NBC broadcast a version of the show during the 1981–82 season.

THE BEST LITTLE WHOREHOUSE IN TEXAS

Book by Larry L. King and Peter Masterson

Music and lyrics by Carol Hall

Opened June 19, 1978

1,639 Performances, after an off-Broadway run at the Entermedia Theatre

46th Street Theatre

Directed by Peter Masterson and Tommy Tune

Choreographed by Tommy Tune

Produced by Universal Pictures

Cast: Carlin Glynn (Mona Stangley); Henderson Forsythe (Sheriff Ed Earl Dodd); Pamela Blair (Amber); Joan Ellis (Shy); Delores Hall (Jewel); Clint Allmon (Melvin P. Thorpe/Farmer); Jay Garner (Traveling Salesman/C.J. Scruggs/Chip Brewster/Governor); Susan Mansur (Doatsey Mae); Bradley Clayton King (Leroy Sliney); Edna Milton (Miss Wulla Jean); Don Crabtree (Edsel Mackey); J. Frank Lucas (Mayor Poindexter/Sen. Wingwoah); Lisa Brown (Imogene Charlene/Dawn); Donna King (Linda Lou); Louise Quick-Brown (Ginger); Jan Merchant (Beatrice); Carol Chambers (Taddy Jo); Becky Gelke (Ruby Rae); Marta Sanders (Eloise); Debra Zalkind (Durla); Gerry Burkhardt (Shy Kid); Jay Bursky (Governor's Aide); K. C. Kelly (Slick Dude/Announcer); Tom Cashin (Stage Mgr./Cameraman/Specialty Dancer); Larry L. King (TV Announcer); Craig Chambers (Rio Grande Bandleader).

Four Texans collaborated to create *The Best Little Whorehouse in Texas,* a rollicking musical with a country-western sound. The plot concerns a small-town brothel which is closed down by a zealous, right-wing broadcaster. The citizens object to the shutting down of the house, but despite appeals that go as high as the governor, the brothel finally locks its doors. The house of prostitution was based on a real one, The Chicken Ranch of La Grange, Texas, which was in operation from the 1840s to 1973. The name came

from the fact that livestock, including chicken, would be accepted as payment for services rendered.

Texas journalist Larry L. King wrote an article about the shutting of the Chicken Ranch for *Playboy* magazine. Actor Peter Masterson read the piece in his dressing room while appearing on Broadway in *That Championship Season.* "I thought it would make a good straight play with a strong statement for women," Masterson later told the *Daily News.* "I've always respected people who survived no matter who they are." The actor showed the article to his friend and fellow Texan, songwriter Carol Hall, who thought the material would make a great musical. She introduced Masterson to King, who had not seen a musical since the film version of *Oklahoma!* and was reluctant to have his work transformed for the Broadway stage. Eventually he was persuaded to collaborate on the book with Masterson.

The show was given a workshop production at the Actors Studio with Carlin Glynn, Masterson's wife, as the

Henderson Forsythe as Sheriff Ed Earl in *The Best Little Whorehouse in Texas.*

madam, Miss Mona. Henderson Forsythe played Sheriff Ed Earl, her former lover who must close down her business. Producer Stevie Philips saw the Studio production and, acting on behalf of Universal Studios, she agreed to mount the show off-Broadway and move it to Broadway if it were a success. In return, the authors would grant Universal the film rights.

As *Best Little Whorehouse* was preparing to pull up stakes and move to off-Broadway (at the Eden Theatre), a fourth Texan, Tommy Tune, joined the production team, making his Broadway debut as choreographer and director (with Masterson). Among the highlights of Tune's contributions were "The Angelette March," in which live cheerleaders were flanked by cardboard cut-out girls, and "The Aggie Song," a hoedown of anticipation with the members of a winning football team preparing for a visit to the bawdy establishment. "Hard Candy Christmas" was another popular song from the score. Edna Milton, the real-life former owner of the Ranch, was given a bit part.

There were some objections to the show's advertising. Bus ads reading "Have fun at the *Whorehouse*" were taken down after protests from church groups. Certain television stations would not air the production's commercial because of the 'W' word in the title. On the Tony Awards, some lyrics were bleeped when a number from the show was performed.

Despite timidity in some quarters over the language and subject matter, the production played 1,639 Broadway performances and sent out three national touring companies. The 1982 Universal film version starred Burt Reynolds and Dolly Parton, two performers noted for their sex appeal, but they failed to ignite sparks. The film's score was supplemented by a few new songs by Parton.

THEY'RE PLAYING OUR SONG

Book by Neil Simon

Music by Marvin Hamlisch

Lyrics by Carole Bayer Sager

Opened February 11, 1979

1,082 Performances

Imperial Theatre

Directed by Robert Moore

Choreographed by Patricia Birch

Produced by Emanuel Azenberg

Cast: Robert Klein (Vernon Gersch); Lucie Arnaz (Sonia Walsk); Wayne Mattson, Andy Roth, Greg Zadikov (Voices of Vernon); Helen Castillo, Celia Celnik Matthau, Debbie Shapiro (Voices of Sonia); Philip Cusack (Voice of Phil the Engineer).

After dramatizing his own romance with actress Marsha Mason in *Chapter Two*, Neil Simon brought another real-life relationship to the stage: that of his collaborators, composer Marvin Hamlisch and lyricist Carole Bayer Sager. In *They're Playing Our Song*, Vernon Gersch and Sonia Walsk make a terrific songwriting team but a troubled couple (roughly paralleling the ongoing liaison between Hamlisch and Sager.) At the final curtain, Vernon and Sonia agree to keep making music and seeing each other, but unlike the musical comedy lovers of old, they make no commitment to marriage or even living together.

In another break with tradition, there were only two principal characters, as in *I Do! I Do!*. But Vernon and Sonia are not totally alone, for they are supplemented by six performers representing their "inner voices," a sort of psychological Greek chorus.

Simon was originally planning to collaborate with Hamlisch on a musical version of his 1971 play, *The Gingerbread Lady*. "We had our first meeting," the playwright told the *Chicago Tribune*, "and Marvin was talking about the professional and personal problems he had in living with and collaborating on songs with Carole Bayer Sager. I related to that, because I sometimes work with my wife [Mason and Simon have since divorced]; so when Marvin had gone home, I picked up the phone, called him, and suggested a play, or even better, a musical inspired by but not actually based on his relationship to Carole. . . . We knew, though, that we had to get other voices in there for some of the musical numbers; so we hit upon the idea of introducing the characters' alter-egos."

"Because there are only two central characters, we could start on a low key, instead of the usual bang-up chorus number; and then we were able to work up to the larger numbers involving the six alter egos." (One of the alter egos, Debbie Shapiro, later won a Tony for *Jerome Robbins' Broadway*.)

Robert Klein and Lucie Arnaz were eventually cast in the leads after the first choices, Gilda Radner and John Rubinstein, proved to be unavailable. *They're Playing Our Song* opened new doors for its stars. Arnaz had been known principally as the daughter of Lucille Ball, both in real life and on her television sitcom, while Klein was thought of primarily as a stand-up comic. Both were applauded for their pluck in the difficult task of carrying an entire show almost by themselves. Their roles were later played by Tom Conti and Gemma Craven in London; Tony Roberts and Stockard Channing (among others) in New York; Victor Garber and Ellen Greene in the first road company; and John Hammil and Lorna Luft in the second.

Simon worked with Hamlisch (who later split with Sager) on another musical about a show business couple: *The Goodbye Girl*, which had a moderate run on Broadway in 1993.

SWEENEY TODD, THE DEMON BARBER OF FLEET STREET

Book by Hugh Wheeler, based on the play by Christopher Bond.

Music and lyrics by Stephen Sondheim

Opened March 1, 1979

558 Performances

Uris Theatre

Directed by Harold Prince

Choreographed by Larry Fuller

Produced by Richard Barr, Charles Woodward, Robert Fryer, Mary Lea Johnson, and Martin Richards.

Cast: Len Cariou (Sweeney Todd); Angela Lansbury (Mrs. Lovett); Victor Garber (Anthony Hope); Sarah Rice (Johanna); Merle Louise (Beggar Woman); Edmund Lyndeck (Judge Turpin); Jack Eric Williams (Beadle); Ken Jennings (Tobias Ragg); Joaquin Romaguera (Pirelli); Robert Ousley (Jonas Fogg). Playwright Craig Lucas appeared in the chorus.

Grand Guignol met Broadway musical in *Sweeney Todd, the Demon Barber of Fleet Street*, a black comedy in which the leads are murderers and almost everyone winds up slaughtered by the final curtain. Not since *Chicago* had a musical been so dark and pessimistic. The inspiration for this Broadway bloodbath was the legendary title character, a barber of Victorian London who used his razor to slit the throats of his customers. Once the bodies were stowed away, they were cooked into meat pies by Todd's helper, the diabolical Mrs. Lovett.

Sweeney had been terrifying British audiences since 1847, when George Dibdin Pitt's *A String of Pearls* first played on the London stage. Since that time, numerous versions of the tale have surfaced, including a 1939 film and a 1959 ballet. In 1970, Christopher

Bond wrote a new treatment of the story, depicting Todd as a victim of a corrupt class system. He is driven to his crimes by the injustices dealt him by a lascivious judge with designs on the barber's wife and daughter. Bond's production played the West End in 1974, when it was seen by Stephen Sondheim.

Taken by the theatricality of Bond's adaptation and the new plausibility of the characters' motivations, Sondheim felt that it would make an exciting musical. He contacted producers Richard Barr and Charles Woodward, who were bidding on the American rights for *Sweeney*, and convinced them to let him musicalize it. Sondheim's frequent collaborator, Harold Prince, was brought in to stage the show. It was Prince's idea to use the story as a metaphor for the dehumanizing effects of the Industrial Revolution. To convey this, set designer Eugene Lee re-created a giant factory on the stage of the Uris Theatre. The complexity of Lee's huge set prevented an out-of-town tryout, and the show previewed in New York.

Len Cariou, from the Sondheim–Prince hit *A Little Night Music*, was a coolly obsessed Todd, striking the right balance between stagey melodrama and believability. Angela Lansbury won her fourth Tony Award for her Mrs. Lovett, an amoral Cockney with her own romantic agenda concerning Todd. She shone in "The Worst Pies in London," a comic complaint about her lack of cooking skills. Another highlight was "A Little Priest," a duet for Todd and Lovett cataloguing the various dishes that could be made from their prospective victims.

Angela Lansbury and Len Cariou celebrate their culinary and barbering skills in *Sweeney Todd*.

Sondheim's rich, varied score was punctuated with a pipe organ, for Gothic effect, and a piercing factory whistle to jar the audience and reinforce the atmosphere of industrialism.

The "musical thriller" won eight out of nine Tony Awards, as well as the New York Drama Critics Circle Award. Despite all the prizes and praise from the critics, the show did not earn back its initial investment, and closed in the red. Its uncompromising dark tone attracted a following but was not broadly appealing enough for a wider audience.

Dorothy Loudon and George Hearn took over the leads during the New York run. Lansbury and Hearn headed the national company and played in the television version broadcast on PBS's *Great Performances* series. Hearn won a 1985 Emmy for his Sweeney.

The 1980 London production was not favorably received and closed after four months. In 1984, the New York City Opera incorporated *Sweeney Todd* into its repertory. A scaled-down 1989 revival with Bob Gunton and Beth Fowler had a successful engagement at off-Broadway's York Theatre and later moved to Broadway's Circle in the Square Theatre.

THE ELEPHANT MAN

by Bernard Pomerance

Opened April 19, 1979

916 Performances, after an off-Broadway run at the Theatre of St. Peter's Church.

Booth Theatre

Directed by Jack Hofsiss

Produced by Richmond Crinkley, Elizabeth I. McCann, and Nelle Nugent

Cast: Kevin Conway (Belgian Policeman/Dr. Frederick Treves); Philip Anglim (John Merrick); Carole Shelley (Pinhead/Mrs. Kendal); Richard Clarke (Carr Gomm/Conductor); I.M. Hobson (Ross/Bishop How/Snork), John Neville-Andrews (Pinhead Manager/Policeman/Will/Earl/Lord John); Cordis Heard (Pinhead/Miss Sandwich/Countess/Princess Alexandra); Dennis Creaghan (Orderly); David Heiss (Cellist).

Victorian London provided the setting for both the best musical (*Sweeney Todd*) and the best play (*The Elephant Man*) of the 1978–79 season. Bernard Pomerance's *The Elephant Man* detailed the true story of John Merrick, a victim of neurofibramatosis, a degenerating disease of the skin, bone, and nerve tissue. Bony growths covered his distorted head and body. While earning his bread as a pathetic sideshow attraction, Merrick was "discovered" by Frederick Treves, a prominent physician. After Merrick's heartless manager cuts him loose, Merrick comes to live at London Hospital for six years under Treves's care. There he receives visits by British society including Princess Alexandra, wife of the Prince of Wales. A regular caller is the actress Mrs. Madge Kendal, who becomes increasingly attached to the gentle soul beneath the hideous exterior. In one touching

Philip Anglim as John Merrick and Carole Shelley as Mrs. Kendall share a picnic lunch in *The Elephant Man*.

scene, she bares her breasts to Merrick, only to be interrupted by Treves, who prudishly objects.

Merrick finally dies in 1890, when he falls asleep on his back. He normally slept sitting up, for the weight of his abnormally heavy head would crush his windpipe.

Merrick's deformities were suggested by the contortions of actor Philip Anglim, who wore no special makeup for the role. In one of the opening scenes, a slide projection of the real Merrick was shown on a screen. As Kevin Conway, as Treves, described the condition lecture-style, Anglim twisted his body to become the Elephant Man. "When I landed the part of Merrick," Anglim told *People* magazine, "the question in my mind was whether I was truly equipped to handle it. I mean, it's hard enough when you have to do a part where you walk and talk normally." Anglim's rigorous regimen included jogging, visiting a masseur once a week, going to a gym five hours a week, and exercising before and after the show and during intermission.

Pomerance's play is more than a feel-sorry-for treatment of its subject. It is an examination of hypocrisy and the urge for society to force outsiders to conform. Pomerance, a London-based New Yorker, loosely based his script on Treves's memoirs, which only devoted a chapter to his relationship to Merrick. The play was first produced by Foco Novo, a radical fringe theatre group at London's Hempstead Theatre, in 1978. The favorable British reviews were read by Richmond Crinkley, head of the American National Theatre and Academy (ANTA). He presented the play in New York, under the auspices of the ANTA, as the premiere production in the theatre of St. Peter's Church, an off-Broadway venue below ground on Manhattan's East Side. After the limited off-Broadway engagement, *The Elephant Man* moved to Broadway and won both the Tony Award and the New York Drama Critics' Circle Award for Best Play. There was a boomlet of Elephant Man plays that year, for the suddenly popular material was historical and in the public domain. Eight different dramas about John Merrick were produced in various regional theatres across the country.

Moreover, *The Elephant Man* appeared in a season of plays about physical infirmities. Tom Conti was playing a paralyzed man who is suing for the right to end his existence in *Whose Life Is It, Anyway?*, and Constance Cummings struggled with the aftereffects of a stroke in *Wings*. Anglim lost the Tony to Conti, while Carole Shelley (Mrs. Kendal) won in a tie with Cummings.

Merrick was later played by Jack Wetherall, Bruce Davison, Jeff Hayenga, rock star David Bowie, Benjamin Hendrickson, and Mark Hamill. Anglim, and later Hayenga, headed the national tour, and David Schofield, who originated the role, re-created it when the production returned to London.

David Lynch directed a 1980 movie based on Merrick's life, but it was not a film of Pomerance's play, which was presented on television during the 1981–82 season. Conway and Anglim repeated their roles for the TV version, and Penny Fuller, who played Mrs. Kendal, won an Emmy for her performance.

PETER PAN

by J.M. Barrie

Music by Moose Charlap; additional music by Jule Styne

Lyrics by Carolyn Leigh; additional lyrics by Betty Comden and Adolph Green

Opened September 6, 1979

551 Performances

Lunt-Fontanne Theatre

Directed and choreographed by Rob Iscove

Produced by Zev Bufman and James M. Nederlander

Cast: Sandy Duncan (Peter Pan); George Rose (Capt. Hook/Mr. Darling); Marsha Kramer (Wendy/Jane); Alexander Winter (John); Jonathan Ward (Michael); Beth Fowler (Mrs. Darling); Arnold Soboloff (Smee); Maria Pogee (Tiger Lily); Neva Rae Powers (Wendy Grown-up); Maggy Gorrill (Liza/Ostrich); James Cook (Nana); Jon Vandertholen (Starkey); Trey Wilson (Cecco); Steve Yuhasz (Mullins); Gary Daniel (Jukes).

Peter Pan, the flying elfin spirit who lives in Never-Never Land, had been played by many actresses, but the one who was most identified with the role was Mary Martin, star of the 1954 musical stage version and three subsequent television broadcasts. When Sandy Duncan rose, or rather flew, to meet the challenge of Martin's memory in a 1979 revival, many were skeptical. But she far outdistanced Martin's 152 onstage performances.

J.M. Barrie first presented the captivating character of the little boy who refuses to grow up in a novel, *The Little White Bird* (1902). The play about him premiered in London in 1904. In the tradition of British pantomimes, the leading juvenile role (Peter) was played by a woman, Nina Boucicault.

In 1954, a musical version of the play was produced as a vehicle for Martin. Jerome Robbins was director and choreographer, and a score was written by Moose Charlap and Carolyn Leigh. The show was having trouble in San Francisco, and the more experienced team of Jule Styne, Betty Comden, and Adolph Green were drafted to provide six additional songs. Comden and Green also made revisions to Barrie's original dialogue. With an improved book and score, Martin flew onto Broadway and into the hearts and imaginations of children of all ages. The Broadway run was a limited one because of the producer's exclusive agreement with NBC, which was to broadcast a performance live from its Brooklyn studios. The network didn't want any stage performances to take away potential viewers. This television edition was so popular it was broadcast, again live, in 1956, and then in a videotaped version in 1960.

Martin's portrayal of Peter was considered the definitive one until producer Zev Bufman was impressed by Sandy Duncan in her nightclub act. He proposed starring her in a Broadway production, but she couldn't think of any show that appealed to her. Bufman suggested *Peter Pan*, but the rights were controlled by Michael Bennett, who was planning a production of his own. At Bufman's entreaties, Bennett released the rights and Duncan was airborne. The revival was initially staged by Rob Iscove, the director of Duncan's nightclub act. He was later relieved of those duties and succeeded by Ron Field (but Iscove received the official credit).

Whereas Martin combined elements of mischievous child and seductive adult woman in her encounters with Peter's nemesis, Captain Hook, Duncan was all-boy. Some reviewers missed the androgynous quality, but all delighted in Duncan's joyful performance.

Earlier versions of *Peter Pan* included the first New York production (1905), which starred Maude Adams as Peter; a 1924 revival, featuring Marilyn Miller and two songs by Jerome Kern; and a 1950 edition headlined by

Jean Arthur as Pan and Boris Karloff as Captain Hook, with five songs by Leonard Bernstein.

The "I'm Flying" number was also included in *Jerome Robbins' Broadway* (1989), with Charlotte D'Amboise as Peter. In 1990, former Olympic gymnast Cathy Rigby dismounted from the balance beam and took off for Never Never Land in yet another revival of the 1954 version.

EVITA

Book and lyrics by Tim Rice
Music by Andrew Lloyd Webber
Opened September 25, 1979
1,567 Performances
Broadway Theatre
Directed by Harold Prince
Choreographed by Larry Fuller
Produced by Robert Stigwood

Cast: Patti LuPone (Eva); Mandy Patinkin (Che); Bob Gunton (Peron); Jan Ohringer (Peron's Mistress); Mark Syers (Magaldi).

After their triumph with *Jesus Christ Superstar*, Andrew Lloyd Webber and Tim Rice wrote another all-sung show about an influential world figure: *Evita*, a.k.a. Eva Perón, enigmatic first lady of Argentina, who rose from poverty to wield enormous power through her husband, President Juan Perón. Called a saint by some and a dictator by others, she died of cancer, in 1952, at the age of thirty-three.

Bob Gunton as Juan Perón and Patti LuPone as his wife plot to take over Argentina's government in *Evita*.

In 1973, Tim Rice heard the last few minutes of a documentary on Eva Perón over his car radio. Fascinated by the brief glimpse he got of her, Rice began researching her life. He went to his partner Lloyd Webber and proposed writing a musical on her. Lloyd Webber was reluctant to work a show about such a controversial figure and wanted to finish their current project, a musical based on some of the *Jeeves* stories by P.G. Wodehouse. Rice continued his investigation into Evita's history, even taking a trip to Argentina, while Lloyd Webber completed *Jeeves* with Alan Ayckbourn, who wrote the libretto.

After the unsuccessful *Jeeves* opened and closed, Lloyd Webber turned his attention to *Evita*. As they had with *Jesus Christ Superstar* and *Joseph and the Amazing Technicolor Dreamcoat*, the team presented the *Evita* score as a record album before it was brought to the stage. Julie Covington sang the title role and the album became a number-one seller in Europe. "Don't Cry for Me, Argentina," Evita's farewell to her country, was a hit single.

The authors wanted Harold Prince to stage the show because of his work on *Cabaret*, which had also addressed political issues. Prince explained to the *San Francisco Examiner* how he came into the project: "Years ago, Tim and Andrew brought me the demo of their record and asked me what I thought. I didn't know what the hell to make of it, but I was impressed. . . . So I wrote a long letter about my reactions with many suggestions and criticisms.

"I didn't hear from them for more than a year after that letter and thought they were deeply offended by my remarks. Then one day, they showed up in my office and said they were ready to discuss the opera as a stage piece. They thought that I had been criticizing the record all this time. I told them I was so committed with other projects that I wouldn't be able to direct it for at least a year and a half and suggested that they might want to get somebody else, while the record was hot. They said they'd wait."

For the first time, Prince went to London to stage a show. Using simple devices such as film clips, posters, and banners, Prince transformed *Evita* from album to striking stage production. In one scene, Juan Perón's rise to power is depicted by five generals playing musical chairs. The British production, starring Elaine Paige, was one of the biggest successes of the decade, running 2,900 performances. It made the transatlantic transfer to Los Angeles and San Francisco before tackling Broadway. For the American version, Evita became tougher and less sympathetic as portrayed by Patti LuPone. The character of Che Guevera, who acted as a Greek chorus, was played by Mandy Patinkin and was harsher in his commentary.

Some critics expressed reservations, but the New York version won seven Tony Awards, ran for nearly four years, and sent out three touring companies. The motion picture rights for *Evita* have changed hands many times. At one time, director Oliver Stone was to film it, with Meryl Streep in the lead. Then Madonna was considered for the lead. At publication time, the project was still in limbo.

SUGAR BABIES

Sketches by Ralph G. Allen, based on traditional burlesque material.

Music by Jimmy McHugh

Lyrics by Dorothy Fields, Al Dubin; additional music and lyrics by Arthur Malvin

Opened October 8, 1979

1,208 Performances

Mark Hellinger Theatre

Conceived by Ralph G. Allen and Harry Rigby

Directed and choreographed by Ernest Flatt

Sketches directed by Rudy Tronto

Produced by Terry Allen Kramer and Harry Rigby

Cast: Mickey Rooney, Ann Miller, Ann Jillian, Scot Stewart, Tom Boyd, Peter Leeds, Jack Fletcher, Jimmy Matthews, Sid Stone, Bob Williams.

During the 1979–80 Broadway season, in addition to revivals of *Peter Pan*, *The Most Happy Fella*, *West Side Story*, *Oklahoma!*, and *Morning's at Seven*, there were three shows which traded heavily on the entertainment forms of earlier times. One was *The 1940s Radio Hour*, which recreated a song-filled broadcast from that decade and had a moderate run. Another, *A Day in Hollywood/A Night in the Ukraine*, paid tribute to movie musicals and Marx Brothers films. The third was *Sugar Babies*, a quintessential burlesque show.

Like Mike Todd's *Star and Garter*, *Sugar Babies* was inspired by the burlesque shows from 1900 to 1930 which had featured baggy-pants comics, variety acts, and elaborate production numbers with plenty of long-legged chorus girls, but no strippers. (The dancers had removed a few garments, but hadn't started baring their all until the '30s and '40s). The ribald humor was suggestive, but not blatant.

Even the oldest audience members at *Sugar Babies* were probably too young to remember the early days of burlesque. But most probably had sentimental recollections of the two stars, Mickey Rooney and Ann Miller. The pair had starred separately in numerous Metro-Goldwyn-Mayer film musicals in the '30s and '40s. Rooney usually played a brash juvenile and Miller a hard-as-nails tap dancer. The two stars had attended the same professional children's school, but this was the first time they had worked together. Miller had been on Broadway in *George White's Scandals* during the 1939–40 season and had played *Mame* over twenty-five years later, but Rooney was making his legitimate stage debut. He was comfortable with the material, though, for his father, Johnny Yule, had been a burlesque comic. Rooney cavorted in the innuendo-laden sketches while Miller acted as his straight woman and showed off her legs and remarkable tap skills in the production numbers. They also joined for a memorable medley at the piano.

This low-down, raucous revue had the unlikeliest of origins: a scholarly paper. The work was by Ralph G. Allen, professor of theatre at the University of Tennessee and artistic director of the Clarence Brown Theatre in Knoxville. Allen, a collector of burlesque sketches (he had about 5,000 of them), delivered his paper on burlesque to a conference of theatre historians at Lincoln Center in November of 1977.

Among those attending the lecture was producer Harry Rigby, a nostalgia specialist who had been involved in the revivals of *No, No, Nanette* and *Irene*. He contacted the professor and suggested they create a new burlesque show based on Allen's extensive collection of material. The score consisted of Jimmy McHugh songs from the era, including "I Can't Give You Anything but Love" from *Blackbirds of 1928*. In addition, there were six previously unpublished McHugh tunes with new lyrics by Arthur Malvin, who also wrote four totally new songs.

During the run, dog trainer Bob Williams, juggler Michael Davis, ventriloquist Ron Lucas, and Chaz Chase, whose act consisted of munching light bulbs and other inedibles, were given the specialty spot just before the closing number. Carol Channing and Robert Morse headed a touring version which was retailored for their talents, but it closed after its Boston engagement. Miller and Rooney headed their own touring company once the New York engagement closed.

Ann Miller and Mickey Rooney pay tribute to burlesque in *Sugar Babies*.

THE 1980S

Broadway went into mourning at the dawn of the '80s, when the Morosco, Bijou, and the Helen Hayes theatres were razed to make way for the Marriott Marquis Hotel. Since that time, most of the remaining theatres in the Times Square district have been designated as landmarks and cannot be destroyed. ✯ Because of soaring costs and subsequent high ticket prices, production continued to dwindle on Broadway during the decade. There were sixty-six attractions produced during the 1979–80 season and only thirty-six in 1989–90. Musicals were especially hard hit. During the 1984–85 season, the Tony Awards were forced to drop three categories (Actor and Actress in a Musical and Choreography) because of a lack of suitable nominees. Since there were fewer outstanding shows, musicals that were financial and critical failures, like *Harrigan 'n' Hart, The News, The Wind in the Willows, Legs Diamond*, and *Welcome to the Club* received Tony nominations in order to fill out the categories. ✯ In the field of straight drama, conditions were not much better. A playwright had a tough time getting works produced on Broadway. America's prize-winning playwrights, such authors as David Mamet, Sam Shepard, Christopher Durang, Wendy Wasserstein, A.R. Gurney, and Terrence McNally turned more often than not to off-Broadway and the regional theatres for support. ✯ The regional stage grew in popularity as a venue for new plays, replacing the financial risks of out-of-town tryouts with developmental workshops in nonprofit venues. Theatres such as Actors Theatre of Louisville, Yale Repertory Theatre, Old Globe Theatre of San Diego, and Seattle Repertory Theatre supplied New York with numerous productions, including *Crimes of the Heart, Agnes of God, Master Harold and the Boys, I'm Not Rappaport*, and *Fences*. ✯ The British influence was less strongly felt in the drama, but with composer Andrew Lloyd Webber and producer Cameron MacKintosh leading the way, the Brits made themselves a force to be reckoned with in the musical field. London hits like *Cats, Les Misérables, Starlight Express*, and *Phantom of the Opera*, most of them featuring scores by Lloyd Webber and spectacular physical productions put together by Mackintosh, became the top money-makers. ✯ For many the greatest theatrical experience of the decade, if not a lifetime, was another British import: the Royal Shakespeare Company's eight-hour staging of Charles Dickens's *The Life and Adventures of Nicholas Nickleby*. The entire narrative of the 800-page novel was brought to vivid life on the stage of the Plymouth Theatre in 1981.

CHILDREN OF A LESSER GOD

by Mark Medoff

Opened March 30, 1980

887 Performances

Longacre Theatre

Directed by Gordon Davidson

Produced by Emanuel Azenberg, the Shubert Organization, Dasha Epstein, Ron Dante, and Mark Taper Forum

Cast: Phyllis Frelich (Sarah Norman); John Rubinstein (James Leeds); Lewis Merken (Orin Dennis); William Frankfather (Mr. Franklin); Scotty Bloch (Mrs. Norman); Julianne Gold (Lydia); Lucy Martin (Edna Klein).

The world of the deaf was brought to Broadway with *Children of a Lesser God*, Mark Medoff's Tony-winning play which examines assumptions about the hearing-impaired. The comedy-drama focuses on the romance between speech therapist James Leeds and Sarah Norman, a deaf employee of the school where James works. James attempts to teach Sarah lip-reading and speech, advising that she will never advance beyond her cleaning job without these skills. Unlike Helen Keller in *The Miracle Worker*, Sarah has no triumphant moment of breaking through her silence. She stubbornly refuses to learn speech, saying in sign language that hearing people don't bother to learn her means of communication, so why should she learn theirs? Her perspective on the world is just as valid as his, only different, she argues: "Deafness isn't the opposite of hearing, it's a silence full of sounds."

Their marriage is sorely tested when Sarah becomes involved with a students' rights group which is suing the school for not hiring deaf and hearing-impaired therapists. Refusing to be seen as handicapped, or as the "child of a lesser god," Sarah leaves James, who still wants her to speak. The play ends on an uncertain note as the lovers try to find a space where the worlds of sound and silence can meet.

Playwright Medoff, whose previous credits included the off-Broadway hits *When You Comin' Back, Red Rider?* (1974) and *The Wager* (1974), met Phyllis Frelich, an actress and co-founder of the National Theatre for the Deaf, in 1977. He promised he would write a play for her. In January of 1979, Medoff became chairman of the New Mexico State University drama department. He invited Frelich and her husband to join him in Las Cruces, where they would develop the script of *Children* in the department's Playwrights Lab. For five months, playwright and actress worked on the play, changing and reshaping it on a day-to-day basis. Medoff's agent sent it out to various producers and theatres.

Children was presented that fall at the Mark Taper Forum in Los Angeles, under the direction of Gordon Davidson. Frelich starred with John Rubinstein, who had to learn not only his own part, but Frelich's as well, since his character had to interpret her sign language for the audience. The successful engagement led to a Broadway transfer, another example of regional theatre feeding the New York stage.

Some reviewers criticized the conflicts between James and Sarah as implausible and strained, but they praised the powerful staging and performances. Tonys went to Medoff, Rubinstein, and Frelich, whom Edwin Wilson of the *Wall Street Journal* called "a remarkable actress who can express more tenderness or rage in her sign language than most people do with their voices." Peter Evans and Linda Bove were James and Sarah on the national tour.

The show was brought to the screen in 1986, with William Hurt and Marlee Matlin, a hearing-impaired actress who had a supporting role in the Chicago production of the play. She won a Best Actress Oscar for her performance. Unlike other films on deafness, (*Johnny Belinda, The Miracle Worker, The Heart Is a Lonely Hunter*), this one cast the deaf characters' roles with deaf or hearing-impaired performers. Medoff has also insisted that all productions of *Children* employ such actors for the appropriate roles.

MORNING'S AT SEVEN

by Paul Osborn

Opened April 10, 1980

564 Performances

Lyceum Theatre

Directed by Vivian Matalon

Produced by Elizabeth I. McCann, Nelle Nugent, and Ray Larsen

Cast: Teresa Wright (Cora Swanson); Elizabeth Wilson (Aaronetta Gibbs); Nancy Marchand (Ida Bolton); Maureen O'Sullivan (Esther Crampton); Maurice Copeland (Theodore Swanson); Gary Merrill (David Crampton); Richard Hamilton (Carl Bolton); David Rounds (Homer Bolton); Lois de Banzie (Myrtle Brown).

If not for a hit revival in 1980, Paul Osborn's *Morning's at Seven* would have slipped through the cracks of American theatre and been consigned to endless summer stock and amateur productions. This gentle comedy looks with humor at the infirmities of old age and the restrictions of small-town life.

The story centers on four sisters, all in their sixties and seventies and living near each other in a Midwestern suburb. Ida and her husband Carl have a grown son Homer still living with them. The house next door is shared by Cora and her spouse Theodore, called Thor, and her unmarried sister Aaronetta. The eldest sister, Esther, occasionally visits against the wishes of her husband David, who considers his in-laws morons. When Homer announces he's marrying Myrtle, his fiancée of seven years, and Cora tells Thor she wants a home of her own away from Aarrie, the characters find their staid, placid existences turned upside down.

The title is taken from a Robert Browning poem: "Morning's at seven/God's in his heaven/All's right with the world." But all is not right for the sisters as they squabble like children and try to make sense of their long lives.

The original production in 1939 was directed by Joshua Logan, starred Dorothy Gish, and ran only 44 performances. A 1955 off-Broadway revival featuring Tom Bosley and June Walker fared slightly better, with 125 performances.

Director Vivian Matalon mounted a well-received production of the play at the Academy Festival Theatre in Lake Forest, Illinois, in 1978. The setting was shifted from 1939 to 1922. Veteran actresses Maureen O'Sullivan, Teresa Wright, and Elizabeth Wilson starred. Producer Nelle Nugent saw the Illinois *Morning's* and fell in love with it. With her partner Elizabeth I. McCann and a third producer, Ray Larsen, she brought it to Broadway. Most of the Lake Forest cast remained; Nancy Marchand was added as Ida.

Critics praised the ensemble work of the cast. Walter Kerr of the *New York Times* said, "If you wanted to show someone what a repertory companmy should look like, the Lyceum would be the place to take them." The playwright, then 78, told the *Times*, "This production brought out a lot of human qualities that weren't stressed before—before, it was played all for laughs."

It was Osborn's first hit after *The World of Suzie Wong* in 1958. The author was principally known for his adaptations of the works of others, including *On Borrowed Time* (1938) and *A Bell for Adano* (1944), for the stage, and *The Yearling, East of Eden,,* and *South Pacific,* for films.

During the Broadway run, Kate Reid replaced Nancy Marchand. A touring version, with most of the original cast, failed to draw audiences in Boston, so the producers discontinued the tour. A second company playing smaller cities had a better run.

Copyright © 1984 by Martha Swope

(Top row, left to right) Richard Hamilton, Lois de Banzie, Elizabeth Wilson, Gary Merrill, (bottom row) Kate Reid (who replaced Nancy Marchand), David Rounds, Teresa Wright, Maurice Copeland,, and Maureen O'Sullivan in the hit revival of *Morning's at Seven.*

BARNUM

Book by Mark Bramble

Music by Cy Coleman

Lyrics by Michael Stewart

Opened April 30, 1980

854 Performances

St. James Theatre

Directed and choreographed by Joe Layton

Produced by Judy Gordon, Cy Coleman, Maurice Rosenfeld, and Lois F. Rosenfield

Cast: Jim Dale (P.T. Barnum); Glenn Close (Charity Barnum); Marianne Tatum (Jenny Lind); William C. Witter (Ringmaster/Julius Goldschmidt/James A. Bailey); Terrence V. Mann (Chester Lymman/Humber Morrisey); Terri White (Joice Heth); Kelly Walters (Amos Scudder/Edgar Templeton); Catherine Carr (Lady Plate Balancer); Barbara Nadel (Lady Juggler); Edward T. Jacobs (Chief Bricklayer); Andy Teirstein (White-faced Clown); Dirk Lumbard (Sherwood Stratton); Sophie Schwab (Mrs. Sherwood Stratton); Leonard John Crofoot (Tom Thumb); Karen Trott (Susan B. Anthony); Steven Michael (One-Man Band); Bruce Robertson (Wilton); Robbi Morgan (Lady Aerialist).

If ever there was a razzle-dazzle musical, *Barnum* was it. The skimpy book by Mark Bramble, set from 1835 to 1880, fleetingly touched on highlights of the life of circus producer Phineas T. Barnum. A master showman and "Prince of Humbug" who brought sideshow attractions into towns all over America, he eventually created "The Greatest Show on Earth."

The real flash of the show was provided by Joe Layton's diverting production numbers. Using the circus as a starting point, the story was told in terms of a three-ring big-top spectacle, with a ringmaster announcing each act. (Similar shows-within-shows have been *Stop the World—I Want to Get Off*, with its circus metaphor; *Pippin*, in which strolling players enact the hero's biography; and *Chicago*, which turned a murder trial into vaudeville entertainment.) Jugglers, acrobats, tumblers, and papier-maché elephants bounced, flew, and twirled across David Mitchell's circus tent set. Theoni V. Aldredge's costumes were a riot of color. A lively band marched up the aisles of the theatre.

The only plot points were provided by the desire of Barnum's wife, Charity (played by a little-known Glenn Close), to live quietly in the suburbs, and the hero's brief romantic affair with one of his attractions, Jenny Lind (Marianne Tatum), the "Swedish Nightingale."

Jim Dale triumphed in the lead role, winning the Tony as Best Actor in a Musical. In addition to singing and dancing, he walked across the stage on a tightrope, rode a unicycle, and jumped on a trampoline to a high balcony. "Is there anything that Jim Dale can't do?" asked Frank Rich in his *New York Times* review.

Jim Dale as *Barnum* explains to wife Glenn Close that there is nothing between him and Jenny Lind (played by Marianne Tatum, at left).

David Merrick was scheduled to produce the musical, but withdrew to do *42nd Street* instead. The show's lyricist, Michael Stewart, contemplated co-producing with the composer, Cy Coleman, but decided not to take on the extra responsibility. Judy Gordon, an off-Broadway producer with only a few credits, had expressed interest in presenting an evening of Coleman songs. The composer demurred from such a retrospective revue, but persuaded Gordon to join him as a co-producer of *Barnum*.

Gordon and Coleman visited Irving and Kenneth Feld, the current producers of the Ringling Brothers and Barnum & Bailey Circus, which grew from Barnum's original enterprise. After auditioning *Barnum* for the Felds, the circus producers came up with the necessary bankroll for the musical.

The exhausting title role was later played by Tony Orlando and Mike Burstyn in New York, Michael Crawford in London, and Stacy Keach on tour.

A DAY IN HOLLYWOOD/A NIGHT IN THE UKRAINE

Book and lyrics by Dick Vosburgh; additional lyrics by Jerry Herman

Music by Frank Lazarus; additional music by Jerry Herman

Opened May 1, 1980

588 Performances

John Golden Theatre

Directed by Tommy Tune

Choreographed by Tommy Tune and Thommie Walsh

Produced by Alexander H. Cohen and Hildy Parks

Cast: David Garrison (Serge B. Samovar); Priscilla Lopez (Gino); Frank Lazarus (Carlo); Peggy Hewett (Mrs. Pavlenko); Kate Draper (Nina); Stephen James (Constantine); Niki Harris (Masha); Albert Stephenson (Sascha).

Hollywood musicals and Marx Brothers comedies were given an affectionate tribute in the "double feature" musical *A Day in Hollywood/A Night in the Ukraine*. The first half of the evening was set in the lobby of the legendary Grauman's Chinese Theatre, in Hollywood, into whose sidewalk movie stars would imprint their feet and hands (in wet cement) for posterity. A corps of ushers glides in and out of the theatre to perform excerpts from song-and-dance extravaganzas of the silver screen. In addition to existing cinematic songs by Hoagy Carmichael, Frank Loesser, E.Y. Harburg, and Harold Arlen, new songs were written by Frank Lazarus and Dick Vosburgh. There was also a medley from little-known Hollywood tunesmith Richard A. Whiting, whose output included "The Good Ship Lollipop," "Hooray for Hollywood," and "Beyond the Blue Horizon."

The *Ukraine* section is a take-off on Anton Chekhov's short play *The Bear*, as it might have been performed by the Marx Brothers. Groucho is a shyster lawyer, while Chico and Harpo work on the grounds of the Russian estate where the story is laid. There is even the traditional Margaret Dumont matron for Groucho to razz, and a pair of juvenile lovers to croon a ballad. Composer Frank Lazarus, who appeared onstage as an usher in *Hollywood*, was the piano-playing Chico character in *Ukraine*.

The show was a hit in London and was brought to Broadway by producers Alexander H. Cohen and his wife and partner, Hildy Parks. For the New York run, Jerry Herman (*Hello, Dolly!*, *Mame*) was hired to write three new songs, and Tommy Tune restaged the production. Tune cleverly reused old material in stylish variations. Every Hollywood tribute has a section of great movie dancers; Tune gave this cliché a fresh angle by placing his two dancers on a catwalk above the stage so that only their feet and legs were visible. In this "Famous Feet" number, audiences were able to identify Fred Astaire and Ginger Rogers, Dick Powell and Ruby Keeler, and even Mickey and Minnie Mouse just by their characteristic movements and footwear.

In another highly praised number, the ushers tap-danced while reciting the rules of the stringent Hollywood Production Code, which forbade the use of such words as "hot," "goose," and "alley cat" when used "in a vulgar sense."

Tune and his co-choreographer Thommie Walsh won a Tony for their inventive steps. In addition, Priscilla Lopez was named Best Featured Actress by the Tony voters for her impersonation of the mute, skirt-chasing Harpo.

Not everyone was delighted with this reappearance of the Marx Brothers. The family of the brothers sued for infringement of copyright, and the case was settled out of court.

42ND STREET

Book by Michael Stewart and Mark Bramble, based on the novel by Bradford Ropes.

Music and lyrics by Harry Warren and Al Dubin; additional lyrics by Johnny Mercer and Mort Dixon

Opened August 25, 1980

3,486 Performances

Winter Garden Theatre

Directed and choreographed by Gower Champion

Produced by David Merrick

Cast: Jerry Orbach (Julian Marsh); Tammy Grimes (Dorothy Brock); Wanda Richert (Peggy Sawyer); Lee Roy Reams (Billy Lawlor); Carole Cook (Maggie Jones); Joseph Bova (Bert Barry); Karen Prunczik (Annie); Danny Carroll (Andy Lee); Robert Colson (Oscar); Don Crabtree (Abner Dillon); James Congdon (Pat Denning); Ginny King (Lorraine); Jeri Kansas (Phyllis); Stan Page (Mac/Thug/Doctor); Ron Schwinn (Thug).

No one has shown a better sense of publicity than producer David Merrick. On the opening night of *42nd Street*, the stage version of the Warner Brothers movie musical, Merrick pulled the biggest publicity stunt of his career. First, the producer delayed the opening night many times, claiming a messenger from God would give the right date. At one preview, he cancelled the entire performance when he heard that there was an uninvited critic in the audience.

Finally, the official opening came, and the show was a smash. After a hiatus of five years, Merrick had returned to Broadway in triumph. Gower Champion's inventive direction and choreography revitalized the familiar story of the neophyte chorus girl going on for the leading lady at the last minute and shooting to stardom. The glittering opening-night audience rose to its feet and cheered. After the company took its bows, Merrick came onto the stage. When the crowd quieted down, the producer softly said, "This is a tragic moment." A few people laughed, thinking he was joking, but Merrick was serious. "Gower Champion died this afternoon," he said. Jerry Orbach, who had just spent the evening playing a driven, Merrick-like impressario, gave the command to lower the curtain as the real producer burst into tears.

Of course, Merrick could have waited until after the audience had left to inform the company and could have later issued a press release. But by publicly and dramatically making his announcement, he ensured national news coverage for the show. Everyone would now flock to see Champion's last production.

The idea for the putting *42nd Street* on stage belonged to Michael Stewart, who had written the books for *Bye, Bye, Birdie* and *Hello, Dolly!*, both staged by Champion. He acquired the rights to the original novel by Bradford Ropes and took the concept to Merrick. Stewart collaborated with Mark Bramble (*Barnum*) on the book, which Merrick labelled "Cross-overs and Lead-ins" in the program.

Lee Roy Reams and chorus in "We're in the Money," one of the many elaborate production numbers from *42nd Street*.

(Stewart and Bramble protested and the billing was changed to the more traditional "Book by. . . .") This revealed the emphasis given to Champion's musical numbers, rather than the material linking them.

And what numbers. Four songs were kept from the original film ("Young and Healthy," "You're Getting to Be a Habit with Me," "Shuffle off to Buffalo," and the title tune); nine others from other movie musicals of the same era were added. With the aide of Theoni V. Aldredge's sumptuous 1930s costumes, Robin Wagner's sparkling sets, and Tharon Musser's versatile lighting, Champion reconceived Busby Berkeley's elaborate cinematic capers for the stage.

Merrick spared no expense—and he let the world know that he didn't—to approximate the lavish spectacle that musicals once offered. The curtain rose on the full chorus of more than thirty dancers tapping to the title song. "We're in the Money" was crisp and flashy, with the silver-spangled dancers jumping on dimes the size of New York manhole covers. "Dames" displayed an seemingly endless fashion show. "The Lullaby of Broadway" dramatized the pleas of the cast of the show-within-a-show for the young unknown to take over the lead as she is about to leave town. The grand finale was an elaborate number set amid the marquee lights of yesterday's more vitally active theatre district.

Those dancing feet kept tapping for 3,486 performances, the longest run for an American musical in the '80s. Three national companies toured the country, and a London engagement enjoyed a successful run.

Amy Wright and Jeff Daniels in Lanford Wilson's *The Fifth of July*.

FIFTH OF JULY

by Lanford Wilson

Opened November 5, 1980

511 Performances

New Apollo Theatre

Directed by Marshall W. Mason

Produced by Jerry Arrow, Robert Lussier, and Warner Theatre Productions

Cast: Christopher Reeve (Kenneth Talley, Jr.); Jeff Daniels (Jed Jenkins); Jonathan Hogan (John Landis); Swoosie Kurtz (Gwen Landis); Joyce Reehling (June Talley); Amy Wright (Shirley Talley); Mary Carver (Sally Friedman); Danton Stone (Weston Hurley).

Lanford Wilson examined the aftermath of the 1960s in *Fifth of July*. This Chekhovian comedy-drama concerns what happens after independence has been declared and nothing is left of the fireworks but a faint smell of sulphur. The setting is the Talley family farm in Lebanon, Missouri (the playwright's hometown), over Independence Day weekend, 1977. Ken Talley, a gay paraplegic Vietnam veteran, is considering selling the farmhouse to his former college chums and fellow radicals Gwen and John Landis, who are visiting him. Accompanying them is Weston Hur-

ley, the spaced-out guitarist for Gwen, who is attempting a career as a country and western singer. Also in residence for the weekend are Ken's aunt, Sally Friedman; his sister June; his niece Shirley; and his lover Jed.

The Talleys and their guests reawaken old wounds, and romantic rivalries are brought out in the open. The idealism of the characters' pasts are pitted against the materialism and practicalities of the present. This central conflict is embodied in Ken, who is torn between his desire to return to teaching and his fear of commitment.

Wilson told the *San Francisco Examiner*: "I wanted to write about my Berkeley friends, who had retreated into protective shells after their disenchantment with the sixties. . . . The play challenges them to come out of their shells and become useful human beings again."

Fifth of July was originally produced off-Broadway, in 1978, at the Circle Repertory Company, of which Wilson was a co-founder and a resident playwright. As with his previous *Hot L Baltimore*, he was writing to fit and challenge the talents of the company. William Hurt then starred as Ken, and Nancy Snyder played Gwen. The limited engagement was extended to six months.

Warner Theatre Communications bankrolled a Broadway transfer two years later, but they insisted that stars be cast in order to guarantee a strong box office. The lead role went to Christopher Reeve, who was a big name after playing Superman in the movies. (Hurt was relatively unknown then.) Swoosie Kurtz had long been a favorite of theatre audiences and was just beginning to gain mass recognition through television. She stole the show and won a Tony for her acerbic playing of Gwen.

Reeve was succeeded by Richard Thomas (who also played Ken in the 1982 television adaptation), Michael O'Keefe, Timothy Bottoms, and his brother Joseph Bottoms. Larraine Newman of TV's *Saturday Night Live* took over Swoosie Kurtz's role.

Wilson returned to the Talley clan with *Talley's Folly* (Pulitzer Prize, 1980) and *A Tale Told* (1981) (later rewritten as *Talley and Son* in 1985). Both these plays were set on the same night in 1944, when the young aunt Sally elopes with Matt Friedman, a Jewish accountant.

Wilson's later plays include *Angels Fall* (1982), *Burn This* (1987), and *Redwood Curtain* (1993). Although he is one of America's leading playwrights, *Fifth of July* remains his only Broadway production to exceed 500 performances.

AMADEUS

by Peter Shaffer

Opened December 17, 1980

1,181 Performances

Broadhurst Theatre

Directed by Peter Hall

Produced by the Shubert Organization, Elizabeth I. McCann, Nelle Nugent, and Roger S. Berlind

Cast: Ian McKellen (Antonio Salieri); Tim Curry (Wolfgang Amadeus Mozart); Jane Seymour (Constanze Weber); Nicholas Kepros (Joseph II); Paul Harding (Johann Kilian von Strack); Patrick Hines (Count Orsini-Rosenberg); Louis Turenne (Baron von Swieten); Philip Pleasants (Giuseppe Bonno); Linda Robbins (Teresa Salieri); Caris Corfman (Katherina Cavalieri); Gordon Gould, Edward Zang (The "Venticelli"); Michael McCarty (Priest); Victor Griffin (Salieri's Valet); Haskell Gordon (Salieri's Cook); Martin LaPlatney (Major Domo).

The rivalry between two 18th-century composers in Peter Shaffer's *Amadeus* packed houses in both London and New York. Like his *The Royal Hunt of the Sun* and *Equus*, *Amadeus* illuminated the conflict between an older, rational, and essentially ordinary protagonist and a younger antagonist touched with a divine madness. The composers in this case are Antonio Salieri, court musician to the Austrian emperor Joseph II, and Wolfgang Amadeus Mozart, child prodigy turned musical genius. Shaffer based his drama on claims made by Salieri late in his life that he had poisoned Mozart, who had died in 1791, at the height of his powers, at age thirty-five. The same story had inspired a short story by Pushkin and a one-act opera by Nicolai Rimsky-Korsakov.

The playwright explained the subject's appeal in an interview with *Playbill*: "What seemed to me of totally spellbinding interest and power is the man Salieri, who lives only for his art, is obsessed by art; he regards it as the essence of life, only to discover his own music is mediocre. . . . When he discovers that God has chosen Mozart, instead of himself, given Mozart the gift of genius, he blocks Mozart's advancement and in due course mentally frightens him to death, having physically ruined him first. That is what Salieri meant when he went around claiming to have poisoned Mozart; it was the murder of a spirit, not a body."

When *Amadeus* opened in London at the National Theatre, with Paul Scofield and Simon Callow in the leads, critical reaction was sharply divided. The *Sunday London Times* condemned it as "appalling, a perfectly nauseating—to use a word much loved by Peter Shaffer—pile of s--t." But the daily reviewer of the same paper hailed it as "a near masterpiece." The main bone of contention was the depiction of Mozart. Rather than an angelic child spinning out heavenly music, the composer is portrayed as an ill-mannered boor with a fondness for scatalogical humor.

The author defended his play to *Playbill*, "It's all Mozart, every word of it. I've worked for three years on this material, reading all of his letters, of which there are a great many. He could be highly irascible and tactless, very bumptious and conceited. And yet his work was of a perfection and finish almost unknown before or since."

Critics notwithstanding, *Amadeus* was the National's biggest hit in years. Scores of people were turned away from the box office night after night.

An American production with different British stars was prepared. Scofield was playing Salieri in repertory with *Othello* and did not wish to go New York. He was replaced by Ian MacKellen, while Tim Curry took over the role of Mozart. During a tryout in Washington, D.C., the playwright made a few changes, strengthening Salieri's contribution to the demise of Mozart.

The play's reputation as a hit in London, plus the Broadway audience's love affair with anything British, ensured a long run. *Amadeus* won five Tony Awards, tying *Who's Afraid of Virginia Woolf?* and *A Man for All Seasons* for the most Tonys won by a straight play. John Wood, Frank Langella, David Dukes, and David Birney were among those who subsequently played Salieri. Wood and Mark Hammill starred on tour.

Milos Forman directed the 1984 film version, which won eight Oscars including Best Picture, and Best Actor for F. Murray Abraham's Salieri. Tom Hulce was nominated for his Mozart.

THE PIRATES OF PENZANCE

Book and lyrics by W.S. Gilbert

Music by Sir Arthur Sullivan

Opened January 8, 1981

772 Performances, after an off-Broadway run at the Delacorte Theatre

The Uris Theatre

Directed by Wilford Leach

Choreographed by Graciela Daniele

Produced by Joseph Papp, the New York Shakespeare Festival

Cast: Kevin Kline (Pirate King); Linda Ronstadt (Mabel); Rex Smith (Frederic); George Rose (Maj.-Gen. Stanley); Estelle Parsons (Ruth); Tony Azito (Sergeant); Stephen Hanan (Samuel); Alexandra Korey (Edith); Marcie Shaw (Kate); Wendy Wolfe (Isabel).

After *A Chorus Line* had been running for five years, Joseph Papp needed another popular hit to keep his New York Shakespeare Festival well-financed. Luckily, his somewhat modernized production of the Gilbert and Sullivan operetta *The Pirates of Penzance* became a hit. (The original version had premiered in 1879, in New York—the only Gilbert and Sullivan work to appear first in the United States.)

"I've always loved Gilbert and Sullivan," the producer told the *San Diego Union*. "In school, I was one of the train of little ladies in *The Mikado*. The next year, I was one of the three little maids. I've been talking about a Gilbert and

Sullivan revival for ten years. But I probably wouldn't have done it if Wilford Leach hadn't been so enthusiastic." Leach not only directed this *Pirates* but also contributed to the Henri Rousseau-inspired set design.

To guarantee an audience, Papp recruited several big names from the worlds of rock music and Broadway. "The idea was to get popular singers to play the young people and older British actors to do the other roles," Papp said in the same interview. "We wanted to find the connection between the two cultures and we felt the pop singers would make the production more accessible to our audience."

Top-40 singers Linda Ronstadt and Rex Smith were the gushingly sweet young lovers. Veteran character actor George Rose was the very model of a modern major-general. Patricia Routledge as Ruth, the piratical maid-of-all-work, and Tony Azito as a double-jointed policeman provided laughs. But the show was stolen by Kevin Kline as the bumbling Pirate King. Usually played by a sedentary, middle-aged bass, Kline made the pirate chieftain very active, swinging around the stage and stumbling over his own blade, engaging the orchestra conductor in a sword fight and finally snatching his baton from him. One critic referred to Kline as a combination of Errol Flynn and Inspector Clouseau, Peter Sellers' incompetent film detective. The

Linda Ronstadt and George Rose in *The Pirates of Penzance* in Central Park's Delacorte Theatre, before the production moved to Broadway.

actor won a Tony Award (his second) over the favored Gregory Hines in *Sophisticated Ladies*.

Musical director William Elliott radically reorchestrated Sullivan's score to include synthesizers, adding a somewhat satirical edge, as if to wink at the audience. Songs from two other Gilbert and Sullivan works (*Ruddigore* and *H.M.S. Pinafore*) were added.

After a summer run at the Shakespeare Festival's free outdoor theatre, the Delacorte, *The Pirates of Penzance* set sail for Broadway, where Estelle Parsons replaced Patricia Routledge. Thousands flocked to see if Linda Ronstadt could sing light-operatically. (She underwent special training for the role.)

Most of the original company (save for Angela Lansbury, who substituted for Estelle Parsons) appeared in the 1983 film version.

A national tour of the revival featured Barry Bostwick, Clive Revill, Andy Gibb, Pam Dawber, and Jo Anne Worley. During the Broadway run the leads were later played by Treat Williams, Robby Benson, Karla DeVito, George S. Irving, and Kaye Ballard.

SOPHISTICATED LADIES

Conceived by Donald McKayle, based on the music of Duke Ellington.

Opened March 1, 1981

767 Performances

Lunt-Fontanne Theatre

Directed by Michael Smuin

Choreographed by Michael Smuin, Donald McKayle, and Henry LeTang

Produced by Roger S. Berlind, Manheim Fox, Sondra Gilman, Burton L. Litwin, and Louise Westergaard.

Cast: Gregory Hines, Judith Jamison, Priscilla Baskerville, Hinton Battle, P.J. Benjamin, Gregg Burge, Mercedes Ellington, Phyllis Hyman, Terri Klausner.

The tradition of Broadway tributes to African-American composers continued with *Sophisticated Ladies*, a revue full of the elegant big-band works of Duke Ellington. While the Fats Waller show *Ain't Misbehavin'*, with its ensemble of

The company of *Sophisticated Ladies* before a giant photo of Duke Ellington.

five, approximated an intimate Harlem rent party, *Sophisticated Ladies* re-created an elaborate Cotton Club stage show, complete with a full orchestra led by Ellington's son Mercer and a large cast of singers and dancers, including the composer's granddaughter Mercedes.

Gregory Hines, veteran of numerous Broadway shows, including *Eubie*, another songbook revue devoted to composer Eubie Blake, and Judith Jamison, premier dancer with the Alvin Ailey Dance Theatre, were the stars. Thirty-six of Ellington's songs were featured, including "In a Sentimental Mood," "Mood Indigo," and "It Don't Mean a Thing."

The show was distinguished by its staging: in "Caravan," the dancers, dressed in silver-toned pilot outfits and goggles, formed an Art Deco airplane. Another transportation number featured Hines being carried onstage by a living taxi. The show also knew when to be simple and direct, allowing Ellington's music to speak for itself. Hines crooned "Sophisticated Lady" while the statuesque Jamison, clad in white ermine, sensuously performed a dance solo.

Ellington had had only two scores of his on Broadway: an updated version of the *The Beggars' Opera*, called *Beggars' Holiday* (1946), and *Pousse Café* (1966), a musical version of the Marlene Dietrich film *The Blue Angel*. His *Jump for Joy* and *My People* received popular regional productions, but never reached New York. *Queenie Pie* was unproduced during his lifetime, but was posthumously presented at the Philadelphia Music Theatre Festival in 1986.

Donald McKayle, director and choreographer of *Raisin*, conceived the idea of an evening devoted to Ellington's work. But book trouble plagued the show. McKayle attempted to link the diverse songs and orchestra pieces with a storyline. Several playwrights, including Samm-Art Williams, were drafted in the effort, but none succeeded.

Like *Bubbling Brown Sugar*, *Sophisticated Ladies* found its strength once the book was downplayed. *Brown Sugar* had reduced it to a thin bridge connecting all the numbers; *Ladies* eliminated it altogether. Michael Smuin of the San Francisco Ballet took over the direction from McKayle during tryouts in Washington, D.C. It was his decision to excise the dialogue. He also restaged the show, adding his own choreography and that of tap-dance expert Henry LeTang.

Reviewers were skeptical of the show after a near-failure in Washington, but they welcomed it with open arms once it opened on Broadway. Costume designer Willa Kim and featured performer Hinton Battle won Tony Awards. (It was the first of three for Battle.)

Sophisticated Ladies was reproduced in Los Angeles and on tour with two national companies. It was also taped as one of the first pay per view cable events.

WOMAN OF THE YEAR

Book by Peter Stone, based on the screenplay by Ring Lardner, Jr. and Michael Kanin.

Music by John Kander

Lyrics by Fred Ebb

Opened March 29, 1981

770 Performances

Palace Theatre

Directed by Robert Moore

Choreographed by Tony Charmoli

Produced by Lawrence Kasha, David S. Landay, James M. Nederlander, Warner Theatre Productions, Inc./Claire Nichtern, Carole J. Shorenstein and Stewart F. Lane.

Cast: Lauren Bacall (Tess Harding); Harry Guardino (Sam Craig); Roderick Cook (Gerald); Marilyn Cooper (Jan Donovan); Eivind Harum (Alexi Petrikov); Grace Keagy (Helga); Jamie Ross (Larry Donovan); Daren Kelly (Chip Salisbury); Gerry Vichi (Pinky Peters); Tom Avera (Phil Whitaker); Rex Hays (Ellis McMaster); Lawrence Raiken (Abbott Canfield); Rex Everhart (Maury); Helon Blount (Chairperson/Cleaning Woman); Marian Haraldson (Cleaning Woman); Michael O'Gorman (Floor Manager).

Lauren Bacall followed up her Tony-winning star turn in *Applause* with another musical based on a film, *Woman of the Year*, and won a second Tony. After tackling a role made famous by Bette Davis (Margo Channing in *All About Eve*, the film source for *Applause*), Bacall went after a trademark Katharine Hepburn part. In the 1942 movie *Woman of the Year*, Hepburn was Tess Harding, a political columnist squaring off professionally and romantically with Spencer Tracy as Sam Craig, an earthy sportswriter. (It was their first of eight films together.)

For the musical version, Tess became a Barbara Walters-like television interviewer, and Sam was transformed into a Garry Trudeau-ish cartoonist. In Peter Stone's update, Tess makes some disparaging remarks about "the funnies" on her morning TV show. Sam strikes back by poking fun at Tess in his daily strip. Naturally, they meet, fall in love, marry, and experience career conflicts. After splitting up, they decide to reunite and work out their differences.

The differences in the resolution of the story in the movie and stage versions of *Woman of the Year* indicated the changing roles of women. Producer Lawrence Kasha explained to the *New York Times*: "In the movie, the implication at the end is that she's going to settle down and be Mrs. Housewife. We're not doing that. No one gives up a career; they make room for each other in their lives."

Sam was played by Harry Guardino, a nonsinger whose only previous musical experience was a role in the short-lived *Anyone Can Whistle*. In spite of the limited vocal abilities of both leads, they clicked both onstage and, reportedly, off.

The show itself was a potpourri, with everything thrown in. An animated cartoon cat danced with Harry Guardino. Bacall cavorted with the chorus boys in a big production number, as she had in *Applause*. The supporting cast was sprinkled with familiar comic characters like a defecting Russian ballet dancer, a fastidious British private secretary, a Teutonic maid, and an advice-dispensing bartender. There was even going to be an Asian orphan for Tess to adopt, but the character was dropped out of town.

Marilyn Cooper had only one scene as the frumpy current wife of Tess's ex-husband, but she took full advantage of her few moments onstage. In her duet with Bacall, "The Grass Is Always Greener," Cooper stopped the show with her deadpan, nasal delivery and later won a Tony Award for Best Featured Actress in a Musical.

Bacall was followed in the lead by Raquel Welch, Debbie Reynolds, and Louise Troy.

CRIMES OF THE HEART

by Beth Henley

Opened November 4, 1981

535 Performances, after an off-Broadway run at Manhattan Theatre Club

John Golden Theatre

Directed by Melvin Bernhardt

Produced by Warner Theatre Productions, Inc., Claire Nichtern, Mary Lea Johnson, Martin Richards, and Francine LeFrak.

Cast: Lizbeth MacKay (Lenny); Mary Beth Hurt (Meg); Mia Dillon (Babe); Sharon Ullrick (Chick); Raymond Baker (Doc Porter); Peter MacNichol (Barnette Lloyd).

Crimes of the Heart represented the Broadway debut of Beth Henley, a young dramatist who often writes about Southern eccentrics similar to the characters of Eudora Welty and Flannery O'Connor. *Crimes* centers on the three MaGrath sisters of Hazelhurst, Mississippi. Each of them is disaster-prone, as indicated by the description of the time of the play: "Five years after Hurricane Camille."

The eldest sister Lennie has a shrunken ovary and fears becoming a spinster because she can't have children. Middle sister Meg left home for a career as a singer, but wound up with a position in a dog-food factory, followed by a stint in a mental institute. The baby of the family, appropriately named Babe, has brought the clan together by shooting her husband because she "didn't like his looks."

The dialogue is studded with comic references to weird tragedies which explode like land mines. The sisters' mother had hanged herself along with the family cat. A neighbor has a tumor on her bladder. Lennie's pet horse recently expired as a result of being struck by lightning.

While these desperate Southerners could easily have come across as caricatures, Henley endows them with a believable humanity. The audience laughs while feeling sympathy for them. As Frank Rich of the *New York Times* put it, "Such is Miss Henley's prodigious talent that she can serve us pain as though it were a piece of cake."

Crimes premiered at the Actors Theatre of Louisville, where it was a co-winner of the theatre's 1979 Great American Play contest. Kathy Bates, Susan Kingsley, and Lee Anne Fahey were the orignal MaGraths.

The author explained one of her playwriting techniques to the *Wall Street Journal*: "I like to keep my plays in one room and see whether I can make everything happen in one place. Besides, if I keep my plays simple I'll have a better chance of having them produced." The play's single kitchen set and small cast indeed helped it to gain many subsequent productions: *Crimes* appeared in Los Gatos (California), St. Louis, and Baltimore before it was presented by the off-Broadway Manhattan Theatre Club. Lizbeth MacKay, Mary Beth Hurt, and Mia Dillon starred. Along the way to New York, the play had achieved a reputation among actresses for being full of wonderful women's roles.

The MTC production resulted in a Pulitzer Prize and the New York Drama Critics Circle Award before *Crimes* even opened on Broadway.

Crimes remains Henley's only Broadway hit. Her next Broadway play *The Wake of Jamey Foster* (1982) had a brief run. Her subsequent works, *The Miss Firecracker Contest* (1984); *The Lucky Spot* (1987); *The Debutante Ball* (1988); and *Abundance* (1990) were presented off-Broadway by Manhattan Theatre Club.

The MaGrath sisters were played on screen in 1986 by an all-star cast consisting of Diane Keaton, Jessica Lange, and Sissy Spacek.

DREAMGIRLS

Book and lyrics by Tom Eyen

Music by Henry Krieger

Opened December 20, 1981

1,522 Performances

Imperial Theatre

Directed by Michael Bennett

Choreographed by Michael Bennett and Michael Peters

Produced by Michael Bennett, Bob Avian, Geffen Records, and the Shubert Organization.

Cast: Sheryl Lee Ralph (Deena Jones); Jennifer Holliday (Effie Melody White); Loretta Devine (Lorell Robinson); Ben Harney (Curtis Taylor, Jr.); Cleavant Derricks (James Thunder Early); Obba Babatunde (C.C. White); Deborah Burrell (Michelle Morris); Cheryl Alexander (Charlene); Linda Lloyd (Joanne); Vondie Curtis-Hall (Marty); Larry Stewart (Emcee/Mr. Morgan); Joe Lynn (Tiny Joe Dixon/Jerry); Sheila Ellis (Edna Burke); Tony Franklin (Wayne); David Thorne (Frank). Phylicia Ayers-Allen (later Phylicia Rashad) was in the chorus.

After the gigantic success of *A Chorus Line*, director and choreographer Michael Bennett came a cropper with his next production *Ballroom* (1978), which ran a scant 116 performances and lost $2.2 million. He bounced back with *Dreamgirls*, a near-operatic history of a "girl group" not unlike the Supremes. The new show ran for almost four years.

(Left to right) Sheryl Lee Ralph, Cleavant Derricks, Loretta Devine, Deborah Burrell, Ben Harney, Jennifer Holliday, and Obba Babatunde in a tense scene from *Dreamgirls*.

With co-choreographer Michael Peters, set designer Robin Wagner, lighting designer Tharon Musser, and costume designer Theoni V. Aldredge, Bennett created a constantly moving spectacle told almost completely through song and dance.

Bennett, like Harold Prince, was moving the Broadway musical away from the traditional series of scenes and numbers separated by blackouts. Using mobile lighting towers to shift time and place, the director was able to create cinema-style dissolves, cross-fades, montages, jump cuts, and close-ups. The Motown-influenced score by Harry Krieger (composer) and Tom Eyen (lyrics) traced the history of African-American pop music from Detroit's recording studios to Las Vegas's nightclubs.

The show originated as *One Night Only*, under the direction of Eyen, who had worked with Krieger off-Broadway on *The Dirtiest Musical in Town*. Like *A Chorus Line*, *One Night Only* was initially developed in a workshop at the New York Shakespeare Festival. Nell Carter was playing Effie White, the fantastic singer who is pushed out of the group in favor of the more glamorous Deena Jones.

Thanks to *A Chorus Line*, Michael Bennett could now afford to sponsor his own workshops. Carter dropped out to go on to a TV career, and Eyen and Krieger auditioned their material for Bennett in hopes of getting another workshop at Bennett's new theatre and rehearsal complex, 890 Studios. "Michael called me to direct a musical by Alan Menken and Steve Brown called *Battle of the Giants*," Eyen wrote in *Back Stage*. "He became a producer after *Ballroom* in hopes of developing other artists. I listened to the score and told him 'I only direct my own works, and I just happen to have one ready!'. . . He said, 'Let's hear it' and he liked the score. In two weeks, we were in rehearsal with *Dreamgirls* [as it was later titled], with myself directing." To replace Nell Carter, Eyen and Krieger hired Jennifer Holliday, then shaking the roof of the Ambassador Theatre in the gospel musical *Your Arms Too Short to Box with God*. She would eventually do the same for *Dreamgirls* with her searing solo, "And I Am Telling You, I'm Not Going."

There were three subsequent workshops and numerous script revisions at 890 Studios. At one point, Effie was a nurse employed by a wise-cracking senior citizen played by Estelle Getty. Bennett took over the direction from Eyen and guided the show through a difficult tryout in Boston to a triumphant Broadway opening.

In a fiercely competitive year, *Dreamgirls* lost the best musical Tony to *Nine*, staged by Bennett's protégé Tommy Tune. Despite the loss, it outran the rival show.

Dreamgirls was to be the final Broadway show for Michael Bennett. His next project, a musical about a woman's sexuality called *Scandal*, was scuttled after a series of workshops. He was to have staged the world premiere of Tim Rice's *Chess* in London, but withdrew for health reasons. As a revival tour of *Dreamgirls* was playing to acclaim on Broadway in 1987, Bennett died of AIDS.

JOSEPH AND THE AMAZING TECHNICOLOR DREAMCOAT

Music by Andrew Lloyd Webber

Lyrics by Tim Rice

Opened January 27, 1982

747 Performances, after an off-Broadway run at the Entermedia Theatre.

Royale Theatre

Directed and choreographed by Tony Tanner

Produced by Zev Bufman, Susan R. Rose, Melvyn J. Estrin, Sidney Shlenker, and Gail Berman.

Cast: Bill Hutton (Joseph); Laurie Beechman (Narrator); Tom Carder (Pharoah/Ishmaelite); David Ardao (Potiphar/Ishmaelite); Gordon Stanley (Jacob); Robert Hyman (Reuben); Kenneth Bryan (Simeon/Butler); Steve McNaughton (Levi); Charlie Serrano (Napthali); Peter Kapetan (Issachar); David Asher (Asher); James Rich (Dan); Doug Voet (Zebulon); Barry Tarrallo (Gad/Baker); Philip Carrubba (Benjamin); Stephen Hope (Judah); Randon Lo (Mrs. Potiphar).

Although it reached Broadway after their *Jesus Christ Superstar* and *Evita*, *Joseph and the Amazing Technicolor Dreamcoat* was the first collaboration between composer Andrew Lloyd Webber and lyricist Tim Rice. Written in 1967 at the request of a schoolmaster friend, the piece was

Bill Hutton as Joseph and Laurie Beechman as the Narrator in *Joseph and the Amazing Technicolor Dreamcoat*.

originally only twenty-five minutes long and was performed the following year in London by the St. Paul's Junior School boy choir. The brief song cycle retold the Biblical tale of Joseph, who is given a splendid multicolored garment by his father Jacob. Joseph's eleven brothers, feeling envy and hatred, sell him into bondage. He is eventually rescued through his ability to interpret dreams and rises to become the right-hand man of the Elvis Presley-like Egyptian Pharoah.

This musical pastiche borrowed not only from Presley-era rock 'n' roll, but also country and western, calypso, French cabaret, and traditional Broadway song-and-dance. One of the parents in the audience at that first performance was the music critic of the *London Times,* who gave *Joseph* a favorable mention in his column. Consequently, as many productions sprang up as colors in Joseph's coat. The first was a public concert version in Westminster Central Hall. The original running time was expanded to ninety minutes. As with *Jesus Christ Superstar* and *Evita*, an album of the score was produced. A British TV version was aired. Limited-run American productions followed in Washington, D.C., and at the Brooklyn Academy of Music.

In 1981, a new staging opened at the off-Broadway Entermedia Theatre, the launching pad for the off-Broadway–to–Broadway hit *The Best Little Whorehouse in Texas.* The next year, *Joseph* took the same path and transferred to the Royale Theatre. The bouncy, unpretentious score and Tony Tanner's simple, energetic staging offered a refreshing contrast to the spectacle of *Jesus Christ Superstar.*

Bill Hutton as Joseph was succeeded by teen idols Andy Gibb and David Cassidy, as well as Allen Fawcett and Doug Voet. A 1993 revival featuring a fifty-member boy choir starred Michael Damian.

PUMP BOYS AND DINETTES

Music and lyrics by Jim Wann and other members of the original cast.

Opened February 4, 1982

573 Performances, after off-Broadway runs at the Westside Arts and the Colonnades Theatre.

Princess Theatre

Produced by Dodger Productions, Louis Busch Hager, Marilyn Strauss, Kate Studley, Warner Theatre Productions, Inc., and Max Weitzenhoffer.

Cast: John Foley (Jackson); Mark Hardwick (L.M.), Debra Monk (Prudie Cupp); Cass Morgan (Rhetta Cupp); John Schimmel (Eddie); Jim Wann (Jim).

Country music has always been one of the most popular genres in the record industry, but its twangy style has been scarce on Broadway. Aside from *The Best Little Whorehouse in Texas*, *I Love My Wife*, and *Big River*, the only long-running Broadway musical to feature Southern and Southwestern music has been the intimate revue *Pump Boys and Dinettes.*

Set in the Double Cupp Diner in Frog Level, South Carolina, *Pump Boys* is basically an extended cabaret act. The show consists of twenty songs performed and played by four gas station attendants across the street and two waitresses, Rhetta and Prudie Cupp. The book, what there is of it, serves to introduce the tunes, which range from the comic "The Night Dolly Parton Was Almost Mine" to the sincere ballads "Sisters," sung by Rhetta and Prudie, and "Mamaw," about the grandmother of one of the mechanics.

The *New York Times* called *Pump Boys* "a small triumph of ensemble playing." Theatregoers cottoned to the simple show. It was the theatrical equivalent of stopping by with some good ol' boys and gals for a cup of coffee and a piece of pie. There was even a nightly raffle with the winner chosen from the audience. The prize was a car air-freshener.

Jim Wann, who wrote most of the songs, spoke with the *New York Sunday News* about the show's creation: "*Pump Boys* has been going through growing stages. Mark Hardwick [another cast member and writer] and I were working one summer at the Cattleman Restaurant where we were encouraged not to play too loud. Which was okay with us, because then we didn't have to play the kind of song people wanted to sing along with. We could do some of our own tunes, work them out. . . . It was about that time we began

The cast of *Pump Boys and Dinettes.*

to think of it as a theatre piece. The dinettes were already a theatrical entity." Cass Morgan (then Wann's wife) and fellow actress Debra Monk had been contemplating putting together a show about waitresses. They joined with Wann and Hardwick, creating *Pump Boys and Dinettes.*

The ninety-minute show was mounted as a late-night entertainment at the off-Broadway Westside Arts Theatre in July of 1981. In October it moved from there to a commercial run at the Colonnades Theatre, another off-Broadway house, and finally to Broadway's Princess Theatre the following March.

Debra Monk and Mark Hardwick later collaborated with two other performers (Mike Carver and Mary Murfitt) to write and perform *Oil City Symphony* (1987), another revue which enjoyed a long run off-Broadway.

AGNES OF GOD

by John Pielmeier
Opened March 30, 1982
599 Performances
Music Box Theatre
Directed by Michael Lindsay-Hogg
Produced by Kenneth Waissman, Lou Kramer, and Paramount Pictures Productions
Cast: Elizabeth Ashley (Dr. Martha Livingstone); Geraldine Page (Mother Miriam Ruth); Amanda Plummer (Agnes).

A spate of plays and musicals about Catholic priests and nuns opened on and off-Broadway in the early '80s. All dealt with a challenging of the authority of these figures. *Mass Appeal* depicted a jovial priest as a hypocrite who dispenses false hope. *Once a Catholic, Catholic School Girls* and *Do Black Patent Leather Shoes Really Reflect Up?* dwelt on the horrors of a parochial school upbringing. Christopher Durang's cartoonish one-act, *Sister Mary Ignatius Explains It All for You,* exposed the self-righteous teachings of a nun and enjoyed a long run off-Broadway. The musical *Nunsense,* also an off-Broadway hit, satirized its sisters a little more gently.

John Pielmeier's *Agnes of God* had the longest Broadway run of these shows. A psychological drama strongly reminiscent of Peter Shaffer's *Equus,* the play received a mixed critical reaction but was praised for its acting and direction. The title character is a nun accused of murder. A dead baby has been found in the waste basket of her convent room, strangled by the umbilical cord. Agnes recalls nothing of the birth or death of the child. A court psychiatrist, Dr. Martha Livingstone, is appointed to determine if the young woman is competent to stand trial. A battle of wills ensues between the doctor and Mother Miriam Ruth, Agnes' mother superior. The psychiatrist believes there is a rational explanation for the incident, while Mother Miriam Ruth prefers to attribute it to divine conception. In a shattering conclusion, Agnes (like Alan Strang of *Equus*) reenacts the crime while under hypnosis.

Like *Crimes of the Heart, Agnes* was first presented at the Actors Theatre of Louisville. Most reviewers found the play uneven. The questions of faith and miracles were intriguing and potentially profound, but some felt that Pielmeier merely raised them without addressing them. Certain revelations in the second act seemed contrived, and questions about the baby's paternity and murder went unresolved.

Nevertheless, *Agnes* had a two-year run, thanks to the strong performances of the three-woman cast and their replacements. *Time* magazine summed up the critical reaction: "If *Agnes of God* just fails as an example of the playwright's craft, it shines as a demonstration of three actresses' seductive art." Elizabeth Ashley as the chain-smoking psychiatrist and Geraldine Page as the domineering mother superior used every weapon in their actresses' arsenal in their duel. Amanda Plummer lent an eerie ethereal quality to Agnes. She won a Tony as Best Featured Actress in a Play. The same year she was also nominated for Best Actress in a Play for a revival of *A Taste of Honey.*

Diahann Carroll took over for Elizabeth Ashley, who played her role on a national tour. Carrie Fisher, Maryann Plunkett, and Lily Knight played Agnes after Amanda Plummer. Geraldine Page remained with the show through the Broadway run. Jane Fonda, Anne Bancroft, and Meg Tilly were the three antagonists in the 1985 film version, for which Pielmeier wrote the screenplay.

NINE

Book by Arthur Kopit, based on the Federico Fellini film *8½,* as translated and adapted by Mario Fratti.
Music and lyrics by Maury Yeston
Opened May 9, 1982
732 Performances
46th Street Theatre
Directed by Tommy Tune
Choreographed by Tommy Tune and Thommie Walsh
Produced by Michel Stuart, Harvey J. Klaris, Roger S. Berlind, James M. Nederlander, Francine LeFrak, and Kenneth D. Greenblatt.
Cast: Raul Julia (Guido Contini); Karen Akers (Luisa Contini); Anita Morris (Carla); Shelly Burch (Claudia); Taina Elg (Guido's Mother); Liliane Montevecchi (Liliane La Fleur); Laura Kenyon (Lina Darling); Stephanie Cotsirilos (Stephanie Necrophorus); Kate Dezina (Our Lady of the Spa); Kathi Moss (Saraghina); Camille Saviola (Mama Maddelena); Cameron Johann (Young Guido); Jeanie Bowers (Maria); Kim Criswell (Francesca); Collen Dodson (Venetian Gondolier); Louise Edeiken (Giulietta); Nancy McCall (Annabella); Cynthia Meryl (Diana); Rita Rehn (Renata); Lulu Downs (Gretchen von Krupf); Linda Kerns (Heidi von Sturm) Dee Etta Rowe (Olga von Sturm); Alaina Warren Zachary (Ilsa von Hesse); Evans Allen, Jadrien Steele, Patrick Wilcox (Young Guido's Schoolmates).

Federico Fellini's Oscar-winning, semi-autobiographical film *8½* was notched up by a half and served as the basis for the musical *Nine.* Like the film upon which it was based, *Nine* is a dazzling series of images; it relied more on staging than on conventional storytelling. With this show Tommy Tune firmly established himself as a director whose style was defined by arresting stage pictures.

The setting is a Venetian spa where movie director Guido Contini has come to revitalize himself creatively and emotionally. After three flops in a row, he cannot think of an idea for his next picture and is distracted by real and dreamlike intrusions from the women in his life. The show starts with Guido seated in Lawrence Miller's white-tiled set. Gradually, twenty-two females enter, clad in William Ivey Long's black costumes. This visual shock of black on white was just the beginning; other dazzling sequences followed. In a mock Folies-Bergère number, a feather boa stretches into infinity. In an extended montage

Raul Julia and the Pink Ladies in the Grand Canal number from *Nine*.

(reminiscent of the "Loveland" scene from *Follies*) Guido's movie idea becomes a lavish spectacle about Casanova, replete with gondolas, chandeliers, and elaborate gowns.

Maury Yeston, the composer and Yale Professor of Music Theory, first saw *8½* when he was a high school student in 1963. He became fascinated with the film and later set about musicalizing it. He subsequently enrolled in the Broadcast Music, Inc. (BMI) Workshop, a training ground for tunesmiths, and presented three songs from the project there in 1973. He collaborated with Mario Fratti, who translated the film from the Italian and wrote a libretto. The resulting musical was given a 1979 staged reading at the Eugene O'Neill Memorial Theatre Center in Waterford, Connecticut. The reading was well-received and won the first Richard Rodgers Production Award for a new musical developed at the Center.

But *Nine* was not able to make the transition from promising reading to full-fledged production because Fellini was withholding the rights. Katharine Hepburn, who had seen the Waterford staging, wrote to the Italian filmmaker on behalf of Yeston and Fratti. The director acquiesced on the condition that the original film not be mentioned in any of the musical's advertising.

In 1980, Tune was hired to direct the production and, because of creative differences, Fratti was replaced by Arthur Kopit. Raul Julia was cast as Guido. It was Tune's idea to have a cast entirely made up of women, save for Guido and four young boys, who played the director as a child and his three schoolmates. Over 1,000 actresses were auditioned for the available twenty-two roles. The final selections included cabaret singer Karen Akers as Guido's wife, former Folies-Bergère star Liliane Montevecchi as his French producer, Shelly Burch as his leading actress and muse, Taina Elg as his elegant mother, and Anita Morris as his mistress. Morris' provocative number "A Phone Call from the Vatican," which she performed in a skin-tight, flesh-colored suit was judged too salacious for the televised Tony Awards and was axed from the broadcast.

Nine won five Tonys including Best Musical and Best Director. There were rumors that the Tony voters chose *Nine* over *Dreamgirls* to exact revenge on the Shuberts, a sponsor of the latter show, for allowing the Helen Hayes, Bijou, and Morosco Theatres owned by them to be demolished.

The press was split over *Nine*. Douglas Watt of the *News* labelled it "a pretentious, tiresome musical." Most found Tune's production gorgeous but the story cold and uninvolving. The Best Musical Tony kept the audiences coming despite the critic's qualifications.

Bert Convy and, later, Sergio Franchi took over the lead role on Broadway after Julia. Franchi also headed a national tour which changed the locale from a spa to a railway station in order to make hauling the scenery from city to city easier.

TORCH SONG TRILOGY

by Harvey Fierstein

Opened June 10, 1982, after off-Broadway runs at La MaMa, the Richard Allen Arts Center, and the Actors Playhouse.

1,222 Performances

Little Theatre

Directed by Peter Pope

Produced by Kenneth Waissman, Martin Markinson, Lawrence Lane, John Glines, BetMar, and Donald Tick

Cast: Harvey Fierstein (Arnold Beckoff); Estelle Getty (Mrs. Beckoff); Court Miller (Ed); Diane Tarleton (Laurel); Paul Joynt (Alan); Fisher Stevens (David); Susan Edwards (Lady Blues).

Producer John Glines raised eyebrows coast-to-coast when he thanked his lover Lawrence Lane upon accepting the Tony for Best Play for *Torch Song Trilogy*, a play that was something of a shock itself. Written by and starring an unknown actor, three-and-a-half hours long, and dealing sympathetically with gay characters, *Torch Song* had everything going against it. Yet it ran for 1,222 performances, one of the longest runs for a nonmusical in the '80s.

The main character is a flamboyant drag queen, Arnold Beckoff, originally played by the frog-voiced playwright

Harvey Fierstein, author and star of *Torch Song Trilogy*, makes the sign for "I love you."

Harvey Fierstein, who won Tonys for both Best Play and Best Actor. In three stylistically distinct one-act plays that shatter the stereotyped images of homosexuals as lascivious, limp-wristed lunatics, Arnold searches for love and stability.

The first piece, *The International Stud*, is composed of three monologues and two dialogues with Arnold and his bisexual, closeted boyfriend, Ed. A female blues singer uses torch songs to comment on their on-again, off-again relationship. *Fugue in a Nursery* takes place in a giant bed, as Ed and Arnold attempt unions with new lovers, to the accompaniment of onstage musicians.

In the final segment, *Widows and Children First*—a more realistically presented comedy-drama with Neil Simon-ish one-liners—Arnold establishes a family with an adopted son and the returning Ed as his lover. He also confronts his mother, forcing her to accept him as he is.

Fierstein had performed in and written numerous plays off-off-Broadway. The first two *Torch Song* plays were presented at Ellen Stewart's La MaMa E.T.C. (Experimental Theatre Club). *The International Stud* was written in pieces. One scene was written as a monologue for a festival of plays at the Theatre for the New City, while another was a monologue for a proposed floor show Fierstein was writing for himself. The next one-act, *Fugue in a Nursery*, came about when La MaMa had to fulfill a grant program for using instruments, so the play revolved around the musical structure of a fugue. Fierstein then wrote the third play, which was optioned for Broadway.

Glines and his partner Lane, of the Glines, a gay arts organization, asked Fierstein for a play for a gay arts festival. The playwright gave a reading of excerpts from the complete trilogy. They immediately wanted to present all three works, but had to wait until the option on the third play had run out. When *Widows* became available again, the Glines planned to present all three together at the off-Broadway Richard Allen Arts Center. But it couldn't be decided if they should be shown on separate evenings or in one sitting. With the success of the Broadway engagement of the Royal Shakespeare Company's nine-hour *Nicholas Nickleby*, it was determined to promote *Torch Song* as the *Nicholas Nickleby* of off-Broadway. Fierstein condensed all three pieces to fit into one long evening. (Matthew Broderick was in the cast as Arnold's adopted son.) The engagements at the Allen Center and the Actors Playhouse were hits. The subsequent Broadway transfer was a gamble, but it paid off when the Tonys increased the take at the box office.

During the Broadway run, the lead was also played by David Garrison, Jonathan Hadary, and P.J. Benjamin. Donald Corren was Arnold on tour.

Fierstein re-created his role and wrote the shortened screenplay for the 1988 film version. He received third billing behind Anne Bancroft as his mother and Matthew Broderick, who now played his lover. Fierstein wrote another triple bill of one-acts *Safe Sex,* which dealt with the AIDS crisis. The program played on Broadway in 1987, but only ran for a week.

Other extra-long Broadway evenings have included *Strange Interlude* (1928); *Angels in America* (1993); and *The Kentucky Cycle* (1993).

CATS

Music by Andrew Lloyd Webber

Lyrics taken from *Old Possum's Book of Practical Cats* by T.S. Eliot

Opened October 7, 1982

Still running (4,733 performances as of February 6, 1994)

Winter Garden Theatre

Directed by Trevor Nunn

Choreographed by Gillian Lynn

Produced by Cameron Mackintosh, the Really Useful Company, David Geffen, and the Shubert Organization.

Cast: Betty Buckley (Grizabella); Ken Page (Old Deuteronomy); Hector Jaime Mercado (Alonzo); Stephen Hanan (Bustopher Jones/Asparagus/Growltiger); Donna King (Bombalurina); Steven Gelfer (Carbucketty); René Ceballos (Cassandra); René Clemente (Coricopat/Mungojerrie); Wendy Edmead (Demeter); Christine Langner (Etcetera/Rumpleteazer); Bonnie Simmons (Jellylorum/Griddlebone); Anna McNeely (Jennyanydots); Timothy Scott (Mistoffelees); Harry Groener (Munkustrap); Kenneth Ard (Plato/Macavity/Rumpus Cat); Herman W. Sebek (Pouncival); Terrence V. Mann (Rum Tum Tigger); Whitney Kershaw (Sillabub); Reed Jones (Skimbleshanks); Janet L. Hubert (Tantomile); Robert Hoshour (Tumblebrutus); Cynthia Onrubia (Victoria).

Cats was British *wunderkind* Andrew Lloyd Webber's first hit without his former partner, Tim Rice, and it established him as the dominant musical force both on Broadway and in London's West End. By 1983, Lloyd Webber had six productions running simultaneously in New York and London: *Joseph and the Amazing Technicolor Dreamcoat, Evita* and *Cats* in America, and *Evita, Cats* and *Song and Dance* in his native land.

Cats marked the beginning of a wave of British megahits with lots of flashy spectacle and little story. Instead of a narrative, the show is a series of songs and dances, as an ensemble of actors in John Napier's elaborate cat costumes cavort around a junkyard. Each feline is given his or her own moment to meow in the spotlight. There's Macavity, the mystery cat; Skimbleshanks, the railway cat; and Grizabella, the glamour puss who provides the evening's only bit of plot: she is chosen to ascend to "the heavy-side layer," the cats' version of heaven. Singing the show's haunting pop hit "Memory," the formerly elegant but now-frazzled feline (a sort of furry Evita) is led to her reward by the sagacious Old Deuteronomy. This scene provided the show with its most stunning visual effect, as the two are lifted on a giant tire to the upper reaches of the theatre. Later British pop musicals mimicked this device in the crashing chandelier in *Phantom of the Opera* and the helicopter in *Miss Saigon*.

Terrence V. Mann
and feline friends
in *Cats*.

The remarkable source for this fantasy was the Nobel Prize–winning poet T.S. Eliot, whose *The Love Song of J. Alfred Prufrock* and *The Waste Land* are masterpieces of modern poetry. But Eliot, a true cat lover, showed his lighter side when he wrote *Old Possum's Book of Practical Cats*, a collection of verse for children that he first circulated only among friends, then eventually published in 1939. Lloyd Webber originally set these poems to music for the amusement of his friends, much as Eliot had written them.

The composer explained his interest in the poems to *Playbill*: "I suddenly realized there were very musical rhythms in them, an extraordinary rhythm that really is the rhythm of lyrics. The words themselves dictate that certain musical phrases have to be there. . . . I couldn't say why I was drawn to setting the poems; I suppose it was because it was a book I knew very well and I was very much intrigued to see if I could write music to existing words, which I hadn't done before."

The few songs written for weekend afternoons soon grew into a full production. The composer originally intended to present them as a one-act musical. It was to be coupled with *Tell Me on a Sunday*, a one-woman song recital which later became the "song" half of *Song and Dance* (1985). *Cats* expanded into a full evening. When the material in the original Eliot work was exhausted, other Eliot works were used. Then director Trevor Nunn and lyricist Richard Stilgoe supplied additional lyrics. The poet's widow, Valerie Eliot, gave Lloyd Webber a previously unpublished fragment of her husband's work, which was transformed into "Memory." This song gave the show a pop hit when Barbra Streisand and Judy Collins recorded it.

Few thought a musical about dancing cats would be a success, but producer Cameron Mackintosh had instincts that told him otherwise. Along with Lloyd Webber's new production entity, the Really Useful Company, Mackintosh mounted the show in New York and London to a tumultuous public response, despite a somewhat lukewarm press.

The advertising slogan for *Cats* states: "Now and Forever." As of this writing it is the longest running Broadway show still playing, and is outdistanced only by *A Chorus Line* and *Oh! Calcutta!* in total number of performances. It has played all over the world, with companies in every capital, earning in excess of $100 million. The slogan's boast may be an understatement.

ON YOUR TOES

Book by George Abbott, Richard Rodgers, and Lorenz Hart

Music by Richard Rodgers

Lyrics by Lorenz Hart

Opened March 6, 1983

505 Performances

Virginia Theatre

Directed by George Abbott

Choreographed by Donald Saddler, George Balanchine, and Peter Martins

Produced by Alfred de Liagre, Jr., Roger L. Stevens, John Mauceri, Donald R. Seawell, and Andre Pastoria.

Cast: Natalia Makarova (Vera Baronova); Lara Teeter (Junior); Christine Andreas (Frankie Fayne); George De La Pena (Konstantine Morrosine); George S. Irving (Sergei Alexandrovitch); Dina Merrill (Peggy Porterfield); Peter Slutsker (Sidney Cohn); Jerry Mitchell (Joe McCall); Michaela K. Hughes (Miss Pinkerton); Tamara Mark (Anushka); Mary C. Robare (Lola); Eugene J. Anthony (Phil Dolan II/Oscar); Betty Ann Grove (Lil Dolan/Woman Reporter); Philip Arthur Ross (Phil Dolan III/Young Junior); Dirk Lumbard (Stage Manager); Chris Peterson (Dimitri); Don Steffy (Ivan); George Kmeck (Louie); David Gold (Stage Doorman).

George Abbott returned to the hit parade at the age of ninety-five with a revival of *On Your Toes*. It was his 120th production on Broadway. The 1936 show had been the director's first musical. It was the second Broadway musical for choreographer George Balanchine, who became one of the leading forces in the world of ballet. Songwriters Richard Rodgers and Lorenz Hart had conceived of combining the rarefied atmosphere of the classical ballet with the razzmatazz of Broadway. They came up with a story of an ex-hoofer turned music professor attempting to get a Russian ballet company to perform a jazz piece. Along the way, the prima ballerina falls for him and her jealous lover hires a hit man to kill the ex-hoofer during a performance of the ballet, ironically titled "Slaughter on Tenth Avenue."

The material was first presented to Fred Astaire as a film vehicle. When the star rejected it, Rodgers and Hart decided to put it on stage. They hired Abbott, who had only done straight plays up to that point, to co-author the book and stage it. Ray Bolger and Tamara Geva played the leads. Abbott withdrew from the production, and Worthington Miller was the officially credited director. But Abbott served as show doctor during the out-of-town tryout, reworking the staging after a disastrous Boston opening. The show ran for 315 performances in New York—a decent run in 1936.

On Your Toes was the first musical to use serious ballet in its choreography. Agnes de Mille would later make such dancing more organic to a show's plot in *Oklahoma!*, but *Toes* was first in its use of the ballet vocabulary. Balanchine created two extended ballets for the show: "Slaughter on Tenth Avenue" and "Princess Zenobia," a satire on the overserious aspects of ballet companies such as the Ballets Russes, which had recently made a popular American tour.

The musical was revived in 1954 with Bobby Van, Vera Zorina, and Elaine Stritch. Abbott and Balanchine re-created their original production, but most critics found it old-fashioned. In 1983, another revival was mounted, and the new generation of reviewers felt that the show had aged like a fine wine. Abbott and Balanchine were once again slated to participate, but Balanchine fell ill. His steps for "Slaughter" and "Zenobia" were realized by his protégé Peter Martins. Donald Saddler staged the remaining dances, including the title song, a wild challenge number between ballet and Broadway dancers.

The discovery of the production was American Ballet Theatre *premiere danceuse* Natalia Makarova, playing her first speaking role as the haughty Vera Barnova. The ballet dancer displayed sparkling comic talents as well as her flawless ballet technique. She won a Tony Award, and the show was named Best Revival.

Makarova was succeeded by fellow Russian ballerinas Galina Panova and Valentina Kozlova (who co-starred with her husband Leonid Kozlov). Leslie Caron was slated to star in the touring version of the revival, but suffered an injury and alternated performances with Makarova. The tour was cancelled when Caron was hospitalized.

BRIGHTON BEACH MEMOIRS

by Neil Simon

Opened March 27, 1983

1,530 Performances

Alvin Theatre

Directed by Gene Saks

Produced by Emanuel Azenberg, Wayne M. Rogers, and Radio City Music Hall Productions

Cast: Matthew Broderick (Eugene); Elizabeth Franz (Kate); Peter Michael Goetz (Jack); Zeljko Ivanek (Stanley); Joyce Van Patten (Blanche); Jodi Thelen (Nora); Mandy Ingber (Laurie).

Brighton Beach Memoirs was the first in a trilogy of plays by Neil Simon, tracing his entry into manhood from the latter days of the Depression through World War II and into his first foray into comedy writing in the late 1940s. The play is narrated by fifteen-year-old Eugene Morris Jerome, who, like Tom Wingfield of *The Glass Menagerie*, is a stand-in for the author.

The Jerome household in 1937 is a crowded one. In addition to Eugene and his parents and brother, his aunt Blanche and her two daughters are living there after the death of Blanche's husband. There is no real plot; instead, the play offers a snapshot of each family member as he or she deals with economic and emotional hardships. Unlike many of Simon's previous plays, the humor comes less from snappy one-liners than from the situations. Thus, with *Brighton Beach*, critics took another look at the popular playwright, who had time and again called his reputation as a mere joke machine into question. The New York Drama Critics Circle named *Brighton Beach Memoirs* the Best Play that season. Still, Simon was snubbed by the nominating committee for the Tony Awards, which failed to put the comedy in the running for Best Play. The show did win Tonys for Gene Saks's direction and Matthew Broderick's performance as Eugene.

The play opened after a series of disappointments for Simon on Broadway. His last unqualified hit had been the musical *They're Playing Our Song*. This was followed by the moderately successful *I Ought to Be in Pictures* (1980), which enjoyed a run of 324 performances; *Fools* (1981), his shortest-running play (only 40 performances); and a revised version of the musical *Little Me* (1982), which starred Victor Garber and James Coco and had a 35-performance run.

The playwright found his ensemble cast for *Brighton Beach Memoirs* after attending many off-Broadway pro-

ductions. Matthew Broderick was in *Torch Song Trilogy* before it moved to Broadway. Zeljko Ivanek appeared in *Cloud 9*, while Elizabeth Franz was playing the title role in *Sister Mary Ignatius Explains It All for You*. The only performer to have worked with Simon before was Joyce Van Patten.

As usual, the author had many irons in the fire. At the time of *Brighton Beach*'s opening, another Simon play, *Actors and Actresses*, was in an out-of-town tryout, and the film *Max Dugan Returns*, with a Simon screenplay, was in release. In addition to winning the Drama Critics Award, Simon received the honor of having a Broadway theatre named after him: the Alvin Theatre was rechristened the Neil Simon. The honors were tempered with setbacks. During the triumphant year of 1983, *Actors and Actresses* closed on the road, making it the only Simon play never to reach Broadway, and the playwright separated from his wife Marsha Mason.

Matthew Broderick (center) surrounded by the Jerome family of *Brighton Beach Memoirs*: (left to right.) Mandy Ingber, Joyce Van Patten, Jodi Thelen, Elizabeth Franz, Peter Michael Goetz, and Zeljko Ivanek.

Saks directed the 1986 film of *Brighton Beach Memoirs*, starring Jonathan Silverman, who replaced Broderick on Broadway and played in the national tour as Eugene. Bob Dishy, Blythe Danner, and Judith Ivey were featured as the rest of the family.

The play was written at first without a trilogy in mind, but Simon went on with Eugene's story in *Biloxi Blues* (1985) and *Broadway Bound* (1986), both of which also ran over 500 performances.

MY ONE AND ONLY

Book by Peter Stone and Timothy S. Meyer

Music by George Gershwin

Lyrics by Ira Gershwin

Opened May 1, 1983

767 Performances

St. James Theatre

Directed and choreographed by Tommy Tune and Thommie Walsh

Produced by Paramount Theatre Productions, Lester Allen, Francine LeFrak, Kenneth Greenblatt, and Mark Scwartz

Cast: Tommy Tune (Capt. Billy Buck Chandler); Twiggy (Edith Herbert); Denny Dillon (Mickey); Bruce McGill (Prince Nicolai/Achmed); Charles "Honi" Coles (Mr. Magix); Roscoe Lee Browne (Rt. Rev. J.D. Montgomery); David Jackson, Ken Leigh Rogers, Ronald Dennis (New Rhythm Boys); Paul David Richards (Policeman/Stage Doorman); Adrian Bailey (Conductor); Nana Visitor (Flounder); Susan Hartley (Sturgeon); Stephanie Eley (Minnow); Jill Cook (Prawn); Niki Harris (Kipper); Karen Tamburrelli (Anchovie).

My One and Only was originally intended as a revival of the 1927 Gershwin musical *Funny Face*, which featured such sterling songs as "He Loves and She Loves," "'Swonderful," "My One and Only" and the title song. Director Peter Sellars, then twenty-five and the darling of the avant-garde for his productions of operas and classics, wanted to restage the show with Tommy Tune in the lead. Tune had just finished staging *Nine* and was eager to return to performing. He is one of the few directors and choreographers to switch back and forth from either side of the footlights. For his leading lady, Tune suggested Twiggy, the British former supermodel with whom he co-starred in the film *The Boy Friend*. With such a leading man and lady, a distinguished director, and can't-miss songs, the production seemed like a sure thing.

But there is no such thing in show business, and Sellars, with the aid of playwright Timothy S. Mayer, totally revamped the musical, giving it a dark, political slant almost Brechtian in nature. Now called *My One and Only*, the show was transformed from a light and airy lark to a leaden diatribe.

In a panic, the producers fired Sellars and elevated Tune and his co-choreographer Thommie Walsh to directors.

Directors Mike Nichols and Michael Bennett were called in to minister to the sick patient, and Peter Stone rewrote the libretto. Adrianne Lobel's expressionist sets were replaced by those of Tony Walton. During Boston tryouts, Tune made nightly curtain speeches apologizing for the rough nature of the show. (Ironically, *Funny Face* had gone through similar drastic changes during its pre-Broadway tour.)

Only six of the original *Funny Face* songs remained as the Gershwin canon was raided for other tunes. The co-directors realized that the story should merely be an excuse to introduce the musical numbers. Meyer and Stone's book was a featherweight mixture in which Tune, as a Lindbergh-like aviator, romances swimming star Twiggy.

One of the elements that contributed to the show's success was the casting. Not only was there the unusual pairing of the tall Tune and diminutive Twiggy; the chorus was cleverly cast with black males and white females, providing an

Twiggy and Tommy Tune are all decked out in *My One and Only*.

unspoken racial and sexual tension. Veteran dancer Charles "Honi" Coles tapped out of near-obscurity in his Tony-winning featured role, while Roscoe Lee Browne, Denny Dillon, and Bruce McGill provided comic highlights.

In spite of the early production troubles, *My One and Only* scored mightily. *Variety* said, "it may stand as one of the most successful salvage jobs in recent Broadway history." *Newsweek* cheered, "It's as if Lazarus not only came back from the grave, but came back singing and dancing."

Tune won two Tony Awards for his leading performance and his choreography with Walsh, making him the only person to have won Tony Awards in four different categories. His previous wins were for Best Featured Actor in a Musical (*Seesaw*) and Best Director of a Musical (*Nine*).

Sandy Duncan and her husband Don Correia succeeded the two leads on Broadway. Duncan and Tune played them in the national tour.

Crazy for You, another reworked Gershwin show, was also a hit in 1992.

LA CAGE AUX FOLLES

Book by Harvey Fierstein, based on the play by Jean Poiret.

Music and lyrics by Jerry Herman

Opened August 21, 1983

1,761 Performances

Palace Theatre

Directed by Arthur Laurents

Choreographed by Scott Salmon

Produced by Allan Carr, Kenneth D. Greenblatt, Marvin A. Krauss, Stewart F. Lane, James M. Nederlander, and Martin Richards

Cast: Gene Barry (Georges); George Hearn (Albin); John Weiner (Jean-Michel); William Thomas, Jr. (Jacob); Leslie Stevens (Anne); Elizabeth Parrish (Jacqueline); Jay Garner (Edouard Dindon); Merle Louise (Marie Dindon); Brian Kelly (Francis); Walter Charles (Renaud).

While *La Cage Aux Folles* was about a highly unconventional relationship (a middle-aged transvestite and his male lover) for a Broadway musical, it told its story in familiar musical theatre terms, with broad comedy, sentimental moments, and elaborate production numbers. The farcical story turns on Georges and Albin, who run a St.

George Hearn (left, foreground) and Gene Barry with "Les Cagelles" in *La Cage Aux Folles*.

Tropez nightclub as owner and star drag performer. Georges's son from a youthful heterosexual affair has fallen in love with the daughter of a right-wing crusader. When the boy brings his fiancée and her family home to met "the folks," Albin disguises himself as his "mother" and the future in-laws are in for a ride they'll never forget.

La Cage humanized its outlandish homosexual characters, dazzled audiences with glitzy costumes and flashy choreography, and provided an unofficial national anthem for the gay population ("I Am What I Am").

Producer Allan Carr, a former manager for Ann-Margaret, Marvin Hamlisch, and others, saw the original play by Jean Poiret in Paris in 1976. "Even though my French wasn't that good," Carr explained to the *New York Post*, "I knew what was going on onstage and saw that the audience ate it up. I knew I had to have this play and bring it over here." Carr wanted to adapt the comedy into a film to star Tony Curtis and Jack Lemmon, but he learned that the American rights were controlled by David Merrick, who intended it as a vehicle for Zero Mostel.

After Merrick and then British producer Michael White dropped their options on the property, Carr snatched it up, only to learn that a film had already been made. The cinematic *La Cage*, a French-Italian production released in 1978, became a hit and spawned two sequels. Rather than attempt to match the film's success with another movie version, Carr decided to make the play into a stage musical.

Theatre columns soon announced that the American musical edition would be set in New Orleans and go by the title *The Queen of Basin Street*, with Mike Nichols directing, Tommy Tune choreographing, Maury Yeston (*Nine*) composing the score, and Jay Presson Allen (*Forty Carats*) adapting the book. But creative differences among this all-star team arose. The New Orleans idea was totally scrapped, and Carr began again with a new set of collaborators.

Jerry Herman, whose previous Broadway hits included *Hello, Dolly!* and *Mame*, again wrote a popular score with ballads, comedy pieces, and a big number centered on a fabulous female figure surrounded by chorus boys. Only this time, the woman was a man and the chorus (except for two women) were boys in drag.

For the book, Carr chose Harvey Fierstein, who had just won two Tonys for acting and writing *Torch Song Trilogy*, a hit play which also dealt with gay themes. Fierstein wrote the libretto while traveling on the subway from his Brooklyn home to perform in *Torch Song* on Broadway.

Arthur Laurents, author of the books for *Gypsy* and *West Side Story*, was asked to direct, but he was reluctant. He told the *New York Daily News*, "I only liked the movie moderately. I thought it was an amusing comedy, but it was offensive to me in some ways. It was sort of a success-ful middle-class fantasy and I didn't think it would make a good musical. Then I read the play, which I think is worse than the movie. It's a very cheap farce which would die in this country, in my opinion. It has everything for a cheap joke. I think the thing that finally appealed to us was the humanity. It's there in the script, but it really had to be pulled out." The creative team solved the problem by emphasizing the family relationship between the two lovers and the son instead of the bizarre comedy.

Casting the two leads proved difficult. Gene Barry, known mostly for his detective and Western roles on television, played Georges. George Hearn, one of the stage's best singers, donned gowns and high heels to play Albin. Press interviews with the two stars mentioned their wives and families several times so that no one would think for a minute that either of the actors was actually gay.

Two national tours were launched. Walter Charles and Keith Michell headed one, while Keene Curtis and Peter Marshall toplined another.

NOISES OFF

by Michael Frayn
Opened December 11, 1983
553 Performances
Brooks Atkinson Theatre
Directed by Michael Blakemore
Produced by James Nederlander, Robert Fryer, Jerome Minskoff, The Kennedy Center, and Michael Cordon.
Cast: Dorothy Loudon (Dotty Otley); Brian Murray (Lloyd Dallas); Victor Garber (Garry Lejeune); Deborah Rush (Brooke Ashton); Amy Wright (Poppy Norton-Taylor); Paxton Whitehead (Frederick Fellowes); Linda Thorson (Belinda Blair); Jim Piddock (Tom Allgood); Douglas Seale (Selsdon Mowbray).

The definition of *farce* is "an exaggerated comedy based on broadly humorous situations; a play intended only to be funny." British author Michael Frayn wrote *Noises Off* apparently to fit the description perfectly. The title is theatrical jargon for any unwanted sounds that emanate from backstage during a performance. In Act I of this romp, a British company of third-rate actors is ineptly rehearsing for a touring production of a play called *Nothing On*. A clearly dreadful sex farce, it involves an eccentric housekeeper, a pair of adulterous lovers, another couple fleeing a tax audit, Arab sheiks, a drunken burglar, and a plate of sardines. As is typical in farces, there are plenty of doors to slam, stairs to fall down, identities to be mistaken, and beds to jump in and out of.

Act II takes place backstage during a performance of *Nothing On*. The cast has been playing for a month and now hate each other's guts. All hell breaks loose as the farce off-stage parallels the one before the footlights. Act III occurs one month later. After playing in a series of dreary seaside towns with names like Weston-Super-Mare and Stockton-on-Tees, even the semblance of order and harmony has broken down. The onstage performance collapses in a riot of missed cues, misplaced props, and mangled limbs.

Frayn conceived of the play in 1970 when he was backstage at a performance of a farce he had written, which starred Lynn Redgrave and Richard Briers. The play required behind-the-scenes split-second timing and several quick costume changes. "It was funnier from behind than in front," the playwright recalled to *Time* magazine, "and I thought 'One day, I must write a farce from behind.'"

The author sent a rough draft of his rough-and-tumble comedy to Australian director Michael Blakemore, who made several suggestions for improvements. Frayn rewrote most of the script based on the director's ideas. *Noises Off*, staged with Swiss-watch precision by Blakemore, premiered in London in 1982 and was still running when the American edition opened. The fast-paced direction had worn out two British casts, and a third was playing when Blakemore arrived in New York to put the Yankee ensemble through their paces. Of course, though the action onstage appeared to be totally choatic, each movement and line was carefully planned. Broadway cast member Deborah Rush stated that they eventually learned "just how many breaths were required between the opening and closing of a door."

The rigorous pratfalls and antics resulted in some injuries for the ensemble. Top-billed Dorothy Loudon lost twenty-five pounds and suffered two broken toes, two bruised ribs, and a trachea infection from the strain on her voice. "I'm so black and blue I haven't worn a dress for weeks," she told *Time*.

When the original American cast left New York for the West Coast production, a new ensemble was ready for the pandemonium. Carole Shelley, Paul Hecht, Concetta Tomei, and Randle Mell were among the new farceurs. An all-star 1992 film version featured Carol Burnett, Michael Caine, Christopher Reeve, and Julie Hagerty.

THE TAP DANCE KID

Book by Charles Braswell, based on the novel *Nobody's Family Is Going to Change*, by Louise Fitzhugh.

Music by Henry Krieger

Lyrics by Robert Lorick

Opened December 21, 1983

669 Performances

Broadhurst Theatre

Directed by Vivian Matalon

Choreographed by Danny Daniels

Produced by Stanley White, Evelyn Baron, Harvey J. Klaris, and Michel Stuart

Cast: Alfonso Ribeiro (Willie); Hinton Battle (Dipsey); Hattie Winston (Ginnie); Samuel E. Wright (William); Alan Weeks (Daddy Bates); Martine Allard (Emma); Barbara Montgomery (Dulcie); Karen Peskow (Mona); Jackie Lowe (Carole); Michael Blevins (Winslow).

The Tap Dance Kid took the unusual route from novel to TV special to Broadway musical. The title character is Willie, a young boy in an upper-middle-class black family who wants to become a tap dancer. His lawyer father is

(Left to right) Alan Weeks, Alfonso Ribeiro, and Hinton Battle in *The Tap Dance Kid.*

against such a career move, fearing that the boy's ambition is a step backward into racial stereotyping. Thanks to Willie's Uncle Dipsey, a professional dancer himself, Willie is able to realize his dream.

Producer Michel Stuart, a former dancer who had been in the original cast of *A Chorus Line*, told *Playbill* magazine, "[Fellow producer] Evelyn Baron found Louise Fitzhugh's novel *Nobody's Family Is Going to Change* six years ago and turned that into *The Tap Dance Kid* for afternoon TV. It was a nonmusical then, and it won three Emmys. After that success, Evelyn felt, 'Now wait a minute, there's more to be done with this story. It's such a relevant story about what parents can teach their children and children can teach their parents.'" So *The Tap Dance Kid* became a musical.

Baron hired actor Charles Blackwell, who had played the father in the telecast, to write the book and Henry Krieger (*Dreamgirls*) and Robert Lorick for the score. Tony-winning director Vivian Matalon (*Morning's at Seven*) was engaged to direct. (Jerry Zaks directed the national tour.)

An extensive talent search was conducted to find the right young man for the title role. Twelve-year-old Alfonso Ribiero was chosen from more than 1,000 auditioners. "When I tried out for the show," Ribiero said in a *Playbill* interview, "I didn't know how to tap dance at all. It was Vivian who wanted me, so the choreographer Danny Daniels said he would teach me." Ribiero learned his steps well enough to keep up with his co-stars Hinton Battle (who won his second Tony Award for his portrayal of Uncle Dipsey) and Alan Weeks.

Despite a mixed press, the show had an unexpectedly long run, perhaps because of the flashy excerpt shown on the Tony Awards telecast. Such national exposure often aids the box office of musicals which might otherwise close prematurely. The musical also launched a heavy television advertising campaign.

Alfonso Ribiero was later replaced by Savion Glover, who tapped onward to Broadway shows like *Black and Blue* and *Jelly's Last Jam*.

THE REAL THING

by Tom Stoppard
Opened January 5, 1984
566 Performances
Plymouth Theatre
Directed by Mike Nichols

Produced by Emanuel Azenberg, the Shubert Organization, Icarus Productions, Byron Goldman, Ivan Bloch, Roger Berlind, and Michael Cordon

Cast: Jeremy Irons (Henry); Glenn Close (Annie); Kenneth Welsh (Max); Christine Baranski (Charlotte); Peter Gallagher (Billy); Cynthia Nixon (Debbie); Vyto Ruginis (Brodie).

Jeremy Irons uses his cricket bat to explain good writing to Glenn Close in *The Real Thing*.

British playwright Tom Stoppard had dazzled London and Broadway with such witty works as *Rosencrantz and Guildenstern Are Dead* (1967), *Jumpers* (1974), and *Travesties* (1975), many based on elaborate premises and intellectual conundrums. *Rosencrantz and Guildenstern*, for example, followed the exploits of two minor characters from *Hamlet*. *Travesties* toyed with the fact that James Joyce, Tristan Tzara, and V.I. Lenin had all been in Zurich at the same time and presented their unlikely associations with each other. *Rosencrantz* and *Travesties* had won the Tony as Best Play of their respective seasons. But many critics, admiring Stoppard as a clever gamester who devised intricate stageable puzzles, doubted that he could deliver plays about real people. He proved them wrong with *The Real Thing*, his third Tony-winner and longest-running New York production.

Jeremy Irons, star of the Broadway production said to *The New York Times*, "I felt as if someone had said to him, 'Tom, your plays are brilliant, very theatrical, but they have nothing to do with life.' And that he heard that once too often and said, 'I'll write a play that shows I know about life and love, and that I know the difference between life and love in the theatre and life and love in real life.'"

The main characters in *The Real Thing* are Henry, a brilliant playwright not unlike Stoppard, and Annie, an actress who is not as articulate and who operates on a more instinctive level. The two are lovers and cheating on their spouses, both of whom are actors appearing in a brittle comedy by Henry about adultery. Similiar contrasts between "real life" and "stage life" continue throughout the play as Henry and Annie divorce their partners, marry each other, and repeat the cycle of deception, as Annie begins to see another man. During Annie's affair, Henry attempts to hide behind a wall of witticisms, but in a brief shattering scene, the eloquent dramatist is reduced to tears and can only mumble, "Please, please don't." Finally, the couple are able to accept the hurt that goes with love and appreciate "the real thing."

Roger Rees (who had starred in the Royal Shakespeare's production of *Nicholas Nickleby*) and Felicity Kendall played the leads in the original London production, which won the *Evening Standard* Award as Best Play. Mike Nichols saw the play in the West End and persuaded the Shubert Organization and the Nederlanders, rival groups of Broadway theatre owners, to join together in a rare partnership to bring the show to America. The Nederlanders later dropped out, but *The Real Thing* arrived in New York under Nichols' direction and became the biggest nonmusical hit of the 1983–84 season.

By this time in Broadway history, straight plays were rarely able to turn a profit, so major stars were required to ensure a strong box office. Nichols wanted to cast Jeremy Irons (Stoppard's first choice for the London version) and Meryl Streep, who had recently appeared together in the film *The French Lieutenant's Woman*. Irons accepted, but Streep demurred; she was replaced by rising star Glenn Close. Both Irons and Close had solid theatre credentials, but were only just becoming famous through their roles in movies.

The New York production was no carbon copy of the one in London. The West End edition was hampered by confusing slide projections, living tableaux, and elaborate scene changes. Tony Walton's revolving set and Nichols's economical staging eliminated the clutter.

Irons, Close, Christine Baranski (as Henry's caustic ex-wife), Nichols, and the play itself won Tonys. *The Real Thing*'s total of five tied it with *A Man for All Seasons*, *Who's Afraid of Virginia Woolf?*, and *Amadeus* for most Tonys won by a play.

During the New York run, John Vickery and Nicol Williamson replaced Irons, Caroline Lagerfelt and Laila Robbins succeeded Close. Brian Bedford and Sara Botsford played the national tour.

SUNDAY IN THE PARK WITH GEORGE

Book by James Lapine

Music and lyrics by Stephen Sondheim

Opened May 2, 1984

540 Performances

Booth Theatre

Directed by James Lapine

Produced by The Shubert Organization and Emanuel Azenberg

Cast: Mandy Patinkin (Georges/George); Bernadette Peters (Dot/Marie); Barbara Bryne (Old Lady/Blair Daniels); Charles Kimbrough (Jules/Bob Greenberg); Dana Ivey (Yvonne/Naomi Eisen); Brent Spiner (Franz/Dennis); Nancy Opel (Frieda/Betty); Judith Moore (Nurse/Mrs./Harriet Pawling); Kurt Knudson (Mr./Lee Randolph); Cris Groenendaal (Louis/Billy Webster); William Parry (Boatman/Charles Redmond); Robert Westenberg (Soldier/Alex); Melanie Vaughan (Celeste #1/Waitress); Mary D'Arcy (Celeste #2/Elaine); Danielle Ferland (Louise/Boy); John Jellison (Man/Museum Asst.); Michele Rigan (Little Girl); Sue Anne Gershenson (Woman/Photographer).

Stephen Sondheim broke new ground with *Sunday in the Park with George*, a musical rumination on art and those who create it. After an eleven-year collaboration with director Harold Prince (from *Company* in 1970 to *Merrily We Roll Along* in 1981), Sondheim switched partners to work with James Lapine, a director and playwright with numerous off-Broadway credits, such as his plays *Table Settings* (1979) and *Twelve Dreams* (1981) and his staging of *March of the Falsettos* (1981).

Rather than a film, novel or straight play, *Sunday in the Park* was based on a painting: Georges Seurat's huge pointillist masterpiece, "Sunday Afternoon on the Island of La Grande Jatte," a depiction of strolling Parisians rendered in thousands of colored dots. More than just a "painter's bio" like the films *Lust for Life* and *Moulin Rogue*, the musi-

Mandy Patinkin (right, with beard) contemplates his model and lover Bernadette Peters (center) in *Sunday in the Park with George*.

cal explores not only the creation of this work, but the creative process itself. Songs such as "Finishing the Hat," "Putting It Together," and "Move On" detail the compromises, ideals, and motivations of the devoted artist.

After Lapine researched the life of Seurat (1859–1891), who never sold a painting during his brief life, he then discarded the facts to create a fictitious account. Lapine's book follows the French painter's creation of the painting from 1884 to 1886 and his relationship to his mistress and model Dot, whose name is a not-too-subtle reference to Seurat's painting style. As the artist becomes more obsessed with his giant canvas, Dot leaves him for a baker (a man whose work is immediately appreciated by a wider public than Seurat's) and moves to America with Seurat's baby.

With Mandy Patinkin as Georges and Bernadette Peters as Dot, the musical was workshopped at Playwrights Horizons, where this entire story was told in the first act. Exposing it to limited audiences at the off-Broadway theatre's subscribers, the show was refined and reworked. The second act gave the authors trouble. As Sondheim told the *New York Times*, "When we'd fastened on the idea of using Seurat's painting and showing how it was made, for the first act, I was all excited about it

because I thought the second act could be a series of variations or comments on the painting." But Lapine insisted that the first act narrative be continued into the second, or the audience would lose interest.

Several versions of the show's latter half were attempted and abandoned. These included a history of the painting from its first exhibition in France to its acquisition by the Art Insitute of Chicago, its current home. Finally, the authors placed the action in 1984, with Seurat's great-grandson George (without the *s*), played by Patinkin, presenting his kinetic laser sculpture at the Museum of Modern Art. Like his artistic ancestor, he's going through a creative and emotional crisis. In the final scene, the great-grandson returns to the island of the Grand Jatte and is met by the ghost of Dot who again serves as inspiration, joining the two eras and artists.

The rewriting continued as previews began on Broadway, where the first audiences didn't know what to make of this unconventional musical. Their responses were cool. Less than two weeks before the official opening, two lovely ballads, "Children and Art" and "Lesson #8," were added, giving the second act an emotional punch it had previously lacked. Now audiences received the production more warmly.

Critical reaction was divided. Frank Rich of the *New York Times* called it "an audacious, haunting, and . . . touching work." But Clive Barnes of the *Post* whined, "I was nonplussed, unplussed, and disappointed." Many reviewers hailed its innovations, while others found it too self-consciously clever and uninvolving.

Sunday in the Park was nominated for ten Tonys and won two (for Tony Stragies's inventive, pop-up set and Richard Nelson's evocative lighting); the awards that year were swept by *La Cage Aux Folles*. Although *Sunday in the Park* won both the Pulitzer Prize and the New York Drama Critics Circle Award, it was never a big hit at the box office. The production continued for over a year on Broadway, thanks largely to the support of the *New York Times*, which ran numerous features and interviews on the show.

Robert Westenberg and Harry Groener later played the two artists, while Betsy Joslyn and Maryann Plunkett took over Bernadette Peters' role. Late in the run, the production was videotaped with most of the original cast and telecast on cable (Showtime) and on PBS.

BILOXI BLUES

by Neil Simon

Opened March 28, 1985

524 Performances

Neil Simon Theatre

Directed by Gene Saks

Produced by Emanuel Azenberg

Cast: Matthew Broderick (Eugene Morris Jerome); Barry Miller (Arnold Epstein); Bill Sadler (Sgt. Merwin J. Toomey); Brian Tarantina (Roy Selridge); Matt Mulhern (Joseph Wykowski); Alan Ruck (Don Carney); Geoffrey Sharp (James Hennesy); Randall Edwards (Rowena); Penelope Ann Miller (Daisy Hannigan).

Neil Simon continued his trilogy of autobiographical plays with *Biloxi Blues*. The first play, *Brighton Beach Memoirs*, ended with adolescent Eugene Morris Jerome looking uncertainly to the future as his family struggled to survive the Depression and as Europe went to war. *Biloxi Blues* picks up Eugene's story at his entrance into military service at the end of World War II.

The author wrote about the play's gestation: "When I wrote *Brighton Beach Memoirs*, I never intended it to be a trilogy. When it turned out to be so successful, I was encouraged to write a sequel. You don't see many sequels in the theatre. When I thought of what would be the next obvious step in my life, some momentous occasion, it was when I went into the Army. . . . *Biloxi Blues* is Eugene stepping out of New York and the comfort and safety of home into a whole new world."

While in basic training in Biloxi, Mississippi, Eugene loses his virginity, gains a sweetheart, develops his talent as a writer by observing the diverse company of recruits he bunks with, and becomes an adult.

The play was the only long-running nonmusical success of the season and won Simon his first Best Play Tony Award after six nominations. (In 1965, when the Tonys had given separate awards to authors and plays, Simon was named Best Author for *The Odd Couple*, but *The Subject Was Roses* won Best Play.)

As usual, Simon adapted his own script for the 1988 screen edition of *Biloxi*, which starred Matthew Broderick (again as Eugene) and Christopher Walken as the bizarre drill instructor Sgt. Toomey. The film was directed by Mike Nichols, who had staged many of Simon's shows on Broadway, though this was his first Simon film. Jonathan Silverman played Eugene on tour.

Simon was discharged from the Army in 1946 and went to work for a radio comedian, Goodman Ace, as a gag writer, along with his brother Danny. These events were dramatized in the final play of the Simon trilogy *Broadway Bound* (1986).

BIG RIVER

by William Hauptman, based on *The Adventures of Huckleberry Finn*, by Mark Twain.

Music and lyrics by Roger Miller

Opened April 25, 1985

1,005 Performances

Eugene O'Neill Theatre

Directed by Des McAnuff

Choreographed by Janet Watson

Produced by Rocco Landesman, Heidi Landesman, Rick Steiner, M. Anthony Fisher, and Dodger Productions.

Cast: Daniel H. Jenkins (Huckleberry Finn); Ron Richardson (Jim); René Auberjonois (The Duke); Bob Gunton (The King); John Short (Tom Sawyer); Patti Cohenour (Mary Jane Wilkes); John Goodman (Pap Finn/Sheriff Bell); Susan Browning (Widow Douglas/Sally Phelps); Evalyn Baron (Miss Watson/Harmonica Player); Gordon Connell (Mark Twain); William Youmans (Ben Rogers/Hank/Young Fool); Andi Henig (Jo Harper/Joanna Wilkes); Peggy Harmon (Susan Wilkes); Ralph Byers (Judge Thatcher/Harvey Wilkes/Silas Phelps); Carol Dennis (Alice); Jennifer Leigh Warren (Alice's Daughter); Aramis Estevez (Simon); Michael Brian (Dick/Andy/Man in Crowd/Hired Hand); Reathel Bean (Lafe/Counselor Robinson/Hired Hand); Franz Jones (Bill).

Mark Twain's classic 1885 novel *Huckleberry Finn*, had been adapted to film and television numerous times, but a Broadway musical version was not made until a century after the book's publication. Kurt Weill and Maxwell Anderson had attempted a musical, but it remained unfinished at the time of Weill's death. Alan Jay Lerner and Burton Lane started a film musical as a starring vehicle for Gene Kelly and Danny Kaye as the two con men Huck encounters on his journey down the Mississippi. But this project never got beyond the planning stages.

While these veterans had failed to musicalize Twain's epic of Huck's river-raft odyssey from Missouri to Arkansas with the runaway slave Jim, a group of newcomers to Broadway succeeded. The composer, book-writer, director, and most of the producers were making their Broadway debuts. On its journey to hitdom, *Big River: The Adventures of Huckleberry Finn* sailed over the shoals of mixed reviews and big budgets to the safe harbor of a long run.

Big River began in 1982, when husband and wife Rocco and Heidi Landesman went to see country singer and songwriter Roger Miller perform at New York's Lone Star Café. Rocco had turned from teaching drama and criticism at Yale to managing a mutual fund and producing; Heidi was a set designer for off-Broadway and regional theatre. "We had this crazy idea to do something in the theatre with Roger Miller," Rocco told the *New York Times*. "And Heidi said, 'Why not *Huck Finn*,' knowing it's my favorite book."

The couple approached Miller after his performance and, many meetings later, persuaded him to compose the score for a musical, *Huck Finn*. In 1983, Mr. Landesman signed on William Hauptman, a fellow Yale graduate, to write the libretto. On the basis of Hauptman's adaptation, Robert Brustein, who had taught both men as students at Yale, put *Big River* on the schedule of the American Repertory Theatre, in Cambridge, Massachusetts. Des McAnuff, artistic director of the La Jolla Playhouse in California, was hired to stage the musical.

The cast of *Big River*.

As the April 1984 production date loomed closer, Miller had yet to pen one song for the score. Brustein bristled and pushed for getting a new tunesmith, either James Taylor or Carly Simon. But Rocco Landesman believed in Miller and visited the songwriter at his New Mexico ranch. "We would just walk through the fields," Miller said to the *Times*, "and Rocco would tell me I could do it. I grew to totally trust him. He did a wonderful job of diplomacy and of artistic urging. I didn't want to let him down."

Miller came through with eight songs for the Cambridge production. There followed a second mounting at McAnuff's La Jolla Playhouse in the summer. Further songs were added and adjustments made in the libretto.

William Hauptman's book managed to fit in almost all the incidents of Twain's fulsome novel but toned down some of its darker aspects. Miller's rambling, country-flavored songs aurally captured the muddy riverbank world, while Heidi Landesman's flexible, versatile set, dominated by a twisting Mississippi River, did the same visually.

Several established producers offered to take *Big River* to New York, but the Landesmans and their cohorts decided to take the plunge themselves. The show received mostly favorable notices, but an extremely tepid review from the almighty *New York Times* dampened the production's chances for longevity. But box office receipts increased every week, and after two months the show was playing to capacity. The Tony Awards helped push *Big River* into hit country.

The choices for the 1984–85 Tonys were slight. There were only three new musicals running at the time: *Big River*, *Grind*, and *Leader of the Pack*. Three Tony categories had to be eliminated (Actor and Actress in a Musical and Choreography) because of a lack of worthy candidates. *River* won seven out of ten awards, including Best Musical, Best Featured Musical Actor (Ron Richardson as Jim), and Best Score. "This is a pretty good deal," exclaimed Miller upon accepting his award.

Ron Richardson played Jim on tour; Brian Lane Green was Huck.

I'M NOT RAPPAPORT

by Herb Gardner

Opened November 19, 1985

890 performances

Booth Theatre, after an off-Broadway run at the American Place Theatre

Directed by Daniel Sullivan

Produced by James Walsh, Lewis Allen, and Martin Heinfling

Cast: Judd Hirsh (Nat); Cleavon Little (Midge); Gregg Almquist (Danforth); Liann Pattison (Laurie); Jace Alexander (Gilley); Cheryl Giannini (Clara); Steve Ryan (Cowboy).

"There is life after Frank Rich," quipped playwright Herb Gardner as he picked up the Best Play Tony Award for his comedy *I'm Not Rappaport*. Rich, the powerful *New York Times* critic, had not favorably reviewed Gardner's whimsical play about two fiesty old men sharing a park bench and a friendship. Despite the thumbs-down from the *Times*, *Rappaport* garnered enough good word-of-mouth to move from its off-Broadway run at the American Place Theatre to Broadway's Booth Theatre.

The two main characters of the play are Nat, a Jew and former left-wing activist, and Midge, an African-American building superintendent. Both are hiding out in a secluded area of Central Park. Midge is avoiding the chairman of the building committee where he works. He knows the chairman is going to force him to retire, because the building is being converted into a co-op and the yuppie tenants want a younger super. Nat wishes to escape from his well-meaning daughter, who wants him either to check into a retirement home or move into her home in the suburbs ("Siberia," Nat calls it).

This senior "Odd Couple" pass the time with stories, which frequently consist of Nat's exaggerations. "Not lies—alterations," he explains to Midge, "I make certain alterations. Sometimes the truth doesn't fit, I take in here and let out there."

Nat is something of a Don Quixote as he attempts to save Midge's job by pretending to be a labor lawyer. The two tilt at windmills together as they also take on a neighborhood thug and try to save a formerly drug-addicted young woman from her pusher.

Gardner's previous Broadway outings featured similar nonconformists. His *A Thousand Clowns* (1962) starred Jason Robards as a scriptwriter who turns his back on conventional society but is forced to take a hack-writer's job in television to keep custody of his nephew. This comedy had a run just short of the 500-mark (428 performances). *The Goodbye People*, about a group of dreamers who meet in the middle of winter on Coney Island, was presented twice on Broadway (1968 and 1979) and failed both times. *Thieves* (1974), which details an urban couple's travails, was beset with production problems and closed after a short run.

Like so many plays of the '80s, *I'm Not Rappaport* went the regional route before trying New York. The play premiered at the Seattle Repertory Theatre. When the production moved to the American Place Theatre, forty-ish actors Judd Hirsch and Cleavon Little convincingly portrayed the seventy-ish Nat and Midge. While Frank Rich's review dampened the show's early success, audiences and many other critics found the comedy touching and true in its depiction of the plight of the aged.

In the title role, Judd Hirsch was voted a Best Actor in a Play Tony. Hirsch and Little also headed the national tour; they were later replaced by Vincent Gardenia and Glynn Turman. Paul Scofield and Howard Rollins were

Nat and Midge in London. Hal Linden and Jack Klugman both took over for Hirsch on Broadway, and Ossie Davis succeeded Little.

Hirsch won a second Tony Award in 1992 for *Conversations with My Father*, another comedy-drama written by Gardner.

THE MYSTERY OF EDWIN DROOD

Book, music, and lyrics by Rupert Holmes. Based on the novel by Charles Dickens.

Opened December 2, 1985

608 performances

Imperial Theatre, after an off-Broadway run at the Delacorte Theatre

Directed by Wilford Leach

Choreography by Graciela Daniele

Produced by Joseph Papp, the New York Shakespeare Festival

Cast: George Rose (Chairman/Mayor Sapsea); Betty Buckley (Edwin Drood/Alice Nutting); Cleo Laine (Princess Puffer/Angela Prysock); Howard McGillin (John Jasper/Clive Paget); Patti Cohenour (Rosa Bud/Deirdre Peregrine); George N. Martin (Rev. Crisparkle/Cedric Moncrieffe); Jana Schneider (Helena Landless/Janet Conover); John Herrera (Neville Landless/Victor Grinstead); Joe Grifasi (Bazzard/Phillip Bax); Jerome Dempsey (Durdles/Nick Cricker); Stephen Glavin (Deputy/Master Nick Cricker); Judy Kuhn (Alice/Isabel Yearsley); Donna Murphy (Beatrice/Florence Gill).

Rupert Holmes's *The Mystery of Edwin Drood* is the only long-running show in which the audience gets to pick the ending. The musical whodunnit is based on Charles Dickens' unfinished 1870 novel of the same name. Because Dickens died before revealing the identity of the murderer of the title character, the musical has multiple possible endings as to who the killer is, and also how the lovers pair up at the end. The audience is balloted for their choice of a solution, which is then enacted for them, and it picks who ends up with whom.

The show is framed by a Victorian music-hall performance, led by an enthusiastic master of ceremonies and, following the custom of the period, the lead male role of Edwin Drood is played by a woman. After Drood disappears and is presumed dead, the emcee reviews the suspects among several intriguing characters. These include Rosa Bud, the victim's angelic former fiancée; Princess Puffer, the mysterious owner of a London opium den; Neville Landless, a visitor from Ceylon; his sphinx-like sister Helena; and John Jasper, Edwin's uncle, who secretly desires Rosa.

Holmes was the second pop composer-performer to cross over to Broadway in 1985. Roger Miller had made the

Chairman George Rose (center) asks the audience to chose a murderer among suspects (left to right) Joe Grifasi, Howard McGillin, George N. Martin, Patti Cohenour, Cleo Laine, John Herrera, and Jana Schneider in *The Mystery of Edwin Drood*.

transition earlier in the year with *Big River*. Like Miller, Holmes had been performing in a nightclub when he was approached to write for the stage. Gail Merrifield, Joseph Papp's wife and the director of play development at the New York Shakespeare Festival, saw Holmes's act and sent a note backstage asking if he would like to write a musical for the Festival. *The Mystery of Edwin Drood* was the result.

"In our house we had one of those complete sets of Dickens you can buy by the yard to fill up your bookshelves, and the last one was *The Mystery of Edwin Drood*," Holmes told the *New York Times*. "I remember my father telling me, 'You know, it's not a mystery like the *The Tower Treasure* or one of those,' and it was never finished. That haunted me, the idea that Dickens never finished it."

The notion of finishing the novel had always fascinated the composer, but he decided to leave the final conclusion to the audience. "I just thought, how would anyone have the chutzpah to finish what Charles Dickens couldn't. I thought, well, there doesn't have to be one ending. Let the audience end it. If they don't like it, they chose it."

In addition to writing the songs (including various finales, depending on who was chosen as the killer), Holmes also arranged the score and wrote the book. The show was presented at the Delacorte Theatre in Central Park, as a part of the Shakespeare Festival's 1985 free summer schedule. After some tightening and refocusing, it followed in the footsteps of other Festival musicals such as *Two Gentlemen of Verona*, *A Chorus Line*, and *The Pirates of Penzance*—it went to Broadway. There was only one cast change. George N. Martin took over the role of Reverend Crisparkle from actor-playwright Larry Shue (*The Foreigner*) who had died in a plane crash.

In Central Park, the show was three hours long with jugglers, magicians, and unicyclists playing prior to Act I to get the audience into the jovial music-hall mood. After waiting for the free tickets all day and picnicking, the audience reacted raucously. Once the musical moved inside to the Imperial Theatre, the audience was less inclined to let go and respond. George Rose in his role of master of ceremonies often ad-libbed lines to whip up the stuffier Broadway audience.

The show was a moderate hit, winning five Tonys and running 608 performances. Why didn't it enter the class of such mega-successes as *A Chorus Line*, *La Cage Aux Folles*, and *Les Misérables*? Because it had been a free show, which turned off prospective ticket buyers? Or because it asked audiences to participate rather than just sit back and watch—too much of a challenge?

The title was officially shortened to *Drood* later in the run in order to give a fresh allure to the show. Loretta Swit and Karen Morrow followed Cleo Laine as Princess Puffer on Broadway while '60s pop singer Lulu played it in London. Jean Stapleton and Clive Revill headed a national tour.

Holmes later wrote two nonmusical mysteries, *Accomplice* (1990) and *Solitary Confinement* (1992), both of which failed on Broadway. A film version of *The Mystery of Edwin Drood*, based on the Dickens novel, was made in 1935.

ME AND MY GIRL

Book and lyrics by L. Arthur Rose and Douglas Furber; book revised by Stephen Fry, with contributions by Mike Ockrent.

Music by Noel Gay

Opened August 10, 1986

1,420 Performances

Marquis Theatre

Directed by Mike Ockrent

Choreographed by Gillian Gregory

Produced by Richard Armitage, Terry Allen Kramer, James M. Nederlander, and Stage Promotions, Ltd.

Cast: Robert Lindsay (Bill Snibson); Maryann Plunkett (Sally Smith); Jane Summerhays (Lady Jacqueline Carstone); Timothy Jerome (Herbert Parchester); Jane Connell (Maria, Duchess of Dene); George S. Irving (Sir John Tremayne); Leo Leyden (Sir Jasper Tring); Nick Ulett (Hon. Gerald Bolingbroke); Eric Hutson (Lord Battersby); Justine Johnson (Lady Battersby); Thomas Toner (Charles Heathersett/Butler); Elizabeth Larner (Lady Diss/Mrs. Brown); Gloria Hodes (Mrs. Worthington-Worthington); Susan Cella (Lady Brighton/Lambeth Tart); Kenneth H. Waller (Bob Barking); Larry Hansen (Footman); John Spalla (Pub Pianist); Bill Brassea (Telegraph Boy); Eric Johnson (Constable).

The 1986–87 Broadway season was marked by a British musical invasion. Three hits from London—*Me and My Girl*, *Les Misérables*, *Starlight Express*—set up camp on Broadway. The first of these was a reworked edition of a 1930s show that had never been seen in America before. The story is a variation on Shaw's *Pygmalion*, in which brash Cockney Bill Snibson is found to be the long-lost 14th Earl of Hareford. The upper-crust executors of the previous Earl's will attempt to teach working-class Bill their aristocratic ways in order to make him fit for his new position. But they insist that he give up his true love, Sally Smith, a fishmonger's assistant. In the end, Sally and Bill are reunited and the Cockneys and bluebloods shake hands.

The story was not original and the songs were pleasant but unmemorable. What distinguished the production was the lively staging and the captivating performance by Robert Lindsay, who won the Olivier Award in London and the Tony in New York. Lindsay's cavorting ranged from Gene Kelly-caliber hoofing to Danny Kaye-like clowning.

The original *Me and My Girl* had opened in London, at the Victoria Palace, in December of 1937. The comic Lupino Lane had created the role of the ingratiating bloke Bill in a 1935 production called *Twenty to One*. The comedian scored such a personal success in the role that he hired the authors (composer Noel Gay and librettists L. Arthur Rose and Douglas Furber) to write another show in which he could play Snibson. The resulting musical, *Me and My Girl*, was an even bigger hit and ran for 1,646 performances. It survived being bombed out of two theatres during the Battle of Britain. The dance number "The Lambeth Walk" became an international dance craze. (Mussolini reportedly danced it at the British Embassy.) A film version of the show was released in 1939.

Nearly fifty years later, producer Richard Armitage, the son of Noel Gay, wanted to refurbish his father's show and present it again in London. He searched extensively to find the original script. His investigations took him from the British Museum to country attics. Once unearthed, it was rewritten, like the books of *Irene* and *My One and Only*, and tunes from other shows of the era were interpolated. Comic author Stephen Fry revised the script, and Michael Ockrent directed and contributed to the book revisions.

Armitage's choice for leading man was an unlikely one. Robert Lindsay was chiefly known as a classical actor. Among his impressive credits were playing Edmund to

Maryann Plunkett and Robert Lindsay in *Me and My Girl*.

Laurence Olivier's *King Lear* on television. Armitage saw Lindsay enacting the title role in a Manchester production of *Hamlet*. When Lindsay got extraordinary laughs for his mad scenes, Armitage was convinced he was the right actor. If he could make *Hamlet* funny, the producer reasoned, he could make Bill Snibson hilarious. For the female lead, Emma Thompson was cast.

The refitted *Me and My Girl* opened to acclaim in London's West End in 1985. The Broadway production, with American actress Maryann Plunkett replacing Thompson and an all-American cast supporting Lindsay, opened the new Marquis Theatre.

Lindsay was succeeded on Broadway by Jim Dale and James Brennan. The national tour was headed by Tim Curry, who was followed by Brennan and James Young.

BROADWAY BOUND

by Neil Simon
Opened December 4, 1986
756 Performances
Broadhurst Theatre
Directed by Gene Saks
Produced by Emanuel Azenberg

Cast: Linda Lavin (Kate); Jonathan Silverman (Eugene); Jason Alexander (Stanley); John Randolph (Ben); Philip Sterling (Jack); Phyllis Newman (Blanche).

Neil Simon concluded his autobiographical trilogy with *Broadway Bound*. Following the events of *Brighton Beach Memoirs* and *Biloxi Blues*, *Broadway Bound* continues the story of Simon's alter-ego Eugene Jerome after he has left the service and starts on a comedy writing career with his brother Stanley. But the third play somewhat shifts the focus away from Eugene to his mother Kate. Just as her two sons are leaving their Brooklyn home, her marriage is ending. Her aging father, Ben, has moved into the house to keep her company, but it doesn't decrease her loneliness. Simon told the *Wall Street Journal*, "I didn't know I was writing a tribute to my mother, but I guess I was."

The author further commented on his development as a writer in the same interview: "I continue to learn the craft. In my later plays I began to provide a background, a context for the material. *Brighton* was set against the Depression and what was happening in Europe; *Biloxi* against World War II; and *Broadway Bound* is set in the midst of the war between my father and mother as their marriage disintegrated. I also think my characters interact better than they used to. Before I had a protagonist and an antagonist and the others were there to serve the main characters. Now each character has a life of his own and interacts with all the others. Another thing I've had to learn is to trust straight drama. In the past, if I went too long without getting a laugh, I got scared and put in a joke. These days I rarely think about jokes. The funny thing is, I now get laughs in the straight scenes, not from one-liners, but from characters or the situation." Indeed, character and situation fueled *Broadway Bound*, not jokes; each member of the Jerome family was a fully-realized character.

Linda Lavin, who had previously appeared in Simon's *Last of the Red Hot Lovers*, triumphed in the role of Kate. Broadway's toughest critic, John Simon of *New York* magazine, wrote: "Linda Lavin lets you see her feelings as if at the bottom of a pond, allows you to follow them from repression to expression. And what the surface of a pond can do with reflections of sun and clouds, her face and voice can shimmeringly match." This was particularly evident during a long, beautifully written scene in which Kate relives the high point of her youth: the night she danced with movie star George Raft in a speakeasy. As she relives that magical moment, dancing with Eugene (Jonathan Silverman), the sad housewife becomes the elegant dancer of thirty years ago.

Kate was later played by Elizabeth Franz (who originated the character in *Brighton Beach Memoirs*) and Joan Rivers on Broadway. Carole Shelley headed the national tour. A TV production was broadcast on ABC during the 1991–92 season, with Anne Bancroft, Jerry Orbach, Jonathan Silverman, and Hume Cronyn, who won an Emmy for his performance as the aged Ben.

Simon continued to dramatize his early days of writing comedy in *Laughter on the 23rd Floor* (1993).

LES MISÉRABLES

by Alain Boublil and Jean-Marc Natel, with additional material by James Fenton. Based on the novel by Victor Hugo.

Adapted by Trevor Nunn and John Caird

Music by Claude-Michel Schonberg

Lyrics by Herbert Kretzmer

Opened March 12, 1987

Still running (2,820 performances as of February 6, 1994)

Broadway Theatre

Directed by Trevor Nunn and John Caird

Produced by Cameron Mackintosh

Cast: Colm Wilkinson (Jean Valjean); Terrence Mann (Javert); Randy Graff (Fantine); Judy Kuhn (Cosette); David Bryant (Marius); Michael Maguire (Enjoiras); Frances Ruffelle (Eponine); Leo Burmester (Thenardier); Jennifer Butt (Mme. Thernadier); Donna Vivino (Young Cosette); Branden Danner (Gavroche);

Chrissie MacDonald (Young Eponine); Norman Large (Bishop of Digne/Lesgles); Jesse Corti (Farmer/Drinker/ Courfeyac); Alex Santoriello (Laborer/Montparnasse); John Norman (Innkeeper/Drunk/Pimp/ Jean Prouvaire); Susan Goodman (Innkeeper's Wife/Old Beggar Woman); Paul Harman (Foreman/Combeferre); Ann Crumb (Factory Girl/Young Prostitute); Cindy Benson (Old Woman); Marcie Shaw (Crone); Steve Shocket (Pimp/Fauchelevent/Claquesous); Anthony Crivello (Bamatabois/Grantaire); Joseph Kolinski (Young Man/Feuilly); Marcus Lovett (Babet); Kevin Marcum (Brujon); John Dewar (Joly); Jane Bodle, Joanna Glushak. Kelli James, Gretchen Kingsley-Weihe (Whores/Women Workers).

The British invasion of Broadway continued with *Les Misérables*, a mammoth musical based on Victor Hugo's 1862 novel. Set in France from 1815 to 1832, the show condensed into three and a half hours Hugo's epic tale of the relentless

pursuit of the saintly Jean Valjean by the intractable officer Javert. Hugo had created the character of Valjean, jailed for stealing a loaf of bread to save a starving child, to expose the social ills of his era. *Les Misérables* journeys from Valjean's dank prison and the grimy kitchen of the Thernadiers to the barricades of a student uprising and the sewers of Paris as Javert attempts to get his man. In addition to the Valjean–Javert chase, most of numerous subplots and subsidiary characters of the novel were retained.

Some critics found the show overly sentimental and calculated. Indeed, the show's unashamedly emotional music and lyrics do bring audiences to their feet. "Les

Miz," as it has been nicknamed, is the second longest-running show on Broadway, as of this writing, and has won acclaim all over the world. (*Cats* ranks first among currently playing productions.)

The theatrical sojourn of *Les Misérables* was almost as circuitous as Valjean's. It began in the country of its setting. French writer Alain Boublil had been inspired by the Broadway production of *Jesus Christ Superstar* to create a show of his own along the same lines: using pop-rock music to tell a large, historically significant story. With the collaboration of composer Claude-Michel Schonberg, among others, Boublil's idea became a musical about the

The company of *Les Misérables* in the Act I finale.

French Revolution. Several years later, Boublil and Schonberg wanted to do another show, but were stuck for an idea.

Then Boublil saw Cameron Mackintosh's London revival of *Oliver!*. Seeing the British musical of the Dickens work gave the Frenchman the notion of adapting *Les Misérables*, another dark novel of roughly the same period and of similar themes, to the stage. Boublil and poet Jean-Marc Natal wrote the lyrics, and Schonberg the music. As with many of the Andrew Lloyd Webber and Tim Rice hits, a recording of the score resulted in a production. On the strength of the album, the show was presented in Paris at the Palais de Sports in 1980.

There was not much enthusiasm outside France to mount the production until Mackintosh heard the tape. Bowled over by the intensity of the score, the producer immediately set about putting it on in London. He persuaded Boublil and Schonberg to revamp the score for the English version. Since Boublil was not proficient in English, Mackintosh hired drama critic and poet James Fenton to write lyrics after Alan Jay Lerner turned the position down. Trevor Nunn, who had staged *Cats,* was signed on to direct. Nunn made it a condition that John Caird should co-direct. (Together, the two had directed the famous stage adaptation of Dickens's *Nicholas Nickleby* at the Royal Shakespeare Company, where Nunn was artistic director.) The musical was to be presented at the nonprofit RSC before moving to a commercial West End run.

Fenton proved too slow at supplying lyrics, so another former drama critic, Herbert Kretzmer, was hired to finish the work.

The role of Valjean was much coveted by actors, and international stars Max Von Sydow and Topol auditioned for it. The plum part went to Irish singer Colm Wilkinson. American star Patti LuPone was cast as Fantine after appearing in a revival of *The Cradle Will Rock* in London.

When the production opened at London's Barbican Center in October of 1985, the critical reaction ranged from polite to nasty. "Victor Hugo on the Garbage Dump," read the headline of the *Observer* review—not exactly a money-making notice. But the combined appeal of the staging, singing, and scoring inspired excellent word of mouth. The subsequent transfers to the West End's Palace Theatre and New York's Broadway Theatre were equally well-received by theatregoers.

In New York, two of the original British cast re-created their roles: Colm Wilkinson and Frances Ruffelle, as Eponine. Equity, the actors' union, objected to Wilkinson's playing on Broadway. Mackintosh countered by refusing to open without Wilkinson for leading man. Equity backed down. Mackintosh would later be involved in similar casting controversies for the Broadway productions of *The Phantom of the Opera* and *Miss Saigon.*

STARLIGHT EXPRESS

Lyrics by Richard Stilgoe
Music by Andrew Lloyd Webber
Opened March 15, 1987
761 Performances
Gershwin Theatre
Directed by Trevor Nunn
Choreographed by Arlene Phillips
Produced by Martin Starger and Lord Grade

Cast: Greg Mowry (Rusty); Steve Fowler (Poppa); Robert Torti (Greaseball); Ken Ard (Electra); Reva Rice (Pearl); Jane Krakowski (Dinah); Andrea MacArdle (Ashley); Jamie Beth Chandler (Buffy); Berry K. Bernal (Red Caboose); Janet Williams Adderly (Belle); Michael Scott Gregory (Dustin); Todd Lester (Flat-Top); A.C. Ciulla (Bobo); Philip Clayton (Espresso); Michael Berglund (Weltschaft); William Frey (Turnov); D. Michael Heath (Hashamoto); Sean McDermott (Prince of Wales); Frank Mastrocola (Rocky I); Sean Grant (Rocky II); Ronald Garza (Rocky III); Angel Vargas (Rocky IV); Christina Youngman (Wrench); Nicole Picard (Joule); Mary Ann Lamb (Volta); Gordon Owens (Purse); Branden Danner (Voice of the Boy); Melanie Vaughan (Voice of the Mother).

"Cats on Wheels" and "The Theme Park Musical" were some of the acerbic descriptions certain commentators applied to *Starlight Express*, Andrew Lloyd Webber's musical about anthropomorphized locomotives on a cross-country race. Like its feline predecessor, *Starlight's* emphasis was on stunning special effects and the visual concept, rather than the content, of the show. It also featured a cast of thirty wearing metallic outfits and roller skates in order to impersonate the locomotives. Unlike *Cats*, this railroad musical did have a plot, though it could not boast having T.S. Eliot as its wordsmith.

The story concerns Rusty, a little steam engine with a big heart entering a cross-country race against Greaseball, a muscular diesel-driven vehicle, and Electra, an androgynous electric train. Rusty hopes to impress the fair Pearl, a svelte sidecar.

Lloyd Webber stated to the *New York Times* that "*Starlight* was a small piece blown out of all proportion." The original intention was for the score to accompany a children's animated TV special. Lloyd Webber had always loved trains. "As a composer, I've always been attracted to the sounds of trains," he told the *New York Post*. "They hiss, they rumble, they chug. Wheels bumping over railroad ties have got to be the most evocative sound in the world."

The animated special fizzled, but Lloyd Webber got the idea of making the show a live one when he saw rollerskaters performing difficult tricks in New York's Central Park. Why not put the actors on wheels? The resulting gargantuan production opened in London in 1984. The theatre was augmented with tracks and ramps that allowed the singing trains to zoom up into the balconies and around the orchestra. The press was not impressed, but audiences were dazzled.

The American edition was not as elaborate and confined the performers to the immediate stage area. Nevertheless, the production cost $8 million on Broadway, the most expensive show to date, with $2 million alone going for the set. Reaching speeds of forty miles an hour, the cast whizzed around the stage of the Gershwin Theatre—and suffered numerous injuries.

Designer John Napier won a Tony for his steel-and-chrome costumes, but was not even nominated for his complicated set, which featured a huge revolving suspension bridge. Ironically, he lost to himself for his settings for another British blockbuster *Les Misérables*.

The enormous costs of running the show made it too expensive to realize a profit on Broadway, despite its almost two-year run. In London, where expenses are not as high, the show was a financial as well as a popular hit.

FENCES

by August Wilson
Opened March 26, 1987
526 Performances
The 46th Street Theatre
Directed by Lloyd Richards
Produced by Carole Shorenstein Hayes

Cast: James Earl Jones (Troy Maxson); Mary Alice (Rose); Courtney B. Vance (Cory); Ray Aranha (Jim Bono); Frankie R. Faison (Gabriel); Charles Brown (Lyons); Karima Miller (Raynell).

Fences was August Wilson's second play in a continuing cycle examining the lives of African-Americans in the 20th century. Each play in the cycle takes place in a separate decade. The author's stated intention is to fill in the gaps in black history. Wilson told *American Theatre* magazine, "I'm taking each decade and looking back at one of the most important questions that blacks confronted in that decade and writing a play about it. Put that together and you have a history."

The first produced play in the series was *Ma Rainey's Black Bottom*, which was presented at the Eugene O'Neill Theatre Center and then at Yale Repertory Theatre before opening on Broadway in 1984. Set in the 1920s, the play depicted of a group of jazz musicians between sets at a recording session. Despite winning the New York Drama Critics Circle Award, *Ma Rainey* closed after a middling run of 274 performances.

Fences, Wilson's next play in the cycle, moved ahead to the 1950s and scored a longer run. In *Ma Rainey*, there had been no central character, not even the singer of the title. However, *Fences* had a formidable protagonist in Troy Maxson, a former baseball player. Born too early to take advantage of the advances made by Jackie Robinson, Troy was forced to stay in the Negro Leagues. Now fifty-

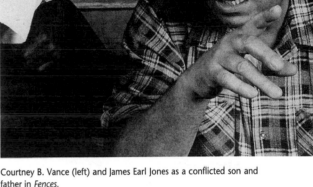

Courtney B. Vance (left) and James Earl Jones as a conflicted son and father in *Fences*.

one and working as a garbage collector, Troy is bitter about his treatment in professional sports—so much so that he will not let his athletically promising son take a football scholarship.

The title refers to a small picket fence Troy is building in his yard, but it also encompasses the barriers he erects between himself and his loved ones. By trying to love and shelter them too much, Troy alienates his son, his wife, and his mentally retarded brother. Set at the advent of the Civil Rights movement, the play shows how the racial discrimination of the previous decades frustrated ambitions to such an extent that it destroys loving families.

Carole Shorenstein Hayes made her solo Broadway producing debut by bringing *Fences* from engagements at the Yale Rep and Chicago's Goodman Theatre to New York. She put $850,000 of her own money in the production, and the investment paid off. Not only did *Fences* cop the Tony, Pulitzer, and a second Critics Circle citation for its author, but it also provided James Earl Jones with the role of a lifetime in Troy. After his burst into stardom in *The Great White Hope*, Jones had performed in Shakespeare, O'Neill, and Steinbeck (as the lumbering giant Lennie in a revival of *Of Mice and Men*), but no production had yet equalled *Hope* in its impact. The actor was acclaimed in *Fences* as being larger than life, filling up the drab dirt-yard setting with great dynamism. Troy's dishonorable actions during the play—he cheats on his wife with a younger woman, who bears his child, and robs his brother of government relief money—in the hands of a lesser actor would have made the character intolerable, but Jones made Troy's humanity the predominant feature of the role. Mary Alice was equally adept as Troy's wife Rose.

Both Jones and Alice won Tony Awards and were succeeded by Billy Dee Williams and Lynn Thigpen during the Broadway run.

Wilson's later plays in his history cycle include *Joe Turner's Come and Gone* (1988), set in the early 1900s; *The Piano Lesson* (1990), which takes place during the 1930s; and *Two Trains Running* (1992), a chronicle of the turbulent 1960s. Like *Ma Rainey* and *Fences*, each of these plays was first produced at regional theatres before moving to Broadway and winning the New York Drama Critics Circle Award. *The Piano Lesson* also received a Pulitzer Prize.

ANYTHING GOES

Book by Timothy Crouse and John Weidman, based on the original book by P.G. Wodehouse and Guy Bolton, Howard Lindsay and Russel Crouse).

Music and lyrics by Cole Porter

Opened October 19, 1987

804 Performances

Vivian Beaumont Theatre

Directed by Jerry Zaks

Choreographed by Michael Smuin

Produced by Lincoln Center Theatre

Cast: Patti LuPone (Reno Sweeney); Howard McGillin (Billy Crocker); Bill McCutcheon (Moonface Martin); Rex Everhart (Elisha Whitney); Anthony Heald (Sir Evelyn Oakleigh); Anne Francine (Mrs. Harcourt); Kathleen Mahony-Bennett (Hope Harcourt); Linda Hart (Erma); David Pursley (Captain); Gerry Vichi (Purser); Stanford Egi (Luke); Toshi Toda (John); Richard Korthaze (minister); Eric Y.L. Chan (Louie).

Lincoln Center Theatre's bubbly revival of Cole Porter's 1934 musical, *Anything Goes*, cemented the theatre's reputation as a producer of shows which could move from the nonprofit sector to the commercial arena. Jerry Zaks, Lincoln Center's resident director, staged the production with zest and ingenuity, making him one of Broadway's most sought-after directors of both plays and musicals.

The production began and ended with the spirit of Porter. As the house light dimmed in Lincoln Center's Vivian Beaumont Theatre, a scratchy recording of the composer singing the title song could be heard. The orchestra then played a jazzy arrangement of the overture. At the finale, a huge picture of Porter descended as if to look down on the merry proceedings from musical comedy heaven. In between these two visitations, the passengers and crew of a luxury liner sailed to Europe on a voyage of mistaken identities and low comedy.

As with many other hit revivals, such as *No, No, Nanette* and *Irene*, the *Anything Goes* book was revised for contemporary audiences. The silly "ship of fools" story was streamlined and the more outdated gags were discarded. Ironically, there were book problems with the first production, in 1934. The original book by British authors P.G. Wodehouse and Guy Bolton had involved a fire on board the ocean liner. The script had to be hastily rewritten when the S.S. *Morro Castle*, an actual ship, caught fire and sank. Wodehouse and Bolton had returned to England, so Howard Lindsay, the show's director, and Russel Crouse, a press agent, were recruited for the job. (This emergency collaboration led to a permanent partnership between them; they later penned *Life with Father*, Broadway's longest-running straight play). The 1987 production's new book was by Timothy Crouse (Russel's son) and John Weidman (son of *Fiorello!* co-author Jerome Weidman). As in the original production, the plot is merely an excuse for the cast to sing such scintillating songs as "I Get a Kick Out of You," "Blow, Gabriel, Blow", and "You're the Top." Some numbers from other Porter shows were added, such as "Friendship" from *DuBarry Was a Lady* and "It's Delovely" from *Red, Hot, and Blue*. "Easy to Love," cut from the first production because the original lead William Gaxton couldn't sing it, was restored for Howard McGillin to warble.

Most reproductions of *Anything Goes* suffered from the indelible memory of Ethel Merman in the original production as the saucy chanteuse–evangelist Reno Sweeney. Patti LuPone, the 1987 Reno, did not attempt to duplicate Merman's brassy style, but brought her own style of belting a song to the show. Bill McCutcheon seemed perfectly cast in the comic role of deadpan gangster Moonface Martin, who is disguised as a minister.

The revival was nominated for ten Tonys and won three (for Best Revival, for Michael Smuin's choreography, and for McCutcheon's supporting performance). It ran for almost two years at the Beaumont, beating the original production's run of 420 performances. Meanwhile Lincoln Center presented its other slated productions in the Mitzi E. Newhouse Theatre, (downstairs from the Beaumont) and in other Broadway theatres.

Leslie Uggams replaced LuPone during the Broadway run and also toured with the production. Rex Smith and Rip Taylor were her traveling co-stars.

The musical was filmed twice, once in 1936 and again in 1956. Both times Bing Crosby starred. Ethel Merman, Charles Ruggles, and Ida Lupino were his shipmates on the first voyage. Jeanmarie, Donald O'Connor, and Mitzi Gaynor were along on the second trip. Also, Ethel Merman re-created her original role in a 1950s TV version, with Frank Sinatra and Bert Lahr.

INTO THE WOODS

Book by James Lapine

Music and lyrics by Stephen Sondheim

Opened November 5, 1987

765 Performances

Martin Beck Theatre

Directed by James Lapine

Choreographed by Lar Lubovitch

Produced by Heidi Landesman, Rocco Landesman, Rick Steiner, M. Anthony Fisher, Frederic H. Mayerson, and Jujamcyn Theatres.

Cast: Bernadette Peters (Witch); Joanna Gleason (Baker's Wife); Chip Zien (Baker); Tom Aldredge (Narrator/Mysterious Man); Robert Westenberg (Wolf/Cinderella's Prince); Danielle Ferdland (Little Red Riding Hood); Ben Wright (Jack); Kim Crosby (Cinderella); Barbara Bryne (Jack's Mother); Joy Franz (Cinderella's Stepmother); Kay McClelland (Florinda); Lauren Mitchell (Lucinda); Edmund Lyndeck (Cinderella's Father); Merle Louise (Cinderella's Mother/Grandmother/Giant); Pamela Winslow (Rapunzel); Chuck Wagner (Rapunzel's Prince); Philip Hoffman (Steward); Jean Kelly (Snow White); Maureen Davis (Sleeping Beauty).

Stephen Sondheim and James Lapine went from the world of modern art in *Sunday in the Park with George* to grown-up fairy tales in *Into the Woods*. The complicated plot connected the traditional stories of Cinderella, Jack and the Beanstalk, Rapunzel, and Little Red Riding Hood with an original story of a baker and his wife who must steal various objects from each of the other characters in order to break the spell of childlessness that the Wicked Witch has placed on them. (The Three Little Pigs and Rumplestiltskin were dropped during the early stages of production.)

Like *Sunday in the Park*, *Into the Woods* had two self-contained acts. Act I is a clever satire on Brothers Grimm–type stories in which everyone, including the Witch, winds up happily ever after. In Act II, the mood turns darker and the characters must pay for their good fortune. The widow of the giant killed by Jack climbs down the beanstalk to seek revenge and wreak havoc on the kingdom. Some commentators saw the giant's wife as a metaphor for the AIDS epidemic, arbitrarily taking lives. But Sondheim and Lapine were addressing larger issues, such as taking responsibility for your actions and putting the interests of the community above those of the individual. "I think the final step in maturity is feeling responsibility for everybody," Sondheim said in a *New York Times* interview. "If I could have written 'no man is an island' I would have. . . . You can't go stealing gold and selling cows for more than they're worth, because it affects everybody else."

Into the Woods, like *Sunday in the Park*, began as a workshop at Playwrights Horizons, but only with a first draft of the book and half the score of the first act. Sondheim originally intended for each character to have his or her own musical style, but this proved too confusing. A remnant of this idea remains in the Witch's rap song. The final form of the score was a series of brief, jaunty tunes which turned darker in the second act.

Bernadette Peters (foreground) and the cast of *Into the Woods* look up in terror at an offstage giant.

After the workshop, *Into the Woods* acquired a brace of producers, including Rocco and Heidi Landesman, who were among those to sponsor *Big River*, another musical based on a classic source about a journey to maturity. The show then traveled to the Old Globe Theatre in San Diego, California, where it received mixed reviews from the Los Angeles newspapers.

After more rewrites and rehearsals, the show began previews for a Broadway opening. Betty Buckley, who had been playing the Witch during the post–San Diego rehearsal period, dropped out and was replaced by Bernadette Peters. It was unusual for this star to be playing an essentially ensemble role. Her name did sell a lot of tickets, helping to achieve a $3.7-million advance.

The show enchanted most of the critics, with the notable exception of the *Times*'s powerful Frank Rich, who had so fiercely supported *Sunday in the Park*. Despite this, the box office was strong and got a big boost when the show won Tonys for Best Score and Book over the more popular *Phantom of the Opera*. Joanna Gleason also won for Best Actress as the sardonic baker's wife. In addition, *Into the Woods* was named Best Musical by the New York Drama Critics Circle and won the Best Original Cast Album Grammy Award.

The Witch was later played by Phylicia Rashad, Betsy Joslyn, Nancy Dussault, and Ellen Foley, who had essayed the role in San Diego. Others appearing in the Broadway replacement company included Dick Cavett, Mary Gordon Murray, and Cynthia Sykes. Murray, Cleo Laine, Charlotte Rae, Rex Robbins, and Kathleen Rowe McAllen toured the country in the national company.

As with *Sunday in the Park*, the original cast returned to the production towards the end of the run for a videotaping of the show for the PBS television *American Playhouse* series.

Sondheim's next musical went even farther afield than *Sunday in the Park* or *Into the Woods*. *Assassins* (1991), with a book by John Weidman, was an odd, revue-like show about people like John Wilkes Booth, who had successfully or unsuccessfully tried to kill United States presidents. It played a limited run off-Broadway at Playwrights Horizons.

THE PHANTOM OF THE OPERA

Book by Richard Stilgoe and Andrew Lloyd Webber, based on the novel by Gaston Leroux.

Music by Andrew Lloyd Webber

Lyrics by Charles Hart and Richard Stilgoe

Opened January 26, 1988

Still running (2,519 performances as of February 6, 1994)

Majestic Theatre

Directed by Harold Prince

Choreographed by Gillian Lynne

Produced by Cameron Mackintosh and the Really Useful Theatre Co.

Cast: Michael Crawford (Phantom); Sarah Brightman (Christine Daae); Steve Barton (Rauol, Victome de Chagny); Judy Kaye (Carlotta Guidicelli); Cris Groenendaal (Monsieur Andre); Nicholas Wyman (Monsieur Firmin); Leila Martin (Madame Giry); David Romano (Ubaldo Piangi); Elisa Heinsohn (Meg Giry); Peter Kevoian (Monsieur Reyer); George Lee Andrews (Don Attilo/Passarino); Kenneth Waller (Monsieur Lefevre); Philip Steele (Joseph Buquet); Beth McVey (Madame Firmin); Richard Warren Pugh (Auctioneer); Jeff Keller (Porter/Marksman); Luis Perez (Slave Master); Barry McNabb (Flunky/Stagehand); Charles Rule (Policeman); Olga Talyn (Page); William Scott Brown (Porter/Fireman); Candace Rogers-Adler (Page); Mary Leigh Stahl (Wardrobe Mistress/Confidante); Rebecca Luker (Princess); Jan Horvath (Innkeeper's Wife).

After the pure spectacle of *Cats* and *Starlight Express*, Andrew Lloyd Webber turned to romance with his musical version of Gaston Leroux's classic 1911 novel *The Phantom of the Opera*. Although the focus of the production was the relationship between the soprano Christine and the facially disfigured composer hiding in the bowels of the Paris Opera, the staging by Harold Prince was as sumptuous and elaborate as any of the other British megahits of the '80s. A slow boat ride through the Opera's underground lake and a crashing chandelier were highlights of a gorgeous production.

Prince had had a string of failures after his direction of Lloyd Webber's *Evita* and Sondheim's *Sweeney*

Michael Crawford has Sarah Brightman under his spell in *The Phantom of the Opera*.

Todd. There followed, in quick succession, *Merrily We Roll Along* (1981), *A Doll's Life* (1982), *Play Memory* (1984), *End of the World* (1984), the off-Broadway revue *Diamonds* (1984); *Grind* (1985); and *Roza* (1987). All were short-lived. Lloyd Webber had offered him *Cats*, but Prince turned it down. The romantic idea of *Phantom* appealed to the director, oddly enough, as an antidote to all the overproduced English spectacle musicals.

Lloyd Webber got the idea of doing his own *Phantom* upon seeing another version on the London stage. This rendition was by Ken Hill and employed excerpts from real operas. The composer thought the material would make an amusing satire of the horror genre, somewhat like *Sweeney Todd*. But upon rereading the original work (which had gone out of print), he was taken in by the romantic angle rather than the scary melodrama and decided to tell the story straight.

For the book and lyrics, he contacted *My Fair Lady* librettist Alan Jay Lerner, who was living in London at the time. But Lerner was in failing health and died before he could begin work. Richard Stilgoe, who contributed to *Cats* and *Starlight Express*, collaborated on the book with Lloyd Webber and provided the lyrics. His work was later augmented by that of Charles Hart.

Lloyd Webber wrote the role of Christine for his wife, Sarah Brightman. After doing the female lead in London, she had to fight for her right to reprise her performance in New York. Actors Equity opposed her appearing in the Broadway production, claiming that she would be denying an American the career-making role. Exceptions to this rule of foreign actors appearing on Broadway could be allowed only in the case of international stars, Equity ruled, but Brightman did not qualify for this status. The composer challenged the ruling, and Brightman was permitted to topline the musical for six months, provided that an American actress was given an equivalent role in a London show. This obligation was fulfilled when American Ann Crumb starred in the British premiere of Lloyd Webber's next musical, *Aspects of Love*.

Phantom scored resoundingly in both New York and London and is still playing at publication time in both cities, as well as in numerous others around the world.

Since Leroux's novel is in the public domain, numerous other *Phantom* musicals have appeared on the horizon before and since the Lloyd Webber version. The most hardy of these features a score by Maury Yeston and a book by Arthur Kopit. Their *Phantom* crops up in numerous regional and touring productions.

Lloyd Webber's *Aspects of Love*, based on David Garnett's novel, was a hit in London, but not on Broadway when it opened there in 1990. The composer followed *Aspects* with a musical retelling of the film *Sunset Boulevard* (1993).

SARAFINA!

by Mbongeni Ngema

Music by Hugh Masekela and Mbongeni Ngema

Opened January 28, 1988

597 Performances

Cort Theatre, after an off-Broadway run at Mitzi E. Newhouse Theatre at Lincoln Center.

Directed by Mbongeni Ngema

Choreographed by Mbonyeni Ngema, and Ndaba Mhlongo

Produced by Lincoln Center Theatre

Cast: Leleti Khumalo (Sarafina); Baby Cele (Mistress It's a Pity); Ntomb'khona Dlamini (Magundane); Khumbuzile Dlamini (Scabba); Pat Mlaba (Colgate); Lindiwe Dlamini (Teaspoon); Dumisani Dlamini (Crocodile); Congo Hadebe (Silence); Nhlanhla Ngema (Stimela Sase-Zola); Mhlanthli Khuzwayo (S'Ginci/Police Sargeant); Nonhlanhla Mbambo (Dumadu); Linda Mchunu (China); Lindiwe Helengwa (Lindiwe); Zandile Hlengwa (Zandile); Siboniso Khumalo (Siboniso); Cosmas Sithole (Timba); Thandani Mavimbela (Priest); Charnele Dozier Brown (Charnele); Mubi Mofokeng (Mubi); Nandi Ndlovu (Mandi); Thandekile Nhlanhla (Thandekile); Pumi Shelembe (Police Lieutenant); Kipzane Skweyiya (Kipzane); Regina Taylor (Regina); Thandi Zulu (Thandi).

Lincoln Center Theatre had two hit musicals on Broadway during the 1987–88 season. One, *Anything Goes*, took place on a luxury liner in the 1930s, where the worst that could happen is being mistaken for a famous gangster or falling in love with the wrong beautiful girl. The locale of the other show, *Sarafina!*, was a school in apartheid-riven South Africa, where black students are accompanied to classes by tanks, soldiers, and attack dogs.

The musical is set in Morris Isaacson High School near Soweto, the site of a real-life student uprising in 1976. Students gathered to protest the use of Afrikaans, the tongue of the ruling white minority, rather than English, as the official language of their lessons. During the year, police and soldiers killed several hundred of the dissident students.

In 1986, composer and director Mbongeni Ngema, who had had two previous productions presented in New York (*Woza Albert!* and *Asinamali*), created a theatre piece about the heroic children. The new show would employ Mbaqanga, the popular music of the South African townships. With the sponsorship of the Committed Artists Company of the Market Theatre of Johannesburg, Ngema recruited twenty-three South African performers, many of them teenagers and amateurs. Under Ngema's tutelage, the young company learned how to sing, dance, and act.

The loose storyline follows the students' efforts to mount a show in honor of the imprisoned leader Nelson Mandela. The children are led by Sarafina, a brave girl who had once been arrested and tortured. Despite government repression, their instructor, Mistress It's a Pity, teaches them about such heroes as Mandela and Steven Biko. As a reminder of the presence of the military, the set is surrounded by barbed wire and the musicians are dressed in khaki. The show climaxes with the students discarding their drab school uniforms and bowlers in favor of colorful African garb.

Gregory Mosher, then artistic director of Lincoln Center Theatre, presented *Sarafina!* on the theatre's Mitzi E. Newhouse stage, in October of 1987. The reception for the company's youthful energy was positive.

After a three-month run at the Newhouse, *Sarafina!* moved to Broadway's Cort Theatre. The production was nominated for five Tonys, including Best Musical and Best Featured Actress in a Musical (Leleti Khumalo in the title role).

This South African show was one of the few Broadway musicals of the 1980s to be made into a film. Khumalo repeated her performance in the 1992 movie version, which starred Whoopi Goldberg.

M. BUTTERFLY

by David Henry Hwang

Opened March 20, 1988

777 Performances

Eugene O'Neill Theatre

Directed by John Dexter

Produced by Stuart Ostrow and David Geffen

Cast: John Lithgow (René Gallimard); B.D. Wong (Song Liling); John Getz (Marc/Man #2/Sharpless); Rose Gregorio (Helga); George N. Martin (M. Toulon/Man #1/Judge); Lindsay Frost (Renee/Woman at Party/Girl in Magazine); Lori Tan Chinn (Comrade Chin/Suzuki/Shu Fang); Alec Mapa, Chris Odo, Jamie H.J. Guan (Kurogo).

Like *Equus* and *Agnes of God*, *M. Butterfly* was a hit psychological drama based on a true story. In 1986, David Henry Hwang, an Asian-American playwright with numerous off-Broadway credits, read a newspaper item about a French diplomat named Bernard Bouriscot who was on trial for treason. He had been engaged in a twenty-year affair with a Chinese actress who, unbeknownst to him, was not only a spy but also a man. Hwang deduced that Boursicot had fallen in love with a stereotyped image of a blushing Asian beauty rather than a real person, since the woman he loved did not even exist. The playwright saw parallels between this bizarre news story and the opera *Madama Butterfly*, by Puccini, in which a Japanese bride kills herself over the American naval officer who marries and then deserts her. The diplomat was seeking another Butterfly, the creation of a sentimental Western mind.

Hwang wanted to make a musical based on this theme and went to producer Stuart Ostrow with the idea. Ostrow was intrigued with the possibilities and bankrolled the project. The result was not a musical, but it did feature a musical score by Lucia Hwong.

In Hwang's finished script, the diplomat is named René Gallimard. Like Dysart in *Equus* and Livingstone in *Agnes of God*, he tells his story through flashbacks. He meets his "Butterfly" in Beijing in 1960. She is Song Liling, a performer with the Peking Opera. Song seduces him, and over

the next two decades obtains information on French and American involvement in the Vietnam War. When Song reveals the truth to Gallimard, preconceived notions about race and gender are turned inside out. Gallimard has become Butterfly, the true lover abandoned by a man.

Ostrow took the bold step of presenting the play directly on Broadway rather than routing it though off-Broadway or regional theatres, which was now the norm for most straight plays in America.

John Dexter, director of the theatrical *Equus*, staged the play with imaginative flair, borrowing elements of the Chinese Opera and the classical Japanese Noh Theatre. His

John Lithgow and B.D. Wong in *M. Butterfly*.

production was enhanced by the striking costumes and set by designer Eiko Ishioka.

John Lithgow, a popular character actor of both stage and screen, created a pitiable Gallimard deceived more by his own insecurities than by a treacherous transvestite. B.D. Wong made a splashy debut as the mysertious Song, winning many awards, including the Tony, Drama Desk, Theatre World, and Outer Critics Circle Awards for his convincing two gender performance.

John Rubinstein, David Dukes, and Tony Randall later played Gallimard. Wong was succeeded by Alec Mapa. Anthony Hopkins played Gallimard in London. David Cronenberg directed the 1993 film with Jeremy Irons and John Lone. Like *Equus*, *M. Butterfly* lost its impact on the screen and was a pale copy of the stage production.

Madama Butterfly would serve as the inspiration of another Broadway hit just three years later, *Miss Saigon*.

RUMORS

by Neil Simon

Opened November 17, 1988

531 Performances

Broadhurst Theatre

Directed by Gene Saks

Produced by Emanuel Azenberg

Cast: Ron Leibman (Lenny Ganz); Jessica Walter (Claire Ganz); Christine Baranski (Chris Gorman), Mark Nelson (Ken Gorman); Joyce Van Patten (Cookie Cusack); Andre Gregory (Ernie Cusack); Ken Howard (Glenn Cooper); Lisa Banes (Cassie Cooper); Charles Brown (Welch); Cynthia Darlow (Pudney).

After reflecting upon his own past in his *Brighton Beach* trilogy, Neil Simon decided to lighten up with *Rumors*, his first attempt at an all-out farce. The hilarity begins when four couples arrive at the palatial estate of the deputy mayor of New York to celebrate the host couple's tenth anniversary. What the guests find is the husband lying in bed with a gunshot wound and the wife nowhere to be found. Complications ensue as the first arrivals attempt to keep the offstage host's condition a secret from the tardier guests. This gives rise to the rumors of the title. In addition, everyone has a physical mishap of some kind. Car doors are slammed on hands, gunshots cause temporary deafness, and fingers are burned on hot trays. There are also gags about mistaken identities, silly names, contemporary crazes (one wife is obsessed with crystals), and the competence (or lack thereof) of elected officials.

All the characters, except for two police officers who come to investigate, are white, upper-class professionals, the same class of citizens who make up the majority of today's Broadway audiences. The play's long run can be partly attributed to theatregoers' age-old zest for seeing people not unlike themselves being made fools of on the stage.

The wild farce played the Old Globe Theatre in San Diego before moving to Broadway. Ron Leibman drew praise as the most manic of the distracted guests. Christine Baranski won her second Tony Award as a lawyer who has just quit smoking and is desperate for a cigarette.

Greg Mulvaney, Alice Playten, Veronica Hamel, Dick Latessa, and Larry Linville were some of the farceurs who replaced the original cast on Broadway. Peter Marshall, Patty McCormick, Heather MacRae, and Kendis Chappell appeared in the touring company.

Some critics were disappointed that Simon had delivered a purely joke-driven play. He resumed writing comedy-drama about people based on his own family with his next play, *Lost in Yonkers* (1991).

BLACK AND BLUE

Conceived by Claudio Segovia and Hector Orezzoli

Music by Duke Ellington, Fats Waller, Benny Goodman, Eubie Blake, and Andy Razaf

Opened January 26, 1989

824 Performances

Minskoff Theatre

Directed by Claudio Segovia and Hector Orezzoli

Choreographed by Cholly Atkins, Henry LeTang, Frankie Manning, and Fayard Nicholas

Produced by Mel Howard and Donald K. Donald

Cast: Ruth Brown, Linda Hopkins, Carrie Smith, Bunny Briggs, Ralph Brown, Lon Chancy, Jimmy Slyde, Dianne Walker, Cyd Glover, Savion Glover, Dormeshia Sumbay, Kyme.

Black and Blue was yet another revue focusing on African-American entertainers and music. It even contained many of the same songs as could be found in *Ain't Misbehavin'*, *Bubbling Brown Sugar*, and *Sophisticated Ladies*. But *Black and Blue* differed from these other "nostalgic" shows in its European perspective.

In the period between the two world wars, many African-American performers like Josephine Baker, Adelaide Hall, and Paul Robeson emigrated to Europe, where they enjoyed celebrity status in place of the second-class citizenship they endured in the States. They starred in elaborate productions and played to adoring audiences fascinated with "le jazz hot." Claudio Segovia and Hector Orezzoli, a pair of Argentinian enterpeneurs residing in Paris, had the idea of recreating the elegant shows in which these black performers had headlined. The pair had had previous successes with such specialty revues as *Tango Argentino* and *Flamenco Puro*, two dance shows which played both Broadway and on international tours.

Black and Blue opened in Paris at the Chatelet Theatre for a limited engagement of eight weeks. It remained for the entire season. The subsequent Broadway production was budgeted at $5 million and the theatregoer could see every penny of it reflected onstage. Costumes were festooned with as many beads, bangles, feathers, and jewels as they could hold. The sets were decorated with yards and yards of drapes and curtains. The large cast featured singers Ruth Brown, Linda Hopkins, and Carrie Smith; veteran hoofers like Bunny Briggs, Jimmy Slyde, Ralph Brown, and Lon Chaney; younger dancers such as Savion and Cyd Glover, and Dormeshia Sumby; and a thirteen-piece onstage orchestra.

Some critics found the lavishness at odds with the blues. Ruth Brown wore a tiara while singing about her second-hand furniture store in "If I Can't Sell It, I'll Keep Sitting on It." Carrie Smith warbled "Am I Blue" on a high swing while the train of her dress fell eighteen feet to the stage. The title number, performed as a heartbreaking lament in *Ain't Misbehavin'*, was a rousing showstopper here. The numbers in *Black and Blue* were not presented for social commentary. William A. Henry III of *Time* magazine suc-

cinctly stated the show's premise: "Infuse a 1940s Harlem nightclub act with a Busby Berkeley film's lavish budget, elbow room and staging style, restrain the raunch and remove the racial bitterness. The result: *Black and Blue*."

The lack of a sharp edge did not prevent the show from running 824 performances and winning three Tonys. Ruth Brown was replaced by LaVern Baker during the New York run. Robert Altman filmed a television version of the show, which was broadcast on PBS in 1993.

JEROME ROBBINS' BROADWAY

Conceived by Jerome Robbins, with numbers by various authors, including Leonard Bernstein, Betty Comden and Adolph Green, Jule Styne, Stephen Sondheim, Richard Rodgers and Oscar Hammerstein II, Jerry Bock and Sheldon Harnick.

Opened February 26, 1989

634 Performances

Imperial Theatre

Directed and choreographed by Jerome Robbins

Produced by The Shubert Organization, Roger Berlind, Suntory International Corp., Bryon Goldman, and Emanuel Azanberg.

Cast: Jason Alexander (The Setter, etc.); Scott Wise (Riff, etc.); Debbie Shapiro (Hildy, Mazeppa, etc.); Faith Prince (Ma, Tessie, etc.); Charlotte d'Amboise (Anita, Peter Pan); Robert La Fosse (Gaby, Tony, etc.); Jane Lanier ("Mr. Monotony" Dancer, etc.); Mary Ellen Stuart (Claire); Nancy Hess (Dolores Dolores/Fruma-Sarah); Michael Kubala (Ozzie/3rd Protean); Joey McNeely (2nd Protean/King Simon); David Lowenstein (1st Workman); Alexia Hess (Maria/Ivy); Nicholas Garr (Bernardo); Donna Di Meo (Graziella/Wendy); Dorothy Benham ("Somewhere" Soloist); Barbara Yeager (Narrator); Susan Kikuchi (Eliza); Linda Talcott (Little Eva/Michael); JoAnn M. Hunter (Topsy); Barbara Hoon (Uncle Thomas); Irene Cho (Angel/George); Mary Ann Lamb (Louise); Steve Ochoa (John); Susan Fletcher (Electra/Golde); Troy Myers (Pontdue); Michael Scott Gregory (Chief of Police); Tom Robbins (Life Guard/Lazar Wolf); Luis Perez ("Mr. Montony" Dancer); Michael Lynch (Motel Kamzoil); Andi Tyler (Tzeitel).

The 1988–89 Broadway season produced no new musicals of note. Mediocre shows such as *Legs Diamond, Welcome to the Club*, and *Starmites* proliferated despite persistent failure and even received multiple Tony nominations due to a lack of competition. It seemed as if the Broadway musical was in serious trouble. The only hit musical at the season's midway point was *Black and Blue*, a Parisian-style revue. *Jerome Robbins' Broadway* was also a backward-looking show, but it was like a sparkling fountain in the desert. The retrospective took a fond glance at the twenty-year Broadway career of the director and choreographer of such hits as *On the Town* (1944) and *Fiddler on the Roof* (1964), after which he retreated to the less-pressured world of ballet. In total, Robbins worked on fifteen Broadway musicals. Nine of these were represented in excerpts. Also included was the "Comedy Tonight" number from *A Funny Thing Happened on the Way to the Forum*, which Robbins had created during out-of-town tryouts for the Sondheim–Gelbart–Shevelove show but did not receive program credit for.

Another such number was "Mr. Monotony," an Irving Berlin specialty song dropped from *Miss Liberty* and then *Call Me Madam*. The remainder of the show was like a visit with old friends: the sailors from *On the Town* cavorting in wartime New York; the bathing beauties and Keystone Kops dashing through the seaside ballet from

The entire company in the closing number from *Jerome Robbins' Broadway.*

High Button Shoes; the rival *West Side Story* gangs clashing; the gaudy strippers of *Gypsy* brassily displaying their individual talents; the colorful "Small House of Uncle Thomas" from *The King and I*; the Russian-Jewish community of *Fiddler on the Roof* celebrating a wedding; and, soaring above it all, the airborne Peter Pan.

The numbers were held together by a narrator character played by Jason Alexander, who slipped into a few of the scenes as Pseudolus, from *Forum*, and Tevye, from *Fiddler*.

Jerome Robbins' Broadway was, in many senses, the biggest show in years. It had the largest cast (sixty-two), the longest rehearsal period (twenty-two weeks), the most lengthy period of previews (seven weeks), the then-highest ticket price ($55), and one of the biggest budgets ($8 million).

The retrospective was originally intended as a much more modest single-performance program, with the dancers in rehearsal clothes, in order to preserve Robbins' work on videotape. Except for the film versions of *West Side Story* and *Fiddler on the Roof*, none of the choreographer's Broadway work had been recorded. One of Robbins' collaborators, librettist Betty Comden, told *Newsweek*: "There was no system of dance notation years ago, and no video to record moves, so dances were lost. They just remained in people's memories." Members of the original casts of the shows, like Nanette Fabray, Comden and her partner Adolph Green, Nancy Walker, and Cris Alexander, came in to help recall details of the numbers as they were first performed.

At Tony Award time, there was a small controversy over whether the show should be considered as a Best Musical or Best Revival nominee, since almost all the material had been seen on Broadway before. Because of the woefully limited number of candidates, the show was nominated and won in the Best New Musical category. Tonys also went to Robbins himself (for Best Director) and cast members Jason Alexander, Debbie Shapiro, and Scott Wise. Alexander's narrator role was later played by Terrence Mann and Tony Roberts.

Like a great many shows of the '80s and '90s, *Jerome Robbins' Broadway*'s production costs were so high that it did not realize a profit.

THE HEIDI CHRONICLES

by Wendy Wasserstein

Opened March 9, 1989

621 Performances

The Plymouth, after an off-Broadway run at Playwrights Horizons

Directed by Daniel Sullivan

Produced by the Shubert Organization, Suntory International Corp., and James Walsh

Cast: Joan Allen (Heidi Holland); Boyd Gaines (Peter Patrone); Peter Friedman (Scoop Rosenbaum); Ellen Parker (Susan Johnson); Anne Lange (Jill, Debbie, Lisa); Joanne Camp (Fran, Molly, Betsy, April); Cynthia Nixon (Becky, Clara, Denise); Drew McVety (Chris, Mark, TV Attendant, Waiter, Ray).

As the 1980s drew to a close, playwright Wendy Wasserstein took a retrospective look at the women's movement through the life and times of art historian Heidi Holland in *The Heidi Chronicles*. Over the course of twenty years and in four cities, Heidi experiences school dances and group encounter sessions, protest marches and power lunches, aerobic classes and the AIDS crisis, frustrated love and adopting a baby.

Joan Allen and Peter Friedman meet at a 1968 mixer in *The Heidi Chronicles*.

Wasserstein was one of many American playwrights accused by *New York Times* critic Benedict Nightengale (an Englishman) of writing "diaper dramas," plays that were largely concerned with authors' unhappy childhoods and unresolved relations with parents; he stated that these dramatists should address social and political issues, as their British counterparts did. Wasserstein answered this charge with *Heidi*, which parallels the heroine's emotional development in a changing world.

The play was written in London on a grant from the National Theatre British American Arts Association. "I didn't write it to be a commercial play," Wasserstein said. "I didn't think people would say, 'A play about a female art historian who becomes sad? Oh, let's go see that. It sounds really hot.' I really wrote it for me."

When manuscript was finished, the author felt it needed further development. "Between my last play, *Isn't It Romantic?* and *Heidi*, I had done a musical called *Miami* that didn't work out. It was exposed to the public and got reviewed too early. I felt that with my next play I wanted to protect it. I didn't want any word of mouth until it was ready."

Heidi then began a journey from regional theatre to off-Broadway that has become typical for most plays on their way to production on Broadway. After an initial reading at Playwrights Horizons, the play was taken to a theatre far from New York, Seattle Repertory Theatre, which had been instrumental in the development of another hit play, *I'm Not Rappaport*. Seattle Rep mounted a workshop production of *Heidi*.

"Then we had another reading in New York and I rewrote it again," Wasserstein recalled. "We then started rehearsals for a full production at Playwrights Horizons. My hopes for it were that it would move off-Broadway.... But Dan Sullivan [the director] said it would work better in a larger house. The theatre at Seattle Rep is actually based on the Plymouth on Broadway, which is where we did move.

In the move there was only one cast change; Cynthia Nixon replaced Sarah Jessica Parker, who had a film commitment. In a Broadway season with very few straight plays, *Heidi* became a hit and won every award available.

Wasserstein accounted for *Heidi*'s popularity: "At the time I wasn't seeing women on the stage. A whole generation of professional women were not being represented and these are people who buy tickets. So I think they were glad to finally see themselves. It appealed to men as well. I used to run into these men in the back of the theatre and they'd say, 'I almost didn't come because I thought it was a girls' play, but, you know, it's really good."

The Heidi Chronicles ran for over a year. Joan Allen originated the title role and was succeeded by Christine Lahti, Brooke Adams, and Mary McDonnell.

GRAND HOTEL: THE MUSICAL

Book by Luther Davis, based upon the novel by Vicki Baum.

Music and lyrics by Robert Wright and George Forrest; additional music and lyrics by Maury Yeston.

Opened November 12, 1989

1,077 Performances

Martin Beck Theatre

Directed and choreographed by Tommy Tune

Produced by Martin Richards, Mary Lea Johnson, Sam Crothers, Sander Jacobs, Kenneth D. Greenblatt, Paramount Pictures, and Jujamcyn Theatres

Cast: David Carroll (Baron Felix Von Gaigern); Liliane Montevecchi (Elizaveta Grushinskaya); Timothy Jerome (Gen. Dr. Preysing); Jane Krakowski (Flaemmchen); Michael Jeter (Otto Kringelein); Karen Akers (Raffaela); John Wylie (Col. Dr. Otternschlag); Rex D. Hays (Rohna); Bob Stillman (Erik); Ben George (Chauffeur); Hal Robinson (Zinnowitz); Mitchell Jason (Sandor); Michael Moinot (Witt); Kathi Moss (Mme. Peepee); Yvonne Marceau (Countess); Pierre Dulaine (Gigolo); David Jackson, Danny Strayhorn (The Jimmys); Charles Mandracchia (Doorman); Suzanne Henderson (Courtesan); Ken Jennings (Georg Strunk); Keith Crowningshield (Kurt Kronenberg); Gerrit de Beer (Hanns Bittner); J.J. Jepson (Willibald); Jennifer Lee Andrews (Hildegarde Bratts); Suzanne Henderson (Sigfriede Holzheim); Lynette Perry (Wolffe Bratts/Maid); Henry Grossman (Ernst Schmidt); William Rydall (Franz Kohl); David Elledge (Werner Holst); Walter Willison (Gunther Gustafsson).

Grand Hotel: The Musical was another step in the development of musicals away from separate song, dance, and dialogue scenes and toward a total integration of the three. It also solidified Tommy Tune's stardom among director-choreographers. Stellar performers were no longer the dominant force in musical theatre. The man or woman behind the scene who put the show in motion was often the main attraction.

In this case, Tune created an intermissionless "theatrical ballet" in which style and staging overcame a weak book and score. The show is based on Vicki Baum's 1927 novel *Menschen im Hotel*, which became a 1930 Broadway play and a classic 1932 MGM film, with John and Lionel Barrymore, Wallace Beery, Joan Crawford, and Greta Garbo. The novel is the first major success in the "intersecting lives" genre, in which several stories and characters revolve around a single setting. The Grand Hotel in Berlin serves as the stopover for five disparate, and desperate, people with time running out. The aristocratic Baron is forced to purloin jewelry to pay off debts. The aging ballerina is losing her talent, while the blustering business executive is losing his empire. The timid clerk has a fatal disease and determines to live his remaining days in luxury. The pretty secretary dreams of going to Hollywood but is saddled with an unwanted pregnancy. These five collide in the lobby, corridors, suites, and ballrooms of the Grand Hotel.

Like Michael Bennett's staging of *Dreamgirls*, Tune's direction was the stage equivalent of cinematic storytelling: short, fast scenes, and endless movement. There was no interruption for set changes, for the only scenery was a row of chairs and a long pole to suggest a bar. Often two or three scenes would occur simultaneously. Musical numbers did-

Lilianne Montevecchi, David Carroll, and Karen Akers are three of the many guests at *Grand Hotel: The Musical*.

n't begin or end in the traditional sense, but flowed into the dialogue and out again without stopping, like a river of rhythm. Dances of the period—the fox trot, Charleston, tango, and bolero—were performed ceaselessly and commented on the action.

Tune had long wanted to do a musical version of *Grand Hotel*, but found out that one had already been mounted. It was called *At the Grand*, with book by Luther Davis and score by George Forrest and Robert Wright (*Song of Norway, Kismet*). It had played in Los Angeles and San Francisco in 1958, with Paul Muni as Kringelein, the dying clerk, and Joan Diener in the role of the ballerina, which had been changed to that of an opera singer in order to suit Diener's talents. *At the Grand* had never reached New York.

Between 1958 and '89, the authors had rewritten the script, and Tune expressed interest in staging it. But he wanted it totally redone. The director decided to develop the show in a New York workshop held in the lobby of the decrepit Hotel Diplomat. The script and score were used as a springboard for improvisations. Scenes and songs were taken apart, put back together, cut, edited, and rearranged.

Collaborators from previous Tune shows, songwriter Maury Yeston and book author Peter Stone, were sum-moned in Boston to augment the Wright–Forrest score and Davis' book. Yvonne Marceau and Pierre Dulaine, founders of the American Ballroom Theatre, were added to the cast as an allegorical couple dancing through the intertwining stories.

Once *Grand Hotel* reached Broadway, reviews were mixed. Most praised Tune's impressionistic, fluid staging, but critics were disappointed by the script. Linda Winer of *Newsday* dismissed the book as "drivel." Frank Rich of the *New York Times* said, "Mr. Tune has built the grandest hotel imaginable in *Grand Hotel*. It would be a happier occasion if so many of its rooms weren't vacant."

The box office was in trouble owing to the cool critical reception. But *Grand Hotel* won five Tonys, including two for Tune and one for Michael Jeter for his heart-tugging turn as Kringelein. Jeter's big Charleston number was shown on the Tony Awards telecast and bolstered the box office for a Broadway run of over two years.

The Baron was played by David Carroll; he was succeeded by Brent Barrett, Rex Smith, and John Schneider. The ballerina was enacted by Lilianne Montevecchi, and later René Ceballos, Cyd Charisse, and Zina Bethune. A national tour starred Montevecchi, Barrett, and Mark Baker as Kringelein.

GYPSY

Book by Arthur Laurents

Music by Jule Styne

Lyrics by Stephen Sondheim

Opened November 16, 1989

582 Performances

St. James Theatre

Directed by Arthur Laurents

Choreographed by Jerome Robbins (re-created by Bonnie Walker)

Producers: Barry and Fran Weissler, Kathy Lewis and Barry Brown.

Cast: Tyne Daly (Rose); Jonathan Hadary (Herbie); Crista Moore (Louise); Tracy Venner (June); Robert Lambert (Tulsa); Barbara Erwin (Miss Crachit/Tessie Tura); Jana Robbins (Mazeppa); Anna McNeely (Electra); Lori Ann Mahl (Agnes); Christen Tassin (Baby June); Kristen Mahon (Baby Louise); Tony Hoty (Uncle Jocko/Kringelein); John Remme (George/Goldstone); Bobby John Carter (Clarence); Jeana Haege (Balloon Girl); Ronn Carroll (Pop/Cigar); Mace Barrett (Weber/Phil); Bruce Moore (Yonkers); Craig Waletzko (L.A.); Ned Hannah (Kansas); Paul Geraci (Flagstaff); Alec Timerman (St. Paul); Jim Bracchitta (Pastey/Bougeron-Cochon); Ginger Prince (Maid).

This was a highly successful revival of the 1959 musical. It even re-created the original choreography by Jerome Robbins. Readers should consult the history of the show on page 154.

CITY OF ANGELS

Book by Larry Gelbart

Music by Cy Coleman

Lyrics by David Zippel

Opened December 11, 1989

878 Performances

Virginia Theatre

Directed by Michael Blakemore

Choreographed by Walter Painter

Produced by Nick Vanoff, Roger Berlind, Jujamcyn Theatres, Suntory International Corp., and the Shubert Organization

Cast: Gregg Edelman (Stine); James Naughton (Stone); Kay McClelland (Bobbi/Gabby); Dee Hoty (Alaura/Carla); René Auberjonois (Irwin S. Irving/Buddy Fidler); Randy Graff (Oolie/Donna); Scott Waara (Jimmy Powers); Rachel York (Mallory/Avril); Shawn Elliott (Munoz/Pancho Vargas); James Cahill (Dr. Mandril/Barber); Keith Perry (Luther Kinglsey/Werner Kriegler); Doug Tompos (Peter Kingsley/Gerald Pierce); Peter David, Amy Jane London, Gary Kahn, Jackie Presti (Angel City 4); Herschel Sparber (Big Six/Studio Guard); Raymond Xifo (Sonny/Studio Guard); Tom Galantich (Officer Pasco/Gene); Carolee Carmello (Margaret/Stand-In); James Hindman (Mahoney/Del DaCosta); Alvin Lum (Yamato/Cinematographer); Evan Thompson (Commissioner Gaines/Shoeshine); Eleanor Glockner (Margie/Anna/Hairdresser); Jacquey Maltby (Bootsie).

While *Grand Hotel* emphasized movement and staging, *City of Angels*, the other new hit musical of the 1989–90

James Naughton and Dee Hoty are gumshoe and gorgeous client in *City of Angels*.

season, stressed the plot and the songs. Larry Gelbart's dazzlingly funny book not only spoofed detective films of the late '40s, but went one step further by profiling the screenwriter of the movie-within-the-play and his personal life.

Composer Cy Coleman, whose diverse output had included such hits as *Sweet Charity, I Love My Wife,* and *Barnum,* contributed a jazzy score for which newcomer David Zippel penned intricately clever lyrics. Coleman had originally wanted to write a score for a show set in the 1940s using the jazz styles of that decade. "I think people are hungry for mainstream American musical language on Broadway," the composer told *Newsweek.* "I did this show out of a sense of frustration. I wanted jazz riffs, tempos, and rhythms that hadn't been heard on Broadway in a long while." He mentioned the idea to Gelbart, whose credits ranged from TV's *MASH* to Broadway's *Sly Fox* and *A Funny Thing Happened on the Way to the Forum,* co-authored with Burt Shevelove. The writer came up with the idea of a private-eye show he tentatively titled *Death Is for Suckers.*

Zippel joined the team at this point, and Gelbart deepened his original concept by adding the story of the writer of the movie detective yarn. The work was now titled *Double Exposure.* The collaborators communicated by fax and Federal Express, since Gelbart was in Los Angeles and Coleman and Zippel were in New York.

Gelbart's finished script, ultimately called *City of Angels,* pitted mystery writer Stine against his fictional creation, the gumshoe Stone, as the former is preparing the screen treatment of his novel, entitled *City of Angels.* Director Michael Blakemore (*Noises Off*) got the idea of dividing the stage, with the movie world of Stone in black and white on one side, and the real-life Hollywood of Stine in full color on the other. The story switched back and forth from the case Stone was cracking and the world of compromises in which Stine must write and rewrite his screenplay. Characters in the real and fictional settings parallel each other. Stone trades blows and quips with shady gangsters and mysterious heiresses, while Stine does battle with shallow movie producers, rapacious starlets, and his own conscience as his story is torn to shreds by the studio.

The score was full of brilliant duets between the film-noir and the "real" characters. In "What You Don't Know About Women," Stine's wife Gabby and Stone's secretary Oolie vocalize about the men in their lives. "You're Nothing Without Me" is a grudge match between the writer and his creation. ("I tell you, you're out of my mind," Stine sings.)

City of Angels opened to mostly favorable reviews. At the Tony Awards, the spoils were divided between *City of Angels* and *Grand Hotel,* with the former winning five, including Best Choreography and Direction and the latter taking six, including Best Score, Book, and the biggest prize of all, Best Musical. *Hotel* was judged the best staged, but *City* was the best written.

Gregg Edelman and James Naughton were replaced by Michael Rupert and Tom Wopat on Broadway. Naughton and Stephan Bogardus played the roles in the Los Angeles company.

THE 1990s

In 1993, Broadway officially celebrated its 100th birthday. Although there had been commercial theatre in New York prior to 1893, that was the year many venues began operating in what is now New York's theatre district, the Times Square area. As Broadway reached its century mark, it was still beset with problems: steeply rising ticket prices, union disputes, dark houses. But production did grow in the '90s, from a mere thirty-four shows in 1988–89 to forty-four in 1991–92. ✭ The British invasion of mammoth musicals continued with *Miss Saigon*. Nostalgia buffs were gratified by *Crazy for You*, a revamping of the Gershwins' 1930 *Girl Crazy*. A smash-hit revival of *Guys and Dolls* seemed to restore some of Broadway's old lustre to the theatre scene. ✭ Among the new American works were Neil Simon's comedy-drama *Lost in Yonkers*; a flashy *Will Rogers Follies*; a gritty *Jelly's Last Jam*; a comfy *The Secret Garden*; a bizarre musical version of *Kiss of the Spider Woman*; and a theatrical retelling of a rock opera, *The Who's Tommy*. This last-named production drew much-needed younger audiences into the theatre by staging a work long popular—as *Jesus Christ Superstar* had been—in its original form as a studio-engineered recording. ✭ Attempts were made at installing a theatre company that would present old and modern classics on Broadway. The Roundabout Theatre Company moved from off-Broadway to on, scoring mightily with mountings of *The Visit, Anna Christie,* and *She Loves Me*. Actor Tony Randall realized a long-held personal goal and formed the National Actors Theatre, which was met, at best, with mixed notices for such productions as *The Crucible* and *Saint Joan*. In a disturbing sign of the recessionary times, Circle in the Square, long a home for the classics, suspended operations due to a lack of funds. Lincoln Center Theatre was responsible for some notable commercial transfers, such as Frank Loesser's *The Most Happy Fella* (a revival), as well as putting new works, such as Wendy Wasserstein's *The Sisters Rosensweig*, on Broadway. ✭ The Broadway Alliance, a consortium of producers, mounted several productions at lower prices. One production was critically praised (*Our Country's Good*), but none of the Broadway Alliance shows has turned a profit or achieved a long run. ✭ Distinctive productions which did not or have yet to run over 500 performances include William Finn's *Falsettos*, a musical dealing with AIDS and homosexuality; Brian Friel's Irish drama *Dancing at Lughnasa*; and two multi-part plays, *Angels in America* and *The Kentucky Cycle*.

SIX DEGREES OF SEPARATION

by John Guare

Opened November 8, 1990

485 Performances, after 185 performances at the Mitzi E. Newhouse Theatre

Vivian Beaumont Theatre

Directed by Jerry Zaks

Produced by Lincoln Center Theatre

Cast: Stockard Channing (Ouisa); James McDaniel (Paul); John Cunningham (Flan); Sam Stoneburner (Geoffrey); Kelly Bishop (Kitty); Peter Maloney (Larkin); David Eigenberger (Hustler); Brian Evers (Detective); Robin Morse (Tess); Gus Rogerson (Woody); Anthony Rapp (Ben); Stephen Pearlman (Dr. Fine); Evan Handler (Doug); Philip LeStrange (Policeman/Eddie); John Cameron Mitchell (Trent); Robert Duncan McNeil (Rick); Mari Nelson (Elizabeth).

Although John Guare's *Six Degrees of Separation* fell short of 500 performances on Broadway, it did play off-Broadway 185 times. But both runs were at Lincoln Center and in the same building; the off-Broadway production took place on a smaller, ground-floor stage, the Mitzi E. Newhouse, and the Broadway production was essentially a continuation of the run on the larger stage upstairs, the Vivian Beaumont Theatre. Thus, most theatre chroniclers would agree that *Six Degrees* reached a hit status of 670 performances.

This "upstairs-downstairs" history could not have been more apt. John Guare's satirical comedy-drama tells of a lofty clutch of wealthy white Upper East Side New Yorkers who are taken in by a young black con artist of a far lower status in society. Named Paul, he is of uncertain origin, but he claims as part of his ploy to be the son of Sidney Poitier. American society's obsession with celebrity and its desperate search for identity is exposed as both the impostor and his victims connect or fail to connect through the charade. (The *Six Degrees* of the title refers to the theory that everyone on Earth is separated from every other person by only six people.)

Guare based his story on a real incident involving one David Hampton, who wormed his way into the homes and pocketbooks of several affluent Manhattanites by saying he was the offspring of the famous film star. Hampton was eventually arrested and jailed for twenty-one months on charges of impersonating Poitier's son (the actor has only daughters—no male progeny) and of stealing money from his unsuspecting hosts.

The playwright explained the play's genesis to the *New York Times*: "I had been in England when it happened. A friend of mine—Osborn Elliott, who was then the dean of the Columbia School of Journalism—and his wife, Inger, visited me and said, 'Have we got a story for you!' It turned out that they were among those taken in by 'David Poitier's' scheme. I had lost touch with the incident, but suddenly, I somehow felt I had to write about it. I bought Sidney Poitier's autobiography at the Strand [Bookstore] and just did it."

The Lincoln Center production opened on June 14, 1990. Hot director Jerry Zaks staged the piece on an empty stage with rapid pacing. Stockard Channing drew praises for her sensitive performance as the disillusioned woman who tries to make sense of the incident. James McDaniel first played Paul, the con artist. The response was so positive that the limited engagement was extended. Kelly Bishop and then Swoosie Kurtz took over for Channing, who had a film commitment. When the production moved to the Beaumont, in November, Channing returned to the cast. Courtney B. Vance replaced McDaniel, who was filming a TV series.

Life imitated art as the play became more popular. Hampton demanded that Guare cut him in on the profits of *Six Degrees*, arguing that it was based on his life. Guare countered that the play was a work of fiction, only suggested by reality. Hampton's subsequent behavior paralleled that of the character in the play. He made numerous phone calls to the author, crashed the *Six Degrees* opening night party, and attempted to bilk several New Yorkers by claiming to be the play's lead actor. Hampton's lawsuit for a share of the *Six Degrees* pie was dismissed. Guare's suit against Hampton for making threatening phone calls was also rejected.

Marlo Thomas played Channing's part in the national tour. Channing did the role in the 1993 film version, with Will Smith, Donald Sutherland, Ian MacKellen, Mary Beth Hurt, and Bruce Davison co-starring.

LOST IN YONKERS

by Neil Simon

Opened February 21, 1991

780 Performances

Richard Rodgers Theatre

Directed by Gene Saks

Produced by Emanuel Azenberg

Cast: Mercedes Ruehl (Bella); Irene Worth (Grandma Kurnitz); Kevin Spacey (Louie); Jamie Marsh (Jay); Danny Gerard (Arty); Mark Blum (Eddie); Lauren Klein (Gert).

Almost thirty years to the day after *Come Blow Your Horn*, his first Broadway hit, opened, Neil Simon's twenty-seventh play, *Lost in Yonkers*, premiered in New York. It won him a long-awaited award.

Like *Horn*, *Yonkers* involves two brothers. Set in 1942, it initially centers on Arty and Jay, aged twelve and fifteen, who are left with their tyrannical German grandmother while their widowed father goes South for a job so he can work himself out of debt. The formidable Grandma Kurnitz has led a hard life and stresses survival above tenderness. Having lost two children, she has emotionally stunted the remaining four: Eddie, the weak-willed father of Arty and

(Left to right) Jamie Marsh, Danny Gerard, Mercedes Ruehl, and Mark Blum in Neil Simon's *Lost in Yonkers*.

Jay; Louie, a small-time gangster; Gert, whose respiratory ailment prevents her from finishing sentences; and Bella, an emotionally arrested young woman with the mind of a child and the body and physical needs of an adult.

Simon began the play as a thirty-five-page draft called *Louie the Gangster*, focusing on the boys' uncle. After many rewrites, the emphasis shifted to Bella, who attempts to escape from the viselike grip of her mother. Bella wishes to marry a similarly impaired usher at a movie theatre. While Simon does tidy up most of the characters' lives by the end, he details Bella's pain and her conflict with Grandma along the way. Mercedes Ruehl, as the touching child-woman Bella, Irene Worth, as the iron grandmother, and Kevin Spacey, as the small-time Louie, all won Tony Awards, as did the play itself. *Yonkers* also won this major American playwright his Pulitzer Prize. Ironically, Simon had stated weeks before that there was no way the prize would not go to John Guare, for *Six Degrees of Separation*.

While not as directly autobiographical as his *Brighton Beach* trilogy, *Yonkers* contains traces of Simon's childhood. He and his brother Danny were farmed out to relatives whenever their parents' combative marriage was on the rocks. His own paternal grandmother was as distant and cold as Grandma Kurnitz. But "*Lost in Yonkers* is invention," the author told *Playbill*. "I remember being terrified of my grandmother, but I barely knew her. I never knew anyone like Louie, but I've known a few Bellas in my time. She was, I suppose, my most familiar reference point."

Ruehl and Worth also appeared in the 1993 film version, with Richard Dreyfuss as Louie. Grandma was also played on Broadway by Mercedes McCambridge, Rose-mary Harris, and Anne Jackson; later Bellas were Jane Kaczmarek, Lucie Arnaz, and Brooke Adams. McCambridge and Adams took the play on tour.

Simon's next two works, *Jake's Women* (1992) and a musical version of his screenplay *The Goodbye Girl* (1993), did not fare well. His comedy *Laughter on the 23rd Floor* (1993), about his early days writing television comedy, opened to mostly positive reviews.

MISS SAIGON

Book by Claude-Michel Schonberg and Alain Boublil

Music by Claude-Michel Schonberg

Lyrics by Richard Maltby, Jr. and Alain Boublil, adapted from the French lyrics by Alain Boublil; additional material by Richard Maltby, Jr.

Opened April 11, 1991

Still running (1,180 performances as of February 6, 1994)

Broadway Theatre

Directed by Nicholas Hytner

Choreographed by Bob Avian

Produced by Cameron Mackintosh

Cast: Lea Salonga (Kim); Jonathan Pryce (The Engineer); Willy Falk (Chris); Hinton Battle (John); Liz Callaway (Ellen); Barry K. Bernal (Thuy); Brian R. Baldomero (Tam); Philip Lyle Kong (Alternate for Tam); Kam Cheng (alternate for Kim); Marina Chapa (Gigi); Sala Iwamatsu (Mimi); Imelda de los Reyes (Yvette); JoAnn M. Hunter (Yvonne); Francis J. Cruz (Owner of the Moulin Rouge/Guard); Eric Chan (Asst. Commissar); Tony C. Avanti (Guard); Thomas James O'Leary (Shultz); Alton F. White (Antoine); Bruce Winant (Reeves); Paul Dobie (Gibbons); Leonard Joseph (Troy); Gordon Owens (Nolen); Matthew Pedersen (Huston); Sean McDermott (Frye).

Miss Saigon alighted on Broadway like a whirlibird, blowing up dustclouds of controversy. Assembled by the creators of *Les Misérables* (composer Claude-Michel Schonberg, lyricist Alain Boublil, producer Cameron Mackintosh), the musical told a similar story of love and compassion amid political turmoil.

The reputation of the authors and the producer for creating large-scale, eye-filling, sentimental musicals preceded them. Audiences in both London and New York flocked to the latest Mackintosh production in anticipation of another spectacle. The team answered with a pop-flavored tragedy complete with the big mechanical gimmick present in every Mackintosh musical: *Cats* had the rising tire; *Phantom* had the crashing chandelier; now, *Miss Saigon* had a helicopter landing at the American embassy at the end of the Vietnam War. By the time *Miss Saigon* got to Broadway, the musical's West End stand had taken in $33 million and the American edition had an advance sale of $36 million.

Boublil and Schonberg's story is a modern version of the Puccini opera *Madama Butterfly*. During the days before the fall of Saigon, in 1975, a Vietnamese village girl, Kim, is forced to become a prostitute. On her first night in a Saigon bar she falls in love with an American soldier, Chris. The two are separated as American troops pull out of the country. Three years later, Chris and Kim are reunited in Bangkok. But Chris has married an American girl, and Kim has borne Chris's son. In order to ensure that the boy is raised by Chris and his wife, Kim commits suicide.

Hovering on the edges of the action is a slimy Eurasian pimp, known only as The Engineer, who manipulates events to his advantage. One of the highlights of the production was The Engineer's paean to Yankee capitalism, "The American Dream," in which he practically made love to a Cadillac.

Boublil and Schonberg wrote the score in Paris, and then took it directly to Mackintosh for a premiere in London, bypassing a French production. Boublil's original French lyrics were adapted to English by Richard Maltby, Jr. and Boublil. London went wild over the show, and an American production seemed like a can't-miss proposition. But the road to Broadway was filled with landmines.

Asian-American performers protested the casting of British actor Jonathan Pryce in the role of the Eurasian pimp, which he had played in London. They stated that the casting of Pryce would be taking away an opportu-

nity from an Asian performer. Actors Equity supported the claim and ruled that Pryce could not repeat his performance in the American production. As he did with *Les Misérables* when Colm Wilkinson was at first refused permission to work on the New York stage, Mackintosh simply threatened to cancel the Broadway edition if his star could not appear in it. Faced with the possibility of losing a multi-million dollar show, Equity backed down and allowed Pryce to play for the first six months of the New York run. (Asian-American actor Francis Ruivivar succeeded him.)

The protests then shifted to the female lead, Lea Salonga, a Filipino native. Salonga was set to play Kim in New York, as she had in London. Equity again ruled that the casting was denying an opportunity for an Asian-American performer. Mackintosh insisted that he had the right to choose his own cast. The matter went to arbitration, with the producer winning. Still, an Asian-American actress, Kam Cheng, performed the role on matinees. Asian-American groups picketed the theatre on opening

The casting of British actor Jonathan Pryce as a Eurasian pimp stirred controversy for the American transfer of the British hit *Miss Saigon*.

night. They not only objected to the casting but to the show's depiction of Asians as either whores or pimps.

Despite the widely publicized controversy—or perhaps because of it—*Miss Saigon* was a major hit. Reviewers were divided. Howard Kissel, of the *Daily News,* complained: "the music is staggeringly banal, the lyrics insultingly predictable." But William A. Henry, of *Time,* said, "If spectators can clear their minds of the hoopla . . . they may find the musical is a cracking good show." But the critics' views did not matter. The show was a pre-sold package with a waiting audience. *Miss Saigon* seems destined to join *Cats, Phantom of the Opera* and *Les Misérables* as a long-time resident of both Broadway and London's West End.

THE SECRET GARDEN

Book and lyrics by Marsha Norman, based on the novel by Frances Hodgson Burnett

Music by Lucy Simon

Opened April 25, 1991

706 Performances

St. James Theatre

Directed by Susan H. Schulman

Choreographed by Michael Lichtefeld

Produced by Heidi Landesman, Rick Steiner, Frederic H. Mayerson, Elizabeth Williams, Jujamcyn Theatres/TV ASAHI, and Dodger Productions

Cast: Daisy Eagen (Mary Lennox); Mandy Patinkin (Archibald Craven); Robert Westenberg (Dr. Neville Craven); Rebecca Luker (Lily); Alison Fraser (Martha); John Cameron Mitchell (Dickon); John Babcock (Colin); Barbara Rosenblatt (Mrs. Medlock); Tom Toner (Ben); Peter Marinos (Fakir); Patricia Phillips (Ayah); Kay Walbye (Rose); Michael De Vries (Capt. Lennox); Drew Taylor (Lt. Peter Wright); Paul Jackel (Lt. Ian Shaw); Peter Samuel (Maj. Holmes); Rebecca Judd (Claire); Nancy Johnson (Alice/Mrs. Winthrop); Terese De Zarn (Jane); Frank DiPasquale (William); Betsy Friday (Betsy); Alec Timerman (Timothy).

Based on Frances Hodgson Burnett's 1911 classic children's novel, *The Secret Garden* provided Broadway with a family musical and little girls with a star role to yearn for. The story centers on Mary Lennox, a lonely and ill-tempered orphan whose parents die during a cholera epidemic while the family is stationed in India. She is sent to live in the Yorkshire moors of England with her cold uncle Archibald Craven, who has ceaselessly mourned the loss of his wife Lily. Mary discovers a secret garden on the Craven estate. With the aid of Archibald's sickly son Colin, the girl cultivates the garden. In so doing, she, Colin and Craven are all brought back to health and vigor.

The Secret Garden was the first hit Broadway musical in which almost all of the creative and design talent were women (producer and set designer Heidi Landesman; librettist Marsha Norman; composer Lucy Simon; director Susan H. Schulman; costume designer Theoni V. Aldredge; and lighting designer Tharon Musser). "It wasn't until the whole team was assembled that we realized it was all women," said Schulman to *Theatre Week.*

Heidi Landesman, who had won two Tonys for producing and designing the set for *Big River,* had first conceived of the show when she was sent a record of a British regional theatre's musical version of *The Secret Garden.* "I very much disliked it," she told *Theatre Week,* "but it made me go back and read the novel, and I got very excited about doing it as a musical."

Landesman contacted her friend Marsha Morman to do the adaptation. The choice of this Pulitzer Prize–winning playwright to pen the book and lyrics for a show based on a children's story seemed an unusual one to many. Not only had she never done a musical before, but her reputation was based on such ultra-serious plays as *Getting Out* (1978), a drama about a woman readjusting to life after prison, and *'night, Mother* (1983), a grim rumination on suicide.

After interviewing six composers, Landesman and Norman hired Lucy Simon, a pop tunesmith and the sister of singers Carly and Joanna Simon. The musical was first presented at the Virginia Stage Company, in Norfolk, Virginia, under the direction of R.J. Cutler. The producers decided that the show needed a new director. They recruited Schulman, who had gained attention with a successful revival of *Sweeney Todd.*

It was not clear that the show would become a hit. Landesman pointed out in an interview that 70 percent of Broadway theatre tickets were purchased by women, and she attributed much of the show's success to its appeal for that audience. Yet Landesman and company realized they would have to do more than draw women who had loved the book when they were girls. The role of Archibald was built up and cast with a star (Mandy Patinkin) in order to strengthen the father–son theme for males in the audience. An additional character, Archibald's brother Neville, who had been secretly in love with Lily, was written into the story.

Schulman also added a chorus of ghosts, representing the spirits of Mary's dead parents and their friends in India. Many critics found these spirits distracting, and their roles were greatly reduced after the reviews came out.

Eleven-year-old Daisy Eagen gave a graceful and natural performance as Mary. She won a Tony for Best Featured Actress in a Musical, making her the second-youngest person to receive the award. (The youngest was Frankie Michaels, who won at the age of ten for *Mame*). Eagen's teary and funny acceptance speech was used in a television commercial for the show, which also helped the production overcome its mixed notices for a long run and a national tour.

Previous British musical versions of *The Secret Garden* were produced in 1983 and 1987. It has appeared as a nonmusical film, in 1949 and again in 1993.

THE WILL ROGERS FOLLIES

Book by Peter Stone

Music by Cy Coleman

Lyrics by Betty Comden and Adolph Green

Opened May 1, 1991

983 Performances

Palace Theatre

Directed and choreographed by Tommy Tune

Produced by Pierre Cossette, Martin Richards, Sam Crothers, James M. Nederlander, Stewart F. Lane, and Max Weitzenhoffer

Cast: Keith Carradine (Will Rogers); Dee Hoty (Betty Blake); Cady Hoffman (Ziegfeld's Favorite); Dick Latessa (Clem Rogers); Paul Ukena, Jr. (Wiley Post); Vince Bruce (Unicyclist/Roper); Jerry Mitchell (Indian of the Dawn); Jillana Urbina (Indian Sun Goddess); Rick Faugno (Will Rogers, Jr.); Tammy Minoff (Mary Rogers); Lance Robinson (James Rogers); Gregory Scott Carter (Freddy Rogers); Gregory Peck (Voice of Mr. Ziegfeld).

The spirit of Florenz Ziegfeld returned to Broadway in *The Will Rogers Follies*, a biographical musical about the beloved cowboy-humorist who headlined Ziegfeld's annual productions. Subtitled *A Life in Revue*, the show presented Rogers's life as a series of vaudeville acts interspersed with elaborate numbers. Rope tricks, dog acts, gorgeously costumed showgirls—just about anything to entertain—was called into play. The story and songs were not especially distinctive; and as he did with *Grand Hotel*, director Tommy Tune took fair-to-middling material and concocted an eye-filling spectacle. He was aided by Tony Walton's set design (a long flight of rainbow-colored stairs); Willa Kim's elegant costumes; and Jules Fisher's versatile lighting.

Cady Hoffman and Keith Carradine
in *The Will Rogers Follies*.

The genesis of the show came when producer Pierre Cossette hired James Lee Burrett to write a musical treatment of Rogers's life with the aim of snaring singer John Denver for the lead. But both Denver's asking price and Burrett's multi-set script proved far too expensive. Then Cossette acquired a new creative team: veterans Cy Coleman, Betty Comden, and Adolph Green for the songs; Tommy Tune to direct; and frequent Tune collaborator Peter Stone for the book.

The main problem was Rogers himself. Apart from his death in a plane crash in 1935, nothing particularly dramatic had happened to him. In researching their subject, Tune discovered Rogers's link to the *Ziegfeld Follies* and decided to use it as the concept for the whole production. "We thought that setting his biography in *The Ziegfeld Follies* would give the material the theatricality his real life lacked," the director told *Theatre Week*.

Lanky film star and songwriter Keith Carradine was hired for the lead in Denver's stead. The star's name attracted almost enough investors to begin workshops and rehearsals. The final backing was supplied by a Japanese broadcasting company in return for the rights to show the musical on Japanese television.

Tune was extremely busy during rehearsals, for he was simultaneously preparing to star in a national touring revival of *Bye, Bye, Birdie* opposite Anne Reinking. Tune's *Birdie* rehearsals and the elaborate staircase set prohibited out-of-town tryouts. The show opened in New York after a series of previews.

The musical was greeted with mixed notices. Frank Rich of the *New York Times* disliked the show's razzle-dazzle concept, stating it was at odds with Rogers's folksy, no-nonsense style. David Richards, the critic for the Sunday edition of the *Times* was more positive: "This is the musical audiences were really waiting for," he cheered in an obvious swipe at the much-ballyhooed *Miss Saigon*.

In a backlash against *Miss Saigon*, *Will Rogers* won six Tonys, including Best Musical, while the British blockbuster copped three. The Tony triumph boosted box office sales. But it didn't save the show from attacks from three different groups.

Some women's groups objected to the production's advertising, which included a giant poster outside the theatre showing chorus girls dressed as brand-bearing cattle. African-American and other minority performers complained to Actors Equity that there were no non-Caucasians in the cast. Native Americans were upset because of a production number in which a near-naked Indian danced on top of a drum; such an act, they said, was sacreligious to them; they also took issue with the depiction of Native Americans in the show, interpreting this as stereotypical. This was especially disturbing, their spokesman said, for

both Rogers and Tune claimed a Native American heritage. The advertising was changed, and three African-American dancers were added to the show, but the Indian dance remained intact.

Country-western singers Mac Davis and Larry Gatlin later replaced Keith Carradine, who took a version of the show on tour. Late in the Broadway run, two cast changes inspired a great deal of publicity and a surge in attendance. Marla Maples, a model known more for being the girlfriend of millionaire Donald Trump than for her experience as an actress, was added to the ensemble. After Maples left the show, and not long before it closed, Mickey Rooney signed on to play Will's father.

CRAZY FOR YOU

Book by Ken Ludwig, based on the original book by Guy Bolton and John McGowan.

Music by George Gershwin

Lyrics by Ira Gershwin; additional lyrics by Gus Kahn and Desmond Carter

Opened February 19, 1992

Still running (822 performances as of February 6, 1994)

Shubert Theatre

Directed by Mike Ockrent

Choreographed by Susan Stroman

Produced by Elizabeth Williams and Roger Horchow

Cast: Harry Groener (Bobby Child); Jodi Benson (Polly Baker); Bruce Adler (Bela Zangler); Michele Pawk (Irene Roth); John Hillner (Lank Hawkins); Jane Connell (Mother); Beth Leavel (Tess); Ronn Carroll (Everett Baker); Stephen Temperley (Eugene); Amelia White (Patricia); The Manhattan Rhythm Kings: Brian M. Nalepka (Moose), Tripp Hanson (Mingo), and Hal Shane (Sam); Stacey Logan (Patsy); Judine Hawkins Richard (Sheila); Paula Leggett (Mitzi); Ida Henry (Susie); Jean Marie (Louise); Penny Ayn Maas (Betsy); Salome Mazard (Margie); Louise Ruck (Vera); Pamela Everett (Elaine); Gerry Burkhardt (Perkins); Casey Nicholaw (Junior); Fred Anderson (Pete); Michael Kubala (Jimmy); Ray Roderick (Billy); Jeffrey Lee Broadhurst (Wyatt); Joel Goodness (Harry).

In the 1991–92 season, the three biggest Broadway musical hits featured scores from previous shows or other sources. The trio consisted of a revival of *Guys and Dolls*; *Jelly's Last Jam*, which utilized the work of jazz pioneer Jelly Roll Morton; and *Crazy for You*, a reworked version of the Gershwins' 1930 *Girl Crazy*. The original *Girl Crazy* marked the dynamic debut of Ethel Merman; the young Ginger Rogers also appeared. It had been filmed twice, in 1932 and 1943.

The story of a spoiled New York playboy going out West and falling in love with a local girl was retained. But instead of saving a college, as in the original, the hero and heroine rescue an old theatre. *Crazy for You* was really a distillation of elements from movie musicals of the '30s and '40s. There was the "Let's put on a show" theme made popular in the films of Mickey Rooney and Judy Garland; the elegance of Fred Astaire and Ginger Rogers's dancing; and Busby Berkeley–style choreography, with bizarre props.

Harry Groener surrounded by chorus girls in *Crazy for You.*

The production was originally set to be a revival of *Girl Crazy.* Roger Horchow, a millionaire in the mail-order catalogue business, had sold his enterprise to Neiman-Marcus for a cool $117 million and set about realizing his lifelong dream of presenting a Gershwin musical on Broadway. His favorite score was *Girl Crazy.* With his partner, Elizabeth Williams, Horchow contacted Mike Ockrent, the British director who had revamped *Me and My Girl* for modern audiences. Ockrent told the *New York Daily News:* "I love those Rogers–Astaire musicals. I love dance, all the shows I've done have had a high dance content. So I said OK . . . if the book was rewritten."

For the rewrite job of the original script by Guy Bolton and John MacGowan, Ockrent contacted Ken Ludwig, a Washington lawyer turned playwright. Ludwig also had an affinity for the period of the show. He had struck it rich with *Lend Me a Tenor,* a successful farce set in the 1930s. Ludwig commented on the *Girl Crazy* libretto to the *Christian Science Monitor:* "Even compared to other books of that period it wasn't very good. In those days, books for musicals tended to be patchy and not have strong plots. And they also tended to rely heavily on stereotypes that

we'd find offensive today." Indeed, Bolton and Mac-Gowan's book had featured a Jewish character named Goldfarb who spoke to the Indians in Yiddish.

The Gershwin estate authorized a new book and allowed Ockrent and Ludwig access to many songs in the Gershwin canon, including several lost numbers which had been unearthed in a New Jersey warehouse. Only five songs from *Girl Crazy* survived to become part of *Crazy for You:* "But Not for Me," "Embraceable You," "Biding My Time" "Could You Use Me?" and Merman's signature tune "I Got Rhythm." The songs from the New Jersey discovery included "Naughty Baby," "Tonight's the Night," and "What Causes That?"

The highlight of the production was Susan Stroman's inventive choreography. Wearing pink tutus, many chorus girls emerged from a too-small car, like clowns in a circus. The Western townfolk tapped on pots, pans, and slate roofs in a joyous expansion of "I Got Rhythm." In "Slap That Bass" dancers became bass fiddles with the aid of lengths of rope.

Broadway went crazy over *Crazy for You,* as did Tokyo and London. James Brennan and Karen Ziemba played the leads in the national tour.

GUYS AND DOLLS

Book by Jo Swerling and Abe Burrows

Music and lyrics by Frank Loesser

Opened April 14, 1992

Still running (759 performances as of February 6, 1994)

Martin Beck Theatre

Directed by Jerry Zaks

Choreographed by Christopher Chadman

Produced by Dodger Producers, Roger Berlind, Jujamcyn Theatres/TV ASAHI, Kardana Productions, and the Kennedy Center for the Performing Arts

Cast: Faith Prince (Miss Adelaide); Nathan Lane (Nathan Detroit); Peter Gallagher (Sky Masterson); Josie de Guzman (Sarah Brown); Walter Bobbie (Nicely-Nicely Johnson); J.K. Simmons (Benny Southstreet); John Carpenter (Arvide Abernathy); Ernie Sabella (Harry the Horse); Timothy Shew (Rusty Charlie); Hershel Sparber (Big Jule); Ruth Williamson (Gen. Matilda B. Cartwright); Steve Ryan (Lt. Brannigan); Michael Goz (Angie the Ox/Joey Biltmore); Eleanor Glockner (Agatha); Leslie Feagan (Calvin); Victoria Clark (Martha); Stan Page (Hot Box MC); Denise Faye (Mimi); Robert Michael Baker (Drunk); Kenneth Kantor (Waiter).

This was a highly acclaimed revival of the Frank Loesser musical. For the history of this show, see page 112 for the original 1950 production.

JELLY'S LAST JAM

Book by George C. Wolfe

Music by Jelly Roll Morton; additional music by Luther Henderson

Lyrics by Susan Birkenhead

Opened April 26, 1992

569 Performances

Virginia Theatre

Directed by George C. Wolfe

Music adapted by Luther Henderson

Choreographed by Hope Clark, Gregory Hines, and Ted L. Levy

Produced by Margo Lion and Pamela Koslow

Cast: Gregory Hines (Jelly Roll Morton); Keith David (Chimney Man); Tonya Pinkins (Anita); Savion Glover (Young Jelly); Stanley Wayne Mathis (Jack the Bear); Ruben Santiago-Hudson (Buddy Bolden); Mary Bond Davis (Miss Mamie); Ann Duquesnay (Gran Mimi); Mamie Duncan-Gibbs, Stephanie Pope, Allison M. Williams (The Hunnies); Brenda Braxton (Too-Tight Nora); Gil Pritchard III (Three Finger Jake); Ken Ard (Foot-in-Yo-Ass Sam); Don Johanson, Gordon Joseph Weiss (Melrose Brothers); Victoria Gabrielle Platt, Sherry D. Boone (Sisters).

Like many previous musicals, *Jelly's Last Jam* celebrated the music of an African-American composer. But unlike *Ain't Misbehavin'*, *Eubie*, and *Sophisticated Ladies*, *Jelly's*

Tony winners Tonya Pinkins and Gregory Hines sing the blues in *Jelly's Last Jam*.

examined the often painful side of the emergence of jazz music from the lives of black people in the early 20th century. This was achieved through a profile of the composer Jelly Roll Morton, the self-proclaimed inventor of jazz. A light-skinned black man, Morton often boasted of his French Creole background and derided other blacks with darker skins. In George C. Wolfe's surrealist book, Morton is summoned to the Jungle Inn, "a lowdown club somewheres 'tween Heaven 'n' Hell," on the last night of his life.

A mystical figure called Chimney Man leads Morton on a review of his life, from his childhood in New Orleans to fame and fortune as a bandleader, pianist, and songwriter, and finally to his lonely last days. Chimney Man forces Jelly to see that by denying his African-American heritage, he has rejected his true self. The musical ends with a riotous New Orleans–style jazz funeral in which Jelly embraces his roots.

As Jelly, Gregory Hines was a spectacular dancer, as always, and he carried off a Best Actor Tony; Tonya Pinkins also won as the woman he loves and loses. Keith David was nominated for his sensuous and menacing Chimney Man.

Producer Margo Lion had initial conceived of presenting Morton's music in a biographical show. She interested Pamela Koslow in the project as a vehicle for her husband Hines. Koslow signed on as co-producer, with Hines as star. An initial workshop of the production, then under the title of *Mister Jelly Lord*, had a sterling cast which included Hines, Lonette McKee, Leilani Jones, and Ben Harney. Stan Latham directed and Ottis Sallid choreographed. Luther Henderson adapted Morton's music for the book by Ken Cavander.

The workshop was positively received by potential investors, but Lion and Koslow were not satisfied with the show. They hired a new high-powered, creative team: Tony-winning director Jerry Zaks (*Six Degrees of Separation*) to stage, and Pulitzer Prize dramatist August Wilson (*Fences*) to write the book. This combination did not work either. Finally, George C. Wolfe, a playwright and director whose *The Colored Museum* had a successful run off-Broadway at the New York Shakespeare Festival, signed on to replace Wilson. Susan Birkenhead, who had collaborated with Wolfe on a revised version of the Duke Ellington musical *Queenie Pie*, came abroad to pen new lyrics to Morton's music as adapted by Henderson. When Zaks bowed out to direct *Miss Saigon* (an assignment which later went to Nicholas Hytner), Wolfe took over the direction as well.

A second workshop version and then a mainstage production of the show, now called *Jelly's Last Jam*, were staged at the Mark Taper Forum in Los Angeles—but without Hines, who was resistant to the choice of the relatively inexperienced Wolfe as director. Obba Babatunde, a Tony nominee for *Dreamgirls*, played the lead role in the Taper production.

When the production was well-received by the L.A. critics and audiences, Hines rejoined the team for another New York workshop of the musical. This third workshop ultimately led to the hit Broadway production. After all the various incarnations and revisions, *Jelly's* was still going through extensive changes. All through previews and right up until up opening night, numbers were cut, restored, and edited.

Gregory Hines, Keith David, and Tonya Pinkins were later replaced by Brian Mitchell, Ben Vereen, and Phylicia Rashad.

Off-Broadway

To many across the country, New York theatre is Broadway. The annual Tony Awards telecast helps to foster this notion, but that flashy event ignores a vital segment of artistic activity which, more than ever, represents the lifeblood of new theatre: Off-Broadway, the cream of New York's small stages beyond the Times Square district. ✯ Companies such as Manhattan Theatre Club, Circle Repertory Company, Playwrights Horizons, Second Stage, and the New York Shakespeare Festival present, by and large, the majority of the dramas, quirky musicals, and innovative revivals, while Broadway producers turn to British megahits, reproductions of old favorites, and the reliable comedies of Neil Simon, for its bread and butter—and then to the hits of off-Broadway or regional stages for other potential successes. ✯ Off-Broadway was born in 1915, when the Washington Square Players began presenting unusual short plays. The group disbanded in 1918 and reformed later to become the Theatre Guild, an influential producing entity. Another important off-Broadway company got its start in 1915, when Susan Glaspell and George Cram Cook founded the Provincetown Players (the Washington Square group had rejected a script they had co-authored). The Players mounted numerous productions, including the early plays of Eugene O'Neill, on Cape Cod and in Greenwich Village. ✯ Various companies came and went over the next few decades (the Neighborhood Playhouse, the Brooklyn Repertory, and the Negro Players, to name a few). In 1952, off-Broadway became recognized as a professional entity when Circle in the Square mounted a revival of Tennessee Williams's *Summer and Smoke* that far surpassed the original Broadway production. As a result, the major newspapers began to cover off-Broadway regularly. ✯ Off-Broadway generated long runs, new American playwrights, such as Edward Albee and Sam Shepard, emerged, and important foreign dramatists—Pirandello, Ionesco, Beckett, and others—gained exposure to American audiences. ✯ During the '60s, off-off-Broadway, the poorer, wilder cousin of off-Broadway, emerged with experimental productions by the Living Theatre, Café Cino, the Open Theatre, and Café La MaMa. More and more hit productions opened downtown and then moved uptown, but many stayed put, too, for the extended engagements they earned.

THE THREEPENNY OPERA

Book and lyrics by Bertolt Brecht; English adaptation by Marc Blitzstein. Suggested by *The Beggar's Opera* by John Gay.

Music by Kurt Weill

Opened September 20, 1955

2,611 Performances

Theatre de Lys

Directed by Carmen Capalbo

Produced by Carmen Capalbo and Stanley Chase

Cast: Scott Merrill (MacHeath); Lotte Lenya (Jenny); Jo Sullivan (Polly Peachum); Beatrice Arthur (Lucy Brown); Frederic Downs (J.J. Peachum); Jane Connell (Mrs. Peachum); Tige Andrews (Streetsinger); Richard Verney (Tiger Brown); John Astin (Readymoney Matt); Eddie Lawrence (Crookfinger Jake); Bernie Fein (Bob the Saw); Joseph Elic (Walt Drearey); Carroll Saint (Rev. Kimball); William Duell (Filch/Messenger); Joan Coburn (Betty); Marion Selee (Molly); Irene Kane (Dolly); Bea Barrett (Coaxer); Rome Smith (Smith); Albert Valentine (1st Constable); Steve Palmer (2nd Constable).

The first long-running off-Broadway hit was *The Three-penny Opera*, Kurt Weill and Bertolt Brecht's dark variation on John Gay's 18th-century musical *The Beggar's Opera*. The original musical was an irreverent satire on English society, showing policemen and judges to be as corrupt as prostitutes and thieves. Chief among the latter is MacHeath, a charming rogue who beds many maidens and schemes his way around the law.

Threepenny tells the same basic story but moves the time ahead to Victorian London and is even more bleak and biting in its depiction of an amoral world. The show had its world premiere in Berlin in 1928. A Broadway production had a brief run at the Empire Theatre in 1933. A new adaptation by Mark Blitzstein was first presented at the Theatre de Lys, a former movie house on Christopher Street in Greenwich Village, on March 10, 1954. It caused a sensation. Lotte Lenya, Weill's widow, repeated her explosive Berlin performance as Pirate Jenny. The 1954 engagement ran for 95 performances, closing because another show was scheduled to play the theatre. *Three-penny* reopened on September 20, 1955 and became the longest-running musical off-Broadway. (The record was later broken by *The Fantasticks* and *Nunsense,* which currently occupy the number one and two spots among off-Broadway musicals). Bobby Darren's jazzy recording of "Mac the Knife" contributed to the show's popularity.

Lenya and Scott Merrill (as MacHeath) were both up for 1956 Tony Awards, with Lenya winning in her category of Featured Actress in a Musical. They are the only performers in an off-Broadway production to be so nominated. As off-Broadway productions proliferated, the Tonys shut them out of competition with Broadway shows.

Broadway revivals of *Threepenny* have included a 1976 adaptation by Ralph Manheim and John Willett, starring Raul Julia and Ellen Greene (307 performances), and a

1989 revival translated by Michael Feingold, starring Sting, Maureen McGovern, and Georgia Brown (65 performances).

Threepenny was filmed in 1931, in Germany, with Lenya and Rudolph Forster, and again in 1964, with Curt Jurgens and Hildegarde Neff.

THE ICEMAN COMETH

by Eugene O'Neill

Opened May 8, 1956

565 Performances

Circle in the Square Theatre

Directed by José Quintero

Produced by Leigh Connell, Theodore Mann, and José Quintero

Cast: Jason Robards, Jr. (Theodore Hickman); Farrell Pelly (Harry Hope); Conrad Bain (Larry Slade); Larry Robinson (Don Parritt); Phil Pheffer (Ed Mosher); Albert Lewis (Pat McGloin); Addison Powell (Willie Oban); William Edmonson (Joe Mott); Richard Abbott (Piet Wetjoen (The General)); Richard Bowler (Cecil Lewis (The Captain)); James Greene (James Cameron (Jimmy Tomorrow)); Paul Andor (Hugo Kalmar); Peter Falk (Rocky Pioggi); Patricia Brooks (Pearl); Gloria Scott Backe (Margie); Dolly Jonah (Cora); Joe Marr (Chuck Morello); Mal Thorne (Moran); Charles Hamilton (Lieb).

Off-Broadway's first nonmusical play to run over 500 performances was a revival of *The Iceman Cometh*, a drama of pipe dreams and moral decay by the Nobel Prize–winning dramatist, Eugene O'Neill. Set in New York at Harry Hope's seedy waterfront bar in 1912, the play depicts man's need for illusion. Declaring himself newly-reformed, salesman Theodore Hickman, or "Hickey" as the regulars call him, shatters each of the barflies' illusions, leaving them with nothing. This five-hour drama was originally produced on Broadway in 1946 and ran 136 performances. Audiences at the end of the war seemed resistant to O'Neill's harsh observations on the human condition.

José Quintero's production launched a reappraisal of the works of O'Neill and of the career of Jason Robards, whose intense performance as Hickey captured the self-loathing behind the salesman's jolly facade. The *Iceman* revival led to a long partnership between Robards and Quintero in presenting the works of O'Neill. That fall they collaborated on the Broadway production of *Long Day's Journey Into Night* (1956). Later Robards–Quintero–O'Neill productions included *Hughie* (1964); *A Moon for the Misbegotten* (1973); *A Touch of the Poet* (1977), and revivals of *Iceman* (1985) and *Long Day's Journey into Night* (1988).

Iceman was presented on TV's *The Play of the Week* in 1960 and filmed in 1973, with Lee Marvin as Hickey. James Earl Jones played Hickey in a 1973 Broadway revival.

THE BOY FRIEND

Music, lyrics, and book by Sandy Wilson
Opened January 25, 1958
763 Performances
Cherry Lane Theatre
Directed by Gus Schirmer
Choreographed by Buddy Schwab
Produced by the New Princess Company

Cast: Ellen McCown (Polly); Bill Mullikin (Tony); Margaret Hall (Hortense); Christina Gillespie (Nancy); Gerrianne Raphael (Maisie); Michele Burke (Fay/Lolita); June Squibb (Dulcie); Neal Kenyon (Pierre); Thom Molinaro (Marcel/Pepe); Jeanne Beauvais (Mme. DuBonnet); Peter Conlow (Bobby Van Husen); Leon Shaw (Percival Browne); David Vaughan (Lord Brucklehurst); Phoebe Mackay (Lady Brucklehurst).

Off-Broadway's third hit was a revival like the first two. But unlike the dark *The Threepenny Opera* and *The Iceman Cometh*, *The Boy Friend* was a feather-light parody with no message for the audience other than "Enjoy yourselves." This take-off on "boy-meets-girl" British musicals of the 1920s opened in London and played Broadway in 1954, introducing a young star named Julie Andrews. The English production ran a phenomenal 2,048 performances; the first New York version lasted 485. The off-Broadway revival outran the latter, playing 763 performances. A short-lived 1970 Broadway remounting featured Judy Carne and Sandy Duncan. Twiggy, Christopher Gable, Tommy Tune, and Glenda Jackson appeared in Ken Russell's 1971 film version.

The Boy Friend was the first of many off-Broadway nostalgia hits: Some—*Leave It to Jane* (1959), *The Boys from Syracuse* (1963)—were revivals; others—*Little Mary Sunshine* (1959), *Curley McDimple* (1967), *Dames at Sea* (1968)—were musicals spoofing genres of bygone eras.

THE CRUCIBLE

by Arthur Miller
Opened March 11, 1958
571 Performances
Martinique Theatre
Directed by Word Baker
Produced by Paul Libin and Word Baker

Cast: Michael Higgins (John Proctor); Barbara Barrie (Elizabeth Proctor); Ann Wedgeworth (Abigail Williams); Ford Rainey (Deputy Governor Danforth); Noah Curry (Rev. John Hale); Wayne Wilson (Judge Hathorne); William Larsen (Rev. Parris); Barbara Stanton (Mary Warren); Sam Greene (The Reader); Janice Meshkoff (Betty Parris); Vinnette Carroll (Tituba); Margaret DePriest (Susanna Walcott); Marjorie Shaffer (Mrs. Ann Putnam); David Metcalf (Thomas Putnam); Mary Gower (Mercy Lewis); Anne Ives (Rebecca Nurse); Burton Mallory (Giles Corey); David Elliott (Francis Nurse); Russell Bailey (Ezekiel Cheever); John Peters (Willard); Marjorie Shaffer (Sarah Good).

The Crucible, Arthur Miller's penetrating drama of the Salem witch trials, had a disappointing run of only 197 performances in its initial Broadway engagement in 1953, despite the presence of Beatrice Straight, Arthur Kennedy, and E.G. Marshall in the cast. Miller wrote the play as an indictment of the bullying anti-communist tactics of Senator Joseph McCarthy, drawing parallels between the hysteria which swept the New England colonies in 1692 and the rabid hunt for subversives in the 1950s. The playwright speculated that the political controversy may have frightened away theatregoers. A 1958 revival was mounted in an arena staging at a converted ballroom in the Hotel Martinique. With the dark cloud of McCarthyism removed from the national landscape, audiences were more appreciative of Miller's taut study of political intimidation.

Subsequent revivals of *The Crucible* have been mounted by the National Repertory Theatre (1964); Lincoln Center Repertory (1972); Roundabout Theatre Company (1990); and National Actors Theatre (1992).

LEAVE IT TO JANE

Book and lyrics by Guy Bolton and P.G. Wodehouse
Music by Jerome Kern
Opened May 25, 1959
Sheridan Square Playhouse
928 Performances
Directed by Lawrence Carra
Choreographed by Mary Jane Doerr
Produced by Joseph Beruh and Peter Kent

Cast: Kathleen Murray (Jane Witherspoon); Art Matthews (Billy Bolton); Angelo Mango ("Stub" Talmadge); Dorothy Stinette (Bessie Tanners); Dorothy Greener (Flora Wiggins); George Segal (Ollie Mitchell); Monroe Arnold (Matty McGowan); Josip Elic ("Silent" Murphy); Jon Richards (Peter Witherspoon); Al Checco (Howard Talbot); Vince O'Brien (Hiram Bolton); Ray Tudor (Harold "Bub" Hicks); Alek Primrose (Hon. Elam Hicks); Eddie O'Flynn (Dick); Austin O'Toole (Jimsey); Ronald Knight (Happy); Carlo Manalli (Jack); Bob Carey (Smitty); Noel Erler (Tom); Gene Bullard (Joe); Lee Thornberry (Sally); Mitzie McWhorter (Cora); Marianne Gayle (Bertha); Lainie Levine (Martha); Patricia Brooks (Josephine); Linda Bates (Louella); Sue Swanson (Sue).

A hit as both a straight play and as a musical, *Leave It to Jane* was a smash once again, forty years after its Broadway run, this time off-Broadway. This campus caper started in 1904 as *The College Widow* by humorist George Ade. Then it was adapted into a musical in 1917 by Jerome Kern, P.G. Wodehouse, and Guy Bolton. That version ran 167 performances, a respectable showing in those days.

The plot is simplicity itself; the campus brain Jane Witherspoon catches the football hero Billy Bolton, while raccoon-coated undergrads plunk ukuleles and waitresses make wisecracks. Wodehouse commented on the revival's popularity in the *New York Herald-Tribune*: "One of the explanations of its success . . . is that the management did not make the mistake of being cute and whimsical."

June Allyson sang songs from the score in *Til the Clouds Roll By* (1946), a film bio of Kern.

THE CONNECTION

by Jack Gelber

Opened July 15, 1959

722 Performances

The Living Theatre

Directed by Judith Malina

Produced by the Living Theatre

Cast: Leonard Hicks (Jim Dunn); Ira Lewis (Jaybird); Warren Finnerty (Leach); Jerome Raphael (Solly); John McCurry (Sam); Gerry Goodrow (Ernie); Freddie Redd (1st Musician); Michael Mattos (4th Musician); Louis McKenzie (1st Photographer); Jamil Zakkai (2nd Photographer); Jackie McLean (2nd Musician); Larry Ritchie (3rd Musician); Henry Proach (Harry); Barbara Winchester (Sister Salvation); Carl Lee (Cowboy).

While drug addiction had been represented on the Broadway stage before, in the 1955 *A Hatful of Rain*, Jack Gelber's *The Connection* brought the topic right into the laps of theatregoers. The "fourth wall" between actors and audiences was broken down in Judith Malina's Living Theatre production. At the beginning of the play, a "producer" announces to the audience that he had brought some real junkies to the theatre and is going to film them for a documentary. Two "cameramen" record the action while the addicts wait for their supplier to show up. There is no conventional plot, as the addicts attempt to hustle the filmmakers and the audience for cash, ruminate on their condition to the accompaniment of onstage jazz musicians, and finally shoot up once the connection arrives.

Most mainstream critics dismissed the play, but Jerry Tallmer of the *Village Voice* championed it by writing about it in weekly columns. Tallmer's persistence built a following for the show and resulted in a long run, the first for an off-Broadway production which was not a revival. The Living Theatre, run by Malina and her husband, Julian Beck, went on to present many avant-garde presentations.

The play was filmed in 1961 with most of the original cast, and there was a 1980 revival starring Morgan Freeman.

LITTLE MARY SUNSHINE

Book, music, and lyrics by Rick Besoyan

Opened November 18, 1959

1,143 Performances

Orpheum Theatre

Directed by Ray Harrison and Rick Besoyan

Choreographed by Ray Harrison

Produced by Howard Barker, Cynthia Baer, and Robert Chambers

Cast: Eileen Brennan (Little Mary Sunshine); William Granham (Cpl. "Big Jim" Warington); John McMartin (Cpl. Billy Jester); John Aniston (Chief Brown Bear); Elizabeth Parrish (Mme. Ernestine Von Liebedich); Elmarie Wendel (Nancy Twinkle); Robert Chambers (Fleet Foot); Ray James (Yellow Feather); Mario Siletti (Gen'l Oscar Fairfax); Floria Mari (Cora); Jana Stuart (Maud); Elaine Labour (Gwendolyn); Rita Howell (Henrietta); Sally Bramlette (Mabel); Jerry Melo (Pete); Joe Warfield (Tex); Arthur Hunt (Slim); Ed Riley (Buster); Mark Destin (Hank).

The junkies of *The Connection* shared the 1959–60 off-Broadway season with the musical-comedy cartoon characters of *Little Mary Sunshine*. While not a revival like other off-Broadway hits such as *The Boy Friend* and *Leave It to Jane*, *Mary* did rely on shows of an earlier era for its inspiration. Rick Besoyan's operetta parody mostly used the 1924 *Rose-Marie* and the subsequent Jeanette MacDonald-Nelson Eddy film as a source. *Rose-Marie*'s Canadian Rockies became the Colorado Rockies and the mounties were replaced by forest rangers. The title heroine was a noble soprano troubled with a heavily mortgaged inn and the unwanted attentions of the villainous Indian, Yellow Feather. She is rescued by hearty baritone Capt. "Big Jim" Warrington. Added to this confection are a displaced Viennese opera star; five young women from a finishing school back East to be paired off with the rangers; a Washington diplomat; a maid who thinks she's Mata Hari; and a tribe of comic Indians.

Eileen Brennan drew rave reviews in the lead. She stated that she modeled her characterization on Walt Disney's Snow White. Brennan went on to Broadway stardom in *Hello, Dolly!* and a later career as a character actress in film and TV. She teamed with Besoyan again in 1963 for *The Student Gypsy*, another (less successful) operetta parody.

William Graham and Eileen Brennan spoof operetta in *Little Mary Sunshine*.

KRAPP'S LAST TAPE

by Samuel Beckett

THE ZOO STORY

by Edward Albee

Opened January 14, 1960

582 Performances

Provincetown Playhouse

Directed by Alan Schneider and Milton Katselas

Produced by Theatre 1960 and Harry Joe Brown, Jr.

Cast: *Krapp's Last Tape*: Donald Davis (Krapp); *The Zoo Story*: William Daniels (Peter); George Maharis (Jerry).

The double bill of one-acts has proved a popular format off-Broadway. The first such evening of short plays to reach hit proportions was a program of Samuel Beckett's *Krapp's Last Tape* and Edward Albee's *The Zoo Story*. Both pieces deal with the isolation of the individual in an uncaring world. In the first play, the only character, a broken-down old writer, replays tape recordings he made as a young man. Krapp alternates reliving the past with recording his last tape as he prepares to die.

The second play is a park-bench encounter between a smug middle-class man and an aimless drifter desperate for human contact. Their meeting turns deadly and changes the lives of both.

Beckett's play had previously been performed at London's Royal Court Theatre, in 1958, with Patrick Magee. *The Zoo Story* had had its world premiere at the Schiller Theatre in Berlin the same year. Alan Schneider, who had directed American productions of Beckett's *Waiting for Godot* and *Endgame*, wanted to mount *Krapp* but needed a second piece to go with it. Producer Richard Barr had acquired the rights to Albee's play. With Clinton Wilder and Albee, Barr formed Theatre 1960 and presented the two plays together. Schneider simultaneously directed *Krapp* and a Washington, D.C., production of Chekhov's *The Cherry Orchard*. Milton Katselas was set to stage *Zoo Story*, but he was fired after two weeks. Barr and Albee took over the direction of *Zoo* but kept Katselas' name on the program.

THE BALCONY

by Jean Genet, translated by Bernard Frechtman

Opened March 3, 1960

672 Performances

Circle in the Square Downtown

Directed by José Quintero

Produced by Circle in the Square and Lucille Lortel

Cast: F.M. Kimball (The Bishop); Nancy Marchand (Irma); Grayson Hall (The Penitent); Sylvia Miles (The Thief); Arthur Malet (The Judge); John Perkins (The Executioner); John S. Dodson (The General); Salome Jens (The Girl); Betty Miller (Carmen); Roy Poole (The Chief of Police); Jock Livingston (The Envoy); Joseph Daubenas (Roger); William Goodwin (The Slave).

French playwright Jean Genet mixed sex, politics, violence, crime, and delusion in a heady brew called *The Balcony*. The play takes place in a brothel, where petty officials enact fantasies of power with hired hookers while a revolution erupts outside. The line between reality and illusion blurs as the bizarre bordello scenes blend with the chaos of the streets.

Genet was familiar with crime and violence, having spent his first thirty years in and out of jails for a variety of felonies. He wrote his first novel in prison in 1942. The success of the novel and later ones prompted a committee of artists, including Jean Cocteau, Pablo Picasso, and Jean-Paul Sartre, to petition for his release which was granted in 1947.

The Balcony was first presented in London, in 1957, at the Arts Theatre. The venue had to be designated as a private club, since the Lord Chamberlain forbade public performances of the play. Genet hated Peter Zadek's staging, saying it reminded him of a Folies-Bergère sketch. The angry playwright created havoc in the theatre on opening night. Half the London critics called it obscene, while the other half hailed it as a masterpiece.

Genet was more satisfied with Peter Brook's 1960 Paris production. Brook was to have directed the New York version at Circle in the Square, but José Quintero stepped in when Brook had a scheduling conflict.

Revivals have been mounted in New York by the CSC Repertory (1976) and the Performance Group (1980) and in London by the Royal Shakespeare Company (1971).

THE FANTASTICKS

Book and lyrics by Tom Jones

Music by Harvey Schmidt

Opened May 3, 1960

Still running (13,974 performances as of February 6, 1994)

Sullivan Street Playhouse

Directed by Word Baker

Produced by Lore Noto

Cast: Jerry Orbach (El Gallo); Rita Gardner (The Girl); Kenneth Nelson (The Boy); William Larsen (The Boy's Father); Hugh Thomas (The Girl's Father); Thomas Bruce (The Old Actor); George Curley (The Man Who Dies); Richard Stauffer (The Mute); Jay Hampton (The Handyman).

The longest-running musical either on or off-Broadway—or anywhere in the world—is *The Fantasticks*, the charming show of romance and magic which opened at the Sullivan Street Theatre in 1960 and is still going strong. The deceptively simple plot involves a pair of young lovers whose fathers pretend to quarrel in order to spur their offspring's union.

The story is derived from *Les Romanesques*, an 1894 play by Edmond Rostand, author of *Cyrano de Bergerac*. Harvey Schmidt and Tom Jones began adapting the piece into a one-act musical while they were both students at the

Jerry Orbach, Rita Gardner, and Kenneth Nelson in the original cast of *The Fantasticks*, the world's longest-running musical.

University of Texas. Originally, their adaptation was an elaborate extravaganza set on a Texas ranch with the boy and the girl living on opposite sides of the Mexican border. It sported the ungainly title of *Joy Comes to Dead Horse*.

The collaborators were forced to rework the piece when *West Side Story* opened with its similar theme of a star-crossed romance. Fellow classmate Word Baker offered Jones and Schmidt the opportunity to mount their new version, called *The Fantasticks*, at Barnard College's Minor Latham Theatre. The new take on the material was presentational, as Baker conjured up the story with deliberate theatrically on a bare stage. Producer Lore Noto saw the show at Barnard and agreed to mount the production off-Broadway if it were expanded to two acts.

Critical reaction was lukewarm, and the production almost closed within a week, but good word of mouth kept the show open.

There have been at least 11,000 productions of *The Fantasticks* in the United States alone, as well as 700 foreign mountings in sixty-eight different countries. Some of the better-known names to have appeared in it are F. Murray Abraham, Anna Maria Alberghetti, Richard Chamberlain, Glenn Close, Bert Convy, Elliott Gould, Robert Goulet, Edward Everett Horton, Liza Minnelli, and John Wood, as well as producer Noto and author Jones (who played the role of the Old Actor under the name of Thomas Bruce).

A 1964 telecast on NBC's *Hallmark Hall of Fame* featured Ricardo Montalban, Bert Lahr, Stanley Holloway, Susan Watson (the original Luisa at Barnard), and John Davidson.

THE BLACKS

by Jean Genet, translated by Bernard Frechtman
Opened May 4, 1961
1,408 Performances
St. Mark's Playhouse
Directed by Gene Frankel
Produced by Sidney Bernstein, George Edgar, and André Gregory

Cast: Roscoe Lee Browne (Archibald Absalom Wellington); James Earl Jones (Deodatus Village); Cynthia Belgrave (Adelaide Bobo); Louis Gossett (Edgar Alas Newport News); Ethel Ayler (Augusta Snow); Helen Martin (Felicity Trollop Pardon); Cicely Tyson (Stephanie Virtue Secret-rose Diop); Godfrey M. Cambridge (Diouf); Lex Monson (Missionary); Raymond St. Jacques (Judge); Jay J. Riley (Governor); Maya Angelou Make (Queen); Charles Gordone (Valet); Charles Campbell (Drummer).

In *The Balcony*, Jean Genet had examined the pervasiveness of role-playing in society. In *The Blacks*, written before *The Balcony* but performed off-Broadway later, the author cast the same topic in racial terms. Subtitled "A Clown Show," the play depicts a group of blacks enacting a ritual rape and murder of a white woman. They are being watched and judged by their white colonial oppressors, who are in reality another group of blacks wearing white masks. The play was first performed in Paris as *Les Nègres* in 1959. The 1961 American production, in a translation by Bernard Frechtman, became the longest-running off-Broadway nonmusical of the decade. It even toured nationally.

The original cast included many performers who would later become some of America's leading actors: James Earl Jones, Roscoe Lee Browne, Louis Gossett, Cicely Tyson, and Godfrey M. Cambridge. Two would gain fame as writers: Maya Angelou Make, who later dropped the surname Make and penned the bestselling autobiography *I Know Why the Caged Bird Sings*, and Charles Gordone, the first African-American author to win the Pulitzer Prize for drama, for *No Place to Be Somebody* (1969).

Maya Angelou and Charles Gordone of *The Blacks* would later attain fame as writers.

THE HOSTAGE

by Brendan Behan

Opened December 12, 1961

545 Performances

One Sheridan Square

Directed by Perry Bruskin

Produced by Norma Frances, Robert Marguiles, and Bell Productions

Cast: Alan Nunn (Pat); Paddy Croft (Meg Dillon); Norman Roland (Monsewer); Kathleen Rowland (Old Ropeen); Marge Burnett (Colette); Rai Saunders (Princess Grace); James Cahill (Rio Rita); Louis Beachner (Mr. Mulleady); Patricia Ripley (Miss Gilchrist); Geoff Garland (Leslie); Jane McArthur (Teresa); William H. Bassett (IRA Officer); Vince O'Connor (Volunteer); Richard Sabol (Russian Sailor); Bill (Bill Johnson).

Irish author Brendan Behan blended bawdy farce with serious drama in *The Hostage*. The title character is a British soldier held captive by the Irish Republican Army in a combination rooming house and brothel. If an Irish lad is hanged for shooting a policeman, the English hostage will be shot. The residents of the house (prostitutes, a spinsterish social worker, and a pair of outlandish homosexuals) provide broad comedy as the deadline for execution approaches.

The play was first written and performed in Gaelic in 1957. Joan Littlewood further developed the play and directed the London premiere at her Theatre Workshop in 1958. A 1960 Broadway staging had a disappointing run of only 127 performances. The off-Broadway revival, mounted just a year later, had a more successful run of 545 performances.

Behan spent most of his early life in prison (or borstal) for his I.R.A. activities. Upon his release he began writing. His first play, *The Quare Fellow* (1956), dramatized his experiences behind bars. He died in 1964 at the age of 41.

A adaptation of Behan's autobiography, *Borstal Boy*, appeared on Broadway in 1970 and won the Tony Award as Best Play.

DIME A DOZEN

Conceived and directed by Julius Monk

Opened October 18, 1962

728 Performances

Plaza 9 Music Hall

Choreographed by Frank Wagner

Cast: Ceil Cabot, Gerry Matthews, Jack Fletcher, Mary Louise Wilson, Rex Robbins, Susan Browning

Dime a Dozen was the most successful in a series of numerically named cabaret revues produced by Julius Monk. The previous entries bore such digital titles as *Four Below, Take Five, Pieces of Eight*, and *Ten-Ish Anyone?*. The songs and sketches satirized a variety of contemporary topics.

Performers launched in other Monk revues and clubs included Pat Carroll, Imogene Coca, Bill Dana, Tammy Grimes, Dorothy Loudon, Jonathan Winters, and the Four Lads.

THE PINTER PLAYS

(*The Dumbwaiter* and *The Collection*)

by Harold Pinter

Opened November 26, 1962

578 Performances

Cherry Lane Theatre

Directed by Alan Schneider

Produced by Caroline Swann

Cast: *The Dumbwaiter*: Dana Elcar (Ben); John C. Becher (Gus); *The Collection*: Henderson Forsythe (Harry); Patricia Roe (Stella); James Ray (James); James Patterson (Bill).

The enigmatic plays of Englishman Harold Pinter were first presented to American audiences off-Broadway. This double bill of *The Dumbwaiter* and *The Collection* was the most successful of these early Pinter productions. Much like Beckett's *Waiting for Godot*, *The Dumbwaiter* concerned two nobodies who must wait—in this case they await instructions from their mysterious employer. *The Collection* detailed a love quadrangle involving two couples, one straight, one gay, neither particularly happy.

Other Pinter plays, such as *The Caretaker* (1961), *The Homecoming* (Tony winner for Best Play, 1967), *Old Times* (1971), and *Betrayal* (1980), were seen on Broadway.

The Dumbwaiter was filmed for ABC-TV with Robert Altman directing John Travolta and Tom Conti. *The Collection* was adapted for television by the BBC and starred Laurence Olivier. It was shown in America on PBS television.

Patricia Roe and James Ray are an estranged couple in *The Collection*, half of a double bill by Harold Pinter.

SIX CHARACTERS IN SEARCH OF AN AUTHOR

by Luigi Pirandello, translated by Paul Avila Mayer

Opened March 8, 1963

529 Performances

The Martinique Theatre

Directed by William Ball

Produced by Theodore Mann and Claude Giroux

Cast: Michael O'Sullivan (Director); Jacqueline Brookes (Stepdaughter); Richard A. Dysart (Father); Joan Croyden (Mother); James Valentine (Son); Angela Wood (Mme. Pace); Anne Lynn (Anne); Alfred Spindelman (Al); Patricia Hamilton (Patsy); David Marguiles (David); Paul Shenar (Paul); David Hersey (Herse); John Higgins (Higgins); Jan Moerel (Jan); Margery Shaw (Marge); Walter Brown (Walt); Gregg Weir (Young Boy); Diana Visco (Young Girl).

Luigi Pirandello, one of Italy's greatest dramatists, often explored the thin line between reality and illusion. In *Six Characters in Search of an Author*, a "fictional" family interrupts a theatre company's rehearsal. These six beg to be put onstage, for their author has abandoned them. The distinction between the "actors" and the "characters" blurs as they argue over who is more real.

The play was written and first performed in Italy in 1921. It appeared in both New York and London the following year and has been revived many times since (1924 and 1931 on Broadway; and during the 1946–47, 1955–56, and 1962–63 seasons off-Broadway). The 1963 revival ran the longest of all these productions. An updating of the play was done by American Repertory Theatre of Cambridge, Massachusetts, and presented in a regional theatre festival at the off-Broadway Joyce Theatre in 1988.

THE BOYS FROM SYRACUSE

Book by George Abbott, based on *The Comedy of Errors*, by William Shakespeare.

Music by Richard Rodgers

Lyrics by Lorenz Hart

Opened April 15, 1963

500 Performances

Theatre Four

Directed by Christopher Hewett

Choreographed by Bob Herget

Produced by Richard York

Cast: Stuart Damon (Antipholus of Syracuse); Danny Carroll (Dromio of Syracuse); Clifford David (Antipholus of Ephesus); Rudy Tronto (Dromio of Ephesus); Ellen Hanley (Adriana); Julienne Marie (Lucianna); Karen Morrow (Luce); Cathryn Damon (Courtesan); Matthew Tobin (Aegeon/Sorcerer); Fred Kimbrough (Duke); Gary Oakes (Sargeant); Jim Pompeii (Tailor/Merchant of Ephesus); Richard Colacino (Merchant of Syracuse); Jeane Deeks (Apprentice/Maid); Richard Nieves (Angelo/Pygamlion); Don Salinaro (Corporal); Zebra Nevins (Fatima); Violetta Landek (Galatea/Courtesan).

This off-Broadway revival of *The Boys from Syracuse*, Rodgers and Hart's adaptation of Shakespeare's mistaken-identity madness, *The Comedy of Errors*, outran the original 1938 Broadway production's run of 235 performances. In both shows, two sets of identical twins cause confusion in ancient Asia Minor. George Abbott, author and director of the first mounting, reported in his memoirs that critics praised everything about the new version except his tired old book. One gag a critic quoted was, "Dozens of men are at my feet," "Yes, I know, chiropodists." Abbott didn't recognize any of these cracks and saw the show to investigate. It turned out that Richard York, the producer of the revival, had interjected his own jokes, hoping they would update the book to 1963 tastes. York removed his interpolations at Abbott's insistence.

Without the "old jokes," the show was even more popular. It went on to win the Vernon Rice and Obie Awards as outstanding musical production off-Broadway.

THE TROJAN WOMEN

by Euripides, translated by Edith Hamilton

Opened December 23, 1963

600 Performances

Circle in the Square Downtown

Directed and choreographed by Michael Cacoyannis

Produced by Theodore Mann

Cast: Mildred Dunnock (Hecuba); Alan Mixon (Talthybius); Carrie Nye (Cassandra); Joyce Ebert (Andromache); Jane White (Helen); Robert Mandan (Menelaus); Rod Steiger (Voice of Poseidon).

This revival of Euripides' The Trojan Women is the only example of classical Greek tragedy to run over 500 performances either on or off Broadway. The play takes place in Troy after the city has fallen to the Greeks. The women mourn as the conquerors come to take them away as slaves. But the gods declare that the victors are doomed as well for having defiled their temples. Greek director Michael Cacoyannis had staged the play at the Spoleto Festival in Italy in July of 1963. Mildred Dunnock was the deposed Queen Hecuba. The Circle in the Square Theatre imported the production for its off-Broadway season that December. The revival won a special citation from the New York Drama Critics Circle. Cacoyannis went on to direct a 1972 film of The Trojan Women which starred four major talents: Katharine Hepburn, Vanessa Redgrave, Irene Papas, and Genevieve Bujold.

THE KNACK (AND HOW TO GET IT)

by Ann Jellicoe

Opened May 27, 1964

685 Performances

The New Theatre

Directed by Mike Nichols

Produced by the Entertainment Theatre Co.

Cast: Brian Bedford (Tom); Roddy Maude-Roxby (Colin); George Segal (Tolen); Alexandra Berlin (Nancy).

Mike Nichols followed up his triumphant Broadway directing debut of Neil Simon's Barefoot in the Park with The Knack at the tail-end of the same season. Ann Jellicoe's wry English comedy tells of two male egos—a cocky lothario and a shy young artist—competing to see who can seduce an awkward girl first. The play was first produced in Cambridge, in 1961, and then in London, at the Royal Court Theatre, in 1962. The Knack eventually had three companies playing simultaneously, in Chicago, in Los Angeles, and off-Broadway. Sam Waterston, and the future authors of Hair, Gerome Ragni and James Rado, were among those who appeared in the New York companies. The 1965 British film version featured Michael Crawford, Rita Tushingham, Ray Brooks, and Donal Donnelly.

A VIEW FROM THE BRIDGE

by Arthur Miller

Opened January 28, 1965

780 Performances

Sheridan Square Playhouse

Directed by Ulu Grosbard

Produced by Ulu Grosbard, Joseph E. Levine, and Katza-Berne Corp.

Cast: Robert Duvall (Eddie); Jeanne Kaplan (Beatrice); Jon Voight (Rudolpho); Susan Anspach (Catherine); Ramon Bieri (Marco); Mitchell Jason (Alfieri); Richard Castellano (Louis); Carmine Caridi (Mike); Gino Morra (Tony); Dan Priest (1st Immigration Officer); Curt Dempster (2nd Immigration Officer); William Corio (Mr. Lipari); Bea Brooks (Mrs. Lipari).

A View from the Bridge was Arthur Miller's second play, after The Crucible, to enjoy a longer run off-Broadway than on. An explosive drama of a Brooklyn longshoreman's excessive attachment to his young niece, Bridge was first presented on Broadway as a one-act play, on a double bill with Miller's A Memory of Two Mondays, in 1955. Van Heflin and Eileen Heckart had headed the cast. It was respectfully received by the press and ran 149 performances.

Director Ulu Grosbard wanted to give the play a second chance. He had staged it at the Gateway Playhouse in Bellport, Long Island, in 1957, using the full-length version Miller had written for the London production. A young Robert Duvall played Eddie, the conflicted dock worker whose unspoken passion for his niece destroys him. Grosbard presented the production for Miller for one performance at the St. Marks Playhouse. The author approved it, and film mogul Joseph E. Levine, who had financed The Knack, another off-Broadway success, put up most of the cash. The revival at the Sheridan Square Playhouse coincided with two other Miller plays—After the Fall and Incident at Vichy—both presented at Lincoln Center the same season.

A 1983 revival starred Tony LoBianco, Rose Gregorio, and Saundra Santiago. Michael Gambon played Eddie in a major 1987 National Theatre production in London.

HOGAN'S GOAT

by William Alfred

Opened November 11, 1965

607 Performances

St. Clement's Church

Directed by Frederick Rolf

Produced by the American Place Theatre

Cast: Ralph Waite (Matthew Stanton); Faye Dunaway (Kathleen Stanton); Roland Wood (John "Black Jack" Haggerty); Cliff Gorman (Petey Boyle); Michaele Myers (Bessie Legg); Grania O'Malley (Maria Haggerty); Barnard Hughes (Father Coyle); John Dorman (Father Maloney); Tom Ahearne (Edward Quinn); Conrad Bain (James "Palsy" Murphy); Luke Wymbs (Bill); Agnes Young (Ann Mulcahy); Teresa Hughes (Josephine Finn); Tom Crane (Boylan); David Dawson (Doctor).

The Irish Brooklyn of the 1890s came alive in William Alfred's blank-verse drama, *Hogan's Goat*. The play depicts the struggle for power between the corrupt mayor of Brooklyn and Matthew Stanton, a rising politician. But Matthew's unchecked ambition and his past relationship with a woman, Agnes Hogan, ruins his career and his marriage to the delicate Kathleen. The playwright, a Harvard history professor, based his play on the tales of his Irish great-grandmother. "She told me many stories about the people around her at that time," the author said in a *New York Times* interview. "And they seemed more alive, even though they were dead, than the people around me, because she was such a wonderful storyteller."

The play was first performed in 1958 at Sanders Theatre in Cambridge, Massachusetts. Alfred rewrote it four times

Robert Hooks and Barbara Ann Teer satirize racist attitudes in *Day of Absence*.

before he was completely satisfied. It came to the attention of the American Place Theatre on a recommendation of poet Robert Lowell, a friend of Alfred's.

Some reviewers disliked the plot, but all were impressed with the eloquent language and the detailed depiction of the rowdy, colorful Brooklyn of a bygone age.

Many in the original cast went on to stardom, including Faye Dunaway, Ralph Waite, Cliff Gorman, Barnard Hughes, and Conrad Bain.

Dunaway re-created her original role in a 1971 PBS telecast, with Robert Foxworth, George Rose, Philip Bosco, and Rue McClanahan.

Cry for Us All, a musical retelling of *Hogan*, had critics and audiences crying for the curtain to come down in 1970. It closed after nine performances.

HAPPY ENDING / DAY OF ABSENCE

by Douglas Turner Ward

Opened November 15, 1965

504 Performances

St. Marks Playhouse

Directed by Philip Meister

Produced by Robert Hooks, Inc.

Cast: Esther Rolle (Ellie/Clubwoman); Frances Foster (Vi/Supervisor/Aide); Robert Hooks (Junie/John/Brush Man); Douglas Turner (Arthur/Mayor/Clan); Lonne Elder (Clem/2nd Citizen/Businessman); Arthur French (Luke/3rd Citizen/Mop Man); Barbara Ann Teer (Mary); Hattie Winston (1st Operator/Doll Woman); Maxine Griffith (2nd Operator); Pamela Jones (3rd Operator); Adolph Caesar (Jackson); Moses Gunn (1st Citizen/Industrialist/Pious/Rastus); Bostic Van Felton (Courier); Mark Shapiro (announcer).

Douglas Turner Ward used pointed satire to draw attention to racial inequality in his duo of one-acts, *Happy Ending* and *Day of Absence*. In *Happy Ending*, two domestics demonstrate to their militant nephew that they are smarter than their wealthy white employers.

Day of Absence reversed the tradition of the old minstrel show in which white performers "blacked up" to play stereotypical black parts. In Ward's play, African-American actors donned white makeup to portray exaggerated Caucasian inhabitants of a Southern town whose black citizens have vanished. The device also echoed the white masks worn by some of the performers in Jean Genet's *The Blacks*.

The original cast included Ward, Robert Hooks, Frances Foster, Lonne Elder (the author of *Ceremonies in Dark Old Men* which Ward later starred in), Hattie Winston, and Adolph Caesar.

In 1968, Ward, Hooks, and Gerald S. Krone founded the Negro Ensemble Company, for years one of the leading off-Broadway theatre companies. In 1970, that company presented *Day of Absence* on a double bill with *Brotherhood*, another satiric one-act by Ward.

THE POCKET WATCH

by Alvin Aronson
Opened January 5, 1966
725 Performances
Actors Playhouse
Directed by Sherwood Arthur
Produced by the New Playwrights Productions Co.

Cast: Rita Karin (Rachel Goldman); Estelle Omens (Freda Goldman); Daniel T. Frankel (Harold Schwartz); Mimi Randolph (Sophie Schwartz); Michael Gorrin (Chaim Goldman); Hy Anzell (Sam Schwartz); C.M. Gampel (Irving Friedman).

Alvin Aronson had only $5,000 and one week of rehearsal to mount his play *The Pocket Watch*. To add to the show's burdens, there was a transit strike and a blizzard to keep theatregoers from making the trek to the Actors Playhouse in Greenwich Village. To make matters even worse, Stanley Kauffman of the mighty *New York Times* panned the play. But Aronson persisted. In addition to having written the comedy-drama, Aronson worked in the box office, ushered, swept out the theatre, threw out the trash, and joined the cast when one of the actors left.

The play managed to survive these initial setbacks and two changes of venue from the Actors Playhouse, first to the Mermaid and then to the similarly-named Maidman Theatre, for a run of 725 performances.

Called "a Jewish *Look Homeward, Angel*" by Jerry Tallmer of the *New York Post*, *The Pocket Watch* naturalistically recorded the doings of three generations of a Roxbury, Massachusetts, family. As in many similar works, there was a nagging, oppressive mother, an overworked father, a spinster sister, and a sensitive son with writing ambitions.

THE MAD SHOW

Book by Larry Siegel and Stan Hart
Music by Mary Rodgers
Lyrics by Marshall Barer, Larry Siegel, and Steve Vinaver
Opened January 10, 1966
871 Performances
The New Theatre
Directed by Steven Vinaver
Produced by Ivor David Balding for the Establishment Theatre Company
Cast: Linda Lavin, MacIntyre Dixon, Dick Libertini, Paul Sand, Jo Anne Worley.

A musical based on *Mad* magazine? Not so unlikely when you consider that a Broadway show based on the adventures of Superman would open the same season, and that *Batman* was a hit television series. Clearly cartoon and comic-book humor were in.

The Mad Show followed the adolescent humor of the publication. Movies, TV shows, and social trends were lampooned in the broadest possible fashion with the visage of Alfred E. Newman grinning down on the proceedings.

The show yields up this trivia note for fans of Broadway: The lyrics for "The Boy from . . . ," a witty take-off on "The Girl from Ipanema," was credited to Norm Deploom, which was a *nom de plume* for Stephen Sondheim. The ditty later showed up in *Side by Side by Sondheim*, a revue of the composer's work.

The revue proved to be remarkably fertile soil: The machine-gun pace of *The Mad Show* could be seen as an influence on NBC's hit variety show *Rowan and Martin's Laugh-In*, which premiered two years later. *Mad Show* alumnus Jo Anne Worley became one of *Laugh-In*'s regular cuckoos. Paul Sand went on to win a Tony for Paul Sills' *Story Theatre* and a TV career playing lovable nebbishes. Linda Lavin leaped from this revue to the musical *Superman* and later stardom. MacIntrye Dixon and Dick Libertini have been seen in numerous quirky roles on screen and stage.

AMERICA HURRAH

by Jean-Claude van Itallie
Opened November 7, 1966
634 Performances
The Pocket Theatre
Directed by Joseph Chaikin (*Interview*) and Jacques Levy (*TV, Motel*)
Produced by Stephanie Sills

Cast: (playing multiple roles) Cynthia Harris, Conrad Fowkes, Ronnie Gilbert, Henry Calvert, Joyce Aaron, James Barbosa, Brenda Smiley, Bill Macy, and Ruth White (Voice of the Motel-Keeper).

Jean-Claude van Itallie presented a savage view of life in the United States with *America Hurrah*, a triple bill of one-acts. In *Interview*, four job applicants are grilled by four interviewers wearing frozen smiles. As the questions and answers build in intensity and tempo, the interview becomes a mad dance of urban *angst*. The bare stage becomes such diverse locales as a subway, an exercise class, a party, an operating room, and psychiatrist's office. In mini-scenes, the actors moved with mechanization, devoid of feeling.

TV takes places in a video viewing room. Three actors play workers who monitor television programs. Five others portray the people on the programs, complete with black lines on their faces to suggest video images. During the course of the play, the TV actors take up more and more of the stage and it becomes impossible to tell the difference between the "real-life" characters and their small screen counterparts.

The final play, *Motel*, is a scathing comment on American violence and tastelessness. Two actors in monstrous doll costumes, portraying a garish couple, trash a motel room while the motel-keeper, also a doll, drones on about the tacky objects in the room. Finally, the vulgar duo dismantle the motel-keeper herself.

The Belgian-born van Itallie developed the plays with the Open Theatre, an avant-garde theatre troupe headed by director Joseph Chaikin. *America Hurrah* had been previously presented in a different form (and without the *TV* play) at Ellen Stewart's Café La MaMa.

Van Itallie, Chaikin, and the Open Theatre collaborated again when they presented the ritualistic drama *The Serpent* (1970).

YOU'RE A GOOD MAN, CHARLIE BROWN

Book, music, and lyrics by Clark Gesner

Opened March 7, 1967

Theatre 80 St. Marks

1,597 Performances

Directed by Joseph Hardy

Choreographed by Patricia Birch

Produced by Arthur Whitelaw and Gene Persson

Cast: Gary Burghoff (Charlie Brown); Bill Hinnant (Snoopy); Reva Rose (Lucy); Bob Balaban (Linus); Skip Hinnant (Schroeder); Karen Johnson (Patty).

You're a Good Man, Charlie Brown, one of off-Broadway's longest-running musicals, was based on Charles M.

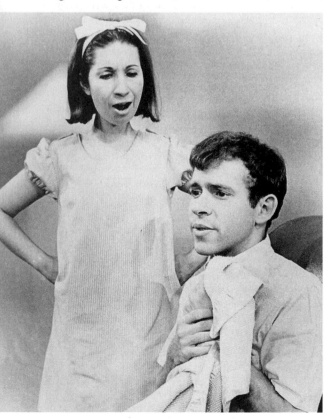

Reva Rose as Lucy and Bob Balaban as Linus in *You're a Good Man, Charlie Brown*.

Schulz's comic strip, *Peanuts*. The cartoon images of perpetual victim Charlie Brown, his human-like dog Snoopy, the crabby Lucy, the blanket-hugging intellectual Linus, and Beethoven-loving Schroeder were immensely popular, seen everywhere from lunch boxes to television specials. Like future megamusicals *Jesus Christ Superstar* and *Evita*, the smaller-scale *Charlie Brown* began life as a record album. Clark Gesner had written a score of songs based on the Peanuts characters, and MGM Records had produced an album. On the basis of the album, producer Arthur Whitelaw persuaded MGM Records to co-finance a stage version.

"We made the show up as we went along," Whitelaw said in an interview. "We cut up all the Charlie Brown books and the kids in the cast brought in their favorite lines." The resulting production was a sort of revue with Gesner's charming songs linked by brief scenes of ordinary childhood incidents. The little show perfectly captured a single day in the life of the Peanuts gang.

Charlie Brown ran for four years at the intimate Theatre 80 St. Marks and even played Broadway in 1971. A second *Peanuts* musical called *Snoopy* played off-Broadway, in 1982, for 152 performances.

SCUBA DUBA

by Bruce Jay Friedman

Opened October 10, 1967

692 Performances

The New Theatre

Directed by Jacques Levy

Produced by Ivor David Balding

Cast: Jerry Orbach (Harold Wonder); Brenda Smiley (Miss Janus); Cleavon Little (Foxtrot); Conrad Bain (Tourist); Rita Karin (Landlady); Judd Hirsch (Thief); Bernard Poulain (Gendarme); Ken Olfson (Dr. Schoenfeld); Christine Norden (Cheyenne); Jennifer Warren (Jean Wonder); Rudy Challenger (Reddington); Stella Longo (Voice of Harold's Mother).

Bruce Jay Friedman had achieved success as the author of two sardonically humorous novels when his first play *Scuba Duba* opened off-Broadway.

The setting of a gorgeous villa in the south of France set the audience up for a light romantic comedy. But what they got was a stinging farce on racial and sexual tensions. The protagonist is Harold Wonder (played by Jerry Orbach), a neurotic white American on vacation. His liberal beliefs are thrown out the window when he fears his wife has run off with a black scuba diver. While waiting for his spouse to return to their rented villa, Harold spends the night spewing racial invective to an empty-headed, bikini-clad party girl. They are interrupted by the scuba diver in question, a French thief, a bigoted American tourist, and Harold's psychiatrist, who is accompanied by his oversexed girlfriend. Finally, Harold's wife Jean arrives. In an ironic twist, it is revealed her lover is not the scuba diver, but a black poet. Harold's worst racial fears are realized when he sees that his black rival is not only his sexual superior, but is more intellectual as well.

The play had something to offend everyone: racial slurs, nudity, myriad sexual references. But the raw jokes were used to starkly address the ambivalent feelings of whites towards blacks.

Judd Hirsch succeeded Orbach. Friedman returned to off-Broadway with *Steambath* (1970), another raunchy and controversial comedy in which heaven is portrayed as a steam room.

CURLEY McDIMPLE

Book by Robert Dahdah and Mary Boylen

Music and lyrics by Robert Dahdah

Opened November 22, 1967

931 Performances

Bert Wheeler Theatre

Directed by Robert Dahdah

Choreographed by Larry Stevens

Produced by The Curley Company

Cast: Bayn Johnson (Curley McDimple); Joyce Nolen (Alice); Paul Cahill (Jimmy); Helon Blount (Sarah); George Hillman (Bill); Norma Bigtree (Miss Hamilton); Gene Galvin (Mr. Gillingwater).

Before nostalgia swept Broadway in the '70s, off-Broadway presented a charming tribute to the '30s with *Curley McDimple*. Just as *Little Mary Sunshine* spoofed the Jeanette MacDonald–Nelson Eddy operettas of the Depression era, *Curley* parodied the Shirley Temple movies of the same period. In addition to a singing and dancing Temple-like tyke, the cast of characters included an Alice Faye heroine, a George Murphy hero, a Bill Robinson tap dancer, and a Margaret Hamilton-ish villainess.

The show was the brainchild of Robert Dahdah, who wrote the songs, co-authored the book, staged the action, produced, and ran the box office. He created *Curley* in reaction to unpleasant experiences he had seeing other off-Broadway shows. In one production, he was sprinkled with urine. At another, the actors spat at the audience. "I wanted to write a play where everyone would come out loving everyone else," he told *Life* magazine, "a valentine to the '30s."

Curley opened in the Bert Wheeler Theatre, actually the converted bar of the somewhat sleazy Dixie Hotel, across the street from the *New York Times* on West 43rd Street. During the run, veteran character actress Butterfly McQueen (now widely remembered for her role in *Gone with the Wind*) joined the cast in a role written especially for her. The show was briefly revived at the Plaza 9 Music Hall in 1972.

YOUR OWN THING

Book by Donald Driver, suggested by *Twelfth Night,* by William Shakespeare.

Music and lyrics by Hal Hester and Danny Apolinar

Opened January 13, 1968

933 Performances

Orpheum Theatre

Directed by Donald Driver

Produced by Zev Bufman and Dorothy Love

Cast: Leland Palmer (Viola); Rusty Thacker (Sebastian); Marian Mercer (Olivia); Tom Ligon (Orson); Danny Apolinar (Danny); John Kuhner (John); Michael Valenti (Michael); Igor Gavon (Purser/Stage Manager); Imogene Bliss (Nurse).

Shakespeare's *Twelfth Night* served as the inspiration for *Your Own Thing*, the "Now-Generation" rock musical. The Bard's brother-and-sister twins were replaced with a '60s sibling singing act. Believing her brother is drowned at sea, the sister poses as a boy and makes a hit in New York's East Village club scene. Confusion ensues as the brother shows up and nobody knows who has been sleeping with whom.

In earlier ventures, songwriters Hal Hester and Danny Apolinar had bad luck in gaining permission to musically adapt a published play. So they decided to take a work in the public domain as the source for their next show. The light bulb went off while an actress friend was reading a synopsis of Shakespeare's plays to Hester. The mistaken sexual-identity plot of *Twelfth Night* fit in perfectly with the long hairstyles and androgynous fashions of the '60s. It became the first off-Broadway show to win the New York Drama Critics Circle Award.

The production employed twelve slide projectors, two movie projectors, and two tape recorders, to create multimedia images of famous personalities such as John Wayne, Queen Elizabeth II, Shirley Temple, the Pope, and Shakespeare himself as a comment on the action.

Two other musicals used *Twelfth Night* as their source: *Love and Let Love*, which played briefly in the same season, and *Music Is* (1976) with book and direction by George Abbott. Both had brief runs.

JACQUES BREL IS ALIVE AND WELL AND LIVING IN PARIS

Conceived by Eric Blau and Mort Shuman

Music and lyrics by Jacques Brel, adapted by Eric Blau and Mort Shuman

Opened January 22, 1968

1,847 Performances

The Village Gate

Directed by Moni Yakim

Produced by 3W Productions

Cast: Elly Stone, Mort Shuman, Shawn Elliott, Alice Whitfield

The songs of Belgian composer and singer Jacques Brel were introduced to a wide American public in the long-running revue *Jacques Brel Is Alive and Well and Living in Paris*. With no plot, the show goes through twenty-six of Brel's songs, ranging from comic numbers ("Timid Frieda") and tender ballads ("Marieke") to stirring social protest ("Sons of," "Next").

The revue was conceived by Eric Blau and Mort Shuman. Blau first heard of Brel when his friend Nat Shapiro, an executive with Columbia Records, played some of the composer's songs. Blau, together with rock songwriter Mort Shuman, did English adaptations of the Brel songs.

Some of the Brel songs wound up in a revue called *O, Oysters!*, co-produced by Blau at the Village Gate in 1961. Elly Stone, Blau's wife, sang the tunes in *Oysters*. Along with Shuman, Shawn Elliott, and Alice Whitfield, she was in the original cast of *Jacques Brel*.

The show ran five and half years at the Village Gate and went on to play Broadway for three months. Stone directed a 25th anniversary production in 1992. The composer—who was indeed living in Paris—did not attend the original production until two years after it had opened. He had refused to visit the United States, in protest of the Vietnam War. Brel died in 1978, at the age of forty-nine.

Stone, Shuman, Joe Maisell, and Brel himself appeared in the 1975 film version.

THE BOYS IN THE BAND

by Mart Crowley

Opened April 15, 1968

1,000 Performances

Theatre Four

Directed by Robert Moore

Produced by Richard Barr and Charles Woodward, Jr.

Cast: Kenneth Nelson (Michael); Frederick Combs (Donald); Cliff Gorman (Emory); Keith Prentice (Larry); Laurence Luckinbill (Hank); Reuben Greene (Bernard); Robert La Tourneaux (Cowboy); Leonard Frey (Harold); Peter White (Alan).

Homosexuality burst out of the closet and onto the stage with Mart Crowley's ribald *The Boys in the Band*. Previous plays had either indirectly touched on the subject or dealt with sensitive protagonists wrongly accused of the love that "dare not speak its name" (*The Children's Hour, Tea and Sympathy*). In *Boys*, the topic was unmistakable. Eight gay men gather for a bitchy birthday party, where the gifts include a male prostitute. An extra guest, the supposedly straight friend of the host, acts as a catalyst for explosive confrontations and *Virginia Woolf*-ish party games.

All of the original cast appeared in the 1970 film, under the direction of William Friedkin. Today, the play would be regarded more as a period piece in which the characters

The cast of *The Boys in the Band*, Mart Crowley's comedy about a gay birthday party.

are seen as negative, unhappy stereotypes unable to cope with a society which despises them. But *Boys* broke ground and numerous gay-themed plays, such as *Torch Song Trilogy* and *Angels in America*, have followed.

DAMES AT SEA

Book and lyrics by George Haimsohn and Robin Miller
Music by Jim Wise
Opened December 20, 1968
575 Performances
Bouwerie Lane Theatre
Directed and choreographed by Neal Kenyon
Produced by Jordan Hott and Jack Millstein

Cast: Bernadette Peters (Ruby): David Christmas (Dick); Tamara Long (Mona Kent); Sally Stark (Joan); Steve Elmore (Henessey/The Captain); Joseph R. Sicari (Lucky).

Bernadette Peters played a Ruby Keeler clone in *Dames at Sea*, a pocket-sized send-up of movie musicals like *The Fleet's In* and *Dames*. Every cliché was used in this story of a struggling chorus girl who goes on for the nasty leading lady and becomes a star.

Dames was originally presented in a one-act revue version at the off-off-Broadway Café Cino in 1966. Robert Dahdah (*Curley McDimple*) directed. Producer Jordan Hott told *Stages* magazine, "Originally, the show was forty-five quite marvelous moments. In expanding it, the authors kept the first twenty minutes and the last twenty minutes intact and got another hour or so in the middle. It was out of shape, didn't work. But I was always confident that we'd be able to make it work."

The rewritten version played the Bouwerie Lane Theatre and then moved to the Theatre de Lys on Christopher Street. The show's unabashed love of the conventions of bygone musicals prefigured the bigger nostalgia hits *No, No, Nanette* and *Irene*.

Bonnie Franklin, Barbara Sharma, Loni Ackerman, Leland Palmer, and briefly, Pia Zadora, followed Peters in the lead during the run. The show also played an additional 170 performances at the Plaza 9 Music Hall.

A televised version in 1972 starred three Annes, Ann-Margaret, Anne Meara, and Ann Miller. After a successful run at the Asolo Theatre, in Florida, a revival of *Dames* played off-Broadway in 1985. The new production, which featured the original producer, director, and set and costume designer, ran 278 performances.

ADAPTATION

by Elaine May

NEXT

by Terrence McNally
Opened February 10, 1969
707 Performances
Greenwich Mews Theatre
Directed by Elaine May
Produced by Lyn Austin, Oliver Smith, and Seymour Vall

Cast: *Adaptation*: Gabriel Dell (Contestant); Paul Dooley (Male players); Carol Morley (Female players); Graham Jarvis (Games Master); *Next*: James Coco (Marion Cheever); Elaine Shore (Sgt. Thech).

The depersonalization of American life, a common theme among playwrights of the '60s, was the subject of *Adaptation / Next*, a double bill of one-acts. *Adaptation* by Elaine May, formerly half of the comedy team of Nichols and May, tells of a man's life as a TV game show with the stage mapped out as a playing board. The unhappy contestant moves from square to square, searching for a prize. He

Bernadette Peters (center) in the nostalgic musical *Dames at Sea*.

never realizes that he can declare himself a winner anytime he wants. *Next* by Terrence McNally is an insightful sketch about an overweight, middle-aged movie theatre manager enduring the humiliation of an army physical exam. After the hiliarous comedy of the inductee attempting every trick in the book to be categorized as an unfit 4-F, the play turns serious as he spills out his anger and frustration at the unlistening female sergeant. James Coco drew plaudits as the nervous inductee and was cast in Neil Simon's *Last of the Red Hot Lovers* as a result.

The same season as *Next*, McNally was represented both on Broadway and off by five other one-act plays: *Eros, Cuba Si, Noon, Witness,* and *Tour.*

OH! CALCUTTA!

Devised by Kenneth Tynan

Sketches by Samuel Beckett, Jules Feiffer, Dan Greenburg, John Lennon, Jacques Levy, Leonard Melfi, David Newman and Robert Benton, Sam Shepard, Clovis Trouille, Kenneth Tynan, Sherman Yellen.

Music and lyrics by the Open Window (Robert Dennis, Peter Schickele, and Stanley Walden)

Opened June 17, 1969

704 Performances

Eden Theatre

Directed by Jacques Levy

Choreographed by Margo Sappington

Produced by Hillard Elkins

Cast: Raina Barrett, Mark Dempsey, Katie Drew-Wilkinson, Boni Enten, Bill Macy, Alan Rachins, Leon Russom, Margo Sappington, Nancy Tribush, George Welbes.

This off-Broadway production, a long-run hit, went on to become the long-running Broadway production during the 1970–71 season (see page 216).

THE EFFECT OF GAMMA RAYS ON MAN-IN-THE-MOON MARIGOLDS

by Paul Zindel

Opened April 7, 1970

819 Performances

The Mercer-O'Casey Theatre

Directed by Melvin Bernhardt

Produced by Orin Lehman

Cast: Sada Thompson (Beatrice); Pamela Payton-Wright (Tillie); Amy Levitt (Ruth); Judith Lowry (Nanny); Swoosie Kurtz (Janice Vickery).

The Effect of Gamma Rays on Man-in-the-Moon Marigolds is Paul Zindel's oddly named, touching drama of a household of women. The bitter, misanthropic Beatrice dominates her two maladjusted daughters Tillie and Ruth. Bookish Tillie is introverted and yearns for knowledge, while the sluttish Ruth is subject to seizures. The title refers to Tillie's science project, in which flowers are exposed to radiation. Just as the marigolds in the experiment are mutated because of the gamma rays, Tillie and Ruth either bloom or wither from the bombardment of Beatrice's twisted love.

Sada Thompson won acclaim as the gin-guzzling, self-centered mother who rarely gets out of her bathrobe. Though the character could have earned the audience's emnity, Thompson got their sympathy. Both the actress and the play won numerous awards, including the Obie and Drama Desk Awards. Zindel also copped the New York Drama Critics Circle Award and the Pulitzer Prize— the play was the second consecutive off-Broadway to take the Pulitzer (after *No Place to Be Somebody*). Broadway was no longer the only home of serious theatre.

Gamma Rays had previously been produced at the Alley Theatre, in Houston (1964), on New York Television Theatre (1966), with Eileen Heckart, and at the Cleveland Playhouse (1969).

Joanne Woodward was directed by her husband Paul Newman in the 1972 film version, which had a screenplay by Zindel. Shelley Winters brought the play to Broadway for a brief run in 1978 after a tour.

Sada Thompson as the misanthropic mother in *The Effect of Gamma Rays on Man-in-the-Moon Marigolds.*

THE DIRTIEST SHOW IN TOWN

by Tom Eyen

Opened June 27, 1970

509 Performances

Astor Place Theatre

Directed by Tom Eyen

Music by Jeff Barry

Produced by Jeff Barry Enterprises, Inc., Ellen Stewart, and Bruce Mailman

Cast: Madeleine le Roux (Blonde); Jennifer Mitchell (Brunette); Sommer Sally (Jet Black); Elsa Tresko (Redhead); Paul Matthew Eckhart (Jonathan); Jeffrey Herman (Cyril); Bradford Riley (Lawrence); Robert Schrock (Blonde Bird-Watcher); Arthur Morey (2nd Sergeant); R.A. Dow (Jiffy Mover); Ellen Gurin (Stoned Angel).

The Dirtiest Show in Town followed in the footsteps of *Oh! Calcutta!* but went even further in its celebration and depiction of sex. This loosely structured revue sported as much nudity as *Calcutta* and explored gay and lesbian unions as well as heterosexual ones. There were no skits or musical numbers per se. A free-form method of staging was employed as one scene blended into another.

Subtitled "A documentary of the destructive effects of air, water, and mind pollution in New York City—not to mention *The Village Voice*," *The Dirtiest Show* made a few political protest statements about urban blight, the Vietnam war, and pollution. But it was mainly concerned with sex.

Created by Tom Eyen (later to write the book and lyrics for *Dreamgirls*) and the Theatre of the Open Eye, the revue moved from its home at Café La MaMa to the Astor Place Theatre. Critical sentiment was sharply divided between outrage and enjoyment. Clive Barnes of the *New York Times* was on the plus side: "This makes *Oh! Calcutta!* seem like *Little Women*—and it's funnier than both." Jeffrey Herman as an effeminate gay Jew and Madeleine LeRoux as a Mae West-ish blonde were singled out for their performances.

The Dirtiest Show in Town also played London and spawned a musical sequel: *The Dirtiest Musical.*

ONE FLEW OVER THE CUCKOO'S NEST

by Dale Wasserman, based on the novel by Ken Kesey.

Opened March 23, 1971

Mercer-Hansberry Theatre

1,025 Performances

Directed by Lee D. Sankowich

Produced by Sankowich/Golyn Productions

Cast: William Devane (Randle Patrick MacMurphy); Janet Ward (Nurse Ratched); William Burns (Chief Borden); James J. Sloyan (Dale Harding); Lawrie Driscoll (Billy Bibbit); William Duff-Griffin (Charles Atkins Cheswick III); Edward Cooper (Frank Scanlon); Danny De Vito (Anthony Martini); William Paterson, Jr. (Aide Williams); John Henry Redwood (Aide Washington); Eve Packer (Nurse Flinn); Jack Aaron (Dr. Spivey); Jeffrey Miller (Aide Turkle); Louie Piday (Candy); Kelly Monaghan (Technician); Sydney Andreami (Sandy).

One Flew Over the Cuckoo's Nest, Ken Kesey's novel of non-conformity in a prison-like mental institution, has gone through many adaptations in different media. It was an Oscar-winning film, starring Jack Nicholson, in 1975, but also a play, which failed when it appeared on Broadway in 1962, with Kirk Douglas in the lead. A 1971 off-Broadway revival of the play restored its reputation, and again proved that off-Broadway could give life to works which deserved a second chance.

Author Dale Wasserman (*Man of La Mancha*) had done the stage adaptation for the original Broadway run. The playwright stated that during out-of-town tryouts, Kirk Douglas wanted the play changed to make his character more sympathetic. Wasserman refused and left the production. The script was retooled by the director, and the Broadway *Cuckoo's Nest* lasted only 82 performances.

Wasserman rewrote the play for future stock and regional productions, of which there were many. One in San Francisco was such a tremendous hit that the producers brought it to off-Broadway; there, it ran over ten times longer than the first Broadway edition. This *Cuckoo's Nest* even survived the collapse of the theatre in which it was playing (the Mercer-Hansberry Theatre) and moved to the Eastside Playhouse. The San Francisco production continued and racked up 1,993 performances.

GODSPELL

Conceived by John-Michael Tebelak

Music and lyrics by Stephen Schwartz

Opened May 17, 1971

2,124 Performances

Cherry Lane Theatre

Directed by John-Michael Tebelak

Produced by Edgar Lansbury, Stuart Duncan, and Joseph Beruh

Cast: Lamar Alford, Peggy Gordon, David Haskell, Joanne Jonas, Robin Lamont, Sonia Manzano, Gilmer McCormick, Jeffrey Mylett, Stephen Nathan, Herb Simon

This musical appeared on Broadway during the 1976–77 season (see page 239.)

EL GRANDE DE COCA-COLA

by Ron House, Alan Shearman, John Neville-Andrews, Diz White, and Sally Willis, based on an idea by Ron House and Diz White.

Opened February 13, 1973

1,114 Performances

Mercer Arts Center

Choreographed by Anna Nygh

Produced by Jack Temchin, Gil Adler, John A. Vacarro, and Low Moan Spectacular

Cast: Ron House (Sr. Don Pepe Hernandez); Alan Shearman (Miguel Hernandez); John Neville-Andrews (Juan Rodriguez); Diz White (Consuela Hernandez); Sally Willis (Maria Hernandez).

Cabaret-style revues continued to provide off-Broadway with many of its hits. One of the longest running of this genre was *El Grande de Coca-Cola*, a one-hour "refreshment" of purposefully bad entertainment performed in gibberish versions of Spanish, French, and German.

The basic premise, as explained in the program, involved Don Pepe Hernandez, a small-time impresario in the town of Trujillo, Honduras. He has promised a parade of international stars, but none have showed. Borrowing money from his uncle, the manager of the local Coca-Cola bottling plant, Don Pepe rents a flea-bitten nightclub and hires his relatives to play the missing talent. Of course, everything goes spectacularly wrong as jugglers drop their clubs, dancers crash into each other, a blind blues singer faces away from the audience, then falls off the stage, and a Toulouse-Lautrec figure fails to get his canvas onto an abnormally large easel.

The revue was developed by a comedy troupe called Low Moan Spectacular, headed by Ron House and Diz White, as they toured Europe.

THE HOT L BALTIMORE

by Lanford Wilson
Opened March 22, 1973
1,166 Performances
Circle in the Square
Directed by Marshall W. Mason
Produced by Kermit Bloomgarden, Roger Ailes, and Circle Repertory Company
Cast: Judd Hirsch (Bill); Trish Hawkins (Girl); Helen Stenborg (Millie); Henrietta Bagley (Mrs. Bellotti); Conchata Ferrell (April); Rob Thirkield (Mr. Morse); Mari Gorman (Jackie); Zane Lasky (Jamie); Anthony Tenuta (Mr. Katz); Stephanie Gordon (Suzy); Jonathan Hogan (Paul Granger III); Louise Clay (Mrs. Oxenham); Burke Pearson (Suzy's John); Peter Tripp (Cab Man); Marcial Gonzalez (Delivery Boy).

The Hot L Baltimore not only signalled the arrival of both a major playwright (Lanford Wilson) and theatre company (Circle Repertory Company), but it also heralded a new source for American plays: off-off-Broadway. The loose amalgamation of theatres, usually former garages, churches, and lofts, had proliferated during the '60s and '70s.

Wilson's touching comedy-drama about the drifting residents in a decrepit Maryland hotel was originally produced in Circle Rep's tiny theatre on the Upper West Side of Manhattan. Critical and audience response was so strong that the production moved to Circle in the Square's Downtown Theatre in Greenwich Village, becoming the first hit play to transfer from off-off-Broadway to off-Broadway. It subsequently won the New York Drama Critics Circle Award for Best American Play, as well as numerous other citations, including several Obie, Outer Critics Circle, and Drama Desk Awards.

Circle Rep followed up *Hot L*'s success the next year with productions of Edward J. Moore's *The Sea Horse* and Mark Medoff's *When You Comin' Back, Red Ryder?*, both of which had respectable off-Broadway runs. The theatre, established

in 1969, maintained a policy of company playwrights writing specifically for the company performers. It moved to a larger space in Greenwich Village in 1974, and went on to become one of the top purveyors of new American works.

Norman Lear (*All in the Family*) adapted *Hot L* into a short-lived ABC sitcom in 1975. Conchata Ferrell was the only member of the original cast to appear in it.

WHAT'S A NICE COUNTRY LIKE YOU DOING IN A STATE LIKE THIS?

Devised by Ira Gasman, Cary Hoffman, and Bernie Travis
Music by Cary Hoffman
Lyrics by Ira Gasman
Opened April 19, 1973
543 Performances
Upstairs at Jimmy's
Directed and choreographed by Miriam Ford
Produced by Budd Friedman
Cast: Betty Lynn Buckley, Sam Freed, Bill La Vallee, Priscilla Lopez, Barry Michlin.

Political satire was rarely seen in the theatre once television had taken over the territory. *What's a Nice Country Like You Doing in a State Like This?* filled the theatrical void for social commentary with sketches and songs on such topics as the current mayoral primaries, the prevalance of pornography and massage parlors, the Nixon cabinet, and crime in the streets. The song "A Mugger's Work Is Never Done" contained the lyrics "What else could I be / With a liberal arts degree?"

The revue played St. Peter's Gate off-off-Broadway and the American Place Theatre's cabaret stage before alighting at its nightclub venue, Upstairs at Jimmy's.

Two future Tony winners Betty Lynn Buckley (*Cats*), who later dropped the Lynn, and Priscilla Lopez (*A Chorus Line*) were featured in the cast.

A second revue by the same authors, *What's a Nice Country Like You Still Doing in a State Like This?*, opened at the American Place Theatre in 1984.

LET MY PEOPLE COME

Music and lyrics by Earl Wilson, Jr.
Opened January 8, 1974
1,327 Performances
The Village Gate
Choreographed by Ian Naylor
Produced and directed by Phil Oesterman
Cast: Christine Andersen, Tobie Columbus, Daina Darzin, Lorraine Davidson, Marty Duffy, Alan Evans, Lola Howse, Joe Jones, James Moore, Ian Naylor, Larry Paulette, Peachena, Jim Rise, Denise Connolley.

Let My People Come was the third in a trio of sexually explicit hit revues of the '70s. Like its predecessors, *Oh!*

Calcutta! and *The Dirtiest Show in Town, People* was a series of songs and sketches dealing with myriad coital positions and variations featuring a sometimes nude cast.

The show's composer and lyricist, Earl Wilson, Jr. (son of a well-known newspaper columnist) had written a previous musical, *A Day in the Life of Just About Everyone,* which failed on Broadway in 1970. Producer and director Philip Oesterman presented a successful regional production of the show. Oesterman contacted Wilson with the idea of doing a musical which celebrated sex as clean and fun rather than naughty and dirty. Wilson wrote forty-four songs in four months, twenty of which wound up in the show.

Let My People Come began performances at the Village Gate on January 8, 1974, but never formally opened. Oesterman felt that negative reviews from prudish critics would kill the show, so the press was never invited to deliver its verdict. The public did instead, keeping the graphic show running for 1,327 performances.

The State Liquor Authority and the Building Commission attempted at various times to stop the revue by revoking the Village Gate's liquor license and citing the club for violations, but *People* kept on coming.

The show did transfer to Broadway's Morosco Theatre in 1976, against the wishes of the League of Broadway Producers and Theatres, who wanted to rid the theatre district of its massage parlors and porno houses. Moreover, the author objected to the Broadway production and requested that his name be removed from the bill. He brought an injuction against Oesterman, stating that he had distorted the original concept. The injunction was not granted and *Let My People Come* ran for 108 performances on Broadway.

VANITIES

by Jack Heifner

Opened March 22, 1976

1,785 Performances

Chelsea Westside Theatre

Directed by Garland Wright

Produced by the Chelsea Theatre Center, Lion Theatre Company, and Playwrights Horizons

Cast: Jane Galloway (Kathy); Susan Merson (Mary); Kathy Bates (Joanne).

The lives of three Texas cheerleaders are revealed in Jack Heifner's *Vanities.* The comedy follows the women from high school during the Kennedy era and through college in the Age of Aquarius to disillusionment in the New York of the '70s.

Author Heifner drew on his own Texas background for his characters. After attending Southern Methodist University in Houston, he came to New York to pursue an acting career. With his fellow alumnus Garland Wright, he

formed the Lion Theatre Company. He penned his first play, *Casserole,* for the company. When this debut work was well received, he gave up acting for writing. His second play, *Vanities,* had a sold-out, six-week engagement at Playwrights Horizons. From there, it had a brief run in a Long Island theatre, then transferred to the Chelsea Westside Theatre. It currently stands as the third-longest nonmusical run in off-Broadway history (after *Perfect Crime* and *Vampire Lesbians of Sodom*).

The initial critical reaction was tepid. "What saved us," Heifner told the *New York Times,* "was the Chelsea's subscription list. It kept us going for a month and a half." The show was aided by ABC, which purchased the rights to the play for a potential television series. The money kept the production going. (Heifner wrote a series pilot, but the show was never picked up.)

Some of the more prominent cast members have included Sandy Duncan, Lucie Arnaz, and Stockard Channing, in Los Angeles; Elizabeth Ashley, Lesley Anne Warren, and Barbara Sharma, in Chicago; and Shelley Hack, Meredith Baxter Birney, and Annette O'Toole in the HBO television version.

THE CLUB

by Eve Merriam

Opened October 14, 1976

674 Performances

Circle in the Square Downtown

Directed by Tommy Tune

Produced by Circle in the Square

Cast: Marlene Dell (Johnny); Gloria Hodes (Bertie); Joanne Beretta (Algy); Carole Monferdini (Freddie); Julia J. Hafner (Bobby); Memrie Innerarity (Maestro); Terri White (Henry).

Eve Merriam made a pointed commentary on sexism with her clever revue *The Club.* Set in an exclusive men's club in the late Victorian era, the show consisted of a group of four elegant gentlemen and the club's employees singing condescendingly and joking about women. A prime song title was "A Woman Is Only a Woman, But a Good Cigar Is a Smoke." Sample quip: "Do you want women to be free?" "Yes, I hate it when they charge." The ironic twist was having these male chauvinists enacted by women. Just as the African-American casts of *The Blacks* and *Day of Absence* had played whites for satiric effect, the company of *The Club* reversed genders.

Merriam explained where she got the idea to the *New York Times:* "I heard a World War I song called 'The Sultan's Harem' and a light bulb came on. I saw four deadpan Art Deco Fred Astaires, all women, singing the song." She then searched for every male chauvinist song and witticism from the 1894–1905 period. "I set *The Club* in the late Victorian period because I think male chauvinism had its flowering in that society," she told the *Times*.

The Club played in a preliminary form at the Westbeth Theatre and then was workshopped at the Lenox Arts Center in Stockbridge, Massachusetts. Tommy Tune made his directorial debut with a stylish staging on a long runway at the Circle in the Square Downtown Theatre.

THE PASSION OF DRACULA

by Bob Hall and David Richmond, based on the novel by Bram Stoker.

Opened September 28, 1977

714 Performances

Cherry Lane Theatre

Directed by Peter Bennett

Produced by the Dracula Theatrical Company

Cast: Christopher Bernau (Count Dracula); Giulia Pagano (Wilhelmina Murray); Brian Bell (Jameson); K. Lyle O'Dell (Dr. Cedric Seward); Michael Burg (Prof. Van Helsing); Alice White (Dr. Helga Van Zandt); K. C. Wilson (Lord Gordon Godalming); Elliott Vileen (Renfield); Samuel Maupin (Jonathan Harker).

It was vampire season: In addition to the Edward Gorey revival of the original Hamilton Deane–John L. Balderston on Broadway and an off-Broadway version at Equity Library Theatre, *The Passion of Dracula* was turning the Cherry Lane Theatre blood red. Coincidentally, the Deane–Balderston *Dracula* had been revived at the same theatre in 1932.

This adaptation of Bram Stoker's classic horror story stressed the psychological subtexts of the tale and added the character of a female Freudian analyst. It also sported scary special effects like bats swooping down over the audience.

The Passion of Dracula, which had originated at the George Street Playhouse, in New Brunswick, New Jersey, opened at midnight under a full moon. The first nighters were given complimentary fangs and Bloody Marys.

Just as they had in New York, the Deane–Balderston *Dracula* and *The Passion of Dracula* played London simultaneously. *Passion* was also filmed for the Showtime cable network and broadcast in 1980.

I'M GETTING MY ACT TOGETHER AND TAKING IT ON THE ROAD

Book and lyrics by Gretchen Cryer

Music by Nancy Ford

Opened June 14, 1978

1,165 Performances

The Public Theatre

Directed by Word Baker

Produced by Joseph Papp, the New York Shakespeare Festival

Cast : Gretchen Cryer (Heather); Joel Fabiani (Joe); Margot Rose (Alice); Betty Aberlin (Cheryl); Don Scardino (Jake); Scott Berry (Piano); Bob George (Drums); Dean Swenson (Bass and Flute); Lee Grayson (guitar).

(Left to right) Betty Aberlin, Gretchen Cryer, and Margot Rose in *I'm Getting My Act Together and Taking It on the Road*.

Gretchen Cryer and Nancy Ford are one of the few female lyricist–composer teams in musical theatre. After varying degrees of success off-Broadway with *Now Is the Time for All Good Men* (1967) and *The Last Sweet Days of Isaac* (1970) and a Broadway failure with *Shelter* (1973), the duo came up with a long-running hit in *I'm Getting My Act Together and Taking It on the Road*.

Written after Cryer had gone through a divorce, the musical addresses the problems women face when they have to make choices and transitions. The show takes place at an audition where Heather, a singer (originally played by Cryer), is performing her new, no-frills nightclub act for a reluctant manager.

The audition is symbolic as well as realistic. Heather is getting not only her singing act together, but her own personal "act" as well. She is preparing to move on with her life after trying to please everyone else. Instead of selling herself to the manager or a potential audience, she wants to express herself through song.

After a six-month run at the New York Shakespeare Festival's Public Theatre, *Act* moved to the Circle in the Square Downtown. Ford later took over Cryer's role, as did another female songwriter, Carol Hall (*The Best Little Whorehouse in Texas*).

SCRAMBLED FEET

by John Driver and Jeffrey Haddow
Opened June 11, 1979
831 Performances
The Village Gate Upstairs
Directed by John Driver
Produced by Jane Adams Vaccaro and Jimmy Wisner
Cast: Evalyn Baron, John Driver, Jeffrey Haddow, Roger Neil, Hermione the Duck.

Scrambled Feet was a lighthearted musical revue satirizing the current Broadway season. The sketches included a wrestling match between the title character of *The Elephant Man* and the paralyzed hero of *Whose Life Is It Anyway?*; "Sham Dancing," a take-off on the busywork nondancers perform in order to look as if they had some terpischorian talent; and "Theatre Party Ladies," in which the three male cast members appeared in drag as female playgoers with a fondness for unwrapping candy and coughing during the performance.

Authors John Driver and Jeffrey Haddow met at Northwestern University. Along with fellow students Evalyn Baron and Roger Neil, they staged the senior show *Reflections in a Golden Bagel*. After graduating, the foursome decided to collaborate on another show and improvised skits in Baron's living room. Driver and Haddow wrote material based on the ad-libbing. After a showcase production at the Shirtsleeves Theatre in New York, the

revue was put on in Chicago, where it poked fun at the fare on Windy City stages. When *Scrambled Feet* moved to New York, the quartet was joined by Hermione the Duck, who played in a sketch about sharing the stage with animals. Like Sandy of *Annie* fame, Hermione was rescued from extinction to become a star. She was purchased from a poultry market just before an appointment with the chopping block.

The revue was filmed for cable in 1984, with three of the original cast (Driver, Haddow, and Neil) and Madeline Kahn in the women's roles.

ONE MO' TIME

Conceived by Vernel Bagneris
Opened October 22, 1979
1,372 Performances
The Village Gate Downstairs
Directed by Vernel Bagneris; additional staging by Dean Irby
Produced by Art D'Lugoff, Burt D'Lugoff, and Jerry Wexler
Cast: Sylvia "Kuumba" Williams (Bertha Williams); Thais Clark (Ma Reed); Topsy Chapman (Thelma); Vernel Bagneris (Papa Du); John Stell (Theatre Owner).

While *Scrambled Feet* was skewering the current theatre scene upstairs at the Village Gate, *One Mo' Time* was celebrating the music of the 1920s black vaudeville circuit downstairs. The small-cast show followed the lead of Broadway hits like *Bubbling Brown Sugar*, *Ain't Misbehavin'*, and *Sophisticated Ladies* by taking old music and revitalizing it with snappy staging and stand-out performances. Unlike these bigger shows, *One Mo' Time* examined the difficulties faced by African-American entertainers, such as Bertha Williams, in white-dominated show business. The action is divided between the stage and dressing room of the Lyric Theatre, in New Orleans, the only venue in the city for blacks to perform and watch. The Lyric, an actual theatre, burned down in 1927; Ma Rainey and Bessie Smith were among those who had played there.

In the show, singer Williams and her troupe of three entertainers belted out familiar period songs like "He's Funny That Way," "Everybody Loves My Baby," and lesser-known tunes like "Kitchen Man" and "I've Got What It Takes." Offstage they confront bigotry, as personified by the white theatre owner who threatens to stop their checks because he was promised six performers instead of four.

Vernel Bagneris was inspired to create the show by the real-life Bertha Williams. He conceived and directed the musical, as well as playing Papa Du, Bertha's manager and a member of the troupe. It was performed in New Orleans by the New Experience Players before moving to New York. Bagneris also starred and directed in the national touring and London productions.

A sequel, *Further Mo'*, played the Village Gate in 1990.

CLOUD 9

by Caryl Churchill

Opened May 18, 1981

971 Performances

Theatre de Lys

Directed by Tommy Tune

Produced by Michel Stuart and Harvey J. Klaris

Cast: Don Amendolia (Joshua/Cathy); Veronica Castang (Maud/Lin); Zeljko Ivanek (Betty/Gerry); Jeffrey Jones (Clive/Edward); E. Katherine Kerr (Ellen/Mrs. Saunders/Betty); Nicolas Surovy (Harry Bagley/Martin); Concetta Tomei (Edward/Victoria).

Actors switch genders and races in Caryl Churchill's wild, carnal romp, *Cloud 9*. Men play women, women play men, and whites play blacks as the playwright comically examines the roles that sex and race play in human relationships. Act I is set in 1880 in a colonial African household, where the proper Victorian exterior of a stiff-upper-lip British family conceals seething lusts. Act II takes place a century later, but the characters have aged only a quarter-century. All the sexual barriers have been dropped, but the anxieties and insecurities remain.

The playwright, who is British, explained the reasons for her flip-flops in the casting to the *New York Sunday News*: "The woman in the first act is a Victorian ideal of a woman, she is a man-made woman, the image projected by men. The black man in that act is a white man's creation as well. That's why white actors play both these roles. It all has to do with sexual oppression, which isn't that different after all."

The play had its beginnings in a workshop at the Joint Stock Company, a British troupe where Churchill was a resident playwright. The Joint Stock method of creating theatre is to have the actors discuss and improvise material on a particular topic, in this case sexual roles. Then the playwright shapes and refines it into a script. After a six-week rehearsal period, *Cloud 9* played a limited engagement at London's Royal Court Theatre, in 1979; at the time, it was coolly received by the critics. The play was then slightly revised, toured to acclaim, and reopened at the Royal Court in 1980. This time the reviewers reversed themselves, and the production was a hit.

It was the second London edition which Michel Stuart, formerly a dancer and now a producer, saw. He bought the American rights and hired his friend Tommy Tune to direct. It was Tune's debut as a nonmusical director, though he had previously worked with another cross-dressed cast, in *The Club*.

Churchill's later plays have covered such diverse topics as feminism (*Top Girls*, 1982), England's agrarian economy (*Fen*, 1983), high finance (*Serious Money*, 1987) and the Romanian revolution of 1989 (*Mad Forest*, 1992).

SISTER MARY IGNATIUS EXPLAINS IT ALL FOR YOU / THE ACTOR'S NIGHTMARE

by Christopher Durang

Opened October 14, 1981

947 Performances

Playwrights Horizons

Directed by Jerry Zaks

Produced by Playwrights Horizons

Cast: Elizabeth Franz (Sister Mary Ignatius/Sara Siddons); Mark Stefan (Thomas); Timothy Landfield (Gary Sullavan/Henry Irving); Polly Draper (Diane Symonds/Meg); Mary Catherine Wright (Philomena Rostovitch/Dame Ellen Terry); Jeff Brooks (Aloysius Benheim/George Spelvin).

Christopher Durang unleashed his bitter, sarcastic humor on the Catholic Church in the one-act play *Sister Mary Ignatius Explains It All for You*. What begins as a parody of a lecture on faith by Sister Mary, a bullying nun, becomes a violent confrontation when some of her disillusioned former students present a bizarre religious pageant. With sharp jabs, Durang punctured holes in the tenets of the church in which he was raised, exposing inconsistencies and intolerance.

The play was first presented at the Ensemble Studio Theatre as a part of their annual one-act marathon.

Elizabeth Franz in *Sister Mary Ignatius Explains It All for You*.

Durang and Elizabeth Franz, who played the murderous title character, won 1980 Obie Awards. In 1981, the work was presented at Playwrights Horizons on a double bill with *The Actor's Nightmare*, which the dramatist wrote specifically to be double cast with Sister Mary. The nightmare refers to the dream performers commonly have of being thrust onstage without knowing which play they are in. In this short sketch, an unlucky young man named George Spelvin speaks lines from Noël Coward's *Private Lives*, Samuel Beckett's *Endgame*, and Robert Bolt's *A Man for All Seasons* and must improvise his way out. The program successfully transferred to a commercial run at the Westside Arts Theatre.

Sister Mary Ignatius was later played by Nancy Marchand, Mary Louise Wilson, and Lynn Redgrave. Durang briefly played George Spelvin.

FORBIDDEN BROADWAY

Concept and lyrics by Gerard Alessandrini

Opened January 15, 1982

2,332 Performances (1982–87 edition); 534 Performances (1988–89 edition); 576 Performances (1990–91 edition)

Palsson's Supper Club

Directed by Gerard Alessandrini

Additional direction by Michael Chapman and Jeff Martin

Produced by Playkill Productions

Cast: Nora Mae Lyng, Wendee Winters, Bill Carmichael, Gerard Alessandrini.

Like *Scrambled Feet* before it, *Forbidden Broadway* satirizes the theatre scene. With wicked zest, lyricist Gerard Alessandrini takes the songs of current shows and adds his own stinging lyrics. Lauren Bacall is "One of the Girls Who Sings Like a Boy" in a parody of her *Woman of the Year* role. *Dreamgirls* became *Screamgirls*. In another sketch, the chandelier from *Phantom of the Opera* battles the helicopter from *Miss Saigon* over who is the best special effect. Liza Minelli, Mandy Patinkin, Patti LuPone, Chita Rivera, and Kevin Kline are just a few of the Broadway stars to have been ribbed.

The author's friends, whom he had often privately entertained with his spoofs, suggested that he perform the mock songs as a mini-revue starring himself and Nora Mae Lyng. The resulting fifteen-minute club spot soon grew into a full revue with four singers and a pianist. Palsson's Supper Club became the in-place to be as theatre folk came to see themselves spoofed.

In various editions—new material had to be inserted as Broadway's offerings changed—*Forbidden Broadway* ran for six years at Palsson's, then moved to Theatre East, where it went on mocking whatever was playing. The last edition closed in 1993. A tenth anniversary version in 1992 featured excerpts from the previous shows.

THE DINING ROOM

by A. R. Gurney, Jr.

Opened February 24, 1982

583 Performances

The Astor Place Theatre

Directed by David Trainer

Produced by Playwrights Horizons

Cast (playing multiple roles): Remak Ramsey, John Shea, W. H. Macy, Lois de Banzie, Ann McDonough, Pippa Pearthree.

Prolific playwright A.R. Gurney, Jr. specializes in chronicling the lives of an endangered species: the upper-middle-class WASP of the Northeastern United States. Long associated with privilege and affluent living, white Anglo-Saxon Protestants found their status shifting in the latter part of the 20th century. Gurney views their adjustment to the changing times with compassion and humor. His longest-running play on the subject is *The Dining Room*, a series of vignettes in the titular room, which comes to symbolize the disappearing elegance and sense of community in all American life. Six actors play sixty different roles, and the scenes go back and forth in time over the course of fifty years. The role of the dining room in the lives of the various families changes from formal meeting place to neglected extra space.

Like *Sister Mary Ignatius*, *The Dining Room* was first done at Playwrights Horizons and later presented in a commercial run at an off-Broadway theatre, the Astor Place Theatre. The play was also telecast on the PBS series *Great Performances*, with most of the original cast.

Other Gurney plays include *The Perfect Party* (1986); *The Cocktail Hour* (1988); *Another Antigone* (1988); and *Later Life* (1993).

LITTLE SHOP OF HORRORS

Book and lyrics by Howard Ashman, based on the film directed by Roger Corman.

Music by Alan Menken

Opened July 27, 1982

2,209 Performances

Orpheum Theatre

Directed by Howard Ashman

Choreographed by Edie Cowan

Produced by WPA Theatre, David Geffen, Cameron Mackintosh, and the Shubert Organization.

Cast: Lee Wilkof (Seymour); Ellen Greene (Audrey); Hy Anzell (Mushnik); Franc Luz (Orin/Bernstein/Snip/Luce/Everybody Else); Ron Taylor (Audrey II Voice); Martin P. Robinson (Audrey II Puppet); Leilani Jones (Chiffon); Jenifer Leigh Warren (Crystal); Sheila Kay Davis (Ronette).

A low-grade science-fiction movie directed by Roger Corman was the surprising source for the fifth-longest run among off-Broadway musicals. *Little Shop of Horrors*, a

Audrey II, the carnivorous plant of *Little Shop of Horrors.*

hilarious spoof of one of Hollywood's sleazier genres, was derived from the 1960 B-picture about a carnivorous plant, in which a young Jack Nicholson had a memorable bit as a masochistic dental patient.

Composer Alan Menken and librettist Howard Ashman decided to musicalize the film after their stage adaptation of Kurt Vonnegut's novel *God Bless You, Mr. Rosewater* had failed. "We were both depressed," Ashman told *Playbill*, "so I decided that the next show we worked on would have to be something *fun*. I suddenly remembered that when I was sixteen, I had written a terrible musical about a man who fell in love with a flower that had opiate powers. I realized that I had subconsciously ripped off *The Little Shop of Horrors.*"

Menken and Ashman used the pop-music sound of early '60s "girl groups," such as the Shirelles, as the inspiration for their score. They even used such a group as a Greek chorus. Martin Robinson of the Muppets designed a giant puppet for the monstrous plant. The musical was first produced at the WPA Theatre and was then transferred to the Orpheum Theatre on Second Avenue.

Ellen Greene, from the original cast, Rick Moranis, Steve Martin, and Vincent Gardenia starred in the 1986 movie of the musical.

TRUE WEST

by Sam Shepard

Opened October 17, 1982

762 Performances

Cherry Lane Theatre

Directed by Gary Sinise

Produced by Harold Thau and Wayne Adams

Cast: John Malkovich (Lee); Gary Sinise (Austin); Sam Schacht (Saul Kimmer); Margaret Thompson (Mom).

Sam Shepard is regarded by many critics as one of the most important playwrights of recent years. His often eerie dramas turn a glaring light on the myths of American life and the fantasies inspired by popular culture. Cowboys, rock stars, movie legends, lonely vagabonds, and impoverished family members crash head-on into each other as they search for a dream to keep them going. Only one of Shepard's many plays, *Operation Sidewinder* (1970), has been done on Broadway. Two of his works, *True West* and *Fool for Love*, began long off-Broadway runs during the 1982–83 season.

True West is about two brothers: Austin, a Hollywood screenwriter, and Lee, a grizzled desert drifter. They clash when Lee is offered a deal to write a "true" western movie based on his experiences. The two gradually switch roles: Lee attempts to write the movie and Austin becomes aimlessly obsessed with toasters. The play ends with the brothers in a stand-off in their war for dominance and identity.

The play was first performed at the Magic Theatre in San Francisco, where the author was resident playwright, in 1980. A New York version was mounted at Joseph Papp's New York Shakespeare Festival with Tommy Lee Jones and Peter Boyle. Director Robert Woodruff quit, and Shepard telephoned Papp to repudiate the production. It closed after the scheduled run of eight weeks. Then the Steppenwolf Theatre of Chicago staged the play, with John Malkovich and Gary Sinise, who also directed. This production gained the playwright's approval, and it moved to an off-Broadway berth at the Cherry Lane Theatre. The *New York Times* called it the "true *True West.*" Malkovich was singled out for his animalistic portrayal of the mangy Lee.

The production was telecast on PBS' *American Playhouse* series. Jim Belushi, Gary Cole, Erik Estrada, and brothers Dennis and Randy Quaid were among those in the New York company to succeed Malkovich and Sinise.

GREATER TUNA

by Jaston Williams, Joe Sears, and Ed Howard
Opened October 21, 1982
501 Performances
Circle in the Square Downtown
Directed by Ed Howard
Produced by Karl Allinson
Cast: Joe Sears, Jaston Williams (The Citizens of Tuna, Texas).

Two actors brought an entire town to life in the quick-change comedy, *Greater Tuna.* Joe Sears and Jaston Williams, who wrote the play in collaboration with their director Ed Howard, enacted ten roles apiece, both male and female. The play depicts a single day in the life of Tuna, Texas, where "the Lions Club is too liberal and Patsy Cline never dies." The zany inhabitants included a dog-poisoning old lady, a book-censoring housewife who thinks *Romeo and Juliet* and *Huckleberry Finn* should be banned for the "dirty words" they contain, a cliché-spouting preacher, and a UFO-spotting alcoholic.

The trio wrote the show when they were stranded in Austin, Texas, at the end of a theatrical tour without means of employment. In order to get work onstage, they penned a production which needed only two actors and a single set. *Tuna* was first presented at Austin's TransAct Theatre. It subsequently played San Antonio, Atlanta, Houston, and Hartford, Connecticut, before opening at the Circle in the Square Downtown in New York. A one-hour version was telecast on the HBO cable network in

Joe Sears (left) and Jaston Williams played the population of a Texas town in *Greater Tuna.*

1984. A sequel, entitled *A Tuna Christmas*, has been performed by Sears and Williams in Los Angeles.

FOOL FOR LOVE

by Sam Shepard
Opened May 26, 1983
1,000 Performances
Circle Repertory Theatre
Directed by Sam Shepard
Produced by Circle Repertory Company
Cast: Ed Harris (Eddie); Kathy Whitton Baker (May); Dennis Ludlow (Martin); Will Marchetti (Old Man).

Fool for Love was Sam Shepard's second long-running play of the 1982–83 season. The fools of the title are May and

Eddie, who, like Lee and Austin of *True West*, seem inextricably bound together. Eddie has chased May to a seedy Mojave Desert motel. At first she threatens to throw him out, since she is expecting a date, but instead she begs him to stay. In eighty intermissionless minutes, the combatants literally bounce off the walls (their thuds were made to reverberate, along with the slamming doors, by the placement of drums just offstage) and come together as they play out their dance of mutual love and loathing.

Shepard directed the original Magic Theatre production, with Ed Harris and Kathy Whitton Baker, in February of 1983. The entire production moved to Circle Repertory Theatre in May and then transferred to the Douglas Fairbanks Theatre on Theatre Row.

Among those who followed the original battling lovers in the New York production were Bruce Willis, Will Patton, Aidan Quinn, Ellen Barkin, and Frances Fisher. Shepard himself played Eddie opposite Kim Basinger in the 1985 movie version, directed by Robert Altman.

Other well-known Shepard plays include *The Tooth of Crime* (1972); *Angel City* (1976); *Curse of the Starving Class* (1977); the Pulitzer Prize–winning *Buried Child* (1978); and *A Lie of the Mind* (1985).

Chip Zien and Christine Rose in Wendy Wasserstein's *Isn't It Romantic?*

ISN'T IT ROMANTIC?

by Wendy Wasserstein
Opened December 15, 1983
733 Performances
Playwrights Horizons
Directed by Gerald Gutierrez
Produced by Playwrights Horizons

Cast: Christine Rose (Janie Blumberg); Lisa Banes (Harriet Cornwall); Chip Zien (Marty Sterling); Betty Comden (Tasha Blumberg); Stephen Pearlman (Simon Blumberg); Jo Henderson (Lillian Cornwall); Jerry Lanning (Paul Stuart); Tom Robbins (Vladimir); Kevin Kline, Swoosie Kurtz, Patti LuPone, Ellis Rabb, Meryl Streep, Jerry Zaks, Timmy Geissler (Telephone Voices).

"I was attempting to write a boulevard comedy, an audience pleaser, like *Mary, Mary*," Wendy Wasserstein recalled about *Isn't It Romantic?*, the story of two best friends, wisecracking writer Janie Blumberg and WASPy Harvard grad Harriet Cornwall, and their adventures in careers and romance in 1980s Manhattan. "It was about two girls on the town in New York, and having Betty Comden in the show provided a comment or historic reference on that," Wasserstein said. Comden, who co-authored the classic New York musical *On the Town* with Adolph Green and Leonard Bernstein, played Janie's tap-dancing mother.

The play was first presented in 1981 at the Phoenix Theatre and got mixed notices. The critics found it promising but too scattered, with too many scenes and too much going on. Wasserstein tightened the script, giving it a cleaner plotline. The newer version opened two years later to raves at Playwrights Horizons. Richard Corliss of *Time* magazine called it one of the year's ten best. The production moved to the Lucille Lortel Theatre for a long run.

Wasserstein explained some of the play's appeal: "It became a show that mothers and daughters would come to. When Janie decides not to marry the doctor, the daughters could say to their mothers 'Now you understand why I didn't marry that guy.'"

THE FOREIGNER

by Larry Shue
Opened November 1, 1984
686 Performances
Astor Place Theatre
Directed by Jerry Zaks
Produced by John A. McQuiggan

Cast: Larry Shue ("Froggy" LeSueur); Anthony Heald (Charlie Baker); Sudie Bond (Betty Meeks); Robert Schenkkan (Rev. David Marshall Lee); Patricia Kalember (Catherine Simms); Christopher Curry (Owen Musser); Kevin Geer (Ellard Simms).

The Foreigner, Larry Shue's gentle comedy of miscommunication, almost didn't make it past the first month. But the determination of the company kept it going for 686 performances. The play takes place in a fishing lodge in the backwoods of Georgia. Englishman Charlie Baker has come to this retreat for complete privacy. In order to avoid communication with the locals, his guide, "Froggy" LeSueur (originally played by Shue) suggests that he pretend to be a native from an unspecified nation who cannot speak or understand English. Because they think he cannot comprehend them, each of the other characters becomes attached to Charlie and unburden themselves to him, with comic results.

The play opened to several bad reviews. The first week of performances, veteran character actress Sudie Bond, who was playing the lodge's landlady, died. The night after Bond's death the theatre's boiler exploded during a performance. Any one of these setbacks might have closed the show, but producer John A. McQuiggan mounted an aggressive campaign for audiences and backers. Thanks to a generous loan from a Texas oilman, *The Foreigner* remained open long enough for good word of mouth to spread.

Shue did get to see his play succeed, but died tragically the following summer in an airplane crash. He was about to appear in the Broadway production of *The Mystery of Edwin Drood*, after having played the role of Reverend Crisparkle in the Central Park version of the musical.

A *Foreigner* national tour starred Bob Denver. Two of Shue's other plays, *The Nerd* and *Wenceslas Square*, were presented in New York posthumously.

PENN & TELLER

Opened April 18, 1985
666 Performances
Westside Arts Theatre
Produced by Richard Frankel and Ivy Properties

Aside from Doug Henning in *The Magic Show*, Penn & Teller are the only purveyors of prestidigitation to achieve a long run on or off-Broadway. Their particularly bizarre brand of escape tricks, illusions, comedy, and magic played for twenty-two months on the downstairs stage of the Westside Arts Theatre. The mismatched pair—Penn is 6'6" and boisterous; Teller is a full foot shorter and remains mute onstage—each disdain the title of magician; they prefer to be called "two eccentric guys who happen to know how to do a few cool things." Teller, for instance, swallowed a series of needles, followed by a length of thread, and then pulled the needles out of his mouth perfectly threaded; he also escaped from a straightjacket while suspended upside down above a bed of spikes before Penn could finish reciting the poem "Casey at the Bat." Penn ate fire and philosophized. All the while, Penn explained how the tricks are done. As he told *People* magazine, "Magicians as a rule have condescended to their audience with this 'I know how to do something you can't do.' We credit the audience with a certain sophistication."

The show played Broadway briefly in 1988. The odd couple of ledgerdemain returned there in 1991 with their new production, *The Refrigerator Tour*, which later played off-Broadway under the title *Penn and Teller Rot in Hell*.

VAMPIRE LESBIANS OF SODOM/ SLEEPING BEAUTY, OR COMA

by Charles Busch
Opened June 19, 1985
2,024 Performances
The Provincetown Playhouse
Directed by Kenneth Elliott
Produced by Theatre-in-Limbo

Cast: *Vampire Lesbians*: Charles Busch (Virgin Sacrifice/Madeleine Astarte); Meghan Robinson (Succubus/La Condessa); Kenneth Elliott (King Carlisle); Theresa Marlowe (Renee Vain/Tracy); Andy Halliday (Etienne/Danny); Tom Aulino (Oatsie Carew); Robert Carey (Ali/P.J.); Arnie Kolodner (Hujar/Zack).

Sleeping Beauty: Charles Busch (Fauna Alexander); Tom Aulino (Ian McKenzie); Meghan Robinson (Enid Whetwhistle); Arnie Kolodner (Craig Prince); Robert Carey (Barry Posner); Kenneth Elliott (Sebastian Lore); Andy Halliday (Miss Thick); Theresa Marlowe (Anthea Arlo).

The second-longest nonmusical run in off-Broadway history began in a tiny bar on the Lower East Side of Manhattan. On a budget of $36, *Vampire Lesbians of Sodom* opened at the Limbo Lounge and quickly attracted a devoted cult following. The one-act comedy, starring the author, Charles Busch, in drag as the leading lady, was a devastating parody of various show-biz genres, ranging from Biblical epics and silent films to glitzy Vegas floor shows.

The Limbo Lounge engagement, initially put on "just for fun," proved so successful that the cast formed their own company (Theatre-in-Limbo) and planned a commercial transfer to an off-Broadway theatre. In order to make for a full-length evening, a curtain-raiser called *Sleeping Beauty, or Coma* was added. The new piece was a modern retelling of the fairy tale, set in the fashion world of mod 1960s London.

Many believe the cause for the double bill's phenomenal run was the bizarre title. It drew in curious theatregoers after the Limbo fans had seen the show several times. The record run for *Vampire Lesbians* remained unbroken till 1992, when *Perfect Crime* surpassed it.

Busch continued to satirize popular culture and classical literature with such works as *Times Square Angel* (1984); *Psycho Beach Party* (1987); *The Lady in Question* (1989); and *Red Scare on Sunset* (1990). In 1993, Busch fictionalized the creation of *Vampire Lesbians* in the novel *Whores of Lost Atlantis*.

NUNSENSE

Book, music, and lyrics by Dan Goggin
Opened December 3, 1985
Still running (3,384 performances as of February 6, 1994)
Cherry Lane Theatre
Directed by Dan Goggin
Choreographed by Felton Smith
Produced by The Nunsense Theatrical Company
Cast: Marilyn Farina (Sister Mary Cordelia); Vicki Belmonte (Sister Mary Hubert); Christine Anderson (Sister Robert Anne); Semina DeLaurentis (Sister Mary Amnesia); Suzi Winson (Sister Mary Leo).

Catholic nuns were seen as narrow-minded harpies in plays like *Agnes of God* and *Sister Mary Ignatius Explains It All for You*, but they were fun-loving entertainers in Dan Goggin's satirical *Nunsense*, the second-longest run among off-Broadway musicals, after *The Fantasticks*.

This may be the only hit musical based on a series of greeting cards. Goggin had designed a line of humorous cards with photographs of actress Marilyn Farina in a nun's habit. Farina would appear in costume at card stores to promote the product, and Goggin would write material for her. This gradually developed into a cabaret act with contributions by Steven Hays. The fifteen-minute act,

called *The Nunsense Story*, included monks as well as nuns and played for thirty-eight weeks at the Duplex, a cabaret in Greenwich Village. Goggin decided to rewrite the act as a full-length musical without the monks (since the nuns were getting all the laughs) and developed it in a workshop at the Baldwin Theatre.

The basic premise of the show was that five nuns were the only survivors of a tragedy at the convent of the Order of Little Sisters of Hoboken, New Jersey ("Little Hobos" for short), for all the others had died of food poisoning when Sister Julia "Child of God" whipped up a batch of tainted vichyssoise. The five survivors were out playing Bingo and now are staging a benefit to raise money to bury their fellow nuns.

The reworked version opened at the Cherry Lane Theatre to an indifferent press, but audiences loved to see the incongruities of the sisters' cavortings. When the Cherry Lane was no longer available, *Nunsense* moved to the Sheridan Square Playhouse and then to the Douglas Fairbanks, on Theatre Row, just west of Times Square.

The singing and dancing sisters were a hit wherever they played. Goggin has stated that at one point there were fifty-six versions playing simultaneously in ten different languages. Among the numerous actresses to have played in its many productions are Alice Ghostley, Pat Carroll, Kaye Ballard, Dody Goodman, Jaye P. Morgan, Phyllis Diller, Peggy Cass, Jo Anne Worley, and even Honor Blackman (*Goldfinger*), in the London version.

A sequel, *Nunsense II: The Second Coming*, has played in some regional theatres.

BEEHIVE

Created by Larry Gallagher
Opened March 11, 1986
600 Performances
The Village Gate Upstairs
Directed by Larry Gallagher
Choreographed by Leslie Dockery
Produced by Betmar and Charles Allen
Cast: Patty Darcy, Alison Fraser, Jasmine Guy, Adriane Lenox, Gina Taylor, Laura Theodore.

Popular female singers of the '60s were the subject of *Beehive*, the musical revue which celebrated women with big voices and big hair. Director Larry Gallagher had put together *Ain't No Mountain High Enough*, a revue of Motown music, at the Manhattan nightspot Sweetwaters. The producer Charles Allen enjoyed the production so much that he asked Gallagher to put on another show.

So Gallagher assembled an evening of songs made famous from 1960 to 1969 by various female groups and soloists. He named his show after the popular piled-up hairdo of the period. A cast of six conveyed the essences of such diverse vocalists as Annette Funicello, Brenda Lee, Connie Francis, Diana Ross, Janis Joplin, and Tina Turner. A narrator named Wanda provided commentary on the changing role of women during the turbulent decade. Gallagher told *Playbill*: "One of the things that attracted me to this era was that it marked the beginning of the Women's Movement." The songs progress from lighthearted ditties about boyfriends to cries like Aretha Franklin's for "R-E-S-P-E-C-T." The show's success led to a commercial transfer at the Village Gate.

The show had an unusually extensive wardrobe for off-Broadway. There were fifty costumes and thirty-five wigs. The production used fifteen cans of hairspray every week.

DRIVING MISS DAISY

by Alfred Uhry
Opened April 15, 1987
1,195 Performances
Playwrights Horizons
Directed by Ron Lagomarsino
Produced by Playwrights Horizons
Cast: Dana Ivey (Daisy Werthan); Morgan Freeman (Hoke Coleburn); Ray Gill (Boolie Werthan).

Alfred Uhry's Pulitzer Prize–winning play *Driving Miss Daisy* details the twenty-five-year relationship between a crochety, Jewish Southern woman and her black chauffeur. Miss Daisy Werthan is forced by her son Boolie and her insurance company to hire Hoke Coleburn as her driver. The growing friendship between Miss Daisy and Hoke parallels the burgeoning Civil Rights movement. Both Dana Ivey and Morgan Freeman won Obie Awards.

Uhry based his play on his own grandmother and her driver. But playwright Henry Denker disputed *Miss Daisy*'s origins when he brought a plagiarism suit against Uhry. The plaintiff claimed that Uhry had lifted his story from Denker's 1980 play *Horowitz and Mrs. Washington*, about a Jewish man and his black nurse. The case was dismissed, with the judge ruling that there was only a surface similarity between the plays.

Frances Sternhagen succeeded Ivey, and Earle Hyman and Arthur French took over for Freeman in the New York company. *Miss Daisy* played widely, with companies in Chicago (with Sada Thompson, Ellen Burstyn, Dorothy Loudon, and Charlotte Rae playing the lead) and on tour (Julie Harris and Rosemary Prinz headed separate road editions).

Freeman re-created his stage role in the 1989 film version, which won four Oscars, including Best Picture and Best Actress (Jessica Tandy as Miss Daisy).

Dana Ivey and Morgan Freeman out for a spin in *Driving Miss Daisy*.

PERFECT CRIME

by Warren Manzi

Opened June 3, 1987

Still running (2,788 performances as of February 6, 1994)

Courtyard Playhouse

Directed by Jeffrey Hyatt

Produced by the Actors Collective

Cast: Catherine Russell (Margaret Thorne Brent); Perry Pirkkanen (Inspector James Ascher); Warren Manzi (W. Harrison Brent); John Sellars (Lionel McAuley); W. MacGregor King (David Breuer).

How did a murder mystery by an unknown playwright, with no stars in the cast, and with only so-so reviews become the longest-running drama in off-Broadway history? That's the mystery of *Perfect Crime*, a complicated thriller with a devoted following and enormous staying power.

Author Warren Manzi wrote the play while playing Mozart on Broadway in *Amadeus*. The script was optioned for Broadway by producer Morton Gottlieb, and Mary Tyler Moore was offered the lead role of a female psychiatrist who may or may not have killed her husband. But Manzi and Gottlieb had artistic differences, and the option was dropped. The playwright decided to present the play himself with the Actors Collective, a theatre company to which he belonged. The initial production of *Perfect Crime* was a showcase presentation at the Courtyard Playhouse, in Greenwich Village. The budget was $6,000, and the play ran three hours and ten minutes. Critics dismissed it as convoluted and confusing. But a commercial production, capitalized at $65,000, was launched. Manzi did constant rewrites, sometimes during performances. Catherine Russell, who had played the psychiatrist since the show's opening, told the *Daily News*: "In the beginning, I'd be given two-page rewrites during intermission to be put in Act II." The running time was finally cut down to one hour and fifty minutes.

Somehow the play caught on. Mystery fans followed the show as it moved from theatre to theatre. The McGinn/Cazale, Harold Clurman, and 47th Street Theatres all played host to *Crime*. Even with the rewriting, some were still mystified by the complicated plot. A special hotline number was set up for those with questions.

STEEL MAGNOLIAS

by Robert Harling

Opened June 19, 1987

1,126 Performances

Lucille Lortel Theatre

Directed by Pamela Berlin

Produced by Kyle Renick, WPA Theatre

Cast: Margo Martindale (Truvy); Constance Shulman (Annelle); Kate Wilkinson (Clairee); Betsy Aidem (Shelby); Rosemary Prinz (M'Linn); Mary Fogarty (Ouiser).

"Laughter through tears is my favorite emotion," says Truvy, the owner of the Louisiana beauty parlor where Robert Harling's *Steel Magnolias* is set. The play offers plenty of both as six Southern belles go through weddings, divorces, births, and deaths while gossiping, joking, and getting their coifs perfected. *Magnolias* could easily have been a sudsy soap opera or a campy bitch-fest, but Harling avoided both extremes by sympathetically portraying both the strengths and faults of his women.

Magnolias began as a short story written by Harling about his diabetic sister, who, like the character Shelby in the play, died two years after giving birth. The piece became a stage work as the dialogue became sassy and sizzling and the location settled on a makeshift hair salon in a converted garage. Harling, an actor and model, took his script to his agent, who submitted it to several theatres and told him not to expect much. No one produces "first plays." This conventional wisdom was proved wrong when the off-Broadway WPA Theatre picked it up. After revisions by Harling, it was given a mainstage production and then a commercial transfer to the Lucille Lortel Theatre.

The hit off-Broadway production spawned companies in Chicago (which featured Anne Francis and Marcia Rodd), Los Angeles (Carole Cook, Barbara Rush, Ronnie Claire Edwards, and Dana Hill), a London production (with Rosemary Harris and Joely Richardson), and a touring edition.

The all-star 1989 movie version with Sally Field, Dolly Parton, Shirley MacLaine, Olympia Dukakis, Daryl Hannah, and Julia Roberts, opened up the story to include the men in the ladies' lives.

FRANKIE AND JOHNNY IN THE CLAIR DE LUNE

by Terrence McNally

Opened October 14, 1987

533 Performances

Westside Arts Theatre

Directed by Paul Benedict

Produced by Steven Baruch, Thomas Viertel, Richard Frankel, and Jujamcyn Theatres/Margo Lion

Cast: Kathy Bates (Frankie); Kenneth Welsh (Johnny); Dominic Cuskern (Voice of Radio Announcer).

Terrence McNally's *Frankie and Johnny in the Clair de Lune* begins in the dark with the sounds of two people making love. The playwright begins his tale of romance where most similar stories end, in bed. From this point on, the overeager Johnny spends the rest of the night attempting to convince suspicious Frankie that they have a future together. The two are not glamorous or conventionally attractive. Johnny is a fry cook and Frankie a waitress at the same restaurant. The playwright sympathetically deals with a pair of wounded, ordinary souls desperate for and frightened of love.

McNally wrote the play specifically for F. Murray Abraham and Kathy Bates, who played it in a workshop version at Manhattan Theatre Club's Stage II. Abraham then received a film role and was replaced by Kenneth Welsh for the play's full production on MTC's mainstage and subsequent commercial run at the Westside Arts Theatre.

The leads were later played by Bruce Weitz and Carol Kane, and then Tony Mustane and Bonnie Franklin. McNally wrote the screenplay for the 1991 film version, titled *Frankie and Johnny*, which "opened-up" the play to include all the characters and locations mentioned in the stage version. Ironically, Michelle Pfeiffer and Al Pacino—two highly attractive stars—were cast as the ordinary pair.

A SHAYNA MAIDEL

by Barbara Lebow
Opened October 29, 1987
501 Performances
Westside Arts Theatre/Downstairs
Directed by Mary B. Robinson
Produced by K & D Productions, Margery Klain, and Robert G. Donnalley, Jr.
Cast: Melissa Gilbert (Rose Weiss); Gordana Rashovich (Lusia Weiss Pechenik); Paul Sparer (Mordechai Weiss); Jon Tenney (Duvid Pechenik); Cordelia Richards (Hanna); Joan MacIntosh (Mama).

A Shayna Maidel is Yiddish for "a pretty girl." It's also the title of Barbara Lebow's drama of the Holocaust and Jewish identity. The play is set in 1946 New York. The main characters are two sisters, Lusia, a Holocaust survivor just

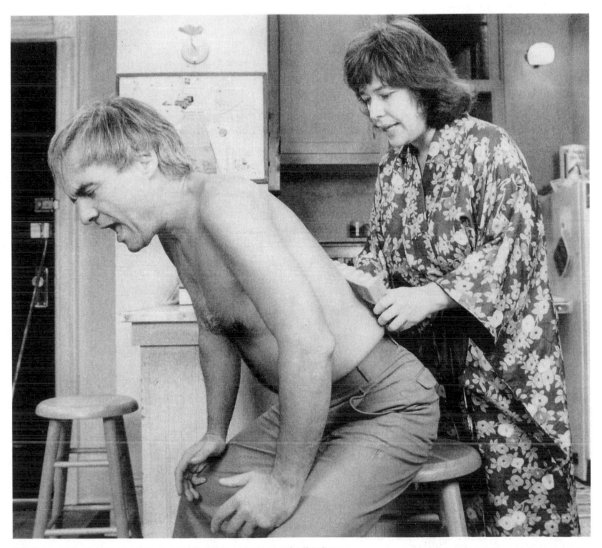

Kathy Bates attempts to cool off Kenneth Welsh in *Frankie and Johnny in the Clair de Lune*.

arrived in the country, and Rose, who was brought over to America as a child and is totally assimiliated. Rose is so Americanized that she assumes a Gentile name at work and doesn't let anyone know she's Jewish. Lebow traces the sisters' growing friendship, as Lusia attempts to find her missing husband and come to terms with the horrors she has endured in Europe, and Rose embraces her religious background.

A Shayna Maidel was first presented at Atlanta's Academy Theatre and voted by the American Theatre Critics Association to be one of the best new plays presented in a regional theatre. Productions at the Philadelphia Drama Guild, Hartford Stage, and at the off-Broadway Westside Arts Theatre followed. Gordana Rashovich, of the Hartford production, played Lusia in New York. Melissa Gilbert was Rose.

The play was filmed under the title of *Miss Rose White* and presented on TV's *Hallmark Hall of Fame* in 1992. The special won an Emmy, as did Amanda Plummer, who played Lusia. Kyra Sedgwick, Maximilian Schell, and Maureen Stapleton co-starred.

OIL CITY SYMPHONY

by Mike Carver, Mark Hardwick, Debra Monk, and Mary Murfitt
Opened November 3, 1987
626 Performances
The Circle in the Square Downtown
Directed by Larry Forde
Produced by Lois Deutchman, Mary T. Nealon, and David Musselman.
Cast: Mike Carver, Mark Hardwick, Debra Monk, Mary Murfitt.

For *Oil City Symphony*, the Circle in the Square Downtown Theatre was converted into a high school gym, with a basketball hoop, balloons, pennants, and colored streamers. The occasion was the fictional reunion of four classmates from Oil City High School and a satiric celebration of middle-of-the-road music, mores, and manners. Every night, a member of the audience was chosen to be Miss Reeves, the group's old music teacher, and everyone got up to do "The Hokey Pokey." Once the eighty-minute show was over, the cast would join the audience in the lobby for cookies and lemonade.

Cast members Mike Hardwick and Mike Carver had met while performing in the show *Diamond Studs*. They decided to put together a two-piano act about a high school reunion and add two women. Hardwick had appeared in *Pump Boys and Dinettes* with Debra Monk, who joined the ensemble as a drummer. Mary Murfitt, a versatile musician whose instruments included the violin, flute, and saxophone, auditioned for the remaining female slot.

The quartet tried the show out as a Christmas event at the South Street Theatre on West 42nd Street and then played Dallas, before opening off-Broadway.

During the run, the title was shortened to *Oil City* to avoid confusion. Some theatregoers thought they were going to attend a serious symphony concert.

TAMARA

by John Krizanc, based on a concept by Richard Rose and John Krizanc.
Opened December 2, 1987
1,036 Performances
The Park Avenue Armory
Directed by Richard Rose
Produced by Moses Znaimer

Cast: Sara Botsford (Tamara de Lempicka); Lally Cadeau (Luisa Baccara); Cynthia Dale (Carlotta Bara); Roma Downey (Emilie Pavese); Patrick Horgan (Gian Francisco de Spiga); Marilyn Lightstone (Aelis Mazoyer); Leland Murray (Dante Fenzo); Frederick Rolf (Gabriele d'Annunzio); August Schellenberg (Aldo Finzi); Jack Wetherall (Mario Pagnutti).

Called "a living movie" by its producer, *Tamara* elevated the concept of audience participation to new heights. Rather than sitting and watching the play unfold before them in a straightforward narrative, audience members followed actors around a representation of a ten-room villa as different scenes occurred simultaneously in different parts of the "house."

The unique presentation takes place during a weekend in 1927, when Polish painter Tamara de Lempicka visits the palatial home of Italian poet and politician Gabriele d'Annunzio. She thinks the purpose of her trip is to paint her host's portrait, while he has designs of a seductive nature. Sexual and political intrigue among the staff and other guests, who include a mad pianist and soldiers in Mussolini's fascist army, kept theatregoers hopping from room to room.

Canadian author John Krizanc was inspired by a book of paintings by the real Tamara. The book included pages of a diary kept by a housekeeper recording the painter's stay at the villa. The play was first presented at a Toronto theatre festival by a group called the Necessary Angel Company. Television executive Moses Znaimer saw the production and mounted a commercial run in Toronto as well as in Mexico City, Los Angeles (with Oscar-winner Anjelica Huston in the title role), and New York.

For the New York *Tamara*, Znaimer rented the Park Avenue Armory from the Army, gave the audience an intermission champagne buffet from the four-star restaurant Le Cirque, and charged $75–$125 a ticket. Film star Elke Sommer was among those who appeared during the off-Broadway run.

TONY 'N' TINA'S WEDDING

Devised by Nancy Cassaro and Artificial Intelligence

Opened February 6, 1988

Still running (1,1947 performances as of February 6, 1994)

Washington Square Church

Directed by Larry Pellegrini

Produced by Joseph Corcoran, Daniel Corcoran, Mark Campbell.

Cast: Nancy Cassaro (Valentina Lynne Vitale Nunzio); Mark Nasser (Anthony Angelo Nunzio); Moira Wilson (Connie Mocogni); Mark Campbell (Barry Wheeler); Elizabeth Dennehy (Donna Marsala); James Altuner (Dominic Fabrizzi); Patricia Cregan (Marina Gulino); Eli Ganias (Johnny Nunzio); Susan Varon (Josephine Vitale); Thomas Michael Allen (Joseph Vitale); Jacob Harran (Luigi Domenico); Jennifer Heftler (Rose Domenico); Elizabeth Herring (Sister Albert Maria); Chris Fracchiolla (Anthony Angelo Nuzio, Sr.); Jeannie Moreau (Madeline Monroe); Denise Moses (Grandma Nunzio); Jack Fris (Michael Just); Phil Rosenthal (Father Mark); Kevin A. Leonidas (Vinnie Black); Joanna Cocca (Loretta Black); Mickey Abbate (Mick Black); Tom Hogan (Timmy Sullivan); Vincent Floriani (Sal Antonucci); Michael Winther (Donny Dulce); Kia Colton (Celeste Romano); Charlie Terrat (Carlo Cannoli); Towner Gallaher (Rocco Caruso).

Audience participation goes even further with *Tony 'n' Tina's Wedding* than it had with *Tamara*. In the latter, theatregoers watched the action; in *Tony 'n' Tina*, they are actual participants in a wedding. The event begins at a church, where the audience attends the union of Valentina Vitale and Anthony Nunzio, complete with gum-chewing bridesmaids. Next, the cast pours into limousines while the audience walks the two blocks to a restaurant where the reception is held. Characters mingle with the playgoers, who eat baked ziti and even dance with the cast.

Original cast members Nancy Cassaro and Mark Nasser first played their roles when they were students at Hofstra University. "We were outcasts in the drama department," Cassaro told the *Newark Star-Ledger*, "and one time we were doing improvisations of a young couple having a fight. They became so real that the dorm master called, wondering what was the matter. It snowballed and we enlisted other friends who created other characters." Cassaro and Nasser, together with a group of other actors, formed Artificial Intelligence, a comedy theatre troupe. *Tony 'n' Tina* grew out of their improvisations. Additional companies have played Los Angeles, Philadelphia, Toronto, Baltimore, and Atlantic City.

OTHER PEOPLE'S MONEY

by Jerry Sterner

Opened February 16, 1989

990 Performances

Minetta Lane Theatre

Directed by Gloria Muzio

Produced by Jeffrey Ash and Susan Quint Gallin

Cast: James Murtaugh (William Coles); Arch Johnson (Andrew Jorgenson); Kevin Conway (Lawrence Garfinkle); Scotty Bloch (Bea Sullivan); Mercedes Ruehl (Kate Sullivan).

Wall Street came to off-Broadway with *Other People's Money*, a cat-and-mouse comedy-drama of hostile corporate takeovers. Jerry Sterner's play pitted investor-raider Lawrence Garfinkle (a.k.a. "Larry the Liquidator") against business lawyer Kate Sullivan, both financially and sexually, as they battle over the fate of a conservative New England company Larry has his eye on.

Sterner, a former real estate investor, based the play on his experience as a shareholder of a Michigan company that received a hostile takeover bid in 1985. After selling his shares to the raider, Sterner visited the company town and found it empty.

The play was premiered at the American Stage Company, in Teaneck, New Jersey. A second production at Hartford Stage was transferred to off-Broadway's Minetta Lane Theatre.

Many major players in the financial world came to see the show. After a slow start, the production had a bull market with a run of more than two years. The play attracted a large number of stockbrokers and analysts, a group not normally associated with theatregoing. The New York success was not repeated on the road. A national tour starring Tony LoBianco closed early in Detroit.

Danny De Vito, Penelope Anne Miller, and Gregory Peck starred in the 1991 film version.

FOREVER PLAID

Conceived by Stuart Ross

Opened May 20, 1990

Still running (1,655 performances as of February 6, 1994)

Steve McGraw's

Musical direction by James Raitt

Directed by Stuart Ross

Produced by Gene Wolsk

Cast: Stan Chandler (Jinx); David Engel (Smudge); Jason Graae (Sparky); Guy Stroman (Francis).

Just as *Beehive* celebrated the female singers of the '60s, *Forever Plaid*, another nostalgic revue with its roots in cabaret, spoofed and paid tribute to the male groups of the '50s. The Plaids are a quartet on the order of The Four Freshmen, The Hi-Lows, and The Four Lads. It seems they were killed back in 1964, in a collision with a busload of convent girls who are on their way to see the Beatles on *The Ed Sullivan Show*. A benevolent diety allows them one night on Earth to perform the show they were headed for almost thirty years earlier. "Three Coins in the Fountain," "Moments to Remember," and the melodies made famous by Perry Como made up the Plaids repertoire.

The musical was conceived, written, and directed by Stuart Ross, who used his Visa credit card to its maximum for the $8,000 he needed to purchase lights, costumes, and a set for a small-scale production. Seeing the show at the nightclub Steve McGraw's, Broadway producer Gene Wolsk recognized the huge market for '50s nostalgia, and he raised $150,000 to budget a regular open run at McGraw's. Wolsk's instincts were right, and a national audience came to hear mellow sounds of the '50s. President George Bush was among the production's biggest fans, inviting the quartet to perform at the White House. In addition to the still-playing New York run, there have been long-running Plaids singing in San Diego, Minneapolis, Boston, Denver, and numerous other cities.

BEAU JEST

by James Sherman

Opened October 10, 1991

Still running (974 performances as of February 6, 1994)

The Lamb's Theatre

Directed by Dennis Zacek

Produced by Arthur Cantor, Carol Ostrow, and Libby Adler Mages

Cast: Laura Patinkin (Sarah Goodman); John Michael Higgins (Chris); Tom Hewitt (Bob); Larry Fleischman (Joel); Rosyln Alexander (Miriam); Bernie Landis (Abe).

Producer Arthur Cantor came across a long-running hit by reading the *Wall Street Journal*'s review of a Chicago production of a comedy called *Beau Jest*. The play was about a Jewish girl who hires a Gentile actor to pose as her boyfriend for the benefit of her Orthodox parents. The reviewer opined that the play was more than a one-joke sitcom, as the plot summary suggested, but was really a warm family comedy. Cantor got on a plane to the Windy City and caught that evening's performance at the Victory Garden Theatre. He liked what he saw and immediately contacted Chicago-based playwright James Sherman for the rights.

The subsequent off-Broadway production at the Lamb's Theatre was not hailed by the press. "We got one rave from Howard Kissel in the *News*," Cantor told *Playbill*, "two patronizing reviews from other newspapers and a really blistering pan from Clive Barnes in the *New York Post*." In the first eight weeks, the show lost $50,000. But word of mouth and theatre groups began to build an audience for the comedy, and it began to turn a profit. As of this writing, *Beau Jest* is still keeping theatregoers laughing.

TUBES

by Blue Man Group (Matt Goldman, Phil Stanton, and Chris Wink)

Opened November 17, 1991

Still running (914 performances as of February 6, 1994)

Astor Place Theatre

Directed by Marlene Swartz

Produced by Mark Dunn and Makoto Deguchi

Three men with bald heads and blue skin splash paint on drums and create brilliant rainbows as they pound away. The blue maniacs invite a member of the audience onstage for a feast of Twinkies and cream begins to ooze out of their chests. They stuff Cap'n Crunch cereal into their mouths and make music with their amplified chomping. Another theatregoer is brought to the stage, taken into the wings and emerges with his head encased in an orange Jello mold. Such are the avant-garde antics of Blue Man Group and their weirdly wonderful performance piece, *Tubes*.

The sketches occasionally take deliberate aim at a specific target, such as the art world, which comes in for a skewering when a Blue Man spits out paint onto a canvas and slaps a price tag on the result. But most of the pieces are only meant to entertain. "We are trying to create an art playground," one of the troupe told *Time* magazine.

The trio comprises Matt Goldman, Phil Stanton, and Chris Wink. They formed the group in 1988 and began performing on the streets of New York. In 1991, they performed a shorter version of *Tubes* at Café La MaMa, which won them an Obie Award. A commercial run at the Astor Place Theatre followed.

OLEANNA

by David Mamet

Opened October 25, 1992

513 Performances

Orpheum Theatre

Directed by David Mamet

Produced by Frederick Zollo, Mitchell Maxwell, Alan J. Schuster, Peggy Hill Rosenkranz, Ron Kastner, Thomas Viertel, Steven Baruch, and Frank and Woji Gero

Cast: William H. Macy (John); Rebecca Pidgeon (Carol).

Pulitzer prize–winning playwright David Mamet (*Glengarry Glen Ross*) tackled the hot topic of sexual harassment with his atom bomb of a play *Oleanna*. In a small college office, a pompous professor and his vacuous female student engage in a battle of wills in which power shifts rapidly from one to the other. The title of this controversial work is ironically taken from a folk song about a utopian community. The play sparked much discussion and argument; some audience members interpreted it a backlash against feminism. The playwright directed the cast, consisting of his wife Rebecca Pidgeon, and William H. Macy.

The army of producers (which outnumbered the cast) considered moving the drama to Broadway but decided that off-Broadway, with its less expensive venues, would be the wiser economic decision. Because of the production's low overhead (tiny cast, one spare set), *Oleanna* was able to run fifteen months and earn an estimated return of $1 million. Productions in regional and foreign theatres proliferated.

APPENDIX

THE PULITZER PRIZE WINNERS FOR DRAMA

1916–17
No Award

1917–18
Why Marry?, by Jesse Lynch Williams

1918–19
No Award

1919–20
Beyond the Horizon, by Eugene O'Neill

1920–21
Miss Lulu Bett, by Zona Gale

1921–22
Anna Christie, by Eugene O'Neill

1922–23
Icebound, by Owen Davis

1923–24
Hell-Bent fer Heaven, by Hatcher Hughes

1924–25
They Knew What They Wanted, by Sidney Howard

1925–26
Craig's Wife, by George Kelly

1926–27
In Abraham's Bosom, by Paul Green

1927–28
Strange Interlude, by Eugene O'Neill

1928–29
Street Scene, by Elmer Rice

1929–30
The Green Pastures, by Marc Connelly

1930–31
Alison's House, by Susan Glaspell

1931–32
Of Thee I Sing, by George S. Kaufman, Morris Ryskind, and Ira Gershwin.

1932–33
Both Your Houses, by Maxwell Anderson

1933–34
Men in White, by Sidney Kingsley

1934–35
The Old Maid, by Zoë Akins

1935–36
Idiot's Delight, by Robert E. Sherwood

1936–37
You Can't Take It with You, by Moss Hart and George S. Kaufman

1937–38
Our Town, by Thornton Wilder

1938–39
Abe Lincoln in Illinois, by Robert E. Sherwood

1939–40
The Time of Your Life, by William Saroyan

1940–41
There Shall Be No Night, by Robert E. Sherwood

1941–42
No Award

1942–43
The Skin of Our Teeth, by Thornton Wilder

1943–44
No Award

1944–45
Harvey, by Mary Chase

1945–46
State of the Union, by Howard Lindsay and Russel Crouse

1946–47
No Award

1947–48
A Streetcar Named Desire, by Tennessee Williams

1948–49
Death of a Salesman, by Arthur Miller

1949–50
South Pacific, by Richard Rodgers, Oscar Hammerstein II, and Joshua Logan

1950–51
No Award

1951–52
The Shrike, by Joseph Krumm

1952–53
Picnic, by William Inge

1953–54
The Teahouse of the August Moon, by John Patrick

1954–55
Cat on a Hot Tin Roof, by Tennessee Williams

1955–56
The Diary of Anne Frank, by Frances Goodrich and Albert Hackett

1956–57
Long Day's Journey into Night, by Eugene O'Neill

1957–58
Look Homeward, Angel, by Ketti Frings

1958–59
J.B., by Archibald MacLeish

1959–60
Fiorello!, by Jerome Weidman, George Abbott, Sheldon Harnick, and Jerry Bock

1960–61
All the Way Home, by Tad Mosel

1961–62
How to Succeed in Business Without Really Trying, by Abe Burrows, Willie Gilbert, Jack Weinstock, and Frank Loesser

1962–63
No Award

1963–64
No Award

1964–65
The Subject Was Roses, by Frank Gilroy

1965–66
No Award

1966–67
A Delicate Balance, by Edward Albee

1967–68
No Award

1968–69
The Great White Hope, by Howard Sackler

1969–70
No Place to Be Somebody, by Charles Gordone

1970–71
The Effect of Gamma Rays on Man-in-the-Moon Marigolds, by Paul Zindel

1971–72
No Award

1972–73
That Championship Season, by Jason Miller

1973–74
No Award

1974–75
Seascape, by Edward Albee

1975–76
A Chorus Line, by Michael Bennett, James Kirkwood, Nicholas Dante, Marvin Hamlisch, and Edward Kleban

1976–77
The Shadow Box, by Michael Cristofer

1977–78
The Gin Game, by D.L. Coburn

1978–79
Buried Child, by Sam Shepard

1979–80
Talley's Folly, by Lanford Wilson

1980–81
Crimes of the Heart, by Beth Henley

1981–82
A Soldier's Play, by Charles Fuller

1982–83
'night, Mother, by Marsha Norman

1983–84
Glengarry Glen Ross, by David Mamet

1984–85
Sunday in the Park with George, by Stephen Sondheim and James Lapine

1985–86
No Award

1086–87
Fences, by August Wilson

1987–88
Driving Miss Daisy, by Alfred Uhry

1988–89
The Heidi Chronicles, by Wendy Wasserstein

1989–90
The Piano Lesson, by August Wilson

1990–91
Lost in Yonkers, by Neil Simon

1991–92
The Kentucky Cycle, by Robert Schenkkan

1992–93
Angels in America: Millennium Approaches, by Tony Kushner

THE ANTOINETTE PERRY (TONY) AWARDS

Presented annually by the American Theatre Wing and the League of American Theatres and Producers. Categories varied until 1948–49. From 1948–49 on, winners are listed in the following order:

Plays
Play; Actor in a Play; Actress in a Play; Featured Actor in a Play; Featured Actress in a Play

Musicals
Musical; Actor in a Musical; Actress in a Musical; Featured Actor in a Musical; Featured Actress in a Musical

1946–47

Performances
Ingrid Bergman (*Joan of Lorraine*); Helen Hayes (*Happy Birthday*); José Ferrer (*Cyrano de Bergerac*); Frederic March (*Years Ago*)

Debut Performance
Patricia Neal (*Another Part of the Forest*)

Musical Performance
David Wayne (*Finian's Rainbow*)

1947–48

Play
Mister Roberts

Performances
Judith Anderson (*Medea*); Katharine Cornell (*Antony and Cleopatra*); Jessica Tandy (*A Streetcar Named Desire*); Henry Fonda (*Mister Roberts*); Paul Kelly (*Command Decision*); Basil Rathbone (*The Heiress*)

Musical Performance
Grace and Paul Hartman (*Angel in the Wings*)

Debut Performance
June Lockhart (*For Love or Money*); James Whitmore (*Command Decision*)

1948–49

Plays
Death of a Salesman; Rex Harrison (*Anne of the Thousand Days*); Martita Hunt (*The Madwoman of Chaillot*); Arthur Kennedy (*Death of a Salesman*); Shirley Booth (*Goodbye, My Fancy*)

Musicals
Kiss Me, Kate; Ray Bolger (*Where's Charley?*); Nanette Fabray (*Love Life*)

1949–50

Plays
The Cocktail Party; Sidney Blackmer (*Come Back, Little Sheba*); Shirley Booth (*Come Back, Little Sheba*)

Musicals
South Pacific; Ezio Pinza, Mary Martin, Myron McCormick, Juanita Hall (all for *South Pacific*)

1950–51

Plays
The Rose Tattoo; Claude Rains (*Darkness at Noon*); Uta Hagen (*The Country Girl*); Eli Wallach (*The Rose Tattoo*); Maureen Stapleton (*The Rose Tattoo*)

Musicals
Guys and Dolls; Robert Alda (*Guys and Dolls*); Ethel Merman (*Call Me Madam*); Russell Nype (*Call Me Madam*); Isabel Bigley (*Guys and Dolls*)

1951–52

Plays
The Fourposter; José Ferrer (*The Shrike*); Julie Harris *I Am a Camera*); John Cromwell (*Point of No Return*); Marian Winters (*I Am a Camera*)

Musicals
The King and I; Phil Silvers (*Top Banana*); Gertrude Lawrence (*The King and I*); Yul Brynner (*The King and I*); Helen Gallagher (*Pal Joey*)

1952–53

Plays
The Crucible; Tom Ewell (*The Seven-Year Itch*); Shirley Booth (*The Time of the Cuckoo*); John Williams (*Dial M for Murder*); Beatrice Straight (*The Crucible*)

Musicals
Wonderful Town; Rosalind Russell (*Wonderful Town*); Thomas Mitchell (*Hazel Flagg*); Hiram Sherman (*Two's Company*); Sheila Bond (*Wish You Were Here*)

1953–54

Plays
The Teahouse of the August Moon; David Wayne (*The Teahouse of the August Moon*); Audrey Hepburn (*Ondine*); John Kerr (*Tea and Sympathy*); Jo Van Fleet (*The Trip to Bountiful*)

Musicals
Kismet; Alfred Drake (*Kismet*); Dolores Gray (*Carnival in Flanders*); Harry Belafonte (*John Murray Anderson's Almanac*); Gwen Verdon (*Can-Can*)

1954–55

Plays
The Desperate Hours; Alfred Lunt (*Quadrille*); Nancy Kelly (*The Bad Seed*); Francis L. Sullivan, Patricia Jessel (both for *Witness for the Prosecution*)

Musicals
The Pajama Game; Mary Martin (*Peter Pan*); Walter Slezak (*Fanny*); Cyril Ritchard (*Peter Pan*); Carol Haney (*The Pajama Game*)

1955–56

Plays
The Diary of Anne Frank; Paul Muni (*Inherit the Wind*); Julie Harris (*The Lark*); Ed Begley (*Inherit the Wind*); Una Merkel (*The Ponder Heart*)

Musicals
Damn Yankees; Ray Walston, Gwen Verdon, Russ Brown (all for *Damn Yankees*); Lotte Lenya (*The Threepenny Opera*)

1956–57

Plays
Long Day's Journey into Night; Frederic March (*Long Day's Journey into Night*); Margaret Leighton (*Separate Tables*); Frank Conroy (*The Potting Shed*); Peggy Cass (*Auntie Mame*)

Musicals
My Fair Lady; Rex Harrison (*My Fair Lady*); Judy Holliday, Sydney Chaplin (both for *Bells Are Ringing*); Edith Adams (*L'il Abner*)

1957–58

Plays
Sunrise at Campobello; Ralph Bellamy (*Sunrise at Campobello*); Helen Hayes (*Time Remembered*); Henry Jones (*Sunrise at Campobello*); Anne Bancroft (*Two for the Seesaw*)

Musicals
The Music Man; Robert Preston (*The Music Man*); Gwen Verdon, Thelma Ritter (tie, both for *New Girl in Town*); David Burns, Barbara Cook (both for *The Music Man*)

1958–59

Plays
J.B.; Jason Robards, Jr. (*The Disenchanted*); Gertrude Berg (*A Majority of One*); Charles Ruggles (*The Pleasure of His Company*); Julie Newmar (*The Marriage-Go-Round*)

Musicals
Redhead; Richard Kiley, Gwen Verdon (both for *Redhead*); Russell Nype, Pat Stanley (both for *Goldilocks*); Special Award to the cast of *La Plume de Ma Tante*

1959–60

Plays
The Miracle Worker; Melvyn Douglas (*The Best Man*); Anne Bancroft (*The Miracle Worker*); Roddy McDowall (*The Fighting Cock*); Anne Revere (*Toys in the Attic*)

Musicals
Fiorello!, *The Sound of Music* (tie); Jackie Gleason (*Take Me Along*); Mary Martin (*The Sound of Music*); Tom Bosley (*Fiorello!*); Patricia Neway (*The Sound of Music*)

1960–61

Plays
Becket; Zero Mostel (*Rhinoceros*); Joan Plowright (*A Taste of Honey*); Martin Gabel (*Big Fish, Little Fish*); Colleen Dewhurst (*All the Way Home*)

Musicals
Bye, Bye, Birdie; Richard Burton (*Camelot*); Elizabeth Seal (*Irma La Douce*); Dick Van Dyke (*Bye, Bye, Birdie*); Tammy Grimes (*The Unsinkable Molly Brown*)

1961–62

Plays
A Man for all Seasons; Paul Scofield (*A Man for All Seasons*); Margaret Leighton (*Night of the Iguana*); Walter Matthau (*A Shot in the Dark*); Elizabeth Ashley (*Take Her, She's Mine*)

Musicals

How to Succeed in Business Without Really Trying; Robert Morse (*How to Succeed . . .*); Anna Maria Alberghetti (*Carnival*), Diahann Carroll (*No Strings*), tie; Charles Nelson Reilly (*How to Succeed . . .*); Phyllis Newman (*Subways Are for Sleeping*)

1962–63

Plays

Who's Afraid of Virginia Woolf?; Arthur Hill, Uta Hagen (both for *Who's Afraid of Virginia Woolf?*); Sandy Dennis (*A Thousand Clowns*); Alan Arkin (*Enter Laughing*)

Musicals

A Funny Thing Happened on the Way to the Forum; Zero Mostel (*A Funny Thing Happened . . .*); Vivien Leigh (*Tovarich*); David Burns (*A Funny Thing Happened . . .*); Anna Quayle (*Stop the World—I Want to Get Off*)

1963–64

Plays

Luther; Alec Guinness (*Dylan*); Sandy Dennis (*Any Wednesday*); Hume Cronyn (*Hamlet*); Barbara Loden (*After the Fall*)

Musicals

Hello, Dolly!; Bert Lahr (*Foxy*); Carol Channing (*Hello, Dolly!*); Jack Cassidy (*She Loves Me*); Tessie O'Shea (*The Girl Who Came to Supper*)

1964–65

Plays

The Subject Was Roses; Walter Matthau (*The Odd Couple*); Irene Worth (*Tiny Alice*); Jack Albertson (*The Subject Was Roses*); Alice Ghostley (*The Sign in Sidney Brustein's Window*)

Musicals

Fiddler on the Roof; Zero Mostel (*Fiddler on the Roof*); Liza Minnelli (*Flora, the Red Menace*); Victor Spinelli (*Oh, What a Lovely War*); Maria Karnilova (*Fiddler on the Roof*)

1965–66

Plays

Marat/Sade; Hal Holbrook (*Mark Twain Tonight!*); Rosemary Harris (*The Lion in Winter*); Patrick Magee (*Marat/Sade*); Zoë Caldwell (*Slapstick Tragedy*)

Musicals

Man of La Mancha; Richard Kiley (*Man of La Mancha*); Angela Lansbury, Frankie Michaels, Beatrice Arthur (all for *Mame*)

1966–67

Plays

The Homecoming; Paul Rogers (*The Homecoming*); Beryl Reid (*The Killing of Sister George*); Ian Holm (*The Homecoming*); Marian Seldes (*A Delicate Balance*)

Musicals

Cabaret; Robert Preston (*I Do! I Do!*); Barbara Harris (*The Apple Tree*); Joel Grey, Peg Murray (both for *Cabaret*)

1967–68

Plays

Rosencrantz and Guildenstern Are Dead; Martin Balsam (*You Know I Can't Hear You When the Water's Running*); Zoë Caldwell (*The Prime of Miss Jean Brodie*); James Patterson (*The Birthday Party*); Zena Walker (*A Day in the Death of Joe Egg*)

Musicals

Hallelujah, Baby!; Robert Goulet (*The Happy Time*); Patricia Routledge (*Darling of the Day*), Leslie Uggams (*Hallelujah, Baby!*), tie; Hiram Sherman (*How Now, Dow Jones?*); Lillian Hayman (*Hallelujah, Baby!*)

1968–69

Plays

The Great White Hope; James Earl Jones (*The Great White Hope*); Julie Harris (*Forty Carats*); Al Pacino (*Does a Tiger Wear a Necktie?*); Jane Alexander (*The Great White Hope*).

Musicals

1776; Jerry Orbach (*Promises, Promises*); Angela Lansbury (*Dear World*); Ronald Hogate (*1776*); Marian Mercer (*Promises, Promises*)

1969–70

Plays

Borstal Boy; Fritz Weaver (*Child's Play*); Tammy Grimes (*Private Lives*); Ken Howard (*Child's Play*); Blythe Danner (*Butterflies Are Free*)

Musicals

Applause; Cleavon Little (*Purlie*); Lauren Bacall (*Applause*); René Auberjonois (*Coco*); Melba Moore (*Purlie*)

1970–71

Plays

Sleuth; Brian Bedford (*The School for Wives*); Maureen Stapleton (*The Gingerbread Lady*); Paul Sand (*Story Theatre*); Rae Allen (*And Miss Reardon Drinks a Little*)

Musicals

Company; Hal Linden (*The Rothschilds*); Helen Gallagher (*No, No, Nanette*); Keene Curtis (*The Rothschilds*); Patsy Kelly (*No, No, Nanette*)

1971–72

Plays

Sticks and Bones; Cliff Gorman (*Lenny*); Sada Thompson (*Twigs*); Vincent Gardenia (*The Prisoner of Second Avenue*); Elizabeth Wilson (*Sticks and Bones*)

Musicals

Two Gentlemen of Verona; Phil Silvers (*A Funny Thing Happened on the Way to the Forum*); Alexis Smith (*Follies*); Larry Blyden (*A Funny Thing Happened . . .*); Linda Hopkins (*Inner City*)

1972–73

Plays

That Championship Season; Alan Bates (*Butley*); Julie Harris (*The Last of Mrs. Lincoln*);

John Lithgow (*The Changing Room*); Leora Dana (*The Last of Mrs. Lincoln*)

Musicals

A Little Night Music; Ben Vereen (*Pippin*); Glynis Johns (*A Little Night Music*); George S. Irving (*Irene*); Patricia Elliott (*A Little Night Music*)

1973–74

Plays

The River Niger; Michael Moriarty (*Find Your Way Home*); Colleen Dewhurst, Ed Flanders (both for *A Moon for the Misbegotten*); Frances Sternhagen (*The Good Doctor*)

Musicals

Raisin; Christopher Plummer (*Cyrano*); Virginia Capers (*Raisin*); Tommy Tune (*Seesaw*); Janie Sell (*Over Here*)

1974–75

Plays

Equus; John Kani, Winston Ntshona (shared Best Actor Award for two one-acts, *Sizwe Banzi Is Dead* and *The Island*); Ellen Burstyn (*Same Time, Next Year*); Frank Langella (*Seascape*); Rita Moreno (*The Ritz*)

Musicals

The Wiz; John Cullum (*Shenandoah*); Angela Lansbury (*Gypsy*); Ted Ross, Dee Dee Bridgewater (both for *The Wiz*)

1975–76

Plays

Travesties; John Wood (*Travesties*); Irene Worth (*Sweet Bird of Youth*); Edward Herrmann (*Mrs. Warren's Profession*); Shirley Knight (*Kennedy's Children*)

Musicals

A Chorus Line; George Rose (*My Fair Lady*); Donna McKechnie, Sammy Williams, Carole (later Kelly) Bishop (all for *A Chorus Line*)

1976 77

Plays

The Shadow Box; Al Pacino (*The Basic Training of Pavlo Hummel*); Julie Harris (*The Belle of Amherst*); Jonathan Pryce (*Comedians*); Trazana Beverly (*for colored girls who have considered suicide / when the rainbow is enuf*)

Musicals

Annie; Barry Bostwick (*The Robber Bridegroom*); Dorothy Loudon (*Annie*); Lenny Baker (*I Love My Wife*); Dolores Hall (*Your Arms Too Short to Box with God*)

1977–78

Plays

Da; Barnard Hughes (*Da*); Jessica Tandy (*The Gin Game*); Lester Rawlins (*Da*); Ann Wedgeworth (*Chapter Two*)

Musicals

Ain't Misbehavin'; John Cullum (*On the Twentieth Century*); Liza Minnelli (*The Act*); Kevin Kline (*On the Twentieth Century*); Nell Carter (*Ain't Misbehavin'*)

1978–79

Plays

The Elephant Man; Tom Conti (*Whose Life Is It Anyway?*); Constance Cummings (*Wings*), Carole Shelley (*The Elephant Man*), tie; Michael Gough, Joan Hickson (both in *Bedroom Farce*)

Musicals

Sweeney Todd; Len Cariou, Angela Lansbury (both for *Sweeney Todd*); Henderson Forsythe, Carlin Glynn (both for *The Best Little Whorehouse in Texas*)

1979–80

Plays

Children of a Lesser God; John Rubinstein, Phyllis Frelich (both for *Children of a Lesser God*); David Rounds (*Morning's at Seven*); Dinah Manoff (*I Ought to Be in Pictures*)

Musicals

Evita; Jim Dale (*Barnum*); Patti LuPone, Mandy Patinkin (both for *Evita*); Priscilla Lopez (*A Day in Hollywood/A Night in the Ukraine*)

1980–81

Plays

Amadeus; Ian McKellen (*Amadeus*); Jane Lapotaire (*Piaf*); Brian Backer (*The Floating Light Bulb*); Swoosie Kurtz (*Fifth of July*)

Musicals

42nd Street; Kevin Kline (*The Pirates of Penzance*); Lauren Bacall (*Woman of the Year*); Hinton Battle (*Sophisticated Ladies*); Marilyn Cooper (*Woman of the Year*)

1981–82

Plays

The Life and Adventures of Nicholas Nickleby; Roger Rees (*The Life and Adventures of Nicholas Nickleby*); Zoë Caldwell (*Medea*); Zakes Mokae (*Master Harold . . . and the Boys*); Amanda Plummer (*Agnes of God*)

Musicals

Nine; Ben Harney, Jennifer Holliday, Cleavant Derricks (all for *Dreamgirls*); Liliane Montevecchi (*Nine*)

1982–83

Plays

Torch Song Trilogy; Harvey Fierstein (*Torch Song Trilogy*); Jessica Tandy (*Foxfire*); Matthew Broderick (*Brighton Beach Memoirs*); Judith Ivey (*Steaming*)

Musicals

Cats; Tommy Tune (*My One and Only*); Natalia Makarova (*On Your Toes*); Charles "Honi" Coles (*My One and Only*); Betty Buckley (*Cats*)

1983–84

Plays

The Real Thing; Jeremy Irons, Glenn Close (both for *The Real Thing*); Joe Mantegna (*Glengarry Glen Ross*); Christine Baranski (*The Real Thing*)

Musicals

La Cage Aux Folles; George Hearn (*La Cage Aux Folles*); Chita Rivera (*The Rink*); Hinton Battle (*The Tap Dance Kid*); Lila Kedrova (*Zorba*)

1984–85

Plays

Biloxi Blues; Derek Jacobi (*Much Ado About Nothing*); Stockard Channing (*A Day in the Death of Joe Egg*); Barry Miller (*Biloxi Blues*); Judith Ivey (*Hurlyburly*)

Musicals

Big River; No awards for best actor or actress in a musical; Ron Richardson (*Big River*); Leilani Jones (*Grind*)

1985–86

Plays

I'm Not Rappaport; Judd Hirsch (*I'm Not Rappaport*); Lily Tomlin (*The Search for Signs of Intelligent Life in the Universe*); John Mahoney, Swoosie Kurtz (both for *The House of Blue Leaves*)

Musicals

The Mystery of Edwin Drood; George Rose (*The Mystery of Edwin Drood*); Bernadette Peters (*Song & Dance*); Michael Rupert, Bebe Neuwirth (both for *Sweet Charity*)

1986–87

Plays

Fences; James Earl Jones (*Fences*); Linda Lavin, John Randolph (both for *Broadway Bound*); Mary Alice (*Fences*)

Musicals

Les Misérables; Robert Lindsay, Maryann Plunkett (both for *Me and My Girl*); Michael Maguire, Frances Ruffelle (both for *Les Misérables*)

1987–88

Plays

M. Butterfly; Ron Silver (*Speed-the-Plow*); Joan Allen (*Burn This*); B.D. Wong (*M. Butterfly*); L. Scott Caldwell (*Joe Turner's Come and Gone*)

Musicals

Phantom of the Opera; Michael Crawford (*Phantom of the Opera*); Joanna Gleason (*Into the Woods*); Bill McCutcheon (*Anything Goes*); Judy Kaye (*Phantom of the Opera*)

1988–89

Plays

The Heidi Chronicles; Philip Bosco (*Lend Me a Tenor*); Pauline Collins (*Shirley Valentine*); Boyd Gaines (*The Heidi Chronicles*); Christine Baranski (*Rumors*)

Musicals

Jerome Robbins' Broadway; Jason Alexander (*Jerome Robbins' Broadway*); Ruth Brown (*Black and Blue*); Scott Wise, Debbie Shapiro (both for *Jerome Robbins' Broadway*)

1989–90

Plays

The Grapes of Wrath; Robert Morse (*Tru*); Maggie Smith (*Lettice and Lovage*); Charles Durning (*Cat on a Hot Tin Roof*); Margaret Tyzack (*Lettice and Lovage*)

Musicals

City of Angels; James Naughton (*City of Angels*); Tyne Daly (*Gypsy*); Michael Jeter (*Grand Hotel*); Randy Graff (*City of Angels*)

1990–91

Plays

Lost in Yonkers; Nigel Hawthorne (*Shadowlands*); Mercedes Ruehl, Kevin Spacey, Irene Worth (all for *Lost in Yonkers*)

Musicals

The Will Rogers Follies; Jonathan Pryce, Lea Salonga, Hinton Battle (all for *Miss Saigon*); Daisy Eagan (*The Secret Garden*)

1991–92

Plays

Dancing at Lughnasa; Judd Hirsch (*Conversations with My Father*); Glenn Close (*Death and the Maiden*); Larry Fishburne (*Two Trains Running*); Brid Brennan (*Dancing at Lughnasa*)

Musicals

Crazy for You; Gregory Hines (*Jelly's Last Jam*); Faith Prince (*Guys and Dolls*); Scott Waara (*The Most Happy Fella*); Tonya Pinkins (*Jelly's Last Jam*)

1992–93

Plays

Angels in America: Millennium Approaches; Ron Leibman (*Angels in America*); Madeline Kahn (*The Sisters Rosensweig*); Stephen Spinella (*Angels in America*); Debra Monk (*Redwood Curtain*)

Musicals

Kiss of the Spider Woman; Brent Carver, Chita Rivera, Anthony Crivello (all for *Kiss of the Spider Woman*); Andrea Martin (*My Favorite Year*)

NEW YORK DRAMA CRITICS CIRCLE AWARDS

1935–36

Best American Play
Winterset

1936–37

Best American Play
High Tor

1937–38

Best American Play
Of Mice and Men

Best Foreign Play
Shadow and Substance

1938–39

Best American Play
No award

Best Forcign Play
The White Steed

1939–40

Best American Play
The Time of Your Life

1940–41

Best American Play
Watch on the Rhine

Best Foreign Play
The Corn Is Green

1941–42

Best American Play
No award

Best Foreign Play
Blithe Spirit

1942–43

Best American Play
The Patriots

1943–44

Best American Play
Jacobowsky and the Colonel

1944–45

Best American Play
The Glass Menagerie

1945–46

Best Musical
Carousel

1946–47

Best American Play
All My Sons

Best Foreign Play
No Exit

Best Musical
Brigadoon

1947–48

Best American Play
A Streetcar Named Desire

Best Foreign Play
The Winslow Boy

1948–49

Best American Play
Death of a Salesman

Best Foreign Play
The Madwoman of Chaillot

Best Musical
South Pacific

1949–50

Best American Play
The Member of the Wedding

Best Foreign Play
The Cocktail Party

Best Musical
The Consul

1950–51

Best American Play
Darkness at Noon

Best Foreign Play
The Lady's Not for Burning

Best Musical
Guys and Dolls

1951–52

Best American Play
I Am a Camera

Best Foreign Play
Venus Observed

Best Musical
Pal Joey

Special Citation
Don Juan in Hell

1952–53

Best American Play
Picnic

Best Foreign Play
The Love of Four Colonels

Best Musical
Wonderful Town

1953–54

Best American Play
Teahouse of the August Moon

Best Foreign Play
Ondine

Best Musical
The Golden Apple

1954–55

Best American Play
Cat on a Hot Tin Roof

Best Foreign Play
Witness for the Prosecution

Best Musical
The Saint of Bleecker Street

1955–56

Best American Play
The Diary of Anne Frank

Best Foreign Play
Tiger at the Gates

Best Musical
My Fair Lady

1956–57

Best American Play
Long Day's Journey into Night

Best Foreign Play
The Waltz of the Toreadors

Best Musical
The Most Happy Fella

1957–58

Best American Play
Look Homeward, Angel

Best Foreign Play
Look Back in Anger

Best Musical
The Music Man

1958–59

Best American Play
A Raisin in the Sun

Best Foreign Play
The Visit

Best Musical
La Plume de Ma Tante

1959–60

Best American Play
Toys in the Attic

Best Foreign Play
Five Finger Exrercise

Best Musical
Fiorello!

1960–61

Best American Play
All the Way Home

Best Foreign Play
A Taste of Honey

Best Musical
Carnival

1961–62

Best American Play
The Night of the Iguana

Best Foreign Play
A Man for All Seasons

Best Musical
*How to Succeed in Business
Without Really Trying*

1962–63

Best Play
Who's Afraid of Virginia Woolf?

Special Citation
Beyond the Fringe

1963–64

Best Play
Luther

Best Musical
Hello, Dolly!

Special Citation
The Trojan Women

1964–65

Best Play
The Subject Was Roses

Best Musical
Fiddler on the Roof

1965–66

Best Play
*The Persecution and Assassina-
tion of Marat as Performed by the
Inmates of the Asylum of Charen-
ton Under the Direction of the
Marquis de Sade*

Best Musical
Man of La Mancha

1966–67

Best Play
The Homecoming

Best Musical
Cabaret

1967–68

Best Play
*Rosencrantz and Guildenstern
Are Dead*

Best Musical
Your Own Thing

1968–69

Best Play
The Great White Hope

Best Musical
1776

1969–70

Best Play
Borstal Boy

Best American Play
*The Effect of Gamma Rays on
Man-in-the-Moon Marigolds*

Best Musical
Company

1970–71

Best Play
Home

Best American Play
The House of Blue Leaves

Best Musical
Follies

1971–72

Best Play
That Championship Season

Best Foreign Play
The Screens

Best Musical
Two Gentlemen of Verona

Special Citations
Sticks and Bones and *Old Times*

1972–73
Best Play
The Changing Room
Best American Play
The Hot L Baltimore
Best Musical
A Little Night Music

1973–74
Best Play
The Contractor
Best American Play
Short Eyes
Best Musical
Candide

1974–75
Best Play
Equus
Best American Play
The Taking of Miss Janie
Best Musical
A Chorus Line

1975–76
Best Play
Travesties
Best American Play
Streamers
Best Musical
Pacific Overtures

1976–77
Best Play
Otherwise Engaged
Best American Play
American Buffalo
Best Musical
Annie

1977–78
Best Play
Da

Best Musical
Ain't Misbehavin'

1978–79
Best Play
The Elephant Man
Best Musical
Sweeney Todd, the Demon Barber of Fleet Street

1979–80
Best Play
Talley's Folly
Best Foreign Play
Betrayal
Best Musical
Evita
Special Citation
Peter Brook's Le Center Internationale de Créations Théatricales for its repertory

1980–81
Best Play
A Lesson from Aloes
Best American Play
Crimes of the Heart
Special Citations
Lena Horne: The Lady and Her Music and *The Pirates of Penzance*

1981–82
Best Play
The Life and Adventures of Nicholas Nickleby
Best American Play
A Soldier's Play

1982–83
Best Play
Brighton Beach Memoirs
Best Foreign Play
Plenty

Best Musical
Little Shop of Horrors
Special Citation
The Young Playwrights Festival

1983–84
Best Play
The Real Thing
Best American Play
Glengarry Glen Ross
Best Musical
Sunday in the Park with George
Special Citation
Samuel Beckett for the body of his work

1984–85
Best Play
Ma Rainey's Black Bottom

1985–86
Best Play
A Lie of the Mind
Best Foreign Play
Benefactors
Special Citation
The Search for Signs of Intelligent Life in the Universe

1986–87
Best Play
Fences
Best Foreign Play
Les Liaisons Dangereuses
Best Musical
Les Misérables

1987–88
Best Play
Joe Turner's Come and Gone
Best Foreign Play
The Road to Mecca
Best Musical
Into the Woods

1988–89
Best Play
The Heidi Chronicles
Best Foreign Play
Aristocrats
Special Citation
Bill Irwin for *Largely New York)*

1989–90
Best Play
The Piano Lesson
Best Foreign Play
Privates on Parade
Best Musical
City of Angels

1990–91
Best Play
Six Degrees of Separation
Best Foreign Play
Our Country's Good
Best Musical
The Will Rogers Follies
Special Citation
Eileen Atkins for her performance in *A Room of One's Own)*

1991–92
Best Play
Dancing at Lughnasa
Best American Play
Two Trains Running

1992–93
Best Play
Angels in America: Millenium Approaches
Best Foreign Play
Someone Who'll Watch Over Me
Best Musical
Kiss of the Spider Woman

BIBLIOGRAPHY

In addition to the following books, research material was provided by the extensive clipping files of the Billy Rose Theatre Collection of the New York Public Library at Lincoln Center.

Abbott, George. *Mister Abbott.* New York: Random House, 1963.

Atkinson, Brooks. *Broadway* (Revised Edition). New York: Limelight Editions, 1970, 1974.

Bacall, Lauren. *Lauren Bacall, By Myself.* New York: Alfred A. Knopf, 1979.

Behr, Edward. *The Complete Book of Les Misérables.* New York: Arcade Publishing, 1989.

Bell, Marty. *Broadway Stories: A Backstage Journey Through Musical Theatre.* New York: Limelight Editions/Sue Katz and Associates, 1993.

Berle, Milton (with Haskell Frankel). *Milton Berle: An Autobiography.* New York: Delacorte Press, 1974.

Best Plays series. Boston: Small, Maynard (1920–25); New York: Dodd, Mead and Company (1916–1919, 1926–88), Applause Theatre Books (1988–1992).

Bragg, Melvyn. *Rich: The Life of Richard Burton.* London: Hodder & Stoughton, 1988.

Burrows, Abe. *Honest Abe: Is There Really No Business Like Show Business?.* Boston, Toronto: Little, Brown and Company, 1980.

Carey, Gary. *Judy Holliday: An Intimate Life Story.* New York: Seaview Books, 1982.

Cohn, Art. *The Nine Lives of Michael Todd.* New York: Random House, 1958.

Coward, Noël. *Autobiography.* London: Methuen, 1986.

Crawford, Cheryl. *One Naked Individual: My 50 Years in the Theatre.* New York: The Bobbs-Merrill Company, Inc., 1977.

De Mille, Agnes. *And Promenade Home.* Boston: Little, Brown, 1958.

Farber, Donald C. and Viagas, Robert. *The Amazing Story of The Fantasticks, America's Longest-Running Play.* New York: Citadel Press, 1991.

Flinn, Denny Martin. *What They Did for Love: The Untold Story Behind the Making of A Chorus Line.* New York: Bantam Books, 1989.

Gibson, William. *The Seesaw Log.* New York: Alfred A. Knopf, 1959.

Goldstein, Malcolm. *George S. Kaufman and His Life, His Theatre.* New York: Oxford University Press, 1979.

Gordon, Max (with Lewis Funke). *Max Gordon Presents.* New York: Bernard Geis and Associates, 1963.

Gottfried, Martin. *All His Jazz: The Life and Death of Bob Fosse.* New York: Bantam Books, 1990.

———. *Broadway Musicals.* New York: Harry N. Abrams, Inc., 1979.

———. *More Broadway Musicals.* New York: Harry N. Abrams, Inc., 1991.

Grafton, David. *Red, Hot & Rich: An Oral History of Cole Porter.* New York: Stein & Day, 1987.

Green, Stanley. *Broadway Musicals Show by Show* (Third Edition). Milwaukee: Hal Leonard Publishing Corp., 1990.

Guernsey, Otis L., Jr. (ed.). *Broadway Song & Story: Playwrights/Lyricists/Composers Discuss Their Hits.* New York: Dodd, Mead & Company, 1985.

Hanson, Bruce K. *The Peter Pan Chronicles: The Nearly One-Hundred-Year-History of the Boy Who Wouldn't Grow Up.* New York: Birch Lane Press, 1993.

Holtzman, Will. *Judy Holliday.* New York: G.P. Putnam and Sons, 1982.

Henderson, Mary C. *Theater in America: 200 Years of Plays, Players, and Productions.* New York: Harry N. Abrams, Inc., 1986.

Ilson, Carol. *Harold Prince: From The Pajama Game to Phantom of the Opera and Beyond.* New York: Limelight Editions, 1992.

Kasha, Al and Joel Hirschhorn. *Notes on Broadway: Intimate Conversations with Broadway's Greatest Songwriters.* New York: Simon and Schuster, 1985, 1987.

Kazan, Elia. *Elia Kazan: A Life.* New York: Alfred A. Knopf, 1988.

Kreuger, Miles. *Show Boat: The Story of a Classic American Musical.* New York: Da Capo Press, Inc. 1977.

Laufe, Abe. *Anatomy of a Hit: Long-Run Plays on Broadway from 1900 to the Present Day.* New York: Hawthorn Books, Inc., 1966.

———. *Broadway's Greatest Musicals: The New Illustrated Revised Edition.* New York: Funk & Wagnalls, 1969, 1970, 1973, 1977.

Lerner, Alan Jay. *The Street Where I Live.* New York: W.W. Norton and Company, 1978.

Lewis, Robert. *Slings and Arrows: Theatre in My Life.* New York: Stein and Day, 1984.

Little, Stuart W. *Enter Joseph Papp: In Search of a New American Theatre.* New York: Coward, McCann and Geoghegan, Inc., 1974.

Loesser, Susan. *A Most Remarkable Fella: Frank Loesser and the Guys and Dolls in His Life, A Portrait by His Daughter.* New York: Donald I. Fine, Inc., 1993.

Logan, Joshua. *Josh: My Up and Down, In and Out Life.* New York: Delacorte Press, 1976.

Mandelbaum, Ken. *A Chorus Line and the Musicals of Michael Bennett.* New York: St. Martin's Press, 1989.

———. *Not Since Carrie.* New York: St. Martin's Press, 1991.

Meredith, Scott. *George S. Kaufman and His Friends.* Garden City, N.Y.: Doubleday and Company, Inc., 1974.

Merman, Ethel (with Ellis, George). *Merman.* New York: Simon and Schuster, 1978.

Mordden, Ethan. *Better Foot Forward: The History of the American Musical Theatre.* New York: Grossman Press, 1976.

———. *Broadway Babies: The People Who Made the American Musical.* New York: Oxford University Press, 1983.

———. *Rodgers and Hammerstein.* New York: Harry N. Abrams, Inc., 1992.

Nathan, George Jean. *The Theatre Book of the Year (from 1942–43 to 1949–50).* New York: Alfred A. Knopf.

New York Times Directory of the Theatre. New York: Arno Press, 1973.

Peyser, Joan. *Bernstein: A Biography.* New York: Ballantine Books, 1987.

Prince, Harold. *Contradictions: Notes on Twenty-Six Years in the Theatre.* New York: Dodd, Mead, & Co., 1974.

Richards, Stanley (ed.). *Best Mystery and Suspense Plays of the Modern Theatre.* New York: Dodd, Mead, & Co., 1971.

Robbins, Jhan. *Front Page Marriage.* New York: G.P. Putnam's Sons, 1982.

Rodgers, Richard. *Musical Stages: An Autobiography.* New York: Random House, 1975.

Schneider, Alan. *Entrances: An American Director's Journey.* New York: Viking, 1986.

Schwartz, Charles. *Cole Porter: A Biography.* New York: Dial Press, 1977.

Shapiro, Doris. *We Danced All Night: My Life Behind the Scenes with Alan Jay Lerner.* New York: William Morrow and Co., 1990.

Skinner, Cornelia Otis. *Life with Lindsay and Crouse.* Boston: Houghton Mifflin Co., 1976.

Spoto, Donald. *The Kindness of Strangers: The Life of Tennessee Williams.* New York: Ballantine Books, 1985.

Teichmann, Howard. *George S. Kaufman: An Intimate Portrait.* New York: Atheneum, 1972.

Theatre World series. New York: The Guide Printing Co., (1944–46); Stuyvesant Press Corp. (1946–48); Greenberg Publisher (1948–57); Chilton Books (1957–64); Crown Publishers, Inc. (1964–90); Applause Theatre Books (1990–91).

Viagas, Robert, Baayork Lee, and Thommie Walsh (with the entire original cast of *A Chorus Line*). *On the Line.* New York: William Morrow and Co., Inc., 1990.

Woll, Allen. *Black Musical Theatre: From Coontown to Dreamgirls.* Baton Rogue: Louisiana State University Press, 1989.

Wright, William. *Lillian Hellman: The Image, The Woman.* New York: Simon and Schuster, Inc., 1986.

Zadan, Craig. *Sondheim & Co. (Second Edition, Updated).* New York: Harper & Row, 1974, 1986, 1987, 1989.

INDEX OF TITLES

PHOTO CREDITS

David Sheward is the Managing Editor and Theatre Critic for *Back Stage*, the performing arts weekly newspaper. A member of the Drama Desk, his articles and reviews have also appeared in *Theatre Week, Street News*, and *The New York Native*. He has acted in and directed numerous off-off-Broadway, regional, community, and university productions. This is his first book.